HISTORICAL DICTIONARIES OF U.S. HISTORICAL ERAS

Jon Woronoff, Series Editor

1. *From the Great War to the Great Depression*, by Neil A. Wynn, 2003.
2. *Civil War and Reconstruction*, by William L. Richter, 2004.
3. *Revolutionary America*, by Terry M. Mays, 2005.
4. *Old South*, by William L. Richter, 2006.
5. *Early American Republic*, by Richard Buel Jr., 2006.
6. *Jacksonian Era and Manifest Destiny*, by Terry Corps, 2006.
7. *Reagan–Bush Era*, by Richard S. Conley, 2007.
8. *Kennedy–Johnson Era*, by Richard Dean Burns and Joseph M. Siracusa, 2008.
9. *Nixon–Ford Era*, by Mitchell K. Hall, 2008.
10. *Roosevelt–Truman Era*, by Neil A. Wynn, 2008.
11. *Eisenhower Era*, by Burton I. Kaufman and Diane Kaufman, 2009.
12. *Progressive Era*, by Catherine Cocks, Peter C. Holloran, and Alan Lessoff, 2009.
13. *Gilded Age*, by T. Adams Upchurch, 2009.

Historical Dictionary of the Progressive Era

Catherine Cocks
Peter C. Holloran
Alan Lessoff

Historical Dictionaries of
U.S. Historical Eras, No. 12

The Scarecrow Press, Inc.
Lanham, Maryland • Toronto • Plymouth, UK
2009

SCARECROW PRESS, INC.

Published in the United States of America
by Scarecrow Press, Inc.
A wholly owned subsidiary of
The Rowman & Littlefield Publishing Group, Inc.
4501 Forbes Boulevard, Suite 200, Lanham, Maryland 20706
www.scarecrowpress.com

Estover Road
Plymouth PL6 7PY
United Kingdom

British Library Cataloguing in Publication Information Available

Library of Congress Cataloging-in-Publication Data

Cocks, Catherine, 1967–
    Historical dictionary of the Progressive Era / Catherine Cocks, Peter Holloran,
Alan Lessoff.
        p. cm. — (Historical dictionaries of U.S. historical eras ; no. 12)
    Includes bibliographical references.
    ISBN-13: 978-0-8108-5349-2 (cloth : alk. paper)
    ISBN-10: 0-8108-5349-3 (cloth : alk. paper)
    ISBN-13: 978-0-8108-6293-7 (eBook)
    ISBN-10: 0-8108-6293-X (eBook)
    1. United States—History—1865–1921—Dictionaries. 2. United States—
Politics and government—1865–1933—Dictionaries. 3. Progressivism (United
States politics)—Dictionaries. I. Holloran, Peter. II. Lessoff, Alan. III. Title.
E661.C63 2009
973.803—dc22   2008041295

Contents

Editor's Foreword

The Progressive Era is a period in American history from the 1890s until World War I. The exact range is questionable and historians often disagree, although 1890 and 1920 seem reasonable boundaries. There is, however, more agreement on what happened during this crucial period and what gives it the right to the name "progressive": the realization of serious problems that had to be resolved and major movements bringing improvement and reform in multiple fields, including equality of sex, race, and religion and a general cleansing of the political processes and government, with increased fairness and justice. Improvements were being made in all fields—political, economic, social, cultural, scientific, and religious. And although people realized there were still a lot of problems in the United States, another major phenomenon of the Progressive Era was a feeling that Americans had little to learn from other countries but much to teach them, which embroiled the country in various wars and ushered in its own form of imperialism.

All of these changes made the Progressive Era one of the most exciting periods in American history and one whose impact is still felt, which makes this a particularly important (and larger) volume in the Scarecrow series on U.S. political eras. The chronology indicates significant events and the introduction situates the era's position and meaning in the rest of American history. The dictionary contains entries on both the negative and the positive faces of the era, including corruption and influence of bosses, segregation and race riots, waste, and frustration as well as the movements for reform and uplift, new legislation and constitutional amendments, crucial court rulings, and cultural ferment. During this time many people played an exceptional role, whether as presidents or congressmen, advocates or organizers, teachers or social scientists, inventors or business people, writers or musicians. Nonetheless, so much has been written about this period that the bibliography remains an invaluable starting point for those interested in further reading.

Impressively large and informative, this *Historical Dictionary of the Progressive Era* was amazingly written by just three authors: Catherine Cocks, Peter Holloran, and Alan Lessoff. Formerly a professor at various universities, Dr. Cocks is now in publishing and has written *Doing the Town: The Rise of Urban Tourism in the United States, 1859–1915.* Peter Holloran is associate professor of history at Worcester State College and a specialist on 19th-century cultural history. Along with the *Historical Dictionary of New England* in a related series, he has written *Boston's Wayward Children: Social Services for Homeless Children.* Alan Lessoff is professor of history at Illinois State University and a specialist in U.S. urban history. He is the author of *The Nation and Its City: Politics, "Corruption," and Progressive in Washington, D.C., 1861–1902* and since 2004 has served as the editor of the *Journal of the Gilded Age and Progressive Era.*

Jon Woronoff
Series Editor

Acronyms and Abbreviations

AAA	American Automobile Association
AALL	American Association for Labor Legislation
AAU	Amateur Athletic Union
AAUP	American Association of University Professors
AAUW	American Association of University Women
ACA	American Civic Association
ADL	Anti-Defamation League
AEA	American Economic Association
AFL	American Federation of Labor
AIA	American Institute of Architects
AMA	American Medical Association
ARU	American Railway Union
ASCAP	American Society of Composers, Authors, and Publishers
ASE	American Society of Equity
ASHA	American Social Hygiene Association
ASL	Anti-Saloon League
AT&SF	Atchison, Topeka, and Santa Fe Railroad
AT&T	American Telephone and Telegraph
AUAM	American Union against Militarism
BIA	Bureau of Indian Affairs
BSA	Boy Scouts of America
COS	charity organization societies
CU	Congressional Union
FTC	Federal Trade Commission
GEB	General Education Board
GE	General Electric Company
GFWC	General Federation of Women's Clubs
GM	General Motors Corporation

GSA	Girl Scouts of America
HIAS	Hebrew Immigrant Aid Society
ICC	Interstate Commerce Commission
ILGWU	International Ladies' Garment Workers' Union
IRT	Interborough Rapid Transit
IWW	Industrial Workers of the World
KKK	Ku Klux Klan
KOL	Knights of Labor
MIT	Massachusetts Institute of Technology
MPPC	Motion Picture Patents Company
NAACP	National Association for the Advancement of Colored People
NACW	National Association of Colored Women
NAM	National Association of Manufacturers
NAOWS	National Association Opposed to Woman Suffrage
NAWSA	National American Woman Suffrage Association
NBS	National Bureau of Standards
NCAA	National Collegiate Athletic Association
NCC	National Conservation Commission
NCCC	National Conference of Charities and Correction
NCCP	National Conference on City Planning
NCF	National Civic Federation
NCL	National Consumers' League
NCLC	National Child Labor Committee
NEA	National Education Association
NFU	National Farmers' Union
NHA	National Housing Association
NICB	National Industrial Conference Board
NMA	National Medical Association
NML	National Municipal League
NNBL	National Negro Business League
NPS	National Park Service
NPRL	National Progressive Republican League
NTA	National Tuberculosis Association
NWP	National Woman's Party

PPA	Planters' Protective Association
SAI	Society of American Indians
SAT	Scholastic Aptitude Test
SEB	Southern Education Board
SLP	Socialist Labor Party
SO	Standard Oil
SP	Southern Pacific Railroad
SPA	Socialist Party of America
SSC	Southern Sociological Congress
SSWSC	Southern States Woman Suffrage Conference
STD	Sexually transmitted disease
SVM	Student Volunteer Movement
TIAA	Teachers Insurance and Annuity Association
UBO	United Booking Office
UDC	United Daughters of the Confederacy
UMW or UMWA	United Mine Workers of America
USBA	United States Brewers' Association
USDA	United States Department of Agriculture
USGS	United States Geological Survey
USPHS	United States Public Health Service
VNS	Visiting Nurses Service
WCTU	Woman's Christian Temperance Union
WFM	Western Federation of Miners
WTUL	Women's Trade Union League
YMCA	Young Men's Christian Association
YWCA	Young Women's Christian Association

Chronology

1887   **8 February:** Congress enacted the Dawes Allotment Act, mandating the dissolution of Native American reservations.

1888   **January:** Edward Bellamy published *Looking Backward.* **17 October:** Thomas A. Edison filed for a patent for the Kinetoscope.

1889   **18 September:** Jane Addams and Ellen Gates Starr founded a settlement house in Hull Mansion on Chicago's West Side.

1890   The Census Bureau announced the closing of the frontier. **May:** A merger between rival organizations created the National American Woman Suffrage Association. **2 July:** Congress passed the Sherman Antitrust Act. **1 October:** Congress passed an act creating Yosemite National Park. **November:** Charles Scribner's Sons published Jacob Riis's *How the Other Half Lives.* **29 December:** A botched effort to disarm a group of Sioux Ghost Dance followers resulted in a massacre by U.S. troops of 150 Indians near Wounded Knee Creek, South Dakota.

1891   **15 December:** James Naismith invented basketball.

1892   **1 January:** The new federal immigration center opened at Ellis Island, New York. **22 February:** A convention to organize a national People's (or Populist) Party met at St. Louis. **15 April:** Thomson-Houston and Edison General Electric merged to form the General Electric Company. **5 May:** Congress enacted the Geary Act, extending the ban on Chinese immigration for another 10 years; it was made permanent in 1902. **28 May:** John Muir founded the Sierra Club. **5–6 July:** A company attempt to break a strike at the Carnegie Steel Company plant at Homestead, Pennsylvania, prompted a deadly battle between strikers and private security forces. **23 July:** Lithuanian-born anarchist Alexander Berkman attempted to assassinate Carnegie Steel executive

Henry Clay Frick in his office in Pittsburgh. **1 October:** The University of Chicago held its first classes. **8 November:** Democrat Grover Cleveland became the first president returned to office after having earlier lost re-election, defeating Republican president Benjamin Harrison and Populist candidate James B. Weaver.

1893   17 January: With support from U.S. sailors at Honolulu, American settlers overthrew Queen Liliuokalani, proclaimed a Republic of Hawaii, and began to negotiate annexation to the United States. **3 March:** Congress established the Dawes Commission to negotiate dissolution of tribal governments in the Indian Territory. **9 March:** Newly inaugurated President Cleveland withdrew the Hawaiian annexation treaty, signed in the last days of the Harrison administration, and advocated restoration of the deposed queen. **1 May–30 October:** The Columbian Exposition took place in Chicago. **4 May:** Collapse of the National Cordage Company set off the Panic of 1893. **24 May:** Ohio temperance advocates founded the Anti-Saloon League. **26 June:** Condemning their trials as riddled with errors and distortions, Illinois governor John Peter Altgeld pardoned the surviving men convicted in the 1886 Haymarket bombing. **12 July:** Frederick Jackson Turner delivered his famous essay, "The Significance of the Frontier in American History," during the Columbian Exposition. **28 October:** A deranged office seeker, Patrick Pendergast, murdered Chicago mayor Carter Harrison Sr. on the evening before the Columbian Exposition's closing ceremonies. **30 October:** Relying on Republican votes, President Cleveland achieved Senate passage of the repeal of the 1890 Sherman Silver Purchase Act, a move that bitterly divided the majority Democrats over the currency issue. **12 November:** English reformer William T. Stead delivered his "If Christ Came to Chicago" address, prompting formation of the Chicago Civic Federation.

1894   25–26 January: Meeting at Philadelphia, the National Conference for Good City Government agreed to establish the National Municipal League. **March:** The Lexow Committee of the New York State Senate began its sensational investigation of police corruption in New York City. **25 March:** Coxey's Army left Massillon, Ohio, on its highly publicized unemployment march on Washington, D.C. **29 April:** Police arrested Coxey and several followers for trespassing on the Capitol grounds, ending their protest. **11 May:** In response to the firing of union leaders, workers at the Pullman Palace Car Company south of Chicago went on strike. **26 June:** American Railway Union leader Eugene V. Debs ordered a boycott of Pullman cars in support of the six-week-old Pullman Strike. **3 July:** Federal troops moved into Chicago to break the Pullman boycott, sparking days of rioting.

1895 **21 January:** In an 8–1 decision in *United States v. E. C. Knight Co.*, the Supreme Court sharply limited the application of the Sherman Antitrust Act to manufacturers. **8–20 February:** A syndicate organized by banker J. P. Morgan floated a massive bond issue to replenish dwindling U.S. gold reserves. **8 April:** In *Pollock v. Farmer's Loan and Trust*, a divided Supreme Court ruled the federal income tax unconstitutional. **27 May:** In *In re Debs*, a case stemming from the 1894 Pullman Strike, the Supreme Court unanimously sanctioned court injunctions to break strikes. **Summer:** Sea Lion Park, the first enclosed amusement park, opened at Coney Island, New York. **20 July:** Labeling the United States "master of the situation" in the Caribbean, Secretary of State Richard Olney invoked the Monroe Doctrine against Great Britain in the border dispute between Venezuela and British Guiana. **18 September:** Booker T. Washington delivered his "Atlanta Compromise" speech at the Cotton States Exposition.

1896 The U.S. Postal Office opened 82 test routes for the new rural free delivery service; 8,000 existed by 1902. **January:** The Laboratory School at the University of Chicago opened under the leadership of philosopher John Dewey. **18 May:** Despite an angry dissent by Justice John Marshall Harlan, a 7–1 decision by the Supreme Court in the *Plessy v. Ferguson* case gave constitutional sanction to racial segregation. **16 June:** William McKinley gained first-ballot nomination for president at the Republican convention. **July:** Black women activists met in Washington, D.C., to form the National Association of Colored Women, with Mary Church Terrell as the first president. **8 July:** At the Democratic convention, William Jennings Bryan delivered his "Cross of Gold" speech, setting the stage for his nomination three days later. **16 August:** Gold was found near Dawson in the Canadian Yukon, sparking the Alaska Gold Rush. **3 November:** McKinley won a narrow but clear victory over Bryan, 51 to 47 percent in the popular vote and 271 to 176 in the Electoral College.

1897 **24 July:** President McKinley signed the Dingley Tariff, a high point in the protectionism favored by the Republican Party. **1 September:** Boston began operating the first subway transit system in the United States.

1898 **1 January:** Queens, Brooklyn, and Staten Island joined the Bronx and Manhattan in the consolidation of greater New York City. **9 February:** William Randolph Hearst's *New York Journal* published the De Lôme letter, which made Spain's negotiations with the United States over Cuban autonomy appear insincere. **15 February:** An unexplained explosion sank the USS *Maine* in Havana Harbor, killing 266 men. **19 April:** Congress passed a joint resolution, signed the next day by President McKinley, directing use of force to expel Spanish forces from Cuba. The attached Teller Amendment committed the United States to Cuban independence. **24 April:** Spain declared war on the United States, with the United States reciprocating the next day. **25 April:** In *Williams v. Mississippi*, the Supreme Court unanimously sanctioned the rewriting of state constitutions in the South to disfranchise African Americans; Mississippi had been the first state to do so in 1890. **1 May:** A fleet under Commodore George Dewey defeated the Spanish at Manila Harbor, the Philippines. **1 June:** Congress passed the Erdman Act, encouraging arbitration of railway labor disputes. **10 June:** U.S. troops invaded Cuba. **15 June:** The Anti-Imperialist League was founded in Boston. **28 June:** Congress passed the Curtis Act, dissolving tribal governments in the Indian Territory and compelling the residents to accept allotment. **1 July:** The Battle of San Juan Hill, Cuba, took place, largely on nearby Kettle Hill. **3 July:** A U.S. squadron destroyed the Spanish fleet at Santiago Bay, Cuba. **7 July:** President McKinley signed a joint resolution annexing Hawaii. **17 July:** The surrender of Santiago effectively ended Spanish resistance on Cuba. **25 July:** Sixteen thousand U.S. troops, commanded by General Nelson Miles, invaded Puerto Rico. **12 August:** France mediated an armistice ending the Spanish–American War. **13 August:** U.S. troops occupied Manila. **10 December:** American and Spanish negotiators signed the Treaty of Paris, which granted Cuba independence and ceded Puerto Rico, Guam, and the Philippines to the United States.

1899 **22 January:** A Vatican encyclical explicitly condemned the liberal Catholic movement known as "Americanism." **4 February:**

Clashes between Filipino and American forces marked the start of the Philippine–American War. **6 February:** With one vote more than two-thirds, the Senate ratified the Treaty of Paris, thereby annexing the Philippines, Puerto Rico, and Guam. **24 March:** An effusive review by William Dean Howells of Frank Norris's naturalistic novel, *McTeague*, appeared in the magazine *Literature*. **May–July:** The United States participated in the first Hague Conference on international arbitration. **6 September:** The United States issued the first Open Door Note, concerning trade access to China. **13–16 September:** A national conference on the trust issue was held in Chicago, leading to the formation of the National Civic Federation early the next year. **November:** Executive Secretary Florence Kelley published an article explaining the new National Consumers' League in the *American Journal of Sociology*.

1900 **14 March:** The Gold Standard Act went into effect. **3 July:** The United States issued the second Open Door Note to protect Chinese territorial integrity. **August:** The United States sent 2,500 troops to China as part of an international expedition to suppress the Boxer Rebellion. **8 September:** A storm surge from a severe hurricane killed an estimated 6,000 people at Galveston, Texas, with thousands more perishing inland in the deadliest natural disaster in U.S. history. **6 November:** Republican president William McKinley easily won reelection over Democratic nominee William Jennings Bryan. Progressive Republican Robert La Follette was elected to the first of three terms as governor of Wisconsin.

1901 **10 January:** Oil was discovered at the huge Spindletop field near Beaumont, Texas. **25 February:** The world's first billion-dollar corporation, United States Steel, was formed in New York City, the result of a buyout of Andrew Carnegie's steel interests arranged by investment banker J. P. Morgan. **1 March:** Congress adopted the Platt Amendment, asserting U.S. authority to intervene in nominally independent Cuba. **23 March:** An expedition led by Colonel Frederick Funston captured Filipino independence leader Emilio Aguinaldo; armed resistance to U.S. rule remained widespread until mid-1902. **16 May:** In Edinburgh, Scotland, William James delivered the first of the Gifford lectures, which became the 1902 book *The Varieties of Religious Experience*. **29 July:** Prominent democratic leftists, including Eugene V. Debs and Victor Berger, formed the Socialist Party of America.

6 September: Leon Czolgosz, a self-proclaimed anarchist, shot President McKinley at the Pan-American Exposition in Buffalo. **14 September:** Theodore Roosevelt assumed the presidency upon McKinley's death. **16 October:** Roosevelt hosted Booker T. Washington at a White House dinner, sparking a backlash from segregationists. **18 November:** The United States and Great Britain signed the second Hay–Paunceforte Treaty, in which the British renounced involvement in the proposed isthmian canal.

1902   January: The McMillan Plan for Washington, D.C., the nation's first comprehensive urban plan, was displayed at the city's Corcoran Gallery. **28 January:** Andrew Carnegie endowed the Carnegie Institution of Washington. **4 March:** The American Automobile Association was founded. **12 May:** The United Mine Workers began a large-scale strike in the anthracite coal fields of Pennsylvania and West Virginia. **13 June:** Congress passed the Newlands Reclamation Act. **October:** Mediation by the Roosevelt administration helped end the five-month anthracite coal strike.

1903   5 January: The Supreme Court ruling in *Lone Wolf v. Hitchcock* abrogated the diplomatic relationship between the U.S. government and Indian tribes. **January:** An acclaimed issue of *McClure's Magazine*, with reports by Ida Tarbell, Lincoln Steffens, and Ray Stannard Baker, marked the emergence of the muckraking movement in investigative journalism. **14 February:** Congress passed legislation to found the Department of Commerce and Labor, which included a Bureau of Corporations. **19 February:** Congress passed the Elkins Act, forbidding railroad rebates. **18 April:** W. E. B. Du Bois published *The Souls of Black Folk*. **22 May:** Cuba reluctantly accepted the Platt Amendment, passed by Congress in 1901. **1–13 October:** Boston played Pittsburgh in the first baseball world series. **3 November:** With support from the U.S. Navy, Panama launched a successful revolt against Colombia. **18 November:** The Hay–Bunau-Varilla Treaty was signed, granting the United States control of the projected Panama Canal. **19 November:** At a joint meeting of labor unionists and reformers in Boston, the Women's Trade Union League was formed. **17 December:** At Kitty Hawk, North Carolina, the Wright brothers flew the first successful mechanized flight.

1904   14 March: In a 5–4 ruling, the Supreme Court sided with the Roosevelt administration and ordered dissolution of the Northern Securities railroad combine, a major legal victory for antitrust advocates. **14 March:** President Roosevelt proclaimed Pelican Island, Florida, the first federal bird reservation. **25 April:** The National Child Labor Committee was founded in New York City. **15 June:** More than 1,000 people died when the steamboat *General Slocum* caught fire in the East River, New York City's deadliest disaster until 11 September 2001. **8 November:** In the largest landslide in American presidential elections to date, Roosevelt defeated conservative Democrat Alton B. Parker. **6 December:** In his annual message, Theodore Roosevelt articulated the Roosevelt Corollary to the Monroe Doctrine.

1905   16 January: New York City's Committee of Fourteen was founded to strengthen enforcement of liquor and anti-prostitution laws. **January–April:** The United States participated in the Algeciras Conference to settle the German–French dispute over Morocco. **1 February:** The Forest Transfer Act expanded the powers of the Bureau of Forestry, soon renamed the United States Forest Service, and moved the agency from the Interior Department to the Agriculture Department. **25 February:** The first installment of Upton Sinclair's *The Jungle* appeared in the socialist newspaper, *Appeal to Reason*. **17 April:** In a 5–4 decision in *Lochner v. New York*, the Supreme Court declared unconstitutional a New York state law limiting bakers to 10 hours of work per day. **7 July:** A convention in Chicago of labor activists founded the Industrial Workers of the World (IWW). **11–14 July:** At a meeting in Fort Erie, Ontario, black civil rights activists launched the Niagara Movement. **29 July:** Secretary of War William Howard Taft agreed to a memorandum with the Japanese prime minister, Count Katsura, apparently giving U.S. sanction to Japanese control of Korea in exchange for Japan's renouncing interference in the Philippines. **5 September:** In the first successful American mediation of a major international crisis, a treaty signed at Portsmouth, New Hampshire, ended the Russo–Japanese War. **6 September:** The New York state legislature's Armstrong Commission hearings on abuses by the life insurance industry began. **7 October:** Samuel Hopkins Adams exposed fraud in the patent medicine industry in *Collier's Magazine*. **28 December:** The National Collegiate Athletic Association was established; it adopted its current name in 1910. **30 December:** A bomb killed former Idaho governor Frank Steunenberg, an attack blamed on Western Federation of Miners leaders, including "Big Bill" Haywood, who was acquitted in 1907 after a sensational trial.

1906 **14 April:** In a speech deploring "excess" in investigative journalism, President Roosevelt gave "muckraking" its name. **18 April:** Thousands died and perhaps 250,000 people lost their homes when a severe earthquake and ensuing fires destroyed much of San Francisco. **18 May:** Congress passed the Hepburn Act to strengthen the Interstate Commerce Commission. **30 June:** The first major federal consumer protection measures, the Pure Food and Drug Act and the Meat Inspection Act, both became law. **13–14 August:** A notorious shooting incident took place in Brownsville, Texas; the Roosevelt administration's heavy-handed discipline of African American soldiers accused of involvement increased black suspicion of the Republican Party. **22 September:** An attack by a white mob on black neighborhoods began four days of rioting in Atlanta. **29 September:** In the first exercise of the Platt Amendment, the United States declared Secretary of War William Howard Taft provisional governor of Cuba and sent troops to suppress a rebellion there. **14 November:** In Boston, William James delivered the first of eight lectures popularizing Pragmatism. **16 November:** Oklahoma joined the union as the 46th state. **12 December:** President Roosevelt nominated as secretary of commerce and labor Oscar S. Straus, who became the first Jewish cabinet member.

1907 More than 1.3 million people immigrated to the United States, the largest recorded total for a single year until the 1990s. In this year, Bakelite, the first commercially viable plastic, was introduced. **20 February:** Congress established the U.S. Immigration Commission, whose 41-volume report appeared in 1911. **24 February:** The so-called Gentlemen's Agreement limited Japanese migration to the United States. **2 March:** The Roosevelt administration proclaimed large forest reserves in six western states, one day before a new law went into effect sharply restricting the president's authority to set aside forest reserves. **May:** The Russell Sage Foundation underwrote the Pittsburgh Survey. **June–October:** The Second Hague Conference, organized by the Roosevelt administration, met with inconclusive results. **21–22 October:** A run on the Knickerbocker Trust Company sparked the Panic of 1907. **16**

December: The Great White Fleet of the U.S. Navy began a round-the-world cruise that ended on 22 February 1909.

1908 **28 January:** Staunton, Virginia, adopted the first charter providing for a professional city manager. **February:** Robert Henri's show "The Eight" publicized the urban realism of the Ash Can School painters. **24 February:** In *Muller v. Oregon*, the Supreme Court ruled unanimously in favor of an Oregon law limiting working hours for women. **13 May:** Theodore Roosevelt convened the White House Conference on Conservation. **30 May:** Congress passed the Aldrich–Vreeland Act, establishing the National Monetary Commission. **18 June:** William Howard Taft won the Republican presidential nomination on the first ballot, despite demonstrations in favor of a third term for Roosevelt. **8–10 July:** At the Democratic convention in Denver, William Jennings Bryan received his third nomination with the open support of the American Federation of Labor. **14 August:** A white mob frustrated in a lynching attempt began three days of race rioting in Springfield, Illinois. **1 October:** The Ford Motor Company introduced the Model T, which by 1913 was being manufactured on the company's innovative assembly line. **3 November:** In the presidential election, Taft handed Bryan a disappointing defeat, 56.6 to 43 percent in the popular vote and 321 to 162 in the Electoral College. **30 November:** The United States signed the Root–Takahira agreement, recognizing Japanese power in Manchuria. **December:** The Motion Picture Patents Company was created to monopolize U.S. movie production and distribution.

1909 **12 February:** Civil rights activists issued a call on Abraham Lincoln's birthday for the formation of the National Association for the Advancement of Colored People (NAACP). **4 July:** Daniel Burnham's *Plan of Chicago* was published, the high point of the City Beautiful movement. **12 July:** The Sixteenth Amendment, authorizing a federal income tax, was sent to the states, which ratified it by February 1913. **6 August:** President Taft signed the divisive Payne–Aldrich Tariff. **6 September:** Israel Zangwill's play, *The Melting Pot*, began its four-month run on Broadway. **23 November:** New York City textile workers launched a strike known as the Uprising of the Twenty Thousand.

1910 **7 January:** President Taft fired Chief Forester Gifford Pinchot for making public his dispute over conservation policy with Secretary of the Interior Richard Ballinger. **21 January:** An immigrant reception center opened on Angel Island in San Francisco Bay. **8 February:** The Boy Scouts of America was incorporated. **February:** The first volume of *The Fundamentals: A Testimony to the Truth,* from which the Fundamentalist movement took its name, was published. **March:** The Chicago Vice Commission was created to address the problem of prostitution. **19 March:** Led by Nebraska congressman George Norris, 46 progressive Republicans joined with Democrats to strip Speaker of the House Joseph Cannon of much of his control over the House of Representatives. **June:** The Carnegie Foundation for the Advancement of Teaching published the Flexner Report, sparking a national controversy over standards in medical education. **18 June:** Congress passed the Mann–Elkins Act, strengthening the rate-setting powers of the Interstate Commerce Commission. **25 June:** Congress passed the Mann Act, declaring it a federal crime to transport women across state lines for "immoral purposes." **31 August:** Speaking to Civil War veterans in Osawatomie, Kansas, Theodore Roosevelt called for a "New Nationalism." **29 September:** The Committee on Urban Conditions among Negroes, which grew into the National Urban League, was founded in New York City. **1 October:** An explosion at the *Los Angeles Times* building, later traced to labor activists James and John McNamara, killed 20 people. **November:** The first issue of the NAACP's magazine, *The Crisis*, appeared; it was edited by W. E. B. Du Bois. **8 November:** Amid economic concerns and Republican infighting, the Democrats gained 56 seats in congressional elections, taking control of the House of Representatives for the first time since 1895; Missouri's Champ Clark became Speaker. Democrats also gained 10 Senate seats, though Republicans retained control of the upper house.

1911   21 January: Robert La Follette and his allies formed the National Progressive Republican League. **25 March:** A fire at Triangle Shirtwaist Company on New York's Lower East Side killed 146 people, mostly young women workers, prompting a broad effort to improve factory safety regulations. **15 May:** In a unanimous decision ordering the breakup of Standard Oil, the Supreme Court articulated the "rule of reason" to govern antitrust suits. **16 May:** The Mexican Revolution began with the forced resignation of authoritarian president Porfirio Díaz. **October:** The civil rights group Society of American Indians was organized. **26 October:** The Taft administration began antitrust prosecution of the U.S. Steel Corporation. **November:** In a referendum decided by 3,587 votes, California became the first large state to adopt women's suffrage.

1912   January: Max Eastman and Floyd Dell took over as editors of the radical culture magazine, *The Masses.* **January–February:** New Mexico and Arizona were admitted as the last two of the lower 48 states. **12 January:** The "Bread and Roses" strike of textile workers began in Lawrence, Massachusetts. **24 February:** Ex-president Roosevelt formally entered the presidential race. **12 March:** The Girl Scouts of America was founded. **14–15 April:** Approximately 1,500 people died in the sinking of the *Titanic* in the North Atlantic. **April 19:** President Taft signed a bill creating the U.S. Children's Bureau, with Julia Lathrop as the first director. **22 June:** Supporters of Theodore Roosevelt walked out of the Republican Party convention in Chicago and in a breakaway meeting planned a new Progressive Party. **2 July:** After 46 ballots spread over five days, Woodrow Wilson defeated Champ Clark for the Democratic presidential nomination. **6 August:** In Chicago, the National Progressive (or Bull Moose) Party nominated Roosevelt for president. **28 August:** Louis Brandeis and Woodrow Wilson began the collaboration that outlined the "New Freedom." **14 October:** Progressive candidate Theodore Roosevelt delivered a speech in Milwaukee after being shot by a deranged bartender. **5 November:** Democrat Woodrow Wilson was elected president with only 42 percent of the vote but with an overwhelming 435 electoral votes. Democrats increased their House majority by 63 seats, while a gain of 10 Senate seats gave them control of that chamber as well. Socialist Party candidate Eugene V. Debs made his best showing ever, winning 6 percent of the popular vote.

1913   1 January: Parcel post went into effect. **17 February:** The Armory Show of modernist art opened in New York City. **1 March:** Congress overrode President Taft's veto to pass the Webb–Kenyon Act, prohibiting shipment of alcohol into dry states. **18 February:** In a coup that further entangled the United States in its neighbor's turmoil, General Victoriano Huerta proclaimed himself president of Mexico, overthrowing popular revolutionary leader Francisco Madero, who was murdered on 22 February. **28 February:** The Pujo Committee published its report on the so-called Money Trust. **8 April:** Ratification of the Seventeenth Amendment, for the direct election of U.S. Senators, was completed. President Wilson spoke on tariff reform before a joint session of Congress, the first president to address Congress directly in 112 years. **2 May:** The United States became the first great power to recognize Sun Yat-sen's Republic of China. **14 May:** John D. Rockefeller Sr. founded the Rockefeller Foundation with a donation of $100 million. **19 May:** California adopted the Alien Land Act to prevent Japanese and other Asian settlers from buying land. **28 July:** A six-month strike by silk workers in Paterson, New Jersey, collapsed, a devastating blow to IWW efforts in the industrial east. **3 October:** The Underwood–Simmons Tariff became law, lowering import duties and implementing the income tax. **19 December:** Conservationists lost a decade-long controversy with the signing of federal legislation to turn the Hetch Hetchy Valley into a reservoir for San Francisco. **23 December:** Legislation establishing the Federal Reserve System was signed.

1914   5 January: The Ford Motor Company began paying workers an unprecedented $5 per day. **20 April:** Around 20 men, women, and children died when state militiamen and company guards destroyed a tent camp of striking miners at Ludlow, Colorado. **21 April:** In response to a clash on 10 April involving American sailors and in an attempt to prevent arms shipments to the Huerta government, the Wilson administration ordered marines to land at Veracruz, Mexico. **8 May:** Congress passed the Smith–Lever Act, greatly expanding the agricultural extension program. **15 August:** The Panama Canal officially opened. **19 August:** President Wilson declared U.S. neutrality in World War I. **7 September:** Texas celebrated completion of the 50-mile Houston Ship Channel. **26 September:** Congress established the Federal Trade Commission. **15 October:** President Wilson signed the Clayton Antitrust Act. **7 November:** The first issue of the liberal opinion magazine the *New Republic* appeared. **17 December:** Congress passed the Harrison Narcotics Control Act, banning the sale and use of opium and cocaine.

1915   February: In response to a British blockade, Germany began submarine warfare in the North Atlantic. **20 February:** D. W. Griffith's *The Birth of a Nation* had a preview showing in New York City.

4 March: The Seaman's Act, which regulated the working conditions of sailors and was sponsored by Wisconsin senator Robert La Follette, became law. **7 May:** A German submarine torpedoed the British passenger ship *Lusitania*, killing 128 Americans and heightening tensions between the United States and Germany. **8 June:** William Jennings Bryan resigned as secretary of state to protest the Wilson administration's implied threat against Germany over the *Lusitania* affair. **August:** The Texas Rangers and vigilantes killed hundreds and perhaps thousands of ethnic Mexicans in response to the Plan de San Diego and attacks on ranches and railroad stations. **16 August:** Leo Frank was lynched near Marietta, Georgia. **25 November:** On Thanksgiving night on Stone Mountain, Georgia, William J. Simmons led the revived Ku Klux Klan on its first cross burning.

1916 12 February: U.S. envoy Edward M. House and Sir Edward Grey, the British foreign secretary, initialed a memorandum that seemed to commit the United States to the Allies if Germany refused American mediation. **15 March:** In response to Mexican rebel leader Pancho Villa's raids across the U.S. border, General John J. Pershing led 7,000 American troops into Mexico. **3 May:** Germany issued the *Sussex* pledge. **1 June:** The Senate voted 42 to 22 to confirm Louis Brandeis as the first Jewish Supreme Court justice. **3 June:** In a response to the preparedness debate, Congress passed the National Defense Act, authorizing a large expansion of the U.S. Army. **10 June:** The reunited Republican Party nominated Supreme Court Justice Charles Evans Hughes for president. **11 June:** The landmark Federal Highway Act became law. **15 June:** Rallying to the cry, "We didn't go to war!" the Democrats renominated Woodrow Wilson. **17 July:** The Federal Farm Loan Act, meant to ease credit for farmers, became law. **25 August:** President Wilson signed legislation creating the National Park Service. **29 August:** The Wilson administration established the Council of National Defense, and the president signed the Jones Act, committing the United States to the eventual independence of the Philippines. **1 September:** The Keating–Owen Act, the first federal effort to limit child labor, was approved. The Supreme Court overturned this law in 1918. **3 September:** Congress passed the Adamson Act, providing an eight-hour day for workers on interstate railroads. **7 November:** Wilson defeated Hughes, 277 to 254 in the Electoral College and 49 to 42 percent in the popular vote; results from California, the decisive state, remained unclear for two days. The Democrats retained control of the House of Representatives by only six seats.

1917   **9 January:** The German government decided to resume unrestricted submarine warfare as of 1 February, knowing that this action would almost certainly prompt an American declaration of war. **22 January:** In a speech to the Senate, President Wilson called for "peace without victory" and the creation of a League of Nations. **3 February:** Wilson informed Congress that his administration had broken diplomatic relations with Germany. **5 February:** Overriding Woodrow Wilson's second veto, Congress passed the Immigration Act, imposing a literacy test and establishing the Asiatic Barred Zone. **1 March:** The United States released the Zimmerman Telegram, turned over by the British five days earlier. **2 April:** President Wilson called for a declaration of war against Germany, which he received on 6 April, with the first woman member of Congress, Jeanette Rankin of Montana, among the 50 representatives and 6 senators who voted no. **15 June:** The Espionage Act became law, placing sharp limits on criticism of the U.S. war effort. **1 July:** The shooting of two policemen sparked a gruesome race riot in East St. Louis, Illinois. **12 July:** Vigilantes in Bisbee, Arizona, forced 1,186 striking miners into a railroad freight car and abandoned them in the desert; U.S. troops rescued them two days later. **18 December:** Congress passed the Eighteenth Amendment for federal prohibition, which the states would ratify by January 1919.

1918   **5 June:** Congress approved the Nineteenth Amendment, providing that the right to vote shall not be abridged or denied on account of sex, and sent it to the states for ratification.

1920   **26 August:** The Tennessee legislature ratified the Nineteenth Amendment, giving the measure the approval of three-quarters of the states that was required for its enactment.

Introduction

Why study the Progressive Era? Although they disagreed about much else, the two most memorable political figures of the early 20th century concurred on the view that the country in these years wrestled with momentous issues. "When the Constitution was adopted," Theodore Roosevelt noted in his first annual message as president in December 1901, "no human wisdom could foretell the sweeping changes, alike in industrial and political conditions, which were to take place by the beginning of the twentieth century." "This is nothing short of a new social age," Woodrow Wilson observed in a 1912 presidential campaign speech, "a new era of human relationships, a new stage-setting for the drama of life." Unusually thoughtful politicians, Roosevelt and Wilson excelled at articulating in understandable terms the country's situation and its options. Yet the thoughts they expressed about the significance of their age were common currency. The rhetoric of William Jennings Bryan, Robert La Follette, and other major politicians all began with the premise that the United States had entered a dramatically new era whose hazards and possibilities Americans needed to understand in order to build a better society. Similar thoughts animated the "muckraking" journalism, social reform, and public policy writing that count among the memorable products of these years.

After the Civil War ended in 1865, the country transformed from a mainly agricultural and artisanal nation to the world's leading industrial and agricultural power, dominated by huge, ungainly cities. In 1869, as work crews raced through the mountains and across plains to complete the first transcontinental railroad, Americans imagined that the colonizing and settling of the West would remain the country's central endeavor for a very long time. In 1893, historian Frederick Jackson Turner gave his famous speech pondering the frontier's closure. When Roosevelt succeeded the assassinated William McKinley in September

1901, the United States was mired in its first overseas guerrilla war, in the Philippines. The republic had won a claim to this sprawling archipelago during the brief Spanish–American War of 1898, an event that signaled it would henceforth behave like the great power it had manifestly become. Vast changes in communications and transportation, immigration and migration patterns, social mores, gender roles, family structure, class structure, work patterns, business methods, education, intellectual life, religion, the professions, technology, science, medicine, and much else were transforming the scope and feel of people's lives and relationships. As Wilson claimed, "We have come upon a very different age from any that preceded us."

AN AMERICAN VARIANT OF INTERNATIONAL TRENDS

It is easy to exaggerate the speed and thoroughness with which industrialization, urbanization, corporate capitalism, and the cultural changes often labeled "modernization" had altered people's lives and consciousness by the turn of the 20th century. Still, the direction of events was clear. Many Americans feared that the country's growth and transformation since the Civil War had been headlong and heedless. At the turn of the 20th century, disparate Americans argued that the challenge now was to harness the forces that the previous generation had unleashed. How could the country check the power of corporations that operated over a vast area and commanded more resources than state governments? How could it ensure the health and safety of workers and reassure them that they had a stake in the seemingly exploitative industrial system? How could a country that had always encouraged the exploitation of natural resources switch to a conservation ethic as the limits of the land became clear? What would it take to remake dreary, dirty cities into healthful, attractive, and even rewarding places to live? Could politics and government change to cope with urban, industrial conditions and still remain dedicated to principles of popular government developed for a smaller-scale society? What role would women play now that new economic, social, and cultural patterns had made ridiculous the old assumption that they belonged only in the private sphere? How could people raise their children to be moral, responsible individuals amid the disorganization and temptations of modern life? Should society pressure people who differed in appearance or behavior from an assumed standard—immigrants, Native Americans, and African Americans, as well as dissidents—to Americanize for the sake of social coherence? Were such people so hopelessly different that the mainstream should exclude or oppress them, or would the country thrive and hold best to its principles by embracing a pluralist reality?

Such issues animated the movements and people active during the Progressive Era. Progressivism was the American version of a wave of social reform that appeared in all industrializing countries before World War I. Indeed, American progressives were very aware of the international context of their endeavors. In their youth during the late 1800s, thousands of future progressive scholars and activists studied in Germany, then considered the most innovative center for public administration and social science. They attended conferences in and took study trips to Europe and borrowed foreign proposals for settlement houses, unemployment insurance, worker's compensation, urban sanitation, publicly owned utilities, and zoning, to name a few measures. The less appealing aspects of European debates made their way across the Atlantic as well, with Americans drawing upon fashionable notions of race and empire to supplement the country's own racist and expansionist traditions.

Yet as suggested by the term *progressive*—which American reformers came to favor in contrast to European terms such as *social democrat*—Americans from virtually every region and social group remained convinced that the United States was not like decadent, class-ridden Europe. European models needed to be adapted to the exceptional conditions of the American republic. Despite dogged efforts by Eugene Debs and other leaders of the Socialist Party of America to make socialism seem patriotic, the movement never lost its taint of being a foreign import, identified with the millions of European immigrants who arrived in the United States in these years. The anarchism that thrived in pockets around the country was probably even more rooted in American history and culture than socialism, but Americanizers forcefully attacked and discredited these radicals as hopelessly foreign. In international relations, most Americans believed—in spite of the resentment and resistance of those who felt the force of U.S. expansion—that the United States would not be a colonial power but a beacon of economic and political progress.

DIFFUSE AND CONTRADICTORY

The Progressive Era remains a minefield for scholarly interpretation. For one thing, much about the era was not progressive in a sense that later generations would accept. The period featured dismal labor conditions, widespread child labor, and violent strikes. It saw the coalescence of the Jim Crow system of racial oppression, with the acquiescence of the judiciary and the federal government and the support of pseudoscientific racism and eugenics. These years saw the apex of the effort to extinguish Native American tribal lands and cultures. Movements to pressure immigrant groups to Americanize or to stay away gathered steam. Imbued with Victorian moralism and enamored with the new social sciences, progressives regularly sanctioned heavy-handed measures to deal with real or perceived social pathologies, such as juvenile crime, alcohol and drug abuse, sexual misbehavior, and prostitution.

All these tendencies evoked countertendencies; for example, the National Association for the Advancement of Colored People and the Society of American Indians manifested the spirit of the era at least as much as segregation, disfranchisement, and detribalization. Nevertheless, many commentators have made the mistake of assuming that the xenophobic, racist, reactionary, or oppressive movements that thrived in the Progressive Era amounted to the wounded cries of an old order as it was pushed aside by a modern, broadminded, and humane way of organizing society. Figures such as Edward A. Ross and enterprises such as the U.S. Commission on Immigration show how readily progressive social science could provide intellectual respectability to prejudice. *The Birth of a Nation* (1915), the period's most innovative movie, spurred the resurgence of the Ku Klux Klan, which spread its message using modern techniques of mass communication and marketing. Prohibitionists triumphed in 1919 by tying up-to-date organization and public relations to a vision of an uplifted moral order, a version of women's and children's rights, and widespread hostility to business power. One of the most formidable cultural movements of 20th-century America, Protestant fundamentalism, emerged partly as a reaction to the religious modernism and Social Gospel mindset that underpinned progressivism. But fundamentalism was also a product of the times, as in its sophisticated use of stage spectacle and print and visual media to reach the mass of people. Not only did fiery forms of conservatism thrive throughout the Progressive Era, but less strident conservatisms did as well and arguably emerged as winners from the period's struggles. By 1920, the progressive factions within the Republican Party had clearly lost to the Old Guard, which sought to make the party a bulwark of conservatism. The Democrats moved decisively toward being the more reformist of the major parties, but segregationist Democrats would for decades exert a veto power over challenges to the South's system of racial oppression.

Historians rightly debate how progressive the Progressive Era was. But over the decades the most important historiographic disputes have surrounded the origins and character of the political, social, and intellectual movements that do deserve the "progressive" label. Progressivism was an extraordinarily diffuse phenomenon, full of variations and contradictions. It exemplifies a pattern that scholars sometimes attribute to American reform movements generally: progressivism appeared first in municipalities and states and arguably gained its most durable achievements at that level. Reflecting diverse local and regional circumstances, progressivism never developed a coherent ideology, program, or institutional structure, despite concerted efforts to do so in the 1910s by theorists such as the *New Republic*'s Herbert Croly and Walter Lippmann and activists behind the short-lived Progressive Party. Activists and politicians could easily offer progressive arguments on both sides of major issues. The most famous instance came in 1912, when Theodore Roosevelt's New Nationalism asserted big business should be tolerated and regulated, while Woodrow Wilson's New Freedom countered that big business should be broken up in the name of entrepreneurship and competition. Similarly, progressive-style arguments were made on both sides of prohibition, immigration, women's suffrage, and African American rights.

This diffuse, contradictory quality led historian Peter Filene, in a widely read 1970 article, to assert that the "progressive movement" was a myth that should be discarded. Later historians have agreed there is no specific set of beliefs or policies that make up a coherent definition of progressivism. Yet following a 1982 essay by Daniel Rodgers, they have come to accept that what held together these disparate movements was a common way of interpreting and discussing social and political problems—a set of languages rooted in long-standing American attitudes as well as in the international conversation about the challenges posed by urbanization and industrial capitalism. For Rodgers, the interaction of three themes distinguishes progressivism: one, "antimonopolism," the traditional American hostility to concentrated power, now directed at big business; two, "social bonds," the notion that liberal individualism was a fiction and that people were interdependent and responsible for one another; and three, "efficiency," the idea that people could improve society through the systematic application of new technologies, the new social science, and new methods of management and finance. Though subject to criticism, this model offers a plausible way to discern a common thread in the cacophony of groups, proposals, and personalities identified with progressivism.

ACTIVISM PUBLIC AND PRIVATE

A large part of the confusion stems from progressives' ambivalent stance toward government as a vehicle for social change. The efficiency and social justice impulses within progressivism provided arguments for more and better government: for civil service reform, expanded social services, restructured municipal government, state regulatory agencies, and federal agencies such as the Department of Commerce and Labor, the Children's Bureau, the Federal Reserve, and the Federal Trade Commission. Yet the antimonopoly mindset prompted suspicion of centralized, efficient government as opaque and detached from the public. Progressives worried about how heavily to depend on government when pursuing their agendas. Louis Brandeis and Woodrow Wilson drew upon these fears in developing the New Freedom critique of Roosevelt's New Nationalism. Ironically, Wilson's approach to mobilization for World War I proved the era's main example of heavy-handed government and government cooperation with big business. Nonetheless, this antiauthority impulse played out in movements to open up government and infuse it with direct democracy through devices such as initiatives, referendums, recalls, direct primaries, direct election of senators, and the income tax. Some of the era's most novel ideas, evident in the works of political scientist Charles Beard and urban affairs expert Frederic Howe, addressed how to make government more professional and democratic at the same time.

Students of U.S. history err when they conceive of progressivism as mainly a precursor to the New Deal of the 1930s and the Great Society of the 1960s, both of which were unambiguously pro-government. Progressivism stood for systematic intervention in social and political problems, but progressives tended to pursue such intervention through the public or private sector based on the situation. With only intermittent misgivings, progressives drew on the philanthropy of their supposed demons in big business to underwrite research at universities such as the University of Chicago, think tanks such as the Brookings Institution, museums, hospitals, public health and social services agencies, and similar endeavors. The string of institutions adorned with names such as Carnegie and Rockefeller count among the most influential products of the era.

The wide-ranging activities of women reformers admirably illustrate this flexibility. Reform movements organized and led by women played an enormous role in Progressive Era efforts to improve urban life, labor conditions, education, child welfare, public health, and other issues. In cities across the country, women's reform began with civic or charitable clubs, grouped loosely in such movements as the charity organization societies and eventually organized into the General Federation of Women's Clubs. Another strand of activity began with idealistic, educated young women like Jane Addams and Ellen Gates Starr, who sought private funding to establish settlement houses intended to serve and uplift working-class people. Some of these women, such as Julia Lathrop and Florence Kelley, became convinced that only government could deal with certain issues—for example, factory safety, juvenile justice, and consumer protection—and they sought positions with sympathetic city or state governments, such as that of Illinois in the 1890s under reform Democratic governor John Peter Altgeld.

This sense that government was now managing matters that had been the traditional purview of women led to the notion known as "municipal housekeeping," the idea that women now had to enter politics as an extension of the duties they fulfilled as wives and mothers. Women's groups took the initiative in pressuring city governments to provide adequate social services, health and safety measures, and education. Alhough women could vote in only a few western states, across the country they began campaigning against elected officials who faltered in these areas. These activities reinforced the accelerating campaign for women's suffrage, based on the expectation that legislators and other elected officials would be more receptive to women's issues if women had a voice in government. In the classic Progressive Era pattern, women's reform activities eventually percolated up to the federal level, for example, in the 1912 establishment of the Children's Bureau. Still, women reformers avoided exclusive reliance on government, maintaining independent organizations such as Kelley's National Consumers' League or the Women's Trade Union League. Women organized and sustained one of the largest membership organizations of the era, the Woman's Christian Temperance Union, which did as much to make women's political activism acceptable as it did to promote its signature issue, prohibition.

Progressivism's diffuse character and activists' willingness to work through the public or private sector, depending on circumstances, greatly compound the distortion that plagues every attempt to center the story of a historical era around national politics. One could more adequately discuss the Progressive Era by focusing on regions, states, and cities and ignoring national politics than the reverse. The alliance between Hull House and the social scientists and education reformers of the University of Chicago, the plans for urban beautification that came together in the City Beautiful movement, the social reform mayoralties of Hazen Pingree in Detroit and Tom Johnson in Cleveland, the Wisconsin Idea of using university-based experts to formulate public policy, the Rockefeller-funded campaigns across the South to eradicate hookworm and expand elementary education, Westerners' fierce battles over water, forests, minerals, and railroads—all are absolutely crucial to any understanding of progressivism.

Another major difficulty in characterizing these decades is that the term *Progressive Era* emphasizes the political, public policy, and institutional responses to economic and social change rather than those changes themselves and their impact on people's material situation and personal experience. Industrialism, urbanization, corporate enterprise, large-scale immigration, consumerism, mass communications and marketing, and popular entertainment and culture continued to evolve even as progressive reformers set out to harness them. Although connected to political events, these economic, social, and cultural trends followed a distinct timeline and logic that require a different kind of history. The reform movements and political fights of the Progressive Era make this a decisive time of change in the role of government in society and indeed in American notions of society and social responsibility. Still, most people experienced the Progressive Era at a more intimate level—in the way they made a living and lived, related to one another, educated and amused themselves, in what they ate and the items they used in daily life, and in their thoughts and beliefs about the world and God. With some exceptions, Americans have generally insisted upon regarding economic, technological, and cultural change as inherently progressive and desirable. Americans in the Progressive Era overall remained loyal to this long-standing assumption. The era was noteworthy, however, for the way that disparate groups throughout the country started a conversation over the costs of progress and the ways that society should reckon with these costs. In myriad ways in their own lives, ordinary people had chances to embrace the promise but also confront the defects of this very different age.

THE GILDED AGE AND THE PROGRESSIVE ERA

Scholars have no consensus about when to start and end the Progressive Era. This volume begins in the late 1890s, though with some attention to earlier events, particularly those related to the Panic of 1893 and the ensuing depression, events that reshuffled the country's politics and dramatized the social and economic problems that accompanied development. The book ends in 1917 with U.S. intervention in World War I, which allows coverage of the most significant events commonly associated with the Progressive Era. Some historians extend the period to 1920, to account for the many ways that the war effort and the immediate postwar period were extensions of progressivism. Although most historians accept 1917 or 1920 as plausible ending dates, some note that certain progressive themes, such as women's reform, urban governmental restructuring, and city planning, continued or even came to fruition in the 1920s.

In general, when to start the Progressive Era causes more disputes among historians than when to end it. A case can be made for erasing the conventional distinction between the Gilded Age (ca. 1865–1898) and Progressive Era altogether and thinking in terms of a "long Progressive Era," in the words of historian Rebecca Edwards, that encompasses the entire half century between 1870 and 1920 and treats as one process American industrialization and responses to it. This perspective has the shortcoming that it pushes aside contemporaries' sense that a turning point occurred around the turn of the century. The virtue of pushing back the origins of progressivism is to underscore the fact that all the major social and political ideas and institutional structures that sustained progressivism had their origins in the Gilded Age, a period of intense intellectual and political ferment as well as a wave of cultural institution-building that matched in scope changes in business organization.

The 1862 Morrill Act made a matter of national policy the creation of state universities with a public service orientation. The 1876 founding of Johns Hopkins University signaled the advent of the German innovation of the research university. The universities and traditional liberal arts colleges proved fertile ground for the intense religious and philosophical debates that yielded two indispensable foundations of American progressive thought: the Social Gospel, with its stress on humanitarianism and social service; and pragmatism, with its elevation of empiricism over theory and its call for engagement with the world. The state universities were coeducational from the start, while the private universities only reluctantly added women's divisions. The new women's colleges, such as Vassar, Wellesley, and Bryn Mawr, all founded between 1861 and 1885, fostered lively debates over women's role in society and created networks of dedicated women activists. Secondary and primary education also experienced vigorous movements for restructuring and reinvigoration well before John Dewey's celebrated founding of the laboratory school at the University of Chicago in 1896.

Boston's Public Library (opened 1854), Museum of Fine Arts (founded 1870), and Symphony Orchestra (founded 1881) were early examples of cultural institutions intended to uplift cities and encourage civic pride in communities that even business elites thought were too devoted to mundane commercialism. Impressed by the romantic design principles of famed landscape architect Frederick Law Olmsted, urban civic leaders pushed for parks, boulevards, monuments, and other physical embellishments. By the 1890s, a cadre of professional municipal engineers had emerged, experts in water supply, sewerage, street and bridge construction, and other elements of urban infrastructure. In principle, civil service had gained a foothold at the federal level and in many states and cities, though it struggled against the deep-rooted habits of machine politics and the spoils system. By the 1890s, urban reformers argued that simply defeating the political bosses at the polls was inadequate; they had to find systematic ways to deliver the basic services that bosses provided haphazardly through influence peddling and connections. Durable innovations in municipal government, finance, and city planning, however, only took shape in the Progressive Era proper under the auspices of groups such as the Bureau for Municipal Research, the National Municipal League, and the National Conference on City Planning. Even then, machine politics remained strong, and social reformers like Belle Moskowitz and Frances Perkins realized that they had much to learn from once-despised bosses such as Tammany Hall's Charles Murphy and Alfred Smith about how to listen to and work with the urban poor.

Analogous efforts to upgrade state government and expand state-level business regulation were underway during the late 1800s, especially in northeastern states such as Massachusetts and midwestern states such as Wisconsin, Illinois, and Iowa. Despite the hard-fought partisan battles that seemed to paralyze national politics during the Gilded Age, the federal government expanded steadily, with agencies such as the U.S. Geological Survey, the Agriculture Department, and the Smithsonian Institution transforming Washington into a major center for the natural and social sciences.

Plentiful examples support the view of the Progressive Era as a culmination of movements begun earlier. With the merger that created the National American Woman Suffrage Association in 1890 and the founding of the Anti-Saloon League in 1893, the basic institutions and ideas behind women's suffrage and prohibition were in place. By the mid-1890s, journalists Jacob Riis and Henry Demarest Lloyd, idolized as pioneers by the muckrakers of the 1900s, used metropolitan daily newspapers and mass-circulation magazines to expose poverty, despair, and business abuses. Agrarian movements such as the National Grange, the Farmer's Alliance, and the Populists formulated a range of ideas between the 1870s and the 1890s that progressives later espoused, including railroad regulation, antitrust, banking and tax reform, farmers' cooperatives, and agricultural credit.

POLITICAL UPHEAVAL OF THE 1890s

The roots of progressivism, therefore, had sunk deeply at the local and state level before figures as diverse as Addams, Bryan, La Follette, and Roosevelt pushed progressive issues and ideas into national politics. But national events and personalities structured how people perceived the era and its issues. A narrative of events from a national perspective is therefore in order.

In 1892, with Grover Cleveland regaining the presidency after a four-year hiatus and clear victories in both houses of Congress, the Democrats fully controlled the national government for the first time since the Civil War. Sharp defeats in the 1890 and 1892 elections had staggered the Republicans, while the agrarian-oriented People's (or Populist) Party fretted over its inability to expand from its Great Plains stronghold into the Midwest, as well as its failure to overcome the Democrats' grip—enforced with fraud, race baiting, and violence—on the South. Although the Populists won 22 electoral votes for presidential candidate James B. Weaver in 1892, along with 11 House seats, the party faltered against the duopoly of the Democrats and Republicans.

Democratic optimism collapsed into recrimination when the economic crisis of 1893 hit within months after Cleveland's inauguration. Allied with the party's East-Coast, hard-money wing, Cleveland took heroic measures to maintain the gold standard in the face of massive runs on U.S. gold reserves, a course of action that culminated in the repeal of the Sherman Silver Purchase Act in October 1893 and the administration's 1895 arrangement with a syndicate led by banker J. P. Morgan to replenish dwindling gold reserves. These actions alienated the party's agrarian, inflationist wing; these primarily southern and western Democrats henceforth heaped impressive rancor and abuse on their party's president. Meanwhile, the Cleveland administration responded to depression-related labor strife with a heavy hand and little political sense. In May 1894, the administration sanctioned the forceful breakup of the ragtag unemployment march known as Coxey's Army at the U.S. Capitol. Then in July, the administration sent troops to Chicago to break the Pullman Strike, over the strenuous objections of Illinois governor John Peter Altgeld and Chicago mayor John Hopkins, both pro-labor Democrats.

Regrouping while the Democrats feuded, the Republicans retook both houses of Congress in 1894, their gain of 117 House seats amounting to the largest swing in congressional strength in U.S. history. Sensing opportunity, the Republicans in 1896 put together the best organized national campaign to date. For its presidential nominee, the party turned to Ohio governor William McKinley, a stolid politician identified with the gold standard, the protective tariff, and an evenhanded approach to labor-management conflict. After a stormy convention, the Democrats settled upon 36-year-old Nebraskan William Jennings Bryan, whose justly famed "Cross of Gold" convention speech signaled the arrival of a charismatic new personality. Though anxious that Bryan's emphasis on the currency issue would divert attention from other measures, the Populists agreed to support him, effectively ending their existence as a separate political force. While Bryan toured the country energetically, McKinley and his campaign manager, Cleveland businessman Marcus Hanna, countered with a "front porch" campaign, the steadiness and dignity of which highlighted Republican charges that Bryan was a wild western radical. McKinley won by a clear margin, 51 to 47 percent in the popular vote and 271 to 176 votes in the Electoral College. The strong Republican showing across the Northeast and Midwest and its sweep of all of the 20 largest cities except New Orleans have led historians to label this election a turning point, the Realignment of 1896.

Victory hid for the moment fissures in the Republican coalition. By the mid-1890s, it was clear that the Republicans had repudiated any concrete commitment to African American rights, divesting the party of moral authority while angering hitherto loyal black voters. Like the Democrats, the Republicans struggled with religious divisions in key states such as Ohio and Wisconsin, where evangelical factions drove away voters with efforts to legislate their views on public education and drinking practices. The small-town businessmen and professionals who were the party's pillars had difficulty adapting to the country's increasingly urban, cosmopolitan character. Italian, Polish, and Russian Jewish immigration was too much even for an upper-class sophisticate like Henry Cabot Lodge, once a youthful idealist but in the Progressive Era a voice for extreme anti-immigrant sentiment. Most tellingly, the party failed to shift gears from its customary policy of promoting industrial development to meet new demands for the regulation of big business and the protection of society and the environment from capitalism's abuses.

The last Civil War veteran to become president, McKinley embodied his party's contradictions. With Hanna and secretary George Cortelyou, McKinley developed an innovative administrative and public relations operation on behalf of a presidency with an inert domestic policy. His signal domestic achievements, the Dingley Tariff of 1897 and the Gold Standard Act of 1900, adhered to decades-old Republican dogma. McKinley spoke vaguely of the need to address the trust issue, while Supreme Court decisions eviscerated the Interstate Commerce Commission and the Sherman Antitrust Act. If not for the economy's fortuitous recovery and the unifying effect of the Spanish–American War of 1898, the Republicans might have descended far sooner into the bickering over domestic policy that undermined the party between 1909 and 1912.

McKinley's situation entering the 1900 election campaign illustrated the lucky streak that had over the years prompted political rivals to fume in frustration. Whether by design or accident, he presided over a booming economy with low unemployment and high farm prices. Gold from the Klondike and South Africa poured into the treasury, draining the currency issue of relevance. After some hesitation, the president embraced an imperialist policy that brought the nation the colonies of Puerto Rico, Guam, Hawaii, and the Philippines, along with a protectorate over Cuba. Renominated by the Democrats, Bryan tried to use the anti-imperialist sentiment that had almost led the Senate to refuse to ratify the 1898 Treaty of Paris ending hostilities between Spain and the United States. With the slogan "Full Dinner Pail" on its side, the Republican campaign apparatus overwhelmed Bryan. Traditional voter loyalties helped keep McKinley's victory within bounds, 292 electoral votes to 155 for Bryan and 52 percent of the popular vote to Bryan's 46 percent.

Six months into his second term, McKinley's luck ran out. On September 6, 1901, while shaking hands at the Pan-American Exposition in Buffalo, he received bullet wounds to the chest and stomach that killed him a week later. The shooter, the American-born child of Polish immigrants, Leon Czolgosz, told the police he was Fred Nieman, or "Nobody," appropriate since this ne'er-do-well was so pitiful that even the anarchists to whom he offered allegiance rebuffed him. But Czolgosz's claim to be avenging the poor against the complacent powerful was useful to social and labor reformers, who pointed to him as the price of inaction.

ROOSEVELT AS CATALYST AND SYMBOL

The politician who made the most of this threat of disorder was the slain president's successor, Theodore Roosevelt ("TR"), at 42 the youngest president in the country's history. "That damned cowboy," as Hanna termed him, had received the 1900 vice-presidential nomination in part because Republican leaders recognized the usefulness of his irrepressible personality and status as a hero of the Spanish–American War and in part because the New York State Republican machine wanted to kick its uncontrollable governor upstairs. The most vibrant intellect in the presidency since Thomas Jefferson, Roosevelt had absorbed a swirl of ideas about governmental and social reform during his stints as a New York state assemblyman, federal civil service commissioner, and New York City police commissioner. A major promoter of the self-reliant masculinity embodied in the cowboy myth, he was the first president born in New York City and, in the end, an urban cosmopolite with a streak of noblesse oblige that grated on rivals such as Robert La Follette.

Roosevelt upgraded the symbolic and practical power of the presidency. With innovative news management techniques, he made the presidency into what he called a "bully pulpit," articulating national issues and rallying people. Endorsing the "efficiency" theme within progressivism, he worked to enhance the expertise and professionalism of federal departments, pushing, for example, the creation of the Department of Commerce and Labor and the Bureau of Corporations, along with the expansion of the U.S. Forest Service under his ally, Gifford Pinchot.

Largely agreeing with his party's concession of the South to the Democrats, Roosevelt took few risks to fight segregation and lynching or otherwise appeal to blacks. He instead sought to make permanent the Republican gains of the 1890s among urban workers. In unguarded moments he could spout outrageous racial epithets and stereotypes wrapped in fashionable social Darwinism, but in public he portrayed himself as a friend of hardworking, responsible immigrants, though a scourge of slackers and agitators. An unabashed believer in the superiority of Anglo-American civilization, Roosevelt argued that immigrants should be welcomed if they intended to live by American rules. He made well-publicized appointments of Catholics to government positions and named the first Jewish cabinet officer, Commerce Secretary

Oscar S. Straus. He fought persistently but unsuccessfully to persuade his party's Old Guard to drop its reflexive defense of corporate property and accept an end to judicial interference in strikes.

Roosevelt's personal popularity and careful organization gained him easy reelection in 1904, making him the first former vice president to win election for himself after taking office through a president's death. His 336 to 140 Electoral College victory was the largest margin since Ulysses S. Grant's reelection in 1872, while his 56- to 38-percent popular margin over the little-known New York judge Alton B. Parker was the largest·popular vote landslide to date. This low point in Democratic fortunes contained the seeds of a comeback, because Parker's crushing defeat discredited old-line conservative Democrats, handing initiative to the Bryanites and Democratic progressives.

In the aftermath of Roosevelt's re-election, the simmering Republican quarrel between Old Guard conservatives and "insurgent" progressives came out in the open. The growing division within the party had long hampered Roosevelt's efforts to maneuver reform legislation through Congress. Landmark measures such as the Newlands Reclamation Act of 1902 depended on jerrybuilt alliances with Democrats. Widespread popular pressure to undo Supreme Court decisions hobbling the Interstate Commerce Commission yielded the Elkins Act (1903) and the Hepburn Act (1906). A series of press revelations and official reports of abuses in the patent medicine and meatpacking industries, culminating in Upton Sinclair's sensational novel, *The Jungle* (1906), made possible the Food and Drug and Meat Inspection Acts of 1906, unprecedented moves by the federal government into consumer protection. But many other proposals failed to make headway.

Stymied in Congress, Roosevelt embarked on a controversial effort to expand the president's discretionary power. Repeatedly, he took contentious actions on his own authority, later asking grudgingly, if at all, for congressional approval. The most famous episodes occurred in foreign affairs. Of TR's several moves to reinforce American hegemony in the Caribbean, the most dramatic was his support for the 1903 Panamanian Revolution, after which he deposited the notorious Hay–Bunau-Varilla Treaty with the Senate, daring senators to refuse control of the route of the isthmian canal on the highly favorable terms he had arranged. After winding down the Philippine War,

Roosevelt became concerned that the aggressive expansionism he had hitherto espoused might have caused the United States to overstretch itself in Asia. The search for a stable Asian balance of power explains his intervention in the Russo–Japanese War, leading to the 1905 Portsmouth Conference, in which the United States for the first time mediated a major international conflict (for which Roosevelt won the Nobel Peace Prize). Working with Secretary of State Elihu Root and Secretary of War William Howard Taft, Roosevelt concluded several agreements in which the United States conceded to the Japanese a free hand in Korea and Formosa (today Taiwan) in exchange for Japan's steering clear of the Philippines. In the so-called Gentlemen's Agreement of 1907, Roosevelt assuaged Japanese anger over San Francisco's attempt to segregate Japanese American children in its schools. Congress supported Roosevelt's foreign policy by doubling the Navy's budget, with the 1907–1909 round-the-world voyage of the Great White Fleet showing off the results. More grudgingly, Congress backed the army reforms set in motion by Secretary of War Root.

In domestic affairs, Roosevelt first displayed his penchant for unilateral activism with his mediation of the 1902 Anthracite Coal Strike. To give teeth to his claim that the federal government could discipline "bad" trusts, the president ordered antitrust prosecutions of the railroad merger known as the Northern Securities Company, as well as big businesses with an irresponsible or bullying public reputation, such as the meatpackers and Standard Oil. However, the president's quarrels with the Old Guard became intractable over conservation, the policy innovation closest to his heart. The notion that the federal government had a duty to manage natural resources flew in the face of Republican dogma on the promotion of western development by private enterprise. TR's conservation policy also annoyed well-connected mining, logging, and ranching interests. When Roosevelt and his chief forester, Gifford Pinchot, used whatever legal interpretations they could muster to set aside 200 million acres of forest and other reserves, Congress retaliated in February 1907 by sharply limiting presidential power to create forest reserves. Although Roosevelt defied this legislation as long as he could get away with it, Congress strangled his subsequent initiatives by denying them funding.

REPUBLICAN FEUDING AND
DEMOCRATIC RESURGENCE

In this divisive atmosphere, Roosevelt threw his prestige behind the presidential candidacy of William Howard Taft. The two men had worked together on colonial, foreign policy, and military matters, on which they mostly agreed and in which Taft's judicious temperament and administrative abilities were assets. But Taft still adhered to the moderate positions Roosevelt had held back in 1901–1902, not the more progressive ones he held by 1908, and this difference would soon cause a split between the two men. Yet despite the party's internal divisions and economic anxiety caused by the Panic of 1907, the Republicans in 1908 once again overwhelmed Bryan and the Democrats. Taft received 321 electoral votes to Bryan's 162 and 52 percent of the popular vote to Bryan's 43 percent. For the indefatigable Bryan, this defeat was especially bitter, as he had run a disciplined campaign on a broad platform that appealed to organized labor and urban liberals, as well as small-town residents and farmers on the Great Plains and in the South.

Lacking Roosevelt's political acumen and popular support, President Taft proved unable to contain the insurgent–Old Guard quarrel. Moreover, he recoiled from his predecessor's claims of discretionary power, leading him to fire Gifford Pinchot during the Ballinger–Pinchot controversy of 1909–1910 and to include in the 1911 antitrust prosecution of United States Steel charges stemming from its 1907 acquisition of Tennessee Coal & Iron, a deal that Roosevelt had personally approved. Taft's term saw many achievements for which he received little credit: constitutional amendments sent to the states for the income tax and direct election of senators, the Children's Bureau, the Bureau of Mines, and the National Monetary Commission, statehood for New Mexico and Arizona, and the Mann–Elkins Act of 1910. In four years, Taft's administration undertook more antitrust suits than Roosevelt had in eight. Yet in the bitter fight over the Payne–Aldrich Tariff of 1909, Taft seemed to throw in his lot with conservative protectionists, for which the insurgents never forgave him. In March 1910, insurgent Republicans in the House sided with Democrats to strip the Old Guard speaker Joseph Cannon of many of his powers, a turning point in congressional history. In that November's congressional elections, the Democrats gained 67 seats to take over the House of Representatives for the first time since the 1893–1895 term. They also gained 10 seats in the Senate, effectively handing the balance of power to liberal Democrats and insurgent Republicans.

By June 1910, when Roosevelt returned from an African safari and world tour, pressure was growing for him to drop his no-third-term pledge and run against his old friend. On a western speaking tour, Roosevelt outlined his New Nationalism, a phrase drawn from Herbert Croly's recent book, *The Promise of American Life*. In the hopes of seizing the party while avoiding TR, insurgent Republican leaders in January 1911 organized the National Progressive Republican League (NPRL), the first national movement to adopt the term *progressive*. But the NPRL's preferred candidate, La Follette, fell by the wayside in February 1911 and Roosevelt campaigned vigorously, nearly sweeping those states that had adopted direct primaries for selecting convention delegates. Nevertheless, Taft entered the June 1912 Republican convention with renomination almost assured.

Charging that the convention was rigged, Roosevelt's supporters walked out and formed the National Progressive Party, soon nicknamed the Bull Moose Party. The Progressives attracted a stellar collection of reform activists and writers. Figures such as settlement house leader Jane Addams, juvenile justice advocate Benjamin Lindsey, and journalist Walter Lippmann threw themselves into the Bull Moose cause with an evangelical spirit that reflected the Social Gospel mindset. The Progressives' platform synthesized reform proposals from women's suffrage, direct primaries, and campaign finance reform to abolition of child labor, unemployment insurance, and wages and hours legislation. But few prominent elected officials openly joined the Progressives, though California governor Hiram Johnson agreed to serve as TR's running mate.

Progressive hopes for a breakthrough hinged on the Democrats' nominating a conservative. But the two main Democratic contenders proved to be Speaker of the House Champ Clark, a Bryanite from Missouri, and the eventual nominee after four days of convention balloting, Woodrow Wilson. With a Ph.D. in government from Johns Hopkins University, the first of the new-style professionals to play a prominent role in American politics, he was already familiar because of his prolific writings on history and politics and his eight years as president of Princeton University. His battle against New Jersey's notorious political machines after his 1910 election to the state's governorship made him a plausible presidential candidate. Aloof to the point of hauteur, with a destructive self-righteous streak, Wilson nonetheless had a magnetic quality because of the clarity, eloquence, and grandeur with which this successful professor could explain issues.

With Taft staying in the race partly to deny votes to Roosevelt and progressive Democrats rallying behind Wilson, the Bull Moose candidate realized that his cause was lost in the short run, but in the long-term his goal was to inject the New Nationalism permanently into national politics and perhaps establish the Progressives as a permanent party. Roosevelt and Wilson embarked on a remarkable campaign of ideas with few precedents in U.S. history. To counter the New Nationalism, Wilson worked with famed progressive lawyer Louis Brandeis to devise an alternate version of progressivism that they called the New Freedom. Wilson, earlier a small-government conservative who respected the Southern states-rights tradition, deplored Roosevelt's pro-government, nationalistic program as un-American. To Wilson, reformers should challenge centralization in both business and government and rededicate the country to the old virtues of individualism, competition, and opportunity. In October, Roosevelt added to his legend by delivering a stirring speech after being shot in the chest by a deluded former bartender. But the November election ended as expected. Against three opponents, including socialist Eugene Debs, who ran his strongest race and gained over 6 percent of the vote, Wilson needed only 45 percent of the popular vote to win 435 electoral votes. Roosevelt won six states for 88 electoral votes, with 29 percent of the popular vote. Reduced to spoiler, Republican Taft held only 25 percent of the votes, less than half his 1908 percentage, for a paltry eight electoral votes.

THE WILSON YEARS AND
THE LEGACIES OF PROGRESSIVISM

In control of the presidency and both houses of Congress, the Democrats had an unusual opportunity to implement measures debated in both parties for a decade. Wilson carefully cultivated relations with congressional Democratic leaders, with whom he shared a Southern, small-town, or middle-class heritage. This meeting of the minds accounts for a huge blot on Wilson's record, acquiescence to segregation in federal departments, where open racism had hitherto been resisted. By fall 1914, Democrats had implemented the income tax, established the Federal Reserve and the Federal Trade Commission, and passed the Clayton Antitrust Act. With the Democrats gaining repute as a plausible reform vehicle, the Progressive Party stagnated and then fell apart when Roosevelt refused renomination and rejoined the Republicans in 1916. After the 1914 midterm elections, meanwhile, the majority Democrats allied with progressive Republicans to back experiments in social welfare, labor, and farm support such as the La Follette Seaman's Act, the Keating–Owen Child Labor Act, the Adamson Act, the Federal Highway Act, and the Federal Farm Loan Act.

Perhaps naively, Wilson intended to remain a domestic president. His appointment of Bryan as secretary of state was partly a reward for the Nebraskan's support at a key moment in the nomination fight. In addition, the president meant to signal to grassroots Democrats in the South and West that the new administration intended to break with Roosevelt's blunt assertions of U.S. power and Taft's dollar diplomacy. A dedicated antimilitarist, Bryan promoted arbitration and "cooling-off" treaties. Yet the traditional presumption of superior American virtue prevented Bryan and Wilson from reflecting carefully on why foreigners were often suspicious of U.S. power and motives. They never found a way to square their "missionary" impulse to spread democracy and free enterprise with their espousal of nonintervention and self-determination. Despite repudiating expansionism in a widely noted speech in Mobile, Alabama, in October 1913, Wilson oversaw a significant increase of American military and political intervention in the Caribbean and Latin America, the highlight of which was his futile meddling in the Mexican Revolution.

Wilson's initial response to the outbreak of the Great War in August 1914, the call to be "impartial in thought as well as in action," fit well with the traditional American desire to remain isolated from Great Power quarrels in Europe. It also suited a nation whose ethnic and political divisions made leaning toward the Allies (Britain, France, and Russia) or the Central Powers (Germany, Austria-Hungary, and the Ottoman Empire) potentially explosive. But from the perspective of Berlin, the claim of neutrality defied the reality of multilayered U.S. financial, commercial, and political ties to Great Britain. These connections, along with American unwillingness to challenge the British blockade of Germany, meant that the United States provided the Allies with billions of dollars' worth of goods and credits even before American entry into the war in 1917, while the flow of goods and capital to Germany dwindled to almost nothing. Strict neutralists followed Bryan in insisting that the proper response to the German declaration of a zone of submarine warfare around Great Britain was to interdict the flow of supplies to the Allies and disclaim responsibility for Americans sailing on Allied ships. When after the *Lusitania* incident of 1915 Wilson made implicit threats against Germany in demanding that the Germans indemnify victims and cease submarine warfare, Bryan resigned. After this, pro-Allied voices within the Wilson administration, such as Edward House and Robert Lansing, gained the upper hand, though the actual decision to intervene resulted from the Germans' January 1917 decision to resume unrestricted submarine warfare.

Nevertheless, the Democratic slogan, "He Kept Us Out of War," used in the hard fought campaign of 1916—in which Wilson narrowly won reelection over the moderate Republican Charles Evans Hughes by 49 to 46 percent in the popular vote and 277 to 254 in the Electoral College— was honest when proclaimed. Wilson even expressed concern that this slogan implied a pledge to which he might not be able to stick.

Most progressives, even prominent followers of the pro-war Roosevelt, recoiled from the carnage of the war. They were distressed by the war's destruction of the optimistic prewar movement for international social and political reform. Numerous midwestern and western progressives followed the isolationist-leaning La Follette into outright opposition to Wilson's war policy. Socialists usually agreed with Debs and the radical press in damning the war as a capitalist monstrosity in which workers had no interest. After much soul searching and argument, however, most leading progressives decided to support U.S. involvement. Wilson's Fourteen Points, highlighted by the League of Nations proposal, swayed many progressives, who hoped that by intervening, the United States could turn the war into a fight for international law and collective security. Others saw wartime mobilization and economic planning as an opportunity to institutionalize progressive policies at the federal level. When John Dewey wove such arguments into a pragmatist case for supporting the war, his former student, Randolph Bourne, reacted with a legendary series of essays accusing Dewey and other progressive intellectuals of perverting pragmatism into rationalization. "War is the health of the state," Bourne declared, an irrational, authoritarian force destructive of the humanitarian, tolerant values that underpinned reform.

Events gave some support to both sides of this quarrel. The war produced numerous experiments in federal oversight of resources, the economy, and labor relations. Yet these experiments crumbled amid the intolerant atmosphere that the war unleashed, especially as sanctioned by the Wilson administration's overwrought response to war critics. It is true that other belligerent governments clamped down on dissent even more heavily than the United States did. Still, the war proved not the apotheosis but the end of the American Progressive Era. In other western countries, embroiled in the war longer and in more devastating ways, the fluid social democracy and liberalism of the prewar years gave way to an era of bitter, strident, violent politics on both the left and right.

Despite the Progressive Era's youthful death in war, its concrete results were immense. If one pushes the timeline forward to the New Deal and takes into account private endeavors as well as government action at the local and state as well as national level, then almost every major progressive proposal for governmental, social, labor, and moral/cultural reform saw at least a temporary trial. The noteworthy exception was universal health insurance, which labor and social welfare progressives had insisted was an indispensable element of an effective social welfare system. Yet in practical operation, successful progressive reforms often dramatized the depth of the challenge of creating a more decent urban-industrial society. Far from inspiring civic-mindedness among the public, direct-democracy measures such as initiatives, referendums, and direct primaries nurtured new forms of shortsighted, special interest politics. Machines and well-connected business interests found ways to dominate commission and city manager municipalities. Attempts to ban alcohol and prostitution seemed to strengthen narrow-minded, oppressive elements in society without noticeably improving people's behavior. Even women's suffrage, the most durable progressive reform brought to fruition by World War I, disappointed proponents who expected women to uplift and humanize politics.

In its disappointments as well as achievements, the Progressive Era set an agenda for modern America. It represents the first major wave of efforts to adapt systematically to the country's new status as a pluralist, urban, industrial, and global power. Of continuing relevance are the ways that participants wrestled with the dilemmas inherent in the three themes identified by historian Daniel Rodgers. How does a society balance the individualism and opportunity called for by the antimonopoly ethic against the capacity of large business corporations to spread material prosperity through mass production and mass distribution? How do public and private institutions achieve efficiency and professionalism while remaining comprehensible and accountable to ordinary people? How can a society foster a sense of interdependence and mutual responsibility among people without creating institutions that promote conformity, control, and repression? While progressive solutions to these dilemmas were often ineffective, one has to credit the reform activists and thinkers of the Progressive Era for opening discussion of these daunting issues and persistently wrestling with them.

The Dictionary

– A –

ABBOTT, EDITH (1876–1957) AND GRACE (1878–1939). Social scientists and reformers. Born in Nebraska, the Abbott sisters exemplified the reform-minded **New Woman** of the era. At the **University of Chicago**, Edith earned a doctorate in economics (1905), Grace a master's degree in political science (1909). The sisters lived at **Hull House** and participated in **reform movements** concerned with labor, industry, **juvenile** justice, **immigration**, and **women**'s **suffrage**. Edith and **Sophonisba Breckinridge** helped professionalize social work by founding the School of Social Service Administration at the University of Chicago in 1920. Grace headed the Immigrants' Protective League and was involved in the **Women's Trade Union League** and **child labor** and penal reform. In 1917, she worked for the **Children's Bureau**, becoming its director in 1921.

ABBOTT, LYMAN (1835–1922). Editor and minister. Born in Massachusetts, he graduated from New York University in 1853 and practiced law before his ordination as a Congregational minister in 1860. He became an exponent of theological **modernism** and the **Social Gospel** after he succeeded Henry Ward Beecher at Brooklyn's Plymouth Church in 1888. He left his pulpit in 1899 to become editor of the *Outlook*, a liberal Protestant magazine. In books such as *The Theology of an Evolutionist* (1897), Abbott argued for the compatibility of Darwinism and Christianity.

ABBOTT, ROBERT S. (1868–1940). Editor and civil rights activist. Born in Georgia, Abbott graduated from the Hampton Institute (1896) before moving to Chicago, where he graduated from Kent

1

College of Law (1899), the only **African American** in his class. In 1905, after several attempts at a legal career, he founded the *Chicago Defender* and made it one of the nation's most popular black newspapers. Abbott proved an effective, creative publisher, a dauntless champion of African Americans, and an important promoter of the **Great Migration**. *See also* JOURNALISM.

ABIKO, KYUTARO (1865–1936). Publisher and labor contractor. After converting to Christianity, Abiko moved from Japan to the United States in 1885 and attended the University of California. In the 1890s, he ran one of the largest labor-contracting agencies in California and published the nation's most widely read Japanese-language newspaper. Despite legal obstacles to Asian naturalization, Abiko encouraged Japanese **immigrants** to take up permanent residence and **Americanize** themselves. Before the passage of the **Alien Land Act** in 1913, he bought large tracts of California farmland and built three colonies for Japanese migrants.

ACADEMIC ASSOCIATIONS. By the late 1800s, the growing acceptance of the Ph.D. as a qualification for **university** professors, the spread of research universities, and the belief that social science could provide an empirical foundation for social reform prompted the formation of professional associations for academics. Social science groups such as the American Historical Association (founded in 1884), the American Anthropological Association (1902), the American Political Science Association (1903), and the American Sociological Society (1905), set standards for scholarship that they disseminated through conferences and journals. An analogous movement in the humanities resulted in groups such as the Modern Language Association (1883) and the American Philosophical Association (1900). The American Chemical Society (1876) was the first discipline-based society in the natural sciences; between 1888 and 1899 organizations emerged in anatomy, botany, mathematics, microbiology, physics, physiology, and zoology.

Many academic associations began with activist ambitions. For example, in the founding platform of the American Economic Association (AEA; 1884), **Richard T. Ely** questioned laissez-faire economics and praised government intervention in the **economy**.

Typical of most academic societies, the AEA soon found that members preferred a focus on disciplinary issues to engagement in public controversy. Similarly, whereas some prominent members of the American Historical Association used history to serve a **progressive** political agenda, the organization concentrated on raising standards for research and education and improving infrastructure that supported historical research, for example, **J. Franklin Jameson**'s efforts in forming the National Archives. *See also* INTELLECTUAL.

ADAMS, BROOKS (1848–1927). Lawyer and historian. Born in Massachusetts, he graduated from Harvard College (1870), studied at Harvard Law School, practiced law in Boston (1872–81), and engaged in diplomacy and reform politics before devoting himself to writing. Like his older brother, **Henry Adams**, he produced ambitious books, the best known being *The Law of Civilization and Decay* (1895), which sought universal historical principles and took a jaundiced view of pluralist democracy and industrial capitalism. He contrasted the martial virtues of the Middle Ages with the flaccid materialism of his times, which he blamed on the excessive influence of bankers and **Jews**. In *America's Economic Supremacy* (1900) and *The New Empire* (1902), he offered a historical justification for **imperialism** as a vehicle for regenerating American culture.

ADAMS, HENRY (1838–1918). Historian and cultural theorist. Great-grandson of the second president and grandson of the sixth, a Harvard College graduate (1858), Adams as a youth embarked on a career in **journalism** and civic affairs, before turning to history and **literature**. He taught medieval history at Harvard and edited the *North American Review* before moving in the 1870s to Washington, D.C. His nine-volume *History of the United States of America during the Administrations of Thomas Jefferson and James Madison* (1889–91) was a landmark in the transition from gentlemanly to professional history, and he served as president of the American Historical Association in 1894.

In the 1890s, despondent over the 1885 suicide of his wife, Adams embarked with his friend, artist John La Farge, on a round-the-world trip, which he followed with periods of study in France. His 1904 work, *Mont-Saint Michel and Chartres*, inspired American interest in medieval culture. His memorable autobiography, *The Education of Henry Adams* (privately printed, 1907, commercially published, 1918), is a grand and at times brooding meditation on modern society. In the political chapters of *Education,* the satirical novel *Democracy* (1880), and journalism and essays, Adams helped to create the image of a venal Gilded Age to which **progressive** reformers reacted.

ADAMS, HENRY CARTER (1852–1921). Economist. From a minister's family in Iowa, with training at Johns Hopkins University and in Berlin, Adams was prominent among a generation of economists who rejected neoclassicism for an institutionalist, policy-oriented approach. After pro-labor views led to his dismissal from Cornell University in 1887, Adams spent his career at the University of Michigan and as head statistician for the **Interstate Commerce Commission**, for which he developed statistical measures used to regulate railroad rates. Adams developed the notion of a "natural monopoly" that provides a rationale for the regulation or public ownership of **utilities**.

ADAMSON ACT (1916). Named for Representative William Adamson, a Georgia **Democrat**, this early example of federal labor legislation was passed in September 1916 under threat of a nationwide railway strike. It mandated the **eight-hour workday** on interstate railroads. The Supreme Court upheld the law in *Wilson v. New* (1917) and thereby established the authority of Congress to pass wages and hours legislation.

ADDAMS, JANE (1860–1935). Social reformer and peace activist. Born in Illinois to a wealthy, reform-minded family, Addams earned the first bachelor's degree given by Rockford Female Seminary in 1881 but then confronted the limits on **women** who wished to pursue professional careers. During a trip to London, she and **Ellen Gates Starr** visited London's pioneer **settlement house**, Toynbee Hall, which inspired the pair to open **Hull House** in one of Chicago's poorest neighborhoods. They soon abandoned their initial goal of cultural uplift in favor of providing social services and advocating political and social reform. In part following the lead of Hull House colleague **Florence Kelley**, Addams gradually involved herself in local, regional, and national campaigns to improve labor relations, eliminate

child labor, assist and **Americanize immigrants**, improve waste removal, abate pollution, set up **juvenile courts**, build **playgrounds**, and abolish **prostitution**, among other projects.

A model for many **New Women** of the early 20th century, Addams played a key role in institutionalizing women's **reform movements** and gaining women professional, salaried positions in new municipal, state, and federal agencies. She served as the first woman president of the **National Conference of Charities and Correction**, a vice president of the **National American Woman Suffrage Association**, a founding member of the **National Association for the Advancement of Colored People**, and an influential member of the **Women's Trade Union League**. She had an important role in the establishment of the **Children's Bureau** and the appointment of **Julia Lathrop** to head the agency. Although at times radical in her approach to social problems, Addams exemplified the selfless, maternal reformer, earning the sobriquet "Saint Jane." Like many female reformers of this era, she never married and had her closest relationships with other women. She wrote her autobiography, *Twenty Years at Hull House* (1910), and was active in **Theodore Roosevelt**'s **Progressive Party**. A pacifist, she endured criticism during World War I for opposing U.S. participation in the war. In 1931, she became the first American woman to win a Nobel Peace Prize.

ADLER, FELIX (1851–1933). Philosopher and reformer. Born in Germany, son of a Reform rabbi who emigrated in 1857 to take the pulpit at New York's prestigious Temple Emanu-El, Adler graduated from Columbia College (1870) and returned to Germany to study for the rabbinate. Exposure to the new biblical criticism at the University of Heidelberg, where he earned a Ph.D. (1873), led him to question even the rationalist theology of the Reform movement. In 1874, Adler left the rabbinate for a professorship of Hebrew literature first at Cornell University, then at Columbia University (1902–33). He gave his thinking institutional form in the Ethical Culture Society, which he founded in 1876. A **Jewish** analogue to more secular versions of the Protestant **Social Gospel**, Ethical Culture stressed moral action as the core of all religion. Though Adler's movement remained small, it became visible in **reform movements**, especially in New York City, where it influenced the formation of Jewish **intellectual** liberalism. *See also* MODERNISM; WISE, STEPHEN S.

ADOLESCENCE. Changes in **education**, employment, and attitudes toward children encouraged a new view of youth as a distinct period of life, especially for boys. Middle-class parents had fewer children, and prosperous families rarely expected them to contribute to the family income from an early age. Children spent a longer time in school as attendance at **high school** and college became more common. Longer schooling heightened age **segregation** while diminishing gender segregation, as girls and boys attended school with each other or in affiliated institutions. While the age of social maturity rose, the age of physical maturity fell thanks to better nutrition and health care and less strenuous work. Changes in the **economy** and employment patterns encouraged both **women** and men to delay marriage and parenthood. Among working-class populations of all races, these changes followed different patterns, with the early end of formal education and entry into the workforce obviously much more common.

The concept of adolescence, particularly as formulated by pioneering psychologist **G. Stanley Hall** in his two-volume work, *Adolescence* (1904–05), focused attention on the teen years as a difficult time characterized by moral immaturity and powerful sexual urges. Hall offered a new model for leading white children into responsible, moral adulthood. Recasting existing mores in a scientific language, Hall drew on the then-fashionable theory of "recapitulation" to argue that children, especially boys, developed from primitives into civilized people. Childhood "savagery" was essential to fortifying boys' moral fiber and capacity for leadership; girls, in contrast, should focus on their role as mothers and abandon higher education and employment. Maturity required sublimation of savage instincts in service to civilized values and institutions, a view later identified with Austrian psychologist Sigmund Freud. This notion of adolescence assumed that nonwhites never achieved full, moral maturity and therefore deserved their social subordination. The formulation of adolescence was closely linked to the social hygiene and **eugenics** movements as well as Christian men's movements like the **Young Men's Christian Association**. The **Boy Scouts** and organized sports similarly attempted to help boys navigate these difficult years. **Department stores** and **advertising** firms identified adolescents as a new market by 1900. Finally, the concept also reflected the professionalization of psychology as a field of study and therapeutic practice.

ADVERTISING. For much of the 19th century, advertising was often disreputable for its association with patent medicines and other scams. Advertisers functioned as brokers, providing space in newspapers and magazines to business. By 1890, advertising agencies such as N. W. Ayer and J. Walter Thompson, now prestigious businesses, created and designed publicity campaigns and bought space in newspapers and **mass-circulation magazines**. Advertising went hand-in-hand with the emergence of a national **economy** increasingly reliant on consumer goods, the decline of home production of food and clothing, and the branding and packaging of goods formerly sold in bulk. New or newly packaged foods, such as breakfast cereals, and personal care products, like soaps, **cosmetics**, and the new **Gillette safety razor**, dominated early national advertising. Although expenditures on advertising rose rapidly in the early 20th century, estimates of just how much money businesses spent are uncertain. By 1910, spending on advertising reached an estimated $600 million per year, and that amount doubled by about 1925. Some businessmen, notably **Henry Ford**, resisted advertising because of its inherent deceptiveness, but national markets and the willingness of others to advertise soon forced him to put significant resources into publicity. Antibillboard campaigns met with mixed success. The ubiquity of advertising by 1920 was one of the signs of the erosion of 19th-century fears about the market and the emergence of a new culture of consumption. *See also* CHAIN STORES; DEPARTMENT STORES; MAIL ORDER.

AFRICAN AMERICANS. The years between 1890 and 1920, labeled by some later scholars as the nadir of American race relations, saw the **disfranchisement** of black men by southern states and the **Supreme Court**'s affirmation of racial **segregation** in *Plessy v. Ferguson* (1896). **Lynching** and **race riots** were the most visible forms of violence that white supremacists used to enforce African American subordination. Racial inequities in law enforcement and sentencing condemned large numbers of African American men to prisons or to brutal, state-run

convict leasing programs. Discrimination in **education**, hiring, promotion, and access to credit; the sharecropping system; and the vicissitudes of global markets in cotton, tobacco, and sugar made it extremely difficult for the majority to escape from poverty.

African Americans did not suffer these outrages quietly. They founded national civil rights organizations such as the **National Association of Colored Women** (1896), the **National Association for the Advancement of Colored People (NAACP)** (1910), and the **Urban League** (1911). Protestant churches organized resistance to racism at the local, regional, and national levels. Black women, unwelcome in many white women's organizations, battled racism, founded **settlement houses**, lobbied for **prohibition** and **women**'s **suffrage**, and ran **public health** and community improvement projects. **Ida B. Wells-Barnett** risked her life to combat lynching. Barred from most white-controlled colleges and **universities**, black Americans developed institutions of higher education such as Howard University (1867), **Tuskegee Institute** (1881), and Spelman College (1881), as well as professional organizations such as the **National Medical Association**. Publications like the *Chicago Defender*, the *Pittsburgh Courier*, the *New York Age*, and the NAACP magazine *The Crisis* circulated nationally. The best-known black leader of the era, **Booker T. Washington**, gained national influence based on relationships with white philanthropists and politicians.

Individually and as families, black Americans responded to the lack of opportunity and heightened racism in the South, where the majority still lived in 1890, by moving to cities in the South and then to the Northeast and Midwest. The **Great Migration** out of the South peaked during World War I. Forced into run-down ghettoes by discriminatory hiring and leasing, African Americans also faced violence from angry white neighbors. Nevertheless, outside the South, African American men could vote and greater tolerance existed for political mobilization. Critics of Washington's Tuskegee Machine, like the *Boston Guardian* editor **William Monroe Trotter** and sociologist **W. E. B. Du Bois** insisted that the pursuit of civil rights have equal priority with economic advancement. Staunch members of the **Republican Party** in the face of the **Democratic Party**'s virulent white supremacy, many black Americans took a strong interest in European **imperialism** in Africa and U.S. expansion in the

Caribbean and the Pacific. Several groups promoted migration to western Africa, **Haiti**, or Mexico as a solution to intractable American racism, but only small numbers left the United States. *See also* ATLANTA COMPROMISE; ATLANTA RIOT; BROWNSVILLE RAID; GRANDFATHER CLAUSE; LITERACY TESTS; POLL TAX; REFORM MOVEMENTS; SPRINGFIELD RIOT; WHITE PRIMARY; *WILLIAMS V. MISSISSIPPI.*

AGUINALDO Y FAMY, EMILIO (1869–1964). Filipino independence leader. Born in a Chinese-mestizo landowning family, Aguinaldo was in exile in Singapore for anti-Spanish activities at the outbreak of the **Spanish–American War** in April 1898. Inconclusive negotiations with American officials led Aguinaldo to believe that the United States would support independence in exchange for help against the Spanish. Transported home on an American ship, he organized a Filipino army allied at first with U.S. forces. Outraged by the U.S. decision to annex the archipelago, Aguinaldo had himself inaugurated president of a Philippine Republic and led the liberation movement during the **Philippine–American War**. Accused of favoring fellow Tagalogs over other ethnic groups and ordering rivals murdered, he proved unable to hold the fragmented independence movement together. Captured by **Frederick Funston** in March 1901, Aguinaldo proclaimed an end to resistance, but fighting continued for another year. He remained a symbol of Filipino nationalism despite a failed campaign for the presidency in 1935 and accusations that he collaborated with Japan during World War II.

ALASKA BOUNDARY DISPUTE. The Alaska Gold Rush of the 1890s highlighted the longstanding uncertainty about the southeastern boundary of Alaska, which controlled sea access to the gold fields in Canada's Klondike region. At stake were not just the gold but also customs fees and licenses, law enforcement, and railroad projects. Complicating the conflict was Canadian impatience with Great Britain's continued oversight of its former colony's **foreign policy**. Secretary of State **John Hay** rejected Canada's offer to arbitrate the claim but arranged a modus vivendi to avoid a crisis during President **William McKinley**'s administration. In March 1902, President **Theodore Roosevelt** sent troops to assert the American interpretation of the boundary. To save face, Britain negotiated the Convention of 1903 with Hay, and Canada agreed to an **arbitration** commission, which in 1903 decided in favor of the U.S. claim despite Canadian protest. The dispute strengthened Anglo–American cooperation at the expense of Canadian claims. *See also* BOUNDARY WATERS TREATY.

ALDRICH, NELSON W. (1841–1915). Politician. Born into a Rhode Island farm family, this wholesale grocer served in the Civil War before becoming active in **Republican Party** politics. Elected to the House of Representatives (1879–81), he also served five terms as a U.S. Senator (1881–1911). After the **Realignment of 1896** gave the Republicans control of Congress, he joined William B. Allison, O. H. Platt, and J. C. Spooner in **modernizing** the party's leadership structure and reorganizing the Senate's committees and legislative procedures. Washington's most formidable voice for big business, with lucrative investments in banking, manufacturing, and **utilities**, Aldrich helped provoke the split between his party's **Old Guard** and the **Insurgents** by resisting railroad regulation measures such as the **Hepburn Act** and defending the protectionism of the **Payne–Aldrich Tariff**. As chair of the Senate Finance Committee, he oversaw the **Gold Standard Act** and the **Aldrich–Vreeland Act**. As chair of the National Monetary Commission, he formulated the central banking proposal that eventually produced the **Federal Reserve Act**. The marriage of his daughter, Abby, to John D. Rockefeller Jr. symbolized the intertwining of corporate capital and the political establishment. David Graham Phillips's "Treason of the Senate" (1906) impugned (probably unfairly) Aldrich's integrity as well as his politics.

ALDRICH–VREELAND ACT (1908). Named for **Nelson Aldrich** and New York congressman Edward Vreeland, this measure, a response to the **Panic of 1907**, made it easier for banks to expand the supply of currency during financial emergencies. It also established the National Monetary Commission, which drafted plans for what became the **Federal Reserve**. *See also* MONEY TRUST.

ALIEN LAND ACT. In 1913, California, home to most of the nation's Asian **immigrants**, passed a law prohibiting land ownership by "aliens ineligible to citizenship." This phrase applied exclusively to immigrants from Asia and the Indian subcontinent because of a long series of U.S. laws and court decisions limiting naturalization to white immigrants and African-descended people. Japanese truck farmers were the target of California's law, but it also prevented Chinese, Korean, and Indian immigrants from owning land. The state later enacted another law that prevented Asian immigrants from owning and leasing land in the name of American-born children or through corporations. A dozen other states enacted similar laws. No other group of immigrants faced such restrictions on naturalization or land ownership.

AMATEUR ATHLETIC UNION (AAU). Founded in 1888 amid disputes over amateur versus professional **athletics**, the AAU served as the governing body for nonprofessional sports such as track and field, cycling, boxing, fencing, gymnastics, and wrestling. **Basketball** came into its purview in 1895, and other sports joined early in the 20th century. The **National Collegiate Athletic Association**, founded to regulate **football**, came into conflict with the AAU about definitions of amateurism, control over sports and competitors, and management of U.S. participation in the Olympic Games, which began in 1896. The AAU stripped track star **Jim Thorpe** of medals he won in the 1912 Olympics because he had played professional **baseball**.

AMERICAN ASSOCIATION FOR LABOR LEGISLATION (AALL). Formed in 1905 as an American branch of the International Association for Labor Legislation, this group organized the efforts of labor economists such as **Adna Ferrin Weber**, **John R. Commons**, and **Isaac M. Rubinow** to draft and lobby for state and federal laws on **workers' compensation** and other **social insurance** measures. With 3,600 members on the eve of World War I, the AALL engaged in a bold but failed campaign to have states adopt universal health insurance laws, based on models from Germany and Britain. *See also* REFORM MOVEMENTS.

AMERICAN ASSOCIATION OF UNIVERSITY PROFESSORS (AAUP). Founded in 1915, this organization sought to bolster the autonomy of professors and their control over academic affairs. The

AAUP championed the right of academics to do research and teach according to professional standards set by **academic associations** rather than by college presidents or boards of trustees. The defense of expertise contributed to the decline of religious and political tests for employment at colleges and **universities**. The AAUP supported the widely shared view that students' minds were immature and professors should be moderate and scientific, avoiding direct political involvement. *See also* DEWEY, JOHN; INTELLECTUAL; ROSS, EDWARD ALSWORTH.

AMERICAN ASSOCIATION OF UNIVERSITY WOMEN. Founded as the Association of Collegiate Alumnae by Marion Talbot in 1882, this organization aimed to raise standards for **women**'s **education**, increase teachers' salaries, and provide fellowships for women who wanted to pursue graduate work in Europe. It also engaged in research and publicity to refute the popular notion that higher education undermined women's reproductive health and led to **race suicide** by making white women reluctant to marry and have children. In the 20th century, the Association of Collegiate Alumnae broadened its campaign against sex discrimination, beginning with a 1913 report on pay equity and job classifications in the federal civil service. In 1921, the Association of Collegiate Alumnae merged with the Southern Association of College Women and renamed itself the American Association of University Women. *See also* NEW WOMAN; UNIVERSITY

AMERICAN CIVIC ASSOCIATION (ACA). Founded in 1904 from the merger of two smaller groups dedicated to parks and urban beautification, this group promoted **City Beautiful** planning and wilderness preservation. Though always small, ACA became familiar through its indefatigable leader, J. Horace McFarland (1859–1948), a horticultural writer and publisher who gave dozens of speeches annually, advised city improvement groups, and produced numerous pamphlets, books, and articles, including a column, "Beautiful America," in the *Ladies' Home Journal*. The ACA lobbied for preservation of Niagara Falls, the Everglades, and **Hetch Hetchy Valley**, as well as for establishment of the **National Park Service**. *See also* CONSERVATION.

AMERICAN FEDERATION OF LABOR (AFL). Founded in 1886, the AFL consisted of affiliated **labor unions** set up for the most part by craft rather than by industry. This structure reflected the sense of status among the white, skilled workers who composed the bulk of membership, as well as the strategy of President **Samuel Gompers** to construct a durable movement around those workers who were easiest to organize and hardest to replace. The cost, as Gompers understood, was weakness among semiskilled workers in mass-production industries. A focus on skilled workers also made the AFL hostile to organizing **women, African Americans**, and new **immigrants**. The AFL's cautious approach enabled it to survive defeats such as the Homestead Strike, internal feuds over **socialism**, and crippling unemployment after the Panic of 1893. During the prosperous decade after 1897, membership expanded from 450,000 in 50 affiliated unions to over two million in one hundred affiliates. By World War I, the AFL represented about 80 percent of organized workers, but less than 10 percent of American wage earners belonged to unions.

In theory, the AFL adhered to "pure and simple" or "business" unionism, meaning it avoided partisan and electoral politics. In practice, local trades councils had long exerted influence in municipal politics. On a national level, growing membership and a more favorable political climate after the 1902 **Anthracite Coal Strike** emboldened the AFL to exert pressure in national elections. Although many issues appeared in **Labor's Bill of Grievances**, the overriding concern was to limit federal court injunctions against strikes. Against the wishes of **Theodore Roosevelt** and the **Republican progressives**, the Republican Party refused to make concrete promises to labor in its platforms. This cold shoulder pushed the AFL toward the **Democratic Party** of **William Jennings Bryan** and **Woodrow Wilson**. The Wilson administration rewarded labor with such measures as the **Clayton Antitrust Act** and the **Adamson Act**. During World War I, Gompers steered the AFL into open cooperation with federal agencies, and membership rose to more than four million between 1916 and 1918, while overall unionization grew to over five million. *See also* INTERNATIONAL LADIES' GARMENT WORKERS' UNION; MITCHELL, JOHN; NATIONAL CIVIC FEDERATION; UNITED MINE WORKERS OF AMERICA.

AMERICAN MEDICAL ASSOCIATION (AMA). Founded in the 1840s, the AMA had long worked to improve medical **education** and regulate the ranks of physicians. At the turn of the century, the combination of changes in medical education, better understanding of the causes of many diseases (germ theory), improved treatments for some diseases, and substantial funding from the **Carnegie Foundation** enabled the AMA to dominate mainstream medicine in the United States. After reorganizing in 1901, the AMA enrolled a majority of physicians as members, numbering 50,000 by 1906. Its newly founded Council on Medical Education began inspecting medical schools in 1906–07. In 1910, the AMA published the **Flexner Report**, a study of medical education that provoked another round of reforms. The AMA played a key role in delegitimizing a range of medical practitioners, from homeopathic physicians to midwives. By imposing higher educational standards and demanding laboratory facilities and training in the new fields of pathology and bacteriology, the AMA contributed to the decline of the number of medical schools and physicians, making doctors' income and status rise significantly. It advocated creation of local and state **public health** boards, participated in efforts to regulate access to **birth control** and criminalize abortion, and opposed the **American Association for Labor Legislation**'s campaign for universal health insurance.

AMERICAN SOCIAL HYGIENE ASSOCIATION (ASHA). Founded in 1913 and underwritten by **John D. Rockefeller**, the ASHA merged physician **Prince Morrow**'s American Federation for Sex Hygiene, a **public health** organization dedicated to preventing sexually transmitted diseases (STDs), with the American Vigilance Association, which focused on abolishing **prostitution**. The new group sponsored municipal vice investigations, devised a model antiprostitution ordinance, funded research on STDs, and promoted sex **education** in schools. Members of ASHA divided sharply between those who favored educating the public about the transmission of STDs and those who advocated suppressing all information about **sexuality**.

AMERICAN SOCIETY OF COMPOSERS, AUTHORS, AND PUBLISHERS (ASCAP). Founded in 1914 largely by publisher

George Maxwell and composer Victor Herbert, this organization sought to protect musical copyright and ensure that songwriters, composers, and **music** publishers received royalties for performances of their work. For an annual fee, concert hall managers and band leaders signed licensing agreements with ASCAP, which distributed revenues to its members. During the 1920s, the popularity of **phonograph** records and radio made ASCAP a formidable institution without whose authorization little music could be recorded or broadcast.

AMERICAN SOCIETY OF EQUITY (ASE). Founded in Indianapolis in 1902, this group, like the **National Farmers' Union**, attempted to organize selling **cooperatives**. Active in the tobacco regions of Kentucky and Tennessee during the **Black Patch War**, its most visible successes occurred in the Midwest and on the plains. By 1920 membership reached 40,000 in Wisconsin, where **Robert M. La Follette**'s **progressive Republicans** enacted **antitrust** exemptions for ASE's dairy marketing associations. It organized an Equity Cooperative Organization to control the marketing of spring wheat on the Minneapolis exchange for farmers in Minnesota, the Dakotas, and Wisconsin, an effort that collapsed in the agricultural depression of the early 1920s.

AMERICAN TELEPHONE AND TELEGRAPH COMPANY (AT&T). This telecommunications giant began in 1885 as the long-distance subsidiary of the original Bell Telephone Company. In 1889, AT&T became the parent of the Bell system, which included local operating companies and Western Electric, the telephone equipment manufacturer. When Alexander Graham Bell's patents expired in the 1890s, regional competitors emerged, with the result that by 1907, AT&T controlled only half of the nation's six million telephones. Connections between regional systems remained ill-coordinated. That year, a syndicate led by **J. P. Morgan** gained control of AT&T and installed as president **Theodore N. Vail**, who had left the company in the 1880s, frustrated over lack of progress toward a universal system under AT&T control.

Vail's relentless campaign to buy out or undercut the independents provoked the threat of **antitrust** prosecution by 1913, leading to an agreement between AT&T and the administration of President **Woodrow Wilson** that the company would cease attacks on independent regional companies and give them full access to AT&T's national wires. AT&T's local operating subsidiaries submitted to state regulation of prices, service, and profits. As a regulated quasi-monopoly, AT&T developed by the early 1920s into the country's largest corporation, a leader in radio as well as telecommunications research. A policy of hiring only female operators also rendered AT&T the country's largest employer of **women**. *See also* INDUSTRIAL RESEARCH LABORATORIES; WELFARE CAPITALISM.

AMERICAN TOBACCO COMPANY. *See* DUKE, JAMES BUCHANAN.

AMERICAN UNION AGAINST MILITARISM (AUAM). In response to signs that the martial spirit of World War I had crossed the Atlantic, a group of **progressive** reformers formed an "anti-militarism" or "anti-**preparedness**" committee that by 1916 called itself the American Union against Militarism. Founders included Paul Kellogg of *Survey*, **Florence Kelley**, and reform publisher **Oswald Garrison Villard**. **Lillian Wald** served as chair, and **Crystal Eastman** as executive secretary. After the United States entered the war in April 1917, divisions between resolute pacifists and qualified supporters of intervention led to AUAM's decline, but before then the activities of its Civil Liberties Bureau laid the foundation for the American Civil Liberties Union.

AMERICANISM. The diverse uses of this term reflected a wide-ranging debate over national identity at a time when emigration from Europe and Asia and class conflict reached historic highs. Groups such as the American Protective Association and the **Ku Klux Klan** used "Americanism" to condemn Catholic and **Jewish** immigrants as inassimilable or insist that they adopt an American culture imagined to be Protestant, white, and centered on small-town, agrarian mores. The appeal of this sense of the term intensified in the years just before and during World War I, when nativist groups gained the support of the federal government. Business leaders used the notion to portray **anarchism**, **socialism**, and labor unions as un-American, attributing them to foreign-born radical workers. Labor activists such as **Eugene V. Debs** in turn condemned wealthy industrialists and corporations as un-American because they were undemocratic elitists.

In contrast, reformers and academics conceived of Americanism as the result of cultural changes whereby obsolete European traditions gave way to **progressive** American practices, but they did not necessarily condemn the cultures of ethnic minorities as inferior or degraded. Immigrant advocates of assimilation such as **Abraham Cahan**, **Mary Antin**, and **Kyutaro Abiko** often encouraged newcomers to adopt the values of their new home without scorning their origins. Left **intellectuals** like **Horace Kallen** used the term to praise the putative openness of the United States to the creative coexistence of multiple cultures within a single nation. Americanism also played a role in debates about literature and the arts, as intellectuals such as **Van Wyck Brooks** and **Randolph Bourne** called for **modernist** arts growing organically from American culture, while others, particularly those centered in New York City's **Greenwich Village**, continued to see Europe as the origin of artistic innovation.

The term *Americanism* could also refer to the view of liberal prelates within the Roman Catholic Church, most prominently Archbishop **John Ireland** and Cardinal **James Gibbons**, that the church should adapt to suit American notions of democracy, openness, and progress. Conservative opponents, who saw the Americanists as undermining the distinctiveness of Catholic practice and teaching, succeeded in 1899 in winning from the Vatican an encyclical condemning "Americanism" by name, which contributed to conservative dominance in the American Catholic Church for the next half-century. *See also* ANTI-CATHOLICISM; IMMIGRATION; *THE MELTING POT*; PLURALISM; SOCIAL DARWINISM.

AMERICANIZATION. Most native-born Americans believed that **immigrants** and **Native Americans** needed to abandon their native cultures and embrace American ways. People disagreed on what exactly Americanization meant, but it included everything from instruction on the Constitution and the political system to classes on how to work, eat, worship, dress, marry, and raise children the way white, native-born, Protestant Americans supposedly did. A U.S. version of the international idea of **modernization**, it assumed the superiority of an idealized Anglo-American culture over other family forms, faiths, and identities. Often it incorporated a hagiographic national history to promote patriotism while discouraging **socialism**, **anarchism**, and other forms of political dissent. Large corporations, such as the **Ford Motor Company**, undertook to Americanize their immigrant employees. **Settlement house** workers, the **Boy Scouts**, **Girl Scouts**, and **compulsory education** focused on Americanizing children. New Jersey was the first state to authorize public school evening classes in citizenship, an idea supported by the **U.S. Chamber of Commerce** and the **U.S. Department of Labor** by 1914 and implemented in 1,200 cities. Lawyer and sociologist **Frances Kellor** established the National Americanization Committee to pursue this goal.

At the same time, Americanization efforts sometimes also enacted the belief that Indians and the foreign-born could and should become full-fledged members of American society. This positive faith in assimilation and democratic citizenship opposed the view propagated through **eugenics** and **social Darwinism** that non-Anglo-Saxon or non-European racial characteristics were immutable and antithetical to American citizenship. Reformers such as **Jane Addams** and intellectuals such as **Franz Boas**, **William James**, **Horace Kallen**, **W. E. B. Du Bois**, and **Randolph Bourne** formulated a **pluralist** understanding of culture against coercive forms of Americanization. *See also* INDIAN EDUCATION.

AMUSEMENT PARKS. The modern amusement park developed out of the midways typical in the great **expositions** of this era. The defining features of amusement parks were the incorporation of machinery, the enclosure of the grounds, and the charging of an admission fee. Roller coasters, Ferris wheels, and other rides mimicked railroads and other machines but converted them to frivolous uses and mocked their dangers. The rides violated normal proprieties, throwing strangers together, lifting women's skirts, and encouraging silly behavior. Parks also incorporated features of earlier amusement grounds: cheap food concessions, piers, beaches, **dance halls**, and bandstands. The parks were one of a variety of commercial sites where working-class youth reshaped **sexual** relationships away from adult supervision. Although parks allowed interethnic mingling among whites, they were **segregated** as a rule, refusing **African American** patronage or allowing it only on a few days each season. The typical park stood at the end of an urban electric **trolley** line. **Coney Island** outside New York City hosted the most widely known parks, such as George Tilyou's Steeplechase Park (1897) and Frederic Thompson's Luna Park (1902), but most large cities had at least one by the early 20th century. By 1919, an estimated 1,500 to 2,000 amusement parks existed. *See also* POPULAR CULTURE.

ANACONDA COPPER. Founded in 1880, this company became the largest U.S. producer of copper. Buying out dozens of small claims, Anaconda owner Marcus Daly built a huge complex of mines, smelters, and lumber operations in Butte, Montana, and nearby towns. By the mid-1890s, the company ran the largest reduction works in the world. Daly sold his stake to **Standard Oil** in 1899 and remained as president of the new Amalgamated Copper Company (renamed Anaconda a few years later). After years of corporate warfare, in 1910 Anaconda consolidated all the Butte mines under its control. By 1916, the company produced over 170,000 tons each year.

Anaconda also owned much of the farmland, railroads, hotels, and public **utilities** in the town of Butte. Thousands of miners and their families flocked there, attracted by the highest industrial wages paid in the United States. The city eventually had about 100,000 residents, most of them initially from other states, Ireland, and Cornwall in Britain; later, Finns, Italians, and Serbs arrived, making the city highly ethnically diverse and mostly Catholic. Until 1912, the Butte Miners Union managed relations between miners and management pragmatically. However, the **Western Federation of Miners**, founded in the town in 1893, took a more radical stance and gained the allegiance of many miners. After 1912, the Butte organization was torn apart by ethnic and class tensions, the arrival of the radical **Industrial Workers of the World**, and an **open shop** drive by Anaconda Copper that culminated in the military occupation of the town in 1917 and the forcible deportation of over a thousand striking miners.

ANARCHISM. Originating in Europe and making itself known to Americans through the Haymarket Riot of 1886 and assassination attempts against European royalty and politicians, this political philosophy emphasized individual freedom through abolition of government and private property. Anarchists eschewed the elaborate taxonomies and blueprints of **socialism** and, partly as a result, could accommodate a wide range of causes. The movement's many factions endorsed everything from assassination, sabotage, and conspiracy to artistic and literary **modernism**. In the United States, anarchism motivated **Alexander Berkman**'s attempted assassination of **Henry Clay Frick** in 1892 and appealed to **Greenwich Village** bohemians and **feminists** and to the **Industrial Workers of the World**. **Emma Goldman** became a leading spokesperson for anarchism as a demand for freedom of speech and **sexuality**, to the dismay of orthodox anarchists, like her partner Berkman. Opponents viewed all anarchists as terrorists, and after 1903, advocacy of anarchist principles was cause for an **immigrant** to be refused entry or deported. Anarchism never developed a large constituency in the United States. *See also* CZOLGOSZ, LEON; REITMAN, BEN.

ANDERSON, MARGARET (1886–1973). Editor. Born and raised in Indiana, Anderson moved to Chicago in 1908, where she worked as a **journalist** and book reviewer until encounters with Floyd Dell and other figures of the **Chicago Renaissance** inspired her in 1914 to found the *Little Review*. Attracting some of the best writers of the era, including Sherwood Anderson, Ben Hecht, Amy Lowell, and **Carl Sandburg**, despite frequent financial and personal turmoil, Anderson built her journal into an important outlet for **modernism**. Her flamboyance, unabashed aestheticism, open lesbian relationships, and stormy friendships with literary figures and political radicals such as **Emma Goldman** made her one of the vivid personalities of the "bohemian" scene in Chicago and New York. Her publication of James Joyce's *Ulysses* in *Little Review* starting in 1918 led to her conviction for obscenity; her memoir, *My Thirty Years War* (1930), offers a vivid account of the Progressive Era's cultural radicalism. *See also* GREENWICH VILLAGE; LITERATURE; *POETRY: A MAGAZINE OF VERSE*.

ANGEL ISLAND. Opened in January 1910, this **immigrant** depot on an island in San Francisco Bay was the West Coast counterpart of **Ellis Island**. Bureau of Immigration officials moved to the island from city docks to prevent immigrants from communicating with people outside the center and to quarantine newcomers with communicable diseases. Despite the Geary Act (1892) barring laborers of Chinese descent and the **Gentlemen's Agreement** (1907) barring those from Japan, a trickle of Asian migration continued, and steerage passengers of Asian descent were required to go through interrogation and medical examination. The fire caused by the 1906 **San Francisco earthquake** destroyed many documents, and so-called paper sons took advantage of this to claim relationships with U.S. residents and therefore their right to enter the country. Imprisoned in the ramshackle detention center with poor food and little to do, some people waited for weeks for answers to their interrogation to be corroborated by American residents. Some recorded their anger and despair in poems carved into the walls. Despite protests, the center remained in service until 1940, when a fire forced its relocation to San Francisco.

ANNEXATION, SUBURBAN. The **progressive** movement for **structural reform**, planning, and improved public works and services reinforced a long-standing practice whereby American cities annexed peripheral regions or towns as they were settled. Chicago's addition of 133 square miles in 1889 and the **New York City consolidation** of 1898 offered dramatic instances of a trend also evident in Boston, Detroit, Pittsburgh, and other cities. By the early 20th century, however, rising **immigration** and **machine politics** made central cities, especially in the industrialized Northeast and Midwest, seem increasingly alien to middle-class suburbanites, who were attaining a level of population and wealth sufficient to support independent town governments offering a range of public services. Suburban resistance to annexation left Philadelphia caged within boundaries set in 1854 and St. Louis within 1876 limits. Prosperous communities such as Evanston and Oak Park repeatedly defeated measures that would have empowered Chicago to annex its residential northern outskirts as it had its industrial south. Only in southwestern states such as Texas, where loose annexation laws prevailed, did municipal boundaries expand with suburban development and the progressive vision of a consolidated metropolis under **commission** or **city manager** rule come close to realization. *See also* TROLLEYS, ELECTRIC.

ANTHRACITE COAL STRIKE (1902). When 50,000 members of the **United Mine Workers** (UMW) went on strike in May 1902 against the anthracite coal mines in eastern Pennsylvania, their cause generated an unusual level of public sympathy despite the dependence of urban dwellers in the Northeast on coal for home heating. Miners endured infamously oppressive wages, hours, and working conditions. The Pennsylvania mines were controlled by a cartel of railroad operators, the most visible of whom, George F. Baer of the Philadelphia and Reading Railway, fit the stereotype of heartless plutocrat. By October 1902, with cold weather looming, mine operators came under intense pressure from President **Theodore Roosevelt**, who forced managers to meet with UMW President **John Mitchell** and to accept arbitration. The arbiters ultimately granted the miners improvements in wages, hours, and working conditions, though not official union recognition. Roosevelt's action represented the first federal intervention on labor's side in a major strike in the industrial era. *See also* LABOR UNIONS; SQUARE DEAL.

ANTI-CATHOLICISM. A prejudice deeply rooted in the historically British, Protestant United States, anti-Catholicism diminished in the late 1800s, due in part to Civil War service by American Catholics, the integration of second- and third-generation Irish and German Catholics into the middle class, and efforts by Catholic **Americanists** and **modernizers** such as Cardinal **James Gibbons**. However, it revived during the Progressive Era in response to the continuing **immigration** of Irish and German Catholics and the growing numbers of Eastern Europeans and Italians entering the country. Immigration restriction groups such as the American Protective Association targeted Catholics. Despite the contributions of Catholics such as Father **John Ryan** to **progressive** reform, the Protestant middle classes identified Catholics with **machine politics** and urban corruption. By World War I, the moralistic strain in progressivism exemplified by **prohibition** fused with **fundamentalism** and aggressive **Americanism** to generate the notion, promulgated by the **Ku Klux Klan**, of a Catholic menace. **Alfred E. Smith**'s rise to prominence and then defeat in the 1928 presidential election illustrated ongoing tensions between acceptance and intolerance of Catholics. Throughout the early 20th century, Catholics protested hostile media portrayals, such as the stereotyped disreputable Irishmen in **vaudeville** and **movies**.

ANTI-DEFAMATION LEAGUE (ADL). Founded by the **Jewish** service organization B'nai B'rith in 1913, the ADL primarily fought anti-Semitism, although it claimed that its target was discrimination against any group. Directed by Illinois lawyer Sigmund Livingston, the league confronted discrimination against Jews in housing, employment, **education**, and recreation as well as negative stereotypes of Jews in the press and a U.S. Army manual during World War I. The **lynching** of **Leo Frank** was the most notorious anti-Semitic act during the Progressive Era. As open anti-Semitism waned in America, the league turned its attention to the situation of Jews abroad and became a fixture in campaigns against racism and right-wing extremism within the United States.

ANTI-IMPERIALIST LEAGUE. This organization formed in Boston in 1898 in response to the proposed annexation of the Philippines after the **Spanish–American War**. With former treasury secretary George S. Boutwell (1818–1905) as its president, the league attracted a host of well-known members. **Andrew Carnegie** and former president Grover Cleveland enlisted as vice presidents, and Samuel Clemens (Mark Twain), **William James**, **Jane Addams**, and **Samuel Gompers** also joined. Within months, the league had a Washington, D.C., headquarters and branches from the East Coast to Chicago and Minneapolis. It secured 50,000 signatures on a petition against the 1898 **Treaty of Paris**. Never able to shake its reputation as a group of genteel northeastern idealists, the organization's support for **Democratic** presidential candidate **William Jennings Bryan** in 1900 divided and weakened it. On the diminished scale, the league survived until 1921, with its main concern being the **Philippines' colonial government**. *See also* FOREIGN POLICY.

ANTIN, MARY (1881–1949). Author. Mary Antin fled to the United States from Russia with her family in 1894. Despite her family's poverty, Antin attended Boston Girls Latin **High School** and as a teenager published an account of their migration. Abandoning Judaism and urging **Americanization**, she married geologist Amadeus

William Grabau and in 1901 moved to New York, where she attended Columbia University, bore a daughter, and continued to write and publish. Her major work, *The Promised Land* (1912), was a classic **immigrant** autobiography that launched her career as a lecturer. Antin separated from her husband during World War I, in which she supported the United States and he Germany. She suffered a nervous breakdown and spent the rest of her life in a Christian community in Massachusetts with her daughter and sisters. *See also* LITERATURE.

ANTIQUITIES ACT (1906). Formulated by archaeologist Edgar L. Hewett (1865–1946), this act formalized the federal practice of preventing development on publicly owned archaeological and historical sites. The act gave the president the right to proclaim such areas "national monuments." When Congress barred the president from creating more forest reserves in western states without its approval, **Theodore Roosevelt** used this law for **conservation** purposes. The **National Park Service** also used the monument category for areas it did not want to have as parks. Devil's Tower in eastern Wyoming, El Morro in western New Mexico, and the Petrified Forest and Montezuma's Castle, both in Arizona, became monuments in 1906. The act contributed to the professionalization of archaeology and the development of tourism in the Southwest.

ANTI-SALOON LEAGUE (ASL). Founded in Ohio in 1893 by Howard Russell, a Congregational minister, the league represented a break with traditional temperance and **prohibition** organizations. Instead of appealing for individual conversion, as did the **Woman's Christian Temperance Union** (WCTU) and smaller men's organizations, or running candidates through the Prohibition Party, the ASL directly lobbied for restrictive legislation. An innovative pressure group, the ASL was run by salaried professionals, not members. Mindful of conflicts that wracked the WCTU and other groups, the ASL remained resolutely nonpartisan and single-issue, with prohibition its primary goal. **Purley Baker** replaced Russell as general superintendent in 1903 and remained until his death in 1924, assisted by **Ernest Cherrington** and **Wayne B. Wheeler**. At its height the ASL was closely associated with major Protestant churches, had affiliates in every state, employed 1,500 full time workers and 50,000 lecturers, and had 16 million subscribers to its newsletter, the *American Issue*. In 1913, the league won passage of the **Webb–Kenyon Act**, its first major national victory. By this year, most of the South and rural areas elsewhere had banned alcohol through the **local option** laws enacted in 31 states. Building on its success, the ASL downplayed state-level activism in favor of a campaign for a constitutional amendment banning alcohol. Aiding the ASL was the passage of the Sixteenth Amendment, which enabled the federal government to levy an **income tax** and made revenue from alcohol taxes less important. The U.S. entry into World War I significantly hastened the progress of the **Eighteenth Amendment**, as prohibitionists argued their cause in the name of wartime food and fuel **conservation** as well as the protection of soldiers from vice. *See also* REFORM MOVEMENTS.

ANTITRUST. This term refers to the movement to bring giant industrial, commercial, and transportation enterprises under government control. Ambiguities plagued the notion of antitrust, beginning with the term *trust* itself. This pejorative nickname gained currency after **Standard Oil**'s notorious 1882 attempt to cloak its consolidation of the oil refining business in the venerable philanthropic device of a trust. Henceforth, the term could refer to big businesses in general, no matter how they came into existence or how they affected competition or society, or it could refer specifically to businesses that conspired to destroy competition or fix prices.

The lack of consensus about what trusts were hampered efforts to address the problems they caused. Among those who favored public action against trusts, two general positions came to dominate public discussion. One line of thought, summed up in **Theodore Roosevelt**'s **New Nationalism** and the **Progressive Party** platform of 1912, accepted big business as a natural and usually beneficial product of industrial development. Government, according to this view, should regulate big business, moving to dissolve only those trusts that demonstrably threatened the public good. **Woodrow Wilson**'s **New Freedom** expressed the contrary idea that the very existence of big business and a federal government powerful enough to regulate it threatened American individualism, opportunity, and dispersed power.

These positions proved less exclusive in practice than proponents insisted. The regulatory approach became visible in transportation, **utilities**, and other enterprises deemed to be either quasi-public or "natural" monopolies because of their heavy fixed investment or strategic importance. Americans eschewed government-run railroads and, with some exceptions, municipal ownership of utilities, in favor of state-level railroad commissions and public utility commissions, which came to exert considerable authority over enterprises whose management remained private. At the federal level, the **Interstate Commerce Commission**, with powers enhanced by measures such as the **Elkins**, **Hepburn**, and **Mann–Elkins Acts**, became a model of balanced regulation for proponents and an avatar of incoherent, overbearing bureaucracy to critics.

In other businesses, the public interest was less direct than in railroads or utilities, but the widespread fear of concentrated, unaccountable corporate power prompted demands for action. State antitrust laws, which supplemented common law strictures against "combinations in restraint of trade," could not deal with corporations whose operations extended across many states. The 1890 Sherman Antitrust Act articulated the principle that big business was a federal concern, but **Supreme Court** decisions such as *In re Debs* (1895) and *United States v. E.C. Knight Co.* (1895) made this law more effective at disciplining **labor unions** on behalf of business than at disciplining business. Between 1890 and 1900, only 18 cases were brought under the Sherman Act.

President Roosevelt breathed life into his version of antitrust by establishing the **Bureau of Corporations** and selectively prosecuting unpopular trusts, the highlight of which was a major victory over a proposed Northwest railroad monopoly in the 1903 *Northern Securities* case. Roosevelt's prosecutions of Standard Oil and **American Tobacco** resulted in 1911 Supreme Court decisions articulating the **rule of reason**, an apparent vindication for Roosevelt's notion of selective prosecution of trusts. President **William Howard Taft,** a lawyer and jurist, rejected the argument that the executive branch had discretion to decide which trusts were "bad" enough to prosecute. Taft brought nearly double the number of antitrust cases in four years as had Roosevelt in eight. Taft's stance against **United States Steel**'s acquisition of the Tennessee Coal and Iron Company helped to precipitate his momentous quarrel with Roosevelt. Despite Wilson's opposition to all trusts during his campaign, under his administration measures such as the **Clayton Antitrust Act** and the establishment of the **Federal Trade Commission** showed that in practice the federal government would regulate, not abolish, large corporations. The legislation of Wilson's **New Freedom** years provided more specificity than had the Sherman Act concerning what amounted to illegal business behavior, establishing the outlines of federal antitrust policy for decades to come. *See also* AMERICAN TELEPHONE AND TELEGRAPH; DU PONT DE NEMOURS, E. I., & COMPANY; ECONOMY; GREAT MERGER MOVEMENT; HOLDING COMPANIES; INTERLOCKING DIRECTORATES; INTERNATIONAL HARVESTER; MONEY TRUST; MORGAN, JOHN PIERPONT; PUJO COMMITTEE; *SWIFT AND COMPANY V. UNITED STATES*.

APPEAL TO REASON. *See* DEBS, EUGENE V.; SINCLAIR, UPTON; SOCIALIST PARTY OF AMERICA.

ARBITRATION TREATIES. Before World War I, advocates of effective international law promoted the idea of submitting disputes between countries to binding arbitration. Two **Hague Conferences** created a framework for this process. In 1904, Secretary of State **John Hay** negotiated 10 bilateral treaties to submit disputes to the Permanent Court of Arbitration, established in 1900, a forerunner of the World Court in The Hague, Netherlands. The U.S. Senate balked at the apparent erosion of its authority over foreign affairs that these treaties represented, and President **Theodore Roosevelt** withdrew them. After the Second Hague Conference in 1907, Secretary of State **Elihu Root** negotiated two dozen such agreements containing enough qualifications that the Senate assented to them. No dispute was ever settled under these treaties. Root also sponsored a 1907 Central American peace conference that led to a short-lived Central American Court of Justice. After leaving the State Department, Root remained a leading advocate of arbitration as American counsel to the Hague tribunal and president of the **Carnegie Endowment for International Peace.** The Senate's resistance to the arbitration treaties that Secretary of State **Philander C. Knox** negotiated with

France and Britain in 1911 proved a foretaste of the bitter postwar debate over the League of Nations. **William Jennings Bryan** envisioned the **cooling-off treaties** he negotiated while secretary of state as a more effective version of Root's agreements. *See also* FOREIGN POLICY.

ARCHITECTURE. American architecture went through important changes in the Progressive Era, mirroring changes in **art**, business, and the professions. As in all the arts, architects and critics continued to debate the relationship between American and European architecture. Despite the prominence of École des Beaux Arts–trained or –influenced practitioners such as **Charles McKim** and **Cass Gilbert**—with their studied adherence to European-derived styles— observers on both sides of the Atlantic agreed that before World War I American architecture had become especially innovative, with an identity independent of Europe. In a business sense, the complexity and expense of downtown commercial building pushed firms such as Chicago's **Burnham** and Root to adopt **organizational** methods similar to those of their corporate clients; successful architects became managers of elaborate businesses employing many specialized technicians.

Like other professions, meanwhile, architects took steps to enhance the authority of their professional organization, the American Institute of Architects (AIA), founded in 1857 and strategically relocated in 1897 to Washington, D.C. AIA officers lobbied to wrestle oversight of federal buildings from federal officials, whom the architects disdained. By the early 20th century, architects distinguished their skills from those of civil engineers, their main professional rivals. Architects also worked closely with **universities** to establish new architecture schools after the Civil War. Beginning with Illinois in 1897, architects gradually persuaded states to legislate licensing standards, and improved municipal building codes also increased demand for their services. Most houses and smaller commercial buildings were still designed by their builders, but even master artisans now often sought guidance from pattern books or standard designs sold by architectural firms located in large cities and publicized in **mass-circulation magazines** such as *Ladies' Home Journal*, which brought attention to **Frank Lloyd Wright**'s Prairie Style, among others. The famous prefabricated, **mail-order** houses sold by **Sears, Roebuck** and a few other firms and shipped in pieces via rail were an extreme version of this practice.

Professional architects of the Progressive Era assailed the eclectic styles of the Gilded Age—Second Empire, Queen Anne, and so on—as evidence of the unsophisticated taste and indifferent skills of their predecessors. Thus, a tragedy of American architectural history—the devaluing and neglect of the eclectic Victorian buildings that filled cities by 1900—originated in part in architects' own efforts to raise their status. Yet major lines of early 20th-century architecture had roots in Victorian developments. For example, though millionaires' mansions such as those lining Fifth Avenue in New York could be gaudy to the point of vulgarity, designs such as Richard Morris Hunt's Breakers (1892) in Newport, Rhode Island, and Biltmore (1888–95), built for the Vanderbilt family in Asheville, North Carolina, validated the formalist neoclassical and neo-Renaissance styles that dominated public building into the 1930s.

Likewise, Gothic and Romanesque revival styles had origins in contemporary European debates, but Americans such as Henry Hobson Richardson (1838–86) gave them original form and content in much-praised works such as Trinity Church in Boston (1877) and the Allegheny County Courthouse (1888) in Pittsburgh. Richardson taught both McKim and his partner **Stanford White**, who despite their Beaux Arts leanings took from Richardson the ideal of well-crafted, expressive buildings appropriate to place, purpose, and epoch. Besides being an influential designer of churches and college campuses, **Ralph Adams Cram**, professor of architecture at the Massachusetts Institute of Technology, provided intellectual justification for an American Gothic revival. On a more popular level, the **Arts and Crafts movement** reflected a rejection of industrialism in preference for historical evocative handicraft elements, as in the Craftsman bungalow houses.

The most strikingly innovative trend was in designs for downtown commercial buildings, represented by the **department store** and especially the skyscraper, a distinctive building type by the late 1800s. Chicago-based architects such as William Le Baron Jenney (1832–1907) and Burnham and Root departed from the tradition of masking downtown office buildings as something else, instead highlighting in both facades and interior layouts the distinctive technology and function of these buildings. Jenney's student, **Louis Sullivan**, earned his reputation as the first major exponent of American **modernism** through buildings and writings that celebrated the possibilities of steel-frame construction, elevators, and **electricity.** Sullivan's apprentice, Frank Lloyd Wright, archetype of the modern celebrity architect, went in another direction by emphasizing not urbanity and technology but an organic relationship between design, materials, and environment.

New York City skyscrapers matched those of the Chicago school in magnificence and technical sophistication, though New York designers were often more inclined than the Chicagoans to evoke historicist forms. New York's **Metropolitan Life Building** (1893–1909) was for a time the world's tallest skyscraper at 50 stories and held 20,000 employees by 1914. Gilbert's **Woolworth Building** (1913) expressed an eclectic American fashion with neo-Gothic, Byzantine, Romanesque, and medieval German elements. This cathedral of commerce was the world's tallest building until 1930, symbolizing American power and wealth.

The United States also gained international recognition in landscape architecture and city planning, following the lead of the great romantic designer, Frederick Law Olmsted Sr. (1822–1903), who in numerous parks and parkways, suburbs, and college campuses created a distinctive vision of a modern city that blended the natural with the majestic. His son, **Frederick Law Olmsted Jr.**, played a leading role in the **City Beautiful** and **City Practical** movements, collaborating with architects Burnham and McKim on Washington, D.C.'s **McMillan Plan**, while helping to organize the **National Conference on City Planning** and the **National Park Service**. Although controversial in the United States and Europe, these approaches to urban design brought American planners, like American architects, to the center of the international debate over modern urbanism. *See also* ANNEXATION, SUBURBAN; GARDEN CITY MOVEMENT; MUNICIPAL HOUSEKEEPING; NATIONAL HOUSING ASSOCIATION; *PLAN OF CHICAGO*; ROBINSON, CHARLES MULFORD; SANITARY ENGINEERING; SUBWAY SYSTEMS; TENEMENT HOUSE ACT; TROLLEYS, ELECTRIC; ZONING.

ARMORY SHOW (1913). Officially called the International Exhibition of Modern **Art**, this enormous show acquired its name because of its venue, New York's 69th Regiment Armory, which was divided into 18 galleries to accommodate 1,300 works. Although two-thirds of the works were by Americans, most attention focused on works by Pablo Picasso, Henri Matisse, Marcel Duchamp, and other Paris-based avant-garde artists, who were receiving their first broad exposure in North America. More than 250,000 people saw the show in New York and later in Chicago and Boston. Well-known critics such as **Kenyon Cox, James Gibbons Huneker**, and even **Theodore Roosevelt** reviewed it during months of press controversy. The show boosted the incipient American **modernism** associated with **Alfred Stieglitz's** Gallery 291 at the expense of the **Ash Can School** and other manifestations of **realism** and **naturalism**. The show also fed the customary denigration of American art as provincial and derivative.

ARMSTRONG COMMISSION (1905). When a feud among directors of the Equitable Insurance Company led to revelations of mismanagement in New York's powerful insurance business, the state legislature formed an investigating committee chaired by state senator William Armstrong. His investigation detailed appalling abuses at Equitable, New York Life, and other firms, ranging from irresponsible sales practices and use of assets for speculative investments to unsavory dealings with state officials. The scandal prompted greater **insurance regulation** by New York and other states as well as a reform movement among companies. The affair brought to prominence the investigation's chief counsel, **Charles Evans Hughes**, elected New York governor in 1906.

ART. During the Progressive Era, American artists had not yet overcome the old notion that their work was provincial and derivative in comparison with that of Europeans. Even so, institutional and **intellectual** developments, as well as stylistic ones, portended the dynamism and influence of American art in the 20th century. By the 1880s, the romantic landscape genre that characterized 19th-century American art—epitomized by Thomas Cole and the Hudson River school or by grandiose painters of the Far West such as Albert Bierstadt—was waning in energy and popularity. The later work of

Cole's apprentice Frederick Church, the last great 19th-century land-scape painter, exhibited a wistful, even nostalgic quality. Ambitious American artists continued to study in Paris and Munich and stayed for long stretches in Europe. John Singer Sargent, Childe Hassam, **Henry O. Tanner**, and Mary Cassatt were influenced by French Impressionism, while James McNeill Whistler participated more in European expressionism and early **modernism** than in any American trend.

Nevertheless, various American artists sought to adapt European forms and aesthetics to U.S. circumstances. During the Gilded Age and Progressive Era, decorative arts thrived, epitomized by the glass work of Louis Comfort Tiffany and John La Farge and in a different way by the **Arts and Crafts movement**. The Beaux Arts movement in **architecture** and the related **City Beautiful** movement, both of which relied on art to express the symbolic program of buildings and public places, supported strong work in public sculpture and mural painting. European training was manifest in the work of sculptors such as **Augustus Saint-Gaudens**, Karl Bitter, and Daniel Chester French and mural painters such as **Kenyon Cox** and Edwin Blash-field, but they all cooperated closely with architects such as **Cass Gilbert** and McKim, Mead, and White to fit customary academic styles to American subjects.

Although the link between formalistic murals, sculpture, and stained glass and American democratic ideas could seem abstract, **realistic** and **naturalistic** genres revealed more directly the goal of conveying a democratic spirit. The urban realists of the **Ash Can School** fused the meticulous observation of one great predecessor, Thomas Eakins, with the commercial illustration work that helped to form another forerunner, Winslow Homer. Indeed, of the participants in the 1908 exhibition **The Eight**, which brought widespread attention to this new urban realism, **Robert Henri**, **John Sloan**, **William Glackens**, and George Luks had all studied at the Philadelphia Academy of Fine Arts, which had a notoriously difficult relation with its former instructor, Eakins. Sloan, Glackens, Luks, and Everett Shinn worked as illustrators in Philadelphia before this circle of young artists relocated to New York City. Some from this group continued to illustrate books and periodicals and drew political cartoons, with Sloan becoming art director of *The Masses*. Seeing themselves as harbingers of a democratic, **socialist** art, the urban realists reacted ambivalently when the 1913 **Armory Show** introduced Americans to Picasso, Matisse, Duchamp, and other avant-garde Paris painters, thereby reopening the old issues of American artistic provincialism and art's accessibility to normal people.

The vanishing western frontier inspired the paintings and sculpture of **Frederic Remington** and Charles M. Russell, while Thomas Moran updated the western landscape tradition for the age of **conservation** and the **National Park Service**. **Native American** crafts began to gain commercial popularity, but the vogue for the desert Southwest as a home and subject for artists only began in the mid-1910s, when art patron **Mabel Dodge** moved her salon from **Greenwich Village** and Provincetown to Taos. The new art of American photography as practiced by **Edward S. Curtis** and others influenced the conservation movement and helped to lead Congress to create national parks. George **Eastman**'s simple Kodak camera established amateur photography as an American craze. **Jacob Riis** and **Lewis W. Hine** showed the potential of photography in documenting social conditions. In contrast, **Alfred Stieglitz** and Edward Steichen emphasized the aesthetic qualities of photography. The energetic Stieglitz made his Gallery 291 a showplace for European modernism and attracted a younger generation of American artists devoted to new European trends. Designer Candace Wheeler and photographer Frances Benjamin Johnston were among the **women** who defied the prejudice that the only purpose of tuition paid by women art students was to support serious male professionals.

Perhaps the most significant development was the upgrading of museums, academies, **university** art programs, and other institutional foundations for art. Midwestern cities such as Chicago, Cleveland, and Toledo joined Boston, New York, and Philadelphia in building impressive, neoclassical museums filled with works gathered from around the world by local civic and business elites. At Harvard University Charles Eliot Norton, the country's first art history professor (1873–97), was a leader of the Arts and Crafts movement, advocated the construction of a new Boston Museum of Fine Arts (1909), and mentored art connoisseur **Bernard Berenson** and his patron **Isabella Stewart Gardner**, who founded one of the period's impressive privately sponsored museums. Elizabeth Hart Jarvis Colt, widow of the arms manufacturer, promoted the art collections of the Wadsworth Athenaeum in Hartford. **Andrew Carnegie** founded the Carnegie Museum of Art in Pittsburgh, while his erstwhile partner **Henry Clay Frick** donated his art collection as the Frick Museum in New York City. Gertrude Vanderbilt Whitney studied at the Art Students League, had a studio in Greenwich Village, and was a generous art patron, and **J. P. Morgan** and other financiers donated funds and collections to New York City's Metropolitan Museum of Art. Popular art, meanwhile, whether **Charles Dana Gibson**'s ubiquitous Gibson girl or *Mutt and Jeff*—the first daily comic strip, introduced in the *San Francisco Chronicle* in 1907—reflected other dimensions of the illustration tradition, sustained by innovations in printing, publishing, and **advertising**. *See also* BELLOWS; GEORGE; HUNEKER, JAMES GIBBONS; YOUNG, ART.

ARTS AND CRAFTS MOVEMENT. This movement originated in Europe in the mid-1800s in reaction to the supposed degradation of labor by industrialization and the perceived shoddiness of machine-made goods. This sensibility spread to the United States through the writings of Englishmen John Ruskin and William Morris. In 1897, culture critic Charles Eliot Norton became founding president of the Boston Society of Arts and Crafts, which, along with the Chicago branch (whose cofounders included **Jane Addams** and **Ellen Gates Starr**), was especially influential. In 1901, Gustav Stickley (1858–1942), who ran a shop in Syracuse, New York, that produced handcrafted furniture loosely based on Shaker designs, began publishing *The Craftsman*, a journal that applied the arts-and-crafts ethic to political, economic, and city planning questions, as well as handicrafts and **architecture**. Although some observers dismissed this movement as a bourgeois fad that resulted mainly in romanticization of handicrafts and a vogue for classes in bookbinding and ceramics, the Arts and Crafts movement did encourage new appreciation for regional styles and had a tangible influence on domestic architecture. The *Ladies' Home Journal* published "simple" house designs, and the **Sears, Roebuck** catalog offered kits to build the "craftsman" houses still visible throughout the nation. The idea of unornamented, comfortable houses built with local materials inspired a generation of architects, most famously **Frank Lloyd Wright**. *See also* MODERNISM.

ASH CAN SCHOOL. A group of artists that formed around the charismatic **Robert Henri** and came to prominence with "**The Eight**" exhibition in 1908, the members earned their name for the deliberately unpolished manner in which they depicted everyday urban scenes. Before relocating to New York around the turn of the century, Henri, **John Sloan**, **William Glackens**, Everett Shinn, and George Luks were among those in the group who studied at the Pennsylvania Academy of Fine Arts, where they absorbed the intense **realism** of Thomas Eakins (1844–1916). Most had also worked as newspaper illustrators, jobs that deepened their interest portraying modern cities. Though lacking the Philadelphia connection, **George Bellows** also became identified with this group. While the Ash Can painters generally had **progressive** attitudes, their **art** was not strictly political. They did not dwell on urban ugliness with the intention of spurring attacks on it. Instead they followed Eakins's idea that in a democracy, artists should seek beauty in the commonplace. *See also THE MASSES*; NATURALISM.

ATCHISON, TOPEKA, AND SANTA FE RAILROAD (AT&SF). Begun in the 1850s, the Santa Fe line became the nation's fourth transcontinental connection in the 1880s with service to San Diego and Los Angeles, breaking **Southern Pacific**'s rail monopoly in California. Excluded by rivals from Colorado's lucrative mining districts, the Santa Fe drew passengers to its longer line through the deserts of New Mexico and Arizona by offering superior service and exotic attractions. Starting in 1876, it contracted with restaurant and tourist promoter Fred Harvey (1835–1901) to provide "Harvey House" lunch rooms staffed by wholesome waitresses known as "Harvey Girls." By the 1890s Harvey had also begun building a luxury hotel chain along the AT&SF's route. Harvey and the railroad used **advertising**, art collecting, guided tours, Pueblo-style architecture, and dramatic natural beauty to promote the Southwest as a tourist destination. Fostering the market for **Native American** crafts, Harvey and the Santa Fe brought Pueblo, Hopi, and Navajo artisans to stations and hotels where tourists could buy their handmade textiles, pottery, and jewelry.

ATHLETICS. At the turn of the century, urbanization, the lengthening of formal **education**, and new ideas about **adolescence** and the **strenuous life** made organized team sports more appealing to Americans. Towns, schools, and companies fielded teams in a variety of sports. The new corporate, consumer culture rewarded loyal teamwork and camaraderie by players and spectators. **Baseball** was the first professional sport and endured protracted battles over unionization and the structure and number of leagues. The racial **segregation** of baseball was typical of organized sports generally; **African American** bicycling star Major Taylor was only able to compete outside the United States. **Basketball** was invented in 1891 at the behest of the **Young Men's Christian Association (YMCA)**, and volleyball started in 1895. **Football** was the most important elite men's college sport and spread to **high schools** during this period. Soccer, rugby, hockey, rowing, and track all had their practitioners; the Boston Athletic Association, founded in 1887, launched the Boston Marathon 10 years later.

Girls and **women** had fewer opportunities than boys and men, but these increased during the Progressive Era. The Boston **Young Women's Christian Association (YWCA)** opened a gymnasium in 1884, and many women's colleges required physical education and offered some competitive sports beginning in the 1890s. High schools and factories also fielded women's teams. Women and girls competed in basketball, track, rowing, swimming, tennis, and golf, but physical educators argued for limiting the physicality, competitiveness, and bodily display of female athletes. Among spectators, men also dominated, but women were never completely absent from the stands, even at less respectable events like boxing and horse racing.

Long a disreputable blood sport, boxing became more respectable in the 1880s, especially after the adoption of the Marquis of Queensberry rules in 1892. Golf and tennis became popular pastimes for the well-to-do. Architect **Stanford White** designed the stately Newport Casino, which hosted the earliest national men's tennis championship (1881–1915); women began competing in 1887. Country clubs proliferated in the suburbs and resort hotels added golf courses; Newport hosted the first U.S. Golf Association men's championship in 1895. Trumping the game's elitism, Francis Ouimet, a caddy from Brookline, Massachusetts, became a hero as the first amateur to win the U.S. Open in 1913. Many cities built public tennis courts, along with **playgrounds** and sports fields during this era. Physical educators implemented calisthenics programs intended to make city children robust and draw them away from **saloons** and **dance halls**. These efforts, along with the increasing emphasis on sports in the YMCA and YWCA, and the founding of the **Boy Scouts**, **Girl Scouts**, and Campfire Girls, as well as the **Sierra Club** for adults, all attest to a growing interest in organized exercise and its role in mental, moral, and physical health.

Bodybuilding attracted many after the German weight lifter Eugen Sandow toured the United States in 1893; his magazine *Physical Culture* had 100,000 subscribers by 1898. Revived in Athens in 1896, the modern Olympics first came to the United States with the 1904 St. Louis games. **Jim Thorpe**'s performance in the 1912 Stockholm Olympics led to a national celebration—and a national outrage when the **Amateur Athletic Union** (AAU, founded in 1888) stripped him of his medals because he had briefly played professional baseball. The AAU and the **National Collegiate Athletic Association** competed to control a range of sports as they tried to police the line between amateur and professional. *See also* POPULAR CULTURE.

ATLANTA COMPROMISE. This term was applied to **Booker T. Washington**'s best-known speech on race relations by his most prominent critic, **W. E. B. Du Bois**. As a result of Washington's lobbying for federal support of Atlanta's 1895 Cotton States **Exposition** and his work on the exposition's Negro Building, organizers invited him to speak at the opening ceremonies. Given the heightened racial tension in the 1890s, inviting an **African American** to address a biracial audience was controversial. Aware that white supremacists hoped for a provocative speech, Washington sought instead to promote friendship between black and white. He urged southern blacks to give up for the foreseeable future any direct challenge to **segregation** and **disfranchisement** and concentrate on gaining economic skills to overcome poverty and backwardness. Whites, he argued, should encourage black efforts in agriculture, commerce, and industry as indispensable to the region's overall development. Washington reassured anxious whites that blacks would not demand social equality as they gained property and wealth. His eloquence relieved the tension that had built around the event, and at first both whites and blacks praised his measured response to racist aggression. By the early 1900s, Du

Bois and other critics were arguing that Washington's stance effectively conceded to whites the right to degrade blacks and that blacks could not advance economically without political and civil rights. *See also* INDUSTRIAL EDUCATION; TUSKEGEE INSTITUTE.

ATLANTA RIOT (1906). This four-day **race riot** began on 22 September 1906, when a mob, agitated by newspaper headlines alleging assaults by black men on white women, moved through the city's **African American** neighborhoods, destroying businesses and homes and dragging people from buildings and streetcars to assault and torture them. More than 10,000 whites from every social class participated. Twenty-six people, of whom 25 were black, were killed, and hundreds more were injured, again mostly black. A vitriolic campaign for **disfranchisement** along with a race-baiting campaign for **prohibition** had heightened racial tensions throughout the summer. The mob's targeting of the black business district and middle-class black neighborhoods made it clear that white supremacists were as intolerant of successful, respectable blacks as of poor or ill-behaved ones. The riot thus did much to discredit **Booker T. Washington's Atlanta Compromise**, pronounced in the city a decade earlier.

AT-LARGE ELECTIONS. This term refers to the principle of electing legislative bodies on a jurisdiction-wide basis, rather than by districts or wards. **Structural reformers** promoted the at-large principle, especially at the municipal level, as a device for defeating the ward **bosses** blamed for **machine politics**. Proponents believed that small, **nonpartisan** councils elected on a citywide basis would be less parochial and more **efficient** than ward-based councils. Critics responded that at-large elections removed municipal politics too far from the public and favored professional and business interests at the expense of working-class or ethnic minority voters. A standard feature of model municipal charters promoted by the **National Municipal League**, at-large city council elections became prevalent in the midwestern, western, and southern cities that adopted **commission** or **city manager** systems. Even some large, eastern cities that retained the mayor-council system, such as Boston, adopted an at-large city council.

AUDUBON SOCIETIES. In 1896, a group of Massachusetts women established a society dedicated to the preservation of birds, following **conservationist** George Bird Grinnell's short-lived effort to do so in the 1880s. Like Grinnell, the women named their organization after naturalist and artist John James Audubon (1785–1851). They publicized the plight of overhunted birds and boycotted fashionable plumed hats and clothing. Members soon participated in annual "bird counts," an important source of data for ornithologists and conservationists. Fifteen other state societies formed by 1899, when the organization's unofficial journal, *Bird Lore*, began publication. In 1905, the state societies incorporated as the National Association of Audubon Societies for the Protection of Wild Birds and Animals (shortened in 1940 to National Audubon Society). Under the leadership of William Dutcher (1846–1920), the society hired wardens to chase plumage hunters and lobbied for state and federal bird sanctuaries and bans on the sale of protected birds' plumage and wild game. It played a key role in the passage of the **Lacey Act** (1900), a 1913 ban on imports of exotic bird plumes, and the adoption of the **Migratory Bird Treaty** (1918) between the United States and Canada.

AUSTIN, MARY HUNTER (1868–1934). Author. Born in Illinois, Austin moved with her widowed mother and siblings to California, where she married Stafford Wallace Austin in 1891 and bore a severely retarded daughter in 1892. Austin taught school and fell in love with the desert landscape, the subject of her first book, *The Land of Little Rain* (1903), and many subsequent writings. **Divorced** in 1914, Austin lived in artists' colonies in Carmel, California; **Greenwich Village**; London; and finally in Santa Fe, New Mexico. She often wrote about the conflict between **women**'s individuality and the institution of marriage, as in *A Woman of Genius* (1912), and played a part in turning **Native American** policy from **Americanization** to cultural preservation. *See also* LITERATURE.

AUSTRALIAN BALLOT. Also known as the "secret ballot," it was a reform to the electoral system in which public officials printed ballots that listed the names of all properly certified candidates. Voters then marked these papers in a curtained booth or some other enclosed place that allowed them to vote without others' knowledge. Originating in Australia in the 1850s and first described to Americans in an 1883 article by reformer Henry George (1839–97), this innovation became popular among groups dissatisfied with entrenched party leaderships. Mainstream politicians gradually came to favor it as well. Customarily, Americans had voted with tickets, often color coded, printed by the parties themselves. This practice encouraged parties to mobilize voters but made voters' choices public knowledge and discouraged "ticket splitting," or voting for candidates of different parties. Especially in places where **machine politics** prevailed, harassment and even bullying by party workers justified the disreputable reputation of polling places, long an argument against **women's suffrage**.

After the adoption of the Australian ballot in Massachusetts and Louisville, Kentucky, in 1888, it spread to virtually every state within a few years. Although six of the last seven states to adopt this method were in the South, scholars have sometimes argued that the secret ballot became a tool of **disfranchisement**, because it in effect imposed a **literacy test** on blacks and poor whites. The system might also have favored middle-class voters in northern cities over **immigrants** with poor English. A more subtle argument is that by making voting a private act, the secret ballot contributed to the decay of the public political culture and the high voter turnouts of the 19th century. *See also* SHORT BALLOT; STRUCTURAL REFORM.

AUTOMOBILE. During the first two decades of the 20th century, the internal combustion–driven vehicle reshaped life and the **economy**. German and French makers were already selling several models by the time that bicycle manufacturers Charles and Frank Duryea launched the commercial production of automobiles in the United States in 1896. Frank Duryea's victory in the first American automobile race (1895) attracted attention to their venture. Until the 1910s, the motor car remained largely a toy for the rich, who could afford mechanics and chauffeurs to repair and manage fragile, unwieldy vehicles. Stunts like Horatio Jackson's wager in 1903 that he could drive from San Francisco to New York City in 63 days excited public interest in the automobile while emphasizing the hazards and poor road conditions.

Nevertheless, even before **Henry Ford** introduced the **Model T** (1908–27) and perfected assembly line production between 1909 and 1914, cars were becoming cheaper and reliable enough that the middle class saw them as an alternative to electric **trolleys**. By 1916, Ford's innovations drove the cost of a basic car down to $345, within reach of small business families and even prosperous skilled workers. By that year, Ford sold over 700,000 Model Ts annually, about half the cars in the United States. The former industry leader, **General Motors**, fell to a distant second, with about 100,000 cars per year, around 10 percent of the market. Amid fierce competition, automobile production expanded into a giant industry centered in Detroit, with employment leaping from fewer than 10,000 in 1900 to more than 200,000 by 1920. Approximately 8,000 cars were registered in the United States in 1900, 450,000 by 1910, and over eight million by 1920.

At the turn of the century, states and cities wrote laws governing the registration of automobiles, the licensing of drivers, and the flow and speed of traffic. Traffic police appeared in the early 1900s, supplemented after 1914 by the electric traffic light, based on the red/green principle borrowed from the railroads. Such regulatory measures received intermittent support from motorist groups, which in their early days represented mainly well-to-do men who resented government meddling in their sport. A partial exception was the American Automobile Association (AAA), founded in 1902, a mass-membership service organization that lobbied state and federal government on behalf of normal drivers.

Public health and traffic concerns had encouraged the widespread paving of urban streets by 1900. Although the **City Beautiful** movement had already provided a rationale for urban parkways, cars encouraged civil engineers to experiment with broad, limited access roads especially suited to automobile traffic. New York's Bronx River Parkway (1907) was an early example. Despite the **Good Roads movement**, most states were slow to construct paved roads outside cities, but the 1896 inauguration of **Parcel Post** service and the 1916 **Federal Highway Act** established a foundation for practical intercity travel by car and truck. *See also* ADVERTISING; POPULAR CULTURE.

AZUSA STREET REVIVAL. From 1906 to 1909, William Joseph Seymour (1870–1922), an **African American** preacher, led a series of interracial revival meetings at a former African Methodist Episcopal Church on Azusa Street in Los Angeles. Seymour, who had studied with Charles Fox Parham (1873–1929), renowned exponent of the Holiness movement, encouraged speaking in tongues, miraculous healings, and other physical manifestations of divine grace. Revivalists from around the country participated in Seymour's services and spread his style and message, which combined traditional white and black forms of ecstatic religious expression. This event marks the appearance of **Pentecostalism** as a distinct religious movement.

– B –

BAILEY, LIBERTY HYDE (1858–1954). Botanist and agricultural reformer. A Michigan native, Bailey became chair of the Horticulture Department at Cornell University in 1888 and dean of the College of Agriculture in 1903. The major exponent during this era of the family farmer as the foundation of democracy, he advocated government measures to counter urban migration by improving rural conditions, for example, through farm **cooperatives** and better infrastructure and **education**. He popularized his views through his magazine, *Country Life in America* (founded in 1901), and books such as *The State and the Citizen* (1908) and *The Holy Earth* (1915). Bailey chaired the **Country Life Commission** (1908).

BAKELITE. Introduced in 1907 by the Belgian-born chemist Leo Baekeland (1863–1944), this phenol formaldehyde was the first commercially viable synthetic plastic. Envisioned as an electrical insulation, it had many industrial and consumer uses. Baekeland's factory already made two million pounds per year by 1916, when World War I showed the material's practicality for dials and casings of radio sets.

BAKER, NEWTON D. (1871–1937). Lawyer and politician. A native of West Virginia and attorney with degrees from Johns Hopkins

University (1892) and Washington and Lee University (1894), Baker moved in 1899 to Cleveland, where he was among the young reformers drawn into politics by Mayor **Tom L. Johnson**, under whom Baker rose to be city solicitor (1903–12), then mayor (1912–16) and leader of the Cuyahoga County **Democratic Party**. As mayor, Baker continued Johnson's **structural** and social reform, overseeing Cleveland's first **home rule** charter and sponsoring a municipal light plant, **dance halls**, and other services and amenities. Although he declined to serve as President **Woodrow Wilson**'s secretary of the interior in 1913, within months after his second term as mayor ended in 1916, Baker joined the cabinet as Secretary of War (1916–21). A vocal critic of **preparedness** with obvious **progressive** credentials, Baker suited Wilson's reelection strategy, but he was fiercely criticized for his opposition to the war after the United States entered it in 1917. *See also* HOWE, FREDERIC C.

BAKER, PURLEY A. (1858–1924). Prohibitionist. An Ohio Methodist minister, Baker was hired by the **Anti-Saloon League (ASL)** in 1894, becoming general superintendent in 1903 and dominating the ASL until his death. An excellent preacher and strong administrator, he guided the organization to some of its greatest legislative successes, including **prohibition** via the **Eighteenth Amendment** in 1918.

BAKER, RAY STANNARD (1870–1946). Journalist and author. Born in Michigan, Baker abandoned law in 1892 for a job with the Chicago *News-Record*, for which he reported on Coxey's Army, the Pullman Strike, and other turmoil during the 1890s depression. In 1898, he joined *McClure's Magazine*, covering the **Spanish–American War** and Germany's rising power. His articles on the 1902 **Anthracite Coal Strike** and **lynching** and racial oppression (published in 1908 as *Following the Color Line*) secured his reputation as a premier investigative **journalist**. In 1906, he became an editor of *American Magazine*, where he launched his "David Grayson" stories, about a bachelor who rejects modern moralism and striving. Disenchanted with **Theodore Roosevelt**, Baker supported **Woodrow Wilson** in the 1912 presidential race and eventually became the politician's official biographer.

BALLINGER–PINCHOT CONTROVERSY. Upon becoming president in 1909, **William Howard Taft** appointed lawyer Richard A. Ballinger (1858–1922) as secretary of the interior. He had by all accounts performed admirably as commissioner of the General Land Office under President **Theodore Roosevelt**, but he believed that Roosevelt and **Gifford Pinchot**, chief of the **Forest Service**, had exceeded their authority in reserving public lands from private exploitation. Pinchot in turn criticized Ballinger for undermining Roosevelt's **conservation** policies and reducing federal supervision of western water power sites. The chief forester also publicized charges that the secretary had lobbied for resolution of claims to Alaskan coal lands in favor of his former clients. In January 1910, Pinchot sent a critical open letter to Senator Jonathan Dolliver, and as a result Taft fired the chief forester. A congressional investigation exonerated Ballinger of the most serious charges, but opponents succeeded in portraying him as a tool of rapacious corporations, leading him to resign in 1911.

BASEBALL. Crystallizing out of a variety of ball games in the 1850s, baseball became the first major, professional spectator sport in the United States by the 1870s. The growing popularity and respectability of baseball—attendance at major-league games doubled between 1903 and 1908—was due in part to its evolution into a big business. This process involved bitter struggles among owners over the number of teams and leagues as well as between owners and players over salaries and contracts, especially the reserve clause, which allowed players to be traded without their consent. National League team owners succeeded in destroying the Players' League (1890), even though it employed the best athletes and drew large crowds. Years later the Base Ball Players' Fraternity won concessions enabling players to see their contracts, standardizing contracts, and giving 10-year veterans the right to look for work with other clubs. Club owners then resolved their differences in the National Agreement of 1903. The American and National Leagues used bribery to destroy the upstart Federal League by 1915.

As the playing circuits, seasons, and number of franchises stabilized, cities transformed parks into regulation fields in which fences and walls separated players from spectators. By 1893, the rules governing pitching, hitting, and the size of the diamond had been settled.

In the 1880s and 1890s, players wore protective gear, such as masks for catchers and gloves for fielders. Before 1910, the rubber-centered "dead ball" and the legality of "trick" pitches favored pitchers. The new cork-centered ball introduced in 1910 shifted the balance to hitters, whose averages increased greatly.

Baseball was dominated by urban men of Irish and German ancestry; southerners like Tyrus "Ty" Cobb and the **Native American Jim Thorpe** were exceptions. Commentators praised baseball for rewarding merit and teaching boys teamwork and individual initiative. However, the National League formally excluded **African American** players at its founding in 1876, and by the 1890s white teams refused to play black teams. Formed in the 1880s and coalescing as the Negro National League in the 1920s, black professional teams enjoyed considerable popularity but earned less than white teams. **Women** had almost no opportunities to play and were also a minority of the spectators. The game spread to **Cuba** and **Puerto Rico** after the **Spanish–American War**. The establishment of the World Series as an annual event in 1905 enhanced the sport's appeal, and in 1909 **William Howard Taft** became the first president to throw the season's first pitch, demonstrating baseball's coronation as the "national pastime." *See also* ATHLETICS; POPULAR CULTURE.

BASKETBALL. In 1891, in response to a request from Luther H. Gulick of the **Young Men's Christian Association (YMCA)** training school in Springfield, Massachusetts, for a sport playable in gymnasiums, Professor James A. Naismith devised a game that used peach baskets nailed to a balcony and that emphasized passing and shooting, not running or physical contact. Players got around the rule preventing them from running with the ball by inventing the dribble (formally allowed in 1898). Five-player teams became standard in 1897–98. Net baskets with a hole in the bottom were approved for championship play in 1912. The sport spread rapidly via YMCAs around the world, and professional games began in the 1890s, but regional leagues were short-lived until the 1920s. "National" championships occurred sporadically beginning in 1897 and became annual events in 1913. The earliest men's intercollegiate games were held in the 1890s, and elite universities established an East Coast league in 1901. The **National Collegiate Athletic Association** assumed oversight of the sport and helped to standardize the rules in 1915. Unlike **baseball** and **football**, basketball quickly became a **women**'s sport, with Smith College students and teachers playing the first recorded women's game in 1893. By 1899, however, women officials instituted new rules designed to prevent running, reduce physical contact, and eliminate most competitive play. They also ensured that women's uniforms were drab and voluminous. By the 1910s, these rules spread to most other sports for women. *See also* ATHLETICS.

BATH HOUSES, PUBLIC. The spread of the germ theory of disease and concerns over **public health** and urban housing conditions prompted a movement to build bath houses in poor areas. **Settlement houses** often took the lead in promoting baths and offered them in their buildings. In 1895, the New York state legislature required all large cities to provide municipal baths. The shower, used first in Germany for soldiers and asylum inmates, was introduced as more **efficient** than the bathtub. After an investigation by **Frederic C. Howe** found that only eight buildings in a district of 4,500 people had bathing facilities in Cleveland, Mayor **Tom L. Johnson** constructed eight municipal bathhouses offering a shower or bath with soap and towel for as little as two cents. By the 1920s, dozens of cities operated public bath houses, but the movement always suffered the taint of a middle-class campaign to clean and uplift the **immigrant** poor. Except when connected to pools or gymnasiums, attendance frequently fell well short of capacity, and by the 1920s more urban housing featured private bathrooms, diminishing the need for public facilities.

BAUM, L. FRANK (1856–1919). Author. Born in New York, Baum dabbled in publishing and the theater and suffered a series of business failures before achieving success as a traveling salesman and buyer for an Illinois **department store**; he launched the trade journal *The Show Window* in the 1890s. After publishing two books of nursery rhymes in the late 1890s, he collaborated with an artist on the design of *The Wonderful Wizard of Oz* (1900), the sales of which enabled him to write full-time. His lavish stage production of the book on Broadway in 1903 and several **movies** produced through the Oz Film Manufacturing Company between 1910 and 1915 were financial failures, and none of his more than 80 other works were as popular as the Oz series. *See also* POPULAR CULTURE.

BEARD, CHARLES A. (1874–1948). Historian and public administration expert. An Indiana native, Beard earned a Ph.D. at Columbia University and served on its faculty (1904–17). With **James Harvey Robinson**, Beard was a leading exponent of the **New History**, which conceived of historical analysis as shaped by social and political concerns; his *Economic Interpretation of the Constitution* (1913) was the most noteworthy example of this approach. By highlighting class and economic interests that influenced the Constitution, he legitimized Progressive Era reforms that seemed to violate long-standing constitutional interpretations. Along with **Frank J. Goodnow**, he worked for municipal **structural reform** through the **National Municipal League** and the **Bureau of Municipal Research**, whose training school he directed after resigning in 1917 to protest Columbia's dismissal of antiwar faculty. His textbooks, *American Politics and Government* (1910) and *American City Government* (1912), synthesized **progressive** thought on public administration, and he promoted adult education through New York's Rand School for Social Science and the New School for Social Research. With his wife, pioneering women's historian Mary Ritter Beard (1876–1958), he wrote popular and at times controversial books on history and politics. *See also* INTELLECTUAL.

BEHAVIORISM. This school of psychology, elaborated by **John Broadus Watson** in books such as *Behavior: An Introduction to Comparative Psychology* (1914) and *Behaviorism* (1925), rejected the study of thoughts, beliefs, and emotions except insofar as they manifested themselves in measurable behaviors and physiological processes. In this way, Watson sought to reduce human psychology to an experimental science. According to behaviorism, people's actions and speech are habits produced by conditioned responses to external stimuli dating from early childhood. Despite its apparent reduction of people to biological mechanisms, this approach became popular among social reformers because it purported to offer a scientific means of evaluating conditions that produced well-socialized adults, thus allowing for systematic, rational child rearing and social reform.

BELASCO, DAVID (1853–1931). Actor and director. Born in San Francisco to Portuguese-**Jewish immigrants**, Belasco began acting professionally as a child and soon became a playwright, stage manager, and director. Moving to New York City in 1882, he staged many successful shows that critics panned as melodrama but praised for their stagecraft. Best remembered for his careful oversight of actors' performances, the **realism** of his sets, and innovations in lighting and sound effects, for example in *Madame Butterfly* (1900), he launched the careers of many well-known actors and playwrights. Belasco also contributed to the formation of the **movie**-production company Famous Players, which became **Paramount**.

BELLOWS, GEORGE (1882–1925). Artist. An Ohio native, Bellows moved to New York in 1904 to study at the New York School of Art, where he absorbed the **realism** of **Robert Henri**. Though not one of **The Eight** who launched the **Ash Can School**, he painted vigorous, at times violent, scenes of city life that epitomized this approach. Well-known works include *The Cliff Dwellers* (1913), a tenement scene from a New York summer night, and *Stag at Sharkey's* (1909), a boxing scene. Bellows taught at the Art Students League and helped organize the **Armory Show** in 1913. *See also* ART.

BERENSON, BERNARD (1865–1959). Art historian and connoisseur. Born Bernhard Valvrojenski to a Lithuanian **Jewish** family, he came to Boston in 1875, where the family adopted its American name. Traveling in Europe after graduating from Harvard College (1887), he became enthralled by Renaissance **art** and developed an extraordinary talent for analyzing works of art. His relationship with Boston collector **Isabella Stewart Gardner**, critic Charles Eliot Norton, and other wealthy patrons led to a legendary art consultation practice, in which he identified works for American buyers at a time when they dominated the international art market. Despite accusations that he engaged in smuggling and took kickbacks from dealers, Berenson shaped major collections and, through his voluminous writings, Americans' view of European culture for generations.

BERGER, VICTOR LOUIS (1860–1929). Editor and politician. Born in Transylvania to a **Jewish** family, Berger emigrated to the United

States in 1878 and settled in Milwaukee, where he engaged in **socialist** politics and became an editor and publisher of the Milwaukee *Leader* (1911–29). A delegate to the People's Party convention in St. Louis (1896), he joined **Eugene V. Debs** in founding the **Socialist Party of America** (1901). An advocate of building a local electoral base and working with the **American Federation of Labor**, Berger's moderate stance led him into factional disputes with Debs and other left-wing Socialists. As a Milwaukee alderman, Berger built the socialists' 1910 victory there into a half-century of influence, a record the party matched in no other U.S. city. In 1911, Wisconsin voters made him the first Socialist to sit in the House of Representatives (1911–13) and continued to send him to Washington despite the government's suppression of his newspaper (1917) and his 20-year prison sentence for opposition to World War I (1919). When the House refused to seat him in 1918 and again in 1920, he won a special election while free on appeal. After the **Supreme Court** overturned his conviction in 1921, Berger was seated in 1923 and served three more terms (1923–29).

BERKMAN, ALEXANDER (1870–1936). Anarchist. The son of Lithuanian **Jews**, Berkman was inspired to become an **anarchist** by his uncle, who was involved in assassinating Russian Czar Alexander II in 1881. Immigrating to the United States in 1888, the young man met **Emma Goldman**, a leading anarchist and his longtime lover and friend. During the 1892 Homestead Strike, he attempted to assassinate Homestead manager **Henry Clay Frick**. After serving 14 years of a 22-year prison sentence, Berkman was released in 1906, after which he lectured, published *Prison Memoirs of an Anarchist*, and edited Goldman's *Mother Earth* (1908–15). Implicated but not convicted in 1914 in a plot to attack **John D. Rockefeller**'s estate and an explosion in a New York tenement that killed four, including three anarchist conspirators, Berkman moved to San Francisco but soon left after becoming embroiled in the Tom **Mooney** case. Convicted in 1917 for protesting U.S. participation in World War I, he served a two-year sentence and was deported to the Soviet Union, along with Goldman and 250 other radicals.

BERLIN, IRVING (1888–1989). Composer. Born Israel Baline in Siberia to **Jewish** parents, Berlin and his family came to New York

City in 1893 following a pogrom. After his father's 1901 death, Berlin left school and supported himself by singing on **Lower East Side** street corners and in **vaudeville** houses and restaurants. Writing his first song in 1907, he had a job with a **music** company on **Tin Pan Alley** by 1909. His first successful solo piece was "Alexander's Ragtime Band" (1911), which launched the trend of borrowing from **African American** musical genres such as **ragtime** and **jazz**. He also wrote songs for the **Ziegfeld Follies**, which adopted as its theme Berlin's "A Pretty Girl Is Like a Melody" (1919), and he composed musical stage shows by 1914, including one starring **Vernon** and **Irene Castle**. In 1919, he incorporated his own publishing company and was a charter member of the **American Society of Composers, Authors, and Publishers**. Highly successful through the 1950s, Berlin composed some 3,000 works, including 21 stage and 17 **movie** musicals, among them *The Jazz Singer* (1927) and *Puttin' on the Ritz* (1929). His songs, such as "Cheek to Cheek" and "White Christmas," were among the best-known works of the 20th century. *See also* POPULAR CULTURE.

BEVERIDGE, ALBERT JEREMIAH (1862–1927). Politician and historian. Born in Ohio, he practiced law in Indianapolis and became a stump speaker for the **Republican Party**. When the **Spanish–American War** began, he attracted attention for highly quotable defenses of **imperialism**. Elected to the Senate (1899–1911), Beveridge sponsored the 1906 **Meat Inspection Act** and campaigned unsuccessfully for a national **child labor** law. As Republicans divided over progressivism, Beveridge identified with the **Insurgents**. After losing his bid for a third term in 1910, he joined the **Progressive Party**. He then ran losing races for Indiana governor in 1912 and the Senate in 1914 and 1922, but he mainly devoted himself to writing on public affairs and history. His four-volume biography, *Life of John Marshall* (1916–19), won the Pulitzer Prize.

BIRTH CONTROL MOVEMENT. The battle over contraception began in the 1870s and heightened in the Progressive Era for many reasons: **women**'s growing economic independence, the campaign to abolish **prostitution**, the **feminist** demand for sexual freedom, and the social hygiene and **eugenics** movements. In the 1870s, many states criminalized abortion and the circulation of birth control information; the federal law identified with **Anthony Comstock** banned "obscene" material—defined to include birth control information and devices—from the mail in 1873. Physicians continued to provide contraceptive devices to their clients, and condoms, diaphragms, and cervical caps were **advertised** in **mail-order** catalogs and sold in urban shops. When sellers came to trial, juries frequently refused to convict. Abortion remained common, particularly for women unable to afford contraceptives. Yet many Americans believed that being able to prevent pregnancy would encourage promiscuity.

Birth control advocates, including **socialist** and **anarchist** women like **Emma Goldman**, believed that access to birth control was essential for women's political empowerment. Perhaps the best-known advocate was **Margaret Sanger**, a New York City **nurse** who distributed contraceptive information beginning in 1914. In 1915, she, Mary Coffin Ware Dennett, and others founded the National Birth Control League. When Sanger fled to Europe to escape a jail sentence for running a birth control clinic, the league (renamed the Voluntary Parenthood League in 1919) turned to lobbying Congress to exempt contraceptives from the Comstock law. Sanger's new organization, the American Birth Control League (later Planned Parenthood), dominated the field from its founding in 1921. *See also* REFORM MOVEMENTS; SEXUALITY.

THE BIRTH OF A NATION (1915). This film, directed by **D. W. Griffith** and starring **Lillian Gish**, was based on Thomas Dixon's 1905 novel, *The Clansman*. Two-and-a-half hours long and costing $60,000 to make, it was the most ambitious, expensive film to that time, embodying Griffith's aim to elevate **movies** out of the realm of cheap entertainment. Tickets cost an unprecedented $2. Its innovative scenarios, narrative structure, camera work, and editing techniques make it a landmark in cinematic history. Its portrayal of the heroic **Ku Klux Klan** saving the defeated white South from unscrupulous carpetbaggers and semi-barbarous **African Americans** distorted history and rationalized **segregation** and **disfranchisement**. The **National Association for the Advancement of Colored**

People succeeded in having it banned in Boston and a few other cities, but President **Woodrow Wilson** praised it after a White House screening. *See also* DUNNING SCHOOL.

BISBEE RAID. Frustrated over wages, the pace of work, and the harassment of **labor union** members, about 3,000 miners in the copper town of Bisbee, Arizona, went on strike on 27 June 1917, with the support of the **Industrial Workers of the World**. Backed by local businessmen, the town sheriff recruited 2,000 men and, early in the morning of July 12, rounded up more than 1,000 strikers and sympathizers from their homes, gave them a chance to renounce the strike, and then shut 1,186 prisoners in freight cars and ran the train through the desert. Instead of leaving the men as planned at the town of Columbus, New Mexico, the vigilantes abandoned them in the desert, where they would have died had not U.S. troops arrived two days later to escort them to Columbus. President Woodrow Wilson sent a commission to investigate, but it concluded that no federal law protected the seized strikers, some of whom eventually won out-of-court settlements for this egregious violation of their civil liberties.

BLACK PATCH WAR (1904–11). This term refers to a protest movement among Kentucky and Tennessee tobacco farmers against large tobacco buyers led by the **American Tobacco Company**. In 1904–05, about 5,000 farmers in the area, called the "black patch" for the dark tobacco grown there, joined a Planters' Protective Association (PPA), intended as a marketing **cooperative** to counter the so-called tobacco trust's power. The organization turned to violence against the tobacco trust's facilities and farmers who sold outside the PPA; **African American** farmers (about 10 percent of the population) were disproportionately targeted. The most spectacular raid occurred in December 1907, when 500 masked men attacked Hopkinsville, Kentucky, prompting state authorities to crack down. A less violent, more successful growers' strike took place in central Kentucky, but both efforts had failed by 1911.

BLATCH, HARRIOT STANTON (1856–1940). *See* NATIONAL AMERICAN WOMAN SUFFRAGE ASSOCIATION; SUFFRAGE.

BOAS, FRANZ (1858–1942). Anthropologist. Born in a **Jewish** family in Germany, Boas earned a doctorate in physics from Kiel University before gaining a reputation as an ethnographer for his study of Eskimo culture on Baffin Island (1883). His interest in **Native American** cultures brought him to the United States in 1887, where he prepared exhibits for the Columbian **Exposition** (1893) and settled in New York as a curator at the American Museum of Natural History and professor at Columbia University. Boas is remembered for attacking the views, rooted in **social Darwinism**, that human societies occupy a hierarchy ranging from primitive to advanced and humans are divided into unequal and largely immutable races. In his writings, especially *The Mind of Primitive Man* (1911), he argued that each culture must be studied empirically without a priori judgment. Moreover, his anthropometric study of **immigrants**, part of the 42-volume report of the **Immigration Commission** (1911), demonstrated that no standard racial features existed, rendering race-based immigration restriction absurd. One of the few white academics to speak out against racism and anti-Semitism, he risked his job to oppose U.S. entry into World War I. A major influence on the discipline of anthropology, Boas did much to promote the rejection of racism and acceptance of cultural **pluralism**. *See also* INTELLECTUAL.

BOK, EDWARD WILLIAM (1863–1930). Editor. The son of Dutch **immigrants** who moved to Brooklyn in 1870, Bok left school at age 13 to help support his family. While working in **advertising**, he also edited a magazine, published volumes of sermons, and founded a newspaper syndicate. Publisher Cyrus H. Curtis hired him to edit a new magazine, the *Ladies' Home Journal*, in 1889. At the helm of this popular magazine for 30 years, Bok became a key figure in the creation of the modern **mass-circulation magazine**. While promoting **pure food and drug** legislation, **conservation** (urging **women** not to wear the feathers of endangered birds on their hats), and other causes, he introduced familiar characteristics of the popular magazine. These included combining features and advertising on a single page; vastly increasing the amount of advertising and making subscriptions a secondary source of income; and promoting a personal relationship between readers and the editor via advice columns and letter writing. *See also* JOURNALISM.

BONNIN, GERTRUDE SIMMONS (ZITKALA-ŠA) (1876–1938).

Native American activist. The daughter of a Yankton Lakota woman and a white trader, Bonnin left her mother's house at age eight for a Quaker mission school dedicated to **Indian education** and **Americanization**, eventually becoming a teacher at the Carlisle Industrial Training School. Estranged from her mother and the Yankton people, she refused to assimilate completely to white society, recording and publishing collections of traditional tales and music as well as several autobiographical articles. In 1911, she joined the **Society of American Indians**, of which she became secretary in 1916. From then until her death, she lobbied for Indian citizenship and civil rights.

BORAH, WILLIAM EDGAR (1865–1940). Politician. An Illinois native, Borah practiced law in Kansas and then Idaho, where he became active in **Republican** politics. His role in prosecuting radical labor leader **"Big Bill" Haywood** and others for allegedly arranging the assassination of a former Idaho governor brought him national notice. After being acquitted of involvement in timber land frauds, he was elected to the Senate (1907–40). Suspicious of both big business and the exercise of federal regulatory power, he made an erratic member of the **Insurgent** faction. He shepherded the Seventeenth Amendment for direct election of **senators** through the Senate (1911–12). Although he supported U.S. entry into World War I, he sharply criticized President **Woodrow Wilson**'s wartime suppression of dissent.

BOSSES, POLITICAL. A central goal of urban progressivism was to eliminate the "boss" from municipal government. This slang term is an anglicized form of the Dutch word for a master artisan, *baas,* and it spread into politics through New York City's **Tammany Hall**. The stereotypical boss was a vulgar political operator of dubious background and morals who maintained power through influence peddling, patronage, and the manipulation of credulous ethnic minority or poor voters through corrupt organizations known as **machines**. Trying to understand the enemy, reformers such as **Jane Addams** and **Frederic C. Howe, muckrakers** such as **Lincoln Steffens,** and political scientists such as Mosei Ostrogorski developed a portrait of the boss that later scholarship to some extent confirmed. The typical urban ward boss, in their view, was an Irish Catholic, like New York's **Big Tim Sullivan**, who headed a political club in an **immigrant** or working-class ward and who controlled nominations to local offices and access to higher officials. Although New Orleans' Martin Behrman and San Francisco's **Abraham Ruef** offer **Jewish** counterexamples, the notion of the urban boss as ethnically Irish reflected a reality rooted in the timing and circumstances of the Irish migration to the United States. The boss gained electoral support by providing assistance ranging from Christmas turkeys and country outings to intervention with employers, landlords, and the courts. With secure support in their wards, bosses placed themselves or their allies in key elected and appointed offices and controlled the many franchises, contracts, and permits that the growth of municipal government produced. Focusing on the city, progressives did little to explain statewide bosses with small-town support, such as **Thomas C. Platt**, or earlier bosses like William M. Tweed who were native-born Americans.

Some **urban liberals**, like **Belle Moskowitz**, sought alliances with high-minded, talented machine politicians, such as **Alfred Smith**. More commonly, progressives tried to displace bosses in the name of **efficiency**, social justice, and a more elevated civic life. Even at their best, bosses used their wards' votes as currency in exchanges with other politicians and business interests in which the public good was beside the point. As New York's Lexow investigation during the 1890s documented, bosses tolerated and even colluded in police graft and organized crime. Progressives believed that **structural reforms** such as **nonpartisan**, **at-large elections** would destroy bossism's base in ward politics. Municipal ownership of **utilities**, city planning, civil service, and **commission** or **city manager** government would substitute above-board, professional dealings between municipalities and the private sector for the machines' connections and favor-trading. Many bosses, however, successfully adapted to such reforms. *See also* CROKER, RICHARD; FITZGERALD, JOHN FRANCIS; MURPHY, CHARLES F.

BOUNDARY WATERS TREATY (1909). This agreement between the United States and Great Britain (which conducted Canada's foreign relations) established an International Joint Commission to oversee navigation, pollution, and other issues on the St. Lawrence

River, Niagara Falls, the Great Lakes, and other waters along the 5,500-mile Canada–U.S. border. Concluded in the aftermath of the **Alaska Boundary Dispute**, the agreement sought to end tension between Canada and the United States. In the same year, the British and the Americans also signed an **arbitration** treaty referring the longstanding dispute over North Atlantic fishing rights to the Permanent Court of Arbitration in The **Hague**. *See also* CHICAGO SANITARY AND SHIP CANAL; FOREIGN POLICY.

BOURNE, RANDOLPH S. (1886–1918). Essayist and **journalist**. Born in New Jersey and hampered since childhood by disability, Bourne won a scholarship in 1909 to Columbia University, where he studied with **John Dewey** and published books and essays in magazines such as the *New Republic* and *The Masses* on a variety of topics: **pragmatism**, **education** reform, the **modernist** attack on genteel Victorianism, youth culture, **feminism**, and psychoanalysis. His *Atlantic Monthly* essay, "Trans-National America" (1916), is a powerful argument for **pluralism**. His passionate essays in *Seven Arts* (1917) assailed **progressives** for their belief that World War I could advance their cause. Bourne died in the postwar influenza epidemic at age 32. *See also* BROOKS, VAN WYCK; INTELLECTUAL.

BOXER REBELLION. In 1899, a Chinese nationalist group called Boxers United in Righteousness (a name referring to their martial arts rituals) began attacking Christian missionaries and Chinese converts southeast of Peking (presently Beijing). Attracting enormous support among rural Chinese resentful of foreign influence, Boxers by 1900 spread their attacks on foreigners, Chinese converts, and people carrying foreign objects even to the streets of Peking itself. Encouraged by the imperial government and angered by Western troop movements, they besieged Peking's foreign legations for two months. In August 1900, 18,000 Japanese and Western troops, including 2,500 American soldiers (many diverted from the **Philippine–American War)**, crushed the rebellion. Western powers then forced the Chinese government to pay damages and sign a punitive peace that U.S. Secretary of State **John Hay** opposed but accepted. For Americans, this affair illustrated the inadequacy of the **Open Door notes** to slow foreign **imperialism** in China. *See also* FOREIGN POLICY.

BOY SCOUTS OF AMERICA (BSA). This organization originated in Great Britain. In 1910, Chicago publisher William Boyce persuaded two naturalists, Ernest Thompson Seton and Daniel Carter Beard, to merge their own boys' organizations into a U.S. group modeled after the British one. Responding to contemporary concerns about **adolescence**, Seton and Beard believed that wilderness activity developed masculine virtues that countered an enervating urban environment. However, they resisted the militaristic **Americanization** mission with which scouting quickly became associated. For this reason, organizers forced Seton out in 1915, ostensibly because he was a Canadian. The clash between an emphasis on pioneering self-reliance and the inculcation of mainstream values persisted in the BSA as it did in the parallel **Girl Scouts** and Campfire Girls.

BRANDEIS, LOUIS DEMBITZ (1856–1941). Lawyer and jurist. Born in Kentucky to a **Jewish** family from Bohemia, Brandeis graduated from Harvard Law School (1877) and established a practice in Boston. A wealthy corporate lawyer by the 1890s, he began taking pro bono cases related to **utilities** regulation, **antitrust**, and **labor unions,** earning the nickname "People's Attorney." He popularized **scientific management** in the course of arguing that railroads should demonstrate greater **efficiency** before receiving rate increases. In *Muller v. Oregon* (1908), he established the constitutional viability of **sociological jurisprudence**. The solution he negotiated to a 1910 New York garment workers' strike helped to establish the **International Ladies' Garment Workers' Union**. In 1912, **Democratic** presidential candidate **Woodrow Wilson** turned to Brandeis to devise a program to counter **Progressive Party** candidate **Theodore Roosevelt**'s **New Nationalism**. The **New Freedom** reflected Wilson and Brandeis's shared distrust of big business and their belief in competition as an economic bulwark of democracy. Although conservatives dissuaded the newly elected Wilson from bringing Brandeis into his cabinet in 1913, the attorney advised Wilson on the **Federal Reserve**, the **Federal Trade Commission**, and other matters. Brandeis meanwhile became active in the Zionist movement and published *Other People's Money* (1914), an account of the **Pujo Committee** hearings. In 1916, Wilson won a four-month battle when the Senate confirmed Brandeis's nomination as the first Jew to serve on the **Supreme Court**. As justice (1916–39), he shaped the constitutional basis for business regulation and supported free expression and the right to privacy. *See also* FRANKFURTER, FELIX; GOLDMARK, JOSEPHINE CLARA; MONEY TRUST.

BRECKINRIDGE, SOPHONISBA (1866–1948). Educator and social worker. A Kentucky native, Breckinridge graduated from Wellesley College (1888) and became the first **woman** admitted to the bar in Kentucky (1892). Finding her home state offered few opportunities for **New Women**, she moved to Chicago, where she earned a Ph.D. in political science (1901) and a law degree (1904) from the **University of Chicago**. A prominent member of the city's reform community who contributed to the **Women's Trade Union League**, the Immigrants' Protective League, and the **National American Woman Suffrage Association**, she often lived at **Hull House**. With **Edith Abbott**, she founded the University of Chicago's social work program. In addition to publishing works in social science and law, she held several prestigious public appointments.

BREWER, DAVID J. (1837–1910). Jurist. Born in Turkey to American missionaries, Brewer became a lawyer in Kansas, served on the Kansas Supreme Court, and held a federal judgeship (1884–90) before being elevated to the **U.S. Supreme Court** (1890–1910). Formed in the legal climate of the late 1800s, with its emphasis on property rights and limited government, Brewer issued pro-business opinions such as *In re Debs* (1895), but he also cast the deciding vote in the *Northern Securities* case and praised **Louis D. Brandeis's sociological jurisprudence** in his *Muller v. Oregon* opinion. Although he acquiesced in **segregation** and **disfranchisement** of **African Americans**, he attacked anti-Asian measures such as the Geary Act and spoke for **women's suffrage**. An advocate of international **arbitration**, Brewer led the commission to resolve the Venezuela Boundary Dispute and criticized **imperialism**.

BRISBANE, ARTHUR (1864–1936). *See* HEARST, WILLIAM RANDOLPH; JOURNALISM; PULITZER, JOSEPH.

BROOKINGS, ROBERT S. (1850–1932). Philanthropist. Brookings grew up in Baltimore and left school at age 16 to move to St. Louis, where he and his brother built their business into a major manufacturer and wholesaler of woodenware. Retiring at age 46, he devoted himself to philanthropy, supervising the building of a new campus for Washington University and reorganizing its medical school in response to the **Flexner Report**. These activities led to his acquaintance with **Andrew Carnegie**, in whose **Carnegie Corporation** and **Carnegie Endowment for International Peace** he became active. An advocate of **efficiency** and expertise, he helped organize the Washington-based Institute for Government Research, founded in 1916 and eventually combined with his Institute of Economics and graduate school for economics and public affairs to form the Brookings Institution, the archetypal Washington think tank.

BROOKS, VAN WYCK (1886–1963). Literary critic and historian. Brooks's youth in a family struggling to keep up appearances after his father's business failure filled him with distaste for the shallow optimism of late 19th-century culture. As a student at Harvard University, he found a framework for his disenchantment in the teachings of **George Santayana** and literary scholar Irving Babbitt (1865–1933). After graduating in 1907, he spent a decade moving between Europe, New York, and California and writing essays and books that portrayed American culture as bifurcated between a crass, materialistic, lowbrow commercialism and an ethereal, excessively feminine, highbrow gentility. In *America's Coming-of-Age* (1915), he lambasted pre-1900 American **literature** as sterile, anemic, or puritanical, excepting only Walt Whitman, whose crude, masculine creativity he saw as a model for democratic American art. He lauded the merger of **modernism, realism,** and social concern in the philosophies of **William James** and **John Dewey** and in the work of writers he labeled "Young Americans," such as **Walter Lippmann** and **Randolph Bourne**. A major critic of Victorianism, Brooks was a fixture in experimental literary magazines such as *Seven Arts*, of which he was an editor. *See also* INTELLECTUAL.

BROWNSVILLE RAID. Around midnight on 13–14 August 1906, a shooting spree on the streets of Brownsville, Texas, killed a bartender and wounded a policeman. Empty shells were found in the street, and residents claimed to have seen armed soldiers. Suspicion fell on a dozen enlisted men from three **African American** companies stationed at the fort in town. Since their arrival two weeks earlier, local hostility toward the black soldiers had escalated to the point that the fort's commanders had imposed a curfew. For lack of solid evidence, no one was indicted, but army investigators demanded that soldiers of the three companies reveal those responsible. When no one gave evidence, President **Theodore Roosevelt** carried out an army recommendation to discharge them all, over 160 men, including six Medal of Honor winners. African Americans and some white newspapers and politicians protested, deploring the denial of due process that would not have happened with white soldiers. In 1972, historical research persuaded President Richard Nixon to exonerate the men posthumously. The one surviving soldier received $25,000. *See also* FORAKER, JOSEPH P.; RACE RIOTS; SEGREGATION.

BRYAN, WILLIAM JENNINGS (1860–1925). Politician, lawyer, and publisher. An Illinois native, Bryan established a law practice in Nebraska, where he won election to Congress as a **Democrat** in 1890 and 1892. An eloquent orator with a gift for expressing rural, midwestern discontents, Bryan quickly rose to prominence during the heyday of populism and came to the 1896 Democratic Party convention an influential critic of President Grover Cleveland's tight money policies following the Panic of 1893. His powerful "Cross of Gold" speech in favor of free silver won him the Democratic presidential nomination and the Populist endorsement, although Gold Democrats deserted him. In a hard-fought campaign, Bryan traveled over 18,000 miles and gave as many as 30 speeches a day, but he lost the critical urban, industrial vote to **Republican William McKinley**. His defeat signaled the **Realignment of 1896**.

Over the next four years, Bryan worked to broaden his appeal. After serving in the **Spanish–American War**, he won the nomination for president in 1900 as a critic of **imperialism** and the gold standard. The return of prosperity, the **Gold Standard Act**, and ratification of the 1898 **Treaty of Paris** robbed his issues of immediacy, and McKinley handed him a second defeat. Bryan earned a considerable living giving speeches and maintained his following by publishing a newspaper, *The Commoner*. When **Theodore Roosevelt**'s crushing 1904 defeat of **Alton B. Parker** discredited the conservative Democrats, Bryan emerged again as the party's leader, and Republican **Old Guard** resistance to **labor unions** gave him opportunity for an alliance with **Samuel Gompers** and the **American Federation of Labor**. Nominated again in 1908, Bryan espoused a multitude of reformist policies, including the **income tax** and **employer liability**. Roosevelt endorsed **William Howard Taft**, however, so Bryan was not able to sell himself as heir to the popular president. He suffered his largest and final loss.

Nevertheless, Bryan continued to be powerful in the Democratic Party. At a key moment in the 1912 convention, he swung his support behind **Woodrow Wilson**, who rewarded him with the post of secretary of state. In this position, Bryan fought to minimize Wall Street control of the **Federal Reserve** and made **arbitration** and **cooling-off treaties** the center of his **foreign policy**. He and Wilson attempted, with mixed results, to build international recognition of the Chinese republic and improve relations with Latin America. When World War I broke out, Bryan resisted Wilson's confrontational response to Germany's submarine warfare. The president's demand for an apology over the *Lusitania* prompted Bryan's resignation in June 1915. Weakened by diabetes, in his last years he focused on **women**'s **suffrage, prohibition**, and a campaign against the teaching of evolution, which as a committed **fundamentalist** he saw as an attack on the spiritual basis of humane action. Under the leadership of "the Great Commoner," the Democratic Party put aside its provincial, antigovernment heritage and moved toward being the more **progressive** of the two major parties.

BRYANT, LOUISE (1885–1936). *See* GREENWICH VILLAGE; REED, JOHN.

BUCK'S STOVE **CASE (1911).** In December 1907, the Buck's Stove and Range Company secured an injunction to force the **American Federation of Labor (AFL)** to cease a boycott in support of a strike against the company. In 1908, a federal court sentenced AFL president **Samuel Gompers, John Mitchell**, and one other union leader to prison for contempt of court because they refused to take Buck's

Stove off the AFL's "We Don't Patronize" list. In 1911, the **U.S. Supreme Court** ruled 9–0 in support of the injunction but reversed the union leaders' convictions on a technicality. Along with the **Danbury Hatters' Case**, this suit helped persuade the AFL to drop its pure-and-simple unionism and engage in electoral politics. *See* LABOR'S BILL OF GRIEVANCES; LABOR UNIONS.

BUFFALO BILL. *See* WILD WEST SHOWS.

BULL MOOSE PARTY. This nickname for the **Progressive Party** came from **Theodore Roosevelt**'s boast that he felt "fit as a bull moose" when reporters asked during the June 1912 **Republican** convention whether he was ready for a fight in the upcoming presidential election. By the time of the Progressive convention in August, the nickname appeared in editorials and cartoons. Convention delegates replaced teddy bears, Roosevelt's previous symbol, with the bull moose in campaign paraphernalia.

BUNTING V. OREGON (1917). This case concerned a mill foreman named Bunting, who was convicted for violating a 1913 Oregon law requiring time-and-a-half pay for work beyond 10 hours in a day. As in *Muller v. Oregon*, **Josephine Goldmark** and **Louis Brandeis** prepared a brief citing research on the social benefits of workday regulations. The **National Consumers' League** published and distributed it under the title *Case for the Shorter Workday* to hundreds of law schools and colleges. The **Supreme Court** affirmed the Oregon law, 5–3, another victory for **sociological jurisprudence**, this time applied to male as well as female workers.

BUREAU OF CORPORATIONS, U.S. Established in 1903 within the **Department of Commerce and Labor**, this agency epitomized President **Theodore Roosevelt**'s approach to **antitrust**. Under Commissioner **James R. Garfield**, the bureau gathered information on business activities that Roosevelt could release or keep secret at his discretion, enabling him to prosecute or embarrass "bad" trusts while negotiating with "good" ones. Early tests of this policy, such as the campaigns against the meatpacking industry and **Standard Oil** and the collaborations with **United States Steel** and **International**

Harvester, fed complaints that Roosevelt's approach was arbitrary and politically biased. In 1915, this agency merged with the **Federal Trade Commission.**

BUREAU OF MUNICIPAL RESEARCH. Founded in 1905 as a branch of the Citizens Union (a New York City reform group) and funded in part by **John D. Rockefeller** and **Andrew Carnegie**, the bureau acquired its name and greater autonomy in 1907. Staffed by experts in finance and public administration (including **Charles A. Beard**), it used the principles of **efficiency** and **scientific management** to improve New York's municipal government. Unlike narrow adherents of **structural reform**, it insisted that the point of improvement was not mere economy but the expansion of social services. The bureau consulted with other cities, which often lured away its employees to staff their own agencies, and even won grudging respect from its frequent target, **Tammany Hall**. *See also* NATIONAL MUNICIPAL LEAGUE.

BURGESS, JOHN W. (1844–1931). Political scientist. A native of Tennessee, Burgess absorbed a Hegelian approach during studies in Germany that he applied to American government and history. A professor at Columbia University, he helped found its political science faculty and the *Political Science Quarterly*. As a Hegelian, he focused on the national state and argued that the United States offered an expression of the Aryan spirit, a perspective that made ethnic and racial diversity seem politically corrosive. Although students such as **Frank J. Goodnow, E. R. A. Seligman**, and **Charles A. Beard** rejected his teachings, Burgess helped to inspire the **Dunning School** of history. The first official exchange professor to Berlin in 1906–07, Burgess advocated German–American amity before U.S. entry into World War I.

BURNHAM, DANIEL H. (1846–1912). Architect and city planner. A New York native whose family prospered after moving to Chicago in 1855, Burnham apprenticed with several Chicago **architecture** firms and in 1873 formed a partnership with John Wellborn Root. After a series of house commissions for Union Stockyards executives, the pair designed office buildings in Chicago's Loop, including innovative skyscrapers such as the Rookery (1886), the Monadnock Building (1891), and the Reliance Building (1895). Their now-demolished Rand-McNally Building (1891) was the world's first all-steel-frame skyscraper. Under Burnham's management, the firm pioneered the office organization that enables architects to handle large-scale commercial projects. After Root's death in 1891, Burnham designed Chicago's Field Museum (1900) and New York's Flatiron Building (1902). As chief of construction for the 1893 Columbian **Exposition**, he oversaw the stunning "White City" design that catalyzed the **City Beautiful** movement. His first opportunity to apply these principles to an actual city came with the 1902 **McMillan Plan** for Washington, D.C., which resulted in his designing the capital's Union Station (1907–08) and his appointment as first chair of the National Commission of Fine Arts in 1910. Planning projects followed in Cleveland, San Francisco, Manila, and other cities, culminating in the 1909 *Plan of Chicago*.

BURNS, LUCY (1879–1966). Suffragist. Born in Brooklyn, Burns graduated from Vassar College (1902) and, as a doctoral student at Oxford University in 1909, became active with the British **women's suffrage** movement. She also met fellow American **Alice Paul**, with whom she returned to the United States in 1912 and became a leader of the **National American Woman Suffrage Association**'s (**NAWSA's**) Congressional Committee in 1913. Burns and Paul brought to the U.S. suffrage movement innovative British tactics, including parades; picketing of antisuffrage politicians, especially the president; and prison hunger strikes. These activities and their establishment of the Congressional Union (CU) angered NAWSA president **Anna Howard Shaw**, who forced them out at the end of 1913. Burns and Paul transformed the CU into the **National Woman's Party** in 1916. Although Paul became better known later, Burns did the behind-the-scenes organizing as well as editing the CU's newspaper; by 1919 she had spent more time in jail than any other U.S. women's suffrage advocate.

BUTLER, NICHOLAS MURRAY (1862–1947). Educator. Born in New Jersey, Butler received his Ph.D. in philosophy from Columbia University (1884) and studied in Paris and Berlin for a year before returning to teach at his alma mater. He became one of the central figures in the overhaul of higher **education** and teacher training in this era. He helped to found Teachers College at Columbia and served on the New Jersey State Board of Education, where he worked to reform school governance and teacher qualifications. Butler played a key role in instituting standard entrance exams for higher education as well. He served as president of Columbia from 1902 until he was forced to retire in 1945. The friend and associate of many prominent politicians, Butler was instrumental in the formation of the **Carnegie Endowment for International Peace**. His advocacy of international **arbitration** earned him a Nobel Peace Prize in 1931. *See also* ROOT, ELIHU B.; UNIVERSITY.

– C –

CAHAN, ABRAHAM (1860–1951). Journalist and author. Fleeing political persecution in Lithuania in 1882, Cahan settled on New York City's **Lower East Side**, where he wrote in Yiddish and English for several newspapers. In 1897, he helped to found the *Jewish Daily Forward* and, after rising to be editor in 1903, transformed it into the most popular Yiddish newspaper of the era. He also wrote **realist** fiction about Eastern European **immigrants**, publishing his first novel, *Yekl, A Tale of the New York Ghetto,* in 1896. His best-known work is *The Rise of David Levinsky,* published in serial form in 1912 and as a book in 1917. Cahan was among the first to translate the works of Russian writers into English. A staunch **socialist**, he favored **Americanization** of immigrants. *See also* JOURNALISM; LITERATURE.

CALKINS, EARNEST ELMO (1868–1964). *See* ADVERTISING.

CANDLER, ASA GRIGGS (1851–1929). *See* COCA-COLA.

CANNON, JOSEPH G. (1836–1926). Politician. A North Carolina native raised in Indiana, Cannon studied at Cincinnati Law School, after which he practiced law in Tuscola, Illinois. After serving as a state's attorney (1861–68), he won election as a **Republican** in 1872 to the

House of Representatives, where he represented Illinois for 46 of the next 50 years, the longest tenure in the House to that time. A strong partisan, blunt to the point of coarseness, he exerted enormous power as House Appropriations committee chair and then as speaker from 1903 to 1911. A traditionalist who fought for protective tariffs and against what he saw as frivolous expenditures, "Uncle Joe" obstructed President **Theodore Roosevelt**'s initiatives from **conservation** to naval expansion. Whereas Roosevelt managed to work with Cannon without alienating Republican **progressives**, President **William Howard Taft** stumbled into an alliance with the speaker, fueling progressive attacks on Taft as a tool of "Cannonism." Cannon's ability to use the speakership to thwart opponents prompted a revolt in March 1910, when 46 Republican **Insurgents** joined with House **Democrats** to strip the speaker of the power to appoint committee chairs and dictate the legislative agenda, a turning point in Congress's history. Cannon's traditionalism also led him to oppose **immigration** restriction as an unjust innovation. *See also* OLD GUARD; NORRIS, GEORGE W.

CARNEGIE, ANDREW (1835–1919). Industrialist and philanthropist. At age 12, Carnegie came with his family to Pittsburgh from Scotland, where his father, a handloom weaver, lost his livelihood to industrialization. The boy worked in factories before finding a position as an office boy and telegraph operator. In 1853, he became secretary and telegrapher to Pennsylvania Railroad executive Thomas A. Scott. When Scott became the Pennsylvania's general superintendent in 1859, Carnegie, still only 22, succeeded him as head of the key Western Division. He left the Pennsylvania Railroad in 1865 to manage his investments, including the Pullman Palace Car Company, along with companies producing bridges, iron, and most importantly, steel. Carnegie built his steel company into a model of the vertically integrated, mass production enterprise. By 1901, when he sold out in the merger that created the **United States Steel Corporation**, his mills produced between one-third and one-half of the steel in the United States—perhaps a quarter of the steel in the world—at an annual profit of $40 million.

Not wishing, despite his success, to repudiate Scottish democratic principles, Carnegie sought to mesh his faith in industrial capitalism with egalitarian politics. On record as a supporter of **labor unions**,

Carnegie authorized his partner **Henry Clay Frick** to take a hard line in the 1892 Homestead Strike, though Carnegie later blamed Frick for the ensuing violence. Carnegie's **social Darwinism** led him to philanthropy as a way to justify his wealth and power. In his 1889 essay "Wealth" (better known as "The Gospel of Wealth"), he asserted that accumulations of wealth provided a trust fund that a responsible capitalist should manage for the improvement of society. Left with wealth in excess of $250 million after the sale of his steel company, Carnegie set out to prove his principle. He donated money to build over 2,800 libraries in the United States and other English-speaking countries. His love of **music** is evident in New York's Carnegie Hall, as well as nearly 7,700 pipe organs he donated to churches around the world. His faith in knowledge and science resulted in a host of scientific and **educational** foundations, beginning with the **Carnegie Institution of Washington**, D.C., in 1902 and culminating with the **Carnegie Corporation** in 1911. A charter member of the **Anti-Imperialist League**, Carnegie crowned his work on behalf of **arbitration** with the **Carnegie Endowment for International Peace** in 1910. He paid for the Peace Palace in The **Hague**, Netherlands, and for Washington's Pan American Union. Carnegie also produced eight books and 63 articles on topics from travel to economics and **foreign policy**. By his death, he had managed to give away nine-tenths of his wealth. *See also* ECONOMY; SCHWAB, CHARLES M.

CARNEGIE CORPORATION OF NEW YORK. In 1911, realizing the futility of personally supervising distribution of his fortune, **Andrew Carnegie**, with help from **Elihu B. Root**, transferred the bulk of his remaining wealth—around $125 million—to what was then the world's largest philanthropic foundation. The Carnegie Corporation at first concentrated on libraries and other favored projects of its founder. Beginning in the 1920s, the foundation became a major underwriter of the natural and social sciences, the arts, and **education** research. In 1913, Carnegie established a similar, though smaller fund for his native United Kingdom.

CARNEGIE ENDOWMENT FOR INTERNATIONAL PEACE. Dissatisfied with **Andrew Carnegie**'s haphazard efforts to promote peace, **Elihu B. Root**, **Nicholas Murray Butler**, and other associates persuaded the philanthropist to consolidate his activities into a single foundation, endowed at $10 million in 1910. With Root serving as president until 1925, when Butler succeeded him, the endowment focused on research and education on international law and economics. The endowment's relative conservatism and its professional, elitist approach seemed inadequate to Carnegie, who in 1914 endowed a religious pacifist organization, the Church Peace Union. *See also* ARBITRATION TREATIES; HAGUE CONFERENCES.

CARNEGIE FOUNDATION FOR THE ADVANCEMENT OF TEACHING. Founded by **Andrew Carnegie** in 1905 with a donation of $15 million and chartered by Congress the following year, this foundation is devoted to **education** reform. To improve the college admission process, it sought standardized measures of student achievement, the most important project along these lines being the Educational Testing Service, creator of standardized college admission tests. It also developed methods of evaluating institutions of higher education and oversaw studies such as the **Flexner Report**, which set standards for medical education. In 1918, the foundation created the highly successful pension program for college and **university** faculty, Teachers Insurance and Annuity Association (TIAA), with a $1 million endowment from Andrew Carnegie.

CARNEGIE INSTITUTION OF WASHINGTON. **Andrew Carnegie** underwrote this philanthropic foundation with a $1 million endowment in 1902, followed by another $12 million by 1910. Independently and through partnerships with **universities**, it supported original research in the sciences through six main programs: Department of Plant Biology (established in 1903 as a desert laboratory), Department of Terrestrial Magnetism (1904), Mount Wilson Observatory (1904), Geophysical Laboratory (1905), and Department of Embryology (1913). It also funded archaeological research in Mexico's Yucatan Peninsula and in the 1920s absorbed the **Eugenics** Record Office into its **genetics** program.

CARRANZA, VENUSTIANO (1859–1920). *See* MEXICAN REVOLUTION.

CARVER, GEORGE WASHINGTON (c. 1864–1943). Scientist and educator. Born a slave in Missouri, Carver was raised by his former owners after his mother was apparently kidnapped by slave raiders toward the end of the Civil War. He struggled to obtain an **education**, eventually earning a master's degree at Iowa State University (1896). His talent for agricultural research led to his appointment as head of the agriculture program at the **Tuskegee Institute** in 1896. There, Carver directed the country's only black-run agricultural experiment station. To strengthen southern **African American** agriculture, Carver encouraged soil **conservation** and promoted alternatives to cotton, particularly sweet potatoes, soybeans, and peanuts. His campaigns to publicize myriad uses for peanuts made him a celebrity in the 1920s and 1930s.

CASTLE, IRENE (1893–1969) AND VERNON (1887–1918). Dancers. British **immigrant** Vernon Castle and New Yorker Irene Castle became symbols of modern life through their success in popularizing ballroom dancing. After coming to the United States in 1906, Vernon became a prominent performer and helped Irene launch her career in 1910; they married in 1911. In addition to performing in musical comedies, they demonstrated dances in cabarets, produced films, published a text on ballroom dancing, and operated a dance school. They popularized the turkey trot, tango, and fox trot. Although they modeled the new ideal of companionate marriage for many, they were about to **divorce** when Vernon died in a flight training accident in 1918. Irene was credited with inventing "bobbed" hair, an important symbol of the **New Woman**. At the height of their stardom, they featured **ragtime** bandleader **James Reese Europe** in their shows.

CATHER, WILLA (1873–1947). Author. Born in Virginia, she moved with her family to Nebraska in 1883, graduated from the University of Nebraska in 1895, and worked as a **journalist**, critic, and teacher in Nebraska, Pittsburgh, and New York City, where she was an editor for *McClure's* (1906–12). Between 1912 and 1920, Cather published four novels and a short story collection. Works such as *O, Pioneers!* (1913) and *My Antonia* (1918) captured attention for their **realism** in depicting ethnic minorities' and **women**'s lives on the Great Plains. In the 1920s, she produced acclaimed writings that featured southwestern settings, narrative experiments, and themes of disaffection and spiritual quest, such as *The Professor's House* (1925) and *Death Comes for the Archbishop* (1927). *See also* LITERATURE.

CATT, CARRIE CHAPMAN (1859–1947). Suffrage leader. Born Carrie Clinton Lane on a farm in Wisconsin, she graduated from Iowa State Agricultural College (1880) and became a teacher, principal, and superintendent of schools before marrying her first husband, Leo Chapman, in 1885. Together they edited a local paper until a lawsuit forced them to move; Leo died in San Francisco shortly thereafter. She became a member of the **Woman's Christian Temperance Union** and, in 1889, was a lecturer and organizer for the Iowa Woman **Suffrage** Association. The following year, the activist participated in the formation of the **National American Woman Suffrage Association (NAWSA)** and married George Catt. In 1892, she moved to New York City and became head of NAWSA's business committee; in 1900–04 she served as the organization's president, resigning to care for her husband, who died in 1905. Under the auspices of the International Woman Suffrage Alliance, which she founded, Catt in 1911 journeyed to meet women in Africa, the Middle East, Asia, and Oceania.

Renewing her suffrage activities upon her return, Catt became president of NAWSA again starting in 1915. She upgraded the group's lobbying efforts in Washington, D.C., while continuing campaigns in states that still did not allow women to vote or restricted their participation. This emphasis on both federal and state action and the centralization of NAWSA's decision making she dubbed the **Winning Plan**. Like her predecessor, **Anna Howard Shaw**, she resisted efforts by **Lucy Burns** and **Alice Paul** to radicalize the movement's tactics. In 1917, although she was a lifelong pacifist and cofounder with **Jane Addams** of the Woman's Peace Party (1915), Catt determined that NAWSA should condone the U.S. entry into World War I, a decision that caused much bitterness. Despite these divisions, under Catt's leadership NAWSA was the key force behind the ratification of the **Nineteenth Amendment** in 1920. After helping to convert NAWSA into the League of Women Voters, she dedicated the rest of her life to working for peace, the League of Nations, and **child labor** reform. *See also* REFORM MOVEMENTS.

CHAIN STORES. This term refers to the new retail enterprises that controlled four or more outlets offering the same goods in different locations with common management and a central buying office. Like **department stores** and **mail-order** houses, chain stores took advantage of the economies of scope and scale becoming prevalent in manufacturing; they could maintain expert buying and marketing departments, along with regional offices that oversaw individual stores. Chains increasingly depended on standard, brand-name goods sold in great quantities at small markups, with stock turnover rates in excess of once per month in a grocery chain, for example.

The prototype chain operation was the Great Atlantic and Pacific Tea Company, or A&P, which controlled over 500 outlets nationally by 1912 and over 14,000 by 1925. In the 1910s, A&P stopped trying to match neighborhood grocers in service to customers and instead began cash-and-carry operations, with perhaps a thousand different items in stock but fewer employees—the origin of the supermarket. In 1916, a Memphis-based chain, Piggly-Wiggly, introduced the self-service grocery, where customers, not clerks, took goods from shelves. Similar firms appeared in dry goods, small household items, and hardware. **Woolworth's**, begun in 1879, offered bins of buttons, notions, and other items priced at five cents or a dime, hence the phrase "five & dime store." Between 1902 and 1923, J. C. Penney grew into a chain of 475 small department stores. Walgreen's, founded in 1909, embodied this trend in the drug business. Chain stores proved especially effective in neighborhood shopping centers in cities and on the main streets of small towns. Although they controlled less than 5 percent of national retail sales in 1919, chains outpaced independent merchants in the 1920s. *See also* ADVERTISING; ECONOMY.

CHAMBER OF COMMERCE, U.S. For decades, American cities and states featured "chambers of commerce" or "boards of trade" whose activities extended beyond economic promotion into civic and political affairs. Expanded federal intervention in the **economy** at the turn of the 20th century prompted calls for a national umbrella organization. In 1912, President **William Howard Taft** called a conference attended by representatives from nearly 400 commercial groups, which resulted in the establishment of the U.S. Chamber of Commerce. Prominent among its founders was **progressive** businessman **Edward**

A. Filene. As befitted its quasi-official origin, the U.S. Chamber at first took more moderate stances on regulation and **labor unions** than the **National Association of Manufacturers** as it attempted to shape the **Federal Reserve** and the **Federal Trade Commission.**

CHAPLIN, CHARLIE (CHARLES SPENCER) (1889–1977). Film actor and director. Born in London to poor music-hall singers, Chaplin spent part of his childhood in orphanages. A performer by age five, Chaplin joined a traveling troupe specializing in comic pantomime in 1908. During a visit to the United States in 1913, he signed a contract with **Mack Sennett**, whose Keystone Studios specialized in slapstick comedy **movies.** Quickly becoming extremely popular, Chaplin moved from company to company, earning ever higher salaries and gaining artistic and financial control over his films. In 1919, he, director **D. W. Griffith**, and film stars Douglas Fairbanks and **Mary Pickford** founded United Artists. Chaplin played the same character in most of his films: "the Tramp," a down-on-his-luck man clad in a too-small jacket, baggy pants, and a bowler hat, carrying a cane and wearing a toothbrush moustache. He transformed a vulgar genre into subtle art, thereby helping to make film a respectable entertainment. His own films combined physical humor with romance and pathos. Chaplin was successful into the 1950s, negotiating the advent of sound and achieving worldwide fame.

CHARITY ORGANIZATION SOCIETIES. *See* REFORM MOVEMENTS; SETTLEMENT HOUSE MOVEMENT.

CHAUTAUQUA MOVEMENT. This adult **education** movement grew out of a summer religious education institute run by Methodist minister John Vincent (1832–1920) at the Lake Chautauqua resort in New York State. In 1878, Vincent organized a correspondence school to provide a college-style experience to adults. People formed local reading circles with booklists featuring noted authors such as **Richard T. Ely** and James Bryce. The monthly *Chautauquan* magazine provided guidance with lessons. Participants could attend eight-week summer sessions at Lake Chautauqua, and those who completed a four-year program received a diploma. Vincent and his educational director, **William Rainey Harper**, recruited as lecturers well-known figures such as **Woodrow Wilson** and **William James.** Chautauqua exposed a multitude of Americans to the **intellectual** ferment behind the **Social Gospel** and progressivism. Enrollment reached into the hundreds of thousands by the 1890s, when nearly three-quarters of the 10,000 reading circles were in towns and villages with fewer than 3,500 people. Independent "daughter" chautauquas also appeared around the country. Starting in 1904, a Chicago impresario organized a traveling chautauqua tent show that featured speakers such as **William Jennings Bryan** and **Robert La Follette.** By 1920, 21 such tent companies traveled on 93 circuits, with an audience estimated at over 35 million.

CHERRINGTON, ERNEST HURST (1877–1950). Prohibitionist. From the family of an Ohio Methodist minister, Cherrington taught school and edited a newspaper before becoming district leader for the Ohio branch of the **Anti-Saloon League** in 1902. He rose quickly, serving as assistant to **Purley A. Baker** before overseeing the creation of the Washington state branch, which achieved a **local option** law there. In 1910, Cherrington became the editor of the ASL's newspaper and director of its publications program. Following the example of the **Woman's Christian Temperance Union**, he founded a publishing company that produced huge quantities of **prohibitionist** literature. After the passage of the **Eighteenth Amendment** in 1918, he favored a dual strategy of promoting temperance internationally while continuing to educate Americans. He lost that battle to **Wayne B. Wheeler**, who favored domestic law enforcement, but Cherrington remained active in temperance reform for the rest of his life.

CHESNUTT, CHARLES W. (1858–1932). Author. Born in Ohio, Chesnutt grew up in North Carolina, where after the Civil War his white grandfather helped his mixed-race father start a grocery business. After working as a teacher and principal, he returned to Cleveland, where he passed the bar exam and started a court reporting business. In 1887, he published a short story in *Atlantic Monthly*, the first work of fiction by an **African American** writer to appear in such a prestigious magazine. Over the next two decades, two collections of short stories and three novels made him the first black fiction writer to publish regularly in **mass-circulation magazines** and with major publishers. His carefully crafted fiction drew upon

realism as well as folk culture and allegory. His 1900 novel, *The House Behind the Cedars*, concerned light-skinned blacks attempting to pass as white, and *The Marrow of Tradition* (1901) took the 1898 **Wilmington Riot** as its launching point. When a 1905 novel failed to make money, Chesnutt focused again on his court reporting business, though he continued to publish and participated in the **National Association for the Advancement of Colored People** and other civil rights groups. *See also* LITERATURE.

CHICAGO DEFENDER. Founded in 1905 by **Robert S. Abbott**, this weekly newspaper aimed at **African Americans** used sensational reporting in the mode of **William Randolph Hearst** to become one of the most widely read black newspapers in the United States. By 1920, circulation reached 230,000, about two-thirds of whom were outside Chicago. Passed around in barbershops and read aloud in churches, the paper, with the slogan *American Race Prejudice Must Be Destroyed* on its masthead, reached at least half a million readers each week. From its northern headquarters, the *Defender* documented **lynching**, **disfranchisement**, **segregation**, **race riots**, and other forms of racial oppression. Distributed (often clandestinely) through the South by Pullman porters, the newspaper became a cherished source of information for southern blacks. By 1915, its encouragement of the **Great Migration** increased southern white efforts to confiscate or ban it. The *Defender* lauded Chicago's opportunities and offered migrants advice on adjusting to northern urban life, but it also reported on housing discrimination and other forms of harassment that confronted African Americans in Chicago. *See also* JOURNALISM.

CHICAGO RENAISSANCE. This term refers to a **literary** movement centered in Chicago during the decade before World War I. Depending on how the movement is defined, it might include earlier Chicago writers such as **Hamlin Garland** or **Theodore Dreiser.** But scholars generally focus on Chicago-based writers with midwestern backgrounds and **naturalistic** or **modernist** styles who came to prominence after 1910, such as **Vachel Lindsay**, **Carl Sandburg**, and **Edgar Lee Masters.** Beyond being home to an established literary magazine, *The Dial*, Chicago at the time featured enthusiastic editors who promoted experimental poetry and fiction: **Margaret**

Anderson of *The Little Review*, Harriet Monroe of *Poetry*, and Floyd Dell of *Friday Literary Review*. Around 1914, personal and professional matters began to scatter this group, to New York's **Greenwich Village** in the case of Dell and Anderson, and Chicago's reputation for literary innovation faded.

CHICAGO SANITARY AND SHIP CANAL. Chicago's location on low land along Lake Michigan created chronic problems of flooding and water-borne disease—cholera, typhus, and dysentery. In the mid-19th century, the city undertook ambitious **sanitary engineering** projects that failed to offset the defects of its site. Between 1892 and 1900, the city sponsored the largest earth-removal project in municipal engineering history, taking over 30 million cubic feet of earth from 40 miles of channel (15 miles of which consisted of solid rock), so that the Chicago River would permanently flow into the Mississippi River system. Intended for commerce as well as drainage, the Chicago Sanitary and Ship Canal became a major link in the waterway system from the St. Lawrence to the Gulf of Mexico. This project brought unintended environmental problems, including a drop in the level of the Great Lakes of between four and six inches, which fueled the ongoing dispute with Canada that resulted in the 1909 **Boundary Waters Treaty**. The canal also sparked precedent-setting lawsuits against Illinois by neighboring states and drew the federal government into urban environmental policy for the first time.

CHICAGO, UNIVERSITY OF. With an endowment from **John D. Rockefeller** and land and buildings donated by local business leaders, this Baptist-affiliated **university** opened in 1892 in the Hyde Park section in south Chicago, replacing a small, Baptist college of the same name that closed in 1886. Under the leadership of **William Rainey Harper**, the new institution combined German-style research and graduate training with emphasis on community involvement and adult education. Harper offered high salaries and low teaching loads to lure academic stars. As head of the philosophy department and founder of the Laboratory School, **John Dewey** identified the university with **educational** innovation and engagement with the **settlement house movement**. Noted reformers (and University of Chicago doctorates) **Edith Abbott** and **Sophonisba Breckinridge**

founded the university's social work program. The sociology department, chaired by **Albion Small** with **Robert Park** on the faculty, devised so many fundamental concepts and methods for researching modern cities and urban life that for most of the 20th century, urban affairs scholars used the term "Chicago School" to signify the standard approach to studying urbanism. *See also* INTELLECTUAL; PRAGMATISM; YOUNG, ELLA FLAGG.

CHICAGO VICE COMMISSION. One of many municipal vice investigations of the era, this group was established by the city of Chicago in March 1910 with 30 members appointed by the mayor. Like New York City's **Committee of Fourteen**, it included representatives from religious groups, law enforcement, medicine, academia, and business, but only two **women**, despite their prominence in the campaign against **prostitution**. Its report, *The Social Evil in Chicago* (1911), condemned regulation and **segregated** vice districts as failures and recommended a permanent agency to combat prostitution, a recommendation that the city failed to implement, though the state created an Illinois Vice Commission. Investigators estimated that 5,000 women worked as prostitutes in the city and showed that they earned as much as four times more per week than most female workers, few of whom garnered a living wage. *See also* AMERICAN SOCIAL HYGIENE ASSOCIATION; MANN ACT; REFORM MOVEMENTS; SEXUALITY; WHITE SLAVERY.

CHILD LABOR. Industrialization and changing ideas about childhood made child factory labor a political issue by the 1870s. While **labor unions** indicted child labor for lowering wages for all workers, middle-class reformers emphasized the damage done to children morally, educationally, and physically. Working-class parents often resisted **compulsory education** and child labor laws because they believed that children should contribute economically, and children's wages were often critical to a family's welfare. Children nevertheless earned very little, teenage female silk spinners bringing home about $130 per year, for example, at a time when reformers estimated that a family needed more than $600 to survive.

Patterns of child labor varied by ethnic group. Italian families were more likely to send children to work to keep the wife and mother at home; among Eastern European **Jews** and **African Americans**, mothers more often worked for wages to keep children in school. Families were more likely to support a son's **education** than a daughter's except among the Irish, whose daughters more often became teachers and **nurses** while sons remained in blue-collar jobs. Reformers focused chiefly on factory wage labor; they did not criticize agricultural or domestic labor, jobs in which children's participation was long-standing and assumed to be healthy. In practice, this emphasis excluded most children of color, as well as many whites, from labor regulation.

Despite opposition, the number of employed children grew steadily through the 1910 census, when an estimated 1.8 million children were in the work force. Over 18 percent of children between 10 and 15 years old were employed. The problem was especially severe in the South, where the proliferation of textile factories caused the number of child factory laborers to triple in the 1890s. In 1904, the **National Child Labor Committee** (**NCLC**) was founded at a convention of the **National Conference of Charities and Correction**. The NCLC lobbied successfully for laws banning employment of children under 14 in most northern and western states but not in the South. Local opposition often made labor laws unenforceable, so the NCLC campaigned for a national law. Congress passed the **Keating–Owen Act** in 1916, but the **Supreme Court** struck it down in *Hammer v. Dagenhart* (1918). An amended law also fell before the conservative court in 1922, and federal efforts to ban child labor regularly failed until the 1930s. Nevertheless, many states retained regulations on the age and hours of workers. *See also* ADOLESCENCE; HIGH SCHOOL; HINE, LEWIS WICKES; MCKELWAY, ALEXANDER JEFFREY; REFORM MOVEMENTS.

CHILDREN'S BUREAU. Established by Congress in 1912 as part of the **Department of Commerce and Labor**, the Bureau resulted from a lengthy campaign by **Florence Kelley** and **Lillian Wald** of the **National Child Labor Committee** for a federal bureau to collect and disseminate information on the care and protection of children. In response to lobbying for a female director, President **William Howard Taft** appointed **Julia Lathrop**, who thus became the first woman to head a federal agency. The bureau gathered and publicized information, compiled lists of state **child labor** laws, studied child mortality figures, and campaigned to improve birth registration. Its pamphlets on health care during pregnancy and infancy outsold all other government publications during the 1910s. The bureau also broke new ground by using exhibits, demonstrations, film, and radio, as well as supplying information for **mass-circulation magazine** advice columns. Testifying to its effectiveness, tens of thousands of letters seeking advice or help poured into the bureau each year. Each letter received a personal reply.

CHILDS, RICHARD S. (1882–1978). Urban reformer. Heir to the family that founded the Bon Ami Company, this Connecticut native attended Yale University and worked in **advertising** before devoting himself to urban **structural reform**. He conceived the notion of a **short ballot** and recruited **Woodrow Wilson**, **Charles Beard**, and other prominent political scientists for his Short Ballot Organization. He also developed the **city manager system** based on an experiment in Staunton, Virginia. Active in the **National Municipal League**, Childs used his considerable public relations skills to promote that group's model **home rule** charter.

CHINESE EXCLUSION ACTS. See ALIEN LAND ACT; ANGEL ISLAND; IMMIGRATION.

CHOPIN, KATHERINE O'FLAHERTY (KATE) (1851–1904). Author. Born in St. Louis, Chopin married into New Orleans Creole society (1870) and lived for a time on a plantation in northwestern Louisiana. After her husband died in 1882, she at first tried managing the family business and then returned to St. Louis, where she published stories set in Creole Louisiana that won national attention as examples of local color fiction. She absorbed **realism** and **naturalism** from French writers such as Guy de Maupassant and Émile Zola, whose treatment of **sexuality** and inner passions was still considered sordid by respectable American critics. Her 1899 novel, *The Awakening*, based loosely on her own experiences, created a scandal because of its candid, nonjudgmental treatment of a married **woman**'s sexual longings. Her reputation faded after her early death from a brain hemorrhage in 1904, but by the 1960s her novel was accepted as a masterpiece that expressed elements of early **feminism**. *See also* LITERATURE.

CITY BEAUTIFUL. This term, borrowed from the **Arts and Crafts movement**, came into use in the late 1890s to describe a set of movements to improve the physical environment of cities and make them more attractive and amenable. It had its roots in the mid-19th-century movement for municipal parks and the romantic landscape architecture of Frederick Law Olmsted Sr. Another source was the nearly 2,500 village and town improvement societies that dedicated themselves to removing billboards and overhead wires, cleaning vacant lots, building **playgrounds**, and planting trees. The Beaux Arts movement in **architecture** and sculpture, meanwhile, fueled campaigns for stately public buildings, formal boulevards, downtown civic centers, and impressive public monuments. Then the 1893 Columbian **Exposition**'s "White City," the central complex of fair buildings created under the direction of **Daniel Burnham,** offered a tangible model of the ideal city that brought together these disparate concerns.

By the early 1900s, proponents such as **Charles Mulford Robinson** and Horace McFarland, leader of the **American Civic Association**, spoke and wrote profusely on urban beautification. The 1902 publication of Washington's **McMillan Plan**, prepared by Burnham, **Frederick Law Olmsted Jr., Charles McKim,** and **Augustus Saint-Gaudens**, signaled the City Beautiful's potential as the basis for the "comprehensive" planning of cities. There followed an outpouring of such plans ranging from sketchy reports to Burnham's exquisite *Plan of Chicago*. But after 1910, even former proponents such as Olmsted Jr. began to argue that the City Beautiful focused too much on public buildings and spaces and did not deal systematically with housing, transportation, **public health**, municipal engineering, **zoning**, and other **City Practical** concerns. As a result, the City Beautiful ideal faded in the 1910s but not before leaving its mark on Chicago; Dallas; Denver; Kansas City; Washington, D.C.; and other cities. *See also* NATIONAL CONFERENCE ON CITY PLANNING.

CITY MANAGER SYSTEM. Also known as the council-manager system, this form of municipal government provides for an elected city council, generally small in size, and an appointed city manager. Progressive Era proponents urged that the council be elected on an **at-large**, **nonpartisan** basis, but numerous manager systems provide for district representation and some for partisan elections. In this system, the mayor chairs the city council and acts as a ceremonial leader, but the manager oversees the day-to-day operations of city departments. Urban affairs experts brought the idea to the United States in the 1890s from Germany, where municipal administration was centralized in the hands of professional administrators. Inspired by an experiment in Staunton, Virginia, **Richard S. Childs** promoted the idea in 1910 as an alternative to the **commission system**, which quickly disappointed advocates of urban **structural reform**. After Dayton, Ohio, became the first large city to adopt the manager plan in 1913, it spread rapidly, and by 1920, over 150 cities had city managers. Despite the counterexamples such as Kansas City, where **machines** found ways to control this system, city manager government was more successful than the commission format in countering **bosses**, though it was accused of being too removed from the public and too favorable to commercial and financial interests. *See also* HOME RULE; NATIONAL MUNICIPAL LEAGUE.

CITY PRACTICAL. Also known as City Functional or City Efficient, this term was given currency by a 1909 speech by **Cass Gilbert** and expressed an approach to urban planning conceived in reaction to the **City Beautiful** emphasis on monuments, civic centers, boulevards, and parks. Focusing instead on projects that would improve a city's **economy**, housing, and **public health**, City Practical proponents argued that urban plans should be based on thorough social and economic data, as in the **Pittsburgh Survey**, and that planning should have a tangible influence on the geography and character of industry, commerce, railroads, roadways, **utilities**, housing, and recreation. Often dressed in the language of **scientific management** and **efficiency**, City Practical planning represented an impulse to put urban environments under rational control, just as **structural reforms** aimed to rationalize city government. At its most idealistic, City Practical planning intersected with the **garden city movement** and the housing advocacy of **Benjamin Marsh**. Because such plans needed the sponsorship of chambers of commerce and local governments, they often emphasized **zoning** or economic development while downplaying social reforms. The activities of **Frederick Law Olmsted Jr.**, John Nolen Sr. (1869–1937), and Harland Bartholomew (1889–1989) helped to make this mindset dominant in American city planning for much of the 20th century. *See also* NATIONAL CONFERENCE ON CITY PLANNING.

CIVIC FEDERATION OF CHICAGO. In response to British **Social Gospel** reformer William T. Stead's call for a "civic church" to combat the social and moral desolation detailed in his book *If Christ Came to Chicago* (1894), commercial and civic leaders in February 1894 formed this organization in an effort to fuse urban **structural reform** with Social Gospel impulses. The organization brought together elite figures such as banker Lyman Gage and Honoré Palmer, civic leader and wife of developer Potter Palmer, with **labor union** leaders and social activists such as **Jane Addams**. The federation underwrote relief for the destitute in the 1890s depression and attempted to mediate the 1894 Pullman Strike. The group exposed ties between **machine politicians** and **utility** monopolies, gambling, **prostitution**, and crime. It detailed inadequacies in food inspection and ran vacation schools for poor children, as well as a street cleaning service intended to demonstrate the lack of **efficiency** in municipal street cleaning. The **National Civic Federation** grew from the Chicago group's 1899 conference on trusts. Although its social reform fervor faded, the federation survived through the 20th century as a public policy institution dedicated to metropolitan Chicago.

CIVIL SERVICE COMMISSION, U.S. This three-member board oversaw implementation of the 1883 Pendleton Act, which established procedures for replacing political patronage in federal employment with a merit-based system. The proportion of federal jobs covered by civil service rules grew steadily after 1883, in part because before leaving office presidents would extend coverage to lock in their own appointees. By 1900, 46 percent of positions (94,839 people) in executive departments enjoyed civil service protection, including the bulk of federal workers in Washington, D.C. Of the 113,161 "unclassified" positions, about three-fourths were in the Postal Service, the customary vehicle for spreading partisan influence around the country. As civil service commissioner, **Theodore Roosevelt** (1889–95) struggled to strengthen the board and publicized political manipulation in the Post Office and other departments. This experience made Roosevelt adept at manipulating patronage when it suited him as president after 1901. Still, by the time he left the White House in 1909, the agency had expanded considerably, with two-thirds of federal employees falling under civil service rules, including a large number of postmasters around the country, a process that **William Howard Taft** would virtually complete during his presidency. With old-fashioned patronage visibly on the wane, presidents from Roosevelt to **Woodrow Wilson** battled Congress over the role of the Civil Service Commission in regulating promotion, pay, and working conditions in federal agencies.

THE CLANSMAN **(1905).** *See THE BIRTH OF A NATION*; KU KLUX KLAN.

CLARK, JAMES BEAUCHAMP "CHAMP" (1850–1921). Politician. A Kentucky native, Clark studied at Cincinnati Law School (1875) and practiced in Missouri. He served as a **Democrat** in the state legislature before his election to the House of Representatives (1893–95 and 1897–1921). A colorful orator with a talent for unifying the fractious Democratic Party, Clark became House minority leader in 1908 and guided Democrats toward supporting **progressive** legislation, which put the party in a position to profit from the **Old Guard–Insurgent** quarrel within the **Republican Party**. When Democrats gained a majority in 1910, he served as speaker, rehabilitating an office undermined by the debacle over **Joseph G. Cannon**. Campaigning for the 1912 Democratic presidential nomination, Clark won a majority of the delegates at the party convention, but this was insufficient to gain the nomination because of the two-thirds rule then in force. Backers of **Woodrow Wilson** ultimately defeated Clark, in part by portraying him as more conservative than his record warranted. After Wilson's election, Clark cooperated in guiding **New Freedom** legislation through Congress, but he opposed **preparedness** and broke with Wilson over conscription.

CLAY, LAURA (1849–1941). Suffragist and farmer. The daughter of well-to-do Kentuckians, Clay supported her career in **women**'s rights by managing a 300-acre farm. Converted to the cause by her parents' bitter **divorce**, she helped found the Kentucky Equal Rights Association in 1888 and served as its president until 1912. An officer of the state branches of the **Woman's Christian Temperance Union** and the **General Federation of Women's Clubs**, she helped to improve Kentucky women's property rights, medical care, and access to higher **education** and to gain the right to vote in school board elections. In the 1890s, Clay became the leading southern member of the **National American Woman Suffrage Association (NAWSA)**. Like most southern white women, she supported the **disfranchisement** of **African Americans**, and in 1913 she became vice president of the **Southern States Woman Suffrage Conference**. In 1919, Clay withdrew from NAWSA as it campaigned for the ratification of the **Nineteenth Amendment**. After ratification, she was active in the state **Democratic Party**.

CLAYTON ANTITRUST ACT (1914). Named for **Democrat** Henry D. Clayton of Alabama, chair of the House Judiciary Committee, this measure sought to put teeth into the 1890 Sherman Antitrust Act by specifying business practices prohibited as anticompetitive, such as price discrimination, exclusive contracts, and **interlocking directorates**. The act also partially acceded to a demand of the **American Federation of Labor** by more or less exempting **labor unions** from **antitrust** laws and limiting federal injunctions against strikes. Although the bill fulfilled a central promise of his **New Freedom** program, President **Woodrow Wilson** gave it tepid support because he had decided to press for creation of the **Federal Trade Commission** as a more promising way to control big business. This allowed Congress to write in various loopholes. Despite its shortcomings, the measure defined the country's basic antitrust policy for most of the 20th century.

COCA-COLA. Concocted from coca leaves, kola nuts, sugar, and carbonated water by pharmacist John Pemberton in 1886, this soft drink was initially promoted as a tonic for neurasthenia, headaches, and hangovers. After Pemberton's death in 1888, Asa G. Candler (1851–1929) gained control of the formula and made the drink widely popular at soda fountains, incorporating the Coca-Cola Company in 1892. A successful Atlanta bottling franchise system and **advertising** helped make "Coke" ubiquitous nationally in the 1910s and 1920s, especially at soda fountains in pharmacy **chain stores**. However, the formula changed over time, as Candler conceded to antidrug pressures in 1903 and removed cocaine. In 1909, the federal government brought a **Pure Food and Drug** suit against the company, forcing a 1918 settlement that reduced the amount of caffeine in the drink. *See also* HARRISON NARCOTICS CONTROL ACT; POPULAR CULTURE.

CODY, WILLIAM "BUFFALO BILL" (1846–1917). *See* WILD WEST SHOWS.

COEUR D'ALENE, LABOR STRIFE AT (1892–1905). By the 1890s, labor conditions at the silver, lead, and zinc mines in the Coeur D'Alene region of northern Idaho were notoriously harsh, and the result was frequent and violent conflict. An 1892 effort by mine owners to lower wages by as much as 50 cents per day provoked a strike that owners sought to break with Pinkerton detectives and private guards. Strikers retaliated by attacking mines, taking guards and strikebreakers prisoner, and threatening to destroy buildings and machinery. The bloody struggle left six dead and prompted intervention by the National Guard, which confined hundreds of miners in stockades. During an April 1899 strike, embittered workers, now affiliated with the **Western Federation of Miners (WFM)**, hijacked a train at gunpoint and dynamited machinery. Idaho's generally pro-labor governor, Frank Steunenberg, sent troops who again imprisoned hundreds of miners in stockades. On 30 December 1905, a bomb planted in the gate to Steunenberg's yard killed the former governor. Revelations that the assassin, Harry Orchard (1867–1954), had been involved in other bombings and murders associated with the WFM led to the indictment of union leaders, including **"Big Bill" Haywood**, on conspiracy charges. *See also* BORAH, WILLIAM EDGAR.

COHAN, GEORGE MICHAEL (1878–1942). Actor, dancer, songwriter, playwright, and producer. Born in Rhode Island to Irish **vaudeville** performers, Cohan began his career as a seven-year-old dancer in the family act. By 1894, he was a successful songwriter and also composed comedic variety show sketches. In 1901, he staged the first Broadway show that he composed, directed, produced, and starred in. By 1920, Cohan and his partner Sam H. Harris produced 46 Broadway shows, many starring the leading stage actors of the day. Cohan also appeared in **movies**. In 1917, he wrote the patriotic songs "You're a Grand Old Flag" and "Over There" to support U.S. entry into World War I. Never a darling of critics though immensely popular with audiences, Cohan moved American **musical** theater away from an operatic emphasis on the exotic toward a vaudevillian emphasis on local color. Comic portrayals of ethnic minorities, slangy urban speech, avid patriotism, and rapid pacing characterized his songs and shows.

COHN, FANNIA (1885?–1962). Labor leader. The daughter of middle-class Russian **Jews**, Cohn became a **socialist** as a young **woman** and in 1904 immigrated to the United States, where she worked as a sleeve maker. In 1909, she was elected to the executive board of a newly formed local of the **International Ladies' Garment Workers' Union (ILGWU)**. In 1916, she became the first woman vice president of a major **labor union** when she was elected to the ILGWU's national executive board. In this position, she established an **education** department to train organizers and integrate women into labor organizing. She remained a visible, if at times contentious, figure in the labor movement the rest of her life.

COLUMBIAN EXPOSITION. *See* AMUSEMENT PARKS; BURNHAM, DANIEL H.; CITY BEAUTIFUL; EXPOSITIONS.

COMMERCE AND LABOR, U.S. DEPARTMENT OF. Congress established this cabinet department in February 1903 after lobbying by President **Theodore Roosevelt**. The department brought together hitherto scattered agencies, among them the Bureau of Standards, the Census Bureau, the Bureau of Navigation, the Coast and Geodetic Survey, the Bureau of Labor, the Bureau of **Immigration**, and the **Bureau of Corporations**. The president's trusted White House secretary, **George B. Cortelyou**, became the first secretary of the new department. In 1906, Roosevelt appointed to this post **Oscar S. Straus**, the first **Jewish** cabinet member. After **Democrats** regained control of Congress in 1910, the **American Federation of Labor** stepped up pressure to create a separate **Department of Labor**, a bill for which President **William Howard Taft** signed before leaving office on 4 March 1913. *See also* NATIONAL CIVIC FEDERATION.

COMMERCE COURT. Created under the 1910 **Mann–Elkins Act**, this rotating panel of five federal judges heard appeals to decisions of the **Interstate Commerce Commission (ICC)**. The court reflected the belief of President **William Howard Taft** and other moderates that expanded federal regulatory power required specialized courts expert in specific economic sectors. **Progressives** resisted this initiative as a judicial check on federal regulatory authority, a sentiment that seemed confirmed when the court overturned nine-tenths of contested ICC decisions during its first year. In 1912, Congress nearly overrode Taft's veto of a bill to abolish the court. Its credibility dissolved in January 1913, when the Senate impeached one of its judges on conflict of interest charges. President **Woodrow Wilson** signed a measure abolishing the Commerce Court in October 1913. *See also* ANTITRUST.

COMMISSION ON INDUSTRIAL RELATIONS. *See* INDUSTRIAL RELATIONS, COMMISSION ON.

COMMISSION SYSTEM. In this form of municipal government, voters elect **at-large** five to seven commissioners, each of whom manages a municipal department, while all the members sit collectively as a city council. Although some 19th-century precedents existed, this format gained popularity in 1901 when Texas made permanent the emergency commission that supervised recovery from the 1900 **Galveston Hurricane**. Houston and Dallas soon adopted similar formats. The system spread to nearly 480 mostly medium-sized and small cities in the Midwest, South, and West by 1920. A few large industrial belt cities, such as Buffalo, Newark, and Jersey City, also adopted it. At first, urban affairs experts endorsed the commission as a device for undermining ward **bosses** while improving **efficiency**, although some, such as **Charles A. Beard**, questioned assigning the legislative functions of a city council to the executive board. By the 1910s, many observers were disenchanted with the way this plan placed inexpert, often part-time business or civic leaders in charge of police, health, or public works. The experience of cities such as Memphis and New Orleans revealed that the fusion of legislative and executive functions in a small, secretive board could enhance a boss's lack of accountability. After 1910, the **city manager system** superseded the commission as the preferred **structural reform**, and beginning in the 1920s the number of commissions dwindled. *See also* NATIONAL MUNICIPAL LEAGUE.

COMMITTEE OF FOURTEEN. Founded in New York City in 1905, this body sought to tighten the city's liquor laws and abolish **prostitution**. Its initial target was New York City's Raines Law (1896), which banned the sale of alcohol on Sundays except to lodgers in hotels of 10 or more rooms, a requirement that was easy for **saloons** connected to **Tammany Hall** to circumvent. Like the **Chicago Vice Commission**, the committee included representatives of major religious groups as well as prominent figures in business, law, and reform, such as **Lawrence Veiller**, police commissioner **William G. McAdoo**, and **settlement house** director **Mary Simkhovitch**. Lasting until 1934, the group played a role in tightening the city's liquor restrictions; enacting the Page Law (1910), which required the fingerprinting and gynecological examination of **women** convicted of selling sex, with those found to carry sexually transmitted diseases incarcerated for up to a year or until cured; and in passing a **red-light abatement** ordinance (1914) and amendments to vagrancy statutes that made it easier for police to incarcerate suspected prostitutes (1915). See also AMERICAN SOCIAL HYGIENE ASSOCIATION; COMSTOCK, ANTHONY; MORROW, PRINCE; SEXUALITY.

COMMONS, JOHN R. (1862–1945). Economist and labor reformer. The son of an unsuccessful Ohio businessman, Commons graduated from Oberlin (1888) but failed to complete his doctoral studies at Johns Hopkins. He nevertheless landed lectureships at several universities, where his **socialist** and **Social Gospel** views and difficulties with teaching undermined his academic career. Between 1899 and 1904, Commons blossomed as a researcher on labor and **immigration** for the **U.S. Department of Commerce and Labor** and the **National Civic Federation**. Appointed professor at the University of Wisconsin (1904–32), he produced landmark histories of American industrialization and the labor movement, collaborated with **Charles McCarthy** on the so-called **Wisconsin Idea**, co-founded the **American Association for Labor Legislation**, provided policy advice to the **National Consumers' League**, supervised the labor sections of the **Pittsburgh Survey**, and participated in the **Commission on Industrial Relations**. Through his writing, policy advice, and teaching, Commons played a central role in shaping 20th-century social policies as well as labor history and institutional economics.

COMMONWEALTH EDISON COMPANY. Formed in 1907 by **Samuel Insull** through the merger of Chicago's two electrical franchises, this company developed organizational, financial, and marketing strategies that enabled the mass **electrification** of households and businesses. Commonwealth Edison devised pricing and other strategies to encourage electrical use during periods of low demand, which subsidized huge generators powerful enough to satisfy peak demand. The **utility** gave inducements to industries (as well as **amusement parks**) that operated at night, while it advertised irons, toasters, and other electric household appliances, sold door-to-door and through an outlet store in Chicago. Commonwealth Edison remained legally separate from the suburban utilities that Insull began to integrate into a regional network by the 1910s. This innovative regional grid prompted Illinois to adopt state-level electrical regulation in 1913.

COMPULSORY EDUCATION LAWS. Massachusetts passed the first law requiring children to attend school in 1852. By 1900, 33 states had such laws, the exceptions being almost entirely in the South, where only Kentucky and West Virginia had statutes on school attendance. Most states required three to four months of schooling per year for six to eight years, and truancy was only sporadically punished. The campaign against **child labor**, changing attitudes toward **adolescence**, and the professionalization of **education** prompted efforts to strengthen these laws and their enforcement. Cities established attendance departments with records on tens of thousands of cases; Chicago's department investigated nearly 6,000 truancy cases per year. Working-class families who needed children's wages often resisted enforcement of school laws. In Wisconsin, Oregon, and other states, efforts to enforce attendance became intertwined with **Americanization** and Protestant hostility toward Catholic parochial schools. By 1918, every state had at least a weak compulsory education law, and truancy enforcement was improving. *See also* ANTI-CATHOLICISM; HIGH SCHOOL.

COMSTOCK, ANTHONY (1844–1915). Reformer. Born in Connecticut, Comstock in 1873 became both the principal agent of the New York Society for the Suppression of Vice and a special agent for the U.S. Post Office to enforce a new ban on mailing "obscene" materials. Comstock worked to suppress popular sexual culture, including sex advice manuals, pornography, **birth control**, and abortion services by raiding and arresting everyone from condom sellers to **art** galleries that displayed nudes. He discouraged circulation of the emerging scientific and **intellectual** discourse on **sexuality**, as well as **literary** and artistic works. Comstock contributed to the passage of stricter state laws against obscenity. But by the early 20th century, **feminism** and the social hygiene and **eugenics** movements challenged his narrow view of sexuality, even as changes in family size, **women**'s roles, and children's economic function undermined the Victorian moralism he championed. President **Woodrow Wilson** appointed him to the International Purity Congress in 1914, but by then the term *Comstockery* became a disparaging label for wrongheaded Puritanism. *See also* COMMITTEE OF FOURTEEN.

CONEY ISLAND. Long a beach retreat for New York City residents, Coney Island became the nation's largest and best-known popular resort in the 1890s. Beginning in 1895, entrepreneurs enclosed their mechanical rides, creating the first **amusement parks**. Sea Lion Park (1895), later transformed into Luna Park (1903) by Frederic Thompson; George Tilyou's Steeplechase Park (1897); and Dreamland Park (1904) sprang up alongside the boardwalk, the beach, and the **dance** pavilion. **Trolley** lines and other mass transit made the resort accessible to working-class day-trippers. Promoters claimed as many as 200,000 patrons per day in the early 20th century. *See also* POPULAR CULTURE.

CONGRESSIONAL UNION. *See* NATIONAL WOMAN'S PARTY.

CONSERVATION. Beginning in the 1870s, a few Americans protested deforestation and the loss of game-animal habitats. At the state level, urban politicians seeking to improve water supplies and various reformers, including **women** in organizations such as the **Audubon Societies**, made environmental quality a political issue. Influential at the national level were elite hunters' groups such as the Boone and Crocket Club, timber company officials, the American Forestry Association, and western irrigators, who enlisted state and federal government to manage timberlands and watersheds. The national leaders of the conservation movement, including **Theodore Roosevelt** and **Gifford Pinchot**, turned to government regulation and trained experts to ensure **efficient** use of national resources. Roosevelt convened the **White House Conference on Conservation** in 1908, which led to the **National Conservation Commission (NCC)** and its three-volume survey of the nation's natural resources. Conservationists came into direct conflict with powerful business interests, especially in the West, the location of most land set aside for conservation in this period. Congress thwarted the forest reserve program promoted by Roosevelt and Pinchot and abolished the NCC in 1909, illustrating the clash between the regulatory mindset and competitive capitalism.

Conservationists found their interests served through federal agencies, including the United States Geological Survey, the **Reclamation Service** (1902), the **U.S. Forest Service** (1905), and the **National Park Service** (1916), and federal laws, including the Forest Reserve Act (1891), the Forest Management Act (1897), the **Newlands Reclamation Act** (1902), and the Weeks Act (1911). Some businesses regarded conservation favorably as well. Major railroads, such as the **Atchison, Topeka, and Santa Fe** and the Great Northern, took an interest in barring industrial development and settlement in order to develop national parks as tourist destinations; Yellowstone (1872), Yosemite (1890), and the Grand Canyon (designated a forest reserve in 1893, a game reserve in 1906, a national monument in 1908, and a national park in 1919) are among the best known. By 1905, federal forest reserves included some 100 million acres, and Americans had begun to prevent extinction of species and limit pollution with state and federal laws such as the **Lacey Act** (1900) and international agreements such as the **Boundary Waters Treaty** (1909) and the **Migratory Bird Treaty** (1916).

A different approach to the environment found its spokesman in **John Muir**, who by the 1890s won recognition for his celebration of the spiritual importance of undeveloped wilderness. He founded the **Sierra Club** in 1892 and played a role in encouraging nationalization of Yosemite and creation of Acadia (1916) and other national parks. Muir's "preservation" approach at times directly conflicted with the conservation approach, as illustrated in the struggle over **Hetch Hetchy Valley**. Both conservationists and preservationists imagined "wilderness" as pristine landscape unspoiled by the human presence and sought to erase the reality of human use from areas designated as wilderness. **Native Americans** and other locals found themselves barred from using resources or living on lands taken for state or federal parks, even as wealthy recreational users began to flock to the areas to sightsee, hunt, and fish. *See also* REFORM MOVEMENTS.

CONSUMER CREDIT. The modern system of consumer credit has its origins in the Progressive Era, as lenders developed various new ways to induce consumers to borrow. Personal debt increased faster than population growth beginning in 1896, but debt per household ranged on average only from 4 to 6 percent of income between 1900 and 1920. Sources of credit began to shift away from friends and family or pawnbrokers and moneylenders to banks, finance companies (**General Motors** was an innovator in this realm, and **automobile** purchases contributed to rising consumer debt levels by the 1920s), **department stores**, loan societies, and credit unions. Department stores created the earliest credit cards, permitting selected customers to pay periodically rather than at the time of purchase. For the less well-off, the installment plan substituted a schedule of payments for the older practice of a single deadline by which the entire borrowed sum had to be repaid. The new, rationalized system of credit permitted more people to enjoy the fruits of mass production, but critics charged it with undermining traditional values of thrift and self-discipline. Older forms of credit, such as a charge account at a local store, persisted in poor urban neighborhoods, the rural South, and company towns, where workers relied on landowners and store managers' often exploitative accounting of their income and spending.

CONVICT LEASING. A practice common in the southern states during the Progressive Era, convict leasing enabled businesses to pay the state for the labor of prisoners. Since Reconstruction, proliferating laws against vagrancy, contract evasion, and petty theft combined with **disfranchisement** and the barring of **African American** men from juries to produce rising numbers of black prisoners, who were far more likely than whites to be sentenced to hard labor. The convicts were leased to private contractors and forced to work without pay under brutal conditions, much as they or their ancestors had during slavery. Frequent illness, injury, and death from overwork, physical punishment, and malnutrition among prisoners and their use for financial and political gain produced chronic scandals and calls for penal reform. In some states, "reform" meant abolishing convict leasing so that counties could use prisoners to build roads, a form of labor essential to the realization of the **Good Roads movement** in the South. *See also* SEGREGATION.

COOLING-OFF TREATIES. Secretary of State **William Jennings Bryan** promoted these pacts, a variant on **arbitration treaties**, during 1913–14. Signatory countries committed themselves to not going to war during a dispute for a year, while an international commission investigated. Of the 30 treaties Bryan negotiated, the U.S. Senate rejected only those with **Panama** and the **Dominican Republic**, while foreign countries failed to ratify six others. Bryan, a lifelong pacifist, distributed to the diplomats involved paperweight plowshares that had been melted from U.S. Army swords. Sadly, World War I demonstrated the irrelevance of these wait-a-year pacts. *See also* FOREIGN POLICY.

COOPERATIVES, FARMERS'. Amid the relative prosperity of the early 1900s but with the agrarian crisis of the 1890s fresh in mind, farmers' efforts to organize cooperatives reached an unprecedented level. The number jumped from around 2,000 in 1900 to over 12,000 by 1920. Cooperatives encouraged members to sell only through the group (thus avoiding middlemen) or hold crops for an advantageous price by offering low-cost storage. Some pressured members to limit production, whereas others offered credit on advantageous terms. Organizations of wheat farmers ran grain elevators; dairy associations managed creameries. Livestock ranchers created breeding and shipping associations. Thousands of cooperatives also purchased farm and household supplies for resale to members, but alternatives such as **mail order** made farmers less interested in this possibility than they were in marketing associations. Encouraged by movements such as the **American Society of Equity** and the **Farmers' Union**, cooperatives thrived in midwestern grain, corn, and dairy regions. The Minnesota Cooperative Creameries Association (1911) maintained its own commission house in New York to handle the butter and milk of 130 local cooperatives. In the West, the California Fruit Growers' Exchange (1905) fought local gluts of perishable fruit and damage caused by shipping. This group's "Sunkist" label became a model for California cooperative brand names such as Diamond Walnut and Sun Maid raisins, both begun in 1912. The Southern Cotton Exchange endeavored to break that region's cycle of overproduction and falling prices. Farming cooperatives also campaigned for expanded federal agriculture programs. *See also* FEDERAL FARM LOAN ACT; WAREHOUSE ACT.

CORTELYOU, GEORGE B. (1862–1940). Public official. A New York City native, Cortelyou became a stenographic reporter and worked for President Grover Cleveland starting in 1895. Despite his **Democratic** affiliation, he kept his job during the administration of **Republican William McKinley**, and by 1900 he had become secretary to the president (more or less the chief of staff) and retained this position into **Theodore Roosevelt**'s administration. Cortelyou brought unprecedented **efficiency** and sophistication to White House operations and public relations. His records, personnel procedures, and methods for handling press releases and briefings created an **organizational** basis for the activist presidency that took shape during the Progressive Era. Roosevelt, impressed by Cortelyou's work in the **Anthracite Coal Strike** negotiations, named him the first secretary of **commerce and labor** (1903–04). In 1904, he became chair of the Republican National Committee and managed Roosevelt's reelection campaign. His fundraising from corporations caused a stir, given Roosevelt's **antitrust** stance. Cortelyou rejoined the cabinet as postmaster general (1905–07) before advancing to secretary of the treasury (1907–09). His handling of the **Panic of 1907** led to short-lived talk of a presidential run. Cortelyou's ties to Roosevelt discouraged President **William Howard Taft** from reappointing him in 1909. He spent his remaining career as a **utilities** executive in New York City.

COSMETICS. The use of rouge and other face paints was associated chiefly with **prostitutes** and actresses at the turn of the century, but many **women** did use face creams, powders, shampoos and hair preparations. Expanded manufacture and sale of these personal-care products was a significant trend, as **advertising** in the **mass-circulation magazines** reveals. Beauty parlors and cosmetic products were among the few businesses that offered women independence and potentially substantial income as sales agents, managers, and business owners. Like industry leaders Elizabeth Arden, Annie Turnbo Malone, Helena Rubenstein, and Madame C. J. Walker, many entrepreneurs began with door-to-door sales of preparations made at home. As in so much of American life, **segregation** characterized this industry. The **African American** branch offered opportunity and autonomy to black women even as it sold the promise of a less "African" appearance with creams to lighten the skin and combs and shampoos to straighten and soften the hair. The white branch sold "natural beauty," insisting that its products were not deceptive face paints but merely the means to bring out a woman's inner beauty. *See also* NEW WOMAN; POPULAR CULTURE; SEXUALITY.

COST OF LIVING. After decades of stagnant or deflating prices, the steady prosperity that began in 1897 combined with falling world gold prices to spark a cycle of inflation that raised the cost of supporting a family by an estimated 35 percent by 1913. Although rising incomes meant that many segments of society experienced improving living standards, sporadic price rises amid uneven income improvements made the "high cost of living" a staple of Progressive Era political debate, as well as a subject of numerous magazine articles, books, and even **movies** such as *The High Cost of Living* (1912), a drama, and *The Cost of High Living* (1916), a comedy. Anxiety over inflation underpinned the era's movements for **antitrust**, railroad regulation, and tariff reform. It provided a launching point for **women's** consumer activism, exemplified by the **National Consumers' League**. *See also* ECONOMY.

COUNTRY LIFE, COMMISSION ON. Formed by **Theodore Roosevelt** in 1908, this panel reflected the anxiety that the allure of the city and the isolation and tediousness of rural life threatened family farms. With **Liberty Hyde Bailey** as chair, this panel included experts in **conservation** and agriculture such as **Gifford Pinchot**. The commission distributed 300,000 questionnaires and held hearings in 30 states before filing a report in early 1909 proposing a host of measures to make family farming more rewarding and attractive. At times echoing the ideas of the populists and the Grange, the proposals ranged from improving rural roads, schools, and health care to increasing federal support of farmers' **cooperatives** and agricultural research and upgrading rural communications, banking, and credit. The commission devoted special attention to the condition of white farm **women**, but it shied away from examining the circumstances of **African Americans**. The commission inspired a durable Country Life movement, and many recommendations materialized, but population movement to the cities continued.

COX, KENYON (1856–1919). Artist and critic. Born in Ohio, Cox absorbed academic style while studying with Jean-Léon Gérôme at Paris's École des Beaux Arts (1879–82) and established himself in New York as a painter, illustrator, and instructor at the Art Students League. He won most recognition for allegorical and historical murals at the Columbian Exposition, the Library of Congress, state capitols in Iowa and Minnesota, and other public buildings. As **art** critic for the *Century*, *Scribner's*, and other magazines, Cox became a key voice for the formal yet expressive styles of the late 19th-century American Renaissance. His biting review in *Harper's* of the 1913 **Armory Show** became noted at the time as a statement of artistic resistance to **modernism**.

CRAM, RALPH ADAMS (1863–1942). Architect. A native of New Hampshire, Cram apprenticed as an architect and then traveled in Europe before founding a partnership in Boston (1890). An Anglo-Catholic, Cram specialized in Gothic Revival designs, among them St. Thomas Episcopal Church on Fifth Avenue and the enormous Cathedral Church of St. John the Divine, both in Manhattan. He also oversaw Gothic Revival construction for **universities** such as Princeton, Rice, and West Point. His prolific writings, echoing his **architecture**, celebrated medieval art and deplored all **modernism**. Cram won much acclaim and, beginning in 1914, chaired both the Boston city planning board and the architecture department at the Massachusetts Institute of Technology. *See also* ARTS AND CRAFTS MOVEMENT.

CRANE, STEPHEN (1871–1900). Author. Born in New Jersey to a pair of moralistic Methodist writers, Crane by 1891 took up a bohemian life while working as a reporter in New York City. His interest in lower Manhattan lowlife led to *Maggie: A Girl of the Streets* (1893), the best-known example of the period's slum fiction genre. Despite being self-published after New York publishers rejected it, the novel gained the attention of **Hamlin Garland** and **William Dean Howells**, who promoted Crane as an exemplar of **realism** and **naturalism**. Newspaper syndication of his Civil War novel, *The Red Badge of Courage* (1894), made Crane a celebrity. Reporting assignments in the West and Mexico provided material for his short stories. Amid failing health and a tumultuous personal life that steadied somewhat after his common-law marriage to a Florida brothel owner, Crane covered the Greco–Turkish and **Spanish–American** wars while producing a stream of memorable prose and poetry. He died of **tuberculosis** in Germany. *See also* LITERATURE.

CRIPPLE CREEK. The 1891 discovery of gold in this mountainous region west of Colorado Springs set off the last great Colorado mineral rush. Within five years, miners, their families, and merchants created a substantial town at Cripple Creek, source of half of the state's gold production. An attempt to extend working hours in the slump that followed the Panic of 1893 prompted the **Western Federation of Miners (WFM)** to call a strike in February 1894. When mine owners hired a small army of "deputies" to seize the mines from the armed strikers, Colorado's Populist governor, Davis Waite (1825–1901), sent in the state militia and arranged for arbitration that sided with the miners. By 1903, when the WFM struck in support of mill and smelter workers, the political situation was less favorable. This time, the state militia supported efforts by mine owners and a vigilante group called the Citizens' Alliance to imprison and deport strikers and sympathizers. To make things worse, two bombings in November 1903 and June 1904 killed a superintendent and a foreman and 13 nonunion miners, respectively. The apparent perpetrator was Harry Orchard (1867–1954), the radical unionist whose 1905 murder of former Idaho governor Frank Steunenberg climaxed the violence at **Coeur d'Alene**. The strike collapsed amid state-imposed martial law. Within two years, nonunion miners earning low wages had replaced organized workers.

THE CRISIS. *See* NATIONAL ASSOCIATION FOR THE ADVANCEMENT OF COLORED PEOPLE; DU BOIS, W. E. B.

CROKER, RICHARD (1843–1922). Politician. Born in Ireland, Croker immigrated to the United States in 1846 with his family. As leader of the Fourth Avenue Tunnel Gang, he managed election-day bullying and repeat voting for **Tammany Hall**, which rewarded him by launching his career as an elected official in the late 1860s, and in 1886, he became Tammany's **boss**. More frank in his embrace of **machine politics** than most bosses, Croker used mandatory assessments from 12,000 city employees and contributions from transit lines and **utilities** to exert unprecedented influence over municipal elections, inserting pliable loyalists with genteel names into the city council and mayoralty. More than any previous Tammany leader, he controlled the city's formidable **Democratic** ward and district bosses, such as **Big Tim Sullivan**. Especially after the Lexow Committee revelations of police graft in the mid-1890s, Croker's Tammany was a byword for corruption and suffered two defeats by **reform movements**, the first by a Good Government movement in 1894 (lasting only until 1897) and the second a crushing defeat in 1901 by a Fusion movement led by **Seth Low**. Having made a fortune by funneling public contracts to businesses in which he had an interest, Croker retired to breed racehorses on his estate in Ireland.

CROLY, HERBERT D. (1869–1930). Editor and author. Croly, a New York City native and the son of prominent **journalists**, attended Harvard College over thirteen years without graduating. Finding work with his father's magazine publications, he rose to be editor (1900–06) of the *Architectural Record*, for which he wrote on urban planning and municipal reform. His book *The Promise of American Life* (1909) issued a forceful call for a **New Nationalism**, in which a strengthened federal government would coordinate solutions to modern society's problems. Only by abandoning the Jeffersonian principle of decentralized, minimal government and accepting a strong, Hamiltonian national state, Croly insisted, could the United States preserve the Jeffersonian vision of democracy in an urban, corporate age. **Theodore Roosevelt** used *The Promise of American Life* as a foundation for the New Nationalism platform of his **Bull Moose** campaign. *Progressive Democracy* (1914) solidified Croly's reputation as a thought-provoking proponent of **progressive** public policy. In the same year, he joined **Walter Weyl** and **Walter Lippmann** in founding the *New Republic*, which under Croly's editorship became the leading magazine of liberal opinion.

CUBA. The **Spanish–American War**, precipitated by the brutal Cuban war for independence that began in 1895, ended with the U.S. military occupation of Cuba and a commitment made by the **Teller Amendment** to leave at the earliest opportune moment. With General **Leonard Wood** as military governor, the U.S. occupiers launched recovery efforts and **education** and **public health** reforms, including **Walter Reed**'s campaign against **yellow fever**. The occupiers hoped to create a viable, pro-American political and economic order. Resentful independence leaders, however, insisted that U.S. intervention had robbed them of victory over Spain, and Cubans of color (who played a critical role in the rebellion) were angry because the U.S. occupiers abetted the desire of white Cuban elites to marginalize them. Despite U.S. pressure, Cubans never accepted **segregation** and **disfranchisement**.

Only the threat of continued occupation persuaded a reluctant Cuban Constitutional Convention to accept the 1901 **Platt Amendment**, under which the United States acquired a naval station at Guantánamo Bay and reserved authority to intervene in the island nation's diplomatic, political, and economic affairs. Following the departure of occupation forces in May 1902, the island remained a political protectorate and an economic colony. Between 1898 and 1920, U.S. investment in Cuba multiplied from $50 million to $500 million, with Havana emerging as a business and tourism satellite of the North American republic. A revolt following a disputed election in December 1905 prompted the first U.S. intervention under the Platt Amendment. In September 1906, after mediation by Secretary of War **William Howard Taft** failed, the United States sent 6,000 troops who stayed three years, until a new Cuban government was in place. Small contingents of U.S. Marines helped the Cuban Army suppress electoral revolts in 1912 and 1917, and the United States retained a token military presence until 1922, by which time the North Americans had become the main target of Cuban nationalist sentiment. *See also* FOREIGN POLICY; ROOSEVELT COROLLARY.

CUMMINS, ALBERT BAIRD (1850–1926). Politician. From a Pennsylvania farm family, Cummins read and practiced law in Chicago and then Des Moines, where he was elected as a **Republican** to the Iowa state legislature (1888–90) and the governorship (1902–08).

Identified with reforms ranging from the abolition of **child labor** to direct election of **senators**, Cummins ranked with **Robert La Follette** among midwestern Republican governors who turned their states into proving grounds for **progressive** policies. His "Iowa idea" of removing tariff protection from businesses dominated by trusts brought him national prominence as an opponent of conservative party leaders such as William B. Allison, whose U.S. Senate seat Cummins won after Allison's death. In the Senate (1908–26), Cummins sided with the Republican **Insurgents** in their rift with President **William Howard Taft**. He participated in formation of the **National Progressive Republican League** and backed **Theodore Roosevelt**'s 1912 presidential candidacy but declined to join the new **Progressive Party**. Generally pro–labor union, he wrote the anti-injunction provisions of the **Clayton Antitrust Act**.

CURTIS, EDWARD SHERIFF (1868–1952). Photographer. Born in Wisconsin, Curtis moved to Seattle in 1887 to open a photography studio. For 30 years beginning in 1895, he photographed **Native Americans** from more than 80 tribes. The project cost more than $1.5 million dollars and resulted in the creation of more than 40,000 images, as well as some of the earliest sound recordings. The photographs reached at first a limited audience through 20 lavishly illustrated, limited-edition portfolios published between 1907 and 1930. Among the photographer's patrons were **Theodore Roosevelt, E. H. Harriman**, and **J. P. Morgan**. Like many Americans, Curtis believed that the military defeat and **Americanization** of Native Americans meant they would soon vanish as distinct peoples. He sought to record for posterity dress and activities he considered traditional while ignoring or erasing evidence of Indians' contemporary lives.

CZOLGOSZ, LEON (1873–1901). Assassin. Born in Detroit to Polish **immigrant** parents, Czolgosz worked in factories from the age of 16, and his experience in an 1893 strike at a Cleveland wire mill helped to radicalize the once devout Catholic, who joined a Polish **socialist** club. In 1898, he suffered an emotional breakdown, after which he quit work to read about **anarchism**, showing special interest in violent acts, such as the 1900 murder of King Humbert I of Italy. He introduced himself to **Emma Goldman** and other anarchist leaders, but they suspected the odd young man of being a government spy. On 6 September 1901, he joined the receiving line at the Pan American **Exposition** in Buffalo, where President **William McKinley** greeted visitors. With a revolver he bought shortly after the August announcement about the president's appearance, he shot McKinley twice as the president reached to shake his hand. When McKinley died eight days later, Czolgosz resisted efforts to assess his sanity and tried to plead guilty. After an eight-hour trial, he was convicted and executed on 29 October. Despite his lack of connection to any anarchist group, Czolgosz's deed fueled public suspicion and suppression of them; Goldman was arrested as a conspirator but released after two weeks.

– D –

DANBURY HATTERS' CASE (1908). Also known as *Loewe v. Lawlor*, this lawsuit arose from efforts by the United Hatters of North America to organize workers at the D. E. Loewe Company. When union secretary Martin Lawlor organized a national boycott, Loewe sued union leaders for damages. The **Supreme Court** in February 1908 ruled unanimously that the union's boycott was a conspiracy in restraint of trade under the Sherman Antitrust Act. This decision helped to persuade the **American Federation of Labor** to engage more actively in partisan politics to secure exemption of **labor unions** from **antitrust** prosecution. The property of the prosecuted unionists remained threatened until 1917, when donations helped to pay the $240,000 in damages. *See also* LABOR'S BILL OF GRIEVANCES.

DANCE HALLS. Like **amusement parks** and nickelodeons, dance halls offered young people (especially young **women**) places removed from oversight by their elders. They were a popular venue for the heterosexual youth social realm that replaced older, gender-segregated or family-supervised forms of recreation. Unmarried women's increased participation in wage labor made commercial amusements accessible to them, but low wages encouraged their reliance on male escorts, sometimes in exchange for sexual favors (the "charity girl" phenomenon). The dances of the period, such as the slow rag, bunny hug, turkey trot, and others known collectively as "tough dancing," encouraged physical contact and sometimes simulated sexual intercourse. This style, the unsupervised interaction among young men and women, the presence of **prostitutes**, and the availability of alcohol troubled many middle-class reformers, who investigated dance halls, prompted police raids, and offered "respectable" alternatives in **settlement houses** and girls' clubs that never attracted large numbers. Reformers in some cities managed to shut down or regulate some halls, but the dance craze continued unabated and contributed to the reshaping of **sexuality** in this era. *See also* ADOLESCENCE; MOSKOWITZ, BELLE LINDNER ISRAELS; POPULAR CULTURE.

DANIELS, JOSEPHUS (1862–1948). Editor and public official. A North Carolina native, Daniels left school at age 18 to edit the first of a series of newspapers. In 1894, he purchased the Raleigh *News and Observer*, which under his editorship became one of the most influential southern **Democratic** newspapers. A supporter of **William Jennings Bryan**, Daniels championed **progressive** causes such as **child labor** reform, **education** reform, **public health**, railroad regulation, and **prohibition**. An adherent of white supremacy like many southern progressives, Daniels deployed his paper in race-baiting campaigns against populism and for **disfranchisement** and **segregation**. **Woodrow Wilson** rewarded Daniels for support in the 1912 presidential campaign with the post of secretary of the navy (1913–21), in which capacity he improved the lot of ordinary sailors but is best remembered for banning alcohol on navy ships in 1914 and closing **Storyville** in 1917. Following the sinking of the *Lusitania*, Daniels advocated naval **preparedness** and, after some reluctance, supported U.S. entry into World War I.

DARROW, CLARENCE (1857–1938). Lawyer. Born in Ohio, Darrow studied at Allegheny College and the University of Michigan Law School before reading law at an Ohio firm. Moving to Chicago in 1887, Darrow gained notoriety as a criminal defense attorney, a passionate civil libertarian, and an opponent of the death penalty.

His dramatic courtroom demeanor, innovations in jury selection, and use of expert witnesses and psychological evidence made him a prototype of the modern crusading defense attorney. In 1894, Darrow began 20 years' work to establish **labor unions**' rights by defending **Eugene V. Debs** from federal charges stemming from the Pullman Strike. In 1902, he was advocate for the **United Mine Workers** in the **Anthracite Coal Strike**. In 1907, he successfully defended **"Big Bill" Haywood** on the charge of conspiring to assassinate former Idaho governor Frank Steunenberg. But organized labor broke with Darrow over the 1911 case of John and James **McNamara**; when Darrow discovered that the brothers were indeed responsible for bombing the *Los Angeles Times* building, he arranged for them to plead guilty to avoid the death penalty. Former ally **Samuel Gompers** then refused to help Darrow defend himself in two jury tampering cases arising from his questionable handling of the case. His reputation damaged, finances depleted, and law firm (of which **Edgar Lee Masters** was also a member) destroyed, Darrow rebuilt his practice in the 1920s, when he represented several famous defendants, most notably in the Scopes trial. In 50 murder cases, none of his clients received the death penalty.

DAVENPORT, CHARLES BENEDICT (1866–1944). Eugenicist. The son of well-to-do New Yorkers, Davenport earned a doctorate in zoology from Harvard University in 1892. Beginning in 1898, as director of the Biological Laboratory of the Brooklyn Academy of Arts and Sciences at Cold Spring Harbor, Long Island, he became a leading practitioner of experimental and statistical biology and promoted the new Mendelian understanding of **genetics**. With funding from the **Carnegie Institution of Washington**, he established a research center in 1904 to study heredity and variation in plants and animals; in 1907, he expanded that focus to include human heredity, a field known as **eugenics**. Like most eugenicists, he endorsed notions of human fitness and unfitness that reflected common class and race prejudices. Thanks to support from the widow of **E. H. Harriman**, the Eugenics Record Office opened at Cold Spring in 1910. Scientists criticized Davenport's human genetics research, but he was very influential in legitimizing eugenics in Germany and the United States, notably for **immigration** restriction and **sterilization**.

DAVIS, RICHARD HARDING (1864–1916). Journalist and author. Born into a literary family in Philadelphia, Davis traveled in the South by age 22 as a correspondent for the *Philadelphia Inquirer*. In 1889, he moved to the *New York Sun* and by age 26 was managing editor of *Harper's Weekly*. In the mid-1890s he became the country's premier war correspondent. His style, which mixed astute, often caustic observation with romance and heroism, shaped American perceptions of international conflicts from the Greco–Turkish War of 1897 through World War I. His reporting on the **Spanish–American War** for *Harper's* and **Joseph Pulitzer**'s *New York Herald* publicized **Theodore Roosevelt**'s **Rough Riders** but also documented the army's scandalous logistics. A fixture in New York's theatrical scene, Davis served as the model for the male counterpart of the popular character the Gibson Girl, whose creator, Charles Dana Gibson, collaborated on illustrated books with Davis. A generation of war correspondents, including Ernest Hemingway, looked to him as a role model. *See also* JOURNALISM.

DAWES ALLOTMENT ACT (1887). Named for Massachusetts senator Henry Dawes and also known as the General Allotment Act or the Dawes Severalty Act, this law was implemented largely during the Progressive Era. It authorized the president to divide **Native American** reservation lands into individually owned "allotments" of 160 acres for each head of household. By transforming Indians into property-owning farmers, Congress hoped to **Americanize** them and end their status as wards of the federal government. Any Indian who accepted an allotment became a U.S. citizen. To prevent Indians from losing their land to whites, the federal government was to hold all land in trust for 25 years.

At first the pace of allotment was slow, but western congressmen won several amendments to make it easier for non-Indians to lease or buy Indian lands. Allotment was extended to all Indians, not just heads of household, and the leasing of Indian lands was permitted (1891). When the nations in the **Indian Territory**, who like the Seneca in New York had initially been exempt, resisted allotment, Congress dissolved their governments and forcibly allotted tribal lands (1898). The trust period for Indians deemed "competent" was shortened (1906), and tribal funds were allowed to be allotted to individuals (1907). Congress intended allotment to open reservation land to white settlers and developers in the belief that tribal governments had controlled far more land than Indian farmers needed. In 1887, Native Americans controlled about 138 million acres, but by 1934, when allotment ended, they held only about 47 million. However, allotment proceeded against the wishes of most Indian people and failed to assimilate them to white norms. Those Indian rights activists who initially welcomed allotment, including **Alice Cunningham Fletcher**, **Francis La Flesche**, **Carlos Montezuma**, and **Charles Eastman**, later found it a curse.

Allotment also failed to make Native Americans economically independent. Colluding with white settlers, Bureau of Indian Affairs agents prevented some Indians from choosing good land during allotment, and non-Indian squatters seized land illegally. Some Native people lacked the experience and equipment needed to farm. Almost none of the allottees could get credit on reasonable terms, and unscrupulous lenders and developers often took advantage of their poverty and unfamiliarity with real estate transactions to defraud them. U.S. citizenship, a goal of the **Society of American Indians**, was also a mixed blessing, as it eliminated federal protections while failing to guarantee that western states would extend voting and other civil rights. The severalty act also promoted the removal of children from their families to receive **Indian education** at boarding schools. The act was repealed in 1934.

DEBS, EUGENE VICTOR (1855–1926). Labor leader and socialist. Born in Indiana to French **immigrants**, Debs went to work for the local railroad at age 14. Although he soon left this job, he was active in the Brotherhood of Locomotive Firemen, becoming the union's national secretary–treasurer in 1880 and the editor of its monthly magazine (1880–94). He also served two terms as Terre Haute's city clerk (1880–84) and a term in the Indiana General Assembly (1885–87) as a **Democrat**. In 1893, Debs took the lead in founding the American Railway Union (ARU), an industrial **labor union** intended to encompass all railroad workers. Membership burgeoned to 150,000 members after a successful strike in the spring in 1894, and Debs backed a request for a nationwide boycott to support the Pullman Strike. After President Grover Cleveland sent troops to break the boycott, Debs and other ARU leaders were convicted of defying a federal court injunction, a decision upheld by the **U.S. Supreme Court**'s controversial 1895 decision, *In re Debs*. The union leader spent May to November 1895 in a county jail for contempt of court. A spellbinding orator, Debs campaigned for **William Jennings Bryan** as a Populist in 1896. The following year, the labor leader announced his support for **socialism**, completing his alienation from the antisocialist **Samuel Gompers** and the **American Federation of Labor**, which had refused to aid the Pullman boycott. After receiving nearly 87,000 votes on a Social Democratic ticket in the 1900 presidential election, Debs helped found the **Socialist Party of America** in 1901. A man of charisma and integrity, he provided an attractive public face for the socialist movement. With him as its presidential candidate, the party's national vote total exceeded 400,000 in 1904 and 1908. The 1908 campaign featured a three-month speaking tour on a chartered train dubbed the Red Special. His political influence peaked in 1912, when he received over 900,000 votes, 6.4 percent of the national total. Afterward, bouts of ill health hampered him, while internal feuds hindered the party's response to serious bids for the labor vote from the **progressive** factions in other parties.

In addition to campaigning for office, he earned a salary as associate editor of *Appeal to Reason* (1907–12). Not tied to any Socialist Party factions and uninterested in theoretical disputes, Debs leaned toward the party's left, participating in the creation of the **Industrial Workers of the World (IWW)** in 1905 but later repudiating the IWW as too violent and impractical. He was often at odds with the "reformist" faction led by **Victor Berger** and **Morris Hillquit**. The U.S. entry into World War I energized Debs, whose speeches denouncing the war as a capitalist enterprise led to his conviction and a 10-year prison sentence under the Espionage Act in 1918. Campaigning from federal prison for the presidency in 1920, Debs received his highest total vote, 913,935, though with **women**'s **suffrage** expanding the electorate, his proportion had shrunk to 3.4 percent. President Warren Harding commuted his sentence on Christmas Day 1921.

DE FOREST, LEE (1873–1961). Inventor. Born in Iowa, de Forest studied at Yale University, eventually earning a Ph.D. in physics in 1899; his dissertation was on radio waves. He then became involved in a succession of firms devoted to wireless communications, but shortage of capital, backers' poor judgment, mismanagement, and de Forest's penchant for encroaching on others' patents (leading to 120 patent lawsuits) tarnished his reputation. In 1906, de Forest invented the "audion," a vacuum tube for transmitting, receiving, and amplifying signals, that was crucial for radio, long-distance telephones, and ultimately for television. However, he left essential improvements to others, particularly Edwin H. Armstrong (1890–1954), with whom de Forest engaged in a rancorous legal battle. De Forest's publicity stunts, including a 1908 broadcast from the Eiffel Tower and experiments in broadcasting live and recorded music, publicized radio years before it became commercially viable in the 1920s. *See also* RADIO ACT.

DELL, FLOYD (1889–1969). *See* CHICAGO RENAISSANCE; *THE MASSES.*

DE LÔME LETTER. See CUBA; SPANISH–AMERICAN WAR.

DEMOCRATIC PARTY. The repudiation of President Grover Cleveland during the depression that followed the Panic of 1893 left this party in its weakest position since the Civil War. The Democrats lost 113 congressional seats in the 1894 midterm elections and had virtually no representation in the Midwest and Northeast. The agrarian, free silver presidential campaign of **William Jennings Bryan** in 1896 made the Democrats competitive in the Mountain West but had little appeal in urban-industrial regions. Although the party made gains in 1898 in the House of Representatives, it held not a single U.S. Senate seat in the Northeast, Midwest, or Pacific Coast by 1899; 22 of the 26 Democratic senators came from the South. A similar pattern held in state and local offices. Bryan's second defeat in 1900 confirmed what scholars call the **Realignment of 1896**. The Democratic Party seemed on the verge of being reduced to an ungainly alliance of southern **segregationists**, southern and Great Plains Bryanite agrarians, western silver interests, and northern urban **machines** such as **Tammany Hall**.

Democrats struggled to devise a comeback strategy. Bryan's faction favored economic and social reform to create a farmer–labor alliance. Party conservatives, however, arranged the 1904 nomination of New York judge **Alton B. Parker**, whose drubbing at the hands of Republican **Theodore Roosevelt** discredited the notion that Democrats should run to the right of the **Republicans**. Parker's 37.6 percent of the popular vote represented the lowest Democratic tally since 1860. Even so, Democrats elected governors in five states taken by Roosevelt, and with Bryanites, **progressives**, and moderates such as **Champ Clark** gaining the initiative, the Democrats gradually dug out of their hole. Between 1904 and 1908, Democratic representation in the House increased from 136 to 172, although the Senate remained two-thirds Republican. The **Insurgent–Old Guard** split within the majority party meant that Roosevelt needed Democratic votes to pass any meaningful reform legislation.

In 1908, Bryan ran for the presidency for a third time on a progressive platform that included direct election of **senators**, **employer liability**, the **income tax**, and an anti-injunction plank that brought the **American Federation of Labor** into open alliance with the Democrats. Although defeated again, Bryan had done much to reshape his party into the more consistently progressive of the two major political organizations. The Republicans' quarrels provided an opportunity for dramatic gains in 1910, when Democrats advanced by 56 House seats to enjoy a majority for the first time since 1893–95. They also gained 10 Senate seats in states such as Ohio, New Jersey, Massachusetts, and New York, as alliances between Democratic machine politicians, **labor unions**, and middle-class reformers fueled what historians label **urban liberalism**. In the South, progressives such as **Hoke Smith** made headway as long as they espoused **segregation** and **disfranchisement**, but the southern party remained vulnerable to antigovernment reactionaries such as **James Vardaman**.

Despite his southern conservative roots, 1912 presidential nominee **Woodrow Wilson** had established enough progressive credentials during his term as New Jersey governor to offer a plausible alternative to Roosevelt's **Progressive Party** candidacy. Wilson's victory, however, was only possible because Roosevelt and **William Howard Taft** split the Republican Party. Under Wilson, the Democrats remained rooted in the South; that region accounted for nearly 85 percent of Democratic electoral votes in the eight presidential elections between 1896 and 1928. Wilson's **New Freedom** proved popular enough with progressives that many former Republicans who had supported Roosevelt's **Bull Moose** campaign in 1912 identified with the Democrats in 1916. Wilson's narrow victory that year nevertheless remained dependent on the South and West, with some labor support. Scholars date the origins of the Democrats' New Deal coalition to the alliance-building of this era.

DENNETT, MARY COFFIN WARE (1872–1947). *See* BIRTH CONTROL; FEMINISM; SEXUALITY.

DEPARTMENT STORES. Spreading to the United States from Paris in the mid-19th century, the department store by the Progressive Era had become a vast palace of commerce, its success founded on the quantity and variety of goods, the one-price policy, newspaper **advertising**, low prices based on huge sales volume, and generous return and exchange policies. Department stores also became some of the earliest **chain stores** as, for example, retailer John Wanamaker built stores in Pittsburgh, St. Louis, Baltimore, New York, and other cities after the success of his flagship in Philadelphia. Luxurious department store buildings enlivened urban central business districts. Using plate glass, lighting, mannequins, and dyes, pioneers like Rowland H. Macy and **L. Frank Baum** created alluring window displays for window shoppers.

Department stores offered **women** new occupations, from cash girl to buyer, the latter one of the highest-ranking and best-paid positions women could aspire to. White women without accents dominated the ranks of sales clerks; women of color and **immigrants** were not hired. Groups such as the **National Consumers' League (NCL)** worried that an expensive dress code, low wages, and contact with wealthy men pushed many clerks into **prostitution**. The NCL conducted campaigns in New York and elsewhere to shorten salesclerks' hours and provide them with stools. For middle-class women, the department store was a place of liberation, although fashion and consumerism created its own feminine orthodoxy. Regular customers received charge accounts (an innovation in **consumer credit**) and home delivery, among other services. Cut-price department stores enabled working-class women to wear styles similar to those of wealthier women. Acquiring "American" hats and clothing was a common rite of passage for newly arrived immigrants. *See also* FILENE, EDWARD A.; POPULAR CULTURE.

DEVINE, EDWARD THOMAS (1867–1948). Social worker and administrator. Born in Iowa, Devine studied with economist **Simon Patten** at the University of Pennsylvania, earning a Ph.D. in economics in 1893. He became the head of New York City's Charity Organization Society (COS) in 1896 and during his 16-year tenure did much to professionalize social work. He launched the **Pittsburgh Survey**, promoted housing reform, was active in the fight against **tuberculosis**, and helped found the New York School of Philanthropy in 1898, serving as its director from 1904. He also transformed the COS journal, *Charities and the Commons*, into a major outlet for social work research; in 1909 Paul Kellogg renamed it *Survey* magazine. In 1906, President **Theodore Roosevelt** appointed Devine to lead American Red Cross relief efforts after the **San Francisco earthquake**; he later managed flood relief in Ohio and U.S. government programs for World War I refugees. A founding member of the **National Child Labor Committee**, he lobbied to create the **Children's Bureau**.

DEWEY, GEORGE (1837–1917). Naval officer. A Vermont native, Dewey graduated from the U.S. Naval Academy (1858) and served in the Civil War. A commodore by 1898, Dewey was assigned command of the Asiatic Squadron (1898) with support from his friend, Assistant Secretary of the Navy **Theodore Roosevelt**, who in February 1898, with the **Spanish–American War** looming, ordered Dewey to prepare an offensive against the **Philippines**, then a Spanish colony. Dewey's fleet steamed to Manila, where on 1 May it destroyed the Spanish Pacific Fleet in a six-hour battle with no loss of American life. Remaining in charge of the fleet through May 1899, Dewey participated in the occupation of Manila, the early American rule in the archipelago, the negotiations with **Emilio Aguinaldo** that helped to spark the **Philippine–American War**, and early actions against the Filipino nationalists. In the United States, he received such a hero's welcome that the **Democratic Party** contemplated nominating him for president in 1900 until injudicious pronouncements and actions derailed his candidacy. Promoted to admiral, Dewey in 1900 became president of the General Board of the Navy and two years later presiding officer of the Joint Army and Navy Board, a forerunner of the Joint Chiefs of Staff. In 1915, Dewey became the first chief of naval operations.

DEWEY, JOHN (1859–1952). Philosopher and educator. Born in Vermont, Dewey graduated from the state university (1879), and after teaching for a few years, earned a Ph.D. at Johns Hopkins University (1884), studying with Charles S. Peirce, **G. Stanley Hall**, and George Sylvester Morris. While serving on the faculty of the University of Michigan, he published his first major works in psychology and philosophy. Gradually abandoning his early neo-Hegelian idealism, he adopted a **naturalistic**, Darwinian approach that understood a person's knowledge and psychology as stemming from efforts to adapt to and shape his or her environment. In 1894, Dewey became chair of the philosophy department at the newly founded **University of Chicago**, where his philosophical and personal commitments led him into **education** theory. He oversaw creation of the **university**'s education program and its Laboratory School (1896), where he and colleagues such as **Ella Flagg Young** developed what was later labeled "progressive education." This approach rested on the belief that, rather than impart a set of skills and ideas, education should inculcate a capacity for continuous learning and openness to novel experiences, ideas, and people. Dewey's involvement with **Hull House** strengthened the link between social activism and academic research that became characteristic of "Chicago School" social science. At the same time, he continued to produce scholarly work in philosophy, becoming a chief exponent of **pragmatism** (which he often labeled "instrumentalism"), the argument that beliefs and ideas are practical tools for understanding and managing one's world.

Differences with university president **William Rainey Harper** came to a head in 1904 with the removal of Dewey's wife, Alice, as principal of the Laboratory School. The scholar moved to Columbia University, where he held a joint appointment in philosophy and at Teachers College (1904–30). As in Chicago, he was involved in **reform movements**, contributing to teachers' unions, the Henry Street **settlement house**, and the **women**'s **suffrage** movement. His support for U.S. intervention in World War I led to quarrels with friends and admirers, including former student **Randolph**

Bourne. A consistent defender of freedom of speech, Dewey helped found the **American Association of University Professors** and the American Civil Liberties Union. His scholarly writings and activism profoundly influenced 20th-century notions of social, psychological, and **intellectual** foundations of democracy and **pluralism**. *See also* JAMES, WILLIAM.

DÍAZ, PORFIRIO (1830–1915). *See* MEXICAN REVOLUTION.

DIPHTHERIA. This contagious bacterial respiratory infection commonly afflicted children in overcrowded, unsanitary neighborhoods and contributed mightily to the high infant and child mortality rates in the United States before 1900. By the early 1890s, European researchers isolated the bacillus responsible and began experiments with antitoxins. Faced with a rise in cases during 1893, the New York City Health Department began widespread diagnostic testing and within a few years produced an effective antitoxin on a large scale for only 10 cents per 100 doses. Research also demonstrated that milk could carry diphtheria, which furthered arguments for systematic inspection and pasteurization. Containment of this dreaded childhood ailment stands as one of the first **public health** triumphs based on the germ theory of disease. *See also* HEALTH AND MEDICINE.

DIRECT PRIMARY. During the 19th century, political parties nominated candidates for local offices and delegates to state conventions through caucuses known as primaries. Though these meetings were open to all party members, **bosses** grew adept at stacking them to yield predetermined slates of candidates. Some jurisdictions, especially in the Midwest, developed the alternate practice of nominating candidates through formal elections known as direct primaries. A central proposal of **Robert La Follette**'s **Wisconsin Idea** was a state law mandating that parties nominate candidates through a direct primary. Wisconsin's passage of a statewide **referendum** in 1904 accelerated a national movement for direct primaries. By 1910, more than 30 states had direct primary laws, and by 1920 nearly all did. In the South, the direct primary enabled disenchanted factions to mount attacks on conservative party establishments, but in the form of the **white primary** it reinforced the **disfranchisement** of **African Americans**. *See also* STRUCTURAL REFORM.

DISFRANCHISEMENT. Twelve states used a variety of laws and state constitutional amendments to disfranchise **African American** men between 1889 and 1910 as part of the process of expelling blacks from politics and imposing **segregation**. Starting with Florida and Tennessee in 1889 and ending with Georgia's disfranchisement amendment in 1908, all 11 former Confederate states implemented race-based voting restrictions of greater or lesser comprehensiveness. The southwestern state of Oklahoma adopted the practice in 1910. White southern politicians, such as **Benjamin Tillman**, **Rebecca Latimer Felton**, and **James K. Vardaman**, heightened the call for disfranchisement with their vicious race-baiting rhetoric. Because the Fifteenth Amendment to the Constitution (1870) barred the restriction of voting rights on the basis of race, southern leaders used several subterfuges: **literacy tests** with "understanding" clauses; a cumulative **poll tax**; lengthy residence requirements; complex pre-election registration; **grandfather clauses**; and denial of voting privileges to men convicted of certain crimes. The **U.S. Supreme Court** affirmed these laws in *Williams v. Mississippi* (1898). Although these measures also disfranchised poor white men, they especially affected black voters because of outright discrimination on top of inequities in **education**, employment, and law enforcement. Moreover, laws mandating **Australian ballots** and multiple-box balloting eroded the ability of illiterate men to vote as they intended. Together, these measures deprived nearly all black men of political rights, enhanced opportunities for fraud, and made it very difficult for third parties such as the Populist Party to convert popular support into electoral victory. *See also* ATLANTA COMPROMISE; LYNCHING; NATIONAL ASSOCIATION FOR THE ADVANCEMENT OF COLORED PEOPLE; NIAGARA MOVEMENT; RACE RIOTS.

DIVORCE. The ability to dissolve a marriage legally increased throughout the 19th and 20th centuries, but it did so unevenly because states determined the laws governing marriage. Although some **women**'s rights advocates deplored easing divorce laws, in practice most divorce-seekers were women. Many saw divorce as an essential part of women's emancipation, in keeping with the recently won rights of married women to own property and retain custody of their children when a marriage ended. Exact statistics on U.S. divorces prior to World War II do not exist. One scholar estimated that divorces increased 2,000 percent between 1867 and 1929, while the number of marriages increased by only 400 percent in the same period. Another calculated that three of every 1,000 marriages ended in divorce in 1890; and by 1920, nearly eight in 1,000 did so. Whatever the number, contemporaries often lamented the increase in divorce, blaming **feminism**, women's **suffrage**, and women's growing social activism generally. Women's rising participation in waged labor also enabled them to seek divorce more readily. Rates of abandonment and separation probably decreased as the option of divorce (which permitted remarriage) became more accessible. The early 20th century also saw the expansion of reasons for which divorce could be granted. Historically only adultery, excessive physical cruelty, abandonment, and sometimes incest were grounds for ending a marriage. In the Progressive Era, the notion of companionate marriage and changing ideas about **sexuality** led growing numbers to seek divorce on the grounds of emotional cruelty and sexual inadequacy. *See also* BIRTH CONTROL.

DODGE, MABEL (1879–1962). Salon hostess. Born into a wealthy Buffalo family, Dodge traveled and lived in Florence, Italy, where she befriended Gertrude Stein and **Bernard Berenson**. Returning to New York City in 1912, Dodge became acquainted with the **Greenwich Village** avant garde through her friend **Hutchins Hapgood**, and her apartment became an influential **intellectual** and artistic salon. Visitors included major figures in American **modernism** as well as political radicals such as **Margaret Sanger**, **Walter Lippmann**, and **John Reed**, with whom she had a legendary affair. She helped finance the **Armory Show**, the **Paterson Strike** pageant, and the **Provincetown Players** while writing on photography and psychoanalysis for *The Masses* and **William Randolph Hearst**'s newspapers. Her equally famous life as a collector and art patron in Taos, New Mexico, began in 1918. *See also* ART; LITERATURE.

DOLLAR DIPLOMACY. Alhough this term was first used by a hostile reporter, President **William Howard Taft** adopted it to describe his administration's hope of reducing military confrontations in Latin America and Asia by strengthening poor countries' economic ties with the United States. Taft and Secretary of State **Philander C. Knox** contrasted their approach with the big stick policy of **Theodore Roosevelt**. However, substituting economic for military influence backfired in **Nicaragua**, where political turmoil and international default resulted by 1912 in a weak government propped up by U.S. Marines and relying on a U.S. army officer and U.S. bankers to manage its finances. Likewise in **Haiti**, Knox persuaded New York bankers to invest heavily, setting the stage for years of U.S. financial and military control. In sum, Latin Americans did not experience Taft's economic **imperialism** as an improvement over Roosevelt's **gunboat** approach and began to spurn his administration's offers of financial help. The dollar diplomacy mindset also animated **Willard Straight**'s controversial efforts to arrange American financing for Chinese railroads. *See also* FOREIGN POLICY; OPEN DOOR NOTES.

DOMESTIC SCIENCE. *See* HOME ECONOMICS.

DOMINICAN REPUBLIC. After the 1871 failure of President U. S. Grant's scheme to annex this Spanish-speaking Caribbean country, the Dominican Republic remained vulnerable, a situation exacerbated by political instability in the wake of the 1899 assassination of the nation's president. By early 1904, the Dominican government had trouble meeting payments on $32 million in foreign debts held mainly by European investors. American enterprises also had a huge stake in the Dominican **economy**. Anxious to avoid a European naval expedition like one against Venezuela after it defaulted on foreign loans in 1902–03, President **Theodore Roosevelt**'s administration asserted U.S. hegemony in the form of the **Roosevelt Corollary** in 1904, and in January 1905 the president sent U.S. Navy personnel to manage the Dominican Republic's customs collection and debt repayment. A hapless Dominican government acceded to this American protectorate in a treaty that the U.S. Senate refused to ratify until 1907. A U.S.-supervised election in November 1914 ended another round of upheaval, but yet another revolution in May 1916 prompted President **Woodrow Wilson**'s administration to send in the U.S.

Marines, who established a military government and occupied the country until 1924. The United States retained control of Dominican customs for decades and only relinquished the authority to intervene militarily in 1941. *See also* FOREIGN POLICY.

DREIER, MARY ELISABETH (1875–1963). Labor activist and suffragist. Born into a wealthy Brooklyn family, Dreier and her sister **Margaret Dreier Robins** devoted their lives to the **Women's Trade Union League (WTUL)** after meeting **labor union** organizer **Leonora O'Reilly**. As WTUL president (1906 to 1914), Dreier participated in major strikes, including one against the **Triangle Shirtwaist Company** in 1909; her arrest for walking the picket line during this event publicized the low wages and harsh working conditions. After the 1911 Triangle Shirtwaist Fire, she served on the **New York State Factory Investigating Commission** and helped to generate important labor legislation. Convinced that women had to have the vote to enact improved working conditions, Dreier became a leader in the New York City **women's suffrage** organization. Never marrying, she supported O'Reilly financially for much of her life and shared a house with fellow activist **Frances Kellor** for nearly 50 years.

DREISER, THEODORE (1871–1945). Author. The 12th of 13 children from an impoverished Indiana family, Dreiser managed one year at Indiana University before becoming an itinerant reporter. In 1900, he submitted to Doubleday, Page editor **Frank Norris** a manuscript that became the novel *Sister Carrie*, whose main characters, a country girl ambitious for urban pleasures and a bourgeois man who leaves his family and embezzles from his employer, are driven by deep impulses with little regard for conventional morality. Shunned when it first appeared, the novel was lauded as a monument of American **naturalism** after its 1907 reissue. By 1904, Dreiser embarked on a successful career as an editor, novelist, and short story writer. In novels such as *Jennie Gerhardt* (1911), *The Financier* (1912), and *The Titan* (1914)—the latter two works based on the career of **Charles Yerkes**—Dreiser used a crude, at times plodding style to good effect in presenting a stark picture of a heartless modern society full of deluded people pursuing empty dreams. *See also* CHICAGO RENAISSANCE; LITERATURE; MODERNISM.

DU BOIS, WILLIAM EDWARD BURGHARDT (W. E. B.) (1868–
1963). Scholar and civil rights leader. A native of western Massachusetts, Du Bois earned bachelor's degrees first at Fisk University (1888) and then at Harvard (1890). After studying in Germany, he became the first **African American** to receive a Harvard Ph.D. in 1895. He taught at Wilberforce University and the University of Pennsylvania, where he researched *The Philadelphia Negro: A Social Study* (1899), a pioneering work in both urban sociology and African American studies. Appointed professor of history and economics at Atlanta University in 1897, Du Bois emerged as a major **intellectual** through his editing of the *Atlanta University Publications* and popular writings such as *The Souls of Black Folk* (1903). An eloquent meditation on the dilemmas of being black in the United States, this book also attacked **Booker T. Washington's Atlanta Compromise** as a concession to **segregation** and **disfranchisement** that was doomed to failure. A relentless champion of civil rights and black intellectual and artistic endeavor, Du Bois organized the **Niagara Movement** and was among those black leaders who founded the **National Association for the Advancement of Colored People (NAACP)**. The founding editor (1910–34) of the NAACP's journal, *The Crisis*, he built it into a widely read magazine of news and literature with an assertive political and cultural stance that heralded the "New Negro" militancy of the 1920s. *See also* JAMES, WILLIAM; PRAGMATISM; UNIVERSITY.

DUKE, JAMES BUCHANAN (1856–1925). Manufacturer. The son of North Carolina farmers, Duke oversaw his family's tobacco products business, in the process transforming social habits by popularizing the cigarette. In the 1880s, he led the firm into the production of machine-rolled cigarettes and seized market share by cutting prices and investing heavily in **advertising**. In 1890, he merged five major cigarette firms to form the American Tobacco Company; 11 years later, he unified the snuff, cigar, and stogie firms into the Consolidated Tobacco Company. In 1902, Duke negotiated a deal with the leading English tobacco firm to form the multinational British-American Tobacco Company. Duke's uniting of his three U.S. companies into American Tobacco prompted a federal **antitrust** suit in 1907, which Duke lost in 1911. He then cut his ties with the tobacco industry to focus on hydroelectric power and contributed large sums to Trinity College (renamed Duke University in 1924), Davidson College, and Furman University. *See also* BLACK PATCH WAR.

DUNCAN, ISADORA (1877–1927). Dancer. The daughter of a San Francisco poet, Duncan emphasized rhythmic gestures and rejected voluminous petticoats and corsets for simple tunics and leggings, insisting that dance should be an expressive art centered on the unrestrained body. Although she believed that her movements exemplified health and morality for the **New Woman**, her critics were horrified at her open display of the female body, the **sexual** freedom implicit in her theory of dance, and her unconventional life: she bore three children out of wedlock to different fathers. All of her children died by 1913, two when the car they were in plunged into the Seine River. Duncan supported herself as a teacher, lecturer, and private performer but enjoyed limited success on the U.S. stage. By 1899, she had a reputation in Europe, where she choreographed dances to the music of the leading classical composers, especially Chopin. After briefly working in the newly founded Soviet Union in 1921 and losing her U.S. citizenship for marrying a Soviet citizen, Duncan moved to France, where she died when her scarf tangled in the wheel of an **automobile** and strangled her. *See also* MODERNISM.

DUNNE, FINLEY PETER (1867–1936). Journalist and humorist. From a Chicago Irish **immigrant** family, Dunne worked as a reporter and editor; by 1892, he was an editor at the *Chicago Evening Post*. That year, he began writing humorous columns in which fictional Irish characters commented on contemporary people and events. In 1893, he introduced Martin Dooley, a worldly **saloon**-keeper whose witty monologues became popular satires of the foibles of the age. After publishing *Mr. Dooley in Peace and in War* (1898) and moving to New York in 1900, Dunne focused his columns on national issues. He also wrote books and articles and served as an editor and columnist for magazines such the *American Magazine*, *Metropolitan*, and *Collier's*. *See also* JOURNALISM.

DUNNING SCHOOL. William A. Dunning (1857–1922) was a professor of history and politics at Columbia University best known for two books, *Essays on the Civil War and Reconstruction* (1897) and *Reconstruction, Political and Economic* (1907). In these and other writings, he highlighted the presumed corruption and incompetence of the pro-Union governments imposed on the Confederate states after their defeat. He implied that failures of Reconstruction arose largely from the vindictive character of Congress's radical **Republicans**, who, he argued, had fanatical, self-serving motives for granting citizenship and suffrage to former slaves. **African Americans**, in Dunning's view, were ill prepared to use their freedom and franchise responsibly so soon after emancipation and perhaps were racially incapable of equal citizenship. Dunning's disparaging portrayal of the Radicals differed little from the views of other scholars of his time, such as **John W. Burgess** and **Woodrow Wilson**, not to mention popular accounts such as the novel *The Clansman* and the **movie** based on it, *The Birth of a Nation* (1915). Dunning, however, attracted many graduate students whose studies of Reconstruction at the state level substantiated their mentor's conclusions. Dunning's students dominated Southern history through the first half of the 20th century, and their work found its way into textbooks and popular narratives, providing an apparent **intellectual** sanction for the **segregation** and **disfranchisement** of blacks.

DU PONT DE NEMOURS, E. I., & COMPANY. Founded in 1801, the Du Pont Company was by 1902 a dominant presence in the American gunpowder industry. In that year, three cousins bought out their older relatives after defeating an attempt to sell the venerable firm outside the family. Of the three, Pierre du Pont, an 1890 graduate of the Massachusetts Institute of Technology, emerged as the guiding force in rejuvenating the firm, with the company adopting modern managerial practices such as cost accounting, market forecasting, **organizational** charts, and **industrial research**. It **modernized** plants and expanded into smokeless powder and dynamite. It integrated vertically by buying mines and building plants while forcing formerly independent sales agents to become company employees. The company purchased its competitors so aggressively as to invite a federal **antitrust** suit, which resulted in partial dissolution in 1912.

By 1914, World War I created an unprecedented demand for the company's products, and it maneuvered the French, English, and

American (after 1917) governments into advantageous contracts in which the purchasers financed plant expansion *and* bought the products at a healthy profit. Total sales between 1914 and 1918 reached $1.1 billion and net profits at least $238 million. Pierre du Pont plowed these profits into other products chemically similar to gunpowder: celluloid, synthetic fabrics, dyes, paints, and varnish. When he resigned as president in 1919, he left behind a diversified, modern chemical products company. *See also* ECONOMY; EFFICIENCY.

– E –

E. C. KNIGHT CO., UNITED STATES V. *See* ANTITRUST; SUPREME COURT, U.S.

***EASTLAND* DISASTER.** *See GENERAL SLOCUM* DISASTER.

EAST ST. LOUIS RIOT (1917). This industrial city of 60,000 in Illinois experienced the first large urban **race riot** to result from the **Great Migration**. The city's **African American** population tripled between 1900 and 1914 and increased still more after the outbreak of World War I. Early in 1917, a major local employer, the Aluminum Ore Company, hired blacks to break a strike launched by an all-white **labor union** affiliated with the **American Federation of Labor**. In response, angry whites drove through black neighborhoods shooting into the houses, whose residents quickly armed themselves. When two white policemen investigated, someone in the crowd shot them to death. The next day, speakers at a protest rally exhorted white men to arm themselves, and with the city police aiding or at least ignoring them, several dozen white men marched into the black sections of town, where they pulled black people off streetcars and set fire to homes. The rioters then shot, stabbed, or beat to death men, women, and children as they attempted to flee. By the time Illinois National Guard troops arrived to quell the mobs, at least 39 blacks and nine whites had died, though some estimates ran higher. Twelve blacks ultimately served prison terms for the murder of the policemen, along with nine whites convicted of homicide and 14 whites convicted of lesser crimes.

EASTMAN, CHARLES (OHIYESA) (1858–1939). Author and reformer. Born in Minnesota to parents of Lakota and Lakota-white ancestry, Eastman was raised in Canada by relatives after his mother's death and his father's imprisonment for participating in a revolt. As a teenager, he joined his father on a farm in the Dakota Territory, converted to Christianity, and gained an American **education**. After graduating from Dartmouth College (1887), he earned a medical degree (1890) and practiced medicine at the Pine Ridge reservation (1890–93), where he witnessed the Wounded Knee massacre. Initially in favor of the **Dawes Allotment Act**, Eastman grew critical of the loss of land that resulted. He took the Bureau of Indian Affairs (at times his employer) to task for its many failures and publicized the appalling conditions found on many reservations. An agent for the **Young Men's Christian Association** (1894–98), he also helped found the **Society of American Indians** in 1911 and remained an activist through the 1920s. He believed that Native Americans did not have to abandon their cultures to be successful in white society. *See also* INDIAN EDUCATION; NATIVE AMERICANS.

EASTMAN, CRYSTAL (1881–1928). Lawyer and reformer. Born in Massachusetts, the daughter of ministers and sister of **Max Eastman**, Eastman graduated from Vassar College (1903) and earned an M.A. in sociology (1904) and a Ph.D. in law (1907). Her investigation of workplace injuries, part of the **Pittsburgh Survey** (1907–08), made her one of the nation's leading experts on labor law and industrial accidents. In 1909, she became the only woman serving on New York's **Employers' Liability** Commission, which formulated the nation's first **workers' compensation** law (1910). Eastman participated in the **women's suffrage** movement, cofounding the Congressional Union with **Lucy Burns** and **Alice Paul** in 1913. A **feminist** and **Greenwich Village** bohemian, she agitated for **birth control** and government support for poor mothers and children. After World War I began in 1914, Eastman became executive secretary of the **American Union Against Militarism** and later helped create the American Civil Liberties Union.

EASTMAN, MAX (1883–1969). Writer and activist. Born in upstate New York, his father and mother both ministers, Eastman graduated from Williams College (1905) and studied at Columbia University (1907–11) under **John Dewey**. In part through the influence of his sister, **Crystal Eastman**, Max became involved with bohemian life in **Greenwich Village**, where he became a **socialist** and **feminist**. His 1911 marriage to actress and artist Ida Rauh (which ended in **divorce**) became fodder for newspaper accounts of Greenwich Village libertinism. Eastman became editor of *The Masses* in 1912 and built the journal into the period's most innovative outlet for left-wing writing and graphics. His eloquent defense against sedition charges during World War I made him a celebrity of the Left. Although he and his codefendants escaped jail, government repression destroyed *The Masses* in 1918. Eastman continued his career as a left **journalist** and traveled in the 1920s to the Soviet Union, where he lost faith in socialism and eventually, in the 1950s, identified with the political right. His memoirs provide vivid accounts of the left-wing bohemia of the 1910s. *See also* MODERNISM; SEXUALITY.

EASTMAN KODAK. In 1888, George Eastman (1854–1932), a manufacturer of photographic plates and experimental roll film, introduced the first camera simple enough for amateur use. The trademark name, Kodak, had no significance other than its being easy to remember and pronounce. The first Kodaks cost $25, which limited their use to the upper middle class, and contained film so complex to load and develop that users had to send the camera to the factory every time they finished the 100 pictures on each roll. In 1892, Eastman and partner Henry A. Strong (1838–1919) reorganized their firm into the Eastman Kodak Company, which by the early 1900s became a vertically integrated, multinational producer of films and cameras.

The invention of celluloid film cartridges that ordinary people could load, combined with improved manufacturing techniques, culminated by 1900 in the Brownie camera, originally intended for children. It cost only $1 and used a 15-cent roll of film. Eastman Kodak combined distinctive **advertising** with an elaborate network of sales offices and authorized dealerships to make the snapshot an everyday part of American and European culture. By the 1910s, the company also dominated the new fields of X-ray photography and **movie** film. The firm's aggressive stance toward competitors and patents invited a 1915 federal **antitrust** suit, which ended six years later in divestment of several ancillary businesses. Eastman experimented with **welfare capitalist** measures such as profit sharing and pensions. He and Strong donated over $100 million to a network of cultural, educational, and medical institutions. Eastman also financed **industrial education** institutions for **African Americans**, such as **Tuskegee Institute**.

ECONOMY. Changes in the economy, business structure and practice, and economic policy were driving issues of the Progressive Era. Indeed, progressivism was largely a product of and a response to the new phase of industrialism that historians label the Second Industrial Revolution (c. 1870–1920). The first phase of industrialization, which spread to the United States from Great Britain before the Civil War, was characterized by numerous small firms engaged in textile, iron, and machine manufacture and using coal or waterpower. By contrast, this new phase of industrialism, which made Germany as well as the United States into formidable powers, featured the mass production of chemically or technically complex products by mechanized, energy-intensive processes. In the case of the telephone and **electricity**, the new industries were by nature elaborate technological systems spread over a large geographic area. Firms such as **Standard Oil**, Carnegie Steel and then **United States Steel**, **Westinghouse** and **General Electric**, **American Telephone and Telegraph**, and **Ford Motor Company** and **General Motors** employed thousands of workers, managers, and engineers spread over numerous plants. Such firms were increasingly integrated in a "horizontal" as well as a "vertical" sense. Horizontal integration meant that a firm dominated a strategic stage of production—for example, Standard Oil's grip on oil refining. Vertical integration entailed investments in the different stages of production from the mining of raw materials to the sale of finished products. As epitomized by **department stores**, **chain stores**, and **mail-order** firms, the distribution of goods went through a phase of consolidation and **organizational** elaboration that paralleled trends in manufacturing.

Small firms with modest capital, operated by their owners and using artisan methods or minimal mechanization, remained crucial, especially in industries that for technical or market reasons did not invite standardization and mass production. Industrial cities such as

New York, Newark, and Philadelphia contained intricate networks of clothing-assembly sweatshops; jewelry, leather, and furniture makers; printers; machinists; and precision-instrument makers, all of whom had to adjust quickly to changes in fashion or had to meet customer specifications.

Despite the persistence of small firms, large manufacturing and transportation companies clearly became the driving force behind the economy. Industrialists such as **John D. Rockefeller** and financiers such as **J. P. Morgan** defended industrial and railroad combines for creating a stable environment for investment and innovation, as evidenced in the emergence of **industrial research laboratories**. But the unprecedented power of big business vis-à-vis government and consumers as well as **labor unions** prompted a fervent **antitrust** movement, which had little tangible effect on the trend toward consolidation. By the end of the **great merger movement** of 1895–1904, around 300 firms controlled 40 percent of the country's manufacturing capital. Public sector innovations such as the **Federal Reserve Act**, the **Federal Trade Commission**, and the **Clayton Antitrust Act** revealed that at least at the federal level, policymakers ended the Progressive Era still compromising between accepting and regulating big business (epitomized by **Theodore Roosevelt**'s **New Nationalism**) and breaking up big business in the name of competition and opportunity (epitomized by **Woodrow Wilson**'s **New Freedom**). Progressive activists such as **Louis D. Brandeis** and economic thinkers such as **Thorstein Veblen** imagined a technocratic alternative in which engineers and professionals used concepts of **efficiency** and **scientific management** to oversee the enterprise more for the public good than for private profit.

By 1910, U.S. industries produced goods with twice the value of those from Germany or Great Britain. The United States soon accounted for one-third of world industrial production. **Immigration** was indispensable to industrial growth. Immigrants provided the semiskilled and unskilled labor to harvest abundant raw materials, build cities, and operate factories. Through the period, labor unions struggled to organize and gain legitimacy against overwhelming corporate power, a suspicious middle class, and a hostile **Supreme Court**.

Foreign trade also changed profoundly, though American economic growth remained driven by domestic demand. Improved communications, transportation, and the nation's growing number of overseas dependencies encouraged Americans to import sugar, coffee, rubber, fruit, and minerals and to export food and manufactures, while the federal government employed tariffs, reciprocity treaties, and other aspects of **imperialism** and **dollar diplomacy** to extend American commerce to Latin America and the Pacific. The United States exported agricultural and industrial products to Europe, while Canada and Asia increasingly relied on U.S. products, resulting in a very favorable balance of trade for America.

By 1890, manufacturing surpassed agriculture in the value of its products, and by 1900, industrial production was double the annual value of farm products. Still, the roughly 300 million acres of cultivated farmland remained crucial to the country's wealth and power. Until 1920, most Americans lived in rural areas, and the *number* of Americans living on farms continued to increase, though rapid urbanization meant that the rural *percentage* steadily dropped. Heavy demand from domestic food processors—themselves highly innovative industrialists—along with the opening of new foreign markets and policies such as the **Newlands Reclamation Act** made the decades after 1890 (the year in which the frontier supposedly closed) a major age of homesteading on the Great Plains and in the Far West. Financially stretched, settling hopefully on marginal land, Plains wheat farmers were vulnerable to the combination of falling prices and drought that would plague them during the 1920s and 1930s. More **modernized** and secure were midwestern and California farmers, who by World War I had adopted new machines, such as tractors, along with new methods to produce corn, grain, fruits, and vegetables, all marketed through **cooperatives**. Despite efforts at mechanization and cooperative marketing, the cotton and tobacco regions of the South remained impoverished, indebted, and conflict-ridden, circumstances that contributed greatly to the **Great Migration** of **African Americans** to the cities and the North. Populism and other agrarian movements of the 1890s influenced Progressive Era farm-support legislation such as the **Federal Farm Loan Act** and the **Warehouse Act** (both 1916) and contributed to the establishment of **rural free delivery**, the **Country Life Commission**, and the **conservation** movement. Initiatives culminating in the 1914 **Smith–Lever**

Act upgraded agricultural research and extension services operated through state land-grant universities.

Measures of economic growth, such as gross national product, productivity, and real wages, generally trended upward during the 1898–1917 period. But memories of the severe depression of 1893–97 lingered and were reprised during the **Panic of 1907**. Movements such as the **Socialist Party of America** and the **Industrial Workers of the World**, along with labor violence from **Coeur d'Alene** to **Lawrence** and **Ludlow**, reminded Americans that not everyone shared the benefits of growth. The inflationary cycle that began after 1897 prompted debate over the **cost of living** and fueled consumerist calls for business regulation. The Panic of 1907 dramatized once again the economy's vulnerability to business cycles as well as its dependence on the formidable Wall Street financiers whom critics labeled the **Money Trust**. This welter of momentous transformations inspired a fertile period in economic thought. **University**-based economists such as **Richard Ely**, **Simon Patten**, and **E. R. A. Seligman**, as well as Veblen, impatiently rejected the static formalism of classical economics and developed an empirical, **pragmatist** approach to understanding corporate enterprise, mass production, and consumer culture and providing rationales for expanded public-sector involvement in economic and labor issues. *See also* ADAMS, HENRY CARTER; ALDRICH–VREELAND ACT; ANACONDA COPPER; BUREAU OF CORPORATIONS, U.S.; COMMERCE AND LABOR, U.S. DEPARTMENT OF; COMMON-WEALTH EDISON COMPANY; DUKE, JAMES BUCHANAN; EDISON, THOMAS A.; GOLD STANDARD ACT; HARRIMAN, EDWARD H.; HILL, JAMES JEROME; HOLDING COMPANIES; INDUSTRIAL RESEARCH LABORATORIES; INTERLOCKING DIRECTORATES; INTERNATIONAL HARVESTER; INTERSTATE COMMERCE COMMISSION; NATIONAL CASH REGISTER; NEW MIDDLE CLASS; PAYNE–ALDRICH TARIFF; TARIFF COMMISSION ACT; UNDERWOOD–SIMMONS TARIFF; UNITED FRUIT COMPANY; UTILITIES, MUNICIPAL OWNERSHIP OF; WARBURG, PAUL M.

EDISON, THOMAS A. (1847–1931). Inventor and entrepreneur. Born in Ohio, Edison grew up there and in Michigan, where his father ran a grain and lumber business. A poor student largely educated by his mother, Edison by age 12 sold newspapers on trains and then became a telegrapher. By the late 1860s, he had launched his famous career as an inventor. He established an "invention factory" at Menlo Park, New Jersey, in 1876 and opened an even larger research-and-development New Jersey operation 11 years later. Edison's team devised the **phonograph** (1877), conceived as a business dictating machine; demonstrated the first durable incandescent bulb with a carbon filament (1879); and devised a generating plant on Pearl Street in lower Manhattan (1882) to supply **electricity** on the direct current (DC) principle. Edison promoted his system against **Nikola Tesla**'s alternating current (AC) system, favored by the **Westinghouse Electric Company**, until the introduction of AC/DC equipment, which former associates such as **Samuel Insull** made the basis for electrification of homes and businesses.

Edison frequently left it to others to manufacture devices and operate enterprises that he and his associates created. Consolidation of his electrical enterprises into the **General Electric Company** in 1892 illustrated this pattern. One exception was **movies**, an industry to which Edison contributed little after the invention of the kinetoscope but which he sought to dominate through patents and the formation in 1908 of the **Motion Picture Patents Company**. With over 1,000 patents in his name, Edison became a folk hero, in part by cultivating his image as a pragmatic lone genius, the Wizard of Menlo Park. Yet perhaps his greatest contribution was to demonstrate the dependence of modern industry on complex technological systems devised by teams of engineers and scientists. His "invention factory" became the model for the **industrial research laboratory**, a routine feature of corporate enterprise by the mid-20th century. *See also* ECONOMY.

EDUCATION. Formal education both expanded and changed at the turn of the twentieth century. The passage of **compulsory education laws**, the movement against **child labor**, and a growing demand for literate and numerate workers contributed to a great expansion of public education, especially **high schools**. The change was most dramatic in the South, which did not have a system of public education before the Civil War. The **Southern Education Board**, the **General Education Board**, and other groups contributed large sums to the public schools in the South. Southern **women** mobilized support for tax increases to sustain the schools. However, racial **segregation** and rural poverty meant that many southerners still had only limited access.

Curricula also changed to meet the perceived needs of an increasingly urban and foreign-born student population. **Progressive** reformers like **John Dewey** called for more practical and democratic education, and administrators like **Ella Flagg Young** attempted to realize those ideals. The **Gary Plan** represented one approach. In many places, vocational or **industrial education, Americanization,** and an ecumenical Protestant Christianity combined in a curriculum that emphasized manual labor and political docility for the working class. This approach was particularly common in schools for **Native American, immigrant,** and **African American** children.

In higher education, changes were even more far-reaching. With a growing, if still small, number of Americans enrolling in postsecondary schools, the **Carnegie Foundation for the Advancement of Teaching** and **university** administrators created the standardized tests that came to regulate college admissions. The public land-grant universities expanded rapidly and led the way in introducing extension and evening classes and in stressing the sciences, engineering, and applied fields. In part because public universities were tax-supported service institutions, they were open to female students from the start, and by the 1920s they enrolled 47 percent of all students on U.S. campuses. Private universities and colleges opened to women more slowly. Women were often directed toward courses in teaching, **home economics,** social work, and **nursing,** careers dominated by women. The elite, private women's colleges founded after the Civil War offered a small proportion of women a rigorous academic education.

Private universities and colleges serving men also changed profoundly in this era, following the path taken by Johns Hopkins University in adapting the German model of faculty research and graduate education to the United States and by Cornell in discarding denominational affiliations and religious tests for employment. Following the model of Harvard, they reduced classical studies and introduced modern languages, sciences, and art into the course offerings, while allowing students greater choice of courses. Some leading institutions also founded affiliated women's colleges but avoided full coeducation. Graduate and professional training grew more formal and required entrants to have a bachelor's degree, even as the Ph.D. became more common among university faculty. Although only institutions in the South were legally segregated by race, many ostensibly open colleges and universities enforced quotas to limit the number of women of any race, **African American, Jewish,** Catholic, and Asian American students. Several institutions, among them **Tuskegee Institute,** Howard University, Morehead University, and Spelman College, catered specifically to African American students. The chief bar to higher education was the cost: in this era before state and federal financial aid, few Americans could afford to attend college. *See also* ACADEMIC ASSOCIATIONS; CHICAGO, UNIVERSITY OF; ELIOT, CHARLES W.; FLEXNER REPORT; INDIAN EDUCATION; NATIONAL EDUCATION ASSOCIATION; WISCONSIN IDEA.

EFFICIENCY. This term, identified most directly with the **scientific management** movement in business promoted by consultants such as **Frederick W. Taylor** and **Frank** and **Lillian Gilbreth,** spread into political discussion and took on a moral connotation that stands as a distinctive element in **progressive** thought. Just as technological and managerial innovations increased the productive capacity of industry, so a more thoughtful, professional organization of governmental institutions could yield great benefits to society. Municipal affairs experts such as **Charles Beard** drew on notions of efficiency when promoting **structural reforms** to city government, such as the **commission** or **city manager** plans, civil service, and budgeting. Urban planners identified with the **City Practical** movement often termed their ideal the "city efficient." Labor economists such as **John R. Commons** viewed industrial efficiency as key to improved wages and living standards for the working class, even if this meant the obsolescence of craft skills that had given workers solidarity and status.

The writings of **Herbert Croly, Walter Lippmann,** and **Thorstein Veblen** contained a vision of social efficiency: social scientists, engineers, public administrators, and other professionals could cooperate to transform the self-interested, short-sighted drift of late 19th-century America into a mastery in which planning would serve humanitarian and civic goals (to invoke the title of Lippmann's 1914

Drift and Mastery). Reformers used the notion of social "efficiency" to argue for **juvenile courts**, intelligence testing, abolition of **child labor**, **education** reform, and other measures that promised to mold children into productive, civic-minded adults. In 1910, **Louis Brandeis** drew on expert advice from Frank Gilbreth and other efficiency experts in the so-called *Eastern Rate Case* before the **Interstate Commerce Commission**. Brandeis's success in denying railroads their requested rate increase, on the grounds that scientific management could save them $1 million per day in operating costs, spread the vogue of efficiency among **antitrust** campaigners and other reformers, a vogue illustrated by the 1911 publication of Taylor's *Principles of Scientific Management* in **Ray Stannard Baker**'s *American Magazine*. The efficiency mindset helps to explain why reform-minded economists and other observers in Europe as well as the United States initially thought the **Ford Motor Company**'s assembly line and **five-dollar day** had momentous social potential. International movements for **modernism** in **architecture** and design, such as Germany's Bauhaus, perpetuated the notion of efficiency as social reform, even as the **Arts and Crafts movement** and **Greenwich Village** intellectuals such as **Randolph Bourne** and **Van Wyck Brooks** formulated a critique of the preoccupation with efficiency as tending toward dehumanizing standardization. *See also* MODERNIZATION; NEW MIDDLE CLASS; NEW NATIONALISM; ORGANIZATIONAL SYNTHESIS.

THE EIGHT. Despite **Robert Henri**'s status as a juror for the National Academy of Design's annual exhibition in 1907, he was unable to persuade the academy to include works by his **realist** and **naturalist** allies and followers **William Glackens**, George Luks (1867–1933), **John Sloan**, and Everett Shinn (1876–1953). In frustration, Henri withdrew his own paintings from the show and helped to arrange an alternative exhibit, which opened in February 1908 in Macbeth Galleries in New York and included the original five plus three painters who worked in different styles but shared the realists' antagonism toward the academy: Maurice Prendergast (1859–1924), Arthur Davies (1862–1928), and Ernest Lawson (1873–1939). The exhibit of this group, which called itself "The Eight," popularized the urban realist **art** dubbed the **Ash Can School**.

EIGHTEENTH AMENDMENT (1918). Passed by Congress in 1917 amid mobilization for World War I, this amendment represented the culmination of **prohibition** campaigns by the **Anti-Saloon League** and the **Woman's Christian Temperance Union**. A "bone-dry" law, the amendment banned the "manufacture, sale, or transportation" of alcohol in the United States, thus including private as well as commercial production and distribution. Twenty-one mostly western and southern rural states already had alcohol restriction laws by 1917, and the passage of the Wartime Prohibition Act in 1918 also encouraged rapid ratification of the amendment. It became law when Nebraskans voted to ratify this constitutional amendment in January 1919 and went into effect in January 1920, supported by the Volstead Prohibition Act. Popularly known as the "noble experiment," prohibition succeeded in greatly lowering Americans' alcohol consumption in the 1920s. Enforcement failures, the growing political influence of urbanites and **immigrants** who had never favored the alcohol ban, and an active political movement in opposition led to its repeal in 1933.

EIGHT-HOUR WORKDAY LAWS. The movement for the eight-hour workday gathered momentum after the Civil War; by 1868, six states and the federal government had enacted laws declaring eight hours a normal workday, but such laws were full of loopholes and erratically enforced. The normal workweek did begin to shorten from an average of 60 hours in 1890 to 55 in 1915. This change was in part attributable to the **American Federation of Labor**, whose affiliates achieved eight- or nine-hour workdays through negotiation with employers in highly organized crafts. **Progressive** politicians such as Toledo's **Samuel Jones** pushed for the eight-hour day for workers under their purview. Beginning in 1908, the **Democratic Party** adopted an eight-hour platform plank to court AFL members. The **United Mine Workers** negotiated for an eight-hour day in 1898, and **Henry Ford** reduced the hours of his workers from nine to eight hours in 1914. Yet 10- and 12-hour shifts remained widespread, including at such prominent businesses as **American Tobacco** and **United States Steel**.

Two famous Supreme Court decisions on work hours, *Lochner v. New York* (1905) and *Muller v. Oregon* (1908), concerned legislation setting a maximum 10-hour shift for bakery workers and **women**, respectively. The 1916 **Adamson Act**, which established an eight-hour day for interstate railroad workers, represented the first durable victory for this venerable movement. After World War I began in 1914, **labor unions** used wartime labor shortages to pressure employers to shorten hours. Between 1915 and 1919, the average workweek decreased to 51 hours and the proportion of workers with a 48-hour week rose to 48 percent. An effective national declaration of eight hours as a standard workday awaited the Fair Labor Standards Act of 1938. *See also* NATIONAL CONSUMERS' LEAGUE.

ELECTRICITY AND ELECTRIFICATION. The telegraph brought electricity into ordinary life decades before the Progressive Era proliferation of practical uses for this form of energy. The 1876 Philadelphia Centennial **Exposition** introduced the telephone, and in the late 1870s brilliant "arc" lights appeared as an alternative to dull gas street lamps. With **Thomas A. Edison**'s demonstration in 1879 of the incandescent bulb, electricity promised to become practical for indoor lighting. Through the 1880s, Edison's direct current (DC) system, which required a large number of small generating plants spread through a city, competed with George **Westinghouse**'s alternating current (AC) system, which allowed high voltage transmission over a long distance from centralized generating plants, potentially connected to regional grids. The rivalry grew so fierce that Edison allegedly helped designers of the first electric chair (installed in a New York state prison in 1888) obtain Westinghouse generators in order to demonstrate AC's hazards. By the early 1890s, German, French, and American technicians (among them **Nikola Tesla**) had devised convertible systems that generated and distributed DC current while transmitting high-voltage AC current. The practicality of giant turbo generators and long-distance transmission helped to persuade Edison to cooperate in the 1892 formation of **General Electric Company**. In 1896, GE consented to a patent pool with Westinghouse, thereby ensuring the two firms' dominance of an industry whose revenues grew from $85 million in 1900 to $500 million by 1920. GE and Westinghouse manufactured motors and equipment for industry and transportation as well as lighting. Streetcar lines in Europe and the Americas quickly converted from horse or cable power to the electric **trolley** after 1888. Electricity powered 98 percent of the country's

30,000 miles of streetcar tracks by 1903. Electric elevators facilitated the upward growth of urban office and apartment buildings. Chicago's 1893 Columbian Exposition showcased marvels such as electric stoves and washing machines, part of an all-electric kitchen featured in the Electrical Building, along with Westinghouse dynamos and Edison's eight-story Tower of Light. A former Edison associate who organized the fair's electrical displays, **Samuel Insull** embarked on his career as a mass supplier of electricity, building **Commonwealth Edison** into an electric-and-gas **utilities** organization covering 32 states. Between 1902 and 1912, the number of Chicago households with electrical service increased from under 5,000 to over 80,000, or about half of the city's middle class. Most American homes, however, would not be electrified until the 1920s and 1930s.

ELIOT, CHARLES WILLIAM (1834–1926). Educator. The son of elite Bostonians, as a young professor at the newly founded Massachusetts Institute of Technology (1865–69), Eliot became involved in the ongoing debate over college curricula and surprisingly was appointed president of Harvard University in 1869. Along with Andrew White at Cornell, **Nicholas Murray Butler** at Columbia, and Daniel Coit Gilman of Johns Hopkins University, Eliot played a key role in developing **universities** in the United States. He strengthened the elective system for undergraduates, supported new courses in the sciences and modern languages, and helped to create standardized admissions tests. He also expanded and improved graduate and professional programs, raised faculty salaries, decreased teaching loads, encouraged research, and increased the role of faculty in governing the university.

Although Harvard itself served men only, beginning in 1879, **women** were admitted to a separate school that became Radcliffe College in 1894. Despite the new vogue for intercollegiate **athletics**, Eliot opposed **football**. Although he supported racial **segregation** and shared the anti-Semitism common to his class, he saw the university as an agent of **Americanization** and did not bar **African Americans** and **immigrants** from becoming students. **W. E. B. Du Bois** was the first African American to earn a Harvard doctorate in 1895. By Eliot's retirement in 1909, Harvard had become the nation's leading university and had a substantial endowment. However, Eliot was probably most famous for supervising publication of *The Harvard Classics*, the "five-foot shelf" of books that every educated person should read. *See also* EDUCATION.

ELKINS ACT (1903). Named for West Virginia senator Stephen B. Elkins, this law expanded the power of the **Interstate Commerce Commission** by outlawing the common practice of railroads giving rebates to favored customers. Any departure from published rates became a misdemeanor for both the railroad and the shipper. President **Theodore Roosevelt** and the railroad companies themselves favored this regulatory bill, because the latter was often pressured by **Standard Oil** and other major shippers to provide such secret discounts. *See also* HEPBURN ACT; MANN–ELKINS ACT.

ELLIS ISLAND. In 1892, the federal government opened a new immigrant reception center on this island in New York Harbor, replacing the city's dockside depot at Castle Garden. The embodiment of the federal government's 1891 assertion of control over **immigration**, the Ellis Island facility processed over 12 million mainly European immigrants before closing in 1954. All steerage passengers faced a physical exam, an inspection of their documents, and an interview with immigration officials before being released to gather their bags and take a boat to the city. About 80 percent of the immigrants spent less than one day there, but those with suspect politics, morals, or health were detained for days or weeks before being allowed to enter or deported. Deportees amounted to about 2 percent of the total, a proportion that grew as new limits were imposed, culminating in the comprehensive immigration restriction laws of the 1920s. Passing through Ellis Island was a frightening bureaucratic hurdle for most immigrants, but often ethnic-minority charities such as the **Hebrew Immigrant Aid Society** provided translators and advice. Ellis Island reopened in 1990 as a museum managed by the **National Park Service**. *See also* ANGEL ISLAND.

ELY, RICHARD T. (1854–1943). Economist. Born in New York, Ely graduated from Columbia University (1876) and earned a Ph.D. from the University of Heidelberg (1879). As a faculty member at Johns

Hopkins University (1881–92) and the University of Wisconsin (1892–1925), he became a prominent critic of laissez-faire economics, for which he proposed substituting a fusion of the empirical, historicist German approach with a social democratic, pro-labor agenda. Infusing his work with **Social Gospel** idealism, Ely also served as founding president of the **American Association for Labor Legislation**. He produced books such as *The Labor Movement in America* (1886), which argued for the insertion of Christian ethics into the capital-labor conflict, along with *The Social Aspects of Christianity* (1889) and *The Social Law of Service* (1896). His 1894 book, *Socialism and Social Reform*, criticized Marxist materialism and argued for a mixture of **socialism** and capitalism in which the public sector ran **utilities** and other "natural" monopolies. These ideas led the Wisconsin Board of Regents to investigate Ely for economic heresy in 1894. His exoneration was a noteworthy assertion of the principle of academic freedom. His views grew less zealous and his writings less provocative over his long career, though in 1904–06, Ely did lure to Wisconsin **John R. Commons** and **Edward A. Ross**, both thought to be radicals. *See also* ACADEMIC ASSOCIATIONS; ECONOMY; WISCONSIN IDEA.

EMPLOYER LIABILITY LAWS. By 1907, 26 states had adopted laws countering the common law "fellow servant" principle, according to which employers were almost never liable for workers' injuries on the job because they could claim that the injury resulted from the negligence of another worker, if not from the injured worker's own negligence. Employer liability laws proved a disappointing means of improving hazardous working conditions because they frequently only applied to railroad workers or miners, and even then, injury cases that got to court tended to drag to an uncertain result. By 1908–09, labor leaders such as **Samuel Gompers** and politicians such as **Theodore Roosevelt** had joined with groups such the **American Association for Labor Legislation**, the **National Civic Federation**, and the **Russell Sage Foundation** to support the alternative principle of **workers' compensation**. *See also* SOCIAL INSURANCE.

ERDMAN ACT (1898). Passed by Congress partly in response to the 1894 Pullman Strike, this law named the federal commissioner of labor and the chair of the **Interstate Commerce Commission** as a national Board of Arbitration to provide voluntary mediation in railroad labor disputes. The law also barred **yellow dog contracts**, blacklisting, and other maneuvers to prevent railroad workers from unionizing. In a 1908 case, *Adair v. United States*, the **U.S. Supreme Court** ruled 7–2 that protecting **labor union** membership as the Erdman Act mandated was a violation of freedom of contract and due process and therefore unconstitutional.

EUGENICS. Coined in 1883 by British scientist Francis Galton, this term came into common use after 1900 among advocates of selective breeding to improve the human race. In 1904, **Charles Davenport** secured a $10-million endowment from the **Carnegie Institution of Washington** to establish an institute for the experimental study of evolution in Cold Spring Harbor, New York. Donations from Mrs. **E. H. Harriman** sustained the institute's work on animal and human **genetics** from 1910 on. Beginning in the 1910s and accelerating after World War I, eugenics campaigns used a variety of methods to encourage the "right" people to procreate in healthy ways. Eugenicists favored the scientific study and frank discussion of **sexuality**, reproduction, and inheritable disease, including sex **education** for children; some advocated easier **divorce** laws. Eugenicists stressed public or national welfare above the individual or local community.

In the United States, eugenicists were most often socially conservative, white, Protestant, professional men who favored **immigration** restriction and **segregation** and opposed **African American** civil rights and the **New Woman**'s desire for higher education, professional careers, and **birth control**. Discounting environmental influences, they argued that tendencies toward crime, sexual immorality, alcoholism, and insanity were hereditary. Some **feminists**, including **Charlotte Perkins Gilman** and **Margaret Sanger**, endorsed eugenics from the belief that rationalization of reproduction would liberate women. Many eugenicists worried about "**race suicide**"—the falling birth rate among the white middle class and the higher fertility among supposedly inferior class and racial groups. Eugenicists sought to bar marriage among those they considered "unfit" and to **sterilize** inmates of public institutions for the feebleminded, many of whom were poor **adolescents** jailed for petty crime and sexual misbehavior.

Eugenic ideas also shaped the race-based immigration restriction laws of the 1920s. *See also* SOCIAL DARWINISM.

EUROPE, JAMES REESE (1880–1919). Conductor and composer. Born in Alabama and educated in the segregated **African American** schools of Washington, D.C., Europe in 1903 moved to New York City, where he composed and conducted for black **musical** theaters. In 1910, he organized the Clef Club, which became a conduit for black musicians seeking bookings in New York's dance and cabaret scene. The club's 125-member orchestra, conducted by Europe, performed works by **African American** composers at venues such as Carnegie Hall. In 1913, he became musical director for the dance team of **Irene** and **Vernon Castle**, with whom Europe helped to popularize **ragtime** dancing. The Castles and Europe together created the fox-trot. With one of the first major recording contracts signed by a black musician, Europe made 10 historic dance recordings for Victor in 1913 and 1914. He in large measure devised orchestral **jazz**, which became a staple of American music in the decade after his death. *See also* JOPLIN, SCOTT; PHONOGRAPH.

EXPOSITIONS. Regional, national, and international expositions celebrated the agricultural, industrial, and cultural progress of their participants, modeled ideal cities and social structures, contributed to the development of new display and merchandising techniques, and encouraged the development of **amusement parks** and organized tourist and leisure services. Despite their businesslike aims, they only occasionally made a profit for their organizers. The Victorian era of world's fairs began in 1851 with London's Crystal Palace exposition and culminated with the San Francisco's Panama–Pacific International and San Diego's Panama–California expositions in 1915. The United States' first international fair was the Centennial Exposition in Philadelphia in 1876. Thereafter the United States competed with European countries to stage the grandest, largest fair of them all. The most successful fair in the United States was the World's Columbian Exposition, held in Chicago in 1893.

Unlike European expositions, the American variety enjoyed relatively little federal or state government financial support. Instead, they relied on the funds and enthusiasm of city and state businessmen and cultural elites. International fairs in this era included Buffalo's Pan-American Exposition (1901), marred by bad weather and the assassination of President **William McKinley** on the grounds, and St. Louis' Louisiana Purchase Exposition (1904). Fairs in the southern states advanced the idea of the New South; at Atlanta's Cotton States and International Exposition in 1896, **Booker T. Washington** made his **Atlanta Compromise** speech. Whereas elite white women often served on auxiliary boards and constructed special "Woman's Buildings" on the grounds to showcase **women**'s achievements, **African Americans** and other racial minorities of both sexes were typically barred from organizing or attending. **Native Americans** often appeared as exhibits or performers in **Wild West shows** that accompanied the fair.

The expositions, like **department stores**, pioneered in the use of **electrical** lighting and special effects. Even more than the other institutions, expositions identified the production and consumption of goods with economic and cultural progress. The entertainment area, known by its name in Chicago—the "midway"—usually contained ethnological exhibits that bolstered contemporary racial prejudices and legitimized the U.S. military and cultural campaigns against Native Americans, Filipinos, and other groups. They also gave entrepreneurs like **Coney Island**'s Frederic Thompson a start in show business and popularized foods such as iced tea, hot dogs, and ice cream cones. *See also* POPULAR CULTURE.

– F –

FAGAN, MARK M. (1869–1955). Politician. Born in New Jersey to a poor Irish family, Fagan broke early with the region's Irish **Democratic machine**. As a **Republican**, he held Jersey City's mayoralty from 1901 to 1906 and again from 1913 to 1915 (the city's first election under the **commission** system), espousing a social reform agenda: public **baths, public health, juvenile courts**, and municipal ownership of **utilities**. Despite New Jersey laws highly favorable to corporations, he attacked the tax advantages enjoyed by railroads and other corporations and became a **progressive** hero after a profile by **Lincoln Steffens** in *McClure's* in 1906. He also promoted corporate tax reform while on the county tax commission (1910–13, 1915–17).

FAIRBANKS, CHARLES WARREN (1852–1918). Politician. A native of Ohio, Fairbanks became a successful railroad lawyer and executive and a leader in Indiana **Republican Party** politics. He won a term in the U.S. Senate in 1897, and his work on negotiating the **Alaska boundary dispute** led residents of that territory to name a town for him. His status as a conservative party regular from a swing state explains his selection as **Theodore Roosevelt**'s running mate in 1904. As vice president (1905–9), Fairbanks played a small role in Roosevelt's administration. Their relations remained cordial despite the feud between Roosevelt and the party's **Old Guard**. Fairbanks chaired the platform committee of the dramatic 1912 Republican convention, in which conservatives allied with **William Howard Taft** pushed Roosevelt into bolting the party. Fairbanks ran again for vice president with **Charles Evans Hughes** in 1916.

FARMER, FANNIE MERRITT (1857–1915). Cook, author, and educator. Born in Boston and partially paralyzed as a child, Farmer enrolled at the Boston Cooking School, an early **home economics** institute, becoming an instructor in 1889 and director in 1894. In 1896, she gained nationwide fame when she published a revised edition of *The Boston Cooking-School Cook Book.* By 1915, about 360,000 copies of this book and its revisions had sold, and reprint editions of 50,000 copies continued to appear. Eventually renamed the *Fannie Farmer Cook Book* and much revised, it remained in print for over a century. Often called "the mother of level measurements," she encouraged cooks to work like scientists, using standardized measuring tools. Unlike many rivals, she cared as much about tastiness as nutritional adequacy. Farmer opened her own cooking school in 1902, wrote more cookbooks, and authored a regular column in the **mass-circulation magazine** *Woman's Home Companion.*

FARMERS' UNION. Formed in Texas in 1902 as the Farmers' Education and Cooperative Union of America by former members of the populist-era Farmers' Alliance, this group (also known as the National Farmers' Union or NFU) promoted buying and selling **cooper-**

atives. Despite an unsuccessful 1905 attempt to raise prices by having farmers withhold their cotton from sale, the union attracted about 111,000 southern farm families by 1908, but its membership fell to fewer than 50,000 families by 1916. It excluded bankers, merchants, lawyers, and others whom it saw as exploiters. Also barred were **African Americans**, some of whom formed the Negro Farmers' Union in 1908. Though many of the union's cooperative ventures failed, it endured into the 1920s and 1930s, when its strength lay in midwestern and plains states and it campaigned for price supports, railroad and banking regulation, and other forms of government intervention. It also acted as a lobby and provided financial services to farmers.

FEDERAL FARM LOAN ACT (1916). Passed in July 1916 and sometimes known as the Federal Land Bank Act or the Rural Credits Act, this law established a network of 12 Federal Land Banks underwritten by government bonds. These banks funded long-term, low-interest mortgages for farmers who joined one of thousands of farm loan associations. Along with the **Warehouse Act**, this measure represented one of the first federal responses to the decades-long demand by agrarian groups for a public system of accessible credit.

FEDERAL HIGHWAY ACT (1916). This act, often called the Federal Aid Road Act or the Bankhead Shackleford "Good Roads" Act, the result of years of lobbying by the rural and recreational interests behind the **Good Roads movement** and the American **Automobile** Association, authorized the Department of Agriculture to spend $75 million as grants-in-aid to state highway departments to cover half the cost of rural road improvements. These roads became the foundation of the federal highway system developed in the 1920s.

FEDERAL RESERVE ACT (1913). This bill, the most significant achievement of President **Woodrow Wilson**'s **New Freedom**, reasserted the federal government's role as central banker for the first time since the 1830s. The Federal Reserve had its origins in the **Panic of 1907**, which dramatized the shortcomings of the National Bank system established during the Civil War, notably its inelastic currency and its tendency to funnel capital and power toward Wall Street. The National Monetary Commission (established by the 1908 **Aldrich–Vreeland**

Act) was chaired by **Nelson Aldrich**, who was sympathetic to New York financial interests. Its report in January 1911 called for a "National Reserve Association," in effect a central bank with 15 branches around the country that could issue currency, buy and sell government securities, and control the discount rate (the interest rate charged to banks). Unlike national banks in other countries, this national reserve would not engage in public banking but deal almost entirely with the government or banks that joined the association.

The Aldrich plan was controversial because it centralized finance and made bankers the dominant force on the regional and national boards of directors. Every imaginable political, financial, and commercial interest debated the proposal, including **William Jennings Bryan** and his followers, and **progressives** such as **Louis D. Brandeis**, whose writings on the **money trust** heightened suspicion of high finance. In 1913, President Wilson made banking reform a priority and supported a revision of the Aldrich plan backed by **Carter Glass**, who chaired the House banking committee. The bill that Congress passed on 23 December 1913 established 12 regional Federal Reserve banks, each governed by a nine-member board, with three members representing local banks, three drawn from local commerce, and three appointed by the Washington-based Board of Governors. These regional banks held the reserves of the national banks in that region, as well as those of state-chartered banks that elected to join. The Secretary of the Treasury and the Comptroller of the Currency sat on the national Board of Governors—commonly known as the "Federal Reserve Board"—along with five presidential appointees, who (in an attempt to ensure **nonpartisanship**) served 10-year terms with staggered starting points. "Federal Reserve notes" became the country's sole paper currency. In concessions to regionalists, the regional reserve banks had considerable autonomy, and the discount rate could vary by region, so that the credit-starved Plains and South could potentially adopt looser credit policies than the Northeast. Nevertheless, in part because of Wilson's cautious appointments to the Federal Reserve Board and the New York reserve bank's control of foreign transactions, Wall Street remained dominant until further reforms during the New Deal. The Federal Reserve Act also facilitated the use of checks in private transactions by enabling the regional reserve banks to act as check clearinghouses for their members. *See also* MORGAN, JOHN PIERPONT; PUJO COMMITTEE; WARBURG, PAUL M.

FEDERAL TRADE COMMISSION (FTC). During his 1912 presidential campaign, **Woodrow Wilson** attacked the idea of a federal commission to regulate big business, a central provision of rival candidate **Theodore Roosevelt**'s **New Nationalism**. Yet by 1914 Wilson and his advisor, **Louis D. Brandeis**, came to believe that a regulatory commission was preferable to strengthening **antitrust** law by creating a detailed list of prohibited business practices, the approach embodied in the **Clayton Antitrust Act**, which was moving through Congress at the same time. The act Wilson signed in September 1914 created the Federal Trade Commission to replace Roosevelt's **Bureau of Corporations**. The FTC board consisted of five members appointed for staggered seven-year terms to encourage **nonpartisanship**. The commission could hear complaints of violations of antitrust laws and initiate its own investigations. Although it could issue cease-and-desist orders, businesses retained the right to appeal FTC rulings to the courts. During its early years, the FTC suffered from internal conflicts and an unclear mission but survived as a major governmental innovation of the Progressive Era. *See also* NEW FREEDOM.

FELTON, REBECCA LATIMER (1835–1930). Reformer and **journalist**. The daughter of Georgia planters, Felton managed her husband's political career for nearly 30 years. Together, the couple criticized the state's conservative **Democratic** leadership and advocated the abolition of **convict leasing**, penal reform, **education** reform, **prohibition**, railroad regulation, and diversification of agriculture. However, they rejected criticism of the New South's fledgling industries and opposed **child labor** laws and **labor unions**. Beginning in 1899, she wrote a column for the *Atlanta Journal* and became one of the South's leading voices for white **women**'s **suffrage**, arguing that giving educated white women the vote would offset the electoral power of **African American** men. Like **Benjamin Tillman**, **James K. Vardaman**, **Tom Watson**, and other demagogues, she promoted **disfranchisement** and **segregation** and advocated **lynching**.

FEMINISM. Adapted from the French, this term came into general use after 1910 to describe a radical, mostly middle-class women's campaign to demand full economic, social, and sexual equality. It sprang from the **women's suffrage** movement but appealed chiefly to socially avant-garde men and women, among whom the **Greenwich Village** bohemians were the best known. Whereas contemporaries in other women's reform movements, such as **settlement houses** and temperance, rooted their constituency and their ideology in "woman's sphere" of motherhood and the home, feminists assumed neither gender solidarity nor the distinctiveness of women's experiences. Instead of bringing women's virtues to the public world, they emphasized women's right to self-fulfillment, advocated **birth control**, and argued for equality between husband and wife. Among the self-identified feminists of the era were lawyer **Crystal Eastman**, labor leader **Rose Pastor Stokes**, and anthropologist Elsie Clews Parsons; economist and **journalist Charlotte Perkins Gilman** rejected the term but was a major theorist of the movement. The **National Woman's Party** (1916) adopted an openly feminist agenda. *See also* BURNS, LUCY, CHOPIN, KATHERINE O'FLAHERTY; DIVORCE; GLASPELL, SUSAN; NEW WOMAN; PAUL, ALICE; SEXUALITY.

FILENE, EDWARD A. (1860–1937). Merchant and philanthropist. Born in Massachusetts to a German-**Jewish** family, Filene and his brother, A. Lincoln Filene, transformed their father's dry goods and women's clothing business into Boston's largest **department store**, covering a city block by 1912. He adopted innovations such as **scientific management** and the bargain basement, which drew working-class customers while promoting the turnover of goods that had not sold elsewhere. A client and ally of **Louis D. Brandeis**, Filene gained prominence as a proponent of **welfare capitalist** reforms such as credit unions, **minimum wages**, paid leave, and employee representation. A founder of the **U.S. Chamber of Commerce**, Filene also participated in an early effort at **City Practical** planning using social and economic data.

FITZGERALD, JOHN FRANCIS (1863–1950). Politician. Born in Boston to Irish Catholic **immigrants**, Fitzgerald built a successful insurance business before winning a seat on Boston's Common Council in 1892, a position he used to consolidate his status as the North End's political **boss**. After a term in the state senate, he served in the House of Representatives (1895–1901), for a time the only Catholic and **Democratic** representative from New England. In 1905, he won the Boston mayoralty despite opposition from rival bosses and patrician reformers. After a raucous term marked by expanded public works and services and charges of corruption, "Honey Fitz" lost his 1907 reelection bid but won a four-year term (1910–14) authorized by a new city charter. In the 1910 campaign, he exploited Irish resentment of Boston's Yankee **Republican** establishment, a tactic that set the tone in Massachusetts politics for decades. In 1914, a rival ward boss, James Michael Curley (1874–1958), coerced Fitzgerald into dropping his reelection bid, and he would not win again in races for the Senate (1916), the House of Representatives (1919), or governor (1922). His daughter Rose's marriage to Joseph P. Kennedy gave rise to the legendary Kennedy political dynasty. *See also* MACHINE POLITICS; URBAN LIBERALISM.

FIVE-DOLLAR DAY. In 1912–13, as the **Ford Motor Company** implemented the first automated assembly line to produce the **Model T** at its Highland Park plant, many workers found the monotony and stress unbearable. The company had to hire 54,000 people per year to maintain a workforce of 13,000, with the company replacing about half its workers each month. Such high turnover was common in industries dependent on unskilled labor. Nevertheless, **Henry Ford** determined to stabilize his workforce and undercut **labor unions** in 1914 by doubling workers' pay to $5 per day—an unprecedented wage for semiskilled and unskilled factory jobs—and by cutting the workday from nine to **eight hours**. So many people applied at the plant that guards turned fire hoses on a crowd of angry, unsuccessful applicants one Detroit winter morning. Realizing that high wages gave Ford leverage over workers, the company established a "sociology department" that investigated employees' private lives and compelled **immigrant** workers to attend English-language and **Americanization** classes. The five-dollar day added to Henry Ford's celebrity, especially because the entrepreneur argued that raising wages made expensive goods such as a Ford

automobile affordable to the working class. *See also* SCIENTIFIC MANAGEMENT; WELFARE CAPITALISM.

FLAGLER, HENRY MORRISON (1830–1913). Businessman. Born in New York, Flagler left school at 14 and with the aid of his mother's family became a merchant. After the Civil War, he became a partner of **John D. Rockefeller**, playing a key role in the railroad rebates and mergers that made **Standard Oil** infamous. By 1886, he had withdrawn from everyday management of the oil company and devoted himself to developing tourism and agriculture in Florida. He built two hotels in St. Augustine and purchased the local railroad before extending his efforts to other areas. His aid to Florida farmers in the severe winter of 1894–95 ensured steady traffic on his railroads. In 1896, he extended his Florida East Coast Railway to Miami and built a hotel, churches, and municipal services there. The **Spanish–American War** and U.S. **imperialism** in the Caribbean strengthened the state's economy and assured Flagler's success. His most ambitious (some said foolish) project was a railroad to Key West, completed in 1912.

FLETCHER, ALICE CUNNINGHAM (1838–1923). Reformer and anthropologist. Born in New York, Fletcher was a pioneer in anthropological fieldwork and an advocate for **Native Americans**. In the early 1880s, after camping among the Lakota and Omaha peoples, she successfully lobbied Congress to prevent removal of the latter to the **Indian Territory**. Instead, Congress mandated allotment of their reservation into individually owned plots, with Fletcher appointed to oversee the process. At first, she supported the **Dawes Allotment Act** (1887) and supervised allotment among the Winnebago and Nez Perce. After witnessing the rapid loss of land and abusive effects of the leasing and competency provisions, she came to regret her stance; she also rejected her initial endorsement of removing Indian children from their families to be raised by whites. Collaborating with her adopted son, **Francis La Flesche**, and other scholars, she published works on the Omaha and Pawnee, contributed to the Bureau of American Ethnology's *Handbook of American Indians North of Mexico* (1907, 1910), and lobbied for the **Antiquities Act** (1906).

FLEXNER REPORT (1910). Funded by the **Carnegie Foundation for the Advancement of Teaching** and conducted by **education** reformer Abraham Flexner (1866–1959), this report detailed shortcomings in medical education. At the time, most medical schools were small proprietary institutions without laboratory facilities, entrance requirements, or rigorous coursework. The report was credited with driving this type of school out of business and strengthening the university-based institutions that required a B.A. and extensive laboratory and practical training. It had the side effect of limiting the number of physicians and access to the profession. Of seven **African American** medical schools, for example, only two survived. *See also* AMERICAN MEDICAL ASSOCIATION; NATIONAL MEDICAL ASSOCIATION; UNIVERSITY.

FOLK, JOSEPH W. (1869–1923). Attorney and politician. Son of a Tennessee lawyer, Folk also became an attorney, and his work in 1900 for a streetcar **labor union** during a transit strike in St. Louis brought him public attention, helping him win the office of city prosecutor. Although elected with support of the **Democratic Party**, he prosecuted city and state officials for taking bribes to assign streetcar and **utilities** franchises and brought down the **machine** of political **boss** Edward Butler. **Lincoln Steffens** wrote about him in *McClure's*, and Folk's reputation as a crusader for public integrity helped him win the Missouri governorship (1905–9). In addition to pursuing corrupt officials and business interests, Folk oversaw a range of social and governmental reforms, including **compulsory education**, **child labor** reform, an **eight-hour** law for miners, the **direct primary**, **initiative**, and **referendum**. He ran twice for the U.S. Senate, but enmity from state power brokers crippled his campaigns. Folk held legal posts in President **Woodrow Wilson**'s administration before returning to his law practice.

FOOTBALL. This sport grew out of an array of games that resulted in three distinct sports by the 20th century: soccer, rugby, and American football, which began to take shape in the 1870s. The standardization of rules occurred through discussions among **university** teams in the eastern United States and Canada, with Yale University's Coach

Walter Camp playing a major role. Elite eastern colleges formed the Ivy League in 1870. Midwestern universities began fielding teams in the 1880s and 1890s, and the game was well-established nationwide by the 1920s. Although **Theodore Roosevelt** celebrated the sport as a way for young men to live the **strenuous life**, university officials periodically banned the game because it was manifestly dangerous. In 1905 the deaths of 18 players prompted a revision of the rules to make the game safer; from these meetings emerged the **National Collegiate Athletic Association (NCAA)**. The new rules had less effect than was hoped, as 33 players died in 1909. In 1912, the NCAA published another set of rules that made the game largely what it remained by the early 21st century. The adoption of helmets and pads also reduced the number of injuries and deaths. As with **baseball** and **basketball**, semi-professional and professional teams soon developed; the most famous professional player of the era was **Jim Thorpe**. However, the major university teams remained far more popular and powerful during this period. *See also* ATHLETICS.

FORAKER ACT (1900). Named for its sponsor, Senator **Joseph Foraker**, this bill organized the government of **Puerto Rico**, ceded to the United States by Spain after the **Spanish–American War**. The president appointed the governor and an executive council, while islanders elected a House of Delegates. Puerto Rico became an unincorporated dependency without the implicit promise of eventual statehood extended to earlier territorial acquisitions or even full rights under the Constitution. Puerto Ricans did not receive U.S. citizenship until 1917. Island-grown sugar received preferential access to American markets but was still subjected to duties domestic producers did not have to pay. This act, passed after bitter and racist debate in Congress, narrowly survived legal challenges in the *Insular Cases*.

FORAKER, JOSEPH P. (1846–1917). Politician. Born into an Ohio farming family, after serving in the Civil War and graduating from Cornell University (1869), Foraker embarked on a law practice in Cincinnati in 1869 and advanced in the **Republican Party**, winning the governor's seat in 1885 and 1887. A supporter of **public health** reform and a consistent opponent of **segregation**, he undercut his political effectiveness by quarreling with members of his own party and alienating supporters through actions such as strict enforcement of Sunday liquor laws. Nicknamed "Fire Alarm Joe" for his robust speaking style, Foraker won a U.S. Senate seat (1897–1909). As a member of the Senate Foreign Relations committee, he advocated the **Spanish–American War** and the annexation of **Hawaii** and the **Philippines**. The **Foraker Act** (1900) established colonial government in **Puerto Rico**. Too volatile for the **Old Guard** Republican leadership, Foraker was also frequently at odds with President **Theodore Roosevelt**, notably over the **Brownsville Raid**. Roosevelt helped scuttle Foraker's presidential ambitions in 1908 and used revelations in the **Hearst** papers of the Ohioan's financial connections to **Standard Oil** to force him to end his campaign for a third Senate term. In 1914, future president Warren G. Harding defeated Foraker's last attempt to regain his Senate seat.

FORD, HENRY (1863–1947). Industrialist. Born into a Michigan farm family, Ford early displayed a remarkable aptitude with engines. By age 15, he was a mechanic and apprentice engineer. He worked as a technician at **Westinghouse Electric Company** in the 1880s before becoming an engineer for the Detroit Edison Company by the mid-1890s. Fascinated with the internal combustion engine, he built his first **automobile** in 1896 and found investors to support his first manufacturing effort in 1899, but this failed in 1900. A year later, he launched the Henry Ford Company, only to be pushed out by investors in 1902; that company evolved into Cadillac Motors. He cofounded the **Ford Motor Company** in 1903, gaining majority control in 1906. Like most early manufacturers, at first he focused on assembling parts purchased from subcontractors, but after 1905 he made his own engines and parts in a quest for a lightweight, inexpensive automobile. Success with the Model N provided capital for the **Model T**, launched in 1908. This achievement made him famous and wealthy, an industrial folk hero on a par with his own hero, **Thomas Edison**. After sponsoring the Peace Ship in 1915, Ford supported U.S. involvement in World War I and increasingly dabbled in politics. In the 1920s and 1930s, his anti-Semitic and anti–**labor union** activities eroded his reputation.

FORD MOTOR COMPANY. Founded in 1903, the third attempt by **Henry Ford** to launch an **automobile** firm, this company competed with several Detroit-based firms to make what had been a luxury item affordable for ordinary consumers. After buying out enough original investors by 1906 to insure majority control, Ford and his mechanics experimented with standardized parts that reduced the need for skilled machinists to craft and assemble each car. Following the Model N, which sold briskly at a relatively low $600, Ford introduced the **Model T** in 1908. Over the next seven years, he and his engineers devised the mass production of Model Ts via an assembly line, an innovation that lowered the price of a Ford car enough so that virtually any family with steady income could afford one.

Contemporaries were astonished by what they called "Fordism," the standardization and mass production of a complex machine, an innovation that required machine tools with unprecedented precision and a shift in technological culture. Previously stamps and lathes had been grouped by type in separate rooms. Ford's engineers realized that by placing machines where they were needed in production, the time and expense involved in hauling parts around a plant could be eliminated. They also realized that mass-produced goods needed to be designed with their manufacture in mind, rather than designed first and then a manufacturing method sought. Ford's methods promised to make the benefits of industrialism available to broader segments of the population. Assembly-line work, however, threatened to reduce workers to automatons. The **five-dollar day** and **welfare capitalism** were Ford's answers to high turnover. After 1916, the company routinely sold half or more of the cars in the United States, but it faltered in the face of considerable marketing and technical challenges in the 1920s. *See also* ECONOMY; MODERNIZATION.

FOREIGN POLICY. The Progressive Era was a decisive period in foreign policy, when the United States emerged as a diplomatic, military, and economic power with enormous influence in the Americas and a presence in other parts of the world. American efforts to activate the dormant Monroe Doctrine and establish a real sphere of influence in the western hemisphere took shape under President Benjamin Harrison's energetic secretary of state, James G. Blaine (1889–92), who laid the groundwork for the Washington-based Pan-American Union while seeking to use **arbitration treaties** and tariff reciprocity to bring Central and South America into an economic and diplomatic alliance under U.S. leadership. Harrison's successor, Grover Cleveland, and his secretaries of state, Walter Q. Gresham (1893–95) and Richard Olney (1895–97), exhibited traditional American caution outside the western hemisphere, as illustrated by the Cleveland administration's repudiation of the controversial movement for **Hawaiian annexation**. But Cleveland's willingness to threaten Great Britain in the 1895 border dispute between British Guiana and Venezuela showed that even this cautious president accepted American power in the Caribbean. Initially taken aback, the British saw the usefulness of ceding dominance in the Americas to a generally friendly United States. The Venezuela dispute set in motion the Anglo–American rapprochement visible in the **Alaska Boundary Dispute** and the **Hay–Paunceforte Treaties**, negotiated by **Republican** Secretary of State **John M. Hay** (1898–1905). Politicians sometimes still played to the Anglophobia of Irish Americans and other **immigrant** groups, but Anglo–American cooperation continued, culminating in U.S. intervention on the Allied side in World War I.

The sequence of events that most clearly demonstrated the new U.S. willingness to use its power began in 1895, when a grueling revolution against Spanish rule broke out in **Cuba**. In marked contrast to the U.S. response to previous Cuban crises, Cleveland and his successor, **William McKinley**, escalated pressure on a reluctant Spain, eventually ordering U.S. intervention to drive the old colonial power out of the hemisphere in the **Spanish–American War** (1898). The mixed performance of the U.S. Army prompted the reforms identified with Secretary of War **Elihu B. Root** (1899–1904). The Navy's stunning success in the Caribbean and the **Philippines** dramatized progress since the 1880s in **modernizing** this branch of the military, efforts escalated by expansionist President **Theodore Roosevelt**, who would flaunt American sea power in the famed voyage of the **Great White Fleet** (1907–9).

Quick, sweeping victory over the Spanish played into the hands of the Republican **imperialist** faction, identified with **Henry Cabot Lodge**, **Albert Beveridge**, and Roosevelt. In keeping with Admiral **Alfred T. Mahan**'s vision of a string of naval bases and colonies to secure American power in the Caribbean and project it across the

Pacific, the expansionists revived demands for annexation of Hawaii, which became an American territory in 1898. After some reluctance, the McKinley administration acceded to calls for annexation of the Philippines, Guam, and **Puerto Rico** in the 1898 **Treaty of Paris**. The outrage of the Filipino independence movement over the U.S. deal with Spain sparked the **Philippine–American War** (1899–1902), a draining guerrilla struggle that gave credence to **anti-imperialist** charges that colonialism undermined U.S. democratic and republican principles. Committed to Cuban independence by the **Teller Amendment** (1898), the United States used the **Platt Amendment** (1901) to make the island nation into a protectorate. The **Foraker Act** (1900) established colonial government in Puerto Rico. The 1899 German–American agreement on **Samoan partition** further enhanced the U.S. presence in the Pacific.

Upon succeeding the assassinated McKinley in September 1901, Roosevelt vigorously pursued American hegemony in the Caribbean, a goal most notoriously illustrated by the heavy-handed diplomacy that in 1903 won control of the route of the **Panama Canal**. U.S. actions in Panama, Cuba, the **Dominican Republic,** and elsewhere led to charges of **gunboat diplomacy**. The 1904 Dominican crisis prompted Roosevelt to articulate a rationale for U.S. activism in the western hemisphere in the form of the **Roosevelt Corollary**.

Chastened in part by the Philippine War, Roosevelt and advisers Hay, Root (who oversaw the State Department in Roosevelt's second term), and **William Howard Taft** (governor of the Philippines in 1901–04 and then secretary of war in 1904–08) pursued a cautious, balance-of-power policy in East Asia. Having failed to stave off Great Power competition over China through the **Open Door notes** and having been drawn into the suppression of the **Boxer Rebellion**, the United States sought to accommodate Japan in the **Taft–Katsura** (1905) and **Root–Takahira Agreements** (1908), as well as the 1907 **Gentlemen's Agreement** on the volatile issue of Japanese immigration to the United States. Concern for the Asian balance of power prompted U.S. mediation of the Russo–Japanese War in the 1905 **Portsmouth Conference**, for which Roosevelt won the 1906 Nobel Peace Prize. The Roosevelt administration also pursued balance-of-power politics elsewhere, for example in the 1906 Algeciras Conference over Morocco. In initiatives such as the **Hague Conferences**, the United States committed itself to a framework of international law, a dream for which Root would continue to work as president of the **Carnegie Endowment for International Peace.** Under President Taft, Secretary of State **Philander C. Knox** tried to replace Roosevelt's belligerence in Latin America with a mutually beneficial **dollar diplomacy.** The mixed results of this policy in **Haiti, Nicaragua,** and the Dominican Republic illustrated the difficulty of finding a cooperative approach. President **Woodrow Wilson**'s first secretary of state, **William Jennings Bryan,** sought to implement anti-imperialism and **internationalism** by repudiating Taft-era dollar diplomacy in China and negotiating 30 **cooling-off treaties.** Wilson and Bryan's moralistic outlook on foreign affairs clashed with their self-proclaimed adherence to nonintervention, and during this administration the United States engaged in a new round of interventions in the Caribbean basin, most dramatically in the **Mexican Revolution,** where events such as the **Veracruz** occupation (1914) and the **Pershing Expedition** (1916–17) reinvigorated deep-rooted Mexican suspicions of the United States. But the outstanding diplomatic crisis of the Wilson years was World War I, where repeated clashes with Germany over U.S. economic ties with the Allies and German submarine warfare eroded Wilson's neutrality policy, ending in U.S. intervention in the European war in April 1917. *See also* AGUINALDO Y FAMY, EMILIO; ALIEN LAND ACT; AMERICAN UNION AGAINST MILITARISM; BAKER, NEWTON D.; BOUNDARY WATERS TREATY; DEWEY, GEORGE; GENERAL STAFF, U.S. ARMY; GOETHALS, GEORGE WASHINGTON; HAY–BUNAU-VARILLA TREATY; HAY–HERRÁN TREATY; HOUSE–GREY MEMORANDUM; *INSULAR CASES*; LANSING, ROBERT; LEAGUE TO ENFORCE PEACE; MACARTHUR, ARTHUR, JR.; MIGRATORY BIRD TREATY; PHILIPPINES, COLONIAL GOVERNMENT OF; PREPAREDNESS; STRAIGHT, WILLARD D.; UNITED FRUIT COMPANY.

FOREST SERVICE, U.S. This agency, founded in 1905, resulted from reorganization of the Department of Agriculture's Bureau of Forestry, a small research and educational agency founded as the Division of Forestry in 1879. The Forest Reserve Act (1891) authorized the president to set aside public forests, a power expanded under the Forest Management Act (1897). In the 1890s, Presidents Benjamin Harrison and Grover Cleveland set aside some 37 million acres, but these remained under control of the General Land Office of the Department of the Interior, which **conservationists** suspected of being allied with logging interests. **Gifford Pinchot**, director of Agriculture's forestry division since 1898, lobbied for transfer of forest reserves to his agency, with support from President **Theodore Roosevelt**. In 1905, Congress authorized the transfer into an expanded agency under Pinchot's direction, renamed the U.S. Forest Service. Pinchot and Roosevelt pursued federal forest conservation so energetically that by 1907 the Forest Service, with a staff of 1,500, controlled 150 million acres in 159 national forests. Regretting the latitude it had given Roosevelt and Pinchot, Congress at that point legislated limits on new forest reserves. The Interior Department retained some jurisdiction over land titles in national forests, which led to the **Ballinger–Pinchot controversy** and Pinchot's dismissal in 1910.

FORTUNE, T. THOMAS (1856–1928). Editor and civil rights activist. Born into slavery in Florida, Fortune gained renown as editor of a series of **African American** newspapers, most prominently the *New York Age*. One of the first black leaders openly to criticize the **Republican Party**'s drift from civil rights, he attempted twice between 1889 and 1898 to found a national advocacy organization. Attracted by the economic self-reliance that **Booker T. Washington** called for in his **Atlanta Compromise** speech, Fortune acted as ghost writer for the famous leader, who in return quietly backed the *Age* financially despite disapproving of the editor's militant opposition to **segregation** and his denunciation of President **Theodore Roosevelt**'s handling of the **Brownsville Raid**. After 1900, Fortune suffered bouts of alcoholism and depression, prompting Washington to arrange Fortune's removal as editor of the *Age* temporarily between 1907 and 1911 and permanently after 1914. He continued to write and briefly edited a newspaper sponsored by the nationalist Marcus Garvey. *See also* JOURNALISM.

4-H CLUBS. These rural youth clubs responded to widespread concern over rural **education** and the dwindling appeal of agriculture to young people. In 1902, Ohio educator Albert B. Graham sponsored an agricultural club for white boys and girls with support from the state Agricultural Experiment Station. Similar clubs soon appeared in other midwestern and southern states. By 1906, Agriculture Department agents cooperated with **George Washington Carver** at **Tuskegee Institute** to organize a parallel movement among rural black youth. Educators in Iowa adopted a three-leaf clover—to signify head, heart, and hands—as a symbol; a fourth leaf—for health—was added by 1911. Attempts to coordinate the state movements gained federal backing in 1914, when the **Smith–Lever Act** provided support through the Agriculture Department's **Cooperative Extension System**. Such clubs existed in virtually every state by 1918 when USDA officials called this movement the "4-H clubs."

FRANK, LEO, LYNCHING OF. On 27 April 1913, the night watchman at the National Pencil factory in Atlanta, Georgia, discovered the body of Mary Phagan, a 13-year-old worker who had been raped and murdered. Suspicion fell on Leo Max Frank (1884–1915), superintendent and part-owner of the factory and the last person known to have seen the girl. Police mishandled and even lost potentially exculpatory evidence, and another suspect, **African American** janitor Jim Conley, provided unsubstantiated testimony that he had over time concealed Frank's alleged sexual activities and on the day of the murder had helped Frank hide Phagan's body. Although born in Texas, Frank came from a prosperous New York **Jewish** family, and the case roused anti-northern hostility and anti-Semitism and provoked nationwide sensationalist press coverage. Crowds cheered prosecutors and warned the jury to convict the businessman or face violence. Convicted, Frank appealed to the Georgia Supreme Court and the **U.S. Supreme Court**, which ruled 7–2 that the mob's pressure on the jury did not violate Frank's constitutional right to a fair trial. In a 1923 ruling, the court adopted dissenting arguments made in the Frank case by Justices **Oliver Wendell Holmes** and **Charles Evans Hughes**, but this came too late to save Frank. In June 1915, days before his scheduled execution, Georgia governor John M. Slaton commuted the businessman's sentence to life in prison. National Guard troops had to defend the executive mansion from a mob intent on **lynching** the governor. Roused in part by **Tom Watson**'s anti-Semitic tirades, armed men broke into the state penitentiary on 16 August 1915, kidnapped Frank, and hanged him. This notorious incident helped inspire formation of the **Anti-Defamation League.**

FRANKFURTER, FELIX (1882–1965). Lawyer and jurist. Born in Austria, Frankfurter emigrated to New York at age 12 with his family. After graduating from New York's City College in 1902 and Harvard Law School in 1906, he worked for another young **progressive** at the start of a long career, Henry L. Stimson, first in the New York U.S. Attorney's office and then as the War Department's counsel for insular affairs when Stimson became secretary of war in President **William Howard Taft**'s administration. After involvement in **Theodore Roosevelt**'s **Bull Moose** campaign in 1912, Frankfurter became the first **Jew** on the Harvard Law School faculty (1914–39). One of the founders of the *New Republic* and a protégé of **Louis D. Brandeis**, he served as counsel to the **National Consumers' League** and argued the *Bunting v. Oregon* case before the **Supreme Court**. During World War I, the lawyer joined President **Woodrow Wilson**'s administration as a specialist on labor issues, investigating the **Bisbee Raid** and the **Mooney Case**. His distinguished career culminated in his appointment to the **U.S. Supreme Court** (1939–62).

FRICK, HENRY CLAY (1849–1919). Industrialist. Born into a Pennsylvania farming family, Frick at age 21 formed a firm to buy fields of bituminous coal, the raw material for producing coke, the fuel required for Bessemer steel manufacture. By the late 1870s, his control of coke had made him a millionaire. In 1882 he formed a partnership with steel magnate **Andrew Carnegie** and became chairman of and a major stockholder in Carnegie's steel operation seven years later. He oversaw the acquisition of factories and ore fields that made Carnegie Steel one of the world's prime examples of vertical integration. However, he is perhaps best known for handling of the 1892 Homestead Strike. The deadly violence between **labor union** supporters and Pinkerton Agency guards hired by Frick to break the strike in July 1892 led to a public outcry. Frick's unyielding stance and his fearless response when **anarchist Alexander Berkman** tried to assassinate him on 23 July made the steel executive the personification of the unrelenting capitalist. The negative publicity created a rift between the partners, and in 1899 Carnegie attempted to push his partner out. Frick countered with a lawsuit that forced the revaluation of Frick's share of Carnegie Steel from $5 million to $31 million. This quarrel set the stage for Carnegie's 1901 sellout, which resulted in the formation of **United States Steel**. Now worth over $100 million, Frick retired to manage his banking and insurance interests and developed a renowned **art** collection in his New York City mansion until his death on 2 December 1919.

FULLER, MELVILLE W. (1833–1910). Jurist. From a family of lawyers in Maine, Fuller too became a lawyer, with a practice in Chicago. President Grover Cleveland nominated the well-known appellate lawyer to be Chief Justice of the **Supreme Court** in 1888. On the court (1888–1910), Fuller gained a reputation as an effective administrator who, with some exceptions, issued pro-business, anti–**labor union** decisions such as *Pollock v. Farmer's Loan and Trust* (1895), *United States v. E. C. Knight* (1895), and the **Danbury Hatters' Case** (1908). A target of **progressive** critics, he resisted President **Theodore Roosevelt**'s pressure to resign and remained in office until his death. Fuller served as U.S. representative on the commission that settled the Venezuela Boundary Dispute and was a member of the Permanent Court of **Arbitration** in The **Hague**.

THE FUNDAMENTALS: A TESTIMONY TO THE TRUTH. This series of 12 pamphlets (1910–15) contained 94 articles by prominent conservative Protestant ministers and theologians defending doctrines such as the inerrancy and historical accuracy of the Bible against the historical and philological analyses that produced **modernist** theology. Although they rejected the Darwinist theory of natural selection, the authors claimed to support modern science, and some of the writers considered evolution God's mechanism for developing life. A California businessman paid to have millions of copies distributed throughout the English-speaking world. The title of the series led conservative Christian groups to call themselves "fundamentalists" by the mid-1920s.

FUNSTON, FREDERICK (1865–1917). Army officer. Born in Ohio and raised in Kansas, Funston attended the University of Kansas after failing to gain entry to West Point and acquired military experience in 1896 as an artillery officer in the **Cuban** revolutionary army. After the outbreak of the **Spanish–American War**, he was commissioned a colonel of Kansas volunteers and sent to the Philippines, where his regiment was stationed at the start of the **Philippine–American War**. Exonerated of charges that he had ordered the execution of prisoners, he won the Medal of Honor and was promoted to brigadier general of volunteers. In March 1901, disguised as a prisoner in the hands of Filipino allies masquerading as rebels, Funston captured nationalist leader **Emilio Aguinaldo**, a daring exploit and the decisive moment in this brutal war. Rewarded with a one-star general's commission in the regular army, he undercut his own career by publicly criticizing the **Philippine colonial government**. His heavy-handed conduct as commander of the Department of the Pacific in the aftermath of the **San Francisco earthquake** embroiled him in yet more controversy, but he redeemed himself with his leadership of American forces in the **Veracruz Incident** and his defense of the border during the **Mexican Revolution**. In line to command American forces in World War I, Funston died suddenly in February 1917.

– G –

GALVESTON HURRICANE (1900). On the evening of 8 September 1900, a hurricane with wind speeds estimated at 125 miles per hour struck Galveston, Texas. A 15.7-foot storm surge shattered or swept away one-third of the city. An estimated 6,000 people died in Galveston and over 4,000 more as the storm plowed inland, the highest death toll from a natural disaster in U.S. history. For over a month after the storm, recovery workers pulled some 70 bodies per day from the debris. The Central Relief Committee, a group of business and civic leaders who oversaw recovery, became the basis of Galveston's **commission** government, an innovation that spread nationwide. With assistance from the Army Corps of Engineers, Galveston constructed a massive seawall and raised streets and buildings five to 20 feet above previous levels in an area of more than 500 city blocks. This storm protection system has enabled Galveston to endure repeated hurricanes without the horror of the 1900 storm. *See also* HOUSTON SHIP CHANNEL; STRUCTURAL REFORM.

GARDEN CITY MOVEMENT. This international movement was inspired by Ebenezer Howard's book *Tomorrow: The Peaceful Path to Real Reform* (1898), republished in 1902 as *Garden Cities of Tomorrow*. The English author called for an end to the concentration of population in industrial cities and the construction of low-density communities of around 30,000 people, where all social classes could have ready access to culture, recreation, nature, and work. This vision was at odds with **City Beautiful** and **City Practical** planning, both of which would upgrade existing cities. The garden city nonetheless caught the attention of urban planners such as **Charles Mulford Robinson** and **Social Gospel** figures like **Josiah Strong.** Demonstration projects planned by the Garden City Association of America (1906) fell victim to the **Panic of 1907**, but other projects were realized between 1910 and 1917, the most influential being Forest Hills Park in Queens, New York, sponsored by the **Russell Sage Foundation.**

GARDNER, ISABELLA STEWART (1840–1924). Art patron. Born into a wealthy New York City family, "Belle" Stewart married John L. Gardner Jr., a Boston shipping and insurance executive, in 1860. Too flamboyant for staid, upper-class Boston, Gardner traveled extensively, befriended authors Charles Eliot Norton and **Henry James** and artists J. M. Whistler and John Singer Sargent (both of whom painted her portrait), and collected **art. Bernard Berenson**, whose travels she sponsored, helped her assemble an impressive collection of Renaissance and Dutch masterpieces. After her husband's death in 1898, she built the Isabella Stewart Gardner Museum, an Italian renaissance palazzo on the Fenway in Boston. It became one of the most coherent and thoughtful of the period's numerous privately funded museums. Mrs. Gardner willed it to the city with the proviso that no changes be made to the collection.

GARFIELD, JAMES R. (1865–1950). Lawyer and public official. An Ohio native and the son of assassinated President James A.

Garfield, "Jim" Garfield shared a law practice with his brother Harry in Cleveland. Active in **Republican Party** politics, he served two terms in the state senate before President **Theodore Roosevelt** appointed him in 1902 to the **U.S. Civil Service Commission**. A member of Roosevelt's so-called **Tennis Cabinet**, Garfield became the first head of the **Bureau of Corporations**, where he oversaw investigations leading to the **Meat Inspection Act** and the **antitrust** prosecution of **Standard Oil**. After serving on the **Keep Commission**, he promoted Roosevelt's **conservation** policies during a term as secretary of the interior (1907–09). An early adherent of the **National Progressive Republican League**, Garfield played a prominent role in Roosevelt's 1912 **Bull Moose** campaign, and in 1914 he ran for Ohio governor on the **Progressive** ticket before rejoining the Republican Party in 1916. Garfield remained active in his party's moderate wing and served Republican administrations on various special commissions through the 1920s and early 1930s.

GARLAND, HAMLIN (1860–1940). Author. Born into a poor farming family in Wisconsin and raised in Iowa and North Dakota, Garland moved in 1884 to Boston, where he lived in poverty while spending his days at the Boston Public Library and contributing to reform and literary magazines. A collection of his stories about the grimness of prairie farm life, *Main-Traveled Roads* (1891), won acclaim as a landmark of American **realism**. This book and *Prairie Folks* (1893) were also literary expressions of midwestern populism, but later fiction with explicitly political themes brought him neither critical nor commercial success. Settling in Chicago in 1894, Garland became a fixture in the city's literary circles and published romantic novels set in the Far West, which sold well but disappointed admirers of his early stories. He rebuilt his reputation as an evocative realist with a series of autobiographical books, beginning with *A Son of the Middle Border* (1917). *See also* CHICAGO RENAISSANCE; LITERATURE.

GARY, ELBERT H. (1846–1927). Lawyer and industrialist. From an Illinois farming family, Gary established a law practice and was elected in 1882 as a county judge. His talents as a corporate lawyer drew Gary into the management of midwestern steel producers as they consolidated during the 1890s. In 1898, he became president of Federal Steel, a $200-million combination backed by **J. P. Morgan** as a competitor to **Andrew Carnegie**. Along with Morgan and **Charles Schwab**, Gary oversaw negotiations that led to the 1901 formation of **United States Steel**, which Gary dominated as chairman (1903–27). A proponent of consolidation and plant **modernization** whose anti–**labor union** stance was partly offset by experiments in **welfare capitalism**, Gary symbolized unrestricted corporate power for many. With over 60 percent of the country's steel industry under his control, Gary maneuvered to avoid **antitrust** prosecution and fiercely fought the federal indictment that followed U.S. Steel's controversial acquisition of Tennessee Coal and Iron in 1907. *See also* GREAT MERGER MOVEMENT.

GARY PLAN. Named after the **United States Steel Corporation** town in which it occurred, the plan was the brainchild of school superintendent William Wirt, who sought to make schools community centers for both parents and children, encourage adult **education**, and bring **industrial education** to the center of the curriculum. Pupils spent half the day in academic classes and half in shops or laboratories. The circulation of children in and out of classrooms, shops, **playgrounds**, and auditoriums meant fewer classrooms and teachers were needed. Appealing to proponents of both **efficiency** and **progressive** education, the Gary Plan was adopted in over 1,000 schools at its height. Its failures, most notably in New York City, led critics to condemn its mechanical vision and the tendency of administrators to emphasize efficiency over effectiveness.

GENERAL EDUCATION BOARD (GEB). Established in 1902 by **John D. Rockefeller**, the foundation's aim was to improve **education**. In its first seven years, Rockefeller gave the GEB over $53 million and directed its efforts primarily toward the South, where it shared personnel and funding with the **Southern Education Board**. The GEB helped improve primary education and opened over 500 **high schools** in the southern states between 1905 and 1920. Annual spending, the average length of the school year, enrollment, and teacher salaries all increased among middle-class, town-dwelling whites. Rural whites saw little improvement and continued to resist

compulsory education and **child labor** laws. The GEB offered little aid to **African American** southerners, deliberately **segregated** in underfunded schools.

GENERAL ELECTRIC COMPANY (GE). Organized in 1892, this company merged two of the three largest American electrical equipment makers at the time: Edison General Electric and Thomson-Houston. Investment banker **J. P. Morgan**, who oversaw the merger, pushed out executives close to **Thomas Edison**. The company maintained major manufacturing plants in Massachusetts, New Jersey, and New York and worked with local **utilities** executives such as **Samuel Insull** to promote consumer and industrial use of electricity. In 1900, the firm consolidated its research at the country's first **industrial research laboratory** in Schenectady, New York. Led by **Willis R. Whitney**, the GE lab became renowned for basic and applied research on lighting, vacuum tubes, x-rays, and other electrical devices. *See also* ELECTRICITY AND ELECTRIFICATION; TROLLEYS, ELECTRIC; WESTINGHOUSE ELECTRIC COMPANY.

GENERAL FEDERATION OF WOMEN'S CLUBS (GFWC). Founded in 1890, the GFWC was an umbrella organization of women's groups, including literary clubs, municipal improvement groups, **women**'s **suffrage** organizations, professional women's leagues, and religious and ethnic associations. The GFWC received a federal charter in 1901 and boasted over one million members by 1910. After the controversy in 1900 over inviting **Josephine St. Pierre Ruffin** to join its board, the GFWC remained **segregated** well into the 20th century. It worked with groups such as the **National Consumers' League** and the **National Congress of Mothers** on issues as diverse as **juvenile courts**, **education**, **pure food and drugs**, **child labor**, and **public health**.

GENERAL MOTORS CORPORATION (GM). Former carriage maker William C. Durant (1861–1947) formed General Motors in 1908 as a **holding company** for his diverse **automobile** businesses, the most prominent of which was Buick, briefly the country's best seller before **Henry Ford**'s **Model T**. Other components of GM included Cadillac, Oldsmobile, and Oakland, in addition to truck building and parts manufacturing firms. More adept at acquiring businesses than coordinating them, Durant lost control of the company in 1910 to a group of Boston and New York bankers. Under James J. Storrow's lackluster management, GM held only 10 percent of the American auto market. Durant, meanwhile, set up the new Chevrolet Company to manufacture inexpensive automobiles to compete with Ford. With backing from the **du Pont** family, he regained GM's presidency in 1916 but failed again to coordinate the company's subsidiaries. In 1920, Pierre du Pont ousted Durant for good and installed Alfred P. Sloan (1875–1966), who implemented organizational changes that enabled GM to surpass Ford.

***GENERAL SLOCUM* DISASTER.** About 15 minutes after the steamship *General Slocum* left the East Third Street pier in Manhattan to sail up the East River on 15 June 1904, a fire in the forward cabin raced through the ship. On board were over 1,300 passengers, mostly **women** and children on a German Lutheran Church outing. A fatal combination of an ill-trained crew, rotten life jackets and fire equipment, and lifeboats wired in place condemned more than 1,000 of them to a gruesome death before the captain beached the ship on an island. The 67-year-old captain, a convenient scapegoat, was sentenced to 10 years in prison, though he was pardoned after three years. The disaster, New York City's deadliest until 11 September 2001, prompted the tightening of safety inspections on U.S. passenger ships. A comparable though less-known disaster occurred in Chicago on 24 July 1915 when the steamship *Eastland*, carrying around 2,500 people on a company picnic, capsized while along a wharf, killing 844.

GENERAL STAFF, U.S. ARMY. Established in 1903, the General Staff counted among the military reforms promoted by President **Theodore Roosevelt** and Secretary of War **Elihu Root** in the aftermath of the disastrous mobilization for the **Spanish–American War**. Modeled on institutions in Germany and other European powers, the General Staff coordinated planning, operations, and supply. Its head, the army chief of staff, replaced the old commanding general as the main military advisor to the secretary of war. In a concession to the entrenched military contracting system, Congress weakened

Root's plan by limiting the General Staff's authority over bureaus responsible for procuring weapons, equipment, and supplies, which contributed to a new round of mobilization and supply problems after the United States entered World War I in 1917.

GENETICS. The growth of American research **universities** occurred amid rapid development in genetics, the branch of biology concerned with heredity. Partly as a consequence, genetics became one of the first natural sciences to which American researchers made significant contributions. At Columbia University, Thomas Hunt Morgan's laboratory established *Drosophila melanogaster*, the fruit fly, as a practical creature for tracing heredity. Morgan's experiments revealed that genetic traits pass from parents to offspring via chromosomes. His Columbia colleague, Edmund Beecher Wilson, and Nettie Maria Stevens of Bryn Mawr College investigated the cellular basis for sex-linked characteristics. Genetics at first provided superficial support for **eugenics**, but by the 1920s revelation of the enormous complexity of genetic inheritance provided the scientific basis for an attack on eugenics as unsound biology.

GENTLEMEN'S AGREEMENT (1907). This agreement between Japan and the United States resulted from U.S. efforts to avert an international crisis over American anti-Japanese sentiment. In 1906, the Japanese government protested a decision by the San Francisco Board of Education to provide a **segregated** school for children of Chinese, Korean, and Japanese ancestry. There were only 93 Japanese pupils in the city, but Japanese **immigrants'** rising numbers and entrepreneurial success provoked white hostility. Acting to avoid confrontation with Japan, a staunch defender of its nationals abroad, President **Theodore Roosevelt** denounced the decision and pressured San Francisco's mayor and school board until they relented. In return, the Japanese government agreed to prevent immigration of laborers to the United States, although the wives and children of men already in the country were still able to enter. Migrants also continued to arrive via Canada and Mexico, and the agreement did not apply to Hawaii, where the Japanese became the largest ethnic group. *See also* FOREIGN POLICY; ROOT–TAKAHIRA AGREEMENT (1908); TAFT–KATSURA AGREEMENT (1905).

GIANNINI, AMADEO PETER (1870–1949). Banker. The son of Italian **immigrants** to California, Giannini was a partner in his stepfather's San Francisco wholesale grocery until age 31, when he began managing his deceased father-in-law's estate, including a small savings and loan society. In 1904, he cofounded the Bank of Italy, which, unlike most banks, aggressively solicited the patronage of small business owners. His success in saving the bank's assets from the fire after the **San Francisco earthquake** (1906) ensured the bank's quick growth, as did its deft handling of the **Panic of 1907.** Taking advantage of a new state banking law in 1909, Giannini acquired smaller banks, transforming them into branches, the first such large-scale operation in the United States. In 1919, he began expanding beyond California, and at his death the renamed Bank of America was the largest commercial bank in the world.

GIBBONS, JAMES (1834–1921). Bishop. Born in Baltimore to Irish Catholic immigrant parents, Gibbons grew up in Ireland and New Orleans before entering a Maryland seminary in 1854. Ordained in 1861, the talented priest rose rapidly and was consecrated the youngest bishop in the entire Roman hierarchy in 1868. In his popular book *The Faith of Our Fathers* (1876) he outlined the position with which he was henceforth identified: that Catholic doctrine was compatible with American democracy, including separation of church and state. As archbishop of Baltimore (1877) and cardinal (1886), Gibbons oversaw expansion of parochial **education** and wrestled with the ethnic divisions that troubled American Catholicism as **immigration** from eastern and southern Europe increased. His defense of **labor unions** and the free press, participation in ecumenical activities, and alliance with liberal Catholics like Bishop **John Ireland** brought Gibbons into conflict with the hierarchy in Rome. In an 1899 apostolic letter, Pope Leo XIII condemned the **Americanist** views of Gibbons and Ireland as potentially heretical. Founding chancellor of Catholic University in Washington, D.C., he did much to erode the country's deeply rooted **anti-Catholicism.**

GIBSON, CHARLES DANA (1867–1944). See DAVIS, RICHARD HARDING; JOURNALISM; MASS-CIRCULATION MAGAZINES; NEW WOMAN.

GILBERT, CASS (1859–1934). Architect. Born in Ohio and raised in Minnesota, Gilbert apprenticed with a St. Paul architect and studied briefly at the Massachusetts Institute of Technology. Starting in 1880, he worked with the famed New York firm McKim, Mead, and White, leaving to open his own practice in St. Paul in 1883. His design for the Minnesota state capitol (1898) gained national attention, as did his New York Customs House, a Beaux Arts masterpiece (1907). His **Woolworth Building** (1913) remained the world's tallest skyscraper until superseded by the Chrysler Building (1930). Active in urban planning, he coined the phrase **City Practical** while president of the American Institute of Architects in 1909. Gilbert remained an exponent of monumental, neoclassical styles long after architectural **modernists** launched their campaign against historical forms and decorated facades. *See also* ARCHITECTURE.

GILBRETH, FRANK (1868–1924) AND LILLIAN (1878–1972). Management consultants. A Maine native, Gilbreth owned a successful construction company in Boston in 1904, when he married Lillian Evelyn Moller, a California native with degrees in **literature**. After moving to New York, Frank grew interested in industrial **efficiency** and **scientific management**, especially after meeting **Frederick Winslow Taylor** in 1907. By 1912, he was a full-time management consultant in partnership with Lillian, who wrote most of the popular management books published under either Frank's name or both their names, beginning with *A Primer of Scientific Management* (1912). She also earned a doctorate in psychology from Brown University and wrote *The Psychology of Management* (1914). At the same time, the Gilbreths raised 12 children in a household run by scientific management principles, an experience recounted in the 1948 bestseller *Cheaper by the Dozen*. They expanded on Taylor's ideas and techniques in a number of ways, most memorably by developing photographic equipment to examine work motions and emphasizing the human element, such as employee benefits.

GILLETTE SAFETY RAZOR. In 1895, King C. Gillette Jr. (1855–1932), a Wisconsin-born salesman and inventor, conceived the idea of a disposable double-edged razor blade to replace the traditional straight razor. Working with MIT engineer William Emery Nickerson, Gillette devised a method for mass producing razor blades from ribbons of steel. Launched in Boston in 1903, the Gillette Company soon produced over 2.4 million blades and 90,000 razor holders per year. Within a decade, Gillette was an internationally known brand name, and its inventor retired to pursue other interests, such as a utopian scheme for a world corporation. A vivid personality, he continued to appear in company **advertising** and was known for innovative marketing. For example, he initially priced the razor holders as high as $5 to imbue them with prestige. He then gave holders away through coupon schemes linked with cigar and gum wrappers. The profit, of course, was in the endless demand for disposable blades, which led to the new fashion of clean-shaven men. *See also* POPULAR CULTURE.

GILMAN, CHARLOTTE PERKINS (1860–1935). Feminist, economist, **journalist**, and novelist. Born in Connecticut, Gilman grew up in poverty after her father abandoned the family. She supported herself as a commercial artist and teacher before marrying in 1884. After bearing a child in 1885, she became severely depressed and was prescribed the so-called rest cure, which required her to avoid reading and writing and to lie completely still. Instead, Gilman abandoned her family and moved to California. Her famous story, "The Yellow Wallpaper," evokes this terrible period. Supporting herself as a writer and lecturer, she studied Darwinism and became convinced that the subordination of **women** prevented human improvement. Like many female activists, she wanted to rebuild society based on nurturing, cooperative values associated with maternal femininity. She despised the excessive sexualization of women and the equation of dependence with sexual attractiveness. Her demand for female autonomy paralleled that of the **Greenwich Village** bohemians, but she did not share their positive view of **sexuality**.

Earning an international reputation with the publication of *Women and Economics* (1898), Gilman produced several more studies of children, the home, work, and religion, and wrote most of her monthly magazine, *The Forerunner* (1909–16). Her writings provided an **intellectual** foundation for **progressive** movements that questioned the customary organization of courtship, the family, childrearing, and housework and that asserted public responsibility for ensuring safe, clean, humane conditions for families and workers. She also published utopian novels, the best known of which is *Herland*, about an all-female society. Rejecting the term **feminism** despite being one of its principal theorists, Gilman sought instead to diminish the force of masculinism in society. Like many white women's rights advocates, she accepted white supremacy, shared a widespread anti-Semitism, and endorsed **eugenics**. *See also* DIVORCE.

GIRL SCOUTS OF AMERICA (GSA). Founded in 1912 by Juliette Gordon Low (1860–1927), based on her experience with the British Girl Guides, the GSA boasted some 15,000 members when it incorporated in 1915. Like the rival Camp Fire Girls, the GSA provided girls with the contact with nature and outdoor activities that boys enjoyed in organizations like the **Boy Scouts**. Encouraging physical fitness and independence, the GSA also taught girls how to be better wives and mothers. Established first in Jim Crow Georgia, the Girl Scouts were initially an all-white organization; **segregated** troops for **African American** girls began in 1917, and not until the 1960s would the troops integrate. Girl Scout cookies first appeared in 1936. *See also* ADOLESCENCE.

GISH, LILLIAN (1893–1993). Actress. Born in Ohio, Lillian de Guiche grew up in her mother's theatrical boardinghouse and began acting as a child. Boarder Gladys Smith, who soon became **Mary Pickford**, introduced her to film director **D. W. Griffith** in 1912, and, renamed Lillian Gish, she worked with the famous director for the next 10 years, starring in *The Birth of a Nation* (1915) and other popular **movies**. Under his guidance, she developed a public persona as a fragile, virginal innocent, but in real life she was a successful film editor, director, and actress throughout her long life.

GLACKENS, WILLIAM J. (1870–1938). Artist. Born in Philadelphia, Glackens worked as an illustrator and reporter for newspapers while attending the Pennsylvania Academy of Fine Arts. He became part of a circle of young **realist** artists that included **John Sloan** and **Robert Henri**. Glackens settled in New York City, where he maintained a studio with another artist from Philadelphia, George Luks (1867–1933). Continuing to work for newspapers and *McClure's* magazine, he went to **Cuba** for the *New York World* to cover the **Spanish–American War** in 1898. Marriage into a wealthy family in 1904 freed him to focus on painting. In 1908, Glackens joined Henri, Sloan, and other transplanted Philadelphians in the New York exhibition of realists and **naturalists** known as **The Eight**. Associated thereafter with the so-called **Ash Can School**, Glackens indeed focused on big city subjects but in a **modernist** style that was more impressionist and colorful and less gritty than that of his fellow urban realists. *See also* ART.

GLADDEN, WASHINGTON (1836–1918). Clergyman and theologian. A Pennsylvania native, Solomon Washington Gladden was ordained a Congregational minister and served as a pastor in Massachusetts and Ohio. By the 1880s, he became nationally known for his prolific writings and organizational work, through which he popularized liberal trends within American Protestantism: theological **modernism**, the reconciliation of science and religion, ecumenicalism, and the **Social Gospel**. Although he opposed **socialism**, he supported **labor unions**. A fierce critic of churches that accepted **John D. Rockefeller**'s "tainted money," he opposed **anti-Catholic** movements such as the American Protective Association.

GLASPELL, SUSAN (1876–1948). Author. An Iowa native, Glaspell worked as a reporter while earning a B.A. from Drake University (1899). After studying briefly at the **University of Chicago**, she lived in Davenport, Iowa, and Chicago while writing critically praised novels, along with short stories for **mass-circulation magazines**. Glaspell married radical editor George Cram Cook in 1913, after which the couple joined New York City's **Greenwich Village** literary scene. After they founded the **Provincetown Players** (1915), Cook managed the company, while Glaspell became the leading playwright along with Eugene O'Neill. Like O'Neill's works, Glaspell's plays were often experimental in form. Her work also drew on **feminism** and psychoanalysis. *See also* CHICAGO RENAISSANCE; LITERATURE; MODERNISM.

GLASS, CARTER (1858–1946). Editor and politician. The son of a Virginia newspaper publisher, Glass left school at age 14, when his family had financial trouble, and worked at a variety of jobs before turning to **journalism**. Owner and editor of the Lynchburg *News* by 1888, he was elected as a **Democrat** to the state senate (1899–1901) and constitutional convention (1901–2). In these offices, he played a prominent role in rewriting Virginia's constitution to **disfranchise African Americans**. In 1902, he was elected to the first of eight terms in the U.S. House of Representatives (1902–18), where as chair of the Banking and Currency Committee, he worked with President **Woodrow Wilson** to devise the 1913 **Federal Reserve Act**. Glass was secretary of the treasury (1918–20) but resigned to take a seat in the Senate (1920–46).

GOETHALS, GEORGE WASHINGTON (1858–1928). Army officer and engineer. Born in Brooklyn to Flemish **immigrant** parents, Goethals graduated second in West Point's class of 1880. Commissioned in the Army Corps of Engineers, he distinguished himself in flood control and navigation work on the Ohio, Cumberland, and Tennessee Rivers, in between assignments as an instructor at West Point and assistant to the Chief of Engineers. In 1903, he joined the army's new **General Staff**. Four years later, President **Theodore Roosevelt** chose him to be chief engineer of the **Panama Canal** and head of the Isthmian Canal Commission. Goethals had responsibility for one of the largest, most expensive, and most complex engineering projects in history. He won the respect of the canal's 30,000 workers, and his completion of the canal under budget and ahead of schedule in August 1914 made him a national hero. President **Woodrow Wilson** appointed Goethals as governor of the Panama Canal Zone (1914–17).

GOLDBERGER, JOSEPH (1874–1929). *See* PUBLIC HEALTH.

GOLDMAN, EMMA (1869–1940). Anarchist and feminist. After a traditional **Jewish** childhood in Lithuania and Russia, Goldman emigrated to the United States with her sister in 1885. While working in sweatshops, she embraced **anarchism**, for which she became the leading American exponent. For her, anarchist freedom implied an across-the-board rejection of the legal, political, economic, and sexual constraints that **women** faced. Supporting herself as a **nurse**

and midwife and a lecturer on anarchism, **feminism**, trade unionism, **birth control**, and **sexuality**, she had two long partnerships with fellow anarchists **Alexander Berkman** and **Ben Reitman**. After Berkman's release from prison for the attempted assassination of **Henry Clay Frick** (1892), which she had helped plot, they published the monthly magazine *Mother Earth* (1906–17). With Reitman, she made controversial national lecture tours (1908–15). **Anthony Comstock** persuaded the U.S. Post Office to ban *Mother Earth* from the mail in 1910 for her essay "The **White Slave** Traffic." Jailed for opposing the draft during World War I, Goldman was deported with Berkman and 250 other radicals to the Soviet Union on her release from jail in 1919. Disillusioned, "Red Emma" and Berkman left Russia in 1921. She spent the rest of her life in Europe and Canada and was buried in Chicago.

GOLDMARK, JOSEPHINE CLARA (1877–1950). Social reformer. The daughter of Austrian **immigrants**, Goldmark graduated from Bryn Mawr College (1898) and taught for a few years before meeting **Florence Kelley** and joining the **National Consumers' League**, for which she became a leading researcher, producing books on **child labor** (1907) and women's labor (1912). The statistical research she did for **Louis Brandeis**'s brief in *Muller v. Oregon* (1908) and other decisions upholding state regulation of workers' hours made her central to the development of **sociological jurisprudence**. In 1912, Goldmark participated in the investigation of the **Triangle Shirtwaist Fire** and helped shape New York State's pioneering industrial safety regulations. She also investigated hospital health conditions and the state of **nursing** education.

GOLD STANDARD ACT (1900). The economic revival following **William McKinley**'s 1896 election to the presidency—along with a rapid expansion in worldwide gold production resulting in part from the **Alaska** gold rush—replenished the U.S. Treasury's gold reserves, depleted during the 1890s depression. This emboldened the **Republicans** in Congress to pass a measure to affirm U.S. commitment to a gold-backed currency, a source of angry debate for years. This March 1900 law contained minor provisions to mollify pro-silver Republicans and inflationist westerners, such as making it easier to charter national banks in small towns and declaring the possibility of remonetizing silver if other countries did so. Despite efforts by **Democratic** presidential candidate **William Jennings Bryan**, the currency issue did not galvanize voters in 1900, as it had during the famous election of 1896.

GOMPERS, SAMUEL (1850–1924). Labor leader. Born in England to Dutch **Jews** who migrated to New York City in 1863, Gompers became a cigar maker as a teenager, joined the Cigarmakers' International Union, and dedicated himself to the labor movement. By the late 1870s, he and Adolph Strasser had built the Cigarmakers into a model **labor union**. In 1881, Gompers won election as the first president of what would become the **American Federation of Labor (AFL)** in 1886, and he was reelected every year until his death except 1894, when conflicts over the AFL's stance on **socialism** and anger at his failure to support the Pullman Strike of that year led to his only defeat.

Although Gompers abandoned his youthful Marxism, he never wavered in his belief that the workplace was the locus of conflict between capital and labor and that the labor movement needed strength to win material gains for workers, by strikes if warranted. Adopting a "pure and simple" or "business" strategy that eschewed electoral politics, Gompers concentrated on organizing white, male, skilled workers, who were in the best position to build effective, durable unions. One cost was acceptance of racial **segregation** in many member unions. Still, after weathering disasters such as the 1892 Homestead Strike as well as Pullman, the AFL under Gompers became the first American labor federation to survive a major depression. Membership in AFL-affiliated unions expanded from 250,000 in 1893 to 1.7 million by 1904.

Anti-labor court decisions such as the **Danbury Hatters' Case** and the judiciary's readiness to issue injunctions against strikes persuaded Gompers to drop his policy of steering clear of politics, as did **progressives'** interest in labor issues and the rhetorical support that reform politicians such as **Theodore Roosevelt** gave organized labor. After the AFL established its headquarters in Washington, D.C., in 1896, Gompers became a familiar figure in national political circles, and in 1900, he was the founding first vice president of the **National**

Civic Federation. Six years later, he challenged the **Democratic** and **Republican** parties to address **Labor's Bill of Grievances**. While **Old Guard** Republicans resisted Gompers's demands, **William Jennings Bryan** guided the Democrats toward pro-labor positions. This tacit alliance between the Democrats and the AFL brought dividends such as the **Clayton Antitrust Act**. The AFL counted 2.4 million members at the time of the U.S. entry into World War I in 1917 and four million by 1920. However, Gompers's strategy of supporting President **Woodrow Wilson**'s war effort failed to insure federal support for the AFL following the war. Defeats during the strike wave of 1919 sent AFL membership into decline, and criticism of Gompers's leadership was growing by the time of his death.

GOODNOW, FRANK J. (1859–1939). Political scientist and educator. Born in Brooklyn, Goodnow briefly practiced law before pursuing an academic career. After studying in Paris and Berlin, he taught public administration at Columbia University for 20 years starting in 1883. In books such as *Politics and Administration: A Study in Government* (1900) and *City Government in the United States* (1904), in his teaching, and in his work with the **National Municipal League** and other civic groups, he endeavored to shift the study of American government away from legalism and formalism and toward empiricism. His best-known contribution was distinguishing between politics, the process by which a society makes policy decisions, and administration, the implementation of those decisions. This distinction provided an **intellectual** foundation for the Progressive Era effort to invigorate municipal democracy and municipal administration. Goodnow advised the government of the new Republic of China (1913–17) and served as president of Johns Hopkins University (1914–29). *See also* STRUCTURAL REFORM.

GOOD ROADS MOVEMENT. This movement began as an alliance between farmers' groups and bicyclists' organizations, such as the League of American Wheelmen, for state and federal action to improve rural roads. By 1910, **automobile** lobbies such as the American Automobile Association joined the campaign, and the National Good Roads Association held conventions and supported publications such as *Good Roads* magazine. In response to this lobbying and the post office's requirements for **rural free delivery**, states established highway commissions and subsidized county road grading and paving. Gaining federal support was more difficult because of longstanding opposition to national involvement in local projects and the conflicting desires of farmers (who wanted farm-to-market and rural postal roads) and automobilists and truckers (who wanted a network of intercity and interstate highways). Still, in 1892 the U.S. Department of Agriculture established an Office of Road Inquiry that in 1905 became the federal Bureau of Public Roads and soon had some 450 employees. Highway bills failed in 1912 and 1914 before Congress finally concurred on the landmark **Federal Highway Act** of 1916.

GORDON, JEAN (1865–1931) AND KATE (1861–1932). Social reformers and suffragists. New Orleans natives, the Gordon sisters launched the Louisiana **women**'s **suffrage** movement and affiliated it with the **National American Woman Suffrage Association (NAWSA)** in 1896. Jean devoted herself to combating **child labor** and helped found a state branch of the **National Consumers' League**, among other activities. Kate served as president of the Louisiana Woman Suffrage Association (1904–13) and held offices in NAWSA (1902–11). In 1911, she resigned in opposition to the campaign to amend the federal constitution to allow women to vote and two years later founded the **Southern States Woman Suffrage Conference** as a states' rights alternative. Both sisters believed that federal control of voter qualifications would undermine the **disfranchisement** and **segregation** of **African Americans**. The Gordons also endorsed **eugenics, sterilization**, and **birth control**.

GORMAN, ARTHUR P. (1839–1906). Politician. A Maryland native, Gorman rose through a succession of political posts until by the late 1870s he was the **boss** of the Maryland **Democratic Party**. Elected to the Senate (1881–99, 1903–6), he chaired his party's caucus and National Executive Committee. During the 1890s depression, his disagreements with President Grover Cleveland over the tariff and other **economic** issues deepened the Democrats' disarray, facilitating the sweeping **Republican** victories of the late 1890s. After resisting the 1898 **Treaty of Paris** ending the **Spanish–American War**, Gorman lost his seat in that year's election but won it back in 1903, quickly regaining his party leadership posts. In 1892 and 1904, Democrats touted him briefly as a presidential candidate, but he undermined his chances in 1904 with an ill-advised attempt to defeat President **Theodore Roosevelt**'s popular treaty to acquire the **Panama Canal** Zone.

GRANDFATHER CLAUSE. First enacted in Louisiana's new constitution in 1898, the clause permitted an illiterate man to vote if he had been able to vote on 1 January 1867, or if his father or grandfather had been eligible at that date. Locating the date before the passage of the Fourteenth (1868) and Fifteenth (1870) amendments to the Constitution ensured that most white but few **African American** men would meet the criteria. Alabama, North Carolina, Georgia, and Oklahoma passed similar measures. All were intended to exempt white men from **disfranchisement** laws. The **Supreme Court** declared the grandfather clause unconstitutional in *Guinn v. United States* (1915). *See also* LITERACY TESTS; POLL TAX; WHITE PRIMARY.

GREAT MERGER MOVEMENT. Historians use this term to signify the first of the periodic waves of corporate consolidations that have characterized the modern American **economy**. More than 2,000 firms disappeared into mergers between 1895 and 1904, including 1,200 companies in 1899 alone. Giants such as **DuPont**, **Eastman Kodak**, and **International Harvester** emerged with a market share of over 70 percent in their respective industries. The most famous firm formed in this merger wave, **United States Steel**, controlled more than 60 percent of the steel market and was the world's first billion-dollar corporation. Economic historians offer several explanations for this trend. Capital-intensive, mass-production firms reacted to the severe depression that followed the Panic of 1893 by trying to create a stable, controlled market for their products. Also, Wall Street investment bankers such as **J. P. Morgan** for the first time undertook the large-scale underwriting of industrial securities. By 1904, 318 firms held 40 percent of the country's industrial assets, and firms controlling more than 50 percent of their industries accounted for one-third of the total value added in manufacturing in the United States. The unprecedented level of concentration energized the Progressive Era

antitrust movement. Notably, about half the consolidations attempted failed. Unlike the **National Biscuit Company** or the American Smelting and Refining Company, American Bicycle and National Cordage fell apart because they brought their organizers no distinct advantage in marketing, production technology, or control of strategic raw materials. *See also* HOLDING COMPANIES; INTERLOCKING DIRECTORATES.

GREAT MIGRATION. Historians use this term to describe the mass migration of **African Americans** out of the rural South, which began slowly in the 1890s, accelerated after 1910, and continued into the 1960s. In 1910, more than 90 percent of blacks lived in the South and fewer than a quarter of southern blacks lived in cities. New Orleans, Memphis, Birmingham, and other southern cities experienced marked increases in African American residents between 1910 and 1920, but the most striking trend was blacks' migration to northern and midwestern cities such as New York, Chicago, and Detroit, with a considerable number also going west. Between 1910 and 1920, Chicago's black population increased from around 44,000 to nearly 110,000, while Detroit's jumped from around 5,700 to nearly 41,000. By opening industrial employment to large numbers of blacks for the first time, World War I accelerated this migration. A combination of sociopolitical factors encouraged migrants, ranging from boll weevil epidemics to the determination to escape **segregation** and the prospect of better jobs and **education** in the urban North. Large numbers of southern whites migrated in the same decades to many of the same destinations.

The consequences of this migration were momentous. In the short term, whites barred African Americans from **labor unions**, skilled jobs, and most decent housing, using both violent and nonviolent means, such as **race riots** and bombings and beatings. Still, African Americans in the North had greater scope for political and economic activity than in the South. Newspapers like the *Chicago Defender* called forthrightly for civil equality and decried racism, and organizations like the **National Association of Colored Women** and the **National Association for the Advancement of Colored People** operated openly, something nearly impossible in the Jim Crow South. Moreover, African Americans became influential players in **Repub-**

lican and **Democratic** politics in some cities. In addition, African American **music** and dance began to transform the nation's tastes as **Tin Pan Alley** songwriters and classical composers incorporated **ragtime** and **jazz** into their work and black entertainers like **James Reese Europe**, George Walker, and Bert Williams reached wide audiences.

GREAT WHITE FLEET. Named by the press for the 16 white-painted battleships that led the fleet, this round-the-world cruise of the most modern elements of the U.S. Navy left Virginia on 16 December 1907 and returned on 22 February 1909 to a personal welcome by President **Theodore Roosevelt**. Initially a training exercise to test the logistics of furnishing coal and supplies to the Atlantic fleet as it sailed to California via the Strait of Magellan, the cruise became at Roosevelt's behest a round-the-world trip with visits to ports in 26 countries. In part a show of force in response to tensions with Japan, this cruise by the world's second-largest navy was also a publicity exercise to demonstrate the results of doubling the U.S. Navy budget and size during Roosevelt's presidency. Crowds feted the fleet when it stopped in Japanese ports, but the gesture may have confirmed Japanese strategists' view of the United States as a threat. Roosevelt nevertheless considered the navy's round-the-world trip one of his signal achievements. *See also* PORTSMOUTH CONFERENCE; ROOT–TAKAHIRA AGREEMENT (1908).

GREENWICH VILLAGE. A working-class neighborhood inhabited largely by Irish and Italian **immigrants** and **African Americans** near the **Lower East Side** of New York City, the Village became home to self-styled "bohemians" as early as the 1890s. After 1900 its reputation drew **artists** and **intellectuals** from across the nation, making it the locus of a culturally and politically radical alternative intelligentsia. Among its better-known residents were lawyer and activist **Crystal Eastman** and her brother, the editor and writer **Max Eastman**; **birth control** advocate **Margaret Sanger**; anarchist **Emma Goldman**; dancer **Isadora Duncan**; artists **John Sloan** and **Alfred Stieglitz**; playwright **Susan Glaspell**; **journalists John Reed** and Louise Bryant; political writers **Walter Lippmann** and **Randolph Bourne**; and writers **Hutchins Hapgood** and Neith Boyce. To a greater extent than the European avant garde, the Village bohemians were open to **Jewish** and **women**'s participation, and the issues of **feminism** and **sexuality** stood at the center of their political ideals. **African Americans** found only a limited welcome in Village circles. Defenders of freedom of speech and supporters of the labor movement, the neighborhood's residents produced journals like *The Masses*, *Seven Arts*, *Mother Earth*, and the *Little Review*. Disrupted by federal repression of dissent during World War I, the Greenwich Village bohemia revived in the 1920s, though veterans of the neighborhood came to dismiss the scene as contrived and even touristy. *See also* DODGE, MABEL; LITERATURE; MODERNISM; PATERSON STRIKE.

GRIFFITH, DAVID WARK (1875–1948). Film director. Born into an impoverished but genteel Kentucky family, Griffith became an actor in 1895 and wrote fiction for **mass-circulation magazines**. After the unsuccessful staging of a play he had written, in 1908 he accepted an invitation to direct **movies** for the production company Biograph. Between 1908 and 1913, he directed some 500 films and, along with others, developed important cinematic techniques, such as dynamic and parallel editing, the close-up, the fade-in and fade-out, the long shot, the keyhole shot, and parallel montage. Discontented with Biograph, he looked for opportunities to create the longer, narratively complex films then being pioneered by French filmmakers. In 1914, he left Biograph to work for Reliance-Majestic and began production of the film for which he is best known, *The Birth of a Nation* (1915). Technically innovative, wildly popular, and highly controversial, the film was a racist retelling of the Civil War and Reconstruction era that justified **segregation, disfranchisement**, and **lynching**. His next film, *Intolerance* (1916), was even more ambitious; braiding four historical tales together in a complex fashion, it was not a popular success but attracted the attention of many filmmakers.

The high cost and technical demands of Griffith's long films contributed to the rise of a movie industry based in Hollywood. He launched the careers of **Mary Pickford** and **Lillian Gish**, and in 1919 he joined Pickford and **Charlie Chaplin** to form United Artists.

Although recognized as a great artist, Griffith was unable to sustain his popularity and financial success in the 1920s. Unlike most early filmmakers, who were urbanites and often European **immigrants**, he was rural and Southern, and he is remembered for using film in innovative ways to promote conservative ideas.

GRINNELL, GEORGE BIRD (1849–1938). *See* CONSERVATION.

GUINN V. UNITED STATES **(1915).** This unanimous **Supreme Court** decision overturned Oklahoma's **grandfather clause** as a blatant violation of the Fifteenth Amendment's prohibition of the use of race as grounds for denying the right to vote. The case was one of the first legal victories for the **National Association for the Advancement of Colored People**, which filed an amicus curiae brief. Its immediate effect was limited, however, because the courts had already sanctioned most other forms of **disfranchisement** in cases such as *Williams v. Mississippi* (1898).

GUNBOAT DIPLOMACY. This term described the tendency to deploy U.S. naval forces to settle political or economic disputes. Especially after the **Spanish–American War**, the navy and marines intervened regularly in Caribbean and Central American countries such as the **Dominican Republic, Nicaragua**, and **Cuba**. In 1902, the navy established a permanent Caribbean Squadron to exert U.S. influence in that troubled region. The **Roosevelt Corollary** of 1904 asserted the threat of military intervention as an element of U.S. policy toward its southern neighbors. Because, starting in his prepresidential years, Roosevelt famously liked to cite the African proverb "Speak softly and carry a big stick," contemporaries sometimes called his approach "Big Stick" diplomacy. Cartoonists regularly depicted Roosevelt striding through the Caribbean or elsewhere brandishing a big club. To support the **Open Door** policy in East Asia, the navy built shallow-draft gunboats suitable for Chinese rivers and routinely sent battleships to visit Chinese ports. President **William Howard Taft** espoused **dollar diplomacy** as a less belligerent alternative. *See also* FOREIGN POLICY.

– H –

HAGUE CONFERENCES. Called by the Russian government, the First International Peace Conference brought delegations from 26 countries, including the United States, to The Hague, Netherlands, in 1899. They discussed arms limitations, the international laws of war, and mechanisms for **arbitration** of international disputes. The conference made little headway on arms control but did lead to establishment of the Permanent Court of Arbitration in The Hague, to which President **Theodore Roosevelt** gave credibility in 1902 by submitting to it a financial dispute with **Mexico** and pressing the British, Germans, and Italians to submit their dispute over Venezuela's debts. Secretary of State **John Hay** (1898–1905) and Roosevelt played a visible role in organizing the Second Hague Conference (1907), to which 44 countries sent delegations. This conference discussed an international court of justice, neutral rights, the conduct of war, and other matters, but this second gathering achieved even less than the first. The United States continued to pursue bilateral arbitration treaties up to World War I, whose outbreak in 1914 doomed the proposal for a third Hague conference in 1915. *See also* CARNEGIE ENDOWMENT FOR INTERNATIONAL PEACE; COOLING-OFF TREATIES; FOREIGN POLICY; INTERNATIONALISM; ROOT, ELIHU B.

HAITI. Haiti's huge international debt, $24 million by 1915, along with periodic rumors that European powers were seeking a naval base there that could threaten the **Panama Canal**, prompted the United States to make the impoverished, chaotic island republic a target of its **dollar diplomacy** and eventually **gunboat diplomacy**. With the support of President **William Howard Taft**, Secretary of State **Philander C. Knox** persuaded four U.S. banks to invest heavily in Haiti in 1910, thus precluding foreign intervention. In 1914–15, Haiti rebuffed a proposal by President **Woodrow Wilson**'s administration to establish a financial protectorate similar to one in the neighboring **Dominican Republic**. Then in July 1915, a crowd dragged Haitian president Vilbrun Guillaume Sam from his refuge in the French legation and tore him to pieces in retaliation for the recent execution of 167 political prisoners. Wilson responded by dispatching the U.S. Marines. They restored order with some violence and oversaw an election in August 1915 that resulted in a government willing to accept American occupation and financial management. The marines remained in Haiti until 1934.

HALL, GRANVILLE STANLEY (1844–1924). Psychologist. Born in Massachusetts, Hall earned his Ph.D. in psychology at Harvard in 1878, studying with **William James**, and continued his studies in Germany until he was hired at Johns Hopkins University (1881–88). He played a significant part in organizing the discipline of psychology, helping found a key journal (1887) and **academic association** (1892). In 1888, he became the first president of Clark University (1888–1920), where he built a model graduate psychology program that stressed empirical, laboratory-based research. Hall's own writing drew on evolutionary theory to argue that each individual recapitulates the stages through which the human race evolved. His two-volume work, *Adolescence* (1904–5), popularized its title as the term for a distinct stage of life. Hall brought psychoanalysts Sigmund Freud and Carl Jung to the United States to speak in 1909.

HAMILTON, ALICE (1869–1970). Physician and reformer. Born in New York City, Hamilton grew up in Indiana, earned her medical degree from the University of Michigan (1893), and studied pathology and bacteriology in Germany and at Johns Hopkins University. As a professor at Northwestern University's **women**'s medical school (1897–1910), she lived in **Hull House** and engaged in social reform. In 1910, she was appointed to an Illinois commission investigating industrial disease, the first such survey in the United States, and a year later she did similar work for the **U.S. Department of Commerce and Labor**. Her studies of lead, rubber, and munitions revealed for the first time how toxic they were to workers. She wrote the authoritative textbook in her field and served as an officer of the American Public Health Association. Despite much sex discrimination, she continued her work as the first woman on the Harvard University medical school faculty (1919–35). *See also* PUBLIC HEALTH; SETTLEMENT HOUSE MOVEMENT; WORKERS' COMPENSATION.

HAMMER V. DAGENHART (1918). In this controversial 5–4 decision, the **U.S. Supreme Court** struck down the **Keating–Owen**

Child Labor Act on the grounds that prohibiting goods manufactured using child labor from interstate commerce overstepped Congress's constitutional authority. The majority insisted that although the protection of children might be a worthy cause, the authority to do so belonged to the states, not the federal government. Dissenters included Louis Brandeis and Oliver Wendell Holmes. Congress responded by passing a heavy tax on goods made with child labor and shipped across state lines, but the Supreme Court overturned this law in 1922. Not until 1941 did the Supreme Court clearly concede Congress's authority to regulate child labor.

HANDY, WILLIAM CHRISTOPHER (1873–1958). Composer, musician, and music publisher. An Alabama native and the son of former slaves, W. C. Handy became intrigued by the African American folk music known as the blues while touring the rural South as a bandleader in the 1890s. In 1905, he moved to Memphis, where he ran a music publishing business and collected, orchestrated, and wrote blues and ragtime songs. His "Mr. Crump" (a 1909 campaign song for Memphis political boss E. H. Crump), became a hit in 1912 under the title "Memphis Blues." His "St. Louis Blues" (1914), a popular standard, helped earn Handy the nickname "Father of the Blues." After moving to New York in 1917, he remained active as bandleader, composer, publisher, and folk music collector. His anthologies of blues songs and spirituals preserved and popularized traditional black music.

HANNA, MARCUS ALONZO (1837–1904). Businessman and politician. Born in Ohio, Mark Hanna ran a successful coal and iron business and by the late 1880s exerted much influence in Ohio's Republican Party. Identifying with the party's pro-business wing, he developed a close personal and political alliance with William McKinley. Hanna raised funds for McKinley's successful 1891 campaign for Ohio governor and then organized a bailout of his friend, who faced personal bankruptcy after the Panic of 1893. As manager of McKinley's 1896 presidential campaign and chair of the Republican National Committee, he oversaw the best-funded, best-organized national campaign to date, raising an unprecedented campaign fund estimated at $3.5 million, largely from business donors appalled by **Democratic** candidate **William Jennings Bryan**. Hanna took in stride the opposition press's brutal caricature of him as "Dollar Mark," the fat capitalist pulling the strings of his puppet nominee. When Hanna refused the position of postmaster general in McKinley's cabinet, the new president arranged for his appointment to the Ohio Senate seat vacated when John Sherman became secretary of state. Hanna narrowly won a full Senate term in late 1897. As manager of McKinley's 1900 reelection campaign, he resisted the nomination of **Theodore Roosevelt** as vice president, but after McKinley's assassination in September 1901, he cooperated with Roosevelt. His support aided the passage of Roosevelt's controversial **Panama Canal** treaty, but as chair of the Republican National Committee, Hanna hampered Roosevelt's attempts to win the party's 1904 presidential nomination quickly and even hinted that he might run for himself. More pro-labor than most businessmen, Hanna used the presidency of the **National Civic Federation** to push for mediation of labor disputes. The first party manager attuned to the age of mass marketing and **advertising**, a symbol for better or worse of the ties between government and business, Hanna was an enormously influential figure when he died of typhoid fever. *See also* REALIGNMENT OF 1896.

HAPGOOD, HUTCHINS (1869–1944). Journalist and writer. An Illinois native, Hapgood earned a B.A. and an M.A. in English from Harvard University, studied in Germany, and taught at the **University of Chicago** before embarking in the late 1890s on a career as a **journalist** for **Lincoln Steffens**'s New York *Commercial Advertiser*, where he worked alongside his brother Norman Hapgood (1868–1937), later an influential magazine editor. Another colleague on the newspaper was Neith Boyce (1872–1951), whom he married in 1899. He gained attention for *The Spirit of the Ghetto* (1902), a vivid portrait of **Jewish immigrant** life on the **Lower East Side** illustrated by Jacob Epstein, later a famous sculptor. Hapgood also published books on lower Manhattan's radical culture, *The Autobiography of a Thief* (1903), *The Spirit of Labor* (1907), and *An Anarchist Woman* (1909). Meanwhile, he and Boyce became fixtures in bohemian **Greenwich Village**. Hapgood's *Story of a Lover* (published anonymously in 1919) and the play *Enemies* (1916), which he cowrote with Boyce and performed for the **Provincetown Players**, revealed the troubles of a **modernist** marriage informed by psychoanalysis and **feminism** and undermined by Hapgood's infidelities. He traveled widely, befriending a range of people from **Emma Goldman** to **Bernard Berenson**.

HARLAN, JOHN MARSHALL (1833–1911). Supreme Court justice. Born in Kentucky, Harlan became a lawyer and, after serving in the Union army during the Civil War, was elected state attorney general. He later joined the **Republican Party**, and his support for Republican presidential candidate Rutherford B. Hayes led to Harlan's nomination to the U.S. Supreme Court (1877–1911). He emerged as a staunch defender of civil liberties and civil rights while the court moved toward a formalistic interpretation of the Constitution that rationalized resistance to business regulation and acquiescence in **segregation** and **disfranchisement**. His most memorable rulings were eloquent dissents in the *Civil Rights Cases* (1883) and *Plessy v. Ferguson* (1896), which he prophesied would have as evil an effect as the infamous *Dred Scott* (1857) decision. The pugnacious justice dissented 316 times in 34 years on the court. His dissents often won ultimate vindication in cases such as *Pollock v. Farmer's Loan and Trust* (1895) and *Lochner v. New York* (1905). Yet Harlan also wrote controversial decisions weakening state authority to regulate railroads and sanctioning **yellow dog contracts**. His value arose from his emphasis on the real-world consequences of judicial reasoning in an age when the judiciary seemed infatuated with abstractions.

HARPER, WILLIAM RAINEY (1856–1906). Educator and biblical scholar. Born in Ohio, Harper earned a doctorate in linguistics at Yale in 1875 at age 19. Over the next 25 years, Harper taught subjects from Hebrew to mathematics, established a journal, and published several books. In 1885, he joined the **Chautauqua** organization, whose **education** system he headed by 1892. After serving as professor of Semitic languages at Yale University (1886–91), Harper accepted the presidency of the new **University of Chicago**. Here, he combined techniques of popular education from his Chautauqua work with the new emphasis on scholarship, research, academic freedom, and graduate training. He also participated in efforts to reform Sunday schools, the Chicago public schools, and theological seminaries. In his biblical scholarship, he sought a middle ground that accepted the new "higher criticism," which historicized the Bible, but rejected **modernism**'s discounting of religious as opposed to scientific or historical explanations for events. *See also* DEWEY, JOHN; SOCIAL GOSPEL; UNIVERSITY.

HARRIMAN, EDWARD H. (1848–1909). Railroad executive. Born in New York, Harriman left school at age 14 to work as an office boy on Wall Street, where in 1870 he purchased a seat on the New York Stock Exchange and gained a reputation as a shrewd investor. From the mid-1880s until after the Panic of 1893, his main project was reorganizing the Illinois Central Railroad; he then gained control of the troubled Union Pacific Railroad (1897–98) and made it profitable. This success encouraged him to acquire other major western lines and integrate them into a coherent system. His purchase of the **Southern Pacific** and Central Pacific railroads in 1901 made him the dominant figure in southwestern transportation. An attempt to do the same in the Northwest led to a bidding war with **James J. Hill** for control of the Burlington and Northern Pacific railroads. When this struggle triggered a Wall Street panic in May 1901, financier **J. P. Morgan** arranged to merge the rival investment groups into the Northern Securities Company, a monopoly on long-distance service between Chicago and the Pacific Northwest. In a precedent-setting victory for **antitrust**, the **U.S. Supreme Court** ordered this combine dissolved in 1904. Despite this setback, Harriman made large donations to **Republican Party** campaigns until 1906, when he and President **Theodore Roosevelt** had an acrimonious falling out. This led to allegations that the president had made improper promises to Harriman in exchange for contributions and, when money was not forthcoming, prompted an **Interstate Commerce Commission (ICC)** investigation of Harriman's operations. In 1913, the Supreme Court sided with the ICC in ordering the Union Pacific to sell the Southern Pacific. The businessman's ruthless reputation was tempered by his philanthropies, including the donation of New York forests to the state. *See also* INTERLOCKING DIRECTORATES; PUBLICITY ACT.

HARRISON, CARTER, II (1860–1953). Politician. A native of Chicago, Harrison was a newspaper editor when his father, Carter Harrison I, five-time Chicago mayor, was assassinated in October 1893. Determined to control his father's **Democratic Party** organization, the son ran for mayor in 1897 on a platform that included improvement of public services and **utilities** regulation, along with toleration of ward **bosses** and the drinking and other minor vices of the city's Irish, German, and Czech voters. His live-and-let-live stance brought enormous popularity, as did his campaigns to bring **trolley** magnate **Charles T. Yerkes** under control. He retired after four two-year terms, but the ineffectiveness of his successors drew him back into the fray. Shortly after winning a four-year term in 1911 over political scientist Charles E. Merriam, Harrison confronted the controversy unleashed by the **Chicago Vice Commission**, whose report documented unsavory connections between the police, Democratic politicians, and the city's estimated 1,000 brothels. Pressured into half-hearted anti-**prostitution** and antivice campaigns that alienated the ward bosses without winning over the middle class, Harrison was defeated in the 1915 party primary and never ran for office again.

HARRISON NARCOTICS CONTROL ACT (1914). This act banned the sale and use of opium and cocaine and their derivatives for nonmedicinal purposes. Its promoter was New York congressman Francis Burton Harrison, a **Democrat** appointed as governor-general of the **Philippines** in 1913. The 1914 law required businesses that produced and sold narcotics to register with the Internal Revenue Service, record sales, and pay a tax. Prior to the passage of such laws, these drugs were readily available over the counter, especially in patent medicines. The typical user was a middle-class white woman whose doctor had advised her to take the drug. Nevertheless, many people associated drug use with unwanted minorities—Chinese **immigrants** in the West and **African Americans** in the South—an attitude that led most states to regulate heroin, cocaine, opium, and morphine by the 1890s and **Coca-Cola** to remove cocaine from its ingredients in 1903. However, state laws controlling narcotics could not control interstate shipment, and the uneven legal landscape enabled users and producers to circumvent draconian laws by moving. The **Pure Food and Drug Act** (1906), which required patent medicines to list ingredients, was the first step toward federal regulation of narcotics. To bring the United States into compliance with international treaties regulating the opium trade, Congress in 1909 banned importation of smoking opium except for certified medical uses. The 1914 act imposed comprehensive internal regulations. Quickly validated by the courts, the law favored punishment over treatment, setting a precedent for the century to follow.

HART, WILLIAM S. (1870?–1946). Actor and film director. Born in New York, Hart became a westerner during his youth in Minnesota, Iowa, Kansas, and the Dakotas. A successful Broadway actor by 1899, he is renowned for playing western heroes in the **movies**, including the 1914 film version of **Owen Wister**'s *The Virginian*. After Hart settled in Los Angeles in 1913, the many silent films he directed and starred in, such as *Hell's Hinges* (1916) and *The Narrow Trail* (1917), established the western movie genre. In later years he worked for **Jesse Lasky** and **Adolph Zukor**, among other major producers. Along with the **Wild West shows**, Hart's romantic narratives— featuring the gun, the horse, and the **saloon** as icons—aimed to recapture the vanishing frontier and define American national character.

HAWAII ANNEXATION (1898). The United States accounted for 99 percent of Hawaiian exports and 76 percent of its imports by 1890, and the U.S.-born minority, especially the powerful companies known as the "Big Five," came to own two-thirds of the sugar-producing land. Native Hawaiians were outnumbered by Japanese, Filipino, and Portuguese **immigrants** brought to work on American-owned plantations. In 1887, the United States acquired exclusive rights to a naval base at Oahu's Pearl Harbor, and American planters forced a new constitution on King Kalakaua that instituted property qualifications for voting and gave Americans in government the right to call U.S. troops to settle disputes with Hawaiian officials. The McKinley tariff of 1890 heightened tensions by disallowing the preferential treatment of Hawaiian sugar in the U.S. market. Hawaiian sugar prices quickly fell from $100 to $60 per ton, sending the kingdom's economy into a tailspin.

To diminish American influence, the new queen, Liliuokalani, proclaimed a new constitution returning power to native Hawaiians in January 1893. American residents then overthrew the queen with support from John L. Stevens, the U.S. minister, and 150 American sailors. Under Sanford Dole, the new Hawaiian government reached an annexation agreement with the lame-duck administration of President Benjamin Harrison. Before the U.S. Senate could vote on the treaty, **anti-imperialist** Grover Cleveland became president, withdrew the annexation treaty, and ordered an investigation of the U.S. role in the 1893 coup. Dole's government declared Hawaii a republic and bided its time, suppressing a counter-coup in 1895.

The **Spanish–American War** fueled annexationist sentiment and dramatized the strategic value of Hawaii for American naval power in the Pacific. Still unable to muster the two-thirds Senate vote to ratify a treaty, President **William McKinley** resorted to a joint resolution, which required only a simple majority in both houses. Despite objections from native Hawaiians and Japan, Congress voted to annex Hawaii on 7 July 1898. Ironically, because the territorial government barred Asian immigrants from voting, native Hawaiian men outnumbered white men among voters. They regularly sent a majority of Home Rule Party candidates to the territorial legislature and elected a Hawaiian delegate to Congress. *See also* FOREIGN POLICY; IMPERIALISM; SAMOA PARTITION.

HAY, JOHN M. (1838–1905). Diplomat and writer. Born in Indiana and raised in Illinois, Hay served President Abraham Lincoln as personal secretary during the Civil War and then held diplomatic posts in Paris, Vienna, and Madrid. After his return home, he built a career as an author, writing poetry, editorials, a 10-volume biography of Lincoln, and a novel about the period's violent conflicts between labor and capital. With **Henry Adams** he formed a famous literary and intellectual circle in Washington, D.C. In 1897, President **William McKinley** appointed Hay ambassador to Great Britain, in which post he secured British neutrality in the **Spanish–American War**. As secretary of state (1898–1905), he supervised diplomacy surrounding the **Philippine War**, issued the **Open Door notes**, and undertook other measures to expand American influence in Asia. His diplomacy led to the **Hay–Paunceforte Treaties** enabling the United States to acquire the **Panama Canal**. An architect of Anglo–American rapprochement, Hay worked to resolve the 1903 **Alaska Boundary Dispute** and resisted popular pressure to side with the Afrikaners in Great Britain's Boer War (1899–1902). *See also* FOREIGN POLICY.

HAY–BUNAU-VARILLA TREATY (1903–04). In November 1903, less than two weeks after President **Theodore Roosevelt** aided Panamanian rebels in securing independence from Colombia, Philippe Bunau-Varilla—the French engineer who represented the new Panamanian government as well as French investors trying to sell the remnants of the French isthmian canal project of the 1880s— concluded a treaty with Secretary of State **John Hay** for a perpetual United States lease of the 10-mile zone surrounding the proposed **Panama Canal**. The terms were similar to those offered to Colombia in the **Hay–Herrán Treaty**. In addition to guaranteeing Panama's independence, the United States would pay $10 million immediately and $250,000 per year after nine years. Roosevelt rode out a storm of criticism for the dubious methods used to secure this agreement, and the U.S. Senate ratified it on 23 February 1904. Beginning in 1936, the United States renegotiated the yearly payment upward on several occasions to satisfy Panamanian national sentiment before finally ceding the canal to Panama in 1999. *See also* FOREIGN POLICY; GUNBOAT DIPLOMACY.

HAY–HERRÁN TREATY (1903). In January 1903, Secretary of State **John Hay** reached an agreement with Tomás Herrán, Colombia's chargé d'affairs in Washington, to grant the United States a 99-year, renewable lease to a six-mile-wide zone surrounding the proposed **Panama Canal**. The U.S. Senate ratified the treaty, 73–5, in March 1903, but the Colombian senate rejected it in August by a vote of 24–0. Colombian lawmakers wanted more money from the United States, as well as limits on U.S. authority within the proposed canal zone. The Colombian rejection set in motion the events that led to the Panamanian revolt and the **Hay–Bunau-Varilla Treaty** three months later.

HAY–PAUNCEFORTE TREATIES (1900–1901). By 1900, Great Britain, in retreat from the dominant diplomatic position it once held in Latin America, was willing to cede to the United States control of the proposed isthmian canal, but doing so entailed revision of the 1850 Clayton–Bulwer Treaty. In February 1900, U.S. Secretary of State **John Hay** and British ambassador Sir Julian Pauncefote concluded a treaty to allow the United States to build and operate the canal alone. When the uncooperative U.S. Senate amended the treaty to authorize the American military to fortify the canal, the British demanded renegotiation. The second Hay–Pauncefote Treaty (1901) committed the United States to maintaining the canal's neutrality but implicitly permitted fortification. This agreement gave the United States a free hand to deal with the two countries who owned the possible canal sites, **Nicaragua** and Colombia (at this point still owner of **Panama**). Great Britain also reduced its West Indian naval fleet, recognizing U.S. supremacy in the Caribbean.

HAYWOOD, WILLIAM D. "BIG BILL" (1869–1928). Labor leader and radical. Born in Salt Lake City, Haywood worked as a miner from age 15 until his early 30s, when he became a full-time **labor union** organizer. In 1896, he joined the **Western Federation of Miners (WFM)** and served as the union's secretary-treasurer during the labor strife that wracked the western mining districts in the early 20th century. In February 1906, Pinkerton Agency detectives kidnapped him from a Denver brothel and brought him to stand trial in Idaho for his alleged role in the assassination of former Governor Frank Steunenberg, a murder that grew out of the labor violence in the **Coeur d'Alene** district. Acquitted in a dramatic trial in which he was defended by **Clarence Darrow** and prosecuted by **William Borah**, Haywood became a left-wing hero and the toast of **Greenwich Village** salons during the 1910s. Expelled from the WFM in 1908, he devoted his energies to the **Industrial Workers of the World (IWW)**, which he had helped to found in 1905, and the **Socialist Party** (1910–13), until the socialists also expelled him for his alleged unwillingness to repudiate violence. He helped to organize the **Lawrence** (1912) and **Paterson** (1913) strikes. During World War I, he and more than 100 other IWW leaders were sentenced to long prison terms under the wartime sedition and espionage acts. When his legal appeals failed in 1921, Haywood fled to the Soviet Union, where he soon died from complications of diabetes and alcoholism.

HEALTH AND MEDICINE. Health care and medicine were transformed intellectually and institutionally in this period. The germ theory of disease began to replace environmental explanations because of advances in medical research and the identification of the cause or etiology of deadly diseases. The **Flexner Report** (1910) led to rising requirements for doctors' education and training. The same process occurred in **nursing**. These changes, the growing safety and prestige of hospitals, and the trend toward professionalization strengthened the **American Medical Association** and delegitimized alternative medical practitioners, especially midwives.

Public health made notable gains in this era, as hitherto weak city and state boards of health gained greater resources and professional staff. The U.S. Public Health Service (1912) employed notable medical researchers **Walter Reed**, Charles Stiles, and Joseph Goldberger, who made breakthroughs against **yellow fever**, hookworm, and pellagra, respectively. Private foundations such as the **Rockefeller Sanitary Commission** and the Rosenwald Fund also funded research and treatment, and nongovernmental organizations like the **National Tuberculosis Association** raised money and promoted healthy practices. Henry Street **settlement house** director **Lillian Wald** founded the Visiting Nurses Service, which provided health care at home to poor city residents, and the American Red Cross expanded into disaster relief and first aid training. Physician **Alice Hamilton** pioneered the field of industrial health. The **Pure Food and Drug Act** and **Meat Inspection Act** (both 1906), as well as increasing municipal funding of **sanitary engineering** projects, made food, water, and medicines safer to consume. Life expectancy rose steadily from 47.3 in 1900 to 59.7 years in 1930.

The era also saw notable failures. The **American Association for Labor Legislation** failed to persuade state legislators to enact compulsory health insurance laws, in part because of opposition from physicians. Doctors also largely accepted the criminalization of **birth control** devices and resisted campaigns to publicize men's infections with **syphilis** and other sexually transmitted diseases, although laws regulating **prostitution** made women and girls liable to compulsory gynecological exams and treatment. *See also* DIPHTHERIA; SOCIAL INSURANCE; TUBERCULOSIS.

HEARST, WILLIAM RANDOLPH (1863–1951). Publisher. Born in San Francisco, Hearst went to work for **Joseph Pulitzer**'s *New York World* after being expelled from Harvard College (1885) and came to admire its sensationalist, mass-market **journalism**. Handed control of the San Francisco *Examiner* (1887) by his father, Senator George Hearst (1820–91), who purchased the paper to promote his political ambitions, the younger Hearst built the newspaper into San Francisco's most popular by 1896. He entered into direct competition with Pulitzer in 1895 when he purchased the *New York Morning Journal*. Deploying his family fortune, Hearst offered huge salaries to lure Pulitzer's stars, such as editor and columnist Arthur Brisbane and Richard Outcault, creator of the *Yellow Kid* comic strip, from which derived the term **yellow journalism**.

The revolution in **Cuba** and the **Spanish–American War** offered Hearst and Pulitzer many opportunities for banner headlines over lurid stories gathered by intrepid reporters whose adventures were part of the news. Critics charged that this sensational reporting inappropriately influenced the public's view of the war. Despite his detractors, Hearst used his east and west coast newspapers as the foundation for the country's largest newspaper chain to date, which at its height accounted for over 10 percent of the daily market and about 25 percent of Sunday sales. At one time or another, he owned 42 newspapers and diversified into magazines ranging from *Good Housekeeping* to *Cosmopolitan*, two news services, and a **movie** company.

A **Democrat** with an **antitrust**, pro-labor stance, Hearst supported the 1896 and 1900 campaigns of **William Jennings Bryan** before developing his own political ambitions. Cooperating with **Tammany Hall**, Hearst served two terms in Congress (1903–7), but his abysmal performance damaged his prospects for higher office, as did a personal life suitable for his newspapers' gossip columns. Still, he had enough credibility that more than 200 newspapers endorsed him for president in 1904, and he won 181 votes at that year's Democratic Party convention. He mounted serious campaigns for mayor of New York City (1905 and 1909) and New York governor (1906), defeated in the latter race by **Charles Evans Hughes**. The publisher made repeated attempts to re-enter politics but exerted most influence through his newspapers.

HEBREW IMMIGRANT AID SOCIETY (HIAS). This **immigrant** advocacy association was organized in New York City in 1881 to assist **Jews**, whose U.S. population increased from 250,000 in 1880 to four million in 1920. HIAS assisted those landing at Castle Garden and after 1892 at **Ellis Island**, where beginning in 1902, it provided translators and in 1911, kosher meals. At its **Lower East Side** headquarters and in chapters in Boston, Philadelphia, Chicago, and other cities, the agency provided meals, advice, shelter, clothing, and comfort. HIAS helped organize the National Conference of Jewish Charities in 1900 and the National Desertion Bureau in 1911 to help immigrants trace missing relatives. The United States' oldest international migration and refugee resettlement agency, HIAS had assisted over 4.5 million immigrants by the early 21st century.

HENRI, ROBERT (1865–1929). Artist. Born Robert Henry Cozad in Cincinnati, he grew up in Nebraska until 1882, when the family had to flee and live under assumed names after his father killed a man in self-defense. Robert kept his French-sounding alias even after his father was exonerated. Absorbing **realism** at the Pennsylvania Academy of Fine Arts (1886–88), Henri spent three years studying in Europe before returning to Philadelphia in 1891 to teach **art** and painting. A magnetic personality, he gathered around him a talented group of young artists and illustrators, including **William Glackens**, **John Sloan**, George Luks, and Everett Shinn. After teaching and exhibiting in Paris in 1896, he joined the faculty of the New York School of Art in 1902. **George Bellows**, Edward Hopper, and Rockwell Kent counted among his students.

Dismayed by the academic style favored by the National Academy of Design, in 1908 Henri invited Arthur B. Davies, Ernest Lawson, Maurice Prendergast, Everett Shinn, Glackens, Luks, and Sloan to join an alternative exhibition called **The Eight**, which showcased the urban realism nicknamed the **Ash Can School**. Convinced that he and his circle were developing a distinctively American contemporary art, Henri broke with many former allies over the inclusion of many works by European **modernists** in the 1913 **Armory Show**. After this, modernism's partisans dismissed him as passé, but Henri continued to teach and produce paintings that won admirers and were collected by museums.

HENRY STREET SETTLEMENT. *See* SETTLEMENT HOUSE MOVEMENT; WALD, LILLIAN.

HEPBURN ACT. Passed by Congress in May 1906 and named for its sponsor, Iowa congressman William P. Hepburn, this law gave the **Interstate Commerce Commission (ICC)** authority to set maximum railroad rates (subject to review by the courts) in response to complaints from shippers and expanded the agency's power to review railroads' financial records. President **Theodore Roosevelt** overcame determined opposition from **Nelson Aldrich** and other **Old Guard** members of his own **Republican Party** to get the bill passed, but it still failed to satisfy Republican **insurgents** such as **Robert La Follette**, who began a campaign to grant the ICC authority to investigate and set railroad rates on its own initiative, which Congress did in the 1910 **Mann–Elkins Act.**

HERRON, GEORGE DAVIS (1862–1925). Minister and radical. Born in Indiana, Herron experienced a religious crisis that prompted him to enter the ministry in 1883. In the early 1890s, his forceful sermons and essays advocating the **Social Gospel** led to his appointment first to a prominent pulpit in Iowa and then to a professorship in "applied Christianity" at Iowa (now Grinnell) College in 1893. For several years, his charismatic teaching and leadership made Grinnell a center for Social Gospel activity. Herron attracted admirers ranging from **Richard Ely** and **Samuel** "Golden Rule" **Jones** to **Washington Gladden** and **Eugene V. Debs**. His growing radicalism and neglect of his teaching had already alienated his colleagues and the trustees at Grinnell when an extramarital affair led to his resignation and contributed to his expulsion from the Congregational Church. Herron remained active in the **Socialist Party** and assisted **Upton Sinclair** during his early struggles as a writer. *See also* SOCIALISM.

HETCH HETCHY VALLEY RESERVOIR. Looking for a dependable supply of water to serve its growing population, the city of San Francisco proposed to the federal government in 1903 to dam the Hetch Hetchy Valley in Yosemite National Park to create a reservoir. President **Theodore Roosevelt** resisted the initial proposal but eventually decided that municipal need was more important than preserving the wilderness. Indeed, inadequate water supplies undercut the battle against fires caused by the **San Francisco earthquake** (1906). **John Muir** and the **Sierra Club** fought the proposal but lost in 1913, when the city won federal legislation to flood the valley. *See also* CONSERVATION; SANITARY ENGINEERING.

HIGH SCHOOL. Public secondary **education** expanded rapidly in this era both in numbers of schools and students, but it did not become a majority experience until the 1920s. In 1900, about 11 percent of 14- to 17-year olds attended secondary schools, and only slightly more than half graduated. By 1930, about 55 percent of 14- to 17-year-olds attended public secondary institutions. The reasons for this nearly 700 percent increase were legal and economic. Beginning in the late 19th century, many states enacted **compulsory education** laws that required children under the age of 14 to attend school; a complementary set of **child labor** laws restricted children's eligibility for employment. Moreover, economic **modernization** heightened demand for a literate and numerate workforce, with men pursuing white-collar, managerial roles and **women** needing a high school education to qualify for the clerical, retail, and teaching jobs open to them. Girls were a majority of high school students by 1900. Secondary education thus gradually ceased to be a class-exclusive experience focused on preparing a few students for college. Although the **National Education Association** was by 1918 insisting that all high school students receive some academic education, many institutions tracked students into business and **industrial education**, according to both student demand and class, gender, and race prejudices. The provision of multiple tracks evaded the call by **progressive** educators like **John Dewey, Ella Flagg Young**, and William Wirt of the **Gary Plan** for active, hands-on, and child-directed learning.

Race and region often determined whether children had access to public high schools. In the South, some 500 high schools opened between 1905 and 1920, due in part to the support of the **Southern Education Board** and the **General Education Board**. **Segregation** meant that mainly white students benefited, and local funding meant that rural students of all races had no or inadequate facilities. In the wake of the Supreme Court's decision in *Cummings v. School Board of Richmond County* (1899) that local governments did not have to provide high schools for **African Americans**, fewer than 60 high schools accepted black students in the southern states by 1916. Bureau of Indian Affairs schools for **Native American** students and segregated schools serving other minority groups typically offered little more than vocational education. Female students of all races were often tracked into **home economics** courses.

The expansion of public high schools from 500 in 1870 to over 10,000 in 1910 also raised questions about who was qualified for higher education. **University** administrators and educational reformers issued an influential report in 1893 calling for standardization of secondary education to rationalize college admissions. In 1899, the College Entrance Examination Board was established to create a single exam for all potential college freshmen, eventually producing the Scholastic Aptitude Test (SAT). These developments constituted the creation of the modern system of public education in the United States. *See also* ADOLESCENCE; CARNEGIE FOUNDATION FOR THE ADVANCEMENT OF TEACHING; NEW MIDDLE CLASS.

HILL, JAMES JEROME (1838–1916). Railroad entrepreneur. The son of Canadian farmers, Hill as a young man worked for railroad and steamship services, eventually becoming general manager and then president of the St. Paul and Pacific Railroad. In contrast to other railroad investors, he worked to promote development in the upper Northwest instead of making a quick fortune by speculating on railroad shares. For instance, in 1900 he sold 900,000 acres of forested land in Washington state to his neighbor, lumberman Frederick Weyerhaeuser (1834–1914), and offered him low shipping rates. In 1890, Hill combined his holdings into a new company, the Great Northern Railway. With the help of financier **J. P. Morgan**, he acquired shares in his chief rival, the Northern Pacific, and ran his lines to Seattle by 1903, thereby creating the nation's fifth transcontinental connection. Five years later he, Morgan, and rival **E. H. Harriman** put together an effective monopoly on northwestern transportation under the rubric of the Northern Securities Company. Even though the **U.S. Supreme Court** ordered the company's dissolution in 1904 because it violated the Sherman Antitrust Act, Hill succeeded in consolidating his hold over rail lines between Minnesota and Seattle. *See also* ANTITRUST.

HILL, JOE (1879–1915). Labor agitator and songwriter. Born Joel Hägglund in Sweden, he grew up in poverty before emigrating to the United States in 1902, where he was a migrant worker; he anglicized his name to Joe Hill during this time. By 1910, he was a well-known member of the **Industrial Workers of the World** and frequently sang protest songs at west coast labor rallies. He also composed songs such as "There Is Power in a Union" and "The Rebel Girl," allegedly inspired by the young radical Elizabeth Gurley Flynn. In January 1914, Hill was arrested in Salt Lake City, Utah, for murdering two people during an armed robbery. When he was convicted on circumstantial evidence, Hill's case became a cause célèbre among U.S. and European radicals, convinced he had been framed because of his politics. Despite pleas from the Swedish government, labor leader **Samuel Gompers**, and President **Woodrow Wilson**, Hill was condemned to death. When on the eve of his execution Hill wired the message, "Don't mourn for me. Organize!" to **"Big Bill" Haywood**, the singing **Wobbly** cemented his status as a working-class martyr. *See also* MOONEY CASE; MUSIC.

HILLQUIT, MORRIS (1869–1933). Lawyer and socialist. Born Moses Hillkowitz to a **Jewish** family in Latvia, he anglicized his name after emigrating to New York with his family in 1886. Settling on the **Lower East Side**, he became manager and editor for a Yiddish **socialist** newspaper, the *Arbeiter Zeitung*, which helped him earn a law degree in 1893. A spokesperson for moderate socialists, he joined **Victor Berger** and **Eugene V. Debs** in 1901 to found the **Socialist Party of America**. His main contribution was as an organizer, a spokesperson, and an attorney, especially on behalf of **immigrant**-dominated unions such as the **International Ladies' Garment Workers' Union**. In 1914, he engaged in a memorable debate with the **American Federation of Labor's Samuel Gompers** before the **Commission on Industrial Relations** over the relative merits of socialism versus Gompers's brand of unionism. During World War I, Hillquit devoted his energies to defending high-profile sedition and espionage cases until sidelined by the **tuberculosis** that eventually killed him. *See also* CAHAN, ABRAHAM.

HINE, LEWIS WICKES (1874–1940). Photographer and social reformer. Born in Wisconsin, Hine attended the **University of Chicago** (1900) but left to teach at the Ethical Culture School in New York City, later earning a degree in education from New York University (1905). Encouraged to use photography, he took his students to photograph **immigrants** arriving at **Ellis Island** and living and working in the city's tenements and sweatshops. In 1906, he took a famous series of photographs of small children at work for the **National Child Labor Committee (NCLC)**. By 1908, he was working as a photographer full-time. In his work for the NCLC, the **Pittsburgh Survey**, the *Survey*, and other leading reform organizations and publications, Hine pioneered a documentary reform tradition in photography. His earnest, dignified images of working people, child laborers, and immigrants illustrated hundreds of articles, reports, poster displays, and lectures between 1908 and 1917. *See also* JOURNALISM.

HITCHCOCK, FRANK H. (1867–1935). Politician and public official. An Ohio native, Hitchcock graduated from Harvard University (1891), studied law, and rose in the federal bureaucracy, becoming chief clerk of the **Department of Commerce and Labor** upon its creation in 1903. A protégé of **George B. Cortelyou**, Hitchcock assisted with **Theodore Roosevelt**'s 1904 presidential campaign and then became Cortelyou's assistant postmaster general during Roosevelt's second term. After serving on the **Keep Commission**, Hitchcock chaired the **Republican Party** national committee and managed **William Howard Taft**'s 1908 presidential election campaign. Criticized for paying excessive attention to the party's **Old Guard** and corporate interests, Hitchcock served as postmaster general (1909–13), where his commitment to **efficiency** turned a chronic deficit into a surplus. He implemented **progressive** initiatives such as **rural free delivery**, **parcel post**, and the **postal savings bank**. In 1912, his ties to Roosevelt made him suspect to Taft, who removed him as party chairman; in 1916 and 1920, he organized presidential campaigns for **Charles Evans Hughes** and **Leonard Wood**.

HITCHMAN COAL & COKE V. MITCHELL (1917). This U.S. Supreme Court decision upheld efforts by a West Virginia coal company to enforce **yellow dog contracts** against workers involved in a unionization campaign by the **United Mine Workers**. Three dissenting justices, **Oliver Wendell Holmes**, **Louis Brandeis**, and John H. Clarke, insisted that, having pressured their workers into renouncing unions, employers had no special claim to legal protection when workers attempted to pressure them into collective bargaining. Pro-labor state legislatures undermined the decision in subsequent years by declaring yellow dog contracts unenforceable. *See also* ERDMAN ACT.

HOAR, GEORGE FRISBEE (1826–1904). Politician. A native of Massachusetts and scion of a long line of politicians, Hoar was active in his state's **Republican Party** from its founding in the 1850s, serving in both the House of Representatives (1869–77) and the Senate (1877–1904). A symbol of principle and rectitude in an era when his party was riven by its ties to corporate interests, he coauthored the **Sherman Antitrust Act** and identified with causes ranging from civil service reform, **Native American** rights, and **women's suffrage** to the fight against the **disfranchisement** of **African Americans**. After supporting the **Spanish–American War**, Hoar broke with his party and opposed the annexation of the Philippines and **Puerto Rico**. His eloquent denunciations of the 1898 **Paris Treaty** brought it to the brink of defeat. He pushed for eventual Filipino independence after the outbreak of the **Philippine–American War** and was chiefly responsible for the committee that investigated war crimes in that struggle. *See also* ANTI-IMPERIALIST LEAGUE.

HOLDING COMPANIES. These entities are business corporations with legal authority to buy and sell stock in other corporations. Most state incorporation laws forbade this practice in the 19th century, but in 1889 New Jersey became the first state to allow the easy formation of companies that could buy and sell stock in corporations formed in other states. The 1890 Sherman Antitrust Act made illegal other common devices for forming industrial combines, so in the following years dozens of enterprises took advantage of the New Jersey statute. The **great merger movement** saw the formation of massive holding companies like **Standard Oil**, with nominal headquarters in New Jersey, though the 1903 *Northern Securities* case instilled some caution. Despite periodic scandals, holding companies remain a common business device. *See also* ANTITRUST; ECONOMY; UNITED STATES STEEL CORPORATION.

HOLLYWOOD. *See* MOVIES.

HOLMES, OLIVER WENDELL, JR. (1841–1935). Jurist and legal theorist. Born in Boston, Colonel Holmes was wounded three times in the Civil War, a wrenching experience that biographers believe sharpened the distrust of ideals and abstractions that shaped his legal thought. Launching a career as a lawyer, he participated in the Metaphysical Club, a circle of young Harvard University **intellectuals** who formulated the principles of **pragmatism**. Holmes applied these principles in his many legal writings to argue that law did not manifest abstract principles of logic or justice but instead evolved along with society. These ideas and his application of them made him a leading figure in the development of legal **realism**.

Appointed to the Massachusetts Supreme Judicial Court in 1882, he wrote over 1,400 opinions in his 20 years on the bench. President **Theodore Roosevelt**, who distrusted Holmes, nonetheless nominated him as associate justice of the **U.S. Supreme Court** in 1902. Indeed, one of Holmes's first consequential opinions was a dissent in the Roosevelt administration's *Northern Securities* case (1904), and the justice frequently expressed contempt for the **antitrust** movement as forcing rigid abstractions on a fluid economy. Over his three decades on the U.S. Supreme Court, Holmes wrote 873 opinions, more than any justice to that time. Although relatively few of these were dissents, reformers admired his sharply worded dissenting opinions in labor law cases such as *Lochner v. New York* (1905), in which he argued that the judiciary needed to recognize the realities of an industrial urban economy. In civil rights, his opinions tentatively put forth the principle that the Fourteenth Amendment (1868) meant that the Bill of Rights applied to the states as well as the federal government. In World War I–era civil liberties cases such as *Schenck v. United States* and *Abrams v. United States*, Holmes developed the "clear and present danger" doctrine that puts the burden of proof on government when limiting free expression.

Lauded in his time by **progressive** intellectuals and legal reformers such as **Walter Lippmann** and **Felix Frankfurter**, Holmes remained an ambiguous figure. His views at times veered toward a bleak **social Darwinism**, and he was as suspicious of Progressive Era humanitarianism as of all other ideals. His insistence that the judiciary defer to legislatures could apply to southern states when they **segregated** and **disfranchised African Americans** as well as to northern states when they expanded worker protection. Holmes's unyielding battle against formalistic law provided a philosophical foundation for the legal and governmental experimentation at the heart of progressive reform. *See also* BRANDEIS, LOUIS D.; SOCIOLOGICAL JURISPRUDENCE.

HOME ECONOMICS. This movement sought to transform housework into a profession through the application of scientific principles. Courses in cooking, sewing, child rearing, and other topics had appeared earlier in a variety of settings, especially in **industrial education**. Efforts to systematize the field culminated in the founding of the American Home Economics Association in 1909; among its leaders were **Ellen Swallow Richards** and Marion Talbot. Although the **National Education Association** and the **National American Woman Suffrage Association** endorsed home economics, the **American Association of University Women** declared it had no place in higher education for **women**. By the time the **Smith–Lever Act** (1914) gave federal support to the field, some 250 universities offered courses in the subject. Although the course of study often amounted to a smattering of science and much housework, this field gave women an entrée into careers in science. Home economists did not challenge the gender division of labor or the reign of the private home. In promoting a new style of cooking based on nutritional principles, they played a role in promoting new prepackaged and processed foods. Their **Americanization** programs sought to convince **immigrants** to abandon stews, pastas, alcohol, and spices in favor of cheap meals with bland foods neatly separated on the plate. *See also* EDUCATION; UNIVERSITY.

HOME RULE. This urban **structural reform** was intended to increase the autonomy of municipal government by ensuring local control over city charters and, to a lesser extent, taxation, debt, and municipal services. The idea originated in the 1870s, when Missouri and California adopted state constitutional provisions that gave the voters in St. Louis and San Francisco the authority to adopt and amend their city charters by referendum. Previously, this had required state legislative action. The rationale was that local control would protect cities from short-sighted or venal interference by state legislatures. By 1900, Washington state and Minnesota had adopted similar measures, which then spread to more than a dozen states during the Progressive Era. Some states gave cities the option of choosing the **commission** or **city manager** systems as an alternative to the customary mayor-council format. Others varied the level of autonomy based on the size of cities. New York State gave New York City and Illinois gave Chicago authority to block special state legislative acts applicable to them. Texas afforded its cities broad ordinance-making and **annexation** powers. Organizations such as the **National Municipal League** and urban affairs experts such as **Frederic Howe** endorsed home rule as encouraging local civic activism. Practical results were mixed, however, as **machine politics** thrived in many home rule cities, while voters often greeted charter reform referenda with apathy. In some states, like Massachusetts, the state legislature opposed home rule in order to retain control of cities dominated by **immigrant** voters and political **bosses**. A countertrend also existed toward strengthening state agencies supervising **public health**, **education**, parks, roads, water supply, and other matters.

HOMOSEXUALITY. *See* SEXUALITY.

HOPE, JOHN (1868–1936). Educator. Born in Georgia to a mixed-race couple, Hope won a scholarship to Brown University and, even though he could have passed for white, devoted himself to **African American education** after his graduation in 1894. A classics professor at Atlanta Baptist College (renamed Morehouse College in 1913), he became the institution's first black president (1906–29) and oversaw its development into a first-rate liberal arts college. With his wife, **Lugenia Burns Hope**, he took a leading role in African American civic activity in Atlanta and national organizations such as the **Young Men's Christian Association** and the National **Urban League**. An early critic of **Booker T. Washington**'s **Atlanta Compromise**, Hope was prominent in the **Niagara Movement** and was counted among the founders of the **National Association for the Advancement of Colored People**. *See also* UNIVERSITY.

HOPE, LUGENIA BURNS (1871–1947). Social reformer. A native of St. Louis, Burns studied business and design and took classes at the Art Institute of Chicago until leaving school in 1893, the same year she met **John Hope**, whom she married in 1897. When the couple moved to Atlanta in 1898, she devoted herself to social welfare work, which had interested her since she encountered Chicago's **settlement house movement**. For a quarter century after its founding in 1908, she headed the Neighborhood Union, Atlanta's leading social welfare agency for **African Americans** and a national model. She engaged in a broad range of civic activities in Atlanta and was prominent in national movements such as the **Young Women's Christian Association**, the **National Association for the Advancement of Colored People**, and the anti-**lynching** movement.

HOUDINI, HARRY (1874–1926). Entertainer. Born Ehrich Weiss in Hungary, Houdini immigrated to Wisconsin in 1878 and became a circus performer and magician in 1882. By 1899, he was performing complex escape stunts for enthusiastic **vaudeville** audiences in the United States, Great Britain, Europe, and Russia. Houdini also re-searched and wrote about his trade and briefly owned and ran a **movie** company. After World War I, he devoted much time to debunking spiritualist mediums. The pressure of staying ahead of competitors and the physical difficulty of his escapes took a toll, but Houdini remained active until 1926, when a Canadian fan, invited to test his strength, punched him in the abdomen and ruptured his appendix, leading to his death several days later. *See also* POPULAR CULTURE.

HOUSE, EDWARD M. (1858–1938). Political adviser. Born in Texas, House was a businessman who entered **Democratic Party** politics as a campaign manager for Texas governor James S. Hogg. Known by the honorific "Colonel," House developed a close friendship with

President **Woodrow Wilson** and acted as his advisor and assistant for appointments, patronage, and legislative strategy. After the outbreak of World War I, House devoted himself to **foreign policy** with unfortunate results, such as the abortive **House–Grey Memorandum**. His differences with Wilson over the Versailles Treaty led to a permanent rift between them in 1919.

HOUSE–GREY MEMORANDUM (1916). This tentative agreement, drafted in February 1916 by **Edward M. House**, President **Woodrow Wilson**'s envoy, and Sir Edward Grey, the British foreign secretary, proposed to bring the United States into World War I on the side of the Allies if the Germans refused American mediation or set unacceptable conditions. Wilson made changes that weakened the proposal, and the British backed away as the war seemed to tilt in their favor in 1916. Moreover, the zealously pro-Ally Colonel House exceeded his instructions in promising U.S. intervention, which Wilson had not yet endorsed.

HOUSTON SHIP CHANNEL. In the late 19th century, Houston and Galveston competed to control burgeoning trade of the Southwest. Harbor improvements overseen by the U.S. Army Corps of Engineers in the 1890s opened Galveston to the period's largest ocean-going freighters, and by 1900 it was the largest cotton port in the nation. But the **Galveston Hurricane** of 1900 dramatized the island city's greatest disadvantage. Houston, unlike its rival, had access to abundant fresh water and offered an attractive junction for railroads, 17 of which ran through the city's four depots by the early 20th century. The presence of railroads and industry gradually built public support for a massive dredging project along the 50 miles of bayou between Houston and the Gulf of Mexico. Constructed with federal and local financing beginning in 1902, the Houston Ship Channel reached a depth of 25 feet by its official opening in 1914 and boasted a turning basin 600 feet wide. Periodically expanded and deepened, the ship channel, oil from **Spindletop** and other wells, cotton, and sugar made Houston the largest city in Texas and the country's third busiest port by 1930.

HOW THE OTHER HALF LIVES **(1890).** *See* MUCKRAKING; RIIS, JACOB.

HOWE, FREDERIC C. (1867–1940). Reformer and urban affairs expert. A Pennsylvania native, Howe earned a doctorate in economics from Johns Hopkins University (1892) and studied law before serving on the Pennsylvania Tax Commission and then joining the Cleveland law firm of Harry and **James R. Garfield**. Influenced by the **Social Gospel** and the reformist teachings of **Richard Ely** and **Woodrow Wilson**, Howe involved himself with the **settlement house movement** and urban **structural reform**. Elected as a **Republican** to the city council (1901–3), he allied with **Democratic** reform mayor **Tom Johnson**, whose proposals for municipal ownership of **utilities** and expanded social services Howe absorbed, along with **City Beautiful** ideas. He synthesized these currents into his book *The City: The Hope of Democracy* (1905) and wrote other influential works. After serving in the Ohio state legislature (1906–8) and on Cleveland's Board of Tax Assessors, he moved to New York City in 1910 to direct the People's Institute (1911–14), an experiment in participatory democracy. Howe's support for Wilson in the 1912 election helped lead to his appointment in 1914 as Commissioner of **Immigration** for the Port of New York, in which capacity he oversaw **Ellis Island** (1914–19). *See also* BATH HOUSES, PUBLIC.

HOWELLS, WILLIAM DEAN (1837–1920). Author, editor, and literary critic. Born in Ohio, Howells largely educated himself while working as a printer, reporter, and editor and publishing his poetry in leading magazines. After writing a campaign biography of Abraham Lincoln, he was appointed U.S. consul in Venice (1861–65) and published a successful collection of sketches titled *Venetian Life* (1866). Returning to the United States, he became an editor at the *Atlantic Monthly* (1866–81), in which capacity he wrote novels and championed **realism**, helping to establish the reputation of **Henry James** and Mark Twain, among others. After Howells left the *Atlantic*, his fiction grew more concerned with the psychological and moral dilemmas of modern urban society. His defense of the **anarchists** prosecuted in the Haymarket affair added the political twist evidenced in such novels as *A Hazard of New Fortunes* (1890) and *A Traveler from Altruria* (1894). As an editor for *Harper's Magazine* (1886–92), he introduced Americans to European writers such as Ivan Turgenev, Émile Zola, and Thomas Hardy and promoted Americans ranging from **Edith Wharton** to **Stephen Crane** and **Frank Norris**. In the 1910s, iconoclastic critics such as **Van Wyck Brooks** dismissed him as the epitome of middle-class, Victorian convention, but Howells's reputation as the dean of American letters recovered in the decades after his death. *See also* LITERATURE; MASS-CIRCULATION MAGAZINES; NATURALISM.

HUERTA, VICTORIANO. *See* MEXICAN REVOLUTION.

HUGHES, CHARLES EVANS (1862–1948). Jurist, politician, and diplomat. Born in New York, Hughes graduated from Brown University (1881) and Columbia Law School (1884) before practicing law in New York City. He came to national attention for serving as counsel to an investigation of the gas and **electric utilities** and the **Armstrong Commission**'s investigation of **insurance**. He defeated **William Randolph Hearst** for governor in 1906, and his moderate **progressive** record made him a plausible **Republican Party** presidential candidate in 1908. However, the stiffly high-minded Hughes grated on President **Theodore Roosevelt**, who supported **William Howard Taft** instead. In 1910, toward the end of Hughes's second term as New York governor, Taft named him to the **U.S. Supreme Court**. Resigning to accept the Republican nomination for president in 1916, Hughes ran a lackluster campaign but nearly unseated President **Woodrow Wilson**, falling short 254–277 in the Electoral College and 46.1 percent versus 49.2 percent in the popular vote. In later decades, Hughes compiled a distinguished record as secretary of state (1921–25) and chief justice of the Supreme Court (1930–41).

HULL HOUSE. Established in Chicago in 1889 by **Jane Addams** and **Ellen Gates Starr**, Hull House was the third **settlement house** founded in the United States after two in New York City, Stanton Coit's Neighborhood Guild (later the University Settlement) on the **Lower East Side** in 1886 and Rivington Street in 1889. A handsome mansion in an **immigrant** neighborhood, Hull House provided social services to its working-class neighbors while serving as a staging ground for a range of **reform movements**. The activists who lived or worked there included some of the most successful **women** of the era: **Edith** and **Grace Abbott, Sophonisba Breckinridge, Al-**

ice Hamilton, Florence Kelley, Julia Lathrop, Mary McDowell, and **Mary Kenney O'Sullivan**. Their connections to the social elite helped them raise the money necessary to support Hull House. The institution's manifold links to Chicago-area social scientists, reform activists, and radicals supplemented the energy and intellectual liveliness of the reformers who lived there and made this settlement a unique and influential social experiment.

HUNEKER, JAMES GIBBONS (1857–1921). Essayist and critic. Born in Philadelphia, Huneker became a **music**, theater, and **art** critic whose writings appeared in the era's leading arts magazines and newspapers, especially the *New York Sun* (1902–17), the *New York Times* (1917–19), and the *New York World* (1919–21). Prolific, broad-minded, and witty, Huneker introduced American readers to new currents in the arts, from the music of Johannes Brahms, Richard Strauss, and Arnold Schoenberg and the writing of Friedrich Nietzsche, Joseph Conrad, and Hendrik Ibsen to the art of Paul Cézanne and the **Ash Can School**. He wrote memorable, shrewd accounts of the **Armory Show** and **Coney Island**. Huneker stood for the iconoclasm and aestheticism later identified with H. L. Mencken and the **modernists** of **Greenwich Village**.

– I –

IF CHRIST CAME TO CHICAGO **(1894).** *See* CIVIC FEDERATION OF CHICAGO.

IMMIGRATION. Some 18.5 million newcomers entered the United States between 1890 and 1920, making up 13.2 percent of the population by the latter year. The era saw an important shift in their origins: before 1890 most had come from northwestern Europe, especially Germany, Ireland, and Great Britain, with a significant number from Scandinavia. Starting in the 1880s, emigration from Italy, Greece, and the Austro–Hungarian and Russian Empires increased dramatically, and these "new immigrants" tended to be **Jewish**, Catholic, or Orthodox Christian. Much smaller but politically significant numbers came from Asia (chiefly Japan after the passage of the Chinese exclusion acts) and the Pacific (Hawaii and the **Philippines**) and settled mostly in the Pacific coast states and Hawaii. The several thousand Koreans were classified as Japanese because Japan controlled Korea in these years. A small number of Hindus and Sikhs came from India. Asian newcomers faced more systematic discrimination than did Europeans. Barred from becoming citizens, Asians could not own land in some states because of **Alien Land** laws, lived in **segregated** neighborhoods, and attended segregated schools. Emigration from Mexico grew rapidly during the **Mexican Revolution** but remained largely a southwestern regional issue. The rising number of immigrants from the Caribbean, especially **Puerto Rico**, **Cuba**, Jamaica, and Barbados, clustered in New York City, New Orleans, and southern Florida. French-speaking migrants from Canada became the largest ethnic minority in New England.

Migration to the United States represented the largest single component of a worldwide movement of people catalyzed by economic **modernization**. Eastern European Jews, the third largest immigrant group in this era, also faced religious and ethnic persecution. Political unrest, U.S. **imperialism**, and the spread of plantation agriculture spurred migration from the Caribbean, Hawaii, and the Philippines. Coming to the United States was often the last stage in a series of moves in search of work. Although many migrants anticipated permanently breaking with their homelands, millions of others planned to save money to buy land or otherwise improve their situation at home. Among some groups, rates of return were as high as one-third or even greater at times. Southern Italians, Balkan peoples, and Greeks especially had reputations as "birds of passage." Most immigrants lived in ethnic enclaves in large northeastern and midwestern cities, though these neighborhoods were neither ethnically homogenous nor isolated. The foreign-born typically worked in factories or sweatshops, construction, dock work, and other low-skilled jobs or did piecework at home. A few groups, especially Scandinavians, settled in rural areas and became farmers, and Mexicans and Asians dominated western and southwestern agricultural labor. The cost of living, seasonal labor patterns, lack of industrial skills, prejudice, and recessions combined to keep most immigrants poor.

Men of nearly all ethnic groups were more likely than women to migrate and become transient laborers. Rural men, such as Mexicans,

Italians, and Irish, found themselves relegated to poorly paid day labor, whereas Swedes, Germans, and English and Welsh men who came with skills in mining, industry, or crafts earned decent wages and joined trade unions. Eastern European Jews, Italians, Greeks, and Syrians were noted for their entrepreneurial bent in the garment industry and small retail. Rarely expected or allowed to migrate alone (the Irish were an exception), **women** were underrepresented among immigrants and had fewer job choices than men. Domestic service was the most available, least desirable, and lowest-paid option, dominated by Irish and Scandinavian women. Many girls worked in factories or sweatshops before they married and afterward took in lodgers or did piecework at home to supplement the family income. All ethnic groups supported community-oriented retail sectors and a small middle class.

In addition to founding mutual aid, ethnic, and religious associations, the foreign-born and their children dominated the large industrial unions such as the **International Ladies' Garment Workers' Union (ILGWU)** and participated in major strikes such as the **Uprising of the Twenty Thousand** (1909) and those in **Lawrence** (1912) and **Paterson** (1913). Excluded from mainland unions, Asians dominated the ethnically divided labor movement in Hawaii. Low rates of naturalization restricted men's involvement in electoral politics, but the **Democratic Party** attracted more newcomers than did the **Republican Party**. **Socialism**, **anarchism**, syndicalism, and other forms of radical politics engaged some immigrants. Immigrant spokespeople such as **Kyutaro Abiko**, **Abraham Cahan**, and **Mary Antin** often urged immigrants to adopt American values, but usually without abandoning their ethnic heritage.

Although many native-born Americans met newcomers with racism, anti-Semitism, **anti-Catholicism**, and efforts to restrict immigration, others asserted that the immigrants benefited the nation economically and socially and advocated everything from aggressive **Americanization** to the development of a **pluralist** society. The United States did not restrict immigration at all until 1875, when the Page Law barred "immoral" Chinese women in the first of the Chinese Exclusion Acts. The increasing regulation of immigration and naturalization during the Progressive Era began in 1891, when Congress took oversight of immigration away from the states and created the Bureau of Immigration, opening a new reception center at **Ellis Island** the following year. Race, health, criminal status, and morals were criteria used to determine entry. In 1903, the Bureau of Immigration became part of the new **Department of Commerce and Labor** and gained stronger deportation powers targeting anarchists and other political radicals. In 1906, Congress systematized naturalization and made knowledge of English a prerequisite for citizenship. In 1907, American women who married foreign citizens lost their U.S. citizenship, and San Francisco's decision to segregate Japanese students led to the **Gentlemen's Agreement**. In these years, courts endorsed the denial of citizenship to Asian immigrants but upheld the Fourteenth Amendment's provision that all persons born on American soil are U.S. citizens. The U.S. **Immigration Commission**'s 41-volume report (1911) called for limits on the number and type of people entering the nation, and the 1917 Immigration Act banned all East and Southeast Asian immigrants and imposed a literacy test. World War I heightened anti-immigrant, especially anti-German, feeling, even though people of German descent were the largest U.S. ethnic group. The Progressive Era movement for immigration restriction culminated in the First or "Emergency" Quota Act of 1921 and the National Origins Act of 1924. *See also* AMERICANISM; ANGEL ISLAND; EUGENICS; MACHINE POLITICS; RACE SUICIDE; URBAN LIBERALISM.

IMMIGRATION COMMISSION, U.S. (1907–1910). This board, also known as the Dillingham Commission after its leader, **Republican** senator William P. Dillingham of Vermont, was created in 1907 to study the impact of **immigration** on American life. Influenced by the **eugenics** movement, the commission's 41-volume report (1911) advocated immigration restriction on the grounds that Southern and Eastern Europeans (a rising proportion of immigrants) were biologically inferior to northwestern Europeans, too culturally different to be **Americanized**, and prone to labor militancy and political radicalism. One report, by anthropologist **Franz Boas**, used anthropometric data to undermine the idea of racial distinctiveness and persistence over time. Testimony gathered from the foreign-born revealed diverse motives for immigration, attitudes toward the United States, and labor conditions, contradicting the report's conclusions.

IMMIGRATION RESTRICTION LEAGUE. This group was founded in 1894 by prominent Bostonians, including Francis A. Walker, president of the Massachusetts Institute of Technology, and A. Lawrence Lowell, president of Harvard University, along with Madison Grant and **Owen Wister**. The league's leading spokesman was **Henry Cabot Lodge**, **Republican** senator for Massachusetts. Its aim was to restrict the immigration of Southern and Eastern Europeans, people said to be more criminal than other immigrants, by requiring a **literacy test**. Voted on by Congress five times in 20 years and vetoed by three presidents, the literacy test finally became law in the Immigration Act (1917).

IMPERIAL VALLEY. In 1891, the Colorado Irrigation (later Development) Company was founded to transform a vast natural basin created by the occasional overflow of the Colorado River into an irrigated field. Dubbed Southern California's "Imperial Valley," the development was initially successful, but the irrigation canals clogged with silt faster than developers could clear them or cut new canals. Then in 1905, floods propelled into the valley tons of water and silt that usually flowed into Mexico's Colorado River delta. Unable to fix the problem, local developers ceded control to **Southern Pacific Railroad** owner **E. H. Harriman**, whose engineers managed to force the Colorado River back into its original course in 1907. In the meantime, the 50-mile long Salton Sea had become a permanent feature of the Imperial Valley.

IMPERIALISM. This term refers to the subordination of one people to another or the conquest and occupation of a weaker political entity by a stronger one. Americans sometimes referred to colonization of the trans-Mississippi West as the creation of a republican "empire," but they were usually more hesitant than contemporaneous Europeans to label the country's territorial ambitions as imperialist. The years surrounding the **Spanish–American** and **Philippine–American Wars** formed a partial exception to this squeamishness. Proponents of the annexation of **Hawaii**, the Philippines, and **Puerto Rico** preferred the less openly aggressive word *expansion*, but they referred to annexed lands as possessions and dependencies. Opponents such as the **Anti-Imperialist League** deliberately employed the word, with its taint of betrayal of the nation's principles. During his 1900 presidential campaign, **William Jennings Bryan** warned of the immorality and corrupting effects of imperialism, to little avail. *See also* DOLLAR DIPLOMACY; FOREIGN POLICY; GUNBOAT DIPLOMACY; PANAMA CANAL.

INCOME TAX. Traditionally, governments relied on customs duties, tolls, excise taxes, property taxes, license fees, and other forms of revenue based on tangible goods or assets. The emergence of a capitalist economy threatened these sources of revenue by shifting wealth toward intangible, difficult-to-measure assets—wages, salaries, bank accounts, securities, and so on. The idea of an income tax—"graduated" so that wealthier people paid higher percentages—appeared in the Renaissance. Great Britain was the first large country to impose a national income tax in 1799. The United States did not consider such a tax until the Civil War, when the Union government imposed a graduated income tax, with a maximum rate at 10 percent, that expired in 1872. The **U.S. Supreme Court** upheld this war measure in 1881, despite the provision of the Constitution that "direct" taxes be apportioned among the states according to population, not wealth or income.

By the 1890s, the nation's continuing reliance on customary forms of taxation prompted widespread resentment. The demand for a graduated income tax spread from the populists into the reformist wings of the Democratic and Republican parties. The 1890s depression exposed the disadvantages of outmoded tax systems at the state and local as well as federal level. With the threat of government default looming, Congress authorized a 2 percent tax on incomes over $4,000 as part of the 1894 Wilson-Gorman Tariff bill. In 1895, in a highly contested 5–4 decision in the *Pollock v. Farmers' Loan and Trust* case, the Supreme Court declared it an unconstitutional "direct" tax.

Over the next decade, **William Jennings Bryan** turned the income tax into a staple demand of the **Democratic Party**, and **Theodore Roosevelt** and the **Insurgents** won over **progressive** factions in the **Republican Party** to the idea. In July 1909, amid the quarrel over the **Payne–Aldrich Tariff** bill, both houses of Congress adopted what became the Sixteenth Amendment by overwhelming votes. At the same time, Congress imposed a corporate income tax, which the

Supreme Court sanctioned in 1911. Gaining state ratification by the time of **Woodrow Wilson**'s inauguration in March 1913, the amendment provided a secure constitutional basis for a graduated tax on large incomes, with a 7 percent maximum written into the **Underwood–Simmons Tariff**. This tax did not extend to middle-income families or become the main source of federal revenue until the 1940s. Beginning with Wisconsin in 1911, 20 states adopted income taxes before 1930.

INDIAN EDUCATION. The practice of compelling **Native American** children to attend white-run schools, often boarding institutions far from their homes, began in the 1870s. As many as 150 such schools existed between 1870 and 1930, run by the Bureau of Indian Affairs or contracted to Christian denominations. In 1900, about half of all Indian children were enrolled in federally sponsored institutions, with nearly 7,500 attending off-reservation boarding schools, 9,600 in boarding schools on reservation lands, and 5,000 in reservation day schools. The federal government limited Indian schools after a 1901 study found that it cost $43 million to educate only 20,000 children.

The goal of the schools was to **Americanize** Indian children. To dramatize this, when children arrived, teachers cut their hair and replaced their clothing with uniforms. They were assigned "American" names and forbidden to speak their native languages or return home, sometimes for years. Poor living conditions and corporal punishment were common. Like many post–Civil War schools for **African Americans**, Indian schools emphasized **industrial education**, personal hygiene, English, and Christianity, as well as some academic subjects. Lacking useful job skills and facing prejudice, few Indian graduates succeeded on white terms in the white world, as the assimilationists hoped. Most returned home, where some used their skill in English and familiarity with American society to become tribal leaders. A few, including **Gertrude Bonnin**, **Charles Eastman**, and **Carlos Montezuma**, became activists for Indian rights at the national level through the **Society of American Indians**. *See also* EDUCATION.

INDIAN TERRITORY. Created in 1820 as a "permanent" home for **Native Americans** forced westward by white settlement, the territory became home to the Cherokees, Creeks, Choctaws, Chickasaws, and Seminoles, with additional tribes resettled there after the Civil War. In 1889, the federal government opened the western part of the region, soon named Oklahoma Territory, to non-Indian settlers. Initially the territory's ten tribes were exempt from the **Dawes Allotment Act**, but in 1893 Congress created the Dawes Commission to negotiate the dissolution of tribal governments. Opposition from Cherokee and Choctaw leaders led Congress to pass the Curtis Act in 1898, dissolving the tribal governments and compelling them to accept allotment. In 1907, Congress abolished the Indian Territory and established Oklahoma as a state.

INDUSTRIAL EDUCATION. There were two strands in the movement to incorporate "industrial" or "vocational" **education** into the American public school curriculum. Many educators recommended such programs for **immigrant**, **African American**, and **Native American** students as a way to train them for manual work and inculcate discipline and obedience. Children incarcerated by **juvenile courts** also encountered industrial curricula in reform schools. Despite the name, students rarely learned skills useful in industries that were expanding at the turn of the century; they more often learned to be carpenters than machinists, if male, and maids, laundresses, or seamstresses rather than machine tenders or stenographers, if female. Large urban school systems often tracked the less-promising pupils into vocational or shop classes, such as metalworking or woodworking (for boys) and sewing or cooking (for girls).

Some reformers, meanwhile, advocated "manual" education for all children in response to the **progressive** educational ideals promoted by **John Dewey**, **Ella Flagg Young**, and **Gary Plan** promoter William Wirt, among others. Teaching both mind and body, they believed, would enable children to learn better, overcome the divide between blue- and white-collar workers, and humanize the industrial work regimen. Among African Americans, industrial education occupied a central place in debates about how to counter **segregation** and **disfranchisement**. The founder of the **Tuskegee Institute**, **Booker T. Washington**, emphasized vocational labor and moral training above intellectual pursuits. Other race leaders, notably **Ida B. Wells-Barnett** and **W. E. B. Du Bois**, urged black Americans to seek academic training and professional careers. *See also* HIGH SCHOOL; INDIAN EDUCATION.

INDUSTRIAL RELATIONS, COMMISSION ON. Appointed in 1913 by President **Woodrow Wilson**, this commission examined labor conditions and the causes of labor strife. Chaired by St. Louis labor attorney Frank P. Walsh, it included economist **John R. Commons**, union representatives recommended by **Samuel Gompers**, and three liberal businessmen; eight of the nine members belonged to the **National Civic Federation**. For a time, **Charles McCarthy** directed the commission's research. The board disintegrated after collecting a huge amount of data and publicizing the abuses that produced incidents such as the **Ludlow Massacre**. Unable to agree on recommendations, the commission produced three separate reports: one signed by Walsh and the labor representatives stressing unionization, collective bargaining, and federal social programs; a second favored by Commons that recommended much greater federal involvement in labor–management relations; and a third signed by the business representatives that argued for a moderate expansion of federal oversight. Despite its quarrels, the commission set the agenda for a generation of labor reform. *See also* AMERICAN ASSOCIATION FOR LABOR LEGISLATION; AMERICAN FEDERATION OF LABOR; SOCIAL INSURANCE; WORKERS' COMPENSATION.

INDUSTRIAL RESEARCH LABORATORIES. At the start of the 20th century, large firms such as **General Electric** (GE), **American Telephone and Telegraph**, and **DuPont** established applied research laboratories. By the early 1920s, over 500 companies supported such labs, employing more than 2,700 scientists and engineers. Several factors spurred business to invest in research and development. The number of available scientists was increasing rapidly, from fewer than a handful in the 1880s to 30 physicists and more than 70 chemists earning doctorates each year by 1917. Huge, vertically integrated corporations commanded unprecedented resources to attract promising scientists, and such businesses depended on collections of patents for complex technological processes whose components had to work together **efficiently**. These companies could not wait for innovations by individual inventors or even **Thomas Edison**'s invention factory. When GE opened the first major industrial laboratory in 1900, director **Willis R. Whitney** focused on finding a durable substitute for the carbon filaments then used in light bulbs. Forty researchers working in concert yielded the tungsten filament, which won GE more than 70 percent of the market by 1914. Companies also invested in science to expand into new markets; the DuPont laboratory, for example, played a key role in transforming the explosives manufacturer into a diversified chemicals producer. Private laboratories became major centers for basic as well as applied research. *See also* ECONOMY.

INDUSTRIAL WORKERS OF THE WORLD (IWW). Founded at a 1905 convention of the **Western Federation of Miners**, the IWW—nicknamed the Wobblies—became the leading American **labor union** to espouse "syndicalism," a form of **socialism** with **anarchist** elements. In the IWW's vision, "one big union" formed by all industrial workers would overturn capitalism through direct action. Initially attractive to many activists disenchanted with the **American Federation of Labor**, including **Eugene V. Debs**, Daniel De Leon, and **"Mother" Jones**, the group's refusal to repudiate violence and sabotage, its loose organization, and its ill-defined strategy reduced it to a core of fewer than 4,000 radical activists by 1908. The Wobblies expressed the mindset of the western farm workers, lumberjacks, and miners who formed it, but led by **"Big Bill" Haywood**, the IWW made persistent efforts to win over semiskilled and unskilled eastern and midwestern **immigrant** workers. In 1906, the IWW organized a sit-down strike at the **General Electric** plant in New York State. Between 1909 and 1913, the group was active among steel workers in Pennsylvania, rubber workers in Akron, and auto workers in Detroit, and it led textile strikes in **Lawrence**, Massachusetts, and **Paterson**, New Jersey. Reaching about 30,000 members in 1912, the group then dwindled again until a surge in membership in 1916–17. The Wobblies' aggressive opposition to World War I provided a pretext for its suppression by federal and state governments. *See also* BISBEE RAID; HILL, JOE.

INITIATIVE. This is a form of legislation in which a percentage of registered voters—generally between 10 and 25 percent—can petition to place a law or constitutional amendment on the ballot. A majority vote secures the law's adoption; a two-thirds vote is usually necessary for an amendment. During the late 1800s, reformers frustrated by **machine politics** and the power of business interests in state and city government saw the initiative as a solution. Populists, unions, the **National Municipal League**, and advocates of **prohibition** and **women's suffrage** all supported it. In 1898, South Dakota became the first state to authorize the initiative and the related **referendum**. **William U'Ren's** campaigns for both measures in Oregon sparked a national movement. By 1918, 22 states had adopted such reforms, and states also authorized cities to adopt initiatives as part of **structural reforms**. By 1910, Oregon labor groups had used the initiative and referendum to repeal the **poll tax** and enact an **employer liability law**. *See also* RECALL.

INSULAR CASES. This designation covers 14 **U.S. Supreme Court** cases asking whether the Constitution, the Bill of Rights, and federal law applied to overseas territories annexed since 1898, particularly **Hawaii**, the **Philippines**, and **Puerto Rico**. As the cases were tried between 1901 and 1904, shifting majorities arrived at the notion that the United States could acquire and govern territory without incorporating it fully. Congress could thus apply to these territories statutes that might not pass constitutional muster in the United States proper. For example, jury trials need not be required in unincorporated territories. The decisions angered **anti-imperialists**, who argued that the Supreme Court had yielded to popular pressure and ratified colonial domination.

INSULL, SAMUEL (1859–1938). Utilities entrepreneur. Born in England, Insull left school at age 14 to work for **Thomas Edison** in London and then in the United States. By 1886, his astonishing talent for business details made him general manager of Edison's electrical manufacturing operations. After the formation of **General Electric** in 1892, he became president of the Chicago Edison Company (merged into **Commonwealth Edison** in 1907). In this position, he developed what became the standard methods for mass-producing and marketing **electricity**. His control of Chicago's transit system and dealings with the municipal government over street lamps and electric **trolley** lines led him to advocate state regulatory commissions, an aim he pursued through membership in the **National Civic Federation**. Emphasizing large generating plants serving diverse customers over an extensive grid, Insull expanded his holdings beyond Chicago and its suburbs around 1910. His companies served most of Illinois and parts of Wisconsin, Indiana, and Ohio by 1917. *See also* HOLDING COMPANIES; UTILITIES, MUNICIPAL OWNERSHIP OF.

INSURANCE, REGULATION OF. The rapid growth of the life, fire, and accident insurance businesses during the late 19th century created pressure for public oversight to simplify and standardize policies and ensure companies held adequate reserves to cover major disasters, as they manifestly did not in the case of the **San Francisco earthquake**. Residents in capital-poor western and southern states charged that the **Money Trust** siphoned off their assets in the form of insurance premiums and sent them to eastern financial centers. The 1905 **Armstrong Commission** confirmed suspicions of irresponsible management and unsavory political dealings by prestigious New York firms. New York State then strengthened regulation of the industry, with other states following suit. In 1907, Wisconsin passed measures backed by Governor **Robert La Follette** to cap insurance premiums and require companies to deposit collateral sufficient to pay potential claims. That same year, Texas required insurance companies to invest within the state 75 percent of reserves on policies written there. While amenable to some regulations, insurance companies resisted these measures; 15 companies left Wisconsin and 14 ceased doing business in Texas. The insurance investigations seem to have shifted public opinion in favor of ongoing state regulation of business. *See also* HUGHES, CHARLES EVANS.

INSURGENTS. The press commonly referred to the **progressive Republican** faction in Congress as "Insurgents" or "the Insurgency" after the 1908 presidential election put in office **William Howard Taft**, who seemed to favor the Republican **Old Guard**. In the Senate, a bloc led by **Robert La Follette** and **Albert Cummins** fought Taft and Republican Senate leader **Nelson W. Aldrich** over matters such as the **Payne–Aldrich Tariff**, banking reform, and railroad regulation. In the House, **George Norris** led a bloc that sided with Democrats in the March 1910 vote to strip Republican speaker **Joseph G. Cannon** of control over the chamber's agenda and committee chairmanships. The quarrel between the Insurgents and the Old Guard contributed to **Democratic Party** gains in the 1910 congressional elections and culminated in the Republican split in 1912. *See also* NATIONAL PROGRESSIVE REPUBLICAN LEAGUE.

INTELLECTUAL. Progressivism reflected the intellectual ferment of the late 1800s and the early 1900s to an impressive degree. Popular progressives such as **Jane Addams** and **Frederic Howe** sought to implement in their activities and explain in their writings ideas that they encountered as students of innovative intellectuals—as with Howe and **Richard Ely**—or through later collaborations—as with Addams and **John Dewey**. **Chautauqua** programs and **mass-circulation magazines** reveal the extent that the **new middle class** embraced an adult **education** ethic that included familiarity with complex new ideas. The very novelty of the social sciences, in combination with the **efficiency** ethic that linked investigation and planning with progress, encouraged the belief that **university**-trained experts should shape policy. The so-called **Wisconsin Idea**, which thrived under Governor **Robert La Follette**, epitomized this quest for an alliance between politicians and socially minded professors such as Ely and **John R. Commons**. An incessant reader who surrounded himself with writers and thinkers, **Theodore Roosevelt** endeavored as president to draw attention to American achievements in **literature** and **art** as well as the natural and social sciences. **Woodrow Wilson** first gained prominence as one of a generation of **university** presidents that also included Columbia's **Nicholas Murray Butler** and Harvard's **Charles W. Eliot** and that embraced a public role as all-purpose authorities pronouncing on matters of current import.

The energy and idealism that accompanied the vast expansion of the institutions that supported intellectual life contributed to the vigor of American thought. Two streams of civic idealism came together in the creation of American universities: the land-grant tradition articulated by public university leaders such as Wisconsin's **Charles Van Hise,** and the German academic ethic of practical knowledge in the service of society that thousands of young American scholars brought back from study in that country. Founders intended Johns Hopkins University (1876) to serve as a model of the German ethic reconfigured for the United States. **William Rainey Harper** added an element of **Social Gospel** humanitarianism in molding the **University of Chicago**. The charters of **academic associations** proclaimed dedication to improving society, while important schools of academic research, such as the **New History** of **James Harvey Robinson** and **Charles Beard**, started from the principle that scholarship must be relevant. **Women**'s colleges provided their students with opportunities for intense debate on how women could serve society. This intensity diffused down to **high schools** and, through organizations such as the **National Educational Association**, to elementary education. American museums of art and science, meanwhile, proclaimed their mission to be not just the preservation and display of objects but also scholarship and popular education.

On the substantive level, intellectuals debated the nature and purpose of scholarship in the aftermath of the period's great revolutions in natural science and social understanding. Darwinian life science—along with momentous transformations in physics, geology, and astronomy, let alone the tumultuous experience of urbanization and industrialization—fundamentally challenged old ideas about the universe, humanity's place in it, and truth and knowledge. In the new science, reality often countered common sense, and truth became contingent, merely the best explanation presently available for the evidence at hand. As developed by Charles Sanders Peirce (1839–1914) and **William James**, the philosophical school known as **pragmatism** explored how people should live and learn in an age in which the evolution of society and knowledge continually challenged received wisdom. Dewey's educational theories began with the pragmatic assumption that teaching children fixed truths was stultifying and useless; children needed to develop mental skills that would enable them to learn constantly and incorporate unexpected facts and experiences.

Among younger scholars, this perspective encouraged a loathing for formalistic theories pronounced by detached scholars, along with a strong inclination toward empiricism and social engagement. The line of legal thought from **Oliver Wendell Holmes** through **Louis Brandeis** and **sociological jurisprudence** began with the idea that legal principles were not eternal but evolved with society. **Progres-**

sive economists such as Ely, **Simon Patten**, **E. R. A. Seligman**, and **Thorstein Veblen** dismissed neoclassical economics as metaphysics, arguing instead for empirical, institutional analyses of how modern business actually dealt with markets, consumers, **labor unions**, and government. Among political scientists such as Beard and **Frank J. Goodnow**, an analogous impulse created distaste for political theory in favor of descriptive analyses of politics and policy making, along with prescriptions for **structural reform**.

The formulaic version of **social Darwinism** popularized by English writer Herbert Spencer and his American follower William Graham Sumner (1840–1910) came under a fierce attack rooted in an evolutionary outlook on society probably closer to the spirit of Charles Darwin than were Spencer's grandiose writings. Sociologists such as **Lester Frank Ward**, Charles Horton Cooley (1864–1929), and **E. A. Ross** argued that communities and societies needed to be seen not as loose collections of competing individuals but as interdependent, organic entities that were capable of cooperation, altruism, and purposeful change. This perspective also meshed with the new European sociology—identified with figures such as Frenchman Émile Durkheim and Germans Georg Simmel and Max Weber—that young Americans encountered during studies abroad. The so-called Chicago school of sociology nurtured by **Robert E. Park** contributed in a distinctive way to this new approach by methodically analyzing modern industrial cities as social organisms with an evolving "ecology." In the hands of social scientists such as Ross, however, Darwinian notions of the evolution of civilization could lead to new forms of rigidity, in which civilizations progressed through fixed stages from lower to higher. By depicting people from supposedly backward civilizations as inferior, modern sociology could rationalize compulsory **Americanization** or restriction of **immigration**, detribalization of **Native Americans**, pseudoscientific racism, and **eugenics**. Anthropologists such as **Franz Boas** reacted by calling for an outlook that treated all cultures in a relative way as worth studying on their own terms. In the hands of Dewey, **Randolph Bourne**, and **Horace Kallen**, this point of view turned into **pluralism**. The body of thought that in some hands justified racism and **segregation** also underpinned creative attacks on it, as represented in the work of **W. E. B. Du Bois**, **James Weldon Johnson**, and others.

The pragmatist notion of contingent truth and multiple perspectives sparked literary and artistic **modernism**, as well as **socialism, anarchism, feminism**, and other forms of cultural and political radicalism. Women's rights theorists such as **Charlotte Perkins Gilman** started from the social Darwinist premise that the subordination of women was a relic of a backward stage of civilization. The **Greenwich Village** bohemians were also imbued with the sense that **modernization** dissolved old certainties, potentially liberating people in terms of psychology and **sexuality**.

The scientific revolutions and social transformations of the 19th and early 20th centuries, of course, most directly assaulted revealed religion. Thus, the intense debates taking place among students and faculties at colleges and universities were as much theological as sociological. An important segment of progressive social scientists remained professed Christians. Academicians and writers with a Social Gospel or Christian socialist mindset, such as Ely, Commons, **Lyman Abbott, George Herron**, and **Walter Rauschenbusch**, accepted the modernist arguments that religion needed to accommodate the new science and that in the modern world, religion's value came from the sense it fostered of human obligation and mutuality. This new religious thought reinforced the lessons of secular social science in encouraging empiricism and engagement. Over time, antimodernist Christians articulated the opposite view that Christian truth as revealed in the Bible endured, despite the challenges of science. Through writings such as *The Fundamentals*, these theologians laid the intellectual foundation for 20th-century conservative Protestant thought.

Amid this ferment in progressive thought, secular forms of conservatism did not generate substantial energy or enthusiasm. In later publications such as *Folkways* (1906), William Graham Sumner departed from his seemingly rigid version of social Darwinism to explore how enduring cultural traditions shaped mindsets and behavior. Thinkers such as **George Santayana** and Irving Babbitt (1865–1933) began to launch aesthetic and moral attacks on modern society as shallow, crass, materialistic, and exploitative, damning progressivism along with corporate capitalism for undermining true civilization. At first, such arguments had their greatest effect on left-wing cultural radicals such as **Van Wyck Brooks**, but over decades they would feed a vibrant strain in conservative criticism of American society. *See also* ADAMS, BROOKS; ADAMS, HENRY; ADAMS, HENRY CARTER; AMERICAN ASSOCIATION OF UNIVERSITY PROFESSORS; AMERICAN ASSOCIATION OF UNIVERSITY WOMEN; BEHAVIORISM; BURGESS, JOHN W.; CROLY, HERBERT D.; DUNNING SCHOOL; ECONOMY; GENETICS; HALL, GRANVILLE STANLEY; JORDAN, DAVID STARR; LIPPMANN, WALTER; MCCARTHY, CHARLES; MÜNSTERBERG, HUGO; "SIGNIFICANCE OF THE FRONTIER IN AMERICAN HISTORY"; SMALL, ALBION; THOMAS, M. CAREY.

INTERLOCKING DIRECTORATES. In this form of business consolidation, investment groups created alliances without formally merging or forming a **holding company**. In exchange for arranging financing, investment banks demanded seats on the board of directors, with the result that a small number of people directed a web of enterprises. Especially during the **great merger movement**, heavily capitalized industries such as railroads reorganized into these directorates. By 1906, seven investment groups controlled two-thirds of the country's railroads, with the alliances of **J. P. Morgan** and **E. H. Harriman** each holding around 25,000 miles of tracks. As the **Pujo Committee** hearings revealed, by 1913 Morgan and Company and three other Wall Street investment banks held 193 director's seats in 68 industrial, transportation, and utility firms and also held many seats on the boards of banking, trust, and insurance companies. This so-called **Money Trust** became a target of **antitrust** advocates such as **Louis D. Brandeis**, and the 1914 **Clayton Act** included ineffective prohibitions on interlocking directorates.

INTERNATIONAL HARVESTER. In 1902, **George Perkins** of **J. P. Morgan** and Company organized this merger of the McCormick Harvesting Machinery Company with four smaller agricultural machinery firms. The country's fourth largest industrial company, with nearly $173 million in assets, an 85 percent market share, 75,000 employees, and $125 million in sales by 1912, International Harvester's control of the market allowed it to diversify into tractors, trucks, and other agricultural machinery. It became a target for **antitrust** prosecution in 1912, but the federal government's battle with the company, which continued until 1927, enabled Harvester to divest itself of three outdated lines while limiting it to one dealer in each town.

INTERNATIONAL LADIES' GARMENT WORKERS' UNION (ILGWU). Founded in 1900 with support from the **American Federation of Labor**, this **labor union** merged many small unions in the manufacture of women's clothing. Although founded by skilled male workers, it was successful in organizing the semiskilled and unskilled **women** of Eastern European **Jewish** and Italian background who made up the majority of the workforce. The union grew rapidly after the 1909 **Uprising of the Twenty Thousand**, the 1910 New York cloak maker's strike, and the 1911 **Triangle Shirtwaist Company Fire**. By 1912, it claimed a membership of 60,000; perhaps 90 percent of the New York garment trade was organized by the ILGWU and the unions in men's clothing. Through the so-called Protocol of Peace (1910), mediated largely by **Louis D. Brandeis**, the union secured limits on some of the worst sweatshop abuses, along with a 54-hour maximum workweek and arbitration mechanisms for worker–employer disputes. Sympathetic to **socialism**, the ILGWU, like other urban-based garment unions, experimented with health care and other social services. With half of its members female by 1916, the ILGWU offered an institutional base for prominent **immigrant** women labor activists, such as **Rose Schneiderman** and **Pauline Newman**.

INTERNATIONALISM. This term described the outlook of those who advocated departing from the traditional American foreign policy of avoiding alliances, Great Power politics, and ventures outside the western hemisphere. Internationalists ranged from outright proponents of *Realpolitik*, military might, and **imperialism**, such as **Theodore Roosevelt** and **Henry Cabot Lodge,** to pacifists such as **Jane Addams** and **Oswald Garrison Villard**, who sought an international movement for peace and social and political justice. Moderate **Republicans**, such as Secretary of War **Elihu Root** and President **William Howard Taft**, promoted the resolution of international disputes through **arbitration** and judicial institutions such as those proposed during the **Hague Conferences**. This moderate internationalism took shape as the **League to Enforce Peace** after the outbreak of the European war in 1914. The **cooling-off treaties** pursued by Secretary of State **William Jennings Bryan** represented another version of this approach. These strands of internationalist thought contributed to the League of Nations proposed by President **Woodrow Wilson** during World War I.

INTERSTATE COMMERCE COMMISSION (ICC). The first modern federal regulatory agency, established by Congress in 1887, the Interstate Commerce Commission was intended to control the huge railroad companies. In its early years, the ICC endeavored to eliminate the price discrimination about which farmers, merchants, and industrialists complained. The Panic of 1893 threw the railroads into financial turmoil, however, magnifying the temptation to defy the ICC and revert to giving rebates and special rates to large, long-haul shippers. By 1898, federal court decisions emasculated the ICC. The return of prosperity after 1897, along with the creation of **interlocking directorates** in the railroad industry, relieved pressure on the companies to secure traffic at any cost, and railroad executives came to see federal regulations as a means of refusing demands by large shippers for price breaks. Regulatory legislation such as the **Elkins, Hepburn,** and **Mann–Elkins Acts** meant that by 1910 the ICC oversaw oil pipelines, express companies, and telephone and telegraph lines as well as railroads and had authority to suspend or deny rate increases and set maximum rates. Between 1905 and 1909, the ICC staff increased from 178 to 527, but critics complained that the agency lacked the capacity to determine fair rates that provided railroads with sufficient revenue to maintain and upgrade their operations. In practice, ICC-approved rates responded to competing pressures from agricultural, mercantile, industrial, labor, and transportation interests. As the economy entered an inflationary cycle in the first decade of the 20th century, the ICC rate-setting process threatened to starve the railroads of capital, a danger evident in 1914, when President **Woodrow Wilson** in effect ordered the commission to grant eastern railroads a 5 percent increase. *See also* ANTITRUST; *NORTHERN SECURITIES V. UNITED STATES.*

IRELAND, JOHN (1838–1918). Archbishop. Born in Ireland, he came to the United States with his family in 1849 and was ordained

224 • IVES, CHARLES

a priest in 1861, rising to bishop (1875) and then archbishop of St. Paul, Minnesota (1888). His support for **labor unions** and temperance, opposition to **segregation** and political corruption, advocacy of the **Americanization** of **immigrants**, and compromises between religious and public **education** earned him a reputation as one of the foremost American liberals in the Catholic hierarchy. However, his opposition to foreign-language schools and the creation of parishes to serve single ethnic groups embroiled him in quarrels with members of his church. During the so-called **Americanism** controversy of the 1890s, the Vatican criticized him for his ecumenical attitude toward other churches and willingness to reconcile Catholic doctrine with American republicanism, including the separation of church and state. Archbishop Ireland oversaw the spread of Catholic institutions in the northern Plains. *See also* ANTI-CATHOLICISM; GIBBONS, JAMES.

IVES, CHARLES (1879–1954). Composer. Born in Connecticut, Ives wrote **music** and played the organ as a teenager. He composed his *First Symphony* while at Yale University, but after graduating in 1898 he worked in life insurance until poor health forced his retirement in 1930. In his spare time, he produced many works that incorporated dissonances, snatches of hymns, marches, **ragtime**, and other innovations. Completed compositions include *The Unanswered Question* (1908), *Three Places in New England* (1903–14), and *Concord Sonata* (1900–14). In 1922, he published a collection of 114 songs. Reflecting the composer's partly self-imposed isolation from the musical world, his music remained little known and rarely played until musical **modernists** discovered him in the 1920s and acclaimed Ives as a precursor.

– J –

JAMES, HENRY, JR. (1843–1916). Author. Born into a wealthy New York City family, he was educated privately and as a young man joined Boston and Cambridge intellectual circles, where he made influential friends, including Charles Eliot Norton, **Oliver Wendell Holmes**, and **William Dean Howells**. Making his reputation with novels such as *The American* (1877), *Daisy Miller* (1878), and *The Portrait of a Lady* (1881), James moved permanently to England in 1876. His fiction often addresses the encounter between decent but naïve Americans and Europe's decadent cultures. Moved by the suffering of his sister Alice, he used **women**'s dilemmas to portray the tension between individual personality and social demands. By the 1890s, his style became more intricate, focusing on characters' shifting perspectives and the indirect revelation of plot through dialogue and mental rumination. His later work was thus the novelistic equivalent of his brother **William James**'s explorations of consciousness. Criticized as convoluted and opaque, novels such as *Wings of the Dove* (1902), *The Ambassadors* (1903), and *The Golden Bowl* (1904) gradually won acclaim as precursors of **modernism**. Although he became a British citizen in 1915 and faced accusations that he had cut himself off from his American roots, James was a pivotal figure in establishing American **literature** as equal to the best European writing. He understood himself to be working in the cosmopolitan **realist** tradition of Flaubert, Turgenev, and George Eliot.

JAMES, WILLIAM (1842–1910). Philosopher and psychologist. Born into a wealthy New York City family and brother to **Henry James**, William traveled frequently with his family and was educated privately. After trying and abandoning art and chemistry, he earned a medical degree in 1869 from Harvard University, where he began teaching in 1872, specializing in physiology, psychology, and philosophy. He joined **G. Stanley Hall** in formulating a psychology free of metaphysics and rooted in physiology. His masterwork, *Principles of Psychology* (1890), helped to win acceptance for psychology as a science. Taking a stance rejected by **behaviorists**, he believed that all mental phenomena were worth studying, even if they could not be defined or measured. His interest in religious states of mind and spiritualism culminated in *The Will to Believe* (1897) and *The Varieties of Religious Experience* (1902). Philosophically, James identified with **pragmatism**, arguing that all important truths arise from the interaction of people with their environments. Truths are therefore multiple and change as an individual has new experiences or encounters new facts. Working in a field also developed by Charles Sanders Peirce and **John Dewey**, James popularized this innovative philosophy through works such as *Pragmatism* (1907), *A Pluralistic Universe* (1909), and *Essays in Radical Empiricism* (1912). A charismatic teacher, he called on his students to eschew abstractions and engage with social problems; among those who responded were **W. E. B. Du Bois** and **Horace Kallen**. *See also* INTELLECTUAL; UNIVERSITY.

JAMESON, J. FRANKLIN (1859–1937). Historian and editor. A native of Boston, Jameson earned the first Ph.D. ever granted by Johns Hopkins University (1882) and taught there for six years before taking professorships at Brown University (1888–1901) and the **University of Chicago** (1901–5). Respected within the profession for his writings on historiography and the American Revolution, he was most influential as the founding managing editor of the *American Historical Review*, which under his leadership (1895–1901, 1905–28) earned a reputation as an exemplary academic journal. As head of the **Carnegie Institution**'s Bureau of Historical Research (1905–28) and the Manuscripts Division of the Library of Congress, he greatly enhanced the resources available to U.S. historians. *See also* ACADEMIC ASSOCIATIONS.

JAZZ. A slang term for sexual intercourse, jazz was first applied to **music** in the mid-1910s. This music combined the **African American** genres of **ragtime**, spirituals, and blues with Euro-American folk music; improvisation was a key feature. It developed initially in New Orleans as dance music in the city's **red-light** district, **Storyville**. Many musicians joined the **Great Migration**, bringing jazz to national notice in the 1920s. *See also* EUROPE, JAMES REESE.

JEWISH DAILY FORWARD. Known as the *Forverts* in Yiddish, this **socialist** newspaper was founded in 1897 for **Jewish** residents of New York's **Lower East Side**. It soon became the country's largest Yiddish daily under the leadership of cofounder **Abraham Cahan**, who served as editor from 1903 to 1951. Softening the paper's politics to match the moderate, pro-labor social democracy of most readers, he also borrowed techniques from the **Hearst** and **Pulitzer** chains, veering at times toward **yellow journalism**. With a circulation of 200,000 at its height around 1917, the *Forward* promoted Yiddish authors while urging **immigrant** Jews to learn English and **Americanize**. Its popular advice column, "Bintl Briv" (Bundle of Letters), poignantly portrayed immigrant Jews' daily struggles. Barely avoiding government suppression for its antiwar stance during World War I, the *Forward* endured with dwindling readership through the 20th century. *See also* JOURNALISM.

JEWS. The Jewish population of the United States was only 250,000 in 1880, when a new wave of **immigration** rapidly increased these numbers. The United States was a popular destination because, although anti-Semitism was common, the nation had no laws limiting where Jews could live or what businesses they could pursue; nor did it exclude them from government and military service, as many European nations did. Between 1870 and 1924, some two-and-a-half million Eastern European Jews crossed the Atlantic, increasing the U.S. Jewish population to four million by 1920. Most of these newcomers, unlike the German Jews already living in the country, came from the Austro–Hungarian and Russian Empires and were more orthodox in religious practice. Yiddish-language institutions from newspapers to theaters multiplied. The largest Jewish neighborhood was on New York's **Lower East Side**, where more than 500,000 lived by 1910, but Jews also settled in large cities throughout the Northeast and Midwest, with smaller groups in cities of the South and West.

Like most immigrants, Jewish newcomers were often poor, but many had experience in the garment industry, which they soon dominated, and in running small businesses. Married Jewish women were more likely to work for wages than were other immigrant women. Along with orthodox believers came many secular Zionists; **socialists**, including **Abraham Cahan**, Daniel DeLeon, and **Morris Hillquit**; and **anarchists**, notably **Emma Goldman** and **Alexander Berkman**. Jews were prominent in the labor movement: **Samuel Gompers** founded the **American Federation of Labor**, while **Fannia Cohn**, **Pauline Newman**, and **Rose Schneiderman** were prominent in the **International Ladies' Garment Workers' Union** and the **Women's Trade Union League**. Middle-class Jews, most of them native-born, were important reformers. **Lillian Wald** founded New York's Henry Street **settlement house**; **Josephine Goldmark** was a major figure in developing **sociological jurisprudence**, researching the briefs that **Louis Brandeis** used to win *Muller v. Oregon* and other cases legitimizing labor regulations. **Felix Frankfurter** eventually joined Brandeis on the **Supreme Court. Franz Boas, E. R. A. Seligman**, and **Walter Lippmann** were among the many Jews to make marks on **intellectual** life and **journalism**, despite discrimination in **university** appointments and admissions. **Bernard Berenson** became a prominent art critic. Boston department store magnate **Edward A. Filene** played a major role in **progressive** politics. Jews also became famous in entertainment: magician **Harry Houdini**, popular songwriter **Irving Berlin**, actors Fanny Brice and Eddie Cantor in the **Ziegfeld Follies**, film moguls such as **Adolph Zukor** and **Jesse Lasky**, and popular novelist Anzia Yezierska.

The rapid spread of Orthodox **education** and synagogues and the emergence of Conservative Judaism were but two manifestations of lively debates over religious belief and practice. The first branch of Judaism founded in the United States, Conservatism, which sought a centrist position between Orthodoxy and Reform, developed its own institutional network between the 1880s and the 1910s. Solomon Schindler was the leading Reform rabbi and Jewish progressive philanthropist in Boston, and **Stephen Wise** led Reformed Jews in New York City. The **Social Gospel** inspired former Rabbi **Felix Adler** to form the Ethical Culture Society. The **Hebrew Immigrant Aid Society** and the **Anti-Defamation League** assisted Jews and fought anti-Semitism.

JITNEYS. Named after a slang term for a nickel, jitneys were **automobiles** whose drivers plied fixed routes and took riders short distances for five cents. Frequently driven by unemployed workers or **women** earning extra money for their families, these cars were more flexible than **trolleys** and cheaper than taxicabs. In operation as early as 1910, jitneys spread quickly; by 1915, there were an estimated 62,000, with as many as 1,000 in San Francisco and 1,500 in Los Angeles, where they carried an estimated 150,000 passengers per day. In Detroit and a few other cities, they appear to have briefly captured as much as half the transit market. In southern cities, the popular black-run services enabled **African Americans** to avoid **segregated** streetcars. Trolley and taxi companies lobbied state and municipal governments to impose license and insurance requirements and onerous regulations that effectively suppressed the jitney business by the 1920s.

JOHNSON, ARTHUR JOHN "JACK" (1878–1946). Boxer. Born in Texas, Johnson learned to box by participating in staged group fights. Gaining national exposure by 1903, the **African American** star lost only once between 1905 and 1915, and then on a technicality. In 1908, he defeated the white heavyweight world champion, Tommy Burns, in Australia. Infuriated white U.S. boxing fans convinced former champion James J. Jeffries to return to the ring to challenge Johnson, whose victory in 1910 led to **race riots** throughout the South but made the boxer a hero to many **African Americans**. His marriage to one white woman and affairs with others deeply offended racist whites. By October 1912, federal authorities twice prosecuted Jackson under the **Mann Act** for having traveled across state lines with his girlfriends. Convicted in 1913, Johnson fled the country and lived abroad for several years, during this time losing the heavyweight title. In 1920, Johnson returned to the United States, served his one-year sentence, and later made a living as a trainer and **vaudeville** actor and lecturer. *See also* ATHLETICS.

JOHNSON, HIRAM W. (1866–1945). Politician. Born in California, Johnson's successful prosecution of San Francisco **boss Abraham Ruef** on graft charges brought him prominence. A **progressive** member of the **Republican Party**, he won election as governor (1911–17) on a platform attacking the **Southern Pacific Railroad**'s influence on state politics. In office, he oversaw reforms comparable to those of **Robert La Follette** in Wisconsin, including strengthening of **utilities** and railroad regulation; civil service and **conservation** measures; electoral reforms ranging from **initiative, referendum**, and **recall** to **women**'s **suffrage**; and **workers' compensation** and **child labor** restrictions. He also supported the **Alien Land Act**, a concession to anti-Japanese sentiment. A founding member of the **National Progressive Republican League**, he followed **Theodore Roosevelt** into the new **Progressive Party** in 1912 and was nominated for vice president. Although the new party won in California, it lost nationwide. Reelected governor in 1914, Johnson rejoined the Republicans in time to win a seat in the U.S. Senate (1917–45), where he remained until his death. *See also* INSURGENTS.

JOHNSON, JAMES WELDON (1871–1938). Activist, author, and songwriter. Born in Florida, Johnson earned B.A. and M.A. degrees from Atlanta University and became a **high school** principal, newspaper publisher, and attorney, one of the few **African Americans** admitted to the bar in this era. By 1900, he moved to New York City and established a songwriting partnership that produced Broadway musicals presenting black **music** and themes. His best-known work was the song "Lift Every Voice and Sing," cowritten with his brother. President **Theodore Roosevelt**, on the advice of **Booker T. Washington** and others, appointed Johnson to serve in the Foreign Service in Venezuela (1906–9) and **Nicaragua** (1909–13). Returning to New York as an editor of the *New York Age*, he published poetry and—anonymously—*The Autobiography of an Ex-Colored Man* (1912), a novel about an African American man "passing" as white. Hired in 1917 as field secretary of the **National Association for the Advancement of Colored People**, Johnson oversaw the anti-**lynching** campaign and organizing drives that made the organization a mass movement with a national constituency.

JOHNSON, TOM L. (1854–1911). Streetcar magnate and politician. Born in Kentucky, Johnson went to work at age 14 for a Louisville streetcar company owned by the **du Pont** family. By the 1880s he controlled streetcar companies in St. Louis, Detroit, Brooklyn, and Cleveland and competed with **Mark Hanna** in the iron, steel, and railroad business. He championed Henry George's **single tax** idea during two terms as an Ohio **Democrat** in the House of Representatives (1891–95). In the mid-1890s, Detroit mayor **Hazen Pingree** fought to drive fares down to three cents while improving service on Johnson's streetcar lines. Impressed as well as defeated by Pingree, Johnson withdrew from the transit business and ran for mayor of Cleveland on a platform of doing there what Pingree had forced him to do in Detroit. As mayor (1901–9), he expanded his program to include parks, **playgrounds**, and **bathhouses**, **City Beautiful** planning, **home rule**, tax reform, a municipal **electric** plant, expanded public services, and more humane treatment of the poor by the police and courts. Even as he won over political **bosses**, Johnson drew into politics young reformers such as **Newton D. Baker**, Sara Bard Field, and **Frederic C. Howe**, whose writings popularized Johnson as the model **progressive** mayor. *See also* TROLLEYS, ELECTRIC; UTILITIES, MUNICIPAL OWNERSHIP OF.

JONES, MARY HARRIS "MOTHER" (1837–1930). Labor activist. Born in Ireland, Jones migrated to Canada with her family in 1852. After losing her husband and four children to **yellow fever**, she became a labor activist in the 1870s. She gained a national profile in the 1890s as the symbol of outraged working-class motherhood. About this time she began to be called "Mother" Jones. An organizer for the **United Mine Workers**, she took the unusual step of working with miners' wives, but she rejected **women**'s **suffrage** and emphasized women's duty to support their men. Prominent in the **Socialist Party of America** and the **Industrial Workers of the World**, she was sentenced to 20 years in prison for her role in West Virginia miners' strikes in 1912–13. Outrage at the jailing of a woman in her seventies led the governor to commute her sentence. Jones promptly went west to support a strike against **John D. Rockefeller**'s Colorado Fuel and Iron Company that culminated in the **Ludlow Massacre** (1914).

JONES, SAMUEL M. (1846–1904). Manufacturer and politician. Born in Wales to a family that emigrated to New York in 1849, Jones began working by age 14. After success in the oil business, he opened a factory in Toledo, Ohio, to manufacture drilling equipment. Influenced by the **Social Gospel** and utopian writers such as Leo Tolstoy and Edward Bellamy, the industrialist endeavored to conduct labor-management relations according to the Golden Rule, earning the nickname "Golden Rule" Jones. He grew wealthy while providing workers above-average wages, an **eight-hour day**, profit-sharing, paid vacations, Christmas bonuses, and other benefits all but unknown at the time. Elected Toledo's mayor as a Republican in 1899, Jones supported parks and **playgrounds**, public **bath houses**, kindergartens and other **education** reforms, municipal ownership of **utilities**, and civil service protections. He fought for penal reforms and allowed lax enforcement of temperance and vice laws. Critics accused him of being soft on crime, and the **Republican Party** abandoned him as too controversial, but he won reelection three times and was the peer of **Tom L. Johnson** and **Hazen Pingree**. After his death on 12 July 1904, **Brand Whitlock** carried on his campaign.

JONES ACT (1916). *See* PHILIPPINES, COLONIAL GOVERNMENT OF.

JOPLIN, SCOTT (1868?–1917). Composer and musician. Born in east Texas, Joplin spent much of his youth as an itinerant musician. After working as a band leader at the Columbian Exposition in Chicago, he settled in Missouri in 1894, where he studied **music** at a local **African American** institution. By 1899, he was publishing **ragtime** compositions. The "Maple Leaf Rag," named for a black social club where he performed, became a bestseller. Moving to St. Louis in 1901 and New York in 1907, Joplin published more successful rags, even as he was frustrated in efforts to win attention for more ambitious works, including two ragtime operas. Dogged by personal and financial difficulties, he died in misery of the effects of **syphilis** in Harlem on 1 April 1917. Except for "Maple Leaf Rag," Joplin made no **phonograph** recordings.

JORDAN, DAVID STARR (1851–1931). Scientist and educator. A New York state native, Jordan taught biology before becoming a **university** administrator. Named president of Indiana University in 1885, he transformed this small state school into a modern research university. Six years later, he moved to California to do the same for the new Stanford University. Having constructed a campus from nothing, he rebuilt it after seeing it destroyed in the 1906 **San Francisco earthquake**. Jordan endorsed **eugenics** and **immigration** restriction and opposed U.S. **imperialism** because he did not want the country to incorporate any more nonwhites. He is perhaps best known for his 1900 firing of sociologist **Edward A. Ross** for alleged radicalism. The Ross incident contributed to the founding of the **American Association of University Professors** and the articulation of the ideal of academic freedom. By 1913, Stanford alumni, led by Herbert Hoover, felt Jordan was a liability and removed him from the presidency.

JOURNALISM. There are many institutional and cultural reasons for the close association between the Progressive Era and the media, especially newspapers and **mass-circulation magazines**. By 1900, publishing was an elaborate business that displayed technological and **organizational** innovation analogous to transformations in the railroads and industries whose abuses **muckraking** reporters exposed. In 1886, the *New York Tribune* became the first newspaper to adopt the new linotype machine, which revolutionized printing by allowing accurate typesetting at rapid speed. Similar changes in lithography and photoengraving lowered the cost of producing illustrated magazines and newspapers. Improved telegraphy supported consortia such as the Associated Press and newspaper and magazine syndicates. **Advertising** revenue allowed publishers to cut prices while freeing them from dependence on political patronage. Press barons such as **William Randolph Hearst** cultivated flamboyant public images, but they were astute operators of far-flung enterprises. Magazine editors such as **Edward W. Bok** and **Samuel S. McClure** honed their skills in dealing with authors and appealing to the public through periods running press syndicates. Syndication allowed a regional figure such as **William Allen White**, editor and publisher of the *Emporia Gazette*, to gain a national audience.

The sensational **yellow journalism** identified with Hearst and rival newspaper chain magnate **Joseph Pulitzer** elaborated on the basic style and content of the urban daily newspaper, as worked out by a previous generation of editors. James Gordon Bennett Jr. (1841–1918), for example, created in the *New York Herald* and his newspaper empire the concise, direct writing style that came to characterize newspapers in the United States. Expanding urban populations bought newspapers from street corner newsstands or newsies, boys who hawked papers on streets, a ubiquitous, often exploitative form of **child labor**. The tabloid format was introduced for the convenience of straphanger passengers on **trolleys** and **subway** trains. By the time of Harry Thaw's trial for the sensational 1906 murder of **Stanford White**, lurid crime reporting had long been a newspaper staple, while the basic tone and structure of urban feature stories and sports writing were also in place.

Most ethnic groups supported their own newspapers, often in foreign languages, like the ***Jewish Daily Forward*** edited by **Abraham**

Cahan. For Irish-Americans, the witty **Finley Peter Dunne**'s satirical column in the *Chicago Evening Post* had a national readership. Among **African Americans**, a weekly press thrived, epitomized by **Robert Abbott**'s influential *Chicago Defender*. **William Monroe Trotter**'s *Boston Guardian* criticized **Booker T. Washington** and his so-called **Tuskegee** machine, as much as **T. Thomas Fortune**'s *New York Age* defended him. Scholar **W. E. B. Du Bois** exerted his greatest contemporary influence as editor of *The Crisis*, magazine of the **National Association for the Advancement of Colored People**.

With a secure circulation base in the **new middle class**, weekly and monthly magazines offered essays on society, public affairs, philosophy and religion, travel, and science, as well as **literature**. As an editor of *Atlantic* and *Harper's*, **William Dean Howells** gained his reputation as a superlative literary critic who drew readers' attention to first-rate U.S. and European **realist** and **naturalist** authors. With their expanded format and engaged readership, magazines such as *McClure's* and *Collier's* became the preferred forum for the investigative journalists that President **Theodore Roosevelt** labeled muckrakers. Despite their gritty reputation, investigative journalists such as **Ray Stannard Baker**, **Ida Tarbell**, and **Lincoln Steffens** were products of a more prosperous, educated press and considered themselves professionals with the high duty of informing the public. **Jacob Riis** offered a model for crusading reporters such as Steffens, as well as for documentary photographers such as **Lewis Hine**, who used photo essays in social reform magazines such as *Survey* to further reform causes.

Socialists and other radicals maintained their own press. **Eugene V. Debs** was closely associated with the Kansas-based weekly *Appeal to Reason*, which first published **Upton Sinclair**'s *The Jungle*. **Emma Goldman** and **Alexander Berkman** used *Mother Earth* to explain their version of **anarchism**. **Greenwich Village** bohemians such as **John Reed** and **Randolph Bourne** found an outlet for political and cultural experimentation in magazines such as *The Masses*, edited by **Max Eastman** and Floyd Dell, with artistic contributions from **John Sloan** and **Art Young**. Under the direction of **Herbert Croly**, **Walter Lippmann**, and **Walter Weyl**, the *New Republic* became a forum for **progressive** thought. The first radio news broadcast in Los Angeles in 1912 foreshadowed the future of the media in the United States, but the printed word in magazines and newspapers was the heart and catalyst of progressivism. *See also* ABBOTT, LYMAN; DAVIS, RICHARD HARDING; HAPGOOD, HUTCHINS; HUNEKER, JAMES GIBBONS.

JUVENILE COURTS. First established in Illinois in 1899, juvenile courts had their origins in children's sessions started in Boston by 1830; such courts existed in nearly all states by 1925. Denver judge **Benjamin Lindsey**, Chicago's **Julian Mack** and the **Hull House** reformers, and Boston judge Harvey H. Baker (1869–1915) were leading proponents. The courts embodied the argument that young criminals should be rehabilitated, not confined with adult offenders to be tutored in crime. Juvenile courts did not offer basic legal rights, such as access to counsel, bail, and jury trials. Instead, social workers, probation officers, and judges decided how to handle each case, often sending children to private or public reform schools, orphanages, or foster homes. In many institutions, children received an **industrial education** and lived in barracks; most of these facilities eventually became little more than juvenile jails. Children processed through the juvenile courts were usually guilty of activities such as scavenging, behaving badly in public, or status offenses like truancy, stubbornness, and neglect. Offenses from playing ball on Sunday to assault and theft were typical for boys; lewd and lascivious carriage (meaning anything from seeing men whom families did not like to **prostitution**) and shoplifting were typical for girls. Inmates of reform schools were liable to compulsory **sterilization** in some states. Some working-class parents used the courts to discipline their children. By 1915, many juvenile courts relied on psychologists and psychiatrists, often in a clinic affiliated with the court. *See also* ADOLESCENCE; REFORM MOVEMENTS.

– K –

KALLEN, HORACE (1882–1974). Philosopher. Born in Silesia to **Jewish** parents and raised in Boston, Kallen earned a B.A. and a Ph.D. at Harvard University, where he absorbed **pragmatism** from

William James. This philosophy encouraged his Zionism and explorations of Jewish history and culture, despite his loss of faith. Taking a position at the University of Wisconsin in 1911, he was repelled by **Edward A. Ross**'s pro-**Americanization**, anti-**immigrant** ideas and developed a philosophical case for cultural **pluralism**, a term he coined in an influential essay, "Democracy versus the Melting Pot," published in the *Nation* (1915). After preparing an anthology of pragmatist writings, *Creative Intelligence* (1917), Kallen left Wisconsin in a dispute over his defense of antiwar dissidents during World War I and became a founding faculty member of New York's New School for Social Research. *See also* BOURNE, RANDOLPH S.; INTELLECTUAL.

KEATING–OWEN CHILD LABOR ACT (1916). The **National Child Labor Committee** spearheaded **progressive** lobbying for congressional action regulating **child labor**. **Republican** senator **Albert J. Beveridge** of Indiana first introduced such a bill in 1907, but not until 1916 did Congress agree on a measure. Sponsored by **Democratic** representatives Edward Keating of Colorado and Robert L. Owen of Oklahoma, this bill prohibited children under the age of 14 from working in mills, factories, and canneries; those under 16 could not work in mines and quarries, at night, or for more than **eight hours** per day. Although the law put federal muscle behind the child labor restrictions for the first time, it was riddled with loopholes and undercut more stringent state laws while excluding children in domestic service, sweatshops, agriculture, and casual street labor. Congress appropriated $150,000 for enforcement by the **Children's Bureau**, where **Julia Lathrop** implemented the law against resistance by manufacturers and parents until the **Supreme Court** ruled it unconstitutional in *Hammer v. Dagenhart* (1918). *See also* MCKELWAY, ALEXANDER JEFFREY; NATIONAL CHILD LABOR COMMITTEE.

KEEP COMMISSION. Officially named the Committee on Department Methods, this panel was established by President **Theodore Roosevelt** in 1905 and chaired by Assistant Secretary of the Treasury Charles H. Keep. With Roosevelt allies **James R. Garfield**, **Frank Hitchcock**, and **Gifford Pinchot** as members, the commission compiled information on the organization, operation, expenses, and pay structures of federal departments with the goal of heightened **efficiency** and **modernization**. Caught in wrangling between Roosevelt and the **Republican Old Guard** in Congress, the commission received a scant $5,000 appropriation and published only seven of its 19 reports. Congress even passed a law forbidding presidents from forming such panels as Roosevelt left office in March 1909. Over time, Congress accepted many reforms recommended by the Keep Commission, including creation of a federal retirement system and the National Archives. *See also* CIVIL SERVICE COMMISSION, U.S.

KEITH & ALBEE. Partners Benjamin F. Keith (1846–1914) and Edward F. Albee (1857–1930) opened a theater in Boston in 1883. Having coined the term **vaudeville** to distinguish their shows from musical variety and burlesque, Keith banned profanity and vulgarity from his shows to avoid censorship and attract a wider audience. This policy and Mrs. Keith's connections to the Catholic Church gave Keith & Albee access to bank loans and public approval, enabling them to acquire more than 400 theaters and hire major stars. By 1906, Keith & Albee ran the largest variety syndicate in the United States. Like other businesses in the era, Keith & Albee strove to expand markets while controlling costs by integrating vertically, founding the United Booking Office of America in 1906 to control theaters and performers. Like other workers, actors responded by trying to form unions, without much success. A rival organization, the United States Amusement Company, formed in 1907 but accepted $250,000 to quit the field. In 1912, Keith & Albee merged with the Orpheum Theater chain to gain access to stages in the West; eventually this chain merged with the Radio Corporation of America (RCA). *See also* POPULAR CULTURE.

KELLEY, FLORENCE (1859–1932). Reformer. A Philadelphia native and the daughter of an influential **Republican** politician, Kelley graduated from Cornell University (1882) and studied law at the University of Zurich, where she met many Russian émigrés and German social democrats and became interested in Marxian **socialism**. Returning to the United States, she settled in New York City with her Russian husband and had three children while working to end **child**

labor. In 1891, her marriage failed and she moved to **Hull House** in Chicago. Here she completed her legal studies at Northwestern University and worked with the Illinois Bureau of Labor Statistics. Her work formed the basis of a sweeping 1893 Illinois law limiting women and children to an **eight-hour** working day, banning sweatshops in tenements, and creating the office of factory inspector, a position to which reform governor John Peter Altgeld appointed her. She was the first woman to hold such a position in the United States or Europe. The state supreme court found the limit on working hours unconstitutional in 1895, and a year later Kelley lost her job when Altgeld was not reelected. She returned to New York in 1899 to found and lead the **National Consumers' League (NCL)** and live in the Henry Street **settlement house**. She also held offices in the **General Federation of Women's Clubs**, the **National Congress of Mothers**, and the **National American Woman Suffrage Association**. Under her guidance, the NCL won major cases on regulation of working hours, including ***Muller v. Oregon*** (1908) and ***Bunting v. Oregon*** (1917). *See also* ADDAMS, JANE; GOLDMARK, JOSEPHINE CLARA; REFORM MOVEMENTS; WOMEN.

KELLOGG, JOHN HARVEY (1852–1943). Health reformer. Born in Michigan to members of the Seventh-day Adventist Church, Kellogg earned a medical degree in 1875 and returned home to edit *Good Health*, through which he promoted a variety of dietary and health reforms, including vegetarianism, abstinence from alcohol, caffeine, and tobacco, drinking plenty of water, thorough mastication of food, and plentiful outdoor exercise. With his **home economist** wife and his brother, he developed cereal products that, along with those of **Charles Post**, transformed the American breakfast. Kellogg's alternatives to meat, including peanut butter, were not as successful as his corn flakes. At his Battle Creek Sanitarium, he offered courses in hygiene, home economics, physical education, and **nursing**; he also launched an Adventist medical college in Chicago in the 1890s. In the 1910s, he endorsed **eugenics** and established the Race Betterment Foundation. The initially radical Kellogg came to be a respected physician, serving on the Michigan State Board of Health and treating many well-known figures.

KELLOGG, PAUL U. (1879–1958). See PITTSBURGH SURVEY; *SURVEY.*

KELLOR, FRANCES ALICE (1873–1952). Reformer. Born in Ohio, Kellor grew up in Michigan, graduated from Cornell Law School (1897), and studied sociology at the **University of Chicago**. She published works demonstrating environmental causes of female criminality and **African American** poverty and revealing problems with employment agencies. Increasingly involved in **Americanization** efforts, she served as director of the New York State Bureau of Industries and Immigration under Governor **Charles Evans Hughes** and helped found the National Americanization Committee. In 1912, Kellor was a delegate to the national convention of the new **Progressive Party** and directed publicity for **Theodore Roosevelt**'s **Bull Moose** campaign. She also cofounded an organization devoted to the **arbitration** of labor and international disputes.

KERN, JOHN WORTH (1849–1917). Politician. Kern grew up in Indiana and Iowa and became an attorney and a prominent pro-labor **Democrat**, serving in a variety of elected offices. Nominated for governor in 1900 and 1904, he lost both times amid **Republican Party** sweeps of Indiana, but his strong performance led to his nomination for vice president with **William Jennings Bryan** in 1908. That race lost, Kern won a seat in the U.S. Senate (1911–17), defeating **Albert J. Beveridge**, and became the Democratic floor leader in 1913. He worked closely with **Woodrow Wilson** to guide **New Freedom** legislation through Congress but failed to win reelection in 1916.

KERN–MCGILLICUDDY ACT. Also known as the Federal Employees' Compensation Act and named for Senate **Democratic** leader **John Worth Kern** and Maine representative Daniel J. McGillicuddy, this 1916 law established **workers' compensation** for federal employees. Drafted with assistance from the **American Association for Labor Legislation**, the law was envisioned as a model for states, especially in its provisions for ongoing medical care for injured workers. *See also* SOCIAL INSURANCE.

KNIGHTS OF COLUMBUS. Founded in 1882 by Father Michael J. McGivney, this organization began as a Catholic fraternal organization and mutual aid society. In the 1890s, the rise of **anti-Catholic** organizations such as the American Protective Association prompted it to loosen membership rules and broaden its mission to include fighting prejudice. Initially dominated by Irish Americans, the Knights adopted an **Americanist** view of the role of Catholicism that proved inviting to Italians, Germans, Poles, and other **immigrant** groups. By the start of World War I, the Knights claimed over 300,000 members and had chapters in every state, other North American countries, and American dependencies such as the **Philippines**. Gradually, the organization also supported adult **education**, aid to veterans, the promotion of Catholic history, and ecumenical outreach to **Jews** and Protestants, including **African Americans**.

KNOX, PHILANDER C. (1853–1921). Lawyer and politician. Born in Pennsylvania, Knox was one of his state's most prominent corporate lawyers by the time his old friend, President **William McKinley**, appointed him as U.S. attorney general (1901–4). After McKinley's assassination, Knox worked with President **Theodore Roosevelt** on landmark **antitrust** cases such as the *Northern Securities* suit. Serving in the U.S. Senate (1904–9), Knox took relatively conservative positions on measures such the **Hepburn Act**. As secretary of state (1909–13) under President **William Howard Taft**, he oversaw much-needed administrative reforms but gained a reputation for being ineffective, largely due to his heavy-handed **dollar diplomacy** and failed efforts to counter Russian and Japanese economic influence in Manchuria. With regard to Latin America, he sold battleships to Argentina and persuaded U.S. bankers to refinance foreign debts in **Haiti** and **Nicaragua**. Knox returned to the Senate in 1917 and played a prominent part in the Republican fight against ratification of the Treaty of Versailles and **Woodrow Wilson**'s League of Nations plan. *See also* FOREIGN POLICY; REPUBLICAN PARTY.

KU KLUX KLAN. Founded in Georgia by William Joseph Simmons in 1915, the Invisible Empire of the Knights of the Ku Klux Klan (KKK) revived the name of a Reconstruction-era secret organization devoted to terrorizing **African Americans** and Union sympathizers.

The reborn Klan espoused a broader agenda, encompassing virulent, often violent **anti-Catholicism**, anti-Semitism, and opposition to **immigration**. Thomas Dixon's 1905 novel, *The Clansman*, and especially **D. W. Griffith**'s film version of this book, *The Birth of a Nation* (1915), contributed to the revival of the organization and its self-image as the savior of the United States from corruption and immorality. Groups such as the Daughters of the Confederacy had lobbied for a generation for a positive rewriting of the South's Lost Cause in the Civil War and Reconstruction that made the Klan seem heroic and not merely a terrorist group, a notion given scholarly sanction by the work of the **Dunning School** and like-minded historians. By the 1920s, the KKK gained strongholds in the Midwest, West, and even the East and became the country's most powerful hate group. *See also* AMERICANISM; LYNCHING; PROHIBITION; RACE RIOTS; SEGREGATION.

– L –

LABOR, U.S. DEPARTMENT OF. In March 1913, Congress passed an act to split the **Department of Commerce and Labor** into separate agencies, reflecting the growing political influence of the **American Federation of Labor** and the conciliatory approach to labor-capital relations of the **National Civic Federation** and **Commission on Industrial Relations**. Former **United Mine Workers** official **William B. Wilson** became the new department's first secretary and asserted responsibility for mediating labor disputes, investigating labor conditions, and overseeing **immigration**. Not until 1916 did Congress designate funds for the U.S. Conciliation Service, after which requests for departmental mediation surged, reaching nearly 1,200 during strife-ridden 1917–18. *See* AMERICAN ASSOCIATION FOR LABOR LEGISLATION; LABOR UNIONS.

LABOR UNIONS. The Progressive Era labor movement operated in the shadow of Gilded Age quarrels over organization and strategy. The Knights of Labor (KOL), founded in 1869 and led by Terence V. Powderly, grew steadily in the 1880s, with 729,000 members in 515 assemblies by 1887. This movement attempted a broad-ranging approach to both organization and program, pushing legislative reforms such as **eight-hour workday laws** and enrolling all types of workers, the skilled and unskilled, **women**, and **African Americans**. Loose organization and an unclear agenda made the Knights vulnerable to ill-coordinated local strikes, and the group was in disarray even before it was unfairly blamed for Chicago's Haymarket Riot in 1886. By 1899, the KOL had declined to only 100,000 members.

Determined to avoid the KOL's mistakes, trade unionists led by New York cigar maker **Samuel Gompers** organized the **American Federation of Labor (AFL)** in 1886. As the name suggests, the AFL was a federation of autonomous unions divided by trade and craft in metalwork, building, printing, and so on. By focusing on skilled workers—easiest to organize and hardest for employers to replace—the AFL succeeded in surviving the disasters of the 1890s, including the Homestead and Pullman strikes and that decade's severe depression. The costs of this strategy were a weak presence among semi-skilled and unskilled workers in strategic industries such as steel and acquiescence to many member unions' discrimination against blacks, women, and **immigrants**. Former **socialists**, Gompers and his allies adopted a strategy of "pure and simple" or "business" unionism that emphasized improved wages and working conditions won through direct negotiation with capitalists. Alienated by the fractious, doctrinaire socialist movement of the 1890s and sensitive to the diverse **Democratic** and **Republican** allegiances of members, Gompers eschewed partisan politics, even after a flexible, effective **Socialist Party** emerged under **Eugene V. Debs** and **Victor Berger**. AFL resistance to alliance with the Socialists largely accounts for the most obvious difference between the U.S. labor movement and those in Great Britain, France, and Germany, the failure of a powerful Labor or Social Democratic party to gain momentum.

For 38 years Gompers shaped the nation's major labor union, expanding the AFL slowly from 140,000 members in 1886 to 275,000 in 1893 and nearly two million by 1910. Whereas employers inveterately harassed more radical movements, such as the **Western Federation of Miners** and the **Industrial Workers of the World (IWW)** with lockouts, blacklists, injunctions, Pinkerton detectives, and strikebreakers, moderate industrialists saw the AFL as a responsible partner. **Marcus Hanna**, for example, worked with Gompers and **John Mitchell** of the **United Mine Workers (UMW)** to make the **National Civic Federation** into a vehicle for cooperative solutions to labor problems. Rival industrialists behind the **National Association of Manufacturers** took an uncompromising stance against all unionism and in favor of the **open shop**. The **Anthracite Coal Strike** of 1902, during which President **Theodore Roosevelt** compelled the intransigent, unpopular coal mine owners to negotiate with the UMW, seemed a harbinger of greater government acceptance of organized labor. But labor–management relations remained tense and frequently violent, with major corporations such as **United States Steel** persistently fighting unionization.

Labor complained bitterly of an unfair legal environment in which the **Supreme Court** regularly struck down even mild protective measures in cases such as *Lochner v. New York* (1905), while sanctioning the use of **antitrust** law to allow injunctions to break strikes and boycotts. These issues pushed the reluctant AFL toward political activism. When Democrats under **William Jennings Bryan** proved more receptive than the Republicans to the program spelled out in **Labor's Bill of Grievances** (1906), the AFL moved toward alliance with the Democrats. This alliance bore fruit in **New Freedom** measures such as the 1914 **Clayton Antitrust Act**, which gave labor limited protection against injunctions, but employers and the conservative judiciary continued to find rationales to limit unions.

Mostly ignored by the AFL, working-class women often adopted a sweeping reform agenda. The **International Ladies' Garment Workers' Union (ILGWU)** (1900) urged the AFL to demand pensions, health, safety, and welfare benefits for the 250,000 needle trade workers. Girls and women produced two-thirds of the nation's clothing in thousands of unregulated sweatshops in New York and other cities, earning five dollars or less for more than 60 hours of work per week. In New York, tens of thousands of **Jewish** and Italian women shirtwaist makers defied Gompers's cautious stance to launch the 1909 **Uprising of the Twenty Thousand**. The **Women's Trade Union League** supported the strike against employers, police, and **Tammany Hall**, and the ILGWU won some concessions. The next year, a cloakmakers' strike by multiethnic workers in New York City was more successful. In the **Lawrence Textile Strike** (1912), 23,000 largely female and immigrant Massachusetts workers—led by

IWW organizers **"Big Bill" Haywood** and Elizabeth Gurley Flynn—gained a rare victory for that radical organization. However, the failure of the 1913 **Paterson Strike** in the New Jersey silk factories ended the IWW's organizing campaign on the East Coast. The **Triangle Shirtwaist Company Fire** in 1911, meanwhile, demonstrated that workers needed safe conditions as well as higher wages, reinforcing the **reform movement** for state regulation of factories.

In 1913, President **Woodrow Wilson** recognized the role of labor unions in the Democratic Party and the country by appointing former UMW leader **William B. Wilson** as the first secretary of the newly founded **U.S. Department of Labor**. Wilson generally supported pro-labor legislation and addressed the AFL convention in Buffalo in 1917. During World War I, Gompers persuaded other labor leaders to support the Wilson administration with a national no-strike policy in exchange for recognition of the **living wage** concept. After the Armistice, the Wilson administration retreated from its friendly wartime stance, discrediting the aging Gompers and sparking a wave of angry strikes in 1919. Despite such setbacks, along with criticism of labor leaders for overlooking women, blacks, and unskilled workers, not developing an independent labor party, and not cooperating with **progressive** and socialist reformers, American workers had made progress by 1920. *See also* AMERICAN ASSOCIATION FOR LABOR LEGISLATION; BISBEE RAID; *BUCK'S STOVE* CASE; *BUNTING V. OREGON*; CHILD LABOR; COEUR D'ALENE, LABOR STRIFE AT; COMMONS, JOHN R.; CRIPPLE CREEK; DANBURY HATTERS' CASE; DARROW, CLARENCE; EMPLOYER LIABILITY LAWS; ERDMAN ACT; HILL, JOE; *HITCHMAN COAL & COKE V. MITCHELL*; INDUSTRIAL RELATIONS, COMMISSION ON; JONES, MARY HARRIS "MOTHER"; LUDLOW MASSACRE; MCNAMARA CASE; MINIMUM WAGE LEGISLATION; *MULLER V. OREGON*; NEWMAN, PAULINE; NEW YORK STATE FACTORY INVESTIGATING COMMISSION; O'REILLY, LEONORA; O'SULLIVAN, MARY KENNEY; SEAMEN'S ACT; TEAMSTERS, INTERNATIONAL BROTHERHOOD OF; WORKERS' COMPENSATION; YELLOW DOG CONTRACT.

LABOR'S BILL OF GRIEVANCES. Developed by the **American Federation of Labor (AFL)** in early 1906, these ten demands, aimed at Congress and President **Theodore Roosevelt**, included calls to limit court injunctions against strikers and exempt **labor unions** from the **antitrust** laws, restrict **convict leasing**, provide federal protection of **seamen**, enforce federal **eight-hour** legislation, and impose tighter limits on **immigration**, especially of Asians. By this departure from the AFL's customary avoidance of electoral politics, the organization hoped to influence both parties in the upcoming congressional elections. In the 1908 national election, however, the **Republicans** pointedly refused to adopt the bill of grievances, while the **Democratic Party** led by **William Jennings Bryan** responded favorably. After Democrats gained control of the House of Representatives in 1910 and then the presidency in 1912, they pursued a legislative program influenced by the AFL's demands, solidifying the nascent alliance between organized labor and the Democrats. *See also* CLAYTON ANTITRUST ACT; GOMPERS, SAMUEL; NEW FREEDOM.

LACEY ACT (1900). Sponsored by Iowa **Republican** congressman John F. Lacey, this act banned the interstate transport of animals or birds killed in violation of state laws. This federal endorsement of state **conservation** laws curtailed the market for illegally killed birds, whose feathers decorated fashionable women's hats. It also enabled the Department of Agriculture to prevent importation of birds, plants, and animals dangerous to farming and to encourage the preservation and restoration of wild and game birds. Upheld by the **U.S. Supreme Court** in 1908, the act remains the oldest federal statute for wildlife protection. It was strengthened in 1916 by the **Migratory Bird Treaty.**

LADIES' HOME JOURNAL. See BOK, EDWARD WILLIAM; MASS-CIRCULATION MAGAZINES.

LAEMMLE, CARL (1867–1939). Filmmaker and businessman. Born in Germany, Laemmle emigrated to Chicago in 1884. Opening a nickelodeon in Chicago in 1906, he soon became a film distributor and, when the supply ran short, produced 300 short films himself by 1910. He moved his company to Hollywood (1915) and renamed it **Universal Studios.** The world's largest **movie** operation by the

1920s, Universal introduced the movie star concept and popularized long feature films with complex narratives.

LA FLESCHE, FRANCIS (1857–1932). Anthropologist. Born in Nebraska on the Omaha reservation, La Flesche attended a Presbyterian-run boarding school. A translator for **Alice Fletcher** during the allotment of Omaha land in the 1880s, he initially supported the **Dawes Allotment Act** but later rejected it when its devastating consequences for **Native Americans** became obvious. Adopted by Fletcher, he lived with her in Washington, D.C., earned a law degree, and worked as a clerk in the Bureau of Indian Affairs until becoming an anthropologist at the Bureau of American Ethnology in 1910. His best-known writings are a memoir of his experience with **Indian education** (1900) and a monumental study of the Omaha tribe, coauthored with Fletcher (1911), as well as an Osage dictionary and recordings of many Osage rituals.

LA FOLLETTE, BELLE CASE (1859–1931). Reformer and editor. Born into a Wisconsin farming family, La Follette in 1885 was the first woman to graduate from the University of Wisconsin Law School. In the 1890s and 1900s, she assisted her husband, **Robert M. La Follette**, in his political career and law practice while raising four children. When they launched the **progressive** *La Follette's Magazine* in 1909, Belle became an editor and columnist, writing on issues from **women**'s rights, **education**, family, and health to penal reform and **segregation**. She also lectured on women's **suffrage** and advocated for peace organizations. After her husband's death, she resisted calls to run for his Senate seat, devoting herself instead to their magazine, renamed *The Progressive* in 1929, and wrote her husband's biography.

LA FOLLETTE, ROBERT M. (1855–1925). Politician. Born in Wisconsin, La Follette graduated from the University of Wisconsin (1879) and became a lawyer in Madison. A champion orator, he rose quickly in the **Republican Party**, serving as district attorney (1880–84) and winning three terms in the U.S. House of Representatives (1885–91) before being defeated in the **Democratic Party** landslide of 1890. During the 1890s, he emerged as a popular critic of the state

Republican **machine**, which he saw as a tool of timber and railroad interests. After two unsuccessful runs for governor, he won his third campaign in 1900 and pressed a broad reform program. **Progressive journalists** such as **Lincoln Steffens** and **Frederic Howe** drew national attention to the Wisconsin governor as a champion of business regulation, worker and consumer protection, **conservation**, a state **income tax**, the **direct primary**, and other measures. In devising legislation and developing policy, he enlisted the aid of University of Wisconsin scholars such as **Richard Ely**, **John R. Commons**, and **Charles McCarthy**, an approach that became known as the **Wisconsin Idea**.

Elected to the U.S. Senate in 1905, La Follette criticized the **Hepburn Act** as too lenient to railroads, which brought him into conflict with both the **Old Guard** party leaders and President **Theodore Roosevelt**. The two men's mutual dislike and rival ambitions hampered efforts to make the Republicans more **progressive**. To gain a national forum, La Follette and his wife, **Belle Case La Follette**, founded *La Follette's Magazine* (1909; later named *The Progressive*).

By 1910, La Follette ranked as the leading Republican **insurgent**. In January 1911, Senate allies helped him found the **National Progressive Republican League**. Although ill health and an untimely public outburst derailed La Follette's own candidacy, he could not bring himself to support Roosevelt, the candidate of the **Progressive Party**. These divisions among Republicans led to the election of Democrat **Woodrow Wilson**, whose **New Freedom** legislative agenda included measures La Follette had long favored; indeed, he allied with Democrats to push through the **Seamen's Act** (1915). Reelected three times (1906–25), "Fighting Bob" persisted as a champion of progressive policies even as his party became increasingly conservative. He attacked U.S. involvement in World War I and the suppression of antiwar dissent with such vehemence that the Wisconsin state legislature censured him and the Senate debated expelling him.

LANSING, ROBERT (1864–1928). Lawyer and diplomat. Born in New York, Lansing graduated from Amherst College (1886), studied law, and became a partner in his father's firm (1889–92). Son-in-law of Secretary of State John W. Foster, he developed an interest in international law and served as counsel for the United States in many **arbitration** cases, including the **Alaska Boundary Dispute**, while representing foreign governments such as Mexico and Russia in Washington, D.C. A founder of the American Society for International Law, he became State Department counsel (1914) and then secretary of state (1915–20) under **Democratic** president **Woodrow Wilson**. Lansing counseled the administration to intervene in the **Mexican Revolution**, the **Dominican Republic**, and **Haiti**. He negotiated the purchase of the Virgin Islands from Denmark in 1917 and signed the 1917 Lansing–Ishi agreement with Japan. Although an architect of the neutrality policy at the start of World War I, Lansing's preference for the Allies and hostility toward Germany and his doubts about Wilson's postwar peace plans led to the secretary's resignation in February 1920. *See also* FOREIGN POLICY; INTERNATIONALISM.

LASKY, JESSE LOUIS (1880–1958). Filmmaker and businessman. Born in San Francisco, Lasky failed as a prospector in the Alaska gold rush, formed a bugle duet with his sister, and then turned to managing other **vaudeville** acts. In 1913, Lasky partnered with his brother-in-law Samuel Goldwyn and director Cecil B. DeMille to found a successful **movie** production company based in Hollywood. In 1916, Lasky Feature Play Company merged with **Adolph Zukor**'s Famous Players, later taking the name of its distribution company, **Paramount Pictures**.

LATHROP, JULIA CLIFFORD (1858–1932). Reformer. Born in Illinois, Lathrop graduated from Vassar College (1880) and worked in her father's law office while campaigning on behalf of **women**'s **suffrage** and other causes. In 1890, she moved to Chicago's **Hull House**. Appointed to the Illinois Board of Charities in 1893, she investigated the state's charitable institutions, visited Europe to study reforms there, and proposed far-reaching changes that enhanced the board's professionalism and power. She devoted her energy to **immigrant** welfare, helped to establish innovative **juvenile courts**, and contributed to the founding of the Chicago School of Civics and Philanthropy. A concerted campaign by women reformers in 1912 convinced President **William Howard Taft** to appoint her to head the new **Children's Bureau**, making her the first female bureau chief in the United States. *See also* CHILD LABOR; MACK, JULIAN; REFORM MOVEMENTS; SETTLEMENT HOUSE MOVEMENT.

LAWRENCE TEXTILE STRIKE (1912). In the early 1900s, about 40,000 people (roughly half the population over age 14) in the city of Lawrence, Massachusetts, worked in textile mills, many of them part of the American Woolen Company. In January 1912, when a state law reducing the work week for **women** and children from 56 to 54 hours went into effect, the American Woolen Company cut pay in proportion, outraging workers who struggled to live on an average weekly pay of $8.76. Within days, 23,000 workers of 40 nationalities, most of them women, went on strike. The **Industrial Workers of the World (IWW)** sent a young organizer, Joseph Ettor, to coordinate the protest, but when he was arrested after a woman striker died in violence largely provoked by police and state militia, the IWW sent in its prominent leaders, including **"Big Bill" Haywood**. A notable feature of this strike was sending workers' children to sympathizers in other cities. On 24 February, police and militia prevented 150 children from being sent to Philadelphia for their protection. The spectacle of children wrestled from their parents and thrown into patrol wagons prompted a congressional investigation. On 12 March, the American Woolen Company gave in to strikers' wage demands. This strike represented a high point for the IWW and helped prompt formation of the **U.S. Department of Labor**. *See also* CHILD LABOR; LABOR UNIONS; PATERSON STRIKE.

LEAGUE TO ENFORCE PEACE. Founded in June 1915 after the *Lusitania* sinking, this organization campaigned for an international organization to conciliate disputes between countries and exert military pressure on aggressor nations. With **William Howard Taft** as its first president, the league represented moderate to conservative **internationalist** opinion. President **Woodrow Wilson** first put forth his idea for a League of Nations in a speech to this group in May 1916. Claiming 300,000 members in 1919, it split apart during the quarrel over U.S. ratification of the Versailles Treaty ending World War I. *See also* ARBITRATION TREATIES; CARNEGIE ENDOWMENT FOR INTERNATIONAL PEACE; FOREIGN POLICY.

LINDSAY, NICHOLAS VACHEL (1879–1931). Poet. An Illinois native, Lindsay studied art in Chicago and New York before devoting himself to poetry. In 1906, he began the first of many tramps around the United States, supporting himself by reciting, lecturing, and selling printed poems. Earning a reputation as an idiosyncratic modern troubadour, he recounted these travels in *Adventures while Preaching the Gospel of Beauty* (1914). His elegy on the Salvation Army's founder, "General William Booth Enters into Heaven," published in *Poetry* in 1913, brought him acclaim. In his celebrated recitals, his performance veered from chanting to revivalist preaching and ragtime. Many well-known poems took a populist stance, as in "Abraham Lincoln Walks at Midnight" (1914) and "Bryan, Bryan, Bryan, Bryan" (1919). Revolted by the 1908 **Springfield Riot**, Lindsay denounced racism, but **W. E. B. Du Bois** dismissed efforts such as the 1914 poem "The Congo" as patronizing. *See also* LITERATURE.

LINDSEY, BENJAMIN B. (1869–1943). Jurist and juvenile justice reformer. Born in Tennessee, he moved with his family to Denver, Colorado, in 1880, where he became a lawyer in 1894. His **Democratic Party** ties led to his appointment in 1901 as a Denver county judge. Persuading the district attorney to refer juvenile cases to him, Lindsey established a separate court based on the assumption that children ran into trouble because of bad influences and deserved sympathy, not punishment. He did away with courtroom formalities and stressed personal dealings with offenders, probation, and ongoing contact with **immigrant** street gangs. Gaining national attention, he soon became the country's most highly regarded expert on **juvenile courts**. An opponent of Denver's **machine** politics, Lindsey ran unsuccessfully for governor as an independent in 1906 and helped organize the **Progressive Party** in 1912. He espoused a range of **reform movements** from **Henry Ford**'s Peace Ship to **women**'s **suffrage**, **birth control**, and easier **divorce** laws. *See also* ADOLESCENCE; LATHROP, JULIA CLIFFORD; MACK, JULIAN.

LIPPMANN, WALTER (1889–1974). Political writer and journalist. From a **Jewish** family in New York City, Lippmann graduated from Harvard University (1910), where he studied with **George Santayana** and **William James**. Taking up reform **journalism** and politics, Lippmann worked briefly for **Lincoln Steffens** and the **Socialist** mayor of Schenectady, New York, and dabbled in the bohemian life of **Greenwich Village**. Here he learned about psychoanalysis, which he fused with **pragmatism**, moderate socialist ideas, and other **modernist** intellectual currents in his first book, *A Preface to Politics* (1912), a widely read critique of **progressive** moralism and call for positive government and social reform. **Herbert Croly**, whose **New Nationalism** expressed similar views, recruited Lippmann as an editor of the *New Republic*, which they quickly built into the period's leading magazine of liberal opinion. Lippmann meanwhile published *Drift and Mastery* (1914), a systematic exposition of the pro-government, technocratic impulse within progressivism. Despite publishing critiques of the **antitrust** views expressed by **Woodrow Wilson** in his 1912 presidential campaign, Lippmann admired much of the **New Freedom** in practice and gradually entered Wilson's circle of informal advisers, after which he had a long career as a syndicated columnist and public affairs writer. *See also* INTELLECTUAL.

LITERACY TESTS. Illiteracy became a rationale for **disfranchisement** and **immigration** restriction in the 1890s. Several southern and southwestern states imposed literacy tests between 1890 and 1910 as a means of preventing **African American** men from registering to vote. These laws often included "understanding" clauses that allowed illiterate men to vote if they could convince a registrar (always white) that they understood a passage of the state constitution. In *Williams v. Mississippi* (1898), the **U.S. Supreme Court** sanctioned such legislation. Although most common in the South, reformers elsewhere at times favored restricting the suffrage to "the better class" through literacy tests. The **Immigration Restriction League** campaigned for a ban on illiterate immigrants in 1895 and achieved its goal with the 1917 Immigration Act. *See also* POLL TAXES; SEGREGATION.

LITERATURE. As with **art** and **intellectual** life, American literature in the Progressive Era represented a culmination of and reaction to trends begun in the Gilded Age. The often romantic regionalism known as the "local color school" remained popular, identified with gifted **women** writers such as Sarah Orne Jewett (1849–1909), author of *The Country of the Pointed Firs* (1896), and Mary Wilkins Freeman (1852–1930), known for *A New England Nun and Other Stories* (1891). Joel Chandler Harris (1848–1908) was the best known of many authors who played on the romance of the Old South, a region that **African American** authors such as Paul Laurence Dunbar (1872–1906) and **Charles W. Chesnutt** presented subtly from an alternative perspective. In *The Awakening* (1899) by **Kate Chopin**, southern regionalism provided a backdrop for a dark story with **naturalist** and **feminist** undertones. In his time, Mark Twain (Samuel L. Clemens, 1835–1910) was known mainly as a regionalist, but one who elevated southern and western humor and vernacular into art. In **Hamlin Garland**'s stories, the Great Plains provided a setting for a bleak **realism**. **Willa Cather** made her reputation with novels of the plains such as *O Pioneers!* (1913), before turning her attention to the Southwest, also the subject of **Mary Austin**'s writing. **Owen Wister**'s *The Virginian* (1902) and Zane Grey's *Riders of the Purple Sage* (1912) created the stereotyped western genre, which quickly migrated into the **movies**. **John Muir** was influential in expanding the **conservation** movement with *The Mountains of California* (1894) and *My First Summer in the Sierra* (1911), while **Theodore Roosevelt** also wrote prolifically about the western frontier.

A champion of many authors and genres, **William Dean Howells** drew attention to realist novelists such as **Edith Wharton** and **Henry James**, who in style and theme aspired to be cosmopolitan and not particularly American. In dense, later novels such as *Wings of the Dove* (1902), James explored shifting perspectives and indirect revelation of plots in ways that qualified him as an early exemplar of **modernism**. Howells also drew attention to American naturalist followers of Émile Zola, especially **Frank Norris**, who in turn promoted **Theodore Dreiser**, whose often crude art conveyed the atmosphere of cities such as Chicago. Garland and Dreiser were major figures in the short-lived **Chicago Renaissance**, which helped establish the modern city as a subject of prose and poetry. **Stephen Crane**'s *Maggie: A Girl of the Streets* (1893) presented a menacing, naturalistic view of the urban underworld. **Jack London** evoked naturalistic themes in prolific writings set in both wilderness and cities.

In the decade before World War I, editors such as **Margaret Anderson**, Harriet Monroe, founder of *Poetry*, and Floyd Dell, later a **Greenwich Village** writer and coeditor of *The Masses*, made Chicago a center for innovative poetry, publishing **Edgar Lee Masters**, **Vachel Lindsay**, and **Carl Sandburg**, among others. The generation of innovative New England– and New York–area poets such as Edward Arlington Robinson, Robert Frost, H. D., and Amy Lowell began to gain attention in the mid-1910s, years when the prominent modernist poets Ezra Pound and T. S. Eliot had just started publishing.

The Progressive Era saw publication of such diverse works on the African American experience as **Booker T. Washington**'s autobiography *Up From Slavery* (1901) and **W. E. B. Du Bois**'s *The Souls of Black Folk* (1903), along with **James Weldon Johnson**'s fictional *Autobiography of an Ex-Colored Man* (1912). **Jewish immigrant** life provided a source for **Abraham Cahan** and **Mary Antin,** while **Hutchins Hapgood**'s *The Spirit of the Ghetto* (1902) offered a sympathetic outsider's portrait of the **Lower East Side**. With his character, Chicago bartender Mr. Dooley, **Finley Peter Dunne** helped turn the urban Irishman from an object of derision into a source of wisdom and humor.

With *How the Other Half Lives* (1890), **Jacob Riis** helped to create one of the period's truly influential genres, **muckraking** reform literature. Crusading **journalists** published many widely read books, a small sample including **Ida Tarbell**'s *History of the Standard Oil Company* (1904), **Lincoln Steffens**'s *The Shame of the Cities* (1904), **Ray Stannard Baker**'s *Following the Color Line* (1906), and David Graham Phillips's *The Treason of the Senate* (1906). **Upton Sinclair**'s *The Jungle* (1906) qualified as muckraking in the guise of a novel. The **Hearst** and **Pulitzer** newspapers made celebrities of correspondents such as **Richard Harding Davis**, while Ring Lardner (1885–1933) was the most distinguished of a generation that made literature out of sports.

Greenwich Village figures George Cram Cook and **Susan Glaspell** promoted modernistic drama through projects such as the **Provincetown Players**, which gave a start to former drifter and sailor Eugene O'Neill. The London Jewish writer **Israel Zangwill** coined a new phrase for cultural diversity with his Broadway play *The Melting Pot* (1908). Broadway also introduced new forms of theater with the multitalented **George M. Cohan** in 1901 and the **Ziegfeld Follies** in 1907. *See also* ADAMS, BROOKS; ADAMS, HENRY; BAUM, L. FRANK; BELASCO, DAVID; BOURNE, RANDOLPH S.; BROOKS, VAN

WYCK; COMSTOCK, ANTHONY; FARMER, FANNIE MER-
RITT; GILMAN, CHARLOTTE PERKINS; HUNEKER, JAMES
GIBBONS; JAMES, WILLIAM; RAUSCHENBUSCH, WALTER;
SANTAYANA, GEORGE; VEBLEN, THORSTEIN.

LITTLE REVIEW. See ANDERSON, MARGARET; CHICAGO RE-
NAISSANCE; MODERNISM.

LIVING WAGE. Popularized in Father **John A. Ryan**'s 1906 book,
A Living Wage: Its Economic and Ethical Aspects, this concept held
that an adult male working a reasonable number of hours per week
had a right to earn enough to house, clothe, and feed a family de-
cently. The assertion of the right to a living wage reflected **Social
Gospel** and social justice concerns, as well as anxiety over the rising
cost of living. Research by Ryan, **socialist journalist** Robert Hunter,
and others demonstrated that between 40 and 60 percent of adult
male workers failed to earn enough to support a family. Low wages
contributed mightily to **child labor**, long hours, and other workplace
abuses. The living wage won support from advocates of **minimum
wage legislation**, **social insurance**, and other public-sector interventions in the labor market. Many **women** reformers supported the idea,
though it implied that women should not participate in waged work.

LOCAL OPTION. This phrase described state laws that enabled towns
and counties to hold special elections to decide whether to ban liquor
sales within their boundaries. These laws, high license fees, and other
regulatory measures became popular in the early 20th century, when
the **Woman's Christian Temperance Union** and the **Anti-Saloon
League** supported them as pragmatic steps toward total **prohibition**.
The number of "dry" localities fluctuated as voters changed their
minds and brewers and **saloon**-keepers fought back, until the **Eighteenth Amendment** banned alcohol nationwide.

LOCHNER V. NEW YORK **(1905).** This controversial 5–4 **Supreme
Court** decision in April 1905 arose from a case in which bakery
owner Joseph Lochner was fined $50 for violating an 1895 New
York state law that limited bakery workers to 10 hours per day or 60
hours per week. Writing for the majority, Justice Rufus Peckham dis-

missed the New York law as an unreasonable and arbitrary violation of the doctrine of substantive due process, which guaranteed freedom of contract unless compelling evidence of risk to **public health** or safety existed. Dissents by Justices **John Marshall Harlan** and **Oliver Wendell Holmes** set precedents for subsequent rulings that upheld labor legislation, such as *Muller v. Oregon* (1908) and *Bunting v. Oregon* (1917). Citing evidence that long hours worked in bakeries posed a health hazard, Harlan insisted that the burden of proof was on the courts to show that a state law to promote social well-being represented an unconstitutional violation of liberty of contract. Holmes argued that neither laissez-faire nor any other economic theory was embedded in the Constitution, and a rational person could easily find grounds within that document to justify the state regulation of hours. *See also* EIGHT-HOUR WORKDAY LAWS; SOCIOLOGICAL JURISPRUDENCE.

LODGE, HENRY CABOT (1850–1924). Politician. Born into a prominent Boston family, Lodge earned his B.A. and law degrees from Harvard before taking the first Ph.D. in political science granted by that institution (1876). A successful scholar, he served in the Massachusetts legislature (1880–81) and gained national attention and the friendship of **Theodore Roosevelt** during the 1880 and 1884 **Republican Party** presidential nominating conventions. Although Lodge was more conservative than Roosevelt on domestic issues, he and the future president shared a vision of the United States as a great power. In the U.S. House of Representatives (1887–93), Lodge fought against the **disfranchisement** of southern **African Americans**. Elected to the Senate (1893–1924), he became its most effective proponent of **imperialism** and the assertion of American national interests in the world, sitting on the Senate Foreign Relations committee (for many years as chair), the committee on the **Philippines**, and the **Alaska Boundary** Commission (1903). When Senator **George F. Hoar** demanded an investigation of war crimes in the **Philippine–American War** in 1902, Lodge led a committee whose hearings he designed to accomplish little. As chair of the Senate **Immigration** committee, member of the **U.S. Immigration Commission** (1907–10), and spokesman for the **Immigration Restriction League**, he advocated a **literacy test** to restrict eastern and southern

European immigrants. Increasingly hostile to President **Woodrow Wilson**, Lodge supported U.S. entry into World War I but led the successful fight against Senate ratification of the Treaty of Versailles that ended the war.

LOEWE V. LAWLOR (1908). *See* DANBURY HATTERS' CASE.

LONDON, JACK (1876–1916). Author. A San Francisco native, London grew up in poverty. The hardships he survived, from working with oyster pirates to sailing with seal hunters, tramping with an offshoot of Coxey's Army, and being jailed for vagrancy, provided material for fiction that won him acclaim, at first through stories in **mass-circulation magazines**. In 1903, *Call of the Wild*, a novel inspired by his adventures in the Alaska Gold Rush, became a bestseller. He kept up a draining schedule of writing, travel, reporting on wars from the Russo–Japanese conflict to the U.S. occupation of **Veracruz**, and hard living. Influenced by **social Darwinism**, **socialism**, **naturalism**, Friedrich Nietzsche, Carl Jung, Rudyard Kipling, and the cult of the **strenuous life**, London wrote on a prodigious variety of subjects, from the Klondike to life at sea and including the English working class (*People of the Abyss* [1903]), totalitarianism (*The Iron Heel* [1908]), his struggles to learn (*Martin Eden* [1909]), and his fight with alcoholism (*John Barleycorn* [1913]). He ran twice on the **Socialist** ticket for mayor of Oakland. *See also* CRANE, STEPHEN; LITERATURE; NORRIS, BENJAMIN FRANKLIN.

LONDON, MEYER (1871–1926). Lawyer and politician. Born in a Russian-held province of Poland, London studied law at New York University after his arrival in the United States in 1891. Admitted to the bar (1896), he dedicated himself to serving the immigrant **Jews** of the **Lower East Side**. Legal counsel for the Workmen's Circle, he also represented textile unions, including the **International Ladies' Garment Workers' Union** in the 1910 negotiations that led to the so-called Protocol of Peace. A founding member of the **Socialist Party of America**, London was a moderate who, unlike **Morris Hillquit**, avoided the factionalism that hampered the party. Elected to two terms in the U.S. House of Representatives (1915–19), he lost his seat to a pro–World War I candidate in 1918. When he was struck and killed by a taxicab in 1926, 50,000 people marched in his funeral parade, and hundreds of thousands lined the streets of the Lower East Side.

LONE WOLF V. HITCHCOCK **(1903).** This unanimous **U.S. Supreme Court** ruling concerned a suit by Kiowa-Comanche landowners to halt implementation of the **Dawes Allotment Act** on their reservation in the **Indian Territory**. Lone Wolf and the other complainants argued that the Treaty of Medicine Lodge (1867) guaranteed no further land cessions without the signatures of at least three-fourths of adult male Kiowa-Comanches. The court rejected this argument as well as vestiges of the old principle that the federal government's relationship with **Native American** peoples was diplomatic and governed by treaties. Congress, the court asserted, had the power to govern Native peoples. The sweeping ruling undermined presidential discretion over allotment as well as provisions of the Dawes Act requiring tribal consent to land sales. As a result, allotment accelerated and Indian communities lost ever greater amounts of land.

LOW, SETH (1850–1916). Politician and university president. Born in Brooklyn, New York, Low won two terms as Brooklyn's mayor (1881–85) as a reform **Republican**, compiling a successful record as an advocate for civil service reform, public **education**, and **home rule**. As president of Columbia University (1890–1901), he oversaw the school's transformation into a modern **university** and its move to a new McKim, Mead, and White campus in upper Manhattan. After working for the consolidation of **New York City**, he lost a race for New York mayor (1897) to **Tammany** candidate Robert Van Wyck, but when one of New York's periodic reactions against Tammany occurred, Low won the office in 1901. Striking voters as aloof and patrician, overly concerned with **efficiency** and Sunday closing laws, he lost his 1903 reelection bid to another Tammany candidate. A prominent opponent of **immigration restriction**, he served as president of the **National Civic Federation** and on the board of trustees of **Tuskegee Institute**. *See also* STRUCTURAL REFORM.

LOWER EAST SIDE. Located below Fourteenth Street and east of the Bowery on Manhattan Island in New York City, this neighborhood was home to some 500,000 eastern European **Jews** by 1910, and the number grew rapidly until World War I cut off European **immigration.** Occupying the most densely populated area of the United States, the residents lived in shabby, crowded tenement houses and worked in small businesses, factories, and sweatshops. They supported an array of Yiddish-language newspapers, such as **Abraham Cahan**'s *Jewish Daily Forward,* as well as theaters, orthodox and conservative synagogues, kosher butcher shops, and other cultural institutions. Novels by Cahan and Anzia Yezierska portrayed the experiences of immigrant Jews and their **Americanizing** children here. Not a ghetto in the sense of the mandatory, homogenous enclaves that existed in Europe, the Lower East Side was always a multiethnic neighborhood. *See also* HAPGOOD, HUTCHINS; INTERNATIONAL LADIES' GARMENT WORKERS' UNION; TENEMENT HOUSE ACT; WALD, LILLIAN.

LUDLOW MASSACRE (1914). In 1913, the **United Mine Workers** began organizing in Colorado's mining communities, areas notorious for years of strife between miners and mine owners. Among the companies refusing to recognize the **labor union** was **John D. Rockefeller**'s Colorado Fuel & Iron Company. About 8,000 miners on strike in the fall of 1913 demanded union recognition, a 10 percent raise, and the enforcement of state hours and safety laws. Evicted from company-owned housing, the strikers and their families spent the winter in tents. Federal mediation failed, and in April 1914, the occasional violence between the state militia and strikers turned into a sustained gun battle that culminated in the soldiers' setting fire to the tents. Ten male strikers and a child died in the battle; two women and 11 children suffocated in a dugout below the burning camp in one of the deadliest labor conflicts in the 20th century. Even after federal troops arrived, Rockefeller continued to refuse mediation, relying on public relations expert Ivy Lee to redeem his reputation. The strike failed in the fall of 1914. *See also* CRIPPLE CREEK; INDUSTRIAL RELATIONS, COMMISSION ON.

LUMMIS, CHARLES FLETCHER (1859–1928). Journalist, author, and editor. Born in Massachusetts, Lummis first achieved national notoriety by walking from Cincinnati to Los Angeles in 1884. After a stroke in 1887, he lived for some time in the **Native American** community of Isleta Pueblo and took an interest in native and Hispanic folklore, archaeology, and historic preservation. Back in California, he founded the Landmarks Club (1895) to preserve the Spanish colonial mission churches and promoted the region via the magazine *Land of Sunshine* (1894; renamed *Out West* in 1900), which published the works of **Mary Austin** and **Jack London**, among other western writers. Along with the **Atchison, Topeka, and Santa Fe Railroad** and the Fred Harvey Company, Lummis was a key figure in popularizing a romantic vision of the Southwest and southern California. The Spanish government knighted him in 1915 for his pioneering folklore collections.

LUSITANIA. On 7 May 1915, a submarine enforcing the German-declared war zone around the British Isles sank this British Cunard Line passenger ship without warning. One hundred twenty-eight Americans were among the 1,198 people who died, out of 1,959 on board. President **Woodrow Wilson** demanded that Germany pay indemnity for the victims and cease to threaten passenger liners. Initially rejecting these demands, German leaders contended that the ocean liner had been carrying contraband armaments and that passengers had received fair warning through New York newspaper advertisements. Wilson's insistence on his demands led Secretary of State **William Jennings Bryan** to resign in protest; in Bryan's view the policy of neutrality required Wilson to protest as well to Great Britain about its armaments shipments and to warn Americans not to sail on British ships that might carry arms. The Germans gradually met most of Wilson's demands, but in the meantime **Robert Lansing**, who favored the Allies, replaced Bryan, and the Wilson administration signaled that a renewal of submarine warfare would probably prompt American entry into World War I. *See also* FOREIGN POLICY.

LYNCHING. The practice of extralegal torture and execution, lynching was a common weapon in the arsenal that white southerners deployed against **African Americans** to impose **segregation** and **disfranchisement**. Beginning in the 1880s, black Americans (mostly men, but also a few women) constituted the majority of victims, although **Jews** such as **Leo Frank**, Mexican Americans and Mexican **immigrants**, Chinese residents, and labor organizers were also targets. Vigilante committees lynched some 100 to 200 people every year between 1882, when the **Tuskegee Institute** began keeping records, and 1903, by which time Jim Crow was solidly established in most of the southern states. Lynching also occurred in other regions and throughout the 20th century, but it reached its height in the South during the Progressive Era.

Although illegal, lynchings were frequently public events advertised in the newspapers and attended by large crowds of white men, women, and children. After being tortured and sometimes castrated, victims might be shot, hanged, or burned at the stake, or suffer a combination of these assaults. Their body parts were sometimes photographed or preserved and displayed as souvenirs and postcards. Contemporaries justified these murders by claiming that the victims had earned a gruesome death by raping white women. Many educated whites regretted the failure of the legal system but gave credence to this rationale. This scenario was central to the plot of **D. W. Griffith**'s film *The Birth of a Nation* (1915), which celebrated the **Ku Klux Klan**'s violent reimposition of white supremacy in the South.

But the facts contradicted the perpetrators' claims. Drawing on accounts in white-owned southern newspapers, **Ida B. Wells-Barnett** demonstrated in the 1890s that most lynching victims were not even charged with rape, and when they were, there was little or no proof to sustain the accusation. Instead, she and later scholars have shown that black victims had often incurred the mob's wrath by challenging Jim Crow through demanding fair wages, running a successful business, or arguing with a white person. Upon its founding in 1910, the **National Association for the Advancement of Colored People** took up the battle against lynching. Although white **progressives** disapproved of extralegal violence, bills banning lynching regularly failed in Congress. The U.S. Senate formally apologized for its refusal to act against lynching in 2005. *See also* RACE RIOTS; WATSON, THOMAS E.

– M –

MACARTHUR, ARTHUR, JR. (1845–1912). Army officer. Born in Massachusetts, MacArthur earned a Medal of Honor (awarded in 1890) for his Civil War service. During the **Spanish–American War**, he participated in the capture of Manila and oversaw the city's occupation. When the **Philippine–American War** broke out in February 1899, he commanded Northern Luzon until succeeding Elwell S. Otis as military governor and commander of the archipelago in May 1900. Combining aggressive warfare against Filipino guerrillas with conciliatory measures for civilians, MacArthur eroded the Filipino resistance. In 1901, he authorized **Frederick Funston** to capture Filipino leader **Emilio Aguinaldo**. MacArthur ceded authority to a civilian administration led by **William Howard Taft** in July 1901, served as an observer with the Japanese army in the Russo–Japanese War (1904–5), and retired as a major general in 1909. His son, General Douglas MacArthur, would gain even greater fame and notoriety in the Pacific during World War II and the Korean War. *See also* PHILIPPINES, COLONIAL GOVERNMENT OF.

MACHINE POLITICS. *Machine* was the term commonly used to describe the organizations run by political **bosses**; it suggested a party held together not by shared principles or interests but by a network of patronage, graft, and favor trading. The stereotyped "machine" was a political party that devoted itself to winning elected office and using power and political connections to enrich members with no overriding policy goals or concern for the public welfare. Most historians cite 1880–1930 as the heyday of urban machine politics. By 1900, political scientists and professional **journalists** had begun to analyze the systemic and social circumstances that produced machines and bosses. According to **muckrakers** such as **Lincoln Steffens** and scholars such as James Bryce, the British author of the influential *American Commonwealth* (1888), machine politics arose from an unfortunate combination of a complex nominating and electoral system; a disengaged, short-sighted, impoverished, or ignorant electorate; and the huge stake that business had in municipal contracts, utility and transit franchises, and licensing and regulation. **Progressives** saw cities, with their **immigrant**, working-class voters, as the primary locus of machines, but later research has shown that citywide organizations such as New York's **Tammany Hall** were rare. Most urban politics still entailed loose alliances of ward bosses. Statewide machines, such as **Thomas Platt**'s Republican operation in New York and **Arthur Gorman**'s Democratic operation in Maryland, showed that rural and small town voters could provide a base for such operations. Because the **Democratic Party** successfully attracted urban, ethnic voters, many believed that this party was especially prone to machine politics, but machine-style **Republican Party** organizations existed in Philadelphia, Pittsburgh, and Cincinnati.

Most progressives condemned machine politics, although some gave ward bosses credit for helping the urban poor, a dimension highlighted—along with unabashed influence peddling—in journalist William Riordan's book, *Plunkitt of Tammany Hall* (1905). Progressives generally argued that a combination of **structural reforms**, **education**, improved social services, and civil service and professionalism in public administration would replace machine politics with civic-minded, effective government. **Direct primaries** and the direct election of **senators** undermined state machines, but urban machines may have been strengthened by reforms such as the **commission** and **strong mayor systems**. In turn, machines sometimes nominated progressives in the belief that the reformers could win elections but the machine could control them, as in the case of Tammany boss **Charles Murphy**'s support for **Robert F. Wagner** and **Alfred E. Smith** or **Woodrow Wilson**'s election as New Jersey governor. At the same time, observers such as **Frederic Howe** noted the tendency of big-city progressives such as Cleveland's **Tom Johnson** to adopt machine tactics and cooperate with machine politicians to achieve electoral or policy goals, a tendency that became a component of **urban liberalism**.

MACK, JULIAN (1866–1943). Judge and juvenile justice reformer. Born in San Francisco and raised in Cincinnati, Mack helped found the *Harvard Law Review* while at Harvard Law School. While teaching law at Northwestern University (1895–1902) and the **University of Chicago** (1902–11), he became involved in charities for eastern European **Jewish immigrants**. Elected a county judge as a **Democrat** in 1903, he implemented **juvenile court** reforms similar to those of **Benjamin Lindsey** in Denver and Harvey H. Baker in Boston. In 1905, Mack rose to the Illinois appellate court and then in 1911 to the U.S. **Commerce Court**; after the latter's abolition in 1913, he became a federal circuit judge, the first Jew to rise so high in the federal judiciary. He helped organize the 1909 White House conference that led to the **Children's Bureau** and also participated in Zionist organizations. *See also* LATHROP, JULIA CLIFFORD.

MAHAN, ALFRED THAYER (1840–1914). Naval officer and military theorist. Born in New York, Mahan became an instructor at military academies after serving in the Civil War. In 1886, while teaching at the Naval War College, he gave a series of lectures that, when published as *The Influence of Sea Power upon History* (1890), generated enormous discussion in Great Britain, Japan, Germany, and the United States. He argued that national political and economic supremacy depended on a strong merchant marine backed by a navy capable of projecting power over the oceans. Mahan in effect called for the **modernization** and expansion of the U.S. Navy and acquisition of overseas naval bases. Although he hesitated to conclude that the United States required overseas colonies, **imperialist** admirers such as Senator **Henry Cabot Lodge** and President **Theodore Roosevelt** did so. After retiring in 1896, Mahan wrote profusely, analyzing the naval arms race of the early 20th century and making a formidable case for the United States to create a "blue water" navy capable of supporting an expansionist foreign policy. Mahan briefly returned to public service, serving on the naval strategy board during the **Spanish–American War** and as a delegate to the first **Hague Conference** in 1899. *See also* FOREIGN POLICY.

MAIL ORDER. Improvements in transportation and postal service enabled the growth of mail-order retail businesses after the Civil War. The first successful catalog-based business was Montgomery Ward, founded in 1872 in association with the National Grange. Competitor **Sears, Roebuck and Co.** (established in 1893) surpassed Montgomery Ward in sales by 1906. Low rates for bulk mailings of periodicals enabled these and other companies to circulate thick, illustrated catalogs that offered rural Americans access to consumer culture and contributed to the spread of **consumer credit**. The establishment of

rural free delivery (piloted in 1896) and **parcel post** (1913) further eased delivery to rural customers. The largest firms' enormous, highly rationalized order fulfillment houses exemplified the national scale and reliance on rapid turnover in retail sales also characteristic of **department** and **chain stores**.

MAINE, USS. *See* CUBA; SPANISH–AMERICAN WAR.

MANN ACT (1910). The White Slave Traffic Act, known by the name of its sponsor, Illinois **Republican** congressman James R. Mann, criminalized transportation of **women** and girls across state lines or national borders and within the District of Columbia for **prostitution** or "any other immoral purpose." Regulation of prostitution had previously fallen under local and state jurisdiction, but the **white slavery** panic of the early 20th century led many U.S. antivice activists to believe that **immigrants** ran a nationwide criminal trust that kidnapped white women for sexual slavery. The forced trafficking of prostitutes, however, was rare in the United States, and federal authorities came to use the law's open-ended "immoral purpose" clause to prosecute consensual adultery and fornication. In *Caminetti v. United States* (1917), the **U.S. Supreme Court** upheld the prosecution of women for transporting themselves across state lines with the intent of having nonmarital sex. Federal Bureau of Investigation agents used the law to harass political dissenters and racial minorities, including boxer **Jack Johnson**, architect **Frank Lloyd Wright**, and **movie** actor **Charlie Chaplin**. Although rarely enforced by the 1960s, the law remained in effect in the early 21st century.

MANN–ELKINS ACT (1910). Named for Illinois **Republican** James R. Mann, chair of the House Interstate and Foreign Commerce Committee, and West Virginia Republican Stephen B. **Elkins**, chair of the Senate Interstate Commerce Committee, this act gave the **Interstate Commerce Commission (ICC)** authority to set railroad rates and suspend rate increases proposed by railroads pending investigation, while placing the burden on railroads to prove the need for the rate hike. The act also strengthened the prohibition against railroads granting rebates or preferable rates to long hauls. Other provisions weakened the ICC's power to investigate railroad finances, loosened restrictions on cooperation among railroads to set rates, and established a **Commerce Court** to which railroads could appeal ICC decisions. The bill also expanded ICC jurisdiction to include interstate telephone, telegraph, cable, and wireless companies. *See also* HEPBURN ACT.

MARSH, BENJAMIN C. (1879–1953). Social worker and housing reformer. Born in Bulgaria to American missionary parents, Marsh earned a B.A. at Grinnell College and did graduate work at the **University of Chicago** and the University of Pennsylvania, where he studied with **progressive** economist **Simon Patten**. As head of the Committee on Congestion of Population organized by **Florence Kelley**, **Mary Simkhovitch**, and **Lillian Wald**, he arranged landmark exhibitions on urban population congestion and slum housing. His 1909 book, *An Introduction to City Planning*, stressed German and British experiments with **zoning**, extension planning, and **garden cities**. He provided the impetus for the 1909 **National Conference on City Planning**, which launched urban planning as a distinct profession. However, Marsh's single-minded focus on social welfare led **Frederick Law Olmsted Jr.** and other planners to push him out of the city planning movement to avoid offending moderate business and civic leaders. In 1912, Marsh left New York, first to report on the Balkan War and later to work as a public-interest lobbyist in Washington, D.C.

MARSHALL, THOMAS R. (1854–1925). Politician. Born in Indiana, Marshall became a lawyer and involved himself in **Democratic Party** politics, winning the Indiana governorship in 1908. He accumulated a **progressive** record while in office (1909–13) with measures for state regulation of railroads and **utilities**, **employer liability** and **child labor** laws, and **local option**. During the grueling 1912 Democratic convention, aides to **Woodrow Wilson** offered Marshall the vice-presidential nomination in exchange for Indiana's support. After the Democrats won the presidency, Marshall became the first vice president to serve two full consecutive terms (1913–21) in nearly a century, performing mostly ceremonial duties as well as presiding over the Senate. His reluctance to assume presidential powers contributed to the political paralysis that followed Wilson's devastating stroke in October 1919.

MASS-CIRCULATION MAGAZINES. In the early 1890s, a new type of magazine emerged, offering the sophisticated appearance and well-edited fiction and features of high-class magazines while relying on **advertising**, a practice until then typical of cheaper publications. Innovators included **women**'s magazines such as **Edward Bok**'s *Ladies' Home Journal*, the *Woman's Home Companion*, and *Good Housekeeping*; fashion magazines like *McCall's*; and general periodicals such as *McClure's*, *Munsey's*, *Saturday Evening Post*, and *Cosmopolitan*. Advertising revenue enabled publishers to cut prices to 10 cents per issue from the 25 or 35 cents charged by magazines relying on subscriptions. The editors of the new journals aggressively sought submissions, flaunted the names of well-known authors, and illustrated the pages generously. Together, regular features, a personal tone in columns, lower cost, and the colorful appearance of these magazines attracted a broad audience, and circulation numbers soon surpassed those of the high-class monthlies, often exceeding one million by the 1920s. Although some mass magazines, notably *McClure's* and the *Ladies' Home Journal*, promoted **progressive** causes, in general these publications encouraged readers to perceive the world in terms of consumption. The mass magazines targeted middle-class white Americans; journals aimed at **African Americans** and other ethnic minorities were rarely successful unless supported by an advocacy group, as with the **National Association for the Advancement of Colored People**'s magazine *The Crisis*. Although foreign-language newspapers thrived, **immigrant** magazines were underfunded and short-lived. *See also* JOURNALISM; MUCKRAKING.

THE MASSES. Founded in 1911 by Piet Vlag, a Dutch **anarchist** living in New York City, this **socialist** magazine came to life in 1912, when **Max Eastman** and Floyd Dell took over as editor and assistant editor, respectively. *The Masses* combined lively political writing with essays on **feminism**, psychoanalysis, and other cultural experiments of interest to **Greenwich Village** bohemians. Despite paying contributors nothing, the magazine attracted writers such as **John Reed** and **William English Walling**. Amy Lowell and **Carl Sandburg** contributed poems and Sherwood Anderson fiction. *The Masses* was renowned for illustrations and cartoons by **John Sloan**, its art editor, and **George Bellows**, Stuart Davis, and **Art Young**.

Although it never had more than 25,000 subscribers, the magazine influenced a generation of radicals and earned national notoriety in 1915 for championing **Margaret Sanger**'s **birth control** campaign. Denied mailing privileges in 1917 because of its opposition to World War I, *The Masses* ceased publication, although two efforts to convict the editors under the wartime Espionage Act failed. *See also* MODERNISM.

MASTERS, EDGAR LEE (1869–1950). Poet. Born in Kansas, Masters was raised in Illinois and attended Knox College. Under family pressure he put aside his literary ambitions to become a lawyer in Chicago, working in the law firm of **Clarence Darrow** (1903–11). Having published his first poetry collection in 1898, he achieved critical acclaim in 1914, with the appearance of a series of free verse poems, autobiographical epitaphs for people buried in a graveyard in a village along the Spoon River. With its experimental form and disturbingly candid portrayal of the flaws and disappointments of its subjects, the poems collected in *Spoon River Anthology* (1915) were landmarks of the **Chicago Renaissance** and signal works of early American **modernism**. By the early 1920s, Masters devoted himself to writing full-time. *See also* LITERATURE.

MCADOO, WILLIAM GIBBS (1863–1941). Lawyer, business executive, and politician. Born in Georgia, McAdoo grew up there and in Tennessee. Moving to New York in 1892, he dealt in railroad securities and practiced law. Between 1901 and 1909, he became a local celebrity by organizing the construction of railroad tunnels under the Hudson River. A **Democratic Party progressive**, he managed the 1912 presidential campaign of **Woodrow Wilson**, who nominated him Secretary of the Treasury (1913–18). McAdoo's years in this post rank among the most consequential in the history of American public finance. He oversaw implementation of the **Federal Reserve**, the **income tax**, the **Underwood–Simmons Tariff**, and the **Federal Farm Loan Act**. During World War I, he coordinated fundraising and supervised the railroads. He married President Wilson's daughter Eleanor in 1914; after the war, he practiced law in California, made a controversial run for president (1924), and served in the Senate (1933–38).

MCCARTHY, CHARLES (1873–1921). Reformer and state official. Born in Massachusetts, McCarthy worked his way through Brown University and then earned a doctorate in political science at the University of Wisconsin, studying with **Richard Ely** and Frederick Jackson Turner. The latter recommended him to be the first director of the state's Legislative Reference Library. Drawing on the expertise of University of Wisconsin faculty, as the **university** president **Charles R. Van Hise** had proposed, the library offered research and bill-drafting services to state legislators and officials. Central to Wisconsin's **progressive** reforms, this agency became a model for progressive efforts in other states and the federal government. In 1912, McCarthy published *The Wisconsin Idea*, promoting an alliance between government and the social sciences. Along with a brief, stormy term in 1914 as research director for the **Commission on Industrial Relations**, McCarthy worked with several federal agencies during World War I. *See also* LA FOLLETTE, ROBERT M.

MCCLURE, SAMUEL S. (1857–1949). Editor and publisher. Born in Ireland, McClure came to the United States in 1866 and grew up in Indiana. After graduating from Knox College (1882), McClure edited the bicycle magazine *The Wheelman* and briefly worked for the *Century* magazine. He then launched the first newspaper syndicate to provide serialized fiction, securing fiction from writers such as Thomas Hardy, Rudyard Kipling, and Émile Zola. In 1892, McClure launched *McClure's Magazine*, a **mass-circulation magazine** whose combination of first-rate content and low price outclassed the competition and earned a circulation of 400,000 by 1900. **Ida Tarbell** established her reputation with popular biographies of Napoleon and Lincoln syndicated in *McClure's*. An installment of her incisive exposé of **Standard Oil** appeared in the famous January 1903 issue alongside an essay from **Lincoln Steffens**'s *Shame of the Cities* series and **Ray Stannard Baker**'s account of a **United Mine Workers** strike. This enormously popular issue marked the advent of the **muckraking** movement. Having attracted authors with creative editing, McClure later repelled them with creative bookkeeping, and by 1906, **William Allen White**, Tarbell, Steffens, and Baker had all moved on; six years later, the publisher lost control of his magazine. He wrote *My Autobiography* (1914) and participated in **Henry Ford**'s quixotic 1915 Peace Ship venture. *See also* JOURNALISM.

MCDOWELL, MARY ELIZA (1854–1936). Settlement house director. Born in Cincinnati, McDowell joined the **Woman's Christian Temperance Union** (WCTU) in the 1880s and rose to prominence as head of the WCTU kindergartens. After working at the **Hull House settlement** in the early 1890s, she became the head of the **University of Chicago** settlement in the **immigrant** neighborhood Back of the Yards, named for its location behind Chicago's sprawling stockyards. Her efforts to close a garbage dump led her to advocate **sanitary engineering** and culminated in the 1914 replacement of open dumps with incinerators and reduction plants.

MCKELWAY, ALEXANDER JEFFREY (1866–1918). Reformer. A Virginia native and Presbyterian minister (1891–97), McKelway entered politics as editor of the *Presbyterian Standard*, in which he advocated **progressive** causes but, like many white southerners, condoned **segregation** and **lynching**. His chief commitment was to ending **child labor**, arguing that children should not be expected to contribute to a family's welfare and that **education** could break the cycle of poverty that trapped poor white southerners. McKelway persuaded the North Carolina legislature to pass a weak child labor law in 1903, after which he became a southern lobbyist and officer for the **National Child Labor Committee**. In 1907, he moved to Washington, D.C., to lobby for a federal child labor law. Friendship with **Woodrow Wilson** gave the reformer a role in policymaking, and he convinced Wilson to sign the **Keating–Owen Act** (1916).

MCKIM, CHARLES F. (1847–1909). Architect. A native of Pennsylvania, McKim attended Harvard University, studied **architecture** at Paris's École des Beaux-Arts (1867–70), apprenticed with Henry Hobson Richardson (1870–78), and then formed a partnership with William Rutherford Mead (1846–1928). In 1879, **Stanford White**, another Richardson apprentice, joined the new firm, now called McKim, Mead, and White. By 1900, it was the most successful architecture partnership in the United States, with over 500 buildings produced during the original partners' lifetimes and thousands to its credit by the time the firm dissolved in the 1960s. A proponent of the so-called Beaux-Arts style, McKim took the lead in several grand neo-classical and neo-Renaissance projects, including the Boston Public Library (1895) and the Morningside Heights campus of Columbia University (1901). His work with **Daniel Burnham** on the 1893 Columbian **Exposition** led to his role in the **McMillan Plan** of 1902 and to his renovation of the White House (1902–3). *See also* CITY BEAUTIFUL.

McKINLEY, WILLIAM (1843–1901). President of the United States. An Ohio native, McKinley rose from private to major during the Civil War and gained the respect of his commander, future president Rutherford B. Hayes, who mentored McKinley during his early political career. As an Ohio lawyer, he entered **Republican Party** politics and served six terms in the U.S. House of Representatives (1877–83, 1885–91). His interest was in economic development, especially the protective tariff. His ouster from Congress during the Democrats' 1890 landslide proved fortuitous. With his friend **Marcus Hanna** as campaign manager, McKinley won the Ohio governor's chair (1891–96). His steady performance after the Panic of 1893, his proven ability to navigate Ohio's rough politics, and his campaigning on behalf of Republican candidates won McKinley the 1896 presidential nomination. Deciding it was futile to try to match the speech-making skills of his opponent, **William Jennings Bryan**, McKinley adopted a dignified "front porch" strategy, in which he greeted a daily parade of citizens at his home. His victory margin of 600,000 votes and 271–176 votes in the Electoral College set in motion the **Realignment of 1896**.

After a campaign unprecedented for its systematic fund-raising and operation, McKinley worked with his secretary **George B. Cortelyou** to develop a systematic approach to governing, a harbinger of the managerial presidency of the 20th century. In domestic policy, the new president pursued few innovations. Despite ambivalence over **imperialism** and antiwar impulses stemming from his Civil War experiences, he steadily increased pressure on Spain over **Cuba**, setting in motion the chain of events leading to the **Spanish–American War**. Accepting an enhanced U.S. presence in the Caribbean and the Pacific as a consequence of the war, he pursued annexation of the **Philip-**

pines, **Puerto Rico**, and Guam, authorized U.S. suppression of the Filipino nationalists and intervention in the **Boxer Rebellion**, and advocated the 1898 **Treaty of Paris** and the 1901 **Platt Amendment**.

The prosperity of 1900 helped McKinley win a second term with an enhanced majority, but then he decided to visit the Pan-American Exposition in Buffalo in September 1901, part of an effort to play a more public role. On 14 September, eight days after being shot by **Leon Czolgosz** while shaking hands in a receiving line, McKinley died, the third president assassinated since 1865. The last Civil War veteran to win the presidency, McKinley represented a transition between the limited government that prevailed in the 1800s and the interventionist public policy of the Progressive Era.

MCMILLAN PLAN. Officially titled the *Improvement of the Park System of the District of Columbia* (1902), this study of the physical layout and appearance of Washington, D.C., was sponsored by the U.S. Senate Committee on the District of Columbia at the initiative of long-time committee chair, Michigan **Republican** James McMillan (1838–1902). Conducting the study were **Daniel Burnham**, who coordinated design of the 1893 Columbian **Exposition**, architect **Charles McKim**, sculptor **Augustus Saint-Gaudens,** and landscape designer **Frederick Law Olmsted Jr.** After six months, the consultants produced a lavishly illustrated report and an exhibit with three-dimensional models and watercolors. The plan recommended making the Mall into a unified, formal park according to Beaux-Arts design principles, removing railroad tracks from the Mall to a new Union Station (eventually designed by Burnham), replacing the slums between Pennsylvania Avenue and the Mall with government buildings, constructing a Lincoln Memorial at the Mall's west end, and creating a system of parks and parkways throughout the city. Although never officially adopted by Congress, this plan guided federal efforts to improve Washington into the 1930s. The first concerted effort to apply **City Beautiful** principles to an actual city, the plan inspired similar projects in cities across the country, many coordinated by Burnham, and marked the advent of comprehensive city planning to the United States. *See also* AMERICAN CIVIC ASSOCIATION; ARCHITECTURE; HOWE, FREDERIC C.; ROBINSON, CHARLES MULFORD.

MCNAMARA CASE. Shortly after midnight on 1 October 1910, an explosion at the *Los Angeles Times* building killed 20 people and injured dozens more. Soon afterward, police found bombs near the homes of fiercely anti–**labor union** *Times* publisher Otis Chandler and the head of a business association engaged in an antiunion campaign. On Christmas day, another explosion damaged a Los Angeles iron works in the midst of a strike. A private detective traced the bombings to two unionists from the Midwest, James McNamara (1882–1941) and his brother John J. McNamara (1876–1941). Labor leaders rallied to the brothers' defense, with the **American Federation of Labor** paying **Clarence Darrow** to defend them. Finding overwhelming evidence that they were guilty, Darrow persuaded James to plead guilty to murder in exchange for a life sentence and John to conspiracy in exchange for 15 years in prison. Darrow's clumsy handling of the case estranged him from the labor movement and led to his being tried twice for jury tampering; one trial ended in acquittal and the other in a hung jury. James McNamara died in San Quentin Prison; after his parole in 1921, John returned to union activity in Indianapolis. Two other unionists later received life sentences for their roles in the bombings, which helped defeat the **Socialist Party**'s strongest campaign to win municipal offices in Los Angeles.

MEAT INSPECTION ACT (1906). Public pressure on Congress to assure the safety of the nation's food supply increased after publication of **Upton Sinclair**'s exposé of the meat packing industry, *The Jungle* (1906), and Charles Edward Russell's **muckraking** articles on the beef trust. Eager to avoid the bad publicity, the nation's largest meat packing firms endorsed federal regulation and helped fashion the law, which passed Congress as an amendment to an Agriculture Department appropriations bill. The inspections and sanitary measures it required were more onerous for small companies than they were for the national corporations, which gained ever larger market share. This act, along with the **Pure Food and Drug Act** (1906) and the work of **Harvey W. Wiley**, manifested a tentative movement by the federal government into consumer protection.

THE MELTING POT. This play, which English **Jewish** writer **Israel Zangwill** (1864–1926) dedicated to **Theodore Roosevelt**, became a

Broadway hit in 1909. In the play, a Russian Jew falls in love with a Christian Russian **settlement house** worker in New York City but leaves when he learns her father was responsible for a pogrom that killed members of his family. They reconcile as the sun shines on the Statue of Liberty. Zangwill's play popularized the "melting pot" as the notion that the mingling of ethnic, religious, and racial groups in the United States produced a composite American citizen shorn of Old World hatreds. In debates over **immigration**, the melting pot represented a liberal position between **pluralism**, with its assertion that immigrants should retain their ethnicity, and **Americanization**, with its insistence that immigrants should assimilate into an Anglo-Saxon norm. The popularity of the melting pot idea reflected the desire of many immigrants to become American without abandoning their ethnic heritage.

METROPOLITAN LIFE BUILDING. Designed to evoke the campanile of St. Mark's Cathedral in Venice, this 50-story building at Madison Avenue and 23rd Street in Manhattan was the world's tallest skyscraper from its completion in 1909 until the opening of the **Woolworth Building** in 1913. Construction of the huge office complex began in 1893. Covering most of a city block, the offices of the Metropolitan Life Insurance Company—then the world's largest insurer—epitomized the scale and complexity of modern corporations. By 1914, 20,000 people entered the firm's offices daily. More than 2,000 of the firm's 3,650 white-collar workers were **women**, a sign of their growing prevalence in clerical work. The building was so large that the company rented 40 percent of it and still had enough room for its operations. *See also* ARCHITECTURE.

MEXICAN REVOLUTION (1910–1917). This cataclysmic upheaval began as a protest against the staged reelection of Porfirio Díaz for his seventh term as president in November 1910. The aging dictator fled the country in May 1911, and reform leader Francisco Madero won the presidency in the November elections. However, violence continued as anger at the dispossession of small ranchers and farmers during the Díaz years boiled over. The United States had a keen interest because there were 50,000 Americans in Mexico, and U.S. investments exceeded $1 billion, amounting to 38 percent of foreign investment in Mexico by 1910. In that year, U.S. citizens owned nearly 27 percent of the land in Mexico and controlled some 60 percent of the mining industry as well as engaging in large-scale ranching and agriculture, real estate, and oil drilling; trade between the two countries amounted to $117 million. The U.S. ambassador to Mexico, Henry Lane Wilson, an admirer of the deposed Díaz, advised President **William Howard Taft** not to support Madero and recommended U.S. intervention to install Díaz or a similar successor. Taft rejected such direct intervention but declined support to Madero's government and ordered U.S. Army troops to engage in maneuvers in Texas and U.S. Navy ships to cruise off Mexican ports in 1912.

Surviving a variety of revolts during 1912, Madero's government fell to a coup by the Díaz supporters in February 1913, with General Victoriano Huerta installed as president. A backer of the coup, Ambassador Wilson refused to act to prevent Huerta from having Madero assassinated, but the ambassador's belief that a new dictatorship would bring peace proved very wrong. Supporters of agrarian rebel Emiliano Zapata continued to resist, while constitutionalist leader Venustiano Carranza raised another rebel force. When President **Woodrow Wilson** took office in January 1913, he removed Ambassador Wilson and renounced his actions. The new administration endorsed democracy as the route to peace in Mexico and refused to recognize the Huerta government.

The denial of U.S. recognition meant that Huerta's rivals could openly organize north of the border and maintain a bustling illegal arms trade. Then in spring 1914, the **Veracruz Incident** led to the U.S. Navy's occupation of this important port, allowing the United States to interdict arms to Huerta at the cost of Wilson's disavowal of U.S. **imperialism**. At the same time, Zapata's army and the constitutionalists were defeating Huerta's forces, forcing the dictator to flee the country in July 1914. Once installed as president, however, Carranza refused to work closely with the suspect United States, and in November 1914, U.S. troops withdrew from Veracruz.

By the end of 1914, Zapata and General Francisco "Pancho" Villa allied against Carranza to demand thorough agrarian reform. U.S. radicals began to acclaim the Mexican revolution as a **socialist** uprising, a view promoted by **John Reed**'s portrait of Villa in *Insurgent*

Mexico (1914). President Wilson, however, withheld recognition until the summer of 1915, when Carranza's victory over his rivals was clear. But this official move did not end U.S. involvement in Mexico's civil war. After Villistas shot 18 American miners in Sonora and then invaded the United States and killed 17 Americans at the army garrison at Columbus, New Mexico, Wilson ordered General **John J. Pershing** into Mexico in March 1916 to destroy Villa's army. Although a beleaguered Mexican government grudgingly allowed it, the **Pershing Expedition** achieved nothing during its 10 months in Mexico except to heighten anti-American sentiment. In 1917, Mexico's new constitution diminished the power of foreign investors, empowered the government to expropriate their property, and promised to nationalize key resources, measures that the United States resisted. The revelation in January 1917 of the Zimmerman telegram exacerbated American fears of an alliance between Germany and Mexico, but war-torn Mexico had little desire for such a venture. As violence gradually subsided after 1917, U.S. trade and investment once again rose rapidly. An enduring result of the war was rising **immigration** from Mexico to the United States. Over one million Mexicans fled the civil war to find peace and work north of the border. Many returned home when the war ended, but by 1920 the number of people of Mexican descent in the United States had tripled to some 600,000. *See also* FOREIGN POLICY; PLAN DE SAN DIEGO.

MIGRATORY BIRD TREATY. Concluded in 1916 between the United States and Great Britain (on behalf of its dominion, Canada), this treaty charged the U.S. and Canadian governments with enforcing limits on the hunting of migratory birds. Expanding on the **Lacey Act** (1900), the treaty grew out of a bill that Congress passed in 1913 to regulate hunting of endangered birds. Concerned that federal courts might find the bill unconstitutional, New York **Republican** senator **Elihu Root** sponsored a resolution directing the Department of State to negotiate with Canada because treaties carry more legal weight in the courts than federal laws. *See also* CONSERVATION.

MINIMUM WAGE LEGISLATION. Like many Progressive Era labor reforms, the notion of a legally mandated minimum wage came to the United States from overseas. After the Australian province of Victoria applied the concept to six low-wage industries in 1896, the experiment spread to New Zealand, Great Britain, and elsewhere. American labor reform groups such as the **National Consumers' League** and the **American Association for Labor Legislation** advocated minimum wage laws, particularly in the "sweated" trades, in which wage levels habitually fell below subsistence. Father **John Ryan**'s writings on the **living wage** made an ethical case for rejecting a market-set price for labor. By 1912, the **Progressive Party** of **Theodore Roosevelt** campaigned for a national minimum wage, and Massachusetts adopted the country's first state minimum wage law, though this statute applied only to certain categories of **women** and **child laborers** and provided only for publication of the names of offending employers. Over the next three years, 10 more states adopted minimum wage laws, also limited to women and minors, though usually with stronger sanctions. A federal minimum wage law was not enacted until the Fair Labor Standards Act of 1938. *See also* EIGHT-HOUR WORKDAY LAWS.

MITCHEL, JOHN PURROY (1879–1918). Reformer and politician. A New York City native, Mitchel graduated from Columbia College (1899) and the New York Law School (1901). In 1906, the New York City corporation counsel recruited him to investigate municipal corruption, a task at which he so excelled that he was called "Young Torquemada." Elected president of the city's Board of Aldermen in 1909 on a "fusion" ticket of **Republicans**, anti-**Tammany Democrats**, and **nonpartisan** reformers, Mitchel cooperated with the **Bureau of Municipal Research** on fiscal and administrative reforms. In 1913, President **Woodrow Wilson** nominated him as collector of the Port of New York. A few months later, Mitchel emerged as mayoral candidate of another reform coalition. In one of their periodic revolts against **machine politics**, city voters elected Mitchel the youngest mayor (1914–17) in New York history by 121,000 votes over the Tammany Hall candidate. In office, the so-called Boy Mayor gained a reputation of catering to business and professional interests at the expense of ethnic, working-class neighborhoods, despite his Irish Catholic background. His investigations of religious charities and his proposal to apply the money-saving **Gary Plan** to New

York's public schools alienated huge constituencies and contributed to his crushing defeat by a Tammany candidate in his 1917 re-election bid. He died during a flight training accident while serving in the Army Air Corps. *See also* STRUCTURAL REFORM.

MITCHELL, JOHN (1870–1919). Labor leader. From an Illinois coal-mining family, Mitchell was orphaned at age six and left school at 12 to work in local mines. While still in his early twenties, he played an important role in the expansion of the **United Mine Workers (UMW)**, helping lead the 1897 strike and becoming UMW national president (1898–1908) and vice president of the **American Federation of Labor** (1898–1914). His cooperation with President **Theodore Roosevelt** in settling the 1902 **Anthracite Coal Strike** solidified his reputation as a labor moderate, a stance that eventually made miners suspicious of his loyalties. After leaving the UMW presidency in 1908, he became a paid official of the **National Civic Federation (NCF)** until 1911, when the UMW demanded that he choose between the NCF and the union. A popular speaker who wrote two books making a case for labor unions, he was commissioner of labor for New York State (1914) and chaired that state's industrial commission (1915–19). *See also* LABOR UNIONS.

MODEL T. The **Ford Motor Company**'s replacement for the popular Model N became available to dealers in October 1908 for between $825 and $1,000, depending on the type of body. Lighter, more powerful, and less repair-prone than other cars in its price range, the Model T became the world's first mass-produced **automobile**, as well as the country's most popular model. In 1912, its $575 price tag fell below the average annual wage. By 1916, buyers paid between $345 and $360 for each of the 377,036 Model Ts sold that year, and an extensive market in used vehicles existed. By this time, Ford accounted for about half of the American domestic market, with 125,000 on New York City streets alone. Although the car also sold well overseas, higher gasoline prices and taxes in Europe favored either luxury vehicles or cars smaller than Ford's workhorse. The last Model T rolled off the production lines in 1927 and sold for $290. In its 19 years of production, the Model T revolutionized automobile ownership and transformed rural life, courtship, and pleasure travel. *See also* GOOD ROADS MOVEMENT; POPULAR CULTURE.

MODERNISM. During the early 20th century, this word signified powerful trends in **intellectual** life, **literature**, the **arts**, and **architecture**. "Modernism" generally refers to intellectual or creative work that in *form* as well as *content* endeavors to account for the cultural, social, and psychological consequences of urban, industrial life or new developments in technology and science. Whereas 19th-century **realism** sought to portray a situation objectively, modernists presumed that objectivity was impossible and even counterproductive. Instead, they endeavored to free themselves from aesthetic and moral conventions and express the subjectivity, partiality, and transience of people's experiences. Progressive Era realist and **naturalist** painting, such as the work of the **Ash Can School**, is not modernist, but the expressionist and cubist styles popularized by the **Armory Show** are. The unreal atmosphere and heavily symbolic characters in Eugene O'Neill's early plays and the stress on thwarted inner life in Sherwood Anderson's *Winesburg, Ohio* stories qualify these works as early examples of American modernism.

Although home-grown philosophical movements such as **pragmatism** and artistic movements such as the **Chicago Renaissance** exhibited elements of modernism, American cultural innovators largely saw it as a European import. New York's **Greenwich Village** became a cauldron for modernist ideas and experiments, with self-styled bohemians espousing explicitly radical forms of personal behavior, especially with regard to **sexuality**. **Alfred Stieglitz**'s Gallery 291, **Mabel Dodge**'s salon, and the **Provincetown Players** were important venues for modernism. **Walter Lippmann**'s writings on the psychological basis of mass politics and **Randolph Bourne**'s cultural **pluralism** represented the application of modernist ideas to political questions.

In architecture and design, modernism took on a different meaning, though the philosophical roots were similar. While in other fields modernists stressed the disruptive, alienating, and ominous aspects of contemporary life, architects and designers seemed to exult in the potential of new technologies and industrial methods. Countering the **Arts and Crafts movement**, modernist designers insisted that streamlined, machine-made forms could be beautiful as well as serviceable to humanity. Although Beaux-Arts-style architects such as **Daniel Burnham** and McKim, Mead, and White often hid their use of innovative building methods behind neo-classical or neo-Renaissance facades, **Louis Sullivan** and **Frank Lloyd Wright** became heroes to modernist architects with designs that emphasized the materials and techniques of buildings as well as their functions.

During the Progressive Era, modernism had another common use: in theological discussion, it signified efforts to reconcile religion with Darwinian biology, geology, archaeology, and the philological and historical analysis of the Bible. Although not all practitioners of the **Social Gospel** were theological modernists, the idea that religion's main use was its inducement to humane action was a common modernist conclusion. The **fundamentalist** movement was a reaction against this perspective on Christianity.

MODERNIZATION. In social science jargon, *modernization* signifies a set of social and cultural changes that scholars posit as accompanying the transition from a rural, subsistence-oriented, agricultural society to an urban, market-oriented, industrial society. The social sciences took shape during urbanization and industrialization in Europe and the United States, and in large measure their basic terminology reflected the attempt to understand these processes. Scholars such as the Englishman Henry Maine, the Germans Ferdinand Tönnies, Georg Simmel, and Max Weber, and Frenchman Émile Durkheim created sets of dichotomies to distinguish premodern, rural folk life from modern, urban, industrial life: community versus society; extended families versus nuclear families; sacred versus secular attitudes toward the world; reliance on tradition versus reliance on reason; ascribed versus achieved status. Such sets of distinctions amounted to a scholarly version of the popular image of urban, industrial capitalism as liberating and invigorating but also alienating and overwhelming.

Thousands of young Americans absorbed the new social sciences while studying in Germany before World War I, so it is not surprising that modernization models quickly pervaded U.S. **universities**. For instance, the innovative sociologists of the "Chicago School" who gathered around **Robert E. Park** at the **University of Chicago** explained the struggles of eastern and southern European **immigrants** and **African American** migrants as a result of their sudden move from premodern communities to the most modern of urban-industrial cities. Similarly, influential historians such as Richard Hofstadter, Samuel Hays, and Robert Wiebe have depicted progressivism as an effort to adjust American institutions and practices to modern, urban conditions. However, later scholars have criticized the model for its inability to explain manifest variations among different urban, industrial societies and to account for the obvious persistence in advanced societies of religion, ethnic consciousness, and other supposedly premodern attitudes and practices. Nevertheless, with the partial exception of **feminist** and cultural or transnational models, modernization remained the most comprehensive available model for explaining the timing of progressivism and the character and concerns of the various **progressive** movements. *See also* EFFICIENCY; NEW MIDDLE CLASS; ORGANIZATIONAL SYNTHESIS.

MONEY TRUST. This term came into common use around 1912 as a result of the **Pujo Committee** hearings, particularly through attorney **Louis Brandeis**'s *Harper's Weekly* articles, republished in 1914 in the book *Other People's Money and How Bankers Use It*. Critics asserted that powerful Wall Street investment firms such as **J. P. Morgan** and Company and Kuhn, Loeb, and Company represented a menacing trust that controlled money itself. As alternatives to New York's financial dominance, Brandeis recommended farmers' and consumers' **cooperatives** and credit unions. Despite such criticism, the **Federal Reserve Act** accommodated Wall Street in its reform of the banking system.

MONTEZUMA, CARLOS (c. 1865–1923). Physician and reformer. Born among the Yavapai people of Arizona and orphaned young, he was captured by Pimas who sold him to a white man in 1871. After growing up as the ward of a Baptist minister in Illinois, he earned a medical degree in 1889 and worked on reservations for the Indian Health Service. Convinced of the evils of the reservation system, he was an outspoken critic of the Bureau of Indian Affairs and a proponent of the **Dawes Allotment Act**. In 1896, he returned to Chicago, where he promoted **Americanization** and full citizenship for **Native**

Americans. Like many Indian activists, he grew disenchanted with allotment and began to see merit in the once-deplored tribal system. Montezuma helped found the **Society of American Indians** and edited the journal *Wassaja* starting in 1916. He spent the last year of his life on the Fort McDowell reservation, where he died of **tuberculosis**.

MOONEY CASE. On 22 July 1916, a bomb exploded in the midst of a **Preparedness** Day parade in San Francisco. Ten people were killed and 40 injured. Suspicion fell on Tom Mooney (1882–1942), a local **socialist** and labor activist, and his colleague, Warren K. Billings (1893–1972). They had previously been implicated in dynamite attacks against the Pacific Gas and Electric Company during a 1913 strike. In that case, Mooney was acquitted, but Billings served two years in Folsom Prison after being caught with a suitcase full of dynamite. For the 1916 bombing, Billings received a life sentence and Mooney a death sentence after trials marred by apparently perjured testimony. As revelations discredited the prosecution's case, Mooney's wife and another labor activist were acquitted of participating in the conspiracy, and labor activists and civil libertarians around the world took up Mooney's cause. In 1918, pressure from President **Woodrow Wilson** helped persuade California's governor to commute Mooney's sentence to life in prison. In 1939, Mooney was pardoned, and Billings' sentence was commuted.

MORGAN, JOHN PIERPONT (J. P.) (1837–1913). Investment banker. Born in Connecticut, J. P. Morgan worked in his father's merchant banking firm before forming a partnership called Drexel, Morgan, and Company in 1871 with Philadelphia's powerful Drexel family; the business was renamed J. P. Morgan and Company in 1895. This firm was the major underwriter of railroad securities and organizer of investment syndicates during the 1870s and 1880s. Morgan used his firm's strategic position to consolidate railroad companies into regional systems less vulnerable to stock speculation, ruinous competition, and price wars. A formidable man with a gruff disposition and a fierce appearance, he fit the populist and **antitrust** stereotype of the imperious international financier. His central position in American finance was particularly evident in 1895, when he organized a bailout of the federal government and salvaged the gold standard, both threatened by a run on the U.S. gold reserves stemming from the Panic of 1893.

Branching into industrial finance, Morgan oversaw the formation of **United States Steel** and **International Harvester**, two of the most dramatic consolidations of the **great merger movement**. His 1901 deal with **James J. Hill** and **E. H. Harriman** to form the Northern Securities Company prompted the landmark antitrust suit (*see NORTHERN SECURITIES V. UNITED STATES*) that established President **Theodore Roosevelt**'s reputation as a trust-buster. The Morgan firm's ability to arrange guarantees for strategic debt-ridden Wall Street interests prevented the **Panic of 1907** from turning into another depression. Such actions only deepened the public anxieties about bankers' power that prompted the **Pujo Committee** investigation of the **Money Trust**. Already ill and fading, Morgan vigorously defended his career in a memorable December 1912 confrontation with Pujo committee counsel **Samuel Untermeyer**. Having spent much of his wealth on a renowned collection of **art** and books, Morgan left a fortune estimated at $68 million. The embodiment of finance capitalism whose firm rivaled such legendary banking houses as the Medicis and the Rothschilds, Morgan died in Rome in 1913. *See also* ECONOMY; FEDERAL RESERVE ACT; HOLDING COMPANIES; INTERLOCKING DIRECTORATES.

MORROW, PRINCE ALBERT (1846–1913). Physician and sex reformer. Born in Kentucky, Morrow earned his medical degree from New York University (1873) and opened a dermatology and syphilology practice in New York City. In addition to translating a key French work on **syphilis**, he used his position as physician for the city prisons and hospitals to gather data and publish studies on sexually transmitted diseases (STDs). Morrow was spokesman for doctors who felt that protecting wives from the health consequences of husbands' intercourse with prostitutes was more important than doctor–patient confidentiality. These doctors often advocated sexual education and blood tests for marriage licenses. Like **women**'s rights activists, Morrow called for an end to the double standard and argued that the medical regulation of **prostitution** had failed to curb STDs. In 1905, he founded the American Society of Sanitary and Moral

Prophylaxis, which was eventually replaced by the **American Social Hygiene Association (ASHA)**. *See also* SEXUALITY.

MOSKOWITZ, BELLE LINDNER ISRAELS (1877–1933). Reformer. Born in New York to **immigrants** from East Prussia, Moskowitz devoted herself to social work among **Jews** on the **Lower East Side**. A **settlement house** worker by 1900, eight years later she led a precedent-setting campaign to regulate **dance halls** to curtail **prostitution**. After her first husband, architect Charles Israels, died in 1911, she worked in the **playground movement** and then as a labor dispute arbitrator for a clothing manufacturer's association, work she continued after marrying in 1914 **progressive** physician Henry Moskowitz (1879–1936). Her work with the **New York State Factory Investigating Commission** brought her into contact with **Alfred E. Smith**, whom she advised on political and social issues in the 1910s and 1920s. *See also* URBAN LIBERALISM.

MOTHERS' PENSIONS. In 1909, reformers who were gathered at the White House Conference on the Care of Dependent Children called on government to enable poor mothers to stay at home with their children instead of having to place them in orphanages while the mothers worked for wages. **Jane Addams**, **Theodore Dreiser**, **Jacob Riis**, and **Booker T. Washington** were among the attendees who saw the orphanage as inhumane and expensive. Between 1911 and 1920, 40 states enacted Mother's Aid laws to provide small pensions to widows and abandoned or **divorced** wives raising children under the age of 14 on their own. The amount paid rarely permitted these **women** to give up paid labor, and states regularly policed recipients' behavior to ensure that only respectable women received help. In some southern states, only white women were eligible. *See also* SOCIAL INSURANCE.

MOTION PICTURE PATENTS COMPANY (MPPC). Established in late 1908, this firm was an effort by **Thomas Edison** and several production companies together with film manufacturer **Eastman Kodak** to monopolize distribution and exhibition of **movies** in the United States. Edison engineered the MPPC by claiming to own the patents for all moving film cameras and threatening to sue other film production companies. Only the Biograph Company, whose camera was not covered by Edison's patents, could withstand the inventor's power and insist on holding an equal number of shares in the new cartel. The MPPC forced production companies to obtain a license and then instituted a system of exchanges that controlled the distribution of films to exhibitors. By 1911, the MPPC's General Film Company owned some 75 percent of U.S. film exchanges, but it was unable to dominate the industry because the costs of making and showing films remained low and the enforcement of patent laws weak. The shift of filming to Hollywood was motivated in part by efforts to escape MPPC surveillance. The resistance of independent filmmakers and the rise of multireel "feature" films undermined the organization. A lawsuit brought in 1912 by William Fox's Greater New York Film Exchange led to an out-of-court settlement but prompted a federal **antitrust** suit that ended with a court-ordered dissolution of the trust in 1915.

MOTT, JOHN R. (1865–1955). Evangelist and ecumenical activist. Born in upstate New York and raised in Iowa, Mott devoted himself to evangelism after attending a conference at evangelist Dwight Moody's academy in Massachusetts. A founder of the **Student Volunteer Movement** and the World's Student Christian Federation, he became a paid organizer for the **Young Men's Christian Association (YMCA)** upon graduation from Cornell University in 1888. In 1901, he took charge of the foreign programs of the YMCA, and by World War I, he had traveled to every continent except Antarctica and emerged as a spokesperson for Protestant interdenominational cooperation, especially in missionary work. During **Woodrow Wilson**'s presidency, Mott participated in diplomatic delegations to **Mexico** and Russia. He summed up his views in books such as *The Evangelization of the World in This Generation* (1900). *See also* SOCIAL GOSPEL.

MOVIES. Along with other entrepreneurs, **Thomas Edison** developed a motion picture camera in the 1880s but found no market for the device, so between 1888 and 1892 he devised the "kinetoscope," a machine with a peephole through which the viewer could see a brief clip after paying five cents. Seeing film's entertainment potential,

Edison's assistant William Dickson formed the American Mutoscope and Biograph Company (renamed Biograph in 1909) in 1895. He and other businessmen set up kinetoscope parlors in big cities and by 1897 sold film clips to the **vaudeville** houses for projection on screens between acts. By 1902, nickelodeons, or storefront movie theaters, opened in working-class, urban neighborhoods and quickly became popular and profitable.

Although the **Motion Picture Patents Company (MPPC)** attempted to monopolize film production and distribution in the early years, it disintegrated by 1915. The low start-up costs and broad appeal of movies enabled working-class and **immigrant** Americans to enter the business as exhibitors and theater owners. Entrepreneurs such as William Fox, **Jesse Lasky, Carl Laemmele**, and **Adolph Zukor** dominated the industry after the demise of the MPPC in 1915. European companies, notably Pathé Frères, initially took as much as 60 percent of the U.S. market (language was no barrier in silent film), but the Europeans' share declined as the U.S. industry organized.

Travel, comedy, striptease, boxing, and trick films dominated the early output. The short, silent films enabled people to come and go, talk, and eat during the performances. This ambience changed as producers and directors such as **D. W. Griffith** and **Mack Sennett** moved beyond filming stage shows to exploit the dramatic and comedic potential of film. By the mid-1910s, multireel features based on plays and novels transformed the industry. Longer duration, complex plots, character development, and new film techniques—including close-ups, cross cutting, keyhole shots, fade outs, and parallel editing—made movies more attractive to middle-class audiences. The longer time needed to create multireel films and their higher cost led to the emergence of film acting as full-time rather than casual work. After 1910, actors were more willing to risk the ire of the theatrical syndicates by working in film. The close-up abetted the star system by making individual actors recognizable. Trade magazines provided personal information about stars by 1911, leading to the fan magazines later in the decade. Actors such as **Mary Pickford, Charlie Chaplin, William S. Hart**, and **Lillian Gish** became celebrities.

The feature film also transformed distribution and exhibition. Short films allowed the high audience turnover and constant change that made nickelodeons in working-class neighborhoods profitable. In contrast, feature films required larger audiences and higher admission prices. The greater dramatic quality of the feature films and lavish new "movie palace" theaters in urban downtown districts attracted middle-class audiences. After a feature's initial launch, an individual or company could buy rights to show it in a certain territory. This distribution system led to the emergence of **Paramount Pictures** and other companies. At the same time, many production companies relocated from eastern and midwestern industrial cities to Hollywood, California, where movie making took on a glamorous association with perpetual sunshine, varied scenery, youth, and **sexuality**.

The effect of the movies on morals and safety became a public concern. Fire was a common danger because the nickelodeons brought together films on flammable nitrate stock, cheap storefronts, large crowds, poor ventilation, and few exits. Efforts to control film content ranged from banning the interstate transport of boxing films to municipal and state boards demanding the excision of violent, criminal, antireligious, and sexually suggestive scenes. One notable effort at censorship occurred on Christmas Eve 1908, when the mayor of New York City ordered all nickelodeons closed. An injunction allowed exhibitors to reopen within a short time, but leading New Yorkers met to formulate a system for censoring films for the public good. The MPPC joined the effort in the hope that by acceding to the new National Board of Censorship (renamed the National Board of Review in 1915), it would confront one rather than hundreds of censorship orders from local boards. But municipalities and states continued to enact their own censorship statutes. Many U.S. film producers cooperated with censors, but others, especially foreign and independent filmmakers, simply declined to submit their films.

Although the movies, like vaudeville, drew European ethnics into the American mainstream as both creators and viewers, other minorities found the industry less hospitable. Movies and **segregation** grew up together, as the tremendous success of D. W. Griffith's racist film *The Birth of a Nation* (1915) demonstrated. Where **African Americans** were admitted, they had to sit in the upper balcony. Black actors and filmmakers found few supporters and small audiences; black characters were typically portrayed by whites in blackface makeup.

One black film producer identified a mere 214 black-owned theaters in the United States in 1913. A few **Native Americans** made the transition from performing in **Wild West shows** to acting in movie westerns. Native American filmmakers appeared only many decades later. Asian and Hispanic Americans faced similarly constricted opportunities. *See also* POPULAR CULTURE.

MR. DOOLEY. *See* DUNNE, FINLEY PETER.

MUCKRAKING. This term refers to the investigative **journalism** that characterized the Progressive Era and inspired much **progressive** reform. Various factors promoted the flowering of investigative journalism in this period, including technological and organizational advances in publishing and the increased education levels, status, and professionalism of journalists. Foreshadowed by the work of **Jacob Riis** and Henry Demarest Lloyd, muckraking reached the height of its vigor in the early 1900s, when writers such as **Lincoln Steffens, Ida Tarbell**, and **Ray Stannard Baker** reported for **mass-circulation magazines** such as *McClure's*. The term "muckraker" came from a speech by President **Theodore Roosevelt** in 1906. Angry about David Graham Phillips's *Treason of the Senate* series in *Cosmopolitan*, Roosevelt asserted that many investigative journalists overemphasized debasing material, as had the "Man with the Muck-Rake" in the 17th-century Christian allegory *The Pilgrim's Progress*. These remarks offended journalists such as Steffens and Baker, who had considered the president an ally and a beneficiary of investigative reports such as Samuel Hopkins Adams's exposés of patent medicine fraud, which contributed to the passage of the **Pure Food and Drug Act**. Muckraking went into a noticeable decline by 1910. *See also* HEARST, WILLIAM RANDOLPH; MCCLURE, SAMUEL S.; SINCLAIR, UPTON.

MUIR, JOHN (1838–1914). Environmentalist. The son of Scottish farmers, Muir migrated with his father to Wisconsin in 1849. He studied geology and botany at the University of Wisconsin and became a naturalist and **journalist**. His visit to the Yosemite Valley of California in 1868 made him an activist seeking to protect beautiful wild places from development. He also participated in scientific expeditions and ran a commercial orchard. Between 1890, when Yosemite became a national park, and 1911, when he failed to prevent the flooding of the **Hetch Hetchy Valley**, he enjoyed significant successes. He founded the **Sierra Club** in 1892 and persuaded President Grover Cleveland to create the first national forests in 1896–97. In 1903, he took president and conservationist **Theodore Roosevelt** camping in Yosemite, winning a powerful ally who established additional national parks, monuments, and forests. Muir's spiritual belief in redemptive wilderness led him to favor preservation of undeveloped areas rather than their **conservation** or management for future resource extraction. *See also* FOREST SERVICE, U.S.; NATIONAL PARK SERVICE.

MULHOLLAND, WILLIAM (1855–1935). Civil engineer. A native of Ireland, Mulholland arrived in the United States in 1874. Taking a laborer's job with the private company that provided Los Angeles's water in 1877, he advanced to superintendent by 1886. When the city of Los Angeles took over the water works in 1902, he remained as superintendent and chief engineer. Determined to secure a sufficient water supply for the rapidly growing city, he oversaw construction of the 233-mile **Owens Valley** aqueduct. Under his leadership, Los Angeles's water supply expanded from one reservoir to 65 reservoirs and storage tanks feeding 3,800 miles of pipes. The water he secured sustained the city's population explosion from around 10,000 people in the early 1880s to 1.25 million in the late 1920s.

MULLER V. OREGON **(1908).** In this decision, the **U.S. Supreme Court** unanimously upheld an Oregon law that limited to 10 the hours **women** could work each day in factories and commercial laundries. The case was a path-breaking victory for **sociological jurisprudence**, because lawyer **Louis Brandeis** relied on social-scientific evidence compiled by **Josephine Goldmark**, research director for the **National Consumers' League**, to demonstrate the physical and moral effects of waged labor on women. The justices agreed that the government could abridge the liberty of the individual in employment contracts to protect women's ability to bear children, supposedly an important resource. This success laid the groundwork for later decisions, such as *Bunting v. Oregon* (1917), extending hours limitations to other workers. *See also* EIGHT-HOUR WORKDAY LAWS; *LOCHNER V. NEW YORK.*

MUNICIPAL HOUSEKEEPING. This term expressed two related ideas that encouraged middle-class **women**'s political activism. Advocates pointed out that industrialization and urbanization had taken many of women's traditional housekeeping and child rearing tasks out of the home, so women had to concern themselves with **sanitary engineering**, **public health**, **social insurance**, **education**, and the **playground movement**, to name a few examples. Many women's organizations, notably the **Woman's Christian Temperance Union** and the **National American Woman Suffrage Association**, used this idea to argue for women's **suffrage**. Another version of this argument arose from the notion that women tended to be more virtuous and **nonpartisan** than men and would sweep corruption from politics once they had the right to vote. Female activists' support for **prohibition** and labor protections and opposition to **prostitution** and **child labor** led reformers to imagine that enfranchisement of women would mean realization of the **progressive** agenda.

MURPHY, CHARLES F. (1858–1924). Political boss. The son of Irish **immigrants** on New York's **Lower East Side**, Murphy ran a **saloon** that provided capital to open a chain of bars, hotels, and other businesses and paved his way into **Tammany Hall** politics. A district leader in the **Democratic Party machine** by the early 1890s, as Tammany reeled from the scandals and defeats of the last years of **Richard Croker**'s leadership, in 1902 Silent Charlie Murphy became the organization's **boss**. Although tolerant of patronage, influence peddling, and similar forms of graft, the laconic, shrewd Murphy pressured the machine to avoid police corruption because it offended Tammany's core working-class constituencies. He rebuilt the organization's credibility by selecting talented mayoral candidates such as George B. McClellan Jr. (1865–1940) and William J. Gaynor (1849–1913). However, the boss's insistence on the impeachment of Governor William H. Sulzer, who turned on Tammany after his 1912 election, contributed to the machine's embarrassing 1913 defeat by **John Purroy Mitchel**'s reform coalition. Murphy nevertheless gained a reputation as the most effective Tammany boss and promoted the careers of young **urban liberals** such as **Robert F. Wagner** and **Alfred E. Smith**.

MÜNSTERBERG, HUGO (1863–1916). Psychologist. Born into a **Jewish** family in Prussia, Münsterberg earned a Ph.D. in psychology (1885) and an M.D. (1887) and taught at the University of Freiburg in Germany. His arguments that consciousness, will, emotions, and other mental phenomena had to be studied in close conjunction with their physiological manifestations brought him to the attention of **William James**, who invited Münsterberg to Harvard University in 1892. There the young scientist took charge of the psychology laboratory and became a formative figure in the emergence of **behaviorism** and applied psychology. He also wrote and lectured for popular audiences, explaining psychological theory and its applications to business, law, **education**, **advertising**, **movies**, and other fields. Probably the best-known German American of the time, his vocal pro-German stance alienated colleagues and even led to charges that he was a German agent after the outbreak of World War I in 1914.

MUSIC. American classical music in the Progressive Era was still strongly influenced by European music. The first symphony orchestras, in New York City (1878), Boston (1881), and Chicago (1891), usually played European compositions. Orchestra and opera companies employed **immigrant** musicians, especially from Germany, origin of innumerable audience members who enthusiastically applauded Richard Wagner. Officials hired European-born conductors such Theodore Thomas (1835–1905), Walter Damrosch (1862–1950), and Arturo Toscanini (1867–1957) to bring attention and credibility to their orchestras. Thomas, who led both the New York Philharmonic (1877–91) and the Chicago Symphony (1891–1905), was a tireless promoter and educator, a participant through much of his career in the American tradition of traveling bands, which brought classical music to smaller cities and towns.

Well-regarded American composers such as Edward MacDowell (1860–1908) worked mostly in European traditions. The Czech composer Antonin Dvořák (1841–1904), who was director of the National Conservatory of Music in New York City (1892–95), courted controversy by encouraging students and performers to incorporate American folklore and **African American** influences into their compositions. The highly original **modernist Charles Ives** did work American musical forms into his compositions, but his music only became widely known starting in the 1920s. Determined to raise American music standards, John Philip Sousa (1854–1932) had a far-reaching influence as conductor of the Marine Corps band and other orchestras. The March King's *Stars and Stripes Forever* became the official U.S. march, but Sousa also composed 15 operettas, toured Europe four times, and made a celebrated world tour in 1910.

The period, meanwhile, saw rapid development of popular and folk genres that would influence the country and the world in the 20th century: musical theater, **vaudeville**, **Tin Pan Alley**, **ragtime**, **jazz**, and blues. Three dominant companies sold half a million **phonographs** by 1897, indicating the emergence of a burgeoning recording industry. Inexpensive instruments sustained the custom of playing at home even after the phonograph became commercially viable in the 1890s. More than one hundred American manufacturers produced 25,000 pianos or organs each year. By 1900, the mechanical piano with music on punched paper rolls or phonographs playing cylinder recordings had appeared. The sale of inexpensive sheet music demonstrated the huge demand for waltzes, polkas, and schottisches, as well as patriotic, sentimental, humorous, and topical songs. Illustrated by original lithographs, sheet music became a new form of **popular culture**, and some topical songs became American standards, like "A Hot Time in the Old Town" (1898) by Theodore A. Metz or "Oh My Darling Clementine" (1884) by Percy Montrose. Katherine Lee Bates (1859–1929) wrote a poem called "America the Beautiful" in 1895, and by 1904 it became a popular patriotic song.

Among the most popular compositions were Tin Pan Alley and Broadway songs by **Irving Berlin**, **George M. Cohan**, and scores of less well-known writers. Popular music also included minstrel songs and ragtime by African American composers such as **Scott Joplin** and **W. C. Handy**. Black performers such as orchestra leader **James Reese Europe** and the vaudeville, musical theater, and recording team of George Walker (1873–1911) and Bert Williams (1874–1922) popularized ragtime and jazz, as well as African American dance. Berlin's hit song "Alexander's Ragtime Band" (1911) demonstrated this spreading influence.

This was an era filled with song in churches, **labor unions**, political rallies, **reform movements**, schools, summer concerts in parks, and every gathering of homesick immigrants. Each ethnic group had its own sentimental ballads, composed in America and lamenting a lost homeland in the old country. The ill-fated **Industrial Workers of the World** troubadour **Joe Hill** composed vivid labor songs, often satirizing or stealing from Salvation Army hymns while providing a model for later generations of folk protest songwriters such as Woody Guthrie. Capitalist **Andrew Carnegie**, meanwhile, expressed his love of music by donating organs to thousands of churches, along with New York's cherished Carnegie Hall (1891) and Carnegie Music Hall in Pittsburgh (1895). *See also* AMERICAN SOCIETY OF COMPOSERS, AUTHORS, AND PUBLISHERS; CASTLE, IRENE AND VERNON; DANCE HALLS; EDISON, THOMAS A.; ZIEGFELD FOLLIES.

– N –

NATION, CARRY (1846–1911). Prohibitionist. Raised in Missouri, Nation founded in the 1890s a branch of the **Woman's Christian Temperance Union (WCTU)** in Kansas, where a statewide **prohibition** law went unenforced. In 1900, she became notorious for replacing the usual WCTU weapons against the **saloon**—prayers and hymns—with rocks and a hatchet. Her actions inspired local activists, who awarded her a medal inscribed "To the Bravest Woman in Kansas" (1901), and prohibitionists often wore lapel pins in the shape of a hatchet, but the WCTU disavowed her tactics. Portrayed in the press as an unwomanly fanatic, she earned her living on the lecture circuit.

NATIONAL AMERICAN WOMAN SUFFRAGE ASSOCIATION (NAWSA). In 1890, the rival American and National Woman Suffrage Associations united to form NAWSA; the renowned Elizabeth Cady Stanton and Susan B. Anthony served as the first presidents. The organization confronted circumstances that some historians label the "doldrums." Between 1870 and 1910, proponents ran 480 state campaigns to achieve a scant 17 **referenda**, of which they won only two. After 1896, when Idaho and Utah adopted **women's suffrage**, no statewide measure would succeed until Washington in 1910 and California in 1911. In 1890, only two major women's organizations supported women's right to vote: the **Woman's Christian Temperance Union** and the **National Association of Colored Women (NACW)**. Despite organizing hundreds of state and local branches in the 1890s, the movement claimed fewer than 9,000 dues-paying members by 1900. One hopeful sign was that a growing number of localities and states granted women partial suffrage, allowing them to vote in elections for the school board or state legislature.

By 1900, new leadership, new organizing tactics, campaigns among college students and working-class women, the inspiration of the British suffrage movement, and greater centralization revived the movement. After 1910, the movement again made progress, especially in western states. In that year, dues-paying members numbered 117,000; by 1915, dues- and non-dues-paying members together amounted to two million. In 1912, **Theodore Roosevelt's Progressive Party** endorsed women's suffrage; the **General Federation of Women's Clubs** signed on in 1914.

As it grew more respectable, the organization increasingly relied on the support of wealthy women donors known as "allies," who bankrolled the campaign but muted radical voices. At times, NAWSA questioned the qualifications of **immigrant** and working-class men for full citizenship rights. The group explicitly endorsed **segregation** and condoned **disfranchisement** of **African American** men in the southern states. African American women formed their own suffrage clubs in at least seven states by the early 20th century. The NACW and the **National Association for the Advancement of Colored People (NAACP)** both had suffrage departments. Leaders such as **Lugenia Burns Hope**, **Mary Church Terrell**, and **Ida B. Wells-Barnett** saw the vote as a means of combating racism as well as sexual abuse of black women by white men.

NAWSA President **Carrie Chapman Catt** (1900–05, 1915–20) worked to transform the organization into a streamlined, professionally managed interest group. The years 1913–14 saw two major schisms. First, the decision to concentrate on a national constitutional amendment, instead of state referenda, alienated many southern white suffragists who, led by **Jean and Kate Gordon**, founded the **Southern States Woman Suffrage Conference** in 1913. Recognizing that conservative southern states were unlikely to enfranchise women on their own, however, most southern white activists remained with NAWSA and accepted the campaign for the federal amendment.

The second schism occurred in a dispute over tactics and the establishment of a rival organization. **Alice Paul** and **Lucy Burns** introduced radical tactics inspired by the British women's suffrage movement: suffrage parades (one upstaged **Woodrow Wilson**'s first inauguration as president), the picketing of politicians who opposed enfranchising women, and prison hunger strikes. In 1914, NAWSA president **Anna Howard Shaw** forced out Burns and Paul because they had founded the Congressional Union (renamed the **National Woman's Party** in 1916).

Returning to the NAWSA presidency in 1915, Catt focused the organization on a federal constitutional amendment via her **Winning Plan**, approved at the 1916 convention. The plan worked more swiftly than expected, largely because of U.S. participation in World War I. Although bitter divisions appeared among female activists over the war, most American women supported it, and their work as **nurses** and ambulance drivers, **conservation**-minded housewives, and workers in factories and fields made men more willing to enfranchise them. In 1919, Congress sent the suffrage amendment to the states, who acted on it quickly. In a cliff-hanger special session in August 1920, Tennessee became the 36th state to ratify the **Nineteenth Amendment**, giving the measure the required three-fourths of states. Turning to voter education and mobilization, NAWSA became the League of Women Voters. *See also* FEMINISM; MUNICIPAL HOUSEKEEPING; NEW WOMAN; WOMEN'S TRADE UNION LEAGUE.

NATIONAL ASSOCIATION FOR THE ADVANCEMENT OF COLORED PEOPLE (NAACP). Founded in 1910 to take up the demand for political and civil equality for **African Americans** that had been voiced by the **Niagara Movement**, the NAACP provided an alternative to **Booker T. Washington**, whose gradualist, nonconfrontational approach lost credibility amid the hardening of **segregation** and **disfranchisement**. After the **Springfield Riot** (1908), white activists, among them **William English Walling, Mary White Ovington**, and publisher Oswald Garrison Villard, cooperated with black activists, among them **W. E. B. Du Bois, Mary Church Terrell**, and **Ida B. Wells-Barnett**, to issue "The Call" on Lincoln's birthday, 12 February 1909. Signed by dozens of prominent figures of both races, this document demanded renewed struggle for equal rights. The Call prompted conferences in 1909 and 1910 that gave birth to the NAACP.

Like so many **progressive reform movements**, the NAACP emphasized public **education** and litigation; it discouraged public protests and emphasized professional leadership rather than mass participation. Leadership was primarily male and initially dominated by whites, who provided funds and expertise in the early years but whose dominance soon became a source of tension. Wells-Barnett and **William Monroe Trotter** refused to join the NAACP because of its white leadership. Attorney **Moorfield Storey** was the first president, and Walling, Ovington, and Villard held other key positions. The first paid black staff member was Du Bois, who became editor of the NAACP journal, *The Crisis*, in 1910. The journal had a circulation of 100,000 by 1918.

Brothers **Joel and Arthur Spingarn** founded the first local branch of the NAACP in New York City in 1911, with more branches appearing in New England, the Midwest, and the West over the next years. The locals were largely led and staffed by African Americans. On his appointment as field secretary in 1916, **James Weldon Johnson** expanded organizing efforts into the South. By 1919, the association had 310 local branches (31 in the South) and more than 90,000 members. Among its early activities, the NAACP picketed **movie** theaters showing **D. W. Griffith**'s film *The Birth of a Nation* (1915), investigated and publicized the horrors of **lynching**, and organized a silent mass protest against the **East St. Louis Riot** (1917). NAACP lawyers, led by Arthur Spingarn, challenged disfranchisement laws, segregation ordinances and restrictive covenants in residential areas, and the unequal treatment of black defendants in the criminal justice system. The association contributed to a notable victory against Oklahoma's **grandfather clause** in *Guinn v. United States* (1915). *See also* GREAT MIGRATION; URBAN LEAGUE.

NATIONAL ASSOCIATION OF COLORED WOMEN (NACW).
This organization was founded in 1896 to bring together the National
Federation of Afro-American Women and the National League of
Colored Women. Two events catalyzed its establishment: the exclusion of **African American** women from the Woman's Pavilion at
the Columbian **Exposition** and black contributors or visitors from
the fair generally; and efforts by the white press to discredit **Ida B.
Wells-Barnett**'s anti-**lynching** lecture tour in the United Kingdom.
Overall concerns were the spread of **segregation** and **disfranchisement** in the South and the nationwide retreat from civil rights. The
organization included most of the prominent female reformers of
the era, including Wells-Barnett, **Josephine St. Pierre Ruffin**, and
Mary Church Terrell. The group opened its doors to white women
even though most white organizations either refused black membership or permitted only segregated locals. The NACW had a largely
middle-class membership that provided day care and kindergartens,
ran **settlement houses** (such as **Lugenia Burns Hope**'s Neighborhood Union in Atlanta), raised money for black schools, founded colleges, opened boarding houses and employment agencies for black
women, worked to improve **public health** and health care in urban
neighborhoods, campaigned against lynching, and promoted **prohibition**. A staunch supporter of **women**'s **suffrage**, the organization
had more than 50,000 members in nearly 30 federations and 1,000
branches by 1916.

NATIONAL ASSOCIATION OF MANUFACTURERS (NAM).
Founded in 1895, this organization initially focused on promoting
foreign trade and reforming federal tariffs. In 1902, fervent anti-**labor unionists** gained control and built NAM into a lobbying and
trade association that opposed **eight-hour**, **child labor**, **minimum
wage**, and other labor protection laws. It promoted antiunion drives
in the name of the **open shop**. By 1914, NAM claimed 3,500
members, with its strength greatest among medium-size and small
manufacturers in the Midwest. Its reputation for intransigence made
it seem reactionary compared with the more cooperative **National
Civic Federation**. NAM joined other business groups in forming the
National Industrial Conference Board in 1916.

NATIONAL ASSOCIATION OPPOSED TO WOMAN SUF-FRAGE (NAOWS). Founded in 1911, the NAOWS united conservative **women** who argued that giving women the vote was neither necessary nor their right and that engagement with politics would turn women into men, tear apart families, contribute to **juvenile** crime, and force more women into the workforce. Rejecting the **municipal housekeeping** view that women would purify politics, the "antis" (as they were known) insisted that women would vote as their husbands did or would be duped by male politicians. NAOWS claimed success between 1911 and 1916, when voters approved only six of 21 state **referenda** on enfranchising women. In the latter year, it had some 350,000 members and enjoyed the support of the **United States Brewers' Association**, the Man-Suffrage Association, and the American Constitutional League. After 1916, it was unable to overcome the momentum that culminated in the **Nineteenth Amendment**.

NATIONAL BISCUIT COMPANY. Formed in 1898 amid the **great merger movement**, this corporation combined three regional baked goods firms into a consortium of 114 bakeries representing $55 million in capital. For a long time, National Biscuit operated much like smaller firms, producing unbranded crackers and cookies that grocers sold in bulk from barrels; over 75 percent of sales consisted of bulk goods into the 1920s. Yet shortly after National Biscuit's merger, founder Adolphus Green (1844–1917) contracted with **advertising** agency N. W. Ayer to launch the archetype of the modern brand-name campaign for a cracker named "Uneeda Biscuit," sold in a recognizable package with a moisture-proof "In-Er-Seal." The goal was to create a direct relationship with consumers, bypassing wholesalers and grocers and allowing the firm to invest in mass production and distribution. With 100 million packages sold by 1900, Uneeda Biscuits remained a leading brand for decades. In the course of 250 patent infringement suits, National Biscuit helped to establish modern trademark law. Uneeda Biscuit's success prompted other familiar brands, such as Barnum's Animal Crackers (1902) and Oreos (1912). Renamed Nabisco in 1971, the company became part of Kraft Foods in 2000.

NATIONAL BUREAU OF STANDARDS (NBS). Founded in 1901, this federal agency was envisioned as a replacement for the Treasury Department's Office of Standard Weights and Measures. Moved to the **Department of Commerce and Labor** in 1903, NBS was a clearinghouse for matters ranging from the operation of grocery scales to the composition of steel rails and the measurement of corrosion in pipes and cables; it had more than 500 employees by 1917. The agency developed standards of measurement, quality, and performance for new technologies such as **electricity**, radio, and aviation. Supporting state efforts to regulate **utilities**, NBS fixed the units of gas and electric heat and light. It also tested materials for other federal agencies and acquired a reputation as a consumer advocate through its campaign for "honest weight" and its popular 1915 publication, *Measurements for the Household*. In 1988, the agency was renamed the National Institute of Standards and Technology. *See also* EFFICIENCY.

NATIONAL CASH REGISTER. This company originated in 1884, when John Henry Patterson (1879–1946) acquired a small firm that made machines to keep track of sales. Patterson's innovative sales techniques to create a market for the cash register, a newfangled device that many shopkeepers did not imagine needing, became standard in many industries. In 1906, National Cash Register introduced an **electric** model devised by famed inventor Charles F. Kettering (1876–1958). Patterson and sales executive and future IBM founder Thomas J. Watson (1874–1956) pursued ruthless strategies that won the company 95 percent of the market by the early 1910s. In 1911, the company employed thousands, had sold a million machines, and claimed to have 270 overseas offices. Then a federal **antitrust** prosecution led to the conviction of Watson and Patterson (overturned in 1914 after the two men organized relief for the Dayton flood of 1913). An early proponent of **welfare capitalism**, National Cash Register offered employee benefits ranging from company picnics to profit sharing and health care.

NATIONAL CHILD LABOR COMMITTEE (NCLC). Founded in 1904 at a conference of the **National Conference of Charities and Correction**, the organization was intended as a clearinghouse for state **child labor** reform efforts. **Alexander McKelway** became a key lobbyist between 1904 and 1918. Among the most effective of the NCLC's public relations tools were **Lewis W. Hine**'s photographs of small, shabby, dirty children dwarfed by the machines they tended. The committee persuaded many northern and western states to ban employment of children under the age of 14, but southern states typically set the age lower. Moreover, state laws often included broad exemption clauses or went unenforced. This situation led the NCLC to campaign for a federal child labor law. In 1912, the NCLC supported creation of the **Children's Bureau**. Backed by some northern manufacturers worried about cheap southern labor and benefiting from McKelway's friendship with President **Woodrow Wilson**, the organization shepherded the **Keating–Owen Act** through Congress in 1916, though the **Supreme Court** overturned this law in *Hammer v. Dagenhart* (1918).

NATIONAL CIVIC FEDERATION (NCF). Organized in 1900 by **Civic Federation of Chicago** secretary Ralph M. Easley (1856–1939), the NCF brought together reform-minded businessmen such as **Samuel Insull** and **George W. Perkins** with **American Federation of Labor** leaders such as **Samuel Gompers** and **John Mitchell** to seek cooperative alternatives to labor–management conflict. An alternative to the hard-line **National Association of Manufacturers**, the group attracted executives of larger corporations in a variety of enterprises, including railroads, banks, and **utilities**. Moderate and conservative politicians who supported union recognition and mediation of labor disputes joined as well, including **Elihu B. Root**, **William Howard Taft**, and **George B. Cortelyou**, all high-ranking members of President **Theodore Roosevelt**'s cabinet. **Republican** senator **Marcus Hanna** was the NCF's first president. **Seth Low**, the third president, joined **Nicholas Murray Butler** and **Charles W. Eliot** among **university** presidents active in the group. By 1912, the NCF had 5,000 members and councils in 24 states. It worked with businesses such as **National Cash Register** to promote **welfare capitalism**, collected information on **immigration** reform, **child labor**, and public ownership of utilities, and lobbied for the 1913 **Newlands Act**, which provided for federal arbitration of railroad labor disputes. The NCF also lobbied for state passage of model bills for **worker's**

compensation, minimum wages, and utilities regulation. The NCF went into decline after alienating many liberals with strident anti-radicalism during World War I. *See also* NEW NATIONALISM; SOCIAL INSURANCE.

NATIONAL COLLEGIATE ATHLETIC ASSOCIATION (NCAA). Responding to the growth of collegiate **football** and the frequency of serious injuries and fatalities among players, more than 60 college presidents met in 1905 to set rules for the sport. Initially named the Intercollegiate Athletic Association, the organization adopted its current name in 1910. The NCAA extended its supervision beyond football, overseeing 11 men's team sports by 1919 but taking little interest in **women**'s sports until much later in the century. The organization represented the desire of **university** administrators to control the commercialization and professionalization of **athletics.** *See also* AMATEUR ATHLETIC UNION; BASKETBALL.

NATIONAL CONFERENCE OF CHARITIES AND CORREC-TION (NCCC). This group first met in 1874 under the name National Conference of Boards of Public Charities to coordinate the movement for state oversight of almshouses, orphanages, reform schools, mental hospitals, prisons, and other social welfare institutions; it renamed itself the NCCC in 1879. Its annual meetings became an important forum for discussion of issues, trends, and innovations in social welfare. By the early 20th century, local charity organization societies (COSs) and activists in the **settlement house** movement brought distinct perspectives to the NCCC, with COS workers preferring surveillance and limited assistance to those deemed worthy and settlement house workers insisting on political solutions to conditions that caused poverty. The election of **Jane Addams** as president in 1905 reflected the group's effort to bring together these perspectives, and they found common ground in the new technique of "casework" in the 1910s. As social workers professionalized, the group renamed itself the National Conference of Social Work in 1917. *See also* NATIONAL CHILD LABOR COMMITTEE.

NATIONAL CONFERENCE ON CITY PLANNING (NCCP). This group grew out of a meeting in May 1909 organized by New York housing reformer **Benjamin C. Marsh** and funded by the **Russell Sage Foundation** to bring together activists in housing, urban environmental reform, and city planning. Members led by **Frederick Law Olmsted Jr.** pushed Marsh out of the leadership in 1910. His ouster reflected a split between housing reform and urban planning in the United States that did not occur in other countries with strong urban planning movements, such as Great Britain and Germany. The NCCP served as a forum for discussing the goals and methods of city planning, including the debate over the **City Beautiful** versus **City Practical** approach. It gave way in 1917 to the American City Planning Institute, which after several mergers and reorganizations emerged as the American Planning Association.

NATIONAL CONGRESS OF MOTHERS. Established in 1897 and later known as the National Parent–Teacher Association (PTA), the organization sought to involve mothers in the public schools. It expanded its scope beyond **education** to include campaigning against **child labor** and for **compulsory education laws**, lobbying for the creation of **juvenile courts** and reformatories, better health services for infants, kindergartens, and **playgrounds**. It was a key example of the idea of **municipal housekeeping**. *See also* CHILDREN'S BUREAU; WOMEN.

NATIONAL CONSERVATION COMMISSION. This expert-led organization grew out of the **White House Conference on Conservation** convened by President **Theodore Roosevelt** in May 1908. Chaired by **Gifford Pinchot** and including well-known conservationists and supportive members of Congress such as Nevada senator **Francis G. Newlands** and Ohio congressman Theodore K. Burton, the commission submitted a three-volume report in December 1908. The most thorough natural resource inventory to date, it summarized views that pro-**conservation** officials had recommended for years: soil conservation, waterway reclamation, flood control, careful oversight of mining and grazing leases on public land, and protection of national forests, where cutting was estimated to exceed growth by as much as 250 percent. Initially funded by the executive branch, the commission ceased to exist in 1909 when Congress, under the lead of the **Republican Party**'s

Old Guard, declined to fund it. *See also* FOREST SERVICE, U.S.; RECLAMATION SERVICE, U.S.

NATIONAL CONSUMERS' LEAGUE (NCL). Founded in 1899 in New York and headed by **Florence Kelley** until she died in 1932, the NCL promoted protective labor legislation for **women** and children. By 1904, it had 64 local branches in large cities outside the South. Its membership was mainly white and middle class. Encouraging shoppers to boycott stores and factories that did not abide by state labor laws, it awarded its "Consumers' White Label" to employers who obeyed the laws, produced their goods on premises, did not require overtime, and did not employ anyone under 16 years of age. The league also lobbied for the 10-hour day for women and **minimum wage** legislation. Director of Research **Josephine Goldmark** collected the information on which **Louis Brandeis** based his arguments in the precedent-setting **Supreme Court** decision *Muller v. Oregon* (1908). By 1919, the NCL had contributed to the passage of minimum wage laws for women in several states. After declining in influence during the 1920s, the NCL survived with a broad consumer protection as well as labor agenda. *See also* CHILD LABOR; SOCIOLOGICAL JURISPRUDENCE; WOMEN'S TRADE UNION LEAGUE.

NATIONAL EDUCATION ASSOCIATION (NEA). Launched in 1857 as the National Teachers' Association, this professional association for teachers adopted its current name in 1870. **Women** made up more than half the membership as early as the mid-1880s, reflecting the feminization of public school teaching. Beginning in 1892 with the appointment of the Committee of Ten on Secondary School Studies, chaired by **Charles W. Eliot**, the NEA campaigned to influence curricula, teacher training, salaries, pensions, working conditions, and state and federal **education** policy. It appointed its first full-time director in 1898, gained a congressional charter in 1906, and opened its Washington, D.C., headquarters in 1917. Responding to women's prominence in the teaching profession, the NEA elected its first female president, **Ella Flagg Young** (1910), passed a resolution calling for women's **suffrage** (1912), and two years later demanded equal pay for equal work (women teachers often earned half as much

John Muir was a well-known nature writer who founded the Sierra Club in 1892 and lobbied for national parks and forest conservation. Photo courtesy of the Library of Congress, LC-USZ62-52000 DLC.

The first girls' basketball team, at the Tulalip Indian School, 1912, including Catherine Edwards (Swinomish, far left), Clara Siddle (Muckleshoot, center holding ball), Maggie Daniels, and Agatha Henry (Suquamish). Basketball was one of the few team sports that women were allowed to play. This and other sports also contributed to Indian schools' goal of assimilating Native American children into the mainstream white culture. Photo by Ferd Brady, courtesy of the Brady Collection, Museum of History and Industry, Seattle.

An early football team, ca. 1895–1910. The lack of pads and helmets contributed to a high number of injuries and fatalities. The National Collegiate Athletic Association grew out of efforts to make the increasingly popular sport safer. Photo courtesy of the Library of Congress, LC-D4-32468 DLC.

The inspection room at Ellis Island, New York, during its heyday between 1910 and 1920. Inspectors quizzed the millions of immigrants about their politics and checked for infectious diseases. Most were permitted to enter the country. Photo courtesy of the Library of Congress, LC-D4-73001 DLC.

Electric trolley in Chicago, Illinois. First run successfully in 1887 in Richmond, Virginia, electric trolleys (or streetcars) quickly spread throughout the United States. The crowds hanging off this one illustrate the high demand for and over-crowding of mass transit in densely populated urban centers. By 1902, Americans took 4.8 billion rides annually. Photo courtesy of the Chicago Daily News *negatives collection, Chicago History Museum, DN-0061371.*

Standard Oil owner and philanthropist John D. Rockefeller. An infamous symbol of corporate greed because of his near-monopoly on oil refining, the devout Baptist donated millions of dollars to education, medical research, and public health campaigns. Photo courtesy of the Chicago Daily News *negatives collection, Chicago History Museum, DN-0051594.*

Prof. W. E. B. DuBois

Professor of Sociology, Atlanta University

Subject: *The Development of a People*

Cover of a Redpath Lyceum Bureau flyer announcing a talk, "The Development of a People," by W. E. B. Du Bois. An outspoken champion of African American civil rights, Du Bois was a socialist, novelist, and essayist who edited the magazine of the National Association for the Advancement of Colored People. Photograph courtesy of the Chautauqua Collection, Special Collections Department, University of Iowa Libraries.

State prisoners excavating the site of a water works in Canon City, Colorado. Convict leasing was most notorious in the South, where disproportionately African American prisoners suffered from overwork and abuse. Photo courtesy of the Western History/Genealogy Department, Denver Public Library.

National Woman's Party (NWP) members picketing the White House during President Woodrow Wilson's second inauguration, 4 March 1917. More radical than the larger National American Woman Suffrage Association, the NWP used direct-action techniques to great effect. Photo courtesy of the National Woman's Party Records, Library of Congress, Manuscript Division.

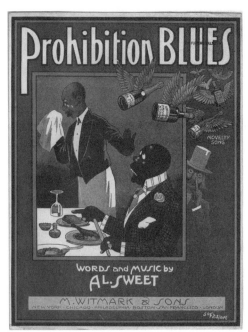

This racist image from 1917 reveals the terrible state of race relations during the Progressive Era. The stereotype of the drunken, dissolute black man was common among whites. This image also suggests the growing association between black Americans and popular music, especially ragtime and jazz. Illustration courtesy of the Rare Book, Manuscript, and Special Collections Library, Duke University.

Carrie Chapman Catt, 28 March 1914. As president of the National American Woman Suffrage Association between 1915 and 1920, Catt implemented the Winning Plan for ratification of the Nineteenth Amendment. Photo courtesy of the Library of Congress, LC-USZ62-28475 DLC.

Eugene V. Debs editing the newspaper Appeal to Reason *in Girard, Kansas, 1909. Presidential candidate of the Socialist Party of America, Debs won 6 percent of the popular vote in 1912. In 1920, he won nearly a million votes despite being in federal prison for opposing WWI and America's involvement in it. Photo courtesy of the Special Collections Department, Cunningham Memorial Library, Indiana State University.*

Chicago garment workers lining up for a protest, 12 December 1910, a year after the Uprising of the Twenty Thousand proved that women could be effective union members. Photo courtesy of the Chicago Daily News *negatives collection, Chicago History Museum, DN-0056264.*

Would-be anarchist Leon Czolgosz shooting President William McKinley at the Pan-American Exposition reception, 6 September 1901. Photograph of a wash drawing by T. Dart Walker, 1905, courtesy of the Library of Congress, LC-USZ62-5377 DLC.

Anarchist and feminist Emma Goldman, 6 March 1934. An outspoken advocate of political and sexual freedom, Goldman was imprisoned and then deported for speaking against the draft during WWI. Photograph by Carl van Vechten, courtesy of the Library of Congress, LC-USZ62-42504 DLC.

Opening game 1916. Bx 112

President Woodrow Wilson throwing the first ball on the opening day of the 1916 baseball season. Played professionally since the 1870s, baseball grew into a stable business enterprise during this era despite player strikes and scandals. Photo courtesy of the Library of Congress, LC-USZ62-9981 DLC.

President Theodore Roosevelt (center) and companions on horseback near Glenwood Springs, Colorado, 1900 or 1905. Roosevelt promoted outdoor living, sports such as football, and at times warfare as antidotes to over-civilization. Photo courtesy of the Western History/Genealogy Department, Denver Public Library.

Massachusetts Senator Henry Cabot Lodge attending the Republican National Convention, 7 June 1916. Lodge was a leading conservative who supported U.S. imperial expansion in Latin America and the Pacific and promoted immigration restrictions. Photo courtesy of the Chicago Daily News *negatives collection, Chicago History Museum, DN-0066443.*

Charles "Boss" Murphy (left) and New York City Sheriff Alfred Smith (right), 5 July 1916. As boss of New York City's Tammany Hall political machine, Murphy rebuilt the organization after revelations of serious corruption led to a string of defeats in 1894–1901. His protégé, Alfred Smith, was a leading urban liberal who forged alliances with progressive reformers. Photo courtesy of the Chicago Daily News *negatives collection, Chicago History Museum, DN-0066548.*

The Culebra Cut, Panama end, in 1908, indicating the scale of construction. Imagined since the 16th century, the Panama Canal was finally completed by the United States in 1914. Theodore Roosevelt's heavy-handed diplomacy, which gave the United States rights to the canal zone, was highly controversial. Photo courtesy of the Chicago Daily News negatives collection, Chicago History Museum, DN-0006154.

Two major leaders of the Mexican Revolution, Alvaro Obregón (right) and Pancho Villa (center), along with U.S. Army General John J. Pershing (left), 27 August 1914. Two years later, Pershing led a campaign into Mexico to punish Villa for the killing of 17 Americans in Columbus, New Mexico. Photograph by Robert Runyon, courtesy of the Robert Runyon Photograph Collection, Center for American History and General Libraries, University of Texas at Austin.

as their male colleagues). Even as **academic associations** and the **American Association of University Professors** (1916) diverted professors, NEA membership grew to over 8,000 by 1917. Unwelcome in the NEA, **African American** educators established the National Association of Colored Teachers in 1904. *See also* HIGH SCHOOL.

NATIONAL HOUSING ASSOCIATION (NHA). Organized in 1910 by **Lawrence Veiller** with help from the **Russell Sage Foundation**, this group gathered information on urban housing conditions while campaigning for stronger building codes and better regulation of health and safety conditions of working-class dwellings, after the model of New York's **Tenement House Act**. The NHA stressed private housing rather than public or cooperative developments and insisted that appropriate regulation would enable urban landlords to make a profit without stinting on construction or maintenance. Real estate interests nonetheless usually resisted the association's model housing law. Even so, by 1920 at least eight states and 40 cities had adopted versions of New York's regulations or the NHA's model law. After peaking at 1,112 members in 1919, the NHA declined until Veiller disbanded it in 1936. *See also* LOWER EAST SIDE; RIIS, JACOB.

NATIONAL INDUSTRIAL CONFERENCE BOARD (NICB). Formed in 1916 by a consortium of employers and trade associations, the most prominent being the **National Association of Manufacturers**, this board collected economic statistics such as wage rates and **cost of living** indexes and published studies of business and labor conditions. Founding director Magnus Alexander (1870–1932) was a prominent **General Electric** engineer with an interest in **welfare capitalism**, **worker's compensation**, and similar reforms. Start-up funds came from **Westinghouse** and **General Motors**, in addition to General Electric. The sponsors intended the NICB as a research and public relations institution favorable to business in a period when suspicions of corporate power were widespread. The board endured as a respected source of domestic and international economic indicators, for example, the Consumer Confidence Index.

NATIONAL MEDICAL ASSOCIATION (NMA). Founded at the Cotton States **Exposition** in Atlanta in 1895, this organization brought together **African American** physicians, who, because of **segregation** and discrimination, were excluded from white-run medical schools, associations, and hospitals. The group enrolled 500 doctors by 1910, around one-third of the country's black physicians. Beginning in 1909, the NMA published the *Journal of the National Medical Association*. When eight of 10 African American medical schools closed in the aftermath of the **Flexner Report**, the NMA campaigned to preserve minority access to medical education and expand the number of black-run hospitals. *See also* AMERICAN MEDICAL ASSOCIATION; HEALTH AND MEDICINE.

NATIONAL MONETARY COMMISSION. *See* ALDRICH, NELSON W.; ALDRICH–VREELAND ACT; FEDERAL RESERVE ACT.

NATIONAL MUNICIPAL LEAGUE (NML). Founded in 1894 and headquartered initially in Philadelphia, this group and its local branches and affiliates emerged as the main research and advocacy organization for urban **structural reform** and **efficiency** in city government. Led by Clinton Rogers Woodruff (1868–1948), the league attracted prominent scholars of public administration, such as **Frank Goodnow** and **Charles Beard**, and publicists for good government, such as **Richard S. Childs**. The NML's first published program (1899) for municipal reform recommended civil service and tax reform, improved budgeting, and careful drafting of **utilities** franchises. Through its model city charters, the NML popularized such innovations as **home rule**, **nonpartisan elections**, and the **strong mayor system**. Woodruff and the NML always regarded the **commission system** with ambivalence, preferring the **city manager system**, especially for medium and small cities. *See also* BUREAU OF MUNICIPAL RESEARCH.

NATIONAL NEGRO BUSINESS LEAGUE (NNBL). Founded in 1900 at the initiative of **Booker T. Washington** and led by Washington's close associate, Emmett Scott (1873–1957), this group supported local leagues of black-owned businesses to promote **African**

American entrepreneurship. This top-down organizational strategy reversed the bottom-up formation of trade associations and **chambers of commerce** among white-owned businesses and reflected the reality that African American businesses were generally small-scale service industries and owner-operated firms catering primarily to a black clientele. With funding from **Andrew Carnegie**, the NNBL grew slowly, with only 278 local chapters in 1915. It became a lightning rod for debates between partisans of Washington and his chief rival, **W. E. B. Du Bois**, because it reflected Washington's approach of giving priority to economic advancement while accommodating **segregation**.

NATIONAL PARK SERVICE (NPS). At its creation in the Department of the Interior in 1916, the NPS assumed control over 14 national parks and 21 national monuments, the former created by acts of Congress and the latter by executive order under the **Antiquities Act**. The NPS was intended to strengthen and rationalize the administration of these lands while redressing the legacy of mismanagement, loss of land, poaching, and souvenir hunting. Only Canada had a similar organization. Stephen Tyng Mather (1867–1930) headed the NPS from 1916 to 1929, raising funds from private donors and drawing on his own fortune when Congress proved reluctant to fund park improvements. Mather attracted visitors to national parks through publicity and development, giving railroads concessions to develop resorts in or near major parks. The Northern Pacific developed and advertised Yellowstone (1872); the Great Northern ran Glacier National Park (1910); and the **Atchison, Topeka, and Santa Fe**–owned resorts on the rim of the Grand Canyon (a national monument in 1908; a park in 1919). The parks' status as recreational resources insulated them from mining, lumbering, and ranching interests. The NPS also barred customary subsistence uses of park lands by **Native Americans** and local whites. However, providing roads, hotels, restaurants, and landscapes and animals (elk but not wolves, for example) that visitors expected conflicted with the preservation of natural environments and species. *See also* CONSERVATION; FOREST SERVICE, U.S.; MUIR, JOHN.

NATIONAL PROGRESSIVE REPUBLICAN LEAGUE (NPRL). Wisconsin Senator **Robert La Follette** organized this forum for

Insurgent Republicans in January 1911. The NPRL's ostensible purpose was to pressure the party to espouse such reforms as direct election of **senators**, **direct primaries**, and "corrupt practices" (today campaign finance) legislation. Its real purpose was to challenge the **Old Guard** for control and deny renomination to President **William Howard Taft**. La Follette and NPRL president Jonathan Bourne, a **progressive** Republican senator from Oregon, recruited such prominent politicians as **Hiram Johnson**, **George Norris**, and **Albert Cummins**, along with writers and activists such as **Ray Stannard Baker**, **Frederic Howe**, **James R. Garfield**, and **Gifford Pinchot**. After the failure of half-hearted efforts to enlist former president **Theodore Roosevelt**, a split emerged between supporters of La Follette for president and advocates of a Roosevelt comeback. The NPRL broke apart during the tumultuous 1912 presidential campaign, when La Follette's candidacy faltered and then, after Taft secured renomination, Roosevelt ran on a separate **Progressive Party** ticket.

NATIONAL TUBERCULOSIS ASSOCIATION (NTA). Founded in 1904 as a clearinghouse for state and city **tuberculosis** prevention societies, the NTA had some 1,300 local branches by the late 1910s. Although mortality from tuberculosis was declining by 1900, it still accounted for 10 percent of all deaths. The state societies and the NTA sponsored lectures and produced pamphlets, posters, exhibits, parades, cartoons, and **movies** exhorting people to improve hygiene, stop spitting in public, and avoid the then-common public drinking cup. Activists also agitated against ornate furnishings and beards, believing both collected germs. These antituberculosis campaigns played a large role in educating Americans about germ theory. *See also* HEALTH AND MEDICINE; PUBLIC HEALTH.

NATIONAL WOMAN'S PARTY (NWP). Founded in 1916, this group had its origins in the Congressional Union, a **women**'s **suffrage** association created by **Alice Paul** and **Lucy Burns** in 1914. The NWP attracted some of the suffrage movement's wealthy backers known as "allies," along with younger, more radical suffragists. Unlike the **National American Woman Suffrage Association**, the NWP pursued an openly **feminist** agenda. Beginning early in

1917, party members picketed the White House, pioneering a now-venerable political practice. After U.S. entry into World War I in 1917, the picketers mocked President **Woodrow Wilson**'s hypocrisy in claiming to fight for democracy abroad while refusing to allow women to vote at home. Arrested and jailed, the protestors followed the example of British suffragists by going on hunger strikes and demanding to be treated as political prisoners. Following the example of British prison officials, American jailors force-fed the activists through tubes in their noses. As in Great Britain, this symbolic rape gained sympathy for the NWP. Even after Wilson shifted to supporting women's suffrage, pickets remained in place until the Senate voted to approve the **Nineteenth Amendment** in 1919.

NATIVE AMERICANS. At the turn of the century, Native American populations in the United States reached historic lows, declining from several million in 1500 to 500,000 in 1900. The **Dawes Allotment Act** (1887) was intended to **Americanize** the remaining Native peoples by destroying their tribal structures and turning communally held reservation lands into privately owned plots. Through this act, with its ill-conceived provisions for selling or leasing so-called surplus lands, Indians lost millions of acres of land to whites and suffered the loss or theft of resources controlled by the Bureau of Indian Affairs (BIA) on their behalf. The abolition of the **Indian Territory** in 1907 further eroded their independence and economic base. The BIA also forced many children to attend boarding schools that provided a special **Indian education** intended to eradicate Native languages and cultural and religious practices.

Even as the United States sought to eliminate Native Americans' collective status as domestic dependent nations (an effort upheld by the **Supreme Court** decision *Lone Wolf v. Hitchcock* in 1903), few gained citizenship rights at the state or federal level. While the majority suffered grinding poverty on reservations, a small number of U.S.-educated Indians turned to protest through the **Society of American Indians**. Activists like **Gertrude Bonnin, Charles Eastman, Carlos Montezuma**, Arthur C. Parker, **Francis La Flesche**, and **Susan La Flesche Picotte** studied and promoted respect for Native cultures and religions, tried to ameliorate poverty, poor health, and demoralization, and agitated for civil rights. Anthropologists such as **Alice Cunningham Fletcher**, Frank Hamilton Cushing, and James Mooney also compiled a record of complex and sophisticated cultures, complemented by the photographs of **Edward Curtis**.

The idea of cultural **pluralism** and a romantic vision of Native Americans led a minority of whites, including novelist **Mary Austin** and publicist **Charles Lummis**, to campaign for Indians' political and cultural rights. Beginning in the 1880s, the **Atchison, Topeka, and Santa Fe Railroad** opened the Pueblo and Navajo homelands to tourism. Many non-Indians came to see Native Americans as natural **conservationists**. Youth organizations such as the **Boy Scouts** and **Girl Scouts** engaged white youth in ersatz Indian rituals. A few Native Americans made a living performing in **Wild West shows** and **movie** westerns. But rates of poverty, disease, alcoholism, and suicide remained high on most reservations.

NATURALISM. A **literary** movement that flourished from the 1890s to World War I, naturalism attempted to depict the brutal, sordid aspects of life unalloyed by notions of morality, beauty, and optimism. To the economic and social circumstances stressed by **realists**, naturalists added an emphasis on irrational desires and innate tendencies toward domination, cruelty, and violence. This dark view of humanity reflected the cultural influence of Darwinism, modern psychology, the **modernist** philosophy exemplified by the German Friedrich Nietzsche (1844–1900), and the literary example of controversial French novelist Émile Zola (1840–1902). Prominent American naturalist writers include **Frank Norris**, **Stephen Crane**, and **Jack London**. Realists such as **Hamlin Garland** and **Theodore Dreiser** also incorporated naturalistic themes.

NEW FREEDOM. **Woodrow Wilson** adopted this term during his 1912 presidential campaign as an alternative to **Theodore Roosevelt**'s call for a **New Nationalism**. With this term, Wilson conveyed his vision of **antitrust** and business regulation as a means of reinvigorating traditional American virtues such as individualism, free enterprise, and self-reliance. According to Wilson, Roosevelt's program leaned too far toward bureaucracy, expert paternalism, and state control. Especially after Wilson published a collection of speeches titled *The New Freedom* (1913), the term came to signify all of his domestic initiatives, even when, as in the case of the **Federal Trade Commission**, they contained elements of the New Nationalism. *See also* BRANDEIS, LOUIS D.

NEW HISTORY. In the early 20th century, this term described what historians later called **progressive** history. Adherents of the New History subscribed to several intertwined tenets. First, historians should emphasize social, cultural, and **intellectual** developments rather than dramatic events or famous people. Second, historical interpretation is by nature relative: as priorities and attitudes change and earlier interpretations are criticized, each generation views the past differently. Third, historians should not be aloof but should use their skills to provide context for contemporary issues. Finally, historians should aim to help citizens understand themselves, their problems, and their prospects. **James Harvey Robinson** articulated this approach in *The New History* (1912) and other writings, but its most prominent practitioner was **Charles A. Beard**.

NEWLANDS, FRANCIS G. (1846–1917). Politician. A Mississippi native raised in Illinois, Newlands practiced law in California and Nevada, where he poured money and energy into water projects, earning a seat in the U.S. House of Representatives (1893–1903) and the Senate (1903–17), first on a pro-silver ticket and later as a **Democrat**. Sponsor of the resolution that led to the annexation of **Hawaii** (1898), he allied with **Theodore Roosevelt** on **conservation** and was the main backer of the 1902 **Newlands Reclamation Act**. A moderate on labor issues, he supported a 1913 bill to enhance federal mediation in railroad labor disputes. During his years in Congress, he developed electric **trolley** lines and suburbs in the Washington, D.C., area and became the main backer of the **McMillan Plan** upon the death of James McMillan in 1902.

NEWLANDS RECLAMATION ACT (1902). Proposed by Nevada **Democratic** congressman **Francis G. Newlands**, this law mandated that proceeds from the sale of public lands in 16 western and southwestern states finance irrigation projects there. The lands were to be sold in 160-acre parcels to individuals (a provision meant to encourage small farms), and state water laws and private rights would remain in effect. The law also prohibited employment of Asian workers and stipulated an **eight-hour day**. The Interior Department created the **Reclamation Service** to implement this law. Despite ostensible successes like the Roosevelt Dam, the act never achieved what Congress intended. Land sales provided too little money to support the proposed projects, speculators rushed in on the heels of bureau engineers, most projects irrigated privately held land rather than public lands sold to small farmers, and the acreage limitation was not enforced. *See also* CONSERVATION; HETCH HETCHY VALLEY RESERVOIR.

NEWMAN, PAULINE (1893?–1986). Labor organizer. The daughter of Lithuanian **Jewish immigrants**, Newman worked in a garment factory at age nine, learning how to hide from **child labor** inspectors. To gain **education** and English skills, she joined a **socialist** reading group and soon became politically active. She joined the **Uprising of the Twenty Thousand** (1909) and became a fundraiser, organizer, and eventually a vice president of the **Women's Trade Union League**. A skilled speaker in English and Yiddish, Newman was the first female organizer for the **International Ladies' Garment Workers' Union**, lectured on behalf of the **Socialist Party**, campaigned for **women's suffrage**, and occasionally worked as a government factory inspector. Like many leading women reformers, Newman had her most enduring relationships with other women, raising an adopted daughter with partner Frieda Miller. *See also* FEMINISM; LABOR UNIONS.

NEW MIDDLE CLASS. The concept of a "new middle class" plays a fundamental part in many interpretations of the Progressive Era, most clearly in the **organizational synthesis**. Scholars use this term to describe the white-collar occupations generated by industrialization, urbanization, **modernization**, the emergence of corporate enterprise, and technological development. Unlike the "old middle class" of self-employed merchants, shopkeepers, master craftsmen, and prosperous farmers, the new managers, professionals, and office and sales clerks earned their living as salaried employees or consultants for large private or public institutions, valued specialized knowledge over general competence, and tended to have more formal **education**. By virtually every measure, the new middle class outstripped the old in size and influence by the early 20th century. By 1910, 20 percent of the labor force was employed in white collar business or clerical positions. Scholars often attribute changing notions of selfhood, success, morality, family, gender, **sexuality**, and so on to the growing influence of the new middle class. *See also* EFFICIENCY; HIGH SCHOOL; UNIVERSITY.

NEW NATIONALISM. Theodore Roosevelt used this phrase—borrowed from **Herbert Croly**'s *The Promise of American Life* (1909)—to describe the reforms he promoted from the time his quarrel with President **William Howard Taft** became public in 1910 through the defeat of his **Bull Moose** presidential candidacy in 1912. Endorsing federal intervention in a wide range of social, economic, and labor issues, Roosevelt called for everything from the **income tax** to **worker's compensation**, **child labor** laws, **conservation**, and tighter corporate regulation. What held the program together was Roosevelt's long-standing insistence that the problems of an urban, industrial, corporate society were of such scale and scope that only the national government could manage them. Collected in a 1910 book titled *The New Nationalism*, his speeches summarized the version of **progressive** reform that stressed the expansion of government authority. **Woodrow Wilson** developed his **New Freedom** as an alternative to Roosevelt's vision. *See also* SQUARE DEAL.

NEW ORLEANS RIOT (JULY 1900). This **race riot**, one of several that occurred in 1900, began when three white police officers and two **African American** men got into a gunfight that ended when one of the men, Robert Charles, killed two officers, wounded the third, and escaped. The hunt for him spawned mobs of white men who first sought to take Charles's companion from jail to **lynch** him but were fended off by the sheriff. They then headed for **Storyville**, the city's **red-light** district, assaulting passersby and shooting, beating, kicking, and burning one black man to death. The riot subsided in the French Quarter and finally ended after police located Charles, burned him out of the apartment where he was hidden, and shot him as he fled. In the process, Charles killed nine white officers and wounded almost 30 others. Whites stomped his corpse to pieces in the street. *See also* LYNCHING.

THE *NEW REPUBLIC*. Financed by the reform banking couple Dorothy and **Willard Straight** and edited by **Herbert Croly**, this weekly magazine became the country's most influential forum for the **New Nationalism** version of progressivism upon its appearance in 1914. Croly and coeditors **Walter Lippmann** and **Walter Weyl** assembled a stellar staff of young, reform-minded writers, including **Felix Frankfurter** and **Randolph Bourne** and attracted such prominent contributors as **Charles Beard**, **John Dewey**, George Bernard Shaw, and H. G. Wells. When the magazine's hero, **Theodore Roosevelt**, declined to enter the 1916 presidential race, the *New Republic* hesitantly supported **Woodrow Wilson**, whose **New Freedom** the editors had earlier disdained. At the same time, the magazine also began to support U.S. entry into World War I on behalf of the Allies, even claiming credit for coining Wilson's slogan "Peace without Victory." *See also* INTELLECTUAL; JOURNALISM.

NEW WOMAN. The phrase and its uses, first in the 1890s and again in the 1910s, referenced a shift in **women**'s economic, educational, and social standing, their increasing public visibility, and their growing political involvement. In **popular culture**, **literature**, and **art**, the New Woman was often represented in terms of her dress—the white-collar working girl's dark skirt and white shirtwaist blouse—and her leisure pursuits. Illustrator Charles Dana Gibson provided the best-known rendering. The reality behind the images of female modernity was more complex, varying by class, ethnicity, and race. Working-class, single women in factory, retail, and clerical jobs gained limited economic independence from families. The growing numbers of women in **high schools**, colleges, and **universities**; clerical work; and the professions reflected the rise of a **new middle class**. Such women were ubiquitous in **progressive** reform movements and integral to the new social service professions. These activities revitalized the women's **suffrage** movement. Culturally, women's patronage of commercial entertainment from **dance halls** to **vaudeville** and **movies** and their participation in organized **athletics** led some to celebrate their liberation and others to mourn their loss of morals. Among **immigrants**, such activities were often blamed on their daughters' too rapid **Americanization**. Declining rates of marriage and fertility and rising rates of **divorce** fostered panics over **race suicide** and produced new medical and **feminist** ideas about **sexuality**, marriage, and child bearing and rearing.

NEW YORK CITY, CONSOLIDATION OF. The most dramatic of the period's urban **annexations** occurred on 1 January 1898, when New York City (encompassing Manhattan and the Bronx) incorporated Staten Island, dozens of villages and suburbs on Long Island comprising the borough of Queens, and the independent municipality of Brooklyn, then the nation's fourth-largest city with 900,000 people. The consolidation promised to systematize the metropolitan region's finances and provide opportunities for more coherent public works, railroad, and port policies. Along with a few villages in the Bronx and Queens, the strongest resistance came from Brooklyn, whose majority Protestant population feared losing power in the giant, **pluralist** city. Even in Brooklyn, however, annexation won an 1894 referendum by 277 votes out of 129,211 cast, mainly because Brooklynites recognized that their narrow tax base could not finance upgrades to municipal services. In 1896, New York **Republican Party** boss **Thomas C. Platt** pushed the consolidation through the state legislature in part because he believed that his party might compete better with **Tammany Hall** in the enlarged city. *See also* LOW, SETH.

NEW YORK STATE FACTORY INVESTIGATING COMMIS-SION. Formed in the aftermath of the **Triangle Shirtwaist Company Fire** of 1911, this commission in three years of operation produced dozens of proposals, 56 of which became law, to improve conditions in the state's factories. Reforms ranged from improved fire safety and enhanced factory inspections to maximum hours legislation for **women** and bans on sweatshops in tenements. In addition, the commission established its leader, state assembly speaker **Alfred E. Smith**, as a major proponent of social and **labor** reform and solidified an alliance between Smith, **Robert F. Wagner**, and reform activists such as **Mary E. Dreier**, **Frances Perkins**, and

Belle Moskowitz. Amid revelations of **Tammany Hall** collusion in factory owners' abuse and negligence, Smith and Wagner pushed the New York machine toward **urban liberalism**.

NIAGARA MOVEMENT. This short-lived organization expressed the dissatisfaction of many **African American** civil rights activists with **Booker T. Washington**'s cautious agenda. Twenty-nine male activists met on 10 July 1905, in Fort Erie, Ontario, Canada, after hotelkeepers in Buffalo, New York, refused to host a black gathering. Women were permitted to join the following year. Organizers **W. E. B. Du Bois** and **William Monroe Trotter** issued a "Declaration of Principles" that demanded civil and political rights and condemned economic discrimination, in sharp contrast to Washington's **Atlanta Compromise** speech. However, the Niagara Movement failed because Washington's opposition led white philanthropists to refuse to fund it, and black leaders were unable to do so. Still, events in 1906–7—among them the **Brownsville Raid** and the **Atlanta Riot**—convinced many that Washington's accommodationism was bankrupt. Although the movement disintegrated by 1908, it was soon replaced by the **National Association for the Advancement of Colored People**. *See also* SEGREGATION; SPRINGFIELD RIOT.

NICARAGUA. Relations between the United States and this Central American republic, strained since William Walker's notorious filibustering expeditions of the 1850s, grew more intertwined during the **imperialist** expansion of the Progressive Era. Until events of 1903 shifted attention toward **Panama**, official studies tended to favor low-lying Nicaragua over mountainous Panama for the projected isthmian canal. In the early 1900s, the United States resisted Nicaraguan dictator José Santos Zelaya's efforts to unite the five Central American republics. In 1909, when Nicaragua executed two Americans found laying mines for antigovernment rebels, President **William Howard Taft** dispatched U.S. forces that protected the rebels until they overthrew Zelaya in 1910. Then, in a vivid instance of **dollar diplomacy**, new president Adolfo Díaz and U.S. Secretary of State **Philander C. Knox** arranged for New York bankers to assume Nicaragua's international debts in exchange for American control of the republic's national bank, railroads, and customs collections.

This deal encouraged a new revolt in 1912, and at Díaz's request the United States sent 2,600 marines, establishing a U.S. military presence that continued with brief interruptions until 1933. President **Woodrow Wilson** and Secretary of State **William Jennings Bryan** tried to replace the bankers' oversight of Nicaraguan finance with a direct protectorate in the Bryan–Chamorro Treaty, but the Senate refused to ratify it until 1916, when it was watered down to granting the United States authority over a never-built second isthmian canal. *See also* FOREIGN POLICY.

NICKELODEON. *See* MOVIES.

NINETEENTH AMENDMENT. This amendment to the U.S. Constitution gave **women** the right to vote. The triumph of the 75-year women's **suffrage** campaign, the measure passed the House of Representatives in 1918 and the Senate in 1919. The required three-fourths of states ratified it in August 1920, when Tennessee became the 36th state to vote in favor. The last state to approve it was Mississippi in 1981. *See also* NATIONAL AMERICAN WOMAN SUFFRAGE ASSOCIATION.

NONPARTISAN ELECTIONS. Omitting the party affiliation of candidates from ballots for municipal elections was one of several **structural reforms**, such as **at-large elections** and the **short ballot**, that proponents argued would undercut **machine politics** and improve the **efficiency** of urban government. In 1888, Louisville became the first large city to adopt this practice, and by the early 20th century a majority of cities with **commission** and **city manager systems** provided for ballots without partisan labels. Nonpartisanship had its greatest success in the West, where parties had shallow roots in local politics, and in the South, where one-party (**Democratic**) rule prevailed. Boston became one of the few large eastern cities to eliminate party labels from its ballots in 1909. During the 1910s, states such as California and Arizona required nonpartisan elections for many municipal and county offices, and Minnesota even adopted nonpartisan ballots for state legislators in 1913. Although most public administration experts who advised the **National Municipal League** endorsed nonpartisan elections for local offices, others, such as **Charles A. Beard**, suggested that voters would tend to favor party candidates anyway, and formats such as the **strong mayor system** could make party government more accountable.

NORRIS, BENJAMIN FRANKLIN (FRANK) (1870–1902). Author. Born in Chicago, Frank Norris grew up in San Francisco and developed a fascination with **social Darwinism** and French novelist Émile Zola's **naturalism** while studying art in Paris and at the University of California and Harvard University. After working as a war correspondent in South Africa (1895–96) and **Cuba** (1898), Norris won praise from editor **William Dean Howells** for his third novel, *McTeague* (1899), a dreary naturalistic story of a self-taught San Francisco dentist overwhelmed by his innate brutish impulses. As a **literary** critic and editor, Norris discovered *Sister Carrie* (1900), the breakthrough novel of another major naturalist, **Theodore Dreiser**. At the time of Norris's early death from peritonitis, he had completed two novels of a trilogy on the grain trade: *The Octopus* (1901), based on a notorious incident involving the **Southern Pacific Railroad**, and *The Pit* (1903), the basis for **D. W. Griffith**'s **movie** *A Corner in Wheat* (1909).

NORRIS, GEORGE W. (1861–1944). Politician. Born in Ohio, Norris became a lawyer and a county attorney and judge in Nebraska, where he was elected to the House of Representatives as a **Republican** (1903–13) and then to the Senate (1913–43). From the start, Norris voted with **progressives** of both parties and frequently criticized railroads and his party leaders. In 1910, he led the **Insurgent** rebellion against Speaker of the House **Joseph G. Cannon**; the following year he became a leader in the **National Progressive Republican League**, supporting first **Robert La Follette** and then **Theodore Roosevelt** for the 1912 presidential nomination, although he refused to join the **Progressive Party**. In the Senate Norris advocated direct election of **senators**, the rights of labor, and public development of natural resources. An ardent isolationist, he voted against U.S. entry into World War I and the Versailles Treaty.

***NORTHERN SECURITIES V. UNITED STATES* (1904).** This landmark **antitrust** case began in a stock market struggle between **James**

J. Hill and **E. H. Harriman** for control of two major railroad lines across the Great Plains: the Chicago, Burlington, and Quincy and the Northern Pacific. In 1901, banker **J. P. Morgan** ended this rivalry by combining Hill's and Harriman's northwestern railroad interests into a **holding company** called the Northern Securities Company. President **Theodore Roosevelt** perceived this combine, which would monopolize long-distance traffic in the Northwest, as the epitome of a menacing concentration of economic power, just what the Sherman Antitrust Act was intended to prevent. Ignoring pressure from Morgan, Roosevelt in 1902 ordered Attorney General **Philander C. Knox** to sue for the company's dissolution. In a 5–4 decision in March 1904, the **U.S. Supreme Court** ordered it dissolved, thereby validating the federal government's authority to break up excessively powerful big businesses. *See also* GREAT MERGER MOVEMENT; SQUARE DEAL.

NURSES AND NURSING. Women played only a small role in extra-familial health care before the Civil War, when thousands of women, the best known being American Red Cross founder Clara Barton, aided wounded and sick soldiers. Most wage-earning nurses remained little more than hospital maids, but between 1870 and 1900, the number of nursing **education** programs expanded tenfold and then tripled in the decade ending in 1910, when about 1,200 such schools existed. Most programs required students to perform menial labor in hospitals for little pay while taking courses on anatomy, physiology, and biology. Once graduated, nurses were frequently required to live at the hospital under strict discipline. Seeking to improve education and working conditions, nurses organized after 1900; the *American Journal of Nursing* began in that year. **African American** nurse Mary Eliza Mahoney founded the National Association of Graduate Colored Nurses in 1908; white nurses followed suit with the whites-only American Nurses Association (1912). **Lillian Wald**'s Visiting Nurses Service was the most highly organized of the **public health** nursing offered by **settlement houses**. These nurses and their supporters established the National Organization for Public Health Nurses in 1912. The creation of the Army (1901) and Navy Nurse Corps (1908) acknowledged the success of nurses in professionalizing their field. *See also* HEALTH AND MEDICINE.

– O –

O'CONNELL, WILLIAM HENRY (1859–1944). Bishop. Born in Massachusetts to Irish **immigrants**, he graduated from Boston College (1881) and entered the priesthood. As bishop of Portland, Maine (1901–6), archbishop of Boston (appointed in 1907), and then cardinal (1911), he **modernized** his dioceses and made them more **efficient**. In Boston, he built new hospitals, churches, schools, colleges, and social service agencies. Unlike many U.S. Catholic bishops, he viewed **Americanism** as a heresy, opposing liberals such as Father **John Ryan** and forbidding Catholics to attend non-Catholic religious ceremonies or join the **Boy Scouts**, **Girl Scouts**, the **Young Men's Christian Association**, and the **Young Women's Christian Association**. He challenged persistent **anti-Catholicism** and exercised considerable influence in the Massachusetts legislature and Congress.

O'HARE, KATE RICHARDS (1876–1948). Socialist. The daughter of Kansas homesteaders, O'Hare became involved in **prohibition** and rescue work with **prostitutes** in the 1890s. A **socialist journalist** and lecturer after 1901, she soon became the leading American **woman** socialist. She headed the Kansas branch of the **Socialist Party of America**, served on the national executive committee, ran unsuccessfully for Congress and the Senate (the first woman to do the latter), and gave more speeches than anyone in the party except **Eugene V. Debs**. Although she sought to broaden the party's program to address farmers and women workers, she kept her distance from women's **suffrage** in the belief that full equality required a social transformation. O'Hare served 18 months in prison for giving an antiwar speech during World War I.

OLD GUARD. During the factional fights in the **Republican Party** that marked **William Howard Taft**'s presidency (1909–13), this term referred to the party's conservatives, especially those in Congress who backed House Speaker **Joseph Cannon** and Senate Majority Leader **Nelson W. Aldrich** in opposition to Republican **Insurgents'** efforts to turn the party in a **progressive** direction.

OLMSTED, FREDERICK LAW, JR. (1870–1957). Urban planner. Born in New York, he was the son of Frederick Law Olmsted Sr. (1822–1933), the defining figure in 19th-century American landscape **architecture**. After graduating from Harvard University in 1894, the young man studied with **Daniel Burnham** and joined his father's firm in 1895. His work as chief landscape architect for Boston's Emerald Necklace park system, which his father had designed, and Washington's **McMillan Plan** (1902), brought him out of his father's shadow and made him a prominent planner in his own right. As founder and president (1899) of the American Society of Landscape Architects, instructor for the nation's first landscape architecture course (at Harvard), organizer of the **National Conference on City Planning**, and founder of the American City Planning Institute (1917), he was influential in the professionalization of urban planning. Initially identified with the **City Beautiful** movement, he increasingly espoused **City Practical** ideas but rejected the social reform–oriented planning advocated by **Benjamin Marsh**. In addition to plans for Detroit, Pittsburgh, New Haven, and other cities, he and his firm designed street systems, parks and parkways, suburbs, and model towns. He helped formulate the 1916 bill creating the **National Park Service** and advised the NPS for 30 years.

OPEN DOOR NOTES. These statements, issued in 1899 and 1900 by Secretary of State **John Hay**, pressured Great Britain, Russia, Germany, Japan, France, and Italy to renounce ambitions to carve China into spheres of exclusive economic and political influence. The first note, circulated in September and November 1899, declared that all areas of China should remain open to business from all countries on an equal basis. In the existing foreign concessions, Hay insisted, the Chinese should retain control of customs collections and apply tariffs equally. Even though the Great Powers, especially Russia, refused to offer firm commitments, in March 1900 Hay announced publicly that the relevant countries had agreed to maintain open access. The **Boxer Rebellion** soon called Hay's effort into doubt by revealing the depth of Chinese distrust of foreigners and raising the possibility that competing countries would use military intervention against the rebellion to establish occupation zones. In July 1900, therefore,

Hay issued a second note demanding that the Great Powers preserve China's territorial integrity. On the surface, the Open Door notes expressed American support for China, but skeptics suggested that the policy epitomized American economic **imperialism**, akin to the **dollar diplomacy** practiced in Latin America. *See also* FOREIGN POLICY.

OPEN SHOP. This term refers to an employer's right to hire workers whether or not they belong to a **labor union**. In contrast, a closed shop requires all job candidates to join a union before employment, and a union shop requires workers to join a union in order to retain their jobs. An antiunion policy, the open shop enabled employers to weaken a union or hire strikebreakers during a strike. It was first used in Dayton, Ohio, in 1900, when 38 firms cooperated to maintain an open shop for two years. The **National Association of Manufacturers** urged other employers to follow this example. *See also* AMERICAN FEDERATION OF LABOR; LABOR'S BILL OF GRIEVANCES.

O'REILLY, LEONORA (1870–1927). Labor organizer. Born to Irish **immigrant** parents in New York City, O'Reilly was a garment worker at age 11 and joined the Knights of Labor and the Working Women's Society in 1886, launching a lifelong career in activism on behalf of waged **women**. With the patronage of wealthy reformers such as **Mary Elisabeth Dreier** and **Margaret Dreier Robins**, O'Reilly ran a cooperative garment factory at the Henry Street **settlement house**, furthered her education, headed a Brooklyn settlement house, and provided education to working women. In 1903, she helped to found the New York branch of the **Women's Trade Union League (WTUL)**, worked as a paid WTUL organizer (1909–14), and participated in the **Uprising of the Twenty Thousand** and the **Triangle Shirtwaist Company Fire** investigation (1911). However, she quit the WTUL in 1915 because of political differences with its wealthy supporters and declining health. An advocate of women's **suffrage**, she was a founding member of the **National Association for the Advancement of Colored People**, attended the 1915 women's peace conference at The Hague, and became an Irish nationalist.

ORGANIZATIONAL SYNTHESIS. Historian Louis Galambos coined this term in a 1970 essay to describe a major line of interpretation of the Progressive Era in which historians use **modernization** theory to explain efforts to reorganize government and business in the name of **efficiency** and professionalism. In this view, progressivism was an effort to adapt the society to urbanization, industrialization, and corporate capitalism, and the impetus for reform came from the **new middle class** of **university**-trained professionals, who reshaped the public and private sectors in its image. Despite some disenchantment with modernization theories, the organizational approach remains influential because it explains important aspects of progressivism, such as the emphasis on **structural reform** and improved public administration, the popularity of social scientific efforts to understand and alleviate social problems, and the technocratic cast of mind evident in **Theodore Roosevelt**'s **New Nationalism** and the writings of **Walter Lippmann** and **Thorstein Veblen**. The organizational synthesis, however, fails to explain the suspicion of centralized power and expert management of society evident in the **antitrust** movement and direct democracy measures such as **initiative**, **referendum**, and **recall**. Nor does it effectively explain the popularity of progressivism among urban **immigrants** and workers, farmers, and small-town people. It likewise fails to account for the criticism of the dehumanizing aspects of industrial society evident in the **Arts and Crafts movement** and literary **modernism**.

O'SULLIVAN, MARY KENNEY (1864–1943). Labor leader. Born in Missouri, O'Sullivan became a bookbinder at age 14 and by 1888 was involved in **labor union** activities. She worked briefly for the **American Federation of Labor** in 1892 but found its commitment to **women** workers shallow, so she turned to female reformers at Chicago's **Hull House** and other **settlement houses**. With their help, she persuaded the Illinois state legislature to enact protective labor laws for women and served as an assistant to the first state factory inspector, **Florence Kelley**. After marrying labor **journalist** Jack O'Sullivan (1894), she moved to Boston. In 1903, she helped to found the **Women's Trade Union League** and recruited sisters **Mary Elisabeth Dreier** and **Margaret Dreier Robins** to the cause.

O'Sullivan became a Massachusetts state factory inspector in 1914, a position she held for 20 years.

OVINGTON, MARY WHITE (1865–1951). Civil rights activist. Born in Brooklyn, Ovington helped to found the Greenpoint **settlement house** in her home town and served as its head resident (1895–1903). Concerned about the situation of **African Americans**, she began corresponding by 1904 with **W. E. B. Du Bois**, worked with local black organizations, lived in an African American residential building, and founded the Lincoln settlement house in Brooklyn, work that led to her book *Half a Man: The Status of the Negro in New York* (1911). In 1908, disturbed by the **Springfield Riot** of that year, she was among the activists who issued "The Call" that led to the founding of the **National Association for the Advancement of Colored People (NAACP)**. Ovington served the NAACP without pay for the next 40 years, mediating conflicts, fundraising, promoting **women**'s **suffrage**, and insisting on racial integration as the organization's ultimate aim.

OWENS VALLEY/LOS ANGELES AQUEDUCT. In 1913, the city of Los Angeles completed a 233-mile aqueduct that funneled water from the fertile Owens River Valley to the coastal city. Chief Engineer **William Mulholland** oversaw the project, which involved the secretive purchase of land in the valley and occurred against the will of most residents, whose livelihoods were destroyed. Among the better-known residents was novelist **Mary Austin**, who left in 1905 when the battle against the aqueduct project was lost. Although cities throughout the country took steps to expand and ensure their water supply in this era, the arid West witnessed the most bitter struggles over water, including this one and San Francisco's flooding of the **Hetch Hetchy Valley**. *See also* SANITARY ENGINEERING.

– P –

PAGE, WALTER HINES (1855–1918). Editor and diplomat. A North Carolina native, Page became a **journalist** and by the late 1880s worked for **mass-circulation magazines**, serving as editor of the

Forum, Atlantic Monthly, and *World's Work,* a public affairs magazine he founded in 1900. His book publishing house, Doubleday, Page, and Company, published writers such as **Theodore Dreiser, Upton Sinclair,** and **Edith Wharton**. Though settled in New York, Page retained a strong interest in the South's social, economic, and racial problems, expressing his views in *The Rebuilding of Old Commonwealths* (1902) and the semiautobiographical *The Southerner* (1909). He drew on his New York connections to raise money for the **General Education Board** and the **Southern Education Board**; he also served on President **Theodore Roosevelt**'s Commission on **Country Life**. Having befriended another expatriate southern reformer, President **Woodrow Wilson**, Page was appointed in 1913 as U.S. ambassador to Great Britain, which he supported after the outbreak of World War I in August 1914, despite the Wilson administration's official neutrality. Even after U.S. entry into the war in 1917, he never regained Wilson's confidence and resigned a few months before his death.

PANAMA CANAL. Spain considered digging a canal across the Isthmus of Panama as early as the 1530s, and an American railroad was completed there in 1855. A French company led by Ferdinand de Lesseps, the builder of the Suez Canal, began construction in 1881 but abandoned the project in 1889. When **Theodore Roosevelt** became president in 1901, U.S. official opinion favored building a canal through **Nicaragua**, as the Isthmian Canal Commission had recommended. For a variety of reasons, including French engineer Philippe Bunau-Varilla's offer to sell the partly dug French canal, Roosevelt and Secretary of State **John Hay** persuaded Congress to grant them authority to negotiate with Colombia, of which Panama was then a province. After the Colombian senate unanimously rejected the resulting **Hay–Herrán Treaty** in August 1903, Roosevelt tacitly encouraged Panama's independence movement. When the rebellion occurred in November, U.S. warships insured its success by hampering Colombian efforts to land troops. With Bunau-Varilla acting as agent for the Panamanian rebels as well as the French canal interests, the United States and the new Republic of Panama signed the **Hay–Bunau-Varilla Treaty** on 18 November 1903. This pact granted the United States control over a 10-mile-wide zone along the proposed route in exchange for payments and a U.S. guarantee of Panamanian independence.

Severely criticized for such unabashed **gunboat diplomacy** by the press, Congress, and members of his cabinet (notably Attorney General **Philander C. Knox**), Roosevelt underscored the canal's importance by becoming the first president to leave the country during his administration in 1906, when he went to Panama and was photographed operating a steam shovel. This trip occurred just as the press published allegations of corruption, mistreatment of the mostly West Indian labor force, and poor sanitary conditions exacerbating the **yellow fever** and malaria that had earlier defeated the French. Indeed, around 5,600 of the approximately 30,000 workers died during the decade required to build the canal. Nevertheless, Colonel **George Goethals** oversaw completion of the canal, widely hailed as an engineering marvel upon its opening in 1914. Fifty miles long, with a series of locks to bring ships over the mountains, the Panama Canal cost $352 million, four times as much as the Suez Canal. The United States transferred control over the canal to Panama in 1999. *See also* DOLLAR DIPLOMACY; FOREIGN POLICY; HAY–PAUNCEFORTE TREATIES; ROOSEVELT COROLLARY.

PANIC OF 1907. This financial crisis, the fourth in 34 years, resulted from a recession, a nearly 50-percent decline from the stock market's peak in 1906, and numerous runs on banks. The precipitating event was the collapse of investor F. Augustus Heinze's effort to corner the copper market in October 1907, which resulted in Heinze's holdings falling $50 million in one day and threatened a number of banks connected to him. On 24 October, Secretary of the Treasury **George B. Cortelyou** designated $25 million to support the market, but not until **J. P. Morgan** organized a group of bankers to restore order did the situation stabilize. In a deal designed to staunch the panic that later caused much controversy, President **Theodore Roosevelt** approved the merger of the financially troubled Tennessee Coal and Iron Company with the Morgan-backed **United States Steel**. With the panic over by February 1908, Congress passed the **Aldrich–Vreeland Act** to establish the National Monetary Commission. Its 30 reports (1909–12) led to the **Federal Reserve Act** of 1913. *See also* ANTITRUST; ECONOMY; MONEY TRUST.

PARAMOUNT PICTURES CORPORATION. Founded in 1914, Paramount was a distribution company for the newly formed film production companies Bosworth, Inc.; Famous Players; and the **Lasky** Feature Play Company. A challenge to the fading **Motion Picture Patents Company**, Paramount kept 35 percent of the proceeds of each **movie**; in exchange, it provided funds for film production and guaranteed a minimum return to the producer. This model prevailed in the 1920s, when Paramount became a major force in the movie industry. *See also* ZUKOR, ADOLPH.

PARCEL POST. Following the enormous popularity of **rural free delivery** (inaugurated in 1896), the **Farmers' Union** and other rural lobbies pressured Congress to enact a law requiring the post office to deliver packages of up to 11 pounds, priced at five cents for the first pound and one cent for each additional pound. Congress complied in 1912, and the new service began on 1 January 1913. Most places in the United States had parcel post service by the 1920s. This expansion of the postal service extended the reach of the **mass-circulation magazines** and helped **mail-order** companies such as Montgomery Ward and **Sears, Roebuck**, whose revenues tripled by 1918. It also encouraged the improvement and paving of thousands of miles of rural roads. *See also* HITCHCOCK, FRANK H.; GOOD ROADS MOVEMENT.

PARIS, TREATY OF (1898). Mediated by France at Spain's request and signed in December 1898, this agreement ended the **Spanish–American War**. Defeated Spain agreed to grant **Cuba** independence while assuming Cuba's heavy debts. Spain ceded Guam, **Puerto Rico**, and, in exchange for a nominal payment of $20 million, the **Philippines** to the United States. Anticipating opposition to the annexation of overseas territories occupied during the war, President **William McKinley** appointed to the five-member American delegation three members of the Senate Foreign Relations Committee, including Delaware **Democrat** George Gray, **Republican** editor Whitelaw Reid, and former secretary of state William R. Day. Indeed, the **Anti-Imperialist League** and its allies attacked the treaty fiercely upon its submission to the Senate. On 6 February 1899, the treaty gained Senate ratification by a 57–27 vote, two more than the two-thirds majority required. At the urging of Democratic leader **William Jennings Bryan**, enough Democrats joined the Republican majority to offset the defection of Republican anti-imperialists **George F. Hoar** (Massachusetts) and Eugene Hale (Maine). The outbreak of the **Philippine–American War** encouraged several wavering senators to back the controversial peace treaty. *See also* AGUINALDO Y FAMY, EMILIO; FOREIGN POLICY; IMPERIALISM; LODGE, HENRY CABOT.

PARK, MAUD WOOD (1871–1955). Suffrage activist. A Massachusetts native, Park taught school before graduating from Radcliffe College (1898). A member of the Massachusetts Women's Suffrage Association, she helped found the College Equal Suffrage League (1900) and a Boston **women's suffrage** league (1901). After helping run the losing 1915 Massachusetts women's suffrage referendum, she moved to Washington, D.C., to run the **National American Woman Suffrage Association**'s **(NAWSA)** Congressional Committee as part of **Carrie Chapman Catt**'s **Winning Plan**. Catt credited Park with lobbying that led to Congress's passage of the **Nineteenth Amendment** in 1919. After women won the right to vote, Park transformed NAWSA into the League of Women Voters and became its first president.

PARK, ROBERT E. (1864–1944). Sociologist. Born in Pennsylvania and raised in Minnesota, he graduated from the University of Michigan (1887) and worked as a **journalist** before studying with **William James** at Harvard University and earning a Ph.D. in philosophy at the University of Heidelberg (1903). At the invitation of **Booker T. Washington**, he joined the faculty at **Tuskegee Institute** (1905–13) and then moved to the **University of Chicago** (1913–33). Using Chicago as a laboratory to study urban land use patterns, city culture, neighborhood life, ethnic groups, race relations, and assimilation, he created with his colleagues the Chicago School of sociology, hugely influential in defining the concepts and methods of urban studies in the 20th century. *See also* INTELLECTUAL.

PARKER, ALTON B. (1852–1926). Politician. Born in New York, Parker practiced law and served on the state supreme court (1885–89) and state court of appeals (1897–1904). In 1904, when **Arthur Gorman**'s candidacy for the **Democratic** presidential nomination fizzled, conservative New York party leaders successfully arranged the obscure Parker's nomination, mainly because of his pro-gold standard views. Free silver Democrats and followers of **William Jennings Bryan** supported Parker mainly from partisan loyalty. When Republican **Theodore Roosevelt** won a landslide victory, Parker returned to his law practice, the last openly conservative candidate ever to gain the Democratic presidential nomination.

PARLIN, CHARLES COOLIDGE (1872–1942). Marketer. Born in Wisconsin, Parlin established a market research division at the Curtis Publishing Company in 1911, the first such organization in the United States. His studies of farm implement, **department store**, and **automobile** firms made him a pioneer in marketing and **advertising**. His successful use of social science techniques to promote the *Saturday Evening Post* prompted U.S. Rubber (1916), Swift Meatpacking (1917), **General Motors** (1919), and other corporations to adopt market research.

PATERSON STRIKE (1913). On 27 January 1913, 800 broad silk mill workers in Paterson, New Jersey, went on strike for improved working conditions and an **eight-hour day**. The recent introduction of new looms had increased each weaver's work with no increase in pay. Ribbon weavers and dye house workers soon joined the strike, and by February the **Industrial Workers of the World (IWW)** was leading 24,000 men, **women**, and children in an industry-wide strike. During the strike more than 1,850 strikers and their supporters were arrested, including **"Big Bill" Haywood** and the young activist Elizabeth Gurley Flynn. The other strike leaders were Adolph Lessig, Carlo Tresca, and Patrick Quinlan. Despite a fund-raising pageant held by **John Reed** in Madison Square Garden that attracted national attention, the strike failed on 28 July 1913. The united mill owners lost $10 million in profits, while the workers lost $5 million in unpaid wages, and some of Paterson's silk manufacturing relocated to Pennsylvania. This defeat marked the end of the IWW's influence in the East. *See* CHILD LABOR; LABOR UNIONS; LAWRENCE TEXTILE STRIKE.

PATTEN, SIMON NELSON (1852–1922). Economist. Born in rural Illinois, Patten studied law at Northwestern University before going to study in Germany. Earning his Ph.D. in 1878, he returned to the United States and, unable to obtain a **university** position, became a secondary school teacher and administrator. Hired by the University of Pennsylvania in 1888, he became a prominent faculty member at the Wharton School, the first business school affiliated with an American university. A cofounder of the American Economics Association, he served as its president (1908–9). In works such as *The New Basis for Civilization* (1907), he became a leading voice among theorists trying to imagine a new culture based on abundance rather than scarcity. Endorsing the **progressive** call for economic and social planning, an expansion of the social safety net, and cooperation instead of competition in business, Patten believed that the new "surplus **economy**" would liberate **women** and lessen the burdens of the working class. He was forced to retire in 1917 because he opposed U.S. entry into World War I. *See* INTELLECTUAL; MODERNIZATION; SOCIAL INSURANCE.

PAUL, ALICE (1885–1977). Women's rights activist. A New Jersey native, Paul graduated from Swarthmore College (1905), studied social work, and earned an M.A. in sociology at the University of Pennsylvania. Moving to Great Britain in 1907, she joined a radical **women**'s **suffrage** organization, was arrested three times while protesting, and was force-fed during a prison hunger strike. Returning to the United States in 1910, she earned a Ph.D. in political science at the University of Pennsylvania (1912) and worked for the **National American Woman Suffrage Association (NAWSA)**. With **Lucy Burns**, she took over NAWSA's Congressional Committee in 1913 and made it a strong lobby for a constitutional amendment enfranchising women. Also in that year, she and Burns drew on their British experience to organize a parade of 5,000 suffragists in Washington, D.C., upstaging President **Woodrow Wilson**'s inauguration. When NAWSA leaders proved reluctant to embrace militant tactics, Paul and Burns founded the independent Congressional Union (CU) in 1914 and were promptly fired. In 1916, the CU became the **National Woman's Party (NWP)**, which gained the support of some of the suffrage movement's wealthy backers and many younger, more radical activists. Like the British activists, Paul and the NWP engaged in public protests that led to their arrest, prison hunger strikes, and force-feeding. After ratification of the **Nineteenth Amendment** in 1920, Paul devoted herself to the Equal Rights Amendment. She survived to play a role in the **feminist** movement of the 1960s.

PAYNE–ALDRICH TARIFF. This 1909 law was the first alteration of the U.S. tariff since 1897 and had its origin in **William Howard Taft**'s promise of tariff revision in his 1908 presidential campaign. Calling Congress into a special session, Taft convinced the House of Representatives to reduce some rates, but protectionists in the Senate increased others. The compromise bill lowered tariffs on 650 imported goods but raised them on 220 items and left 1,150 unchanged. The fierce debate, and Taft's seemingly ineffectual handling of the issue, exacerbated the split in the **Republican Party** between the conservative **Old Guard** and the **progressive Insurgents**, contributing to **Democratic** congressional gains in 1910 and the election of **Woodrow Wilson** in 1912. *See also* ALDRICH, NELSON W.; CUMMINS, ALBERT BAIRD.

PEARY EXPEDITIONS (1886–1909). Robert Edwin Peary (1856–1920), a lieutenant in the U.S. Navy Corps of Civil Engineers, took leave from his official duties to make several expeditions to Greenland (1886, 1891, 1893–95, 1896, 1897, 1898–1902), making valuable scientific observations while he searched for a route to the North Pole. In 1905–6 another expedition sailed north aboard a specially built ice-breaking ship, the *Roosevelt,* and Peary used dog sleds to come within 174 miles of the Pole. After writing *Nearest the Pole* (1907), he made his final journey in 1908. With four Inuits and his **African American** aide, Matthew W. Henson (1866–1955), Peary finally reached the North Pole on 6 April 1909. After a long controversy, a National Geographic Society investigation found that a rival claim by Frederick Cook to have reached the pole in 1891 was a hoax. Peary wrote *The North Pole* (1910) and was promoted rear admiral in 1911. Henson wrote *A Negro Explorer at the North Pole* (1912), with a foreword by Peary and an introduction by **Booker T. Washington**.

PENTECOSTALISM. This evangelical Christian movement places emphasis on direct experience with God through the Holy Spirit, often exhibited through physical manifestations such as speaking in tongues. Appearing at U.S. camp meetings as early as 1867, Pentecostals were present at a North Carolina revival in 1896 and a Topeka event in 1901. However, most mainline Pentecostal denominations trace their roots to the Los Angeles **Azusa Street Revival** (1906), led by an **African American** clergyman, William J. Seymour. The Assemblies of God formed in 1914; white ministers formed the Pentecostal Church of God in Chicago in 1919.

PERKINS, FRANCES (1880–1965). Reformer and government official. Born in Boston, Perkins founded a branch of the **National Consumers' League (NCL)** before graduating from Mount Holyoke College (1902) and becoming a teacher. While director of a Philadelphia association that aided newcomers to the city, she studied economics and sociology with **Simon Patten** at the University of Pennsylvania, then moved to New York to earn a master's degree at Columbia University and head the New York branch of the NCL. In 1911, she was appointed executive secretary for the city–state committee investigating the **Triangle Shirtwaist Company Fire**. She remained in government service for most of her life and is best known as the first **woman** to hold a cabinet post, serving as secretary of labor (1933–45). *See also* URBAN LIBERALISM.

PERKINS, GEORGE W. (1862–1920). Financier. Born in Chicago, Perkins left school at age 15 to be an office boy at the New York Life Insurance Company and advanced over 25 years to first vice president. He joined **J. P. Morgan** & Company in 1901 and, guided by the idea that cooperation was more **efficient** than competition, reorganized the **International Harvester Corporation**, **United States Steel**, and the Northern Securities Company. Retiring in 1910, he supported **Theodore Roosevelt**'s **New Nationalism**, playing a controversial role as organizer and financial backer for the **Progressive Party** in the 1912 presidential race. He later raised $200 million to aid U.S. soldiers in World War I and to support the **Young Men's Christian Association**. *See also* ANTITRUST; GREAT MERGER MOVEMENT; MONEY TRUST.

PERSHING, JOHN J. (1860–1948). Soldier. Born on a Missouri farm, Pershing graduated from West Point (1886) and served in campaigns against the Apache leader Geronimo and at Wounded Knee (1890). While teaching military science at the University of Nebraska (1891–95), he earned a law degree (1893). He then taught at West Point (1897–98). During the **Spanish–American War**, he served in **Cuba** and **Puerto Rico**, and he later fought in the **Philippines** (1903). After holding posts in Washington and Tokyo, Pershing was promoted to brigadier general, at which rank he participated in the suppression of the Moro rebels in the Philippines. At the behest of President **Woodrow Wilson**, the general led the **Pershing Expedition** into Mexico (1916–17). In 1917, Major General Pershing led to France the 1,200,000-man American Expeditionary Force, whose campaigns broke the German war effort. He returned to the United States a hero, earned additional promotions, and published his memoir, *My Experiences in the World War* (1931).

PERSHING EXPEDITION (1916–17). When troops associated with Mexican general Francisco "Pancho" Villa raided Columbus, New Mexico, on 9 March 1916, killing 17 Americans, President **Woodrow Wilson** ordered General **John J. Pershing** to take 12,000 soldiers into Mexico to chastise Villa and protect the border. Preoccupied with ending the **Mexican Revolution**, Mexican president Venustiano Carranza reluctantly allowed the American armed intervention. Pershing's cavalry went 360 miles into Mexico and narrowly missed capturing Villa, but at Carrizal Mexican federal troops fired on the U.S. Army, killing 12 and capturing 23. Pershing experimented with airplanes to carry messages and reconnoiter, but they proved unsuitable in mountainous northwestern Mexico. More successful were new army trucks and trains, which kept the Pershing Expedition supplied despite hostility from the local populace. By August 1916, 48,000 regulars (67 percent of the U.S. Army) and 111,000 National Guardsmen were camped along the border. In February 1917, with U.S. entry into World War I looming, the incursion proving futile, and Carranza demanding its end, Wilson ordered Pershing's troops back to the United States. Despite the mission's failure to capture Villa, American officials claimed it was an important demonstration of the nation's border defenses. *See also* PLAN DE SAN DIEGO; VERACRUZ INCIDENT.

PHILIPPINE–AMERICAN WAR (1899–1902). This conflict between the United States and the first Philippine Republic followed the **Treaty of Paris** that settled the **Spanish–American War**. When the Americans invaded in 1898, Filipino nationalists, who had rebelled against Spain in 1896, at first saw the newcomers as allies who would support independence. After Commodore **George Dewey** returned rebel leader **Emilio Aguinaldo** to Manila in May 1898, the Filipino army worked with the Americans to defeat the remaining Spanish forces. But Spain surrendered Manila to the U.S. commander, not to the rebels, and neither nation recognized the Filipino republic. Having purchased the former Spanish colonies for $20 million in the Treaty of Paris and fearing that the Filipinos could not maintain their independence against Japanese or German **imperialism**, President **William McKinley**'s administration planned to transform the islands into a U.S. colony.

War between Filipino nationalists and the United States began on 4 February 1899. When U.S. troops defeated Filipino regulars by June 1899, the nationalists turned to guerrilla warfare, causing significant American casualties. The U.S. Army responded with a counter-insurgency campaign that was mostly well managed but that included atrocities such as torturing or murdering captives, burning villages, and forcing civilians into concentration camps, where thousands died. Colonel **Frederick Funston** and his Filipino scouts captured Aguinaldo in March 1901, and in April the rebel leader publicly ordered his followers to surrender. But the guerrilla war continued until April 1902, with southern Muslims fighting in what was called the Moro Rebellion until 1913. Reports of U.S. soldiers committing atrocities led Senator **George F. Hoar** to call for an investigation of war crimes, but Senator **Henry Cabot Lodge** prevented the hearings from producing results. Some 1,500 U.S. soldiers died in combat and 3,824 of disease. Filipino deaths from combat and disease can only be estimated, at 16,000 and 250,000, respectively. *See also* FOREIGN POLICY; MACARTHUR, ARTHUR, JR.; TAFT, WILLIAM HOWARD.

PHILIPPINES, COLONIAL GOVERNMENT OF. After the United States defeated Spain in the **Spanish–American War**, President **William McKinley**'s administration, with some hesitation, annexed and directly governed the archipelago, for which the United States paid a nominal fee of $20 million to Spain in the 1898 **Treaty of Paris**. In 1900, with the United States increasingly confident that it would win the grinding **Philippine–American War**, McKinley appointed **William Howard Taft** to chair a commission to organize a colonial government. Taking over from the military government of General **Arthur MacArthur** (1900–01), Taft became an effective and popular civilian governor-general (1901–03), persuading strategic segments of Filipino society to work with the Americans. Under Taft, the U.S. administration disestablished the Catholic Church, bought church land for resale to farmers, made English the official language, established a new judicial system, civil service, police force, and local government, and imported 500 American teachers to reorganize the public schools. Beginning in 1907, the archipelago had a bicameral legislature with an elected Philippine Assembly and an appointed Philippine Commission. In the Jones Act (1916), the United States agreed to grant eventual independence to the Philippines, and an elected senate replaced the commission. *See also INSULAR CASES*.

PHILLIPS, DAVID GRAHAM (1867–1911). *See* MUCKRAKING.

PHONOGRAPH. Seeking a dictation device, **Thomas A. Edison** developed the "phonograph," which engraved the sound pattern on tinfoil, in the late 1870s, around the time that telephone inventor Alexander Graham Bell and Charles Taintor created the "gramophone," which used wax. By the late 1880s, Edison successfully marketed players for these cylinders, which were replaced by disk players after 1912. The first phonograph parlor opened in San Francisco in 1889, charging customers five cents per song, and most cities had coin-operated phonographs in amusement arcades by the 1890s. The first enterprise to market these new devices for home use, the National American Phonograph Company, foundered because of poor sound quality and the Panic of 1893. Four years later, as technology, materials, and business strategy improved, three companies dominated the market: Edison's National Phonograph, the Victor Talking Machine Company, and Columbia. Record sales topped 500,000 units in 1897; by 1914, the 18 companies in the field claimed more than $27 million in sales. The three major firms focused their recording efforts on classical **music**. The many smaller recording companies—more than 100 by 1917—turned to **Tin Pan Alley** songs, **jazz**, **ragtime**, and blues, which rapidly became far more popular than the classical artists. *See also* POPULAR CULTURE.

PICKFORD, MARY (1892–1979). Film star and businesswoman. Born in Toronto, Canada, Gladys Louise Smith began her theatrical career in 1899. In 1907, the teenage actress caught the eye of **David Belasco**, who cast her in a Broadway production and renamed her Mary Pickford. Seeking work in the fledgling **movie** industry, she was hired by **D. W. Griffith** at the Biograph Company and starred in the director's innovative films along with **Lillian Gish**. She worked with **Carl Laemmele** (later head of **Universal Studios**), went back to Griffith, and landed Broadway roles before returning to film with **Adolph Zukor**'s Famous Players. A skilled businesswoman who understood her star power, she earned up to $10,000 a week in the 1910s, usually portraying sweet young girls, epitomized by *Rebecca of Sunnybrook Farm* (1917). Pickford's personal life, including her affair with actor Douglas Fairbanks, whom she married in 1920 after both **divorced** their current spouses, contributed to her celebrity. Fans mobbed their European honeymoon and made the couple the symbol of Hollywood's **sexuality** and glamour. Pickford and her husband joined with Griffith and **Charlie Chaplin** to form United Artists in 1919; she oversaw the company's finances until 1956.

PICOTTE, SUSAN LA FLESCHE (1865–1915). Physician and reformer. Born on the Omaha reservation, the sister of **Francis La Flesche**, Picotte studied medicine with the support of **Alice Cunningham Fletcher** and the Women's National Indian Association. Upon earning her medical degree in 1889, she was the only **Native American** female doctor in the country. She worked as a physician, Presbyterian missionary, **prohibitionist**, and **public health** reformer on the Omaha reservation and in the state of Nebraska. In 1909, Picotte led a delegation to Washington, D.C., to oppose the extension of trust restrictions under the 1887 **Dawes Allotment Act**; she and her colleagues succeeded in compelling the government to give the Omahas direct ownership of their allotments. *See also* SOCIETY OF AMERICAN INDIANS.

PINCHOT, GIFFORD (1865–1946). Conservationist and government official. Born in Connecticut, Pinchot graduated from Yale University (1889) and studied forestry in France. In 1898, Pinchot became director of the Division (after 1900, Bureau) of Forestry in the Department of Agriculture. Sharing with President **Theodore Roosevelt** a fervent commitment to **conservation**, Pinchot lobbied for transfer of the country's burgeoning forest reserves from the Interior Department to his agency, renamed the **U.S. Forest Service** in 1905. He and Roosevelt then rapidly expanded the national forest system while imposing new fees and tightening conditions under which loggers and other businesses could access the federal forests. In 1907, Congress, in retaliation, sharply limited the president's authority to create additional forest reserves. Under President **William Howard Taft**, Pinchot lost influence and finally was fired for his role in the **Ballinger–Pinchot controversy** (1910). Turning to electoral politics, he campaigned for Roosevelt's election on the **Progressive Party** ticket, ran several times unsuccessfully for senator in Pennsylvania, and served twice as governor of that state in the 1920s and 30s. *See also* NATIONAL CONSERVATION COMMISSION; WHITE HOUSE CONFERENCE ON CONSERVATION.

PINGREE, HAZEN S. (1840–1901). Politician. Born in Maine, Pingree moved to Detroit, Michigan, after serving in the Civil War. Elected twice as **Republican** mayor (1889–97), he fought graft, introduced the **eight-hour workday**, advocated municipal ownership of **utilities**, built schools and public **bath houses**, and pursued other reforms. During the depression of the 1890s, he even had 430 acres in city parks plowed to grow potatoes to feed the hungry. He was twice elected governor of Michigan (1897–1901) and demanded that railroads and mines pay their fair share of taxes. Among his peers as **progressive** mayors were **Tom L. Johnson** and **Samuel M. Jones**. Pingree died in office in London after returning from an African safari with **Theodore Roosevelt**.

PITTSBURGH SURVEY. This unprecedented 1907–8 survey of life in the center of U.S. iron and steel production involved some 70 researchers and nearly $50,000 in grants from the **Russell Sage Foundation**. Organized by Paul Kellogg and **Edward Devine** of the New

York Charity Organization Society, the survey produced six reports on steel workers, family life and household management, work accidents, and **women**'s waged labor, among other topics. The reports included photographs by **Lewis Hine** and drawings by artist Joseph Stella. Among the investigators were **John R. Commons, Crystal Eastman**, and **Florence Kelley**. The survey documented the long hours, low wages, and degraded working and living conditions that led to high rates of accidents, disease, and early death. Pittsburgh's people had few parks and poor municipal sanitation and breathed air heavy with coal smoke, while the local rivers served as sewers for human and industrial waste. The survey had almost no effect on life in Pittsburgh. Steel company executives and city leaders dismissed it as excessively negative and, except for demolishing a particularly bad slum, did nothing. However, the survey served as a model for social research, and in recognition of its importance, the journal of the New York Charity Organization was renamed *Survey* in 1909. The survey is also a valuable resource for historians, for it offers a glimpse of life on the factory floor, working-class homes, and women's work.

PLAN DE SAN DIEGO. In February 1915, a manifesto calling for ethnic Mexicans, **African Americans**, and **Native Americans** to unite against non-Mexican whites, massacre the men, and establish an independent republic in the U.S. Southwest came to the attention of south Texas authorities. Hispanics in southern Texas had experienced decades of dispossession and impoverishment, periodically accompanied by violent repression, so many non-Hispanic Texans found it plausible that they would try to extend the **Mexican Revolution** into the state. In August, ethnic Mexican raiders began attacking railroads and Anglo-owned ranches. Killing dozens and forcing thousands to flee, the raiders exchanged fire with American troops several times, often across the international border. Considering all ethnic Mexicans guilty, local Anglo vigilantes and Texas Rangers killed somewhere between 300 and 5,000 people before being restrained by U.S. Army troops. In the atmosphere of terror and revenge, many **lynchings** went unreported, and an accurate count of deaths is now impossible. After the violence ended, Anglo Texans imposed **segregation** and **disfranchisement** in an area once a bastion of ethnic Mexican political participation. *See also* PERSHING EXPEDITION.

PLAN OF CHICAGO **(1909).** Commissioned in 1906 by the Commercial Club of Chicago and published in 1909, this lavishly illustrated volume was the culmination of the **City Beautiful** movement. Knowing he had terminal cancer, **Daniel Burnham**, who oversaw the plan along with his assistant Edward H. Bennett, poured into it ideas gained in earlier work on the 1893 Columbian **Exposition** and the **McMillan Plan**. The plan reorganized the central city around majestic public parks and public places intended to inspire civic pride. Its most visible legacy was the transformation of the Lake Michigan shore, then clogged by railroad lines, into a network of parks, parkways, and museums. In addition to standard City Beautiful proposals for a grand civic center (never built) and forest preserves, parks, and **playgrounds**, Burnham experimented with what became known as **City Practical** schemes, including proposals to improve public transit and reinforce Chicago's status as a railroad hub. The public relations effort to build support for the plan, which included a civics text for eighth graders, a **movie**, and a lecture series, each of which reached at least 150,000 people, became a model for city planners.

PLATT, THOMAS C. (1833–1910). Politician. Born in New York, Platt was a businessman active in the **Republican Party**. As well as serving in the House of Representatives (1873–77) and the Senate (1881, 1897–1909), he was New York State's Republican **boss** during the 1890s. In this role, he pushed the **New York City consolidation** through the state legislature, hoping that his party could use its support in the outlying boroughs to challenge **Tammany Hall** domination of Manhattan. He supported **Theodore Roosevelt** as governor but then backed him for vice president in 1900 largely to remove the feisty challenger from state politics. His power declining, Platt retired in 1909, wrote his autobiography in 1910, and died on 6 March 1910. *See also* MACHINE POLITICS.

PLATT AMENDMENT (1901). This congressional measure solved the problem of what to do about **Cuba** when the **Spanish–American War** ended in 1899 by making the island a quasi protectorate of the United States. Although the **Teller Amendment** promised that the United States would not annex Cuba, **imperialists** argued that this promise had been made in ignorance of Cuba's internal disarray and vulnerability to foreign manipulation. Blocking the imperialists, Connecticut senator Orville Platt attached an amendment to the army appropriations bill in 1901 that gave the United States control over Cuba's foreign relations and empowered the United States to intervene to preserve the island's independence. Under pressure, Cuba agreed to these infringements on its sovereignty and incorporated them into its new constitution. Cuba also promised to lease Guantánamo Bay to the United States and not to incur heavy debts. President **Theodore Roosevelt** withdrew U.S. forces in 1902, but the amendment gave the United States a pretext to intervene in Cuba repeatedly until its abrogation in 1934. *See also* FOREIGN POLICY; GUNBOAT DIPLOMACY; ROOSEVELT COROLLARY; WOOD, LEONARD.

PLAYGROUND MOVEMENT. Beginning in the 1880s, reformers sought to provide working-class urban children with safe spaces to play away from the physical and moral dangers of the streets. In 1906, **Jane Addams** and others associated with the **Young Men's Christian Association** and the physical education movement founded the Playground Association of America (renamed the Playground and Recreation Association of America in 1911). Offering organized **athletics**, child development, psychology, handicrafts, and hygiene, the playgrounds were intended to **Americanize** urban, **immigrant** youth as well as keep them safe. Boston had the nation's first free public outdoor playground (1889), followed by one at the University Settlement in New York City (1890) and another at **Hull House** in Chicago (1894). By 1905, 35 U.S. cities had supervised playgrounds; 13 years later, when one-third of men entering the U.S. Army to serve in World War I were deemed physically or mentally unfit, playground advocates persuaded 33 states to require physical education in the public schools. However, the playgrounds never attracted more than about 4 percent of children within walking distance of them.

PLESSY V. FERGUSON **(1896).** *See* SEGREGATION; SUPREME COURT, U.S.

PLUNKITT OF TAMMANY HALL **(1905).** Transcribed and embellished in 1905 by **journalist** William L. Riordan, this short book explained **machine politics** in the words of **Democratic** state senator George Washington Plunkitt (1842–1924), a district **boss** within **Tammany Hall**. The veteran politician justified the influence peddling that held machines together by distinguishing honest graft (such as purchasing land based on inside information) from dishonest graft (bribery and organized crime). He defended patronage appointments to government jobs while denouncing civil service reform as elitist. Ward bosses, he claimed, provided assistance to the poor in hopes of securing votes, without red tape or social workers' intrusive questions. Candidly and straightforwardly, Plunkitt described and defended his career. By capturing Plunkitt's colorful personality and tracing his activities, Riordan revealed that, however much one might deplore big-city machines, bosses were usually hard-working, dedicated, and in their own way principled.

PLURALISM. This idea long existed in the United States in tension with a celebration of national unity under Anglo-American cultural dominance. By rejecting unifying orthodoxies and celebrating diverse experience, the **pragmatism** of **William James** and **John Dewey** provided a philosophical foundation for the arguments that homogeneity meant stagnation and that the country benefited from its diverse cultures. Pluralism surfaced more explicitly in the cultural relativism championed in the 1910s by anthropologist **Franz Boas**, who demonstrated the lack of a biological basis for race and argued that each culture must be appreciated in its own terms. These academic ideas responded to widespread concerns about **segregation**, **immigration**, **Americanization** and **Americanism**, **imperialism**, and **eugenics**, all of which raised the question of whether the United States could accommodate its diverse and contentious population. The notion of a pluralist society expanded from academia into public debate through writers such as **W. E. B. Du Bois**, **Horace Kallen**, and **Randolph Bourne**. *See also* INTELLECTUAL; *THE MELTING POT.*

POETRY: A MAGAZINE OF VERSE. Founded in 1912 by Chicago literary critic and poet Harriet Monroe (1860–1936), this magazine became the country's major showcase of new and experimental poetry. The magazine gave early exposure to **Chicago Renaissance** poets such as **Carl Sandburg** and **Edgar Lee Masters**, along with

Vachel Lindsay, Amy Lowell, and Robert Frost. In 1915, Monroe recruited the young expatriate poet Ezra Pound as a contributing editor, and he channeled to the magazine his own early work, along with such landmarks of early **modernism** as "The Love Song of J. Alfred Prufrock," by the hitherto unpublished T. S. Eliot. *See also* ANDERSON, MARGARET; LITERATURE.

POLIOMYELITIS. Epidemics of this disease, also known as infantile paralysis, struck the United States repeatedly after the first in 1894. The worst occurred in the northeastern states in 1916, when some 27,000 people sickened and 6,000 died. **Public health** officials resorted to campaigns to clean streets, eliminate flies, and quarantine polio victims, but these tactics had little effect. The spread of modern **sanitary** facilities meant that fewer people regularly encountered the contaminated feces that spread the virus and so fewer developed resistance. Medical researcher Simon Flexner isolated the polio virus in 1908, but a vaccine was not developed until 1955. *See also* HEALTH AND MEDICINE.

POLL TAX. This tax levied on voters was intended to **disfranchise** those who either did not have the money to pay the fee or found it difficult to retain the paperwork proving payment. With the exception of Kentucky and Oklahoma, all of the Southern states levied poll taxes by 1904 as part of the **Democrats'** effort to disfranchise **African American** men and poor white farmers who had supported the Populists. Indeed, because of this tax and measures such as **literacy tests**, convoluted registration procedures, electoral fraud, and anti-black violence, the number of voters fell sharply throughout the South in the early 20th century, and white Democrats solidified their control. *See also* SEGREGATION; *WILLIAMS V. MISSISSIPPI*.

POLLOCK V. FARMER'S LOAN AND TRUST (1895). *See* INCOME TAX.

POPULAR CULTURE. The Progressive Era saw the expansion of commercial popular culture because of innovations in entertainment, communications, technology, and consumer products. Large cities provided the critical mass of consumers to support venues such as

dance halls, musical theaters, **vaudeville** houses, **movie** theaters, **amusement parks**, and **baseball** stadiums. Modern business practices enabled promoters such as vaudeville's **Keith & Albee** profitably to manage far-flung entertainment circuits. Improved publishing and communications methods, along with **advertising** revenues, supported cheap, abundant newspapers, **mass-circulation magazines**, and books. Along with the spread of **electricity**, new devices such as movies, the **phonograph**, and even the **Eastman Kodak** camera enabled the unprecedented recording and dissemination of images and sounds by, to, and for ordinary Americans. Radio, though invented in this era, became a source of entertainment only in the 1920s.

The cosmopolitan urban environment facilitated a fertile, if often tense, interaction among ethnic and racial groups that frequently found expression in popular art and entertainment. In addition to addressing such issues, popular culture was shaped by **immigrants** because they were prominent as entrepreneurs and performers in **athletics**, movies, vaudeville, **Tin Pan Alley**, and other entertainment businesses. The Progressive Era's creativity in **music** is a well-known instance of how the modern urban setting encouraged cultural innovation. In cities such as New York and Chicago, European immigrants — with their own traditions of popular song and their affection for orchestral and opera composers — interacted with **African Americans**, who during the **Great Migration** brought northward **jazz**, **ragtime**, and blues. Phonograph records, club circuits, and sheet music publishers then enabled the results of this interaction to spread across the continent, catalyzing a wholly new musical ferment that people around the world acknowledged as distinctively American. Yet at the same time, black American performers and patrons were routinely denied entrance to or **segregated** within mass entertainment venues.

For many, especially newcomers to the cities, popular culture embodied the attractions of American life. **Adolescents** of immigrant or rural background were particularly quick to adopt new styles and amusements, and their ability to socialize far from the eyes of concerned parents produced changes in **sexuality** and fanned fears of **prostitution** and **juvenile** delinquency. A few **Native Americans** made successful careers in athletics and the **Wild West shows**. Many educated Americans deplored popular culture as commercial, shallow, unaesthetic, repetitive, manipulative, and immoral. Moralists and reformers worried that urban youth would be unable to appreciate refined, uplifting arts. Some observers, such as **Jane Addams** tentatively and **Hutchins Hapgood** more enthusiastically, recognized the vigor and creativity of urban popular culture. Other middle-class reformers advocated team sports such as baseball, **football**, and **basketball** as healthy, pleasurable ways for youths to strengthen their bodies and learn self-discipline and teamwork. But it would be decades before **intellectuals** and cultural analysts considered popular culture worth evaluating on its own terms.

Consumer goods, from **automobiles** to board games, **cosmetics**, brand-name products (Cracker Jacks or **National Biscuit**'s Uneeda brand, the **Gillette Safety Razor**), new foods (Shredded Wheat, **Kellogg** Corn Flakes, **Post**'s Grape-Nuts, ice cream cones, **Coca-Cola**, Moxie), gained general acceptance and transformed Americans' diet and personal hygiene while enhancing their geographic mobility. Shopping venues such as **department stores**, **chain stores**, **Woolworth's**, and **mail-order** catalogs made the ever-increasing stream of consumer goods produced by global industry and agribusiness available to a wide range of consumers, including rural people formerly restricted to the local general store. Writers such as **Theodore Dreiser** treated popular culture and its effects in fiction. Popular culture seemed increasingly to define what it meant to be an American. *See also* ART; COMSTOCK, ANTHONY; CONEY ISLAND; EXPOSITIONS; HOUDINI, HARRY; LITERATURE; MODEL T; SALOON; NEW WOMAN; SEARS, ROEBUCK AND CO.; YELLOW JOURNALISM.

PORTSMOUTH CONFERENCE. When the Russo–Japanese War broke out in 1904, President **Theodore Roosevelt** and many Americans sympathized with Japan. After stunning victories on land and sea, however, the Japanese were near collapse, so they secretly asked Roosevelt to mediate. Russia reluctantly agreed, and both belligerents sent delegates to the U.S. Naval Yard in Portsmouth, New Hampshire, in August 1905, to participate in the first major U.S. effort to mediate a war between Great Powers. Roosevelt's arm twisting produced the Treaty of Portsmouth, which Russia and Japan signed on 5 September 1905. Both nations agreed to evacuate Manchuria, over which much of the war had been fought, and return it to

China, with Japan leasing the Liaotung Peninsula and the South Manchuria Railway and receiving half of Sakhalin Island from Russia, which also recognized Korea as part of Japan's sphere of influence. Expecting more, tax-burdened Japanese rioted, damaging American churches and causing the ruling cabinet to collapse in January 1906. Nevertheless, Japan won the war, solidified control over Korea, and proved itself a dominant power in Asia. The Russians also resented U.S. intervention, believing they could have won the war if fighting had continued. Roosevelt enhanced his reputation as a world leader, preserved the balance of power, and won the Nobel Peace Prize in 1906 for his efforts. *See* FOREIGN POLICY; GREAT WHITE FLEET; ROOT–TAKAHIRA AGREEMENT; TAFT–KATSURA AGREEMENT.

POST, CHARLES WILLIAM (1854–1914). Entrepreneur. Born in Illinois, Post attended the University of Illinois, served in the army, and worked as a cowboy and salesman before becoming general manager of a family-owned plow factory. Post spent some time at **J. H. Kellogg**'s sanitarium in Battle Creek, Michigan, and discovered his calling in Christian Science. In the 1890s, he turned his entrepreneurial energies to promoting **health** through mental suggestion and good foods, beginning with a coffee substitute and then two breakfast cereals, Grape-Nuts (1897) and Post Toasties (1906). Post's business was innovative in producing new processed foods, **advertising** lavishly, boasting an immaculate model factory, and warding off unionization by providing workers low-cost housing and other benefits. A proponent of the **open shop**, he was president of the **National Association of Manufacturers** in 1910–11. After surviving surgery for appendicitis in 1914, Post committed suicide.

POSTAL SAVINGS BANK. In 1861, Great Britain established the first postal savings bank as an alternative to conventional banks, which were inaccessible to the urban working class and unavailable in rural areas. By 1890, 30 countries, including most in western Europe, adopted this system; efforts to set it up in the United States began in 1873. In the 1908 presidential campaign, **Republican** candidate **William Howard Taft** espoused postal savings as a moderate alternative to **William Jennings Bryan**'s then-radical proposal for a national bank deposit guaranty law. After concessions to mollify banking interests and the Republican **Old Guard**, Congress authorized the system in June 1910. Targeted at small savers, the postal savings system was widely available and easy to use but imposed low caps on deposits and interest rates. It expanded during the banking crisis of the 1930s but declined after World War II and was abolished in 1966.

PRAGMATISM. This school of philosophy, associated mainly with **William James** and Charles Sanders Peirce (1839–1914), reflected the consequences of Darwinism and other modern scientific theories for epistemology and psychology. It began with the observation that most useful knowledge is evolving and contingent, subject to revision as new evidence emerges. People should cease worrying about truth in the abstract and instead seek practical propositions that can be refined or replaced to guide concrete actions. During the 1890s and 1900s, James published essays and books offering an accessible theory of pragmatism, arguably the most original, influential American contribution to philosophy. With its radical stress on empirical study and learning through involvement with the world, pragmatism provided a powerful foundation for the new social sciences and **progressive** social reform. Intrigued by the pedagogical implications of pragmatism, **John Dewey** relabeled it "instrumentalism," to underscore the notion that ideas and beliefs offer *instruments* for acting in the world. Children, Dewey argued, learn best by doing, and understanding emerges from applying concepts to directly experienced subject matter. At the **University of Chicago**, Dewey and his colleagues used pragmatism to construct their movement for **education reform**. *See* INTELLECTUAL.

PREPAREDNESS. Even before World War I broke out in August 1914, former president **Theodore Roosevelt** and General **Leonard Wood** urged Americans to anticipate involvement in a European war. Wood organized two "preparedness" camps in 1914 for 245 students from 90 colleges. He invited business and professional men in 1915, and by 1916 over 16,000 men attended 16 one-month and six two-week training courses. In 1917, these men became some of the 200,000 new officers as the army expanded to four million men. In part to ward off criticism of his neutrality policies, President **Woodrow Wilson** supported preparedness in 1915. **Socialists**, the **American Union against Militarism**, and others charged that Wilson's reelection slogan, "He kept us out of war," seemed hypocritical because the administration had begun to train and arm for war. In 1916, Congress passed the Naval Appropriations Act and the National Defense Act to fund military expansion. The infamous Tom **Mooney** case arose over accusations of a plot to bomb a 1916 San Francisco Preparedness Day parade.

PROGRESSIVE. Although it has persisted as the name of the era and its reformist tendencies, *progressive* had only a short vogue among reformers as a description of themselves and their agendas. By the 1890s, reformers in Germany, Great Britain, and France called themselves *progressive*, but their American counterparts still favored *reform*, *radical*, or *liberal*. In the half-decade after 1905, *progressive* became common in the United States for reasons that remain unclear. The term was commonplace by the time that the **National Progressive Republican League** formed in 1911. The **Progressive Party** of 1912 used it with confidence that the public would understand. Writers such as **Herbert Croly** in *Progressive Democracy* (1914) and Benjamin Parke de Witt in *The Progressive Movement* (1915) tried to associate the term with a general set of principles and proposals. Yet by 1916, Croly and his colleagues at the *New Republic* began shying away from it, in part because they saw it as too closely associated with **Theodore Roosevelt**. Their new favorite term, *liberal*, triumphed in later years.

PROGRESSIVE PARTY. Officially called the National Progressive Party but better known as the **Bull Moose** Party, this third party movement was formed in June 1912 by **progressives** who walked out of the **Republican Party**'s convention when the party's **Old Guard** succeeded in securing the renomination of **William Howard Taft** over the more popular **Theodore Roosevelt**. The party attracted reform activists and intellectuals such as **Benjamin Lindsey**, **Gifford Pinchot**, **Walter Lippmann**, and **Jane Addams**, who helped to draft a platform, the "Covenant with the People," that stands out as a statement of the **New Nationalism** version of progressivism. Roosevelt and **Hiram Johnson** were the party's presidential and vice presidential candidates. However, most established politicians hesitated to back the movement. Congressional **Insurgents** behind the **National Republican Progressive League** distrusted Roosevelt and remained loyal to **Robert M. La Follette**, whose candidacy had faltered early in 1912. Progressive **Democrats**, meanwhile, expressed satisfaction with nominee **Woodrow Wilson**. Roosevelt's impressive showing in the 1912 election—winning more than 27 percent of the popular vote (88 electoral votes)—and the election of party members to 13 congressional and about 160 state legislative seats seemed to demonstrate the viability of the Progressive party. Yet despite scattered victories in 1913 local elections, the party stagnated because both Republicans and Democrats supported progressive measures at the state and national levels, including the **Clayton Antitrust Act** and the **Federal Reserve Act**, part of Wilson's **New Freedom**. The Bull Moose vote fell by half in the 1914 congressional elections. The party was already weak when Roosevelt killed it by refusing renomination in 1916 and supporting Republican nominee **Charles Evans Hughes**.

PROHIBITION. The movement to ban alcohol intensified after the Civil War with the formation of the Prohibition Party (1869), the **Woman's Christian Temperance Union (WCTU)** in 1874, and the **Anti-Saloon League (ASL)** in 1893. Temperance activists at first favored propaganda campaigns enlightening people about the evils of drink, along with local, state, and federal regulation of alcohol production and distribution. Prohibitionists believed that the increasing scale of liquor manufacture and the development of national networks of **saloons** controlled by breweries signaled the corruption of American society. Despite the prohibitionists' belief in a "liquor trust," the industry was highly competitive and politically divided. Trade groups such as the **United States Brewers' Association** and the National Wholesale Liquor Dealers' Association failed to enroll even a majority of manufacturers, and brewers often blamed hard liquor for alcohol-related problems.

Prohibitionists also saw **immigration** and urbanization as causes of national demoralization. They blamed immigrants, together with the breweries, for the multiplication of saloons. As the ASL's name suggests, many prohibitionists believed that the collective, public consumption of alcohol among urban, working-class men contributed to a host of social ills, including **machine politics**, gambling, **prostitution**, and poverty. Despite stereotypes, the disproportionate poverty of new arrivals meant that immigrants often drank less per capita than native-born Americans.

Anti-alcohol crusaders were right, however, that most opposition to a ban on alcohol came from urban areas and the working classes, including immigrants. Many working-class Americans, including Irish, German, and Italian immigrants, regarded alcohol as an inoffensive part of family and community life. Most anti-alcohol activists were Protestants, while Catholics and **Jews** tended to oppose prohibition. The greatest support for prohibition came from rural areas dominated by native-born Americans; after 1900 the South was the region most favorable to it. Although the WCTU also blamed immigrant drinkers for national demoralization, it put greater emphasis on drinking as a male pastime leading to the degradation of **women** and children. The WCTU's broad-based activism associated prohibition with **municipal housekeeping** and other efforts to improve the public welfare. Indeed, brewers and distillers opposed women's **suffrage** because they assumed prohibition would result.

From the 1870s, **local option** laws enabling municipalities and counties to regulate alcohol were a key device for extending prohibition. Other temperance measures involved high licensing fees for saloons, state monopolies on alcohol sales, and banning the alcohol sales outright. By 1913, most of the South and rural areas throughout the United States had banned alcohol through local action; about half of all Americans lived in these areas. In that year, Congress passed the **Webb–Kenyon Act**, which prohibited shipping alcohol across state lines into areas where alcohol was illegal. This first major national success led the ASL to orient itself toward a federal constitutional amendment. The passage of the Sixteenth Amendment (1913), which legalized the **income tax**, lessened the importance of alcohol taxes to federal revenue streams and made prohibition fiscally viable. Moreover, the ASL's efforts produced a Congress generally favorable to prohibition in 1916, by which year 19 states had banned alcohol.

Critical to the passage of the **Eighteenth Amendment** was the **preparedness** movement and the war effort. Advocates sought to protect American soldiers from vice by creating dry zones around military bases and portrayed prohibition as a food and fuel conservation measure. In response, Congress approved a measure banning the use of grain in distilling and giving the president the right to determine how much grain brewers could use. Then, in December 1917, Congress sent to the states a draconian "bone-dry" constitutional amendment banning the order, purchase, and sale of alcohol. To the surprise of prohibitionists, the required three-fourths majority of the states ratified the amendment by January 1919, when the Nebraska legislature voted yes. Prohibition went into effect a year later and was repealed in 1933.

PROSTITUTION. Prostitution was a central political issue in the Progressive Era, incorporating anxieties about **sexuality**, changing gender roles, corporate power, **immigration**, urbanization, and disease. Most prostitutes were in their mid-twenties, white, and the native-born daughters of immigrants (few male sex workers existed at this time). In the 1910s, the number of **African American women** in the trade in northern cities rose with the **Great Migration**, while anti-immigration laws decreased the number of foreign-born prostitutes. Until 1900, most prostitutes worked in brothels owned by women, although Asian prostitutes more often served male procurers. Unless they became madams, women usually left the trade after a few years to marry. Contemporary social workers emphasized environmental causes of prostitution, primarily poverty, poor parenting, the lure of urban commercial amusements, and inadequate wages, which led women to depend on better-paid men to attend **dance halls, vaudeville**, and **amusement parks**. Sex work paid much more than other jobs available to working-class women, and the chief risks were violence, disease, and unwanted pregnancy—risks many "respectable" women also faced.

The roots of the period's anti-prostitution activism lie in the years after the Civil War, when a few cities, notably St. Louis, attempted to legalize and regulate commercial sex. The **American Medical Association** endorsed regulation if accompanied by compulsory medical exams and treatment for sexually transmitted diseases (STDs) for sex workers. Like British reformers earlier, U.S. moral reformers and women's rights activists reacted with outrage, regarding regulation as the codification of the double standard. Because there were no effective diagnostics or treatments for **syphilis** and other STDs, compulsory gynecological exams had little purpose except to punish women, and mandatory hospital stays amounted to imprisonment without trial. Public pressure forced St. Louis to repeal its regulatory ordinances within a few years, and only New Orleans then maintained a legal red-light district, the notorious **Storyville**.

In most cities, periodic police raids, arrests, and fines amounted to de facto regulation and taxation. Brothel owners paid police in cash or in kind to ignore their activities, and landlords charged exorbitant rents. **Machine** politicians' links to commercial sex were one element of the corruption that **progressives** hoped to reform. Moral reformers, organized in the American Purity Alliance by 1909, intended to eliminate prostitution altogether. The **American Social Hygiene Association** (1913) favored a **public health** approach, supporting research and sex **education** in the schools. Physicians led by **Prince Morrow** recognized the inefficacy of existing treatments for STDs and rejected regulation. Others, symbolized by **Anthony Comstock**, favored censorship of sexual materials. Women's rights activists portrayed prostitutes as victims of male lust and attempted to rehabilitate them. The native-born Protestants who dominated the movement conjured up a vice trust of male immigrant entrepreneurs, often **Jewish**, who seduced, kidnapped, and coerced native-born, white girls into a life of vice—thus the "**white slavery**" scare, leading Congress to pass the **Mann Act** (1910). Widespread sexual violence against nonwhite women did not concern many reformers.

Nearly 50 cities appointed committees to investigate prostitution between 1900 and 1917, including New York City's Lexow Committee (1894) and **Committee of Fourteen** (1911) and the **Chicago Vice Commission** (1910). **Muckraking journalists** also investigated and publicized the commercial sex trade in the **mass-circulation magazines**. Many cities and states enacted anti-prostitution laws, such as raising the age at which women could legally consent to sex to the mid- and upper teens, rewriting vagrancy statutes so that police could more easily arrest women as suspected prostitutes, hiring a few women police officers to deal with female offenders, and creating special courts for accused prostitutes in which social workers and judges took the place of defense, prosecution, and jury and could impose indefinite sentences. Municipalities also enacted **red-light abatement** laws that allowed citizens to have brothels closed and enabled some institutions to carry out compulsory medical exams and **sterilizations. Juvenile courts** committed girls to reformatories for offenses as trivial as lewd and lascivious carriage, night walking, stubbornness, and waywardness.

The new laws tended to punish working-class women and girls for nonmarital sexual activities, whether paid or unpaid, without holding men to account. The result was not the abolition of sex work but the reorganization of the trade. As police closed down red-light districts in 47 cities by 1916, prostitutes scattered throughout cities, and brothels gave way to street and tenement house prostitution and a greater role for male pimps. The effort to suppress prostitution escalated during World War I, with more than 30,000 "charity girls" (who gave sexual favors in return for meals, clothes, and entertainment) and prostitutes detained and 18,000 incarcerated for mandatory medical care by 1919.

PROTOCOL OF PEACE (1910). *See* BRANDEIS, LOUIS D.; INTERNATIONAL LADIES' GARMENT WORKERS' UNION.

PROVINCETOWN PLAYERS. Founded by the couple George Cram Cook and **Susan Glaspell** in Provincetown, Massachusetts (1915), this amateur summer theater company included many eventually celebrated writers, **Greenwich Village** bohemians, and radicals. The next summer the theater moved into a building owned by radical **journalist** Mary Heaton Vorse. The players produced *Bound East for Cardiff*, Eugene O'Neill's first play, and one-act works by Glaspell and others. The members were interested in the little theater movement, experimental, **modernist** productions that contrasted with conventional commercial Broadway dramas. **John Reed**, Louise Bryant, **Hutchins Hapgood**, artist Marsden Hartley, and poet Edna St. Vincent Millay were also part of the ensemble, which inspired the Playwright's Theatre in New York City and was succeeded in Provincetown by the Experimental Theatre in 1923.

PUBLIC HEALTH. The first large-scale efforts to use federal, state, and municipal power to protect health occurred in response to 19th-century cholera and **yellow fever** epidemics. Congress created the first, short-lived national board of health in the midst of a terrible yellow fever epidemic (1878), but this agency had little power and expired in 1882. The Progressive Era saw the proliferation, strengthening, and centralization of public boards of health, culminating in the founding of the U.S. Public Health Service (USPHS, founded in 1902 as the Marine Hospital Service and renamed in 1912). Large cities led the way in an effort to lower their high mortality rates, which began to fall in the 1870s. By 1890, municipal boards offered vaccinations, food inspection, medical exams for school children, and summer children's health care programs. They also collected statistics on the occurrence of disease despite resistance from some physicians who regarded reporting such information as a violation of patients' privacy. Public health boards were also increasingly staffed by trained physicians with substantial budgets and good biomedical research facilities. By the 1900s, **settlement houses** often offered visiting **nurse** programs of the kind first established by **Lillian Wald**. The professionalization of medicine and nursing and the improvement in medical education spurred by the **Flexner Report** contributed to this development. Yale (1915) and Johns Hopkins University (1916) founded the first degree programs in public health.

Public health efforts also included improvements in **sanitary engineering** and the beginnings of federal regulation of food and drugs in the **Meat Inspection Act** and **Pure Food and Drug Act** (both 1906). The gradual acceptance of germ theory by physicians and the public, advances in bacteriology and epidemiology, and education campaigns run by the **Rockefeller Foundation**, the **Rockefeller Sanitary Commission**, the American Red Cross, the **National Tuberculosis Association**, and other organizations contributed to a decline in morbidity and mortality rates, especially among children. Deaths from cholera, yellow fever, measles, **diphtheria**, and **tuberculosis** declined sharply by 1930.

In other respects this period saw setbacks in public health. Most of the medical care that poor urbanites received came from free or low-cost clinics run by city health boards and settlement houses and visiting nurses. Seeing these services as a threat to their livelihood and professional standing, physicians campaigned against them in favor of doctor-controlled, fee-for-service hospitals. The **American**

Association for Labor Legislation proposed a compulsory health insurance bill modeled on British and German precedents in 1916; although the **American Medical Association** and other doctors' groups initially praised it, they turned against it by 1917, and the measure failed in the states where it was considered.

Public health provisions were strongest in the northeastern states and cities, followed by those in the industrial Midwest, and weakest in the South. City residents enjoyed greater access to health services than did their rural counterparts, and southerners were predominantly rural. Philanthropies such as the Rockefeller Sanitary Commission and the Rosenwald Fund played a key role in improving southerners' health. Creating the field of industrial health, **Alice Hamilton** investigated the problems caused by workplace conditions and succeeded in winning some protections for workers. The provision of health services also varied by race, as **African Americans** and **Native Americans** received poorer or no health care. Public health campaigns sometimes played on middle-class fears that diseased servants, factory workers, and immigrants would spread infection to otherwise clean and careful people, as the permanent incarceration of "Typhoid Mary" Mallon, an immigrant Irish cook and carrier of the bacteria that causes typhoid fever (1915), demonstrated. The 1891 recodification of **immigration** law empowered officials to conduct medical exams on incoming immigrants and deport those with certain diseases. *See also* HEALTH AND MEDICINE; SOCIAL INSURANCE.

PUBLICITY ACT (1910). This federal law culminated a decade of efforts to regulate the financing of political campaigns. Stung by revelations that powerful businessmen, including **J. P. Morgan**, **E. H. Harriman**, and **John D. Rockefeller**, had contributed to his 1904 reelection, **Theodore Roosevelt** called for campaign finance laws in his annual messages in 1905 and 1908. **Elihu Root** formed the National Publicity Law Organization to lobby for public disclosure and regulation of federal campaign spending. The Tillman Act (1907), sponsored by Senator **Benjamin Tillman**, prohibited direct contributions from businesses to political parties and election committees; some states passed similar laws. Intended to close loopholes in the 1907 law, the Publicity Act (also known as the Federal Corrupt Practices Act) required full disclosure of funds contributed and spent in federal campaigns. In 1911, Congress amended the 1907 and 1910 laws to extend disclosure to primary elections, chiefly because in the South the **Democratic** primary was tantamount to the general election. Persisting loopholes undermined the laws, and state and federal attorneys general did not always enforce them.

PUERTO RICO. This Caribbean island, a Spanish colony since Columbus arrived in 1493, had just won autonomy when it was invaded on 25 July 1898 by the U.S. Army during the **Spanish–American War**. **Anti-imperialists** and racists questioned the wisdom of annexing Puerto Rico, but President **William McKinley**, mindful of recent troubles in **Cuba**, wanted to banish Spain from the Americas. Ceded to the United States in the **Treaty of Paris**, the island was under military rule until the **Foraker Act** (1900), which established a civilian government with an elected House of Representatives; the governor, executive council, and a nonvoting delegate to Congress were appointed by the U.S. president. The Jones–Shafroth Act (1917) granted U.S. citizenship to Puerto Ricans, added an elected senate to the legislature, and instituted a local government similar to that of U.S. states. The main industry was agriculture, chiefly sugar; the development of this cash crop by American capitalists after 1898 dispossessed many small farmers, many of whom migrated to the mainland. *See also INSULAR CASES.*

PUJO COMMITTEE (1912). Representative Arsène Pujo (1861–1939), a Louisiana **Democrat**, was a member of the National Monetary Commission (1908–12), created after the **Panic of 1907**. Pujo persuaded Congress to create a committee to investigate the so-called **Money Trust** in 1912. With **Samuel Untermeyer** as committee counsel, Pujo confronted **J. P. Morgan** and other major Wall Street financiers as witnesses and accused them of being a cabal that manipulated capital markets to consolidate a hold over manufacturing, railroads, and other sectors of the **economy**. **Louis Brandeis** publicized the Pujo Committee findings in articles later collected in the book *Other People's Money and How Bankers Use It* (1914). These hearings fueled the movement for the **Federal Reserve** and **Clayton Antitrust Acts**. *See also INTERLOCKING DIRECTOR-ATES.*

PULITZER, JOSEPH (1847–1911). Publisher. Born in Hungary, Pulitzer emigrated to Boston in 1864, served in the Union Army during the Civil War, and then became a reporter for the *St. Louis Westliche Post*, a German-language daily, while studying law. In 1876, he purchased a bankrupt paper that he later merged with another to create the *St. Louis Post-Dispatch*. Buying the *New York World* in 1883, he converted it into a popular newspaper for working-class **Democrats**. By 1898, the fierce competition between Pulitzer's paper and **William Randolph Hearst**'s *New York Journal* encouraged sensational **yellow journalism**. Pulitzer also represented Missouri and New Jersey in the House of Representatives in the 1860s and 1880s. *See also* JOURNALISM.

PURE FOOD AND DRUG ACT (1906). This law banned the sale across state or national borders of adulterated or mislabeled foods and drugs that failed to meet pharmacological and medical standards. Pressure for such a law had built since the 1880s. Despite some hesitancy from the **American Medical Association**, physicians and pharmacists came to support better testing of medicine, while **prohibition** advocates exposed the use of alcohol and narcotics in dangerous, ineffective patent medicines. By the early 1900s, most states had laws on the matter, though many were ineffectual. An inveterate advocate was **Harvey W. Wiley**, long-time chief of the Bureau of Chemistry in the Agriculture Department and a pioneer of the scientific study of food quality and safety. In the early 1900s, Wiley's campaign received a boost from investigations by groups such as the **National Consumers' League**, as well as from Samuel Hopkins Adams's vivid 1905 **muckraking** series in *Collier's*. **Edward Bok** of the *Ladies' Home Journal* braved libel suits from a patent medicine manufacturer to champion the cause. Signed by President **Theodore Roosevelt** on 30 June 1906, the same day as another innovative consumer protection measure, the **Meat Inspection Act**, the Pure Food and Drug Act represented a major extension of federal regulatory power and increased the importance of scientific expertise in public policy. The **U.S. Supreme Court** unanimously upheld it in *Hipolite Egg Company v. United States* (1911). The Agriculture Department's Bureau of Chemistry enforced it for decades until the Food and Drug

Administration was founded in 1930. *See also* HARRISON NAR-COTICS CONTROL ACT.

– R –

RACE RIOTS. White attacks on **African Americans** occurred periodically during the Progressive Era. Anti-Asian riots were less frequent than in previous decades, largely as a result of **immigration** restriction. Anti-black mob violence, along with **lynching**, aided the imposition of **segregation** and **disfranchisement** in the South. Riots also accompanied the **Great Migration** of blacks to northern and midwestern cities. Major riots occurred in **Wilmington** (1898), **New Orleans** (1900), **Atlanta** (1906), **Springfield** (1908), and **East St. Louis** (1917). Whites' belief that African Americans had transgressed racial etiquette often sparked mob violence. Hundreds of black Americans died and tens of thousands more suffered injuries and damage to their homes and businesses, prompting out-migrations that eroded black communities in affected cities. Blacks often fought back, even though police, who frequently abetted white rioters or did little to hinder them, arrested and prosecuted blacks disproportionately. Black determination not to surrender to mob violence played a major role in energizing civil rights activity, including the founding of the **National Association for the Advancement of Colored People**. *See also* BROWNSVILLE RAID; WELLS-BARNETT, IDA B.

RACE SUICIDE. Sociologist **Edward A. Ross** coined this phrase (1901) to name the **social Darwinist** fear that whites were growing overcivilized and might be overwhelmed by so-called lesser races. A crucial symptom was the declining birth rate among native-born white **women**, while birth rates supposedly remained high among **immigrants** and nonwhite women. (In fact birth rates declined in all ethnic groups.) The idea's best-known advocate, President **Theodore Roosevelt**, exhorted white men to engage in the **strenuous life** and do their duty as husbands and fathers. Women should regard motherhood as their highest duty, eschew **birth control**, and avoid diversion by work, **education**, and **feminist** ideas. **Immigration** restriction advocate Madison Grant popularized the idea in his book *The Passing of the Great Race* (1916). Similar ideas had a vogue in Western Europe, where they became part of the mental furniture of fascism. *See also* EUGENICS.

RADIO ACT (1912). Motivated in part by the *Titanic*'s sinking, this act was the first major effort to regulate and professionalize the new wireless industry. Congress mandated licensing of wireless operators and required them to be U.S. citizens, confined stations to particular wavelengths, prioritized distress calls, and recognized the international distress signal, SOS. The act also limited amateur operators to the then-undesirable short wave (200 meters or less) portion of the spectrum, gave the U.S. Navy control of the spectrum between 600 and 1600 meters, and imposed various technical requirements. This law set in motion the American practice of licensing the airwaves, thus promoting the commercialization of radio. *See also* DE FOREST, LEE.

RAGTIME. This genre of **music** featured "ragged time," or syncopated, percussive playing of the instruments, a style that combined **African American** and European musical conventions. First played in brothels and racist "coon" songs in the 1890s, ragtime was popularized by black composers, including **Scott Joplin**, **James Reese Europe**, and Jelly Roll Morton. White musicians such as **John Philip Sousa** and **Tin Pan Alley** composers such as **Irving Berlin** became intrigued by it, as did some classical composers. Ragtime prepared the way for the later popularity of **jazz** and blues.

RAUSCHENBUSCH, WALTER (1861–1918). Theologian. Born in New York, Rauschenbusch was ordained after graduating from the Rochester Theological Seminary (1886). As pastor of the Second German Baptist Church in New York City, he was appalled by poor living conditions and urban injustice and exploitation. Influenced by **socialist** and **single tax** ideas, along with religious **modernism**, he became a major advocate of the **Social Gospel** movement, which he popularized while a professor at Rochester Theological Seminary (1897–1918). His works included *Christianity and the Social Gospel* (1907), *Christianizing the Social Order* (1912), and *A Theology for the Social Gospel* (1917). *See also* GLADDEN, WASHINGTON.

REALIGNMENT OF 1896. The theory of realignment holds that American politics has evolved in phases known as "party systems." Each phase has supposedly featured predictable voting patterns, with the electorate consistently favoring this or that party based on geography, class, ethnicity, and religion. As issues change and new voters enter the political system, existing alliances erode until a political crisis or a hotly contested election overturns the old pattern and creates a new one. Adherents of this theory assert that the period 1892–96 saw such a realignment, in which the even balance between the **Republican** and **Democratic** parties since the 1870s gave way to Republican dominance. The theory posits a number of causes for realignment, among them the agrarian populist revolt, the free silver versus gold standard debate, Democratic infighting over President Grover Cleveland's handling of the Panic of 1893, **William Jennings Bryan**'s 1896 presidential candidacy, state-level fights over temperance, and the growing dominance of **segregationist** Democrats in the South. In this view, Republican **William McKinley**'s victory in the 1896 presidential race ended political stalemate and made possible the Progressive Era's innovations in governmental structure and public policy. However, skeptics insist that the Republican victories had no clear connection to innovative policies, most of which resulted from alliances between Republican **progressives** such as **Theodore Roosevelt** and **Robert La Follette** and reformist Democrats. Skeptics also suggest that the stability of post-1896 politics was an illusion and that voting patterns remained fluid and responsive to new issues, such as the **cost of living** and World War I.

REALISM. In **literature**, this term defined a narrative style and choice of subjects that self-consciously rejected the refined writing and romantic themes of earlier genteel literature. By the 1880s, **William Dean Howells** and **Henry James** exemplified literary realism, though James later developed a subjective style that heralded **modernism**. Realists endeavored to portray contemporary life clearly and honestly. Such landmarks as Howells's *A Hazard of New Fortunes* (1890) sought to capture the tenor of modern urban life and class conflict. By the 1890s, realist authors in this vein, such as **Frank Norris**, **Jack London**, and **Theodore Dreiser**, were shading into **naturalism**. In pictorial **art**, realism began as reaction against the academic school and called for an accurate, as opposed to ideal, depiction of life. In the early 20th century, **Ash Can School** painters **Robert Henri**, **John Sloan**, and their colleagues exemplified this trend. Realistic photography, such as that of **Jacob Riis** and **Lewis W. Hine**, shaded into **muckraking journalism** and was self-consciously opposed to the aestheticized photography championed by **Alfred Stieglitz**.

RECALL. One of the **structural reforms** that **progressives** advocated, recall enables voters to remove an elected officeholder from his or her post. Generally, a certain percentage or number of voters must file a petition for a special election to oust and replace the targeted official. Reformers argued that the public could use recall to punish corruption or limit the power of railroads, banks, and corporations. Recall was always more controversial than **initiative** or **referendum**, and in 1913, only nine states permitted it for state officials. Only 16 states adopted it during the 20th century. Many states, however, permitted municipalities to write recall provisions into **home rule** charters.

RECLAMATION SERVICE, U.S. The Secretary of the Interior created this service to administer the **Newlands Reclamation Act** (1902) and appointed Frederick Newell as its director. Five years later, the agency became independent; it took the name Bureau of Reclamation in 1923. Funded by the sales of western public lands, the service soon had far more projects underway—30 encompassing nearly three million acres of land by 1910—than it could manage. The demand for land was far less and the costs of building dams and tunnels far greater than proponents had forecast. Instead of promoting the distribution of public land for family farms, irrigation projects frequently benefited land already in private hands and encouraged speculation. The section of the law limiting each family to water enough for only 160 acres was rarely enforced, and in any case the service reinterpreted it in 1916 to mean 160 acres each for husband and wife. Early successes such as the Roosevelt Dam underscored the service's technical expertise and the ability of dams to generate **electricity** as well as to provide water. *See also* CONSERVATION.

RED-LIGHT ABATEMENT. First passed by the Iowa state legislature (1909), these laws empowered private citizens to file complaints against buildings used for **prostitution**. A legal hearing followed the issuance of a court order to vacate the property, and owners found guilty of harboring sex workers faced injunctions, fines, and the payment of legal fees. Thirty-one states enacted such laws by 1917 to discourage landlords from allowing tenants to run brothels. Whereas landlords simply evicted prostitutes upon receiving the court order and thus avoided a trial and fine, madams and prostitutes faced increasing difficulties in conducting business, encouraging the rise of pimp-controlled tenement and street prostitution. *See also* STORYVILLE.

REED, JOHN (1887–1920). Journalist. An Oregon native, Reed graduated from Harvard University (1910) and moved to New York's **Greenwich Village**, where he became an editor at *The Masses* and helped to stage a pageant publicizing the **Paterson Strike**. In 1913, he made a name for himself as a war correspondent by traveling with Mexican general Pancho Villa's army and publishing the best-selling *Insurgent Mexico* (1914). A popular figure in free-speech circles and a proponent of **feminism** and modern **sexuality**, Reed conducted highly public affairs with salonnière **Mabel Dodge** and journalist Louise Bryant, whom he married in 1916. He and Bryant helped to found the **Provincetown Players**. Reed's reportage on World War I, *The War in Eastern Europe* (1916), was well received but did not sell. In 1917, he traveled to Russia to report on and participate in the Bolshevik Revolution. When he returned to the United States in 1918, government harassment delayed the writing of his famous book, *Ten Days that Shook the World* (1919). After his trial for criticizing World War I ended in a hung jury, Reed went again to the Soviet Union and, upon his return to the United States, was convicted of smuggling money to support American communists. He died of typhus in Moscow in 1920. *See also* JOURNALISM; MEXICAN REVOLUTION; MODERNISM; SOCIALISM.

REED, WALTER (1851–1902). Physician. Born in Virginia, Reed earned two medical degrees and joined the U.S. Army Medical Department in 1875. After studying bacteriology at Johns Hopkins

Hospital in the early 1890s, he became an instructor at the new Army Medical School and supervised its pathology laboratory. His research on **diphtheria** and typhoid fever improved efforts to prevent or treat these diseases. Following the **Spanish–American War**, he studied **yellow fever** in **Cuba**. Building on the work of Cuban physician Carlos J. Finlay and others, Reed and his coworkers demonstrated the transmission of the fever via the *Aedes aegypti* mosquito. As a result, army and civilian **public health** officials instituted effective preventive measures such as drainage and screening. Reed died after undergoing an appendectomy in 1902.

REFERENDUM. A referendum is a ballot measure to overturn an act of a state legislature or city council. Like the **recall** and **initiative**, the referendum arose from **progressive** reformers' ambition to engage the public directly in government, undermine **machine politics** and corporate influence, and make state and local government more responsive to the popular will. Citizens seeking a vote on a recent law or ordinance need to collect the signatures of a certain percentage of registered voters, usually 5 to 15 percent. In 1897, Nebraska became the first of many states to authorize referenda at the municipal level. In 1898, South Dakota was the first state to allow it statewide. By 1918, more than half the states provided for referenda, although some were nonbinding. Conservative or pro-business legislatures often sought to evade the results of referenda, for example by passing the same measure with different wording or tying up petitions in legal technicalities and court proceedings. In cities such as Los Angeles and San Francisco, where allegations of corrupt influence by **utilities** and **trolley** companies were rife, petitioners and city councils engaged in running battles over franchise ordinances, repealing and repassing them in altered form. Critics claimed that referenda defied the purpose of having a legislature. Others argued that referenda and initiatives cluttered the ballot and endangered civil rights and liberties. *See also* STRUCTURAL REFORM.

REFORM MOVEMENTS. The diffuse character of **progressive** reform and its many variations across cities, states, and regions make generalizations about these movements difficult. For convenience, scholars often divide progressive movements into those dedicated to

structural, social, or moral reform. Obviously, however, movements could have agendas that crossed these categories. For example, the **National Municipal League** and the **Bureau of Municipal Research** saw the reorganization of city government as a precondition for the better delivery of social services and the improved regulation of housing, **public health**, and labor conditions. **Women**'s reform movements such as the **Woman's Christian Temperance Union** adopted a broad agenda that linked social reform, **suffrage**, and women's rights to moral goals such as **prohibition** and the abolition of **prostitution**.

In cities and states, structural reform focused on two often contradictory goals: making government more open and responsive and making it more **efficient** and professional. Through devices such as **home rule**; the **strong mayor, commission**, or **city manager** systems; **at-large, nonpartisan** elections; civil service; and municipal ownership of **utilities**, structural progressives hoped to wean urban voters from parochial, corrupt **machine politics** and focus attention on issues facing the entire city. Cities reorganized according to the **City Beautiful** or **City Practical** principles would be more attractive and prosperous and would also in theory inspire civic pride and public spirit. **Initiative, recall**, and **referendum** would make city and state officials more accountable to the public, while the **income tax** and other revenue reforms would provide a better-funded, fairer government. Though California, Iowa, and other states had similar movements, **Robert La Follette** and the **Wisconsin Idea** summed up a broad program of state-level restructuring that included improved regulation of railroads and corporations and systematic cooperation between politicians and **university**-based experts in formulating public policy.

At the federal level, **Theodore Roosevelt** became identified with efforts to make government more professional and effective, both before his presidency as head of the **U.S. Civil Service Commission** and during his term through agencies such as the **U.S. Department of Commerce and Labor** and the **Bureau of Corporations**, as well as initiatives such as the **Keep Commission**. Roosevelt's **antitrust**, consumer protection, and **conservation** agendas hinged on a more knowledgeable, professional federal government. The creation of the **Federal Reserve** and the **Federal Trade Commission** under

President **Woodrow Wilson** continued this trend. Constitutional amendments for direct election of **senators**, a federal income tax, and women's suffrage all shared in the Progressive Era impulse to make government more open and responsive. Roosevelt's **New Nationalism** program and the platform of the 1912 **Progressive Party** endeavored to sum up the pro-government side of progressivism, with Wilson's **New Freedom** intended as an alternative recognizing the country's decentralist traditions.

Progressive social reform movements were equally varied and worked through both the public sector and private groups. Most progressive social reformers embraced what historian Daniel Rodgers labeled the "social bonds" mindset that emerged in Europe and the United States in response to urbanization, industrialization, and corporate capitalism and that characterized the period's **intellectual** trends and religious thought. Both **Social Gospel** religion and progressive social science argued that individualism was a fiction—people were interdependent and responsible for one another. This perspective was pronounced in women-dominated reform movements such as the **settlement house movement**, the **Women's Trade Union League**, and the **National Consumers' League**, all of which emphasized the responsibility of middle-class women to use their privileged position to serve impoverished and exploited people. This thinking drove movements for abolition of **child labor**, **municipal housekeeping**, and improved public health and **education**, among a myriad of others. Women activists such as **Florence Kelley** and **Josephine Goldmark** cooperated with male reformers such as **Louis Brandeis** and the economists behind the **American Association for Labor Legislation**, as well as with male and female **labor union** organizers in the broad movement for better regulation of work conditions, **social insurance**, the **living wage**, **workers' compensation**, and so on.

Some lines in progressive thought reinforced the movements for the **segregation** and **disfranchisement** of **African Americans**, on the spurious grounds that blacks were backward, ill-disciplined people easily manipulated by southern political **bosses**. But black-run movements such as the **National Association of Colored Women** and the **Urban League** also embodied the social reform impulse in progressivism, as did interracial movements for equal rights and against **lynching** and **race riots** such as the **National Association for the Advancement of Colored People**.

The moral reform impulse in progressivism was and remains controversial. As evidenced in the campaigns against the **saloon** and **white slavery**, reformers at times went well beyond undeniable observations that excess drinking contributed mightily to a host of social pathologies and that prostitution was inseparable from the exploitation and abuse of women and posed public health hazards. In certain permutations, progressivism veered toward an oppressively moralistic vision of an uplifted and purified society. The movements for **Americanization** of **immigrants** and detribalization of **Native Americans** contained an inescapable element of the compulsory uplift of benighted people. Even the **playground movement** could take the fun out of play by stressing physical exercise as a means of teaching self-discipline and responsibility. Part of the enduring influence of **Jane Addams** and **John Dewey** came from their admonitions that heavy-handed attempts to impose Anglo-Protestant morality would alienate the same urban, immigrant working class that reformers purported to help, while eroding the spirit of mutuality and open-mindedness that supposedly animated reform. The trend toward **urban liberalism** in New York and other cities started with the realization that it was more humane and effective to cooperate with working-class ethnics—at times even distasteful **Tammany Hall** politicians—than to deplore their bad habits and preach at them. *See also* ANTI-IMPERIALIST LEAGUE; ANTI-SALOON LEAGUE; AUSTRALIAN BALLOT; BATH HOUSES, PUBLIC; BIRTH CONTROL MOVEMENT; CHICAGO VICE COMMISSION; CIVIC FEDERATION OF CHICAGO; COMMITTEE OF FOURTEEN; COMPULSORY EDUCATION LAWS; EIGHT-HOUR WORKDAY LAWS; EMPLOYER LIABILITY LAWS; FEMINISM; GENERAL FEDERATION OF WOMEN'S CLUBS; GOOD ROADS MOVEMENT; HOME ECONOMICS; INDUSTRIAL EDUCATION; INSURANCE, REGULATION OF; INTERNATIONALISM; JUVENILE COURTS; MEAT INSPECTION ACT; MOTHERS' PENSIONS; NATIONAL AMERICAN WOMAN SUFFRAGE ASSOCIATION; NATIONAL CHILD LABOR COMMITTEE; NATIONAL CIVIC FEDERATION; NATIONAL CONFERENCE OF CHARITIES AND CORRECTION; NATIONAL HOUSING ASSOCIATION; NATIONAL

WOMAN'S PARTY; NIAGARA MOVEMENT; PITTSBURGH SURVEY; PURE FOOD AND DRUG ACT; RED-LIGHT ABATEMENT; ROCKEFELLER SANITARY COMMISSION FOR THE ERADICATION OF HOOKWORM; SANITARY ENGINEERING; SHORT BALLOT; SINGLE TAX; SOCIALISM; SOUTHERN SOCIOLOGICAL CONGRESS; UNEMPLOYMENT INSURANCE; WELFARE CAPITALISM.

REITMAN, BEN (1879–1942). Anarchist. Born in Minnesota to poor immigrant **Jews**, Reitman lived a semi-criminal life as a boy in Chicago, running errands for **prostitutes**. As a young man, he tramped around the country and went to Europe as a merchant seaman. After abandoning his wife and child, he earned a medical degree (1904) with the aid of friendly Chicago physicians. Dedicated to treating tramps, prostitutes, and other outcasts, he opened a "Hobo College" to provide social services and **education** to homeless people. Best known today for his partnership with **anarchist** spokeswoman **Emma Goldman** (1908–15), he managed her lecture tours. Arrested for circulating **birth control** pamphlets at her lecture in Cleveland (1916), Reitman spent six months in prison, the longest sentence served in the United States by a birth control advocate. For Goldman, he embodied working-class **sexuality**, and their famous affair enacted her brand of sexually liberated **feminism**. After Goldman was deported in 1919, he continued to practice medicine in Chicago. *See also* BERKMAN, ALEXANDER.

REMINGTON, FREDERIC (1861–1909). Artist. Born in New York, Remington studied **art** at Yale College and New York's Art Students League, then worked at various jobs until an 1885 trip through the Southwest provided material for him to become a successful illustrator. Subsidized by **mass-circulation magazines**, he traveled throughout the West, supplying images of **Native Americans**, cowboys, cavalrymen, and other western icons. Along with novelist **Owen Wister** and the **movies**, his romanticized paintings and sculpture lamented the vanishing frontier and immortalized the cowboy as a symbol of American masculinity and freedom. Remington gave graphic form to his friend **Theodore Roosevelt**'s idea of the **strenuous life**. A favorite of collectors of western-themed art, Remington produced books including *Pony Tracks* (1895), *Man with the Bark On* (1900), and *The Way of an Indian* (1906). *See also* WILD WEST SHOWS.

REPUBLICAN PARTY. The Progressive Era posed a particular challenge to the Republican Party. Since the party's founding in the 1850s, Republicans had seen themselves as standing for "progress," which in an economic sense meant promotion of domestic industry through protective tariffs; support for railroad construction, river and harbor improvements, and other infrastructure projects; a conservative monetary policy; distribution of mineral and timber resources to private enterprise; and encouragement of rapid western settlement. Arguably, by the 1890s these policies had succeeded too well, because the overriding issue of the Progressive Era was how to control the urban industrialism and corporate capitalism that Republican policies had unleashed.

At the time of the Panic of 1893, the party was reeling from a string of defeats. Protectionism, **antitrust**, the currency, and agrarian discontent contributed to **Democratic** triumphs of 1890 and 1892, but in midwestern states such as Wisconsin, Illinois, Ohio, and Iowa, these setbacks had much to do with volatile ethnocultural issues such as temperance and religion in the schools. Also corrosive was the spread of **segregation** and **disfranchisement**, which gave the Democrats a stronghold in the South while eroding Republican credibility with **African Americans**, who rightly accused the party of Lincoln of abandoning them in 1876 and, especially, after the defeat of **Henry Cabot Lodge**'s Force Bill in 1891. Thereafter, Republicans maintained shell organizations among blacks, because black southern Republicans still counted in selecting delegates for national nominating conventions. But Republicans now avoided real risks on behalf of the old party principle of equal rights.

The disarray among Democrats caused by Grover Cleveland's conservative response to the Panic of 1893 presented Republicans with a comeback opportunity. At that point the more pro-government of the two major parties, Republicans seemed sober and responsible by comparison to squabbling Democrats and angry Populists. Securing strong support in the Northeast and Midwest, Republicans won decisive victories starting with the 1894 congressional elections, when their gain of 117 House of Representatives seats represented the largest shift between parties to that time. **William McKinley**'s 1896 victory over **William Jennings Bryan** in the presidential election, along with the 1898 congressional elections, sealed Republican dominance of national politics. Some historians have labeled the replacement of the highly competitive elections of the Gilded Age by a seemingly stable Republican majority the **Realignment of 1896**.

The return of prosperity in 1897 seemed to vindicate traditional Republican economic policy, but a split emerged within the party over the lessons of the 1890s. The party leadership in Congress—eventually labeled the **Old Guard**—remained pro-business at a time when support for private enterprise was coming to seem conservative and even reactionary. Republican moderates such as **Marcus Hanna** tried through initiatives such as the **National Civic Federation** to carve out a procapitalist position that accommodated **labor unions**. A younger generation of midwesterners and westerners, exemplified by Wisconsin's **Robert La Follette**, experimented with reform at the state level before moving into national politics. Meanwhile, a small, articulate group of nationalistic Republicans, frequently from patrician families in the Northeast and at times strongly **imperialist**, absorbed the case emerging on both sides of the Atlantic for using the public sector to pursue a fair, humane society. **Theodore Roosevelt** had emerged as exemplar of this group by the time McKinley's assassination made him president in 1901.

Roosevelt intended the pro-labor, consumer protection, and antitrust measures he labeled the **Square Deal** to gain support among the urban, ethnic working class without alienating the party's base in the small-town and rural North and Midwest. His personal popularity carried the party to an unprecedented landslide in 1904, after which the underlying **progressive**–conservative split proved impossible to contain. Old Guard leaders such as **Nelson Aldrich** and **Joseph Cannon** thwarted Roosevelt's **conservation** policies and resisted his entreaties that the party espouse proworker measures. By the 1908 election, conservative intransigence had driven the hitherto **nonpartisan American Federation of Labor** into alliance with the Democrats, though the Republican coalition held firm enough to elect **William Howard Taft** over Bryan in the latter's third presidential run. Under Taft, the Republican feud broke into open warfare, with **Insurgent**

Republican progressives behind Representative **George Norris** siding with congressional Democrats in a famous 1910 revolt against the authoritarian Speaker Cannon. The Democrats retook the House later that year.

An accumulation of personal and policy disagreements led Roosevelt to break with his old friend Taft and challenge him for the 1912 presidential nomination. The midwestern Republican progressives, never fully trusting Roosevelt, organized the **National Progressive Republican League** as a vehicle for their natural leader, La Follette. When La Follette's candidacy faltered in early 1912, most of the leading insurgent Republicans kept their distance while Roosevelt's backers formed the breakaway **Progressive Party**. Nominating Roosevelt as president and California governor **Hiram Johnson** as vice president, this splinter movement came in second behind Democrat **Woodrow Wilson** in the 1912 presidential election. But mainstream and conservative Republican leaders had taken a calculated risk that the Progressives would fail to displace them as the second national party and that the Grand Old Party would regroup under conservative control. Indeed, Wilson's **New Freedom** program solidified the Democrats as the more progressive of the two older parties and undermined the rationale for a separate Progressive Party, which fell apart by 1916. The Republican nomination in 1916 of the moderate progressive **Charles Evans Hughes** and the domination of that year's campaign by **preparedness** and World War I hid the reality that progressives had lost the internal struggle and would henceforth be a minority faction among Republicans. An ironic product of the Progressive Era, the shift of the Republicans toward conservatism would have momentous long-term consequences.

RICHARDS, ELLEN SWALLOW (1842–1911). Chemist and home economist. A Massachusetts native, Richards studied chemistry and astronomy at Vassar College, where she earned a B.S. in 1870 and an M.S. in 1873. She then enrolled at the Massachusetts Institute of Technology (MIT), the first female student accepted by an American scientific school. The university resisted allowing a **woman** to pursue a Ph.D. but awarded her a second B.S. in 1873. After much struggle with the prejudice against women scientists, she worked as a chemist for the state of Massachusetts (1872–75) before creating a women's laboratory at MIT, where she worked first as an unpaid instructor and then as a regular instructor from 1884 to her death. With other MIT scientists and the state board of health, she did pioneering studies of water quality and **sanitary engineering**. Her book *Air, Water, and Food from a Sanitary Standpoint* (1892) introduced the word *ecology*. In her later career, Richards devoted her energies to **home economics**, helping to professionalize the field and serving as first president of the American Home Economics Association (1908). This new field enabled her to do on a larger scale what she had done at MIT—give women professional recognition in science and higher **education**. *See also* PUBLIC HEALTH; UNIVERSITY.

RIIS, JACOB AUGUST (1849–1914). Journalist, photographer, and reformer. Born in Denmark, Riis emigrated to the United States in 1870 and spent several years in sometimes dire poverty before becoming a police reporter for the *New York Tribune* (1877–88) and the *New York Sun* (1888–99), where he became an innovator in the investigative reporting later known as **muckraking**. Making urban slums and poverty his specialty, he exposed wretched conditions on the **Lower East Side**, often in lurid, indignant terms intended to shock. His *How the Other Half Lives* (1890) was immediately recognized as a landmark of reform **journalism**, especially for its marriage of vivid prose with shocking photographs. In the 1890s, he turned toward activism on behalf of **tenement house** reform, parks and **playgrounds**, and opportunities for children to visit the countryside. Riis's friendship with **Theodore Roosevelt** when he was president of the New York City board of police commissioners publicized the journalist's reform efforts. A mentor to **progressive** journalists such as **Lincoln Steffens**, Riis wrote *The Children of the Poor* (1892) and *Children of the Tenements* (1903), along with an autobiography, *The Making of an American* (1901). *See also* IMMIGRATION; VEILLER, LAWRENCE T.

ROBINS, MARGARET DREIER (1868–1945). Labor leader. Born in New York, Robins devoted herself to reform after inheriting a fortune in 1898. Partnering with **Frances Kellor** to expose employment agencies that directed **women** into **prostitution**, she established a firm to provide information about safe, respectable lodgings and jobs. In 1904, **Mary Kenney O'Sullivan** recruited her and her sister, **Mary Elisabeth Dreier**, to finance the **Women's Trade Union League (WTUL)**, and Robins became president of the New York branch. After her 1905 marriage to Chicago **Social Gospel** minister Raymond Robins, she ran the Chicago WTUL and served as national WTUL president from 1907 to 1922. In addition to coordinating WTUL support for the **Uprising of the Twenty Thousand** and other strikes, she recruited rich women to provide visibility and financial support for the cause.

ROBINSON, CHARLES MULFORD (1869–1917). Urban affairs writer and planner. A native of New York and an 1891 graduate of the University of Rochester, Robinson worked briefly as a **journalist** but specialized in urban issues after writing a book on the 1893 Columbian Exposition. By the 1901 publication of his book, *Improvement of Towns and Cities*, he was a major publicist and activist in the **City Beautiful** movement. Though lacking the technical skill of **Daniel Burnham** and **Frederick Law Olmsted Jr.**, he produced planning reports for Detroit, Denver, Honolulu, Los Angeles, and other cities. Robinson became secretary of the American Park and Outdoor Art Association and the first professor of civic design at the University of Illinois at Urbana-Champaign.

ROBINSON, JAMES HARVEY (1863–1936). Historian and teacher. Born in Illinois, Robinson earned his B.A. (1887) and M.A. (1888) at Harvard University and earned a Ph.D. in history in Germany (1890). **Simon N. Patten** offered him a position at the University of Pennsylvania in 1891; then he moved to Columbia University (1895–1919). A popular teacher, Robinson encouraged students to read primary sources and worked to improve history textbooks and teaching. He coauthored several works with his former student, **Charles Beard**. Robinson's emphasis on primary documents, social science theory and method, an evolutionary framework, and history's contemporary relevance epitomized the **progressive** approach to history that Robinson named the **New History** in a 1912 book of that title. With Beard, **John Dewey**, **Thorstein Veblen**, and other leading scholars, he founded the New School for Social Research (1919). *See also* INTELLECTUAL.

ROCKEFELLER, JOHN DAVISON (1839–1937). Businessman and philanthropist. Born in upstate New York and raised there and near Cleveland, Ohio, Rockefeller used earnings from his Cleveland wholesale grocery business to enter oil refining, the business in which he became fabulously wealthy. Forming the **Standard Oil Company** in 1870 with **Henry M. Flagler** and other partners, Rockefeller used ruthless methods to consolidate the chaotic oil fields of western Pennsylvania under his auspices. In addition to Standard Oil, Rockefeller invested in other businesses, including mining, transportation, and banks.

A devout Baptist, he frequently donated money to churches, charities, and educational institutions, helping to found the **University of Chicago** and sustain Spelman Seminary (later College) in the 1880s. After 1900, his philanthropy reached an astounding scale, and he did as much to systematize and **modernize** the nonprofit sector as he had earlier done to modernize business. He gave some $540 million to the **General Education Board**, the **Rockefeller Sanitary Commission for the Eradication of Hookworm**, the **Rockefeller Foundation**, the Rockefeller Institute for Medical Research, and the Laura Spelman Rockefeller Memorial. Whereas most recipients accepted Rockefeller's largesse gratefully, **Washington Gladden** dramatically rejected a $100,000 gift to the Congregational Board of Foreign Missions in 1905 as tainted money because of the magnate's reputation. For many Americans, he and banker **J. P. Morgan** personified the evils of corporate capitalism. *See also* ANTITRUST; HOLDING COMPANIES; TARBELL, IDA.

ROCKEFELLER FOUNDATION. Established in May 1913, it grew out of the earlier success of the **Rockefeller Sanitary Commission for the Eradication of Hookworm**. John D. Rockefeller Jr. headed the foundation from its founding until 1940, donating some $350 million during that period. His father, **John D. Rockefeller** Sr., contributed another $182 million. Activities centered on **public health** and medical research, extending the campaign against hookworm, malaria, and **yellow fever** beyond U.S. borders. A major supporter of the **Flexner Report** and the movement to reform medical **education**, the foundation also supported **eugenics**, maternal **health**, sex education, and **birth control**.

**ROCKEFELLER SANITARY COMMISSION FOR THE ERADI-
CATION OF HOOKWORM.** Established in 1909, this commis-
sion aimed to eliminate the hookworm, a parasite endemic in the
South. Hookworms enter the body through the feet or can be ingested
via dirt eating, a common practice among malnourished people. U.S.
Public Health Service researcher Charles W. Stiles persuaded **John
D. Rockefeller**, already interested in southern issues through the
General Education Board, to fund an anti-hookworm campaign.
Despite some initial resistance from southerners wary of northern interference, by 1910 nine states requested funding and assistance; two
more states signed on later. The commission paid local physicians and
lab technicians, bought equipment, and funded travel. Abiding by the
racial etiquette of the Jim Crow South, it employed no black health
workers, but black southerners did receive treatment and prevention
education. In addition to treating the sick, workers educated local
physicians about the disease, gave public lectures, offered treatment
in the public schools, and established free or low-cost clinics. However, people who were treated soon became infected again because
they often could not afford shoes and did not have sanitary ways of
disposing of the bodily wastes that carried hookworm eggs. The U.S.
anti-hookworm campaign ended in 1915, but the new **Rockefeller
Foundation** took the commission's work abroad in 1913. *See also*
HEALTH AND MEDICINE.

ROOSEVELT, THEODORE, JR. (1858–1919). President of the
United States. Born into a prominent New York City family, he graduated from Harvard University (1880) and attended Columbia University law school, dropping out after his election as a **Republican** to
the state assembly (1882–84). Overcome by his wife's death in childbirth and his mother's death the same day, Valentine's Day in 1884,
he left his infant daughter with his sister and moved to a Dakota ranch
(1884–86). As a youth, he had battled asthma and physical weakness
by vigorous self-improvement, and in the west he earned a reputation
as a tough man by living what he later called the **strenuous life**. After
coming in third in a race for New York City mayor in 1886, he retired
to write books on his hunting exploits, along with the multivolume
bestseller *The Winning of the West* (1889–96). Appointed U.S. **civil
service** commissioner (1889–95), he then became president of the

New York City Board of Police Commissioners (1895–97). President **William McKinley** appointed him assistant secretary of the navy (1897–98), giving him the chance to organize Commodore **George Dewey**'s attack on Manila at the opening of the **Spanish–American War**. Resigning his post, he formed the 1st Regiment of the U.S. Volunteers (better known as the **Rough Riders**) and led them in the Battle of San Juan Hill. Returning a war hero, he was elected governor of New York (1899–1900). As governor, irrepressible Roosevelt so thoroughly exasperated Senator **Thomas C. Platt** and the New York State Republican **machine** (which had initially supported him) that they pushed for him to be nominated vice president in 1900 in part to get him out of the way. After the assassination of President William McKinley in 1901, Roosevelt ascended to the Oval Office (1901–9) and moved steadily toward **progressive** policies that irked his party's **Old Guard**.

Revitalizing the **Sherman Antitrust Act** with the *Northern Securities* case, he arbitrated an end to the 1902 **Anthracite Coal Strike** and created a new **Department of Commerce and Labor**. Easily reelected in 1904 with more than 57 percent of the popular votes, he secured passage of the **Pure Food and Drug Act** and the **Meat Inspection Act**, as well as the **Hepburn Act** to strengthen the **Interstate Commerce Commission**. An unabashed **imperialist** in the western hemisphere, he oversaw the seizure of the **Panama Canal** Zone and announced the **Roosevelt Corollary** to the Monroe Doctrine. Determined to engage the United States in great power politics, he supported the **Open Door** in China, mediated the Russo–Japanese War, and ordered the world cruise of the **Great White Fleet** to display the results of his naval expansion program. During his seven years in the White House, Roosevelt expanded the federal government's role in **conservation** through the **Newlands Reclamation Act** (1902) and **Gifford Pinchot**'s **U.S. Forest Service**. With his aide **George B. Cortelyou**, he gave unprecedented attention to the public relations aspect of the presidency, using what he called the "bully pulpit" to rally support for causes ranging from promoting American **art** and **literature** to raising the white birth rate, which he imagined to be teetering toward **race suicide**.

Regretting his promise to not seek election in 1908, he managed the candidacy of his friend, **William Howard Taft**, and then made an extended African safari and tour of Europe. Roosevelt's views became even more liberal after he resumed his political career in 1910, expanding his old **Square Deal** into the **New Nationalism** platform of his 1912 **Progressive Party** campaign for president. This third party split the Republican vote and allowed the **Democratic** candidate, **Woodrow Wilson**, to win. Denied the Republican nomination in 1916 and refusing the Progressive Party's call, Roosevelt campaigned against Wilson and participated in the **preparedness** movement. In failing health, his political career largely over, he traveled and wrote on politics, history, war, and himself until his death.

ROOSEVELT COROLLARY (1904). This series of statements, culminating in a passage in President **Theodore Roosevelt**'s 1904 annual message to Congress, committed the United States to policing the western hemisphere. In effect, Roosevelt asserted that the United States could preemptively intervene in Caribbean and Latin American countries when economic or political troubles might provide occasion for European interference. He claimed this authority as a logical consequence—hence "corollary"—of the principle articulated in the 1823 Monroe Doctrine, of limiting European influence in the Americas. Since the 1895 Venezuela Dispute and especially the 1898 **Spanish–American War**, the United States had grown increasingly aggressive in asserting a military sphere of influence in the Caribbean. In 1904, the Roosevelt administration was particularly anxious about the **Dominican Republic**, whose defaults on international debt payments created the threat of a German and British naval expedition, which had happened in Venezuela as recently as 1902–3. Roosevelt solved the crisis by pressuring the Dominicans into accepting American financial oversight, thus rendering European action superfluous. Latin Americans uniformly loathed the unilateral U.S. claim to protect them. The U.S. State Department renounced the Roosevelt Corollary in 1930, but the North American republic never entirely repudiated the principle behind it. *See also* CUBA; DOLLAR DIPLOMACY; FOREIGN POLICY; GUNBOAT DIPLOMACY; HAITI; NICARAGUA; PLATT AMENDMENT.

ROOSEVELT DAM. *See* RECLAMATION SERVICE, U.S.

ROOT, ELIHU B. (1845–1937). Public official and diplomat. The son of a professor at New York's Hamilton College, from which he graduated (1864), Root became a specialist in corporate law after graduating from New York University Law School (1867). Well known in **Republican** circles in New York, he served as President **William McKinley**'s secretary of war (1899–1904), responsible for consolidating the results of the **Spanish–American War** in **Puerto Rico** and **Cuba**, winning the **Philippine–American War**, and reforming the army after the botched mobilization of 1898. The creation of a **General Staff** and the Army War College were centerpieces of his program to **modernize** the army. Root was secretary of state (1905–9) during **Theodore Roosevelt**'s second term. After a goodwill tour of Latin America in 1906, he negotiated the 1907 **Gentlemen's Agreement** and the **Root–Takahira Agreement** in 1908 with Japan and negotiated several European treaties. His activities on behalf of **arbitration** and The **Hague** process earned him the Nobel Peace Prize (1912). As a Republican senator from New York (1909–15), he sided with party conservatives on domestic matters, breaking with Roosevelt. President **Woodrow Wilson** sent Root as ambassador to Russia (1917) in a futile attempt to support Alexander Kerensky's government. As president of the **Carnegie Endowment for International Peace** (1910–25), Root remained in public service through the 1920s and wrote books on law and politics. *See also* FOREIGN POLICY.

ROOT–TAKAHIRA AGREEMENT (1908). In this agreement, which reflected **Theodore Roosevelt**'s balance-of-power approach in Asia, Secretary of State **Elihu Root** placated Japanese frustration with the results of the **Portsmouth Conference** that had ended the Russo–Japanese War. On 30 November 1908, Japanese ambassador Kogoro Takahira exchanged notes with Root providing that both nations accepted the status quo in the Pacific, in effect conceding Japanese influence in Korea and Manchuria for a Japanese pledge not to interfere with the United States in the **Philippines**. Although this agreement on its surface affirmed the **Open Door** policy, it angered the Chinese because they had not been consulted in this extension of Japanese power in China's northern territories. *See also* FOREIGN POLICY; TAFT–KATSURA AGREEMENT.

ROSENWALD, JULIUS (1862–1932). See SEARS, ROEBUCK AND CO.

ROSS, EDWARD ALSWORTH (1866–1951). Sociologist. An Illinois native, he graduated from Coe College (1886) in Cedar Rapids, Iowa, studied in Berlin, and received a Ph.D. in political economy from Johns Hopkins University (1891). His dismissal from his job at Stanford University (1893–1900) for speaking on public reform issues precipitated a national debate on academic freedom. From the University of Nebraska (1901–6), he moved to the University of Wisconsin (1906–37). His fame rests on 27 books and more than 300 articles. *Social Control* (1906) and *Sin and Society* (1907) became classics of **progressive** social thought. *Social Psychology* (1908) was the first U.S. textbook published in that field, and *The Principles of Sociology* (1920) was the most popular textbook in the discipline. President of the American Sociological Association in 1914, he joined **John Dewey** and others to organize the **American Association of University Professors** (1915). An example of **social Darwinism**, Ross emphasized human interdependence as a basis for social reform, in the manner of **Lester Frank Ward**. Yet, convinced of the superiority of Anglo-Saxons, he coined the term *race suicide*, favored **immigration** restriction, and at times advocated **eugenics** and **prohibition**. *See also* INTELLECTUAL.

ROTARY CLUB. The world's first service club, the Rotary Club was founded in Chicago on 23 February 1905 by Paul P. Harris, a lawyer, and three local businessmen. Harris envisioned it as a **nonpartisan**, nonsectarian club for professional men to share the camaraderie he had known growing up in a small Vermont town. The name derived from the practice of rotating weekly meetings among members' offices, and the club soon adopted the wagon wheel as its emblem. In 1907, the Rotarians began civic service, donating a horse to a poor clergyman and building Chicago's first public lavatory. San Francisco established the second Rotary Club in 1908, and then clubs were chartered in Oakland, Seattle, Los Angeles, and New York City. When the National Association of Rotary Clubs held its first convention in New York City in 1910, Paul Harris was elected president. The slogans "Service Above Self" and "He Profits Most Who Serves

Best" were adopted in 1911. Rotary became an international organization with chartered clubs in Winnipeg (1910) and Dublin (1911). By 1922, clubs were operating on six continents. Membership was opened to business and professional women in 1989.

ROUGH RIDERS. Theodore Roosevelt formed and—along with **Leonard Wood**—led this unit, officially known as the 1st United States Volunteer Cavalry Regiment, in the **Spanish–American War**. Composed of upper-class easterners, New York City policemen, and western cowboys, the 1,000 Rough Riders exemplified Roosevelt's belief that warfare restored the virility weakened by civilization. Portraying his unit as heroes of the seizure of San Juan Hill in **Cuba**, he denigrated as cowards the **African American** 10th U.S. Cavalry, which in fact played a significant role in this minor victory. Suffering a 37 percent casualty rate, the surviving Rough Riders were mustered out in September 1898. Roosevelt's well-publicized exploits helped him win the governorship of New York in 1898 and become the **Republican Party**'s vice presidential candidate in 1900.

RUBINOW, ISAAC M. (1875–1936). Economist. Born in Russia, he immigrated to New York in 1893, trained as a physician, and earned a Ph.D. in economics at Columbia University. Employed by the **Department of Commerce and Labor**, he oversaw a 2,000-page study of European **social insurance** programs (1909). A founding member of the **American Association for Labor Legislation**, Rubinow became his generation's leading expert on **workers' compensation**, **unemployment** and health insurance, and actuarial statistics, as represented in books such as *Social Insurance* (1913). His book *The Quest for Security* (1934) directly influenced the 1935 Social Security Act.

RUEF, ABRAHAM (1864–1936). Politician. Born in San Francisco, from an Alsatian **Jewish** background, he graduated from the University of California (1883), studied at Hastings College of Law in San Francisco, and practiced law (1886–1911). In 1888, he joined the local **Republican machine**, earning a reputation as **Boss** Ruef of the Latin Quarter district. Breaking with the Republicans in 1901, he allied with the Union Labor Party and masterminded the election of the musicians' union leader, Eugene Schmitz, as mayor (1901–7), along with a handpicked board of supervisors. Having accumulated perhaps $500,000 in retainer fees from **trolley** lines, **utilities**, and other companies doing business with the city, he passed along a portion of this income to the supervisors as bribes for street railway franchises, utility rates, permits, and licenses. Brothels, gambling dens, and **dance halls** in the notorious Barbary Coast also allegedly paid bribes to Ruef. Newspaper editor Fremont Older and James D. Phelan, a reformist former mayor, led a campaign to indict him. Convicted of bribery and sent to San Quentin Prison (1911–15), the boss was released after Older obtained his parole.

RUFFIN, JOSEPHINE ST. PIERRE (1842–1924). Editor and reformer. A Boston native, Ruffin first became politically active during the Civil War. After the death in 1886 of her husband, George Lewis Ruffin, the first **African American** graduate of Harvard Law School (1869) and a Boston politician and judge, she published *The Woman's Era* (1890–97), the first monthly for African American women, and edited the *Boston Courant*. The charitable organization she founded, the Woman's Era Club (1893), was a forerunner of the **National Association of Colored Women** (1896), of which she was the first vice president. In 1900, the national **General Federation of Women's Clubs (GFWC)** invited her to join the executive committee. Only when she arrived for the convention did the GFWC leaders realize that she was African American and rescind their invitation. She later helped to establish the Boston branch of the **National Association for the Advancement of Colored People**.

RULE OF REASON. This doctrine, first stated by the **U.S. Supreme Court** in *Standard Oil v. United States* (1911), held that the **Sherman Antitrust Act** only prohibited monopolies, combinations, and contracts that engaged in illegal activity that unreasonably restrained trade. The Court's 8-to-1 decision held that if a large, powerful corporation produced no ill effects, if its bigness resulted from superior **efficiency** or some other honest advantage, it was not illegal. Only Justice **John Marshall Harlan** dissented from this new interpretation. Ex-president and future chief justice **William Howard Taft** defended this decision in *The Antitrust Acts and the Supreme Court*

(1914), and the Court unanimously reaffirmed the Rule of Reason in 1918. *See also* CLAYTON ANTITRUST ACT; UNITED STATES STEEL CORPORATION.

RURAL FREE DELIVERY. The extension of mail delivery into rural areas was the result of a concerted campaign by farmers' groups, **mail-order** houses, and **mass-circulation magazines**. Despite passage of **Tom Watson**'s 1893 bill and congressional appropriations in 1893, 1894, and 1896, not until 1896 did the postmaster general open 82 test routes in 28 states. The service proved wildly popular. In 1898, Congress gave the pilot program $150,000, and the number of routes increased to 8,000 by 1902. Because the Post Office required good roads to implement the service, towns and counties spent some $72 million improving roads and bridges between 1897 and 1908, literally paving the way for a new **parcel post** service in 1913. By 1915, rural mail carriers outnumbered urban ones. *See also* GOOD ROADS MOVEMENT.

RUSSELL SAGE FOUNDATION. This foundation was established in New York City (1907) by Margaret Olivia Sage, the widow of railroad tycoon and financier Russell Sage, with a gift of $10 million. Its purpose is the improvement of social and living conditions in the United States. After gaining national attention by underwriting the **Pittsburgh Survey**, the foundation focused its early work on **social insurance**, labor conditions, penal reform, **health** care, housing, city planning, and the social work profession. Inspired by the **Garden City movement**, the foundation sponsored Forest Hills Park in Queens. Later it supported and published social science research and social policy proposals. *See also* NATIONAL HOUSING ASSOCIATION.

RYAN, JOHN A. (1869–1945). Priest and social reformer. Born in Minnesota, he graduated from St. Thomas College (1892) and St. Paul Seminary (1898), was ordained a Catholic priest, and earned a doctorate from the Catholic University of America (1906). A professor of political science and moral theology at St. Paul Seminary (1902–15) and Catholic University (1915–39), he was for decades the leading social justice advocate in the American Catholic Church, in keeping with Pope Leo XIII's encyclical *Rerum Novarum* (1891). His doctoral dissertation, published in 1906 as *A Living Wage: Its Economic and Ethical Aspects*, popularized the notion that all families deserved an adequate standard of living, a concept behind movements for **minimum wages** and **social insurance**. Skeptical of **socialism**, he gained attention for his friendly debate on this issue with **Morris Hillquit**, published in *Everybody's* magazine (1913–14) and as the book *Socialism: Promise or Menace* (1914). *See also* LIVING WAGE.

– S –

SAINT-GAUDENS, AUGUSTUS (1848–1907). Sculptor. Born in Ireland, Saint-Gaudens emigrated to the United States with his parents in 1848. After studying in New York, Paris, and Rome, he opened a New York studio in 1875. The leading sculptor of the American Beaux Arts period, Saint-Gaudens produced many well-known public sculptures, including the *Adams Memorial* (1890) in Washington's Rock Creek Cemetery and the *Shaw Memorial* (1897) on Boston Common. He was a consultant for **art** at the Columbian **Exposition** of 1893 and the **McMillan Plan** of 1902. His studio in Cornish, New Hampshire (1885–1907), attracted a prominent art colony and became a national historic site after he died there in August 1907.

SALOON. Before **Prohibition**, the saloon served as a club for working-class men and often as an informal bank and employment agency as well. In crowded **tenement** districts, saloons provided meeting space for political, fraternal, and mutual-benefit societies and **labor unions**. Many offered free lunches for the cost of a five-cent beer. Requiring little capital and often supported by breweries, they were attractive business opportunities for men from poorer backgrounds, with the result that in most urban, working-class neighborhoods, several saloons stood on each block. An 1895 survey found an average of one per 317 residents in 95 major cities, but whereas San Francisco had one bar for every 218 residents, Boston had only one per 716 because of high license fees. On a single day in 1899, Chicago police estimated that roughly half the population entered a barroom (without adjusting for repeat visits). Southern states tended to have fewer saloons than the urbanized North. Saloons' character as social space for men apart from families explains much controversy surrounding them. Children often came to buy buckets of beer for the household. Some bars employed barmaids, and others functioned as brothels. Respectable **women** for the most part did not enter saloons, although unmarried women might drink in **dance halls**, and some German American wives and daughters participated in family outings to beer gardens.

A trend toward brewery control of saloons allowed them to become a target of **antitrust** as well as temperance sentiment. Corporate breweries encouraged the proliferation of bars and helped to standardize their furniture, amenities, prices, and products. Saloonkeepers often held prominent positions in ward and city politics, typically as **Democrats**. The **Republicans** were more likely to be "dry" or friendly to prohibition, except in the South, where Democrats led the dry forces. The saloon-keeper's visible place in city neighborhoods explains why many political **bosses** began as tavern owners or managers. With their ties to the corporate interests and political **machines** and their working-class, male atmosphere, saloons provided an inviting target for the aptly named **Anti-Saloon League**. Middle-class, female reform groups such as the **Woman's Christian Temperance Union** denounced saloons as enemies of wholesome family life. Brewers and distillers, in turn, were strong opponents of women's **suffrage**. *See also* LOCAL OPTION; PROSTITUTION; UNITED STATES BREWERS' ASSOCIATION.

SAMOA PARTITION. At the Berlin Conference in 1889, Great Britain, Germany, and the United States attempted to establish a tripartite protectorate over Samoa, where the three powers had competed for influence since the 1870s. This arrangement fell apart when civil war began over succession to the Samoan throne in 1898. Over the next year, Britain renounced interest in the archipelago, which the Germans and Americans then divided between themselves in an agreement signed on 2 December 1899. The U.S. Navy assumed control of Pago Pago and the eastern half of the Samoan island chain, thus acquiring a useful South Pacific coaling station. *See also* FOREIGN POLICY.

SAN FRANCISCO EARTHQUAKE. Early in the morning on 18 April 1906, a huge earthquake, estimated to measure more than 8.0 on the Richter scale, rumbled through the San Francisco area, killing and injuring thousands. People as far away as Los Angeles, southern Oregon, and central Nevada felt the quake. More devastating was the fire fueled by broken gas mains and overturned ovens. It roared through the downtown district for three days, razing much of the central city. San Francisco's inadequate water system could not provide enough water or water pressure to fight the fire effectively, and firefighters only managed to contain it by dynamiting mansions just outside the central area to create a firebreak. Some 200,000 people lost their homes and had to shelter in tents in Golden Gate Park. This disaster gave city officials a potent argument in favor of damming the **Hetch Hetchy Valley** as a municipal reservoir. Rebuilding began at once, despite the usual postdisaster qualms; too many people had invested too much in real estate to abandon the sites. *See also* FUNSTON, FREDERICK; GIANNINI, AMADEO PETER.

SAN JUAN HILL. *See* ROUGH RIDERS; SPANISH–AMERICAN WAR; ROOSEVELT, THEODORE.

SANDBURG, CARL (1878–1967). Poet. Born in Illinois, the son of Swedish **immigrants**, Sandburg served in the U.S. Army in **Puerto Rico** during the **Spanish–American War**, attended Lombard College in his hometown, and spent several years as a tramp, **journalist**, and magazine editor. Joining the **Socialist Party**, he worked as secretary to Milwaukee's Socialist mayor between 1910 and 1912. *Poetry* magazine published his first work in 1914. His book *Chicago Poems* (1916) established Sandburg as a major figure of the **Chicago Renaissance**. Critics compared him to Walt Whitman and praised his knowledge of the land, his enthusiastic evocations of urban grittiness, and his familiarity with common people. A reporter at the *Chicago Daily News* by 1919, Sandburg later won accolades for his multivolume biography of Abraham Lincoln. *See also* LITERATURE; MASTERS, EDGAR LEE.

SANGER, MARGARET (1879–1966). Birth control advocate and eugenicist. The daughter of Irish Catholic New Yorkers, Sanger attended college and trained to be a **nurse** before marrying architect William Sanger in 1902 and having three children. Working as a visiting nurse, she was distressed by poor **women** who reenacted the constant child-bearing that caused her own mother's early death and who suffered often fatal infections caused by botched abortions. This experience and the example of other leftist women, especially **Emma Goldman**, led Sanger to challenge the **Comstock** law that criminalized **birth control**. Her interactions with **Greenwich Village** bohemians and the nascent **feminist** movement convinced her of women's right to enjoy heterosexual intercourse free of the risk of pregnancy, so she opposed the emphasis of many sex reformers on abstinence and continence. Women's **suffrage** and economic rights, she believed, were meaningless if women could not control their fertility. To promote these ideas, in 1912 she wrote a newspaper sex-advice column, only to see several essays banned as obscene. Sanger then published her own newspaper, *The Woman Rebel*, and prepared the pamphlet *Family Limitation* (1914), which described and evaluated contraceptive devices available on the black market. Fearing arrest, she fled to England before the pamphlet was published. Authorities tricked her husband, whom she was soon to **divorce**, into providing a copy of the pamphlet, and he spent a month in jail.

While in England, Sanger met sexologist Havelock Ellis, learned about European birth control campaigns, and advocated fertility control as a solution to overpopulation and poverty. Returning to the United States in 1915, Sanger went on a national lecture tour during which she was arrested several times. In 1916, she helped to open a birth control clinic in Brownsville, Brooklyn, with the aim of training women to use the diaphragm, which did not require the participation of sexual partners or physicians. Police soon shut this clinic and arrested Sanger and the other employees. Her appeal of her conviction led the court to broaden the interpretation of the Comstock law to allow physicians to prescribe birth control to women for medical reasons. In response, Sanger opened clinics staffed by physicians and founded the American Birth Control League (today's Planned Parenthood) in 1921.

Sanger was highly successful in garnering publicity and financial support for her cause. As she moved away from her early **socialism** and became intrigued by **eugenics**, Sanger endorsed the prevention of births among "defective" people, including compulsory **sterilization**. She traveled widely and played a key role in organizing the international birth control movement. She also raised money for research into better contraceptives, including, eventually, the birth control pill. *See also* SEXUALITY.

SANITARY ENGINEERING. Throughout the second half of the 19th century, **public health** experts and civil engineers such as George E. Waring (1833–98) built on the findings of English reformer Edwin Chadwick and others concerning water-borne diseases such as cholera to promote measures to improve water supply, drainage, street paving, household plumbing, garbage collection, and other urban sanitary systems. As a specialty within civil engineering, sanitary engineering expanded after 1884, when the first sanitary chemistry laboratory in the United States, the Lawrence Experiment Station, opened under the direction of Massachusetts Institute of Technology professor William R. Nichols and his colleague **Ellen Swallow Richards**. In 1887, Richards conducted the nation's first study of water quality for the Massachusetts State Board of Health, work that led the state to create the nation's first water quality standards (1886) and the first modern sewage treatment plant in Lowell. Other states soon took similar steps.

Hiram F. Mills earned the nickname "Father of American Sanitary Engineering" for testing the efficacy of filtration as compared to natural oxidation in public water sources. When a typhoid epidemic began in 1893 along the Merrimack River, those Massachusetts cities that adopted Mills's slow sand filters had lower death rates. Theobold Smith, a physician for the U.S. Agriculture Department, made similar advances in combating infectious animal diseases and fecal coliform contamination in the Potomac (1887) and Hudson rivers (1892). Such studies prompted Washington, D.C., and other large cities to build expensive water treatment plants, with dramatic effects on rates of typhoid and other diseases. These efforts exemplify the efforts of Progressive Era scientists and engineers to apply knowledge in practical ways to promote public health and safety. **Women** reformers, attracted to the **municipal housekeeping** aspect of sanitation, played a key role in pressuring cities to address the need for clean water, air, and streets. *See also* CHICAGO SANITARY AND SHIP CANAL; HEALTH AND MEDICINE.

SANTAYANA, GEORGE (1863–1952). Philosopher. Born in Madrid to a Spanish father and an American mother, Santayana came to Boston as a child, graduated from Harvard University (1886), and studied in Berlin before spending 23 years as a Harvard professor. A student of **William James** and Josiah Royce, Santayana participated in the golden age of philosophy at Harvard. Retiring first to England in 1912 and then to Rome in 1920, he became a poet, essayist, playwright, and novelist. An atheist but aesthetically devoted to Catholicism, he regarded Royce's idealistic philosophy with skepticism. His inclination toward **naturalism** and **pragmatism** appear in works such as his five-volume *The Life of Reason* (1905–6). Known for his wit, he is remembered for saying, "Those who cannot remember the past are condemned to repeat it." *See also* INTELLECTUAL.

SCHNEIDERMAN, ROSE (1882–1972). Labor leader. The daughter of Polish **Jews**, Schneiderman immigrated to the United States with her family in 1890. Despite her father's death, she completed the ninth grade before going to work full-time. Attracted to **socialism** and **anarchism**, she became a **labor union** organizer, leading her first strike in 1905 and soon joining the **Women's Trade Union League (WTUL)** and the **International Ladies' Garment Workers' Union**, of which she became a local president. She played a key role in the **Uprising of the Twenty Thousand** in 1909–10. The horrific 1911 **Triangle Shirtwaist Fire**, which she blamed in part on the willingness of male union leaders to compromise safety issues, prompted Schneiderman to become an activist for **women's suffrage**. She was president of the WTUL's New York City branch from 1917 to 1949 and led the national office from 1926 to 1950. In the 1920s and 1930s, she helped to found the American Civil Liberties Union, ran unsuccessfully for the U.S. Senate, and served briefly as a New York state and federal labor official.

SCHWAB, CHARLES M. (1862–1939). Industrialist. Born in Pennsylvania, Schwab became a laborer at **Andrew Carnegie**'s Edgar Thomson Steel Works, rising through the ranks to become manager of the Thomson and Homestead works by 1892. As president of the Carnegie Steel Company, Schwab negotiated with **J. P. Morgan** in the deal that created the **United States Steel Corporation**, of which he became the first president in 1901. Resigning in 1903 to preside over the small Bethlehem Steel Company, Schwab became an advocate of **welfare capitalist** policies such as profit sharing and incentive wages. He won profitable contracts for building submarines during World War I, and President **Woodrow Wilson** recruited him to direct the wartime Emergency Fleet Corporation. Schwab lost his $200-million fortune in the Great Depression and died insolvent. *See also* GREAT MERGER MOVEMENT.

SCIENTIFIC MANAGEMENT. Coined in 1910, this term described an array of efforts to make industrial work processes more **efficient** by replacing experience-based knowledge with technical expertise acquired through scientific study. Its best-known advocate, **Frederick Winslow Taylor**, promised increased profits and greater harmony in the workplace. Taylor's *The Principles of Scientific Management* (1911) was one of the century's most popular business books. Scientific management tended to shift control from blue-collar foremen to white-collar supervisors. The most notorious aspect of scientific management, the time-and-motion study, involved timing a worker's activities with a stopwatch while observing motions he or she made. When businesses tried to use time-and-motion studies to lower piece rates or speed up production, workers reacted negatively and sometimes were able to derail the project. In the 1910s, the **American Federation of Labor** and metalworkers' **labor unions** opposed scientific management's challenge to their control over trade knowledge and work processes. Indeed, few manufacturers attempted to implement Taylor's system in a comprehensive way, although the notion of scientific management became a widespread ideal or slogan. Aimed at the growing ranks of white-collar workers as much as shop-floor employees, scientific management inspired elaborate job descriptions and organizational charts while promoting incentive wages and ergonomics. *See also* BRANDEIS, LOUIS D.; GILBRETH, FRANK AND LILLIAN; WELFARE CAPITALISM.

SCUDDER, VIDA DUTTON (1861–1954). Reformer. Born to missionaries in India, Scudder grew up in Massachusetts. After earning her B.A. and M.A. at Smith College, she was one of the first **women** allowed to study at Oxford University, where she became concerned with issues of class conflict in industrial society. After joining the faculty at Wellesley College (1887–1928), she helped open the Denison **settlement house** in Boston in 1892 and cofounded the **Women's Trade Union League** in 1903. A devout Episcopalian, an advocate of Christian **socialism**, and a pacifist, she joined the **Socialist Party** (1911) and defended the **Lawrence Strike** (1912). Like many professional women in her generation, Scudder never married and spent many years with a female companion, Florence Converse. *See also* SOCIAL GOSPEL.

SEAMEN'S ACT (1915). This act, sponsored by Senator **Robert M. La Follette**, improved the safety, security, and welfare of American merchant seamen. Andrew Furuseth, president of the International Seafarer's Union, and Secretary of Labor **William B. Wilson** helped draft the law. It abolished imprisonment for desertion, reduced penalties for disobedience, regulated pay, limited working hours to 56 per week, and set standards for food, sanitation, lifeboats, unionization, the number of qualified able seamen, and the number who could speak the language of the ship's officers. *See also* NEW FREEDOM; MINIMUM WAGE LEGISLATION.

SEARS, ROEBUCK AND CO. The era's most successful **mail-order** company had its origins in railroad man Richard W. Sears's sale of an unclaimed shipment of watches in 1886. Emulating field leader Montgomery Ward, Sears and his partner, Alvah C. Roebuck, expanded their lines of merchandise and launched a mail-order catalog in 1896. Julius Rosenwald, a Chicago clothing merchant, joined the firm in 1895, reorganizing its shipping department to meet the demand stimulated by Sears's creative **advertising** and low prices. By 1900, the company's sales exceeded those of Montgomery Ward, and in 1909–10, Rosenwald took the company public and then assumed control of it, curbing some of Sears's excesses and eliminating patent medicines from the catalog in 1913. By then, the 750-page Sears catalog—for decades written personally by Sears, who had a knack for wording and features that would appeal to rural and small town dwellers—had become part of the life and folklore of rural America, popularly known as the "wish book." Customers could buy everything from clothing and houses to guns and syringes. The range and quality of goods were better than could be found in most country stores, and **rural free delivery** and **parcel post** extended and lowered the cost of shipments. Mail-order shopping diminished social isolation on the farm and small town and gave rural Americans access to the modern goods that **department stores** provided in cities. However, catalog sales declined along with rural populations, leading Sears to open retail outlets by the late 1920s. Store sales exceeded the mail-order business by 1931, but the catalog survived until 1993. *See also* POPULAR CULTURE.

SECRET BALLOT. *See* AUSTRALIAN BALLOT.

SEGREGATION. The intensification of racial segregation enforced by law and custom was a striking trend of the years from 1893 to 1917, seemingly at odds with the spirit of progressivism but reinforced by certain lines within **progressive** thought. The racial segregation of public institutions and the exclusion of **African Americans** from public and private services and buildings began after the abolition of slavery in 1865 and reflected the desire of blacks for independent, black-run institutions as well as bigotry on the part of whites. As white supremacist politicians took control of southern states after the mid-1870s, they wrote segregation and **disfranchisement** into law, a movement that intensified after the **Supreme Court** struck down the 1875 federal Civil Rights Act in the *Civil Rights Cases* of 1883. African Americans challenged exclusion from railroad and streetcars, schools, hotels, restaurants, hospitals, parks, theaters, and residential districts. Some, like activist **Ida B. Wells-Barnett**, even won cases until the Supreme Court's *Plessy v. Ferguson* decision in 1896 ratified segregation laws under the rubric "separate but equal."

The South's deep economic troubles, ongoing African American challenges to subordination, black migration to southern cities, and political turmoil sparked by the populist challenge to the southern **Democrats**' political monopoly, combined to create an anxious atmosphere conducive to intensified racism. State legislation for segregation and disfranchisement seemed to sanction mob violence against blacks, as manifested in the wave of **lynching** and **race riots** that marred these decades. Although **Booker T. Washington** worked behind the scenes and the **National Association for the Advancement**

of Colored People and other organizations openly contested segregation with a few successes, notably *Guinn v. United States* (1915), the
"separate but equal" doctrine endured until the Supreme Court's 1954
Brown v. Board of Education decision.

The claim that separate facilities for blacks and whites were equal
was almost always a fiction. Barred from voting, impoverished
through discriminatory hiring, lending, and housing practices, and living under the threat of violence, blacks had little leverage to demand
equal treatment. Confined to shabby, crowded, inadequate facilities
(usually side by side with superior "whites only" accommodations),
they could not travel easily and had to defer to whites or risk assault.
Any violation of racial etiquette—not stepping off the sidewalk to let
a white pass, meeting a white's eyes too directly—invited punishment, and African Americans were often arrested, convicted, and
imprisoned for trumped up or petty crimes by the all-white police,
juries, and judges. Black **women** had no legal recourse if raped or
coerced into having sex with a white man, whereas black men faced
torture, castration, and death if even suspected of intimacy with a
white woman. Miscegenation laws banning marriage across the color
line proliferated across the nation and often invoked the "one drop
rule": having a single drop of African blood made a person black and
thus a second-class citizen. Ironically, segregation also encouraged a
small, entrepreneurial middle class to serve black patrons.

Losing hope in the South and lured by the promise of greater
freedom and opportunity in the cities of the Northeast and Midwest,
black Americans began the mass movement known as the **Great Migration**. Outside the Jim Crow South, they met with de facto segregation enforced through discriminatory hiring, lending, and housing
policies as well as violence. Although lynching was less common
outside the South, race riots were a nationwide phenomenon in the
1910s. Because of residential segregation, schools were also largely
segregated. Large black communities such as Chicago's Bronzeville
and New York's Harlem generated pride, some political power, and
business opportunities as well as poverty and violence. Moreover,
outside the South civil rights organizations operated openly and
blacks could vote and elect their own to local office.

Other racial/ethnic groups in the United States also endured segregation that varied in rigidity. Discriminatory housing and hiring

policies kept Chinese, Japanese, Latinos, and **Native Americans** confined to certain city neighborhoods or rural districts and resulted in segregated, decrepit schools. Laws barring interracial marriage named Native Americans and Asians as well as African Americans as undesirable partners for whites; in some states, Asian and African Americans were also barred from marrying each other. The segregation of **Jews** into ghettoes, such as occurred in Eastern European countries, never existed in the United States. Jewish neighborhoods like New York City's **Lower East Side** had no enforced legal status and were neither ethnically homogenous nor closed. However, many elite residential areas, hotels, and clubs barred Jewish membership or home and land ownership, while some **universities** enforced quotas to limit the number of Jewish students.

Women of all races had long faced segregation in schools, hotels, restaurants, workplaces, and entertainment venues, though the separation of the sexes eroded in the early 20th century. Public universities were mostly open to women from the start, and the efforts of the **American Association of University Women** and individuals like **Ellen Swallow Richards** breached barriers blocking women from graduate and professional training. Women worked with men in factories, stores, and offices, though almost always in lesser-status jobs typed by gender. Entertainment venues such as **dance halls**, **vaudeville** shows, nickelodeons, and **amusement parks** became especially visible and controversial sites for interactions between the sexes. *See also* ATLANTA COMPROMISE; CONVICT LEASING; DU BOIS, W. E. B.; EDUCATION; NIAGARA MOVEMENT.

SELIGMAN, EDWIN ROBERT ANDERSON (1861–1939). Economist. Born in New York City into a well-to-do **Jewish** family, Seligman graduated from Columbia College (1879), studied in Europe, and earned a doctorate at Columbia (1885), the same year he cofounded the American Economic Association. For 40 years beginning in 1891, he was a professor of political economy at Columbia, where he became an expert on public finance and taxation and a leading advocate of the **income tax** and **Federal Reserve** system, as well as a moderate voice among economists in favor of the labor movement and redistribution of wealth. Among his philanthropic interests, he assisted Jewish **immigrants**, served as president of the

National **Urban League**, and edited the *Political Science Quarterly* and the *Encyclopedia of the Social Sciences. See also* ECONOMY.

SENATORS, DIRECT ELECTION OF. First proposed in the 1820s, the idea of having voters rather than state legislatures select U.S. senators gathered strength during the late 1800s amid revelations of corporate influence and even bribery in state legislatures. Prominent supporters included populists, **William Jennings Bryan**'s faction among **Democrats**, **Insurgent Republicans** such as **Robert M. La Follette** and **George Norris**, and **structural reform progressives**, along with the **Hearst** newspaper chain and **muckraker** publications. By 1908, both major parties were nominally in favor, but the Senate delayed the required constitutional amendment. **William S. U'Ren**'s campaign in Oregon for state-level action gained widespread attention, and by 1912, 29 states had adopted measures involving either the **direct primary** or the general election. A notorious bribery scandal in the 1909 reelection of Illinois Republican senator William S. Lorimer helped to turn the tide. Still, the vote of Vice President James S. Sherman was required to gain the two-thirds needed to send what became the Seventeenth Amendment to the states in May 1912. The states acted rapidly, with 36 states approving it by 8 April 1913. It took effect in the 1914 election.

SENNETT, MACK (1880–1960). Born Michael Sinnott into an Irish Catholic family in Quebec, Canada, Sennett moved to the United States with his family in 1897. In 1900, he went to New York City, where he played small roles in burlesque and musical theater. In 1908, he worked in the infant **movie** industry, hired at the Biograph Company by director **D. W. Griffith**. Within two years Sennett moved from acting to screenwriting, directing, and producing, heading Biograph's new comedy unit. He moved to Hollywood in 1912 to run the Keystone Film Company, which created brash slapstick comedies. His signature acts were the Bathing Beauty and the rushing, bumbling Keystone Kops, whose antics poked fun at authority figures. Some leading actors and directors, including **Charlie Chaplin**, Mabel Normand, Frank Capra, George Cukor, and Gloria Swanson, started at Keystone. In 1915, Sennett became part of the short-lived Triangle Film Company, which also employed Griffith and Thomas

Ince. Increasingly, audiences and distributors wanted longer, more complex films that relied on plot rather than sight gags, and Sennett's fortunes declined starting in the 1920s, despite recognition of his pioneering role in developing film comedy.

SETTLEMENT HOUSE MOVEMENT. Settlement houses were private social service institutions run by volunteers or social welfare professionals, usually **women** from privileged backgrounds and with a humanitarian or **Social Gospel**–type calling to work with the poor. By living or "settling" among the urban poor, activists hoped to bridge the class divide and provide a conduit for information between the classes. Unlike the male-run British social settlements on which they were modeled, early U.S. settlements generally resulted from the initiative of educated middle-class women who sought an outlet for their energies and talents, given the constrained options that they otherwise faced. Rivington House appeared in New York City in 1889, while **Vida Scudder** and other female college faculty members founded Denison House in Boston in 1892, around the same time that the better-known **Hull House** in Chicago opened under the leadership of **Jane Addams** and **Ellen Gates Starr**. The College Settlements Association formed in 1890 and opened houses in Boston and Philadelphia. In 1895, nurse **Lillian Wald** founded the Henry Street Settlement in New York City and made it an innovator in providing **public health** services. Since white-run settlements usually avoided provoking racism by refusing to serve blacks, black women established their own organizations. **Lugenia Burns Hope**'s Neighborhood Union in Atlanta and **Ida B. Wells-Barnett**'s Negro Fellowship League in Chicago are two examples. Men such as **Graham Taylor** of the Chicago Commons and **Robert A. Woods** of Boston's South End House also participated and lived in the settlements. But women predominated, among them **Grace** and **Edith Abbott**, **Sophonisba Breckinridge**, **Alice Hamilton**, **Florence Kelley**, **Mary Eliza McDowell**, and **Mary White Ovington**.

By 1910, more than 400 settlement houses operated in the United States, and the National Federation of Social Settlements was established in 1911. Starting with the conventional goal of aiding and uplifting the poor and **immigrants**, settlement workers expanded their horizons to include improvement of housing and services in poor neighborhoods and attacks on the debilitating social and economic circumstances that faced the urban working class. Settlement workers campaigned for everything from improvements in **sanitary engineering** to **minimum wage** and maximum hours legislation. Some, including Scudder, Ovington, and Kelley, became **socialists**. Settlement house workers were particularly concerned with the situation of children and working-class girls and women. They opened kindergartens and well-baby clinics and lobbied city governments to establish **playgrounds** for poor children. Reformers sought to provide girls with low-cost, respectable lodging and recreation as an alternative to **dance halls**, **movies**, **vaudeville**, and **amusement parks**. Their fear that women's low wages and the desire for mass-produced finery would lead them into **prostitution** prompted them to establish girls' clubs and to agitate for better pay and working conditions. Protecting girls was especially important for African American reformers, who tried to counter racist stereotypes of black promiscuity and limit the ability of white men to coerce black women.

For the foreign-born, settlement houses sponsored **Americanization** programs, including English classes, courses in **home economics**, and vocational training. Because immigrant parents were unfamiliar with middle-class American standards, the settlement house workers intervened to adjust the "newer races" to American ways. At times, this attitude led these well-intentioned professionals into a confident assault on the working-class family in the name of Americanization. The ethnic neighborhood became a laboratory for the new social sciences. At the same time, some settlement house workers began to see value in cultures previously dismissed as backward and became advocates for a new, **pluralist** vision of American society. They often tolerated racial **segregation** but protested racist stereotypes circulated by the supporters of immigration restriction.

Settlement houses loom large in the tale of Progressive Era reform, but they reached only a tiny fraction of the urban population. Far more working-class people participated in ethnic, religious, fraternal, and labor organizations. The long-lasting effects of this movement were the professionalization of social work, especially as a career for women, and the growth of public and private social services. *See also* REFORM MOVEMENTS.

SEVENTEENTH AMENDMENT. *See* SENATORS, DIRECT ELECTION OF.

SEXUALITY. New understandings of sexuality emerged by the early 20th century for a variety of reasons: the professionalization of medicine, psychiatry, psychology, and biology; **reform movements** focused on **prostitution** and **birth control**; and the challenge to gender roles posed by women's entry into higher **education** and the workforce and by the **feminist** and women's rights movements. The new "sexologists," such as Richard von Krafft-Ebing, Havelock Ellis, and Sigmund Freud, all European experts, argued that sexual desire was a product of biology and child development. In popular discourse, this view translated into the belief that sexuality was a powerful natural urge that had a healthy outlet within heterosexual marriage but that caused physical and social disorders when repressed.

New understandings of sexuality and gender also made sense of changes in family structure, including the decreasing importance of the patriarchal household. By the early 20th century, more men and women lived at least some time on their own or in peer communities. Most American cities and many rural workplaces supported a large and thriving bachelor subculture. In 1890, some 67 percent of all men between the ages of 15 and 34 were unmarried, a rate unmatched in U.S. history until the end of the 20th century. A rapidly expanding commercial sex industry served such men. **Progressives**, especially women, responded with plans to abolish prostitution and prevent the circulation of obscene materials. The **American Social Hygiene Association** promoted a single standard of chastity to prevent the spread of diseases such as **syphilis**. Activists such as **Anthony Comstock** favored censorship; many cities had ordinances enabling the censorship of **movie**, theater, and **vaudeville** performances, and many states legislated confiscation of explicit materials, including birth control information and contraceptive devices. Some physicians advocated premarital blood tests for sexually transmitted diseases and scientific sex education. **Eugenics** encouraged white, middle-class women to procreate, while discouraging the "unfit" from having children, in extreme cases through **sterilization** or imprisonment.

Ideas about sexuality also contributed to the **segregation** and **disfranchisement** of **African Americans,** as white supremacists delegitimized civil rights by insisting that what black men really wanted was sexual access to white women, a myth that justified the **lynching** of thousands of African Americans, mostly men, and made women of color vulnerable to rape. Despite the illegality of contraception and abortion throughout this era, the steady decrease in the birth rate reflected the continuing availability of condoms, diaphragms, spermicidal douches, and other forms of birth control. Abortion remained the most common form of birth control for working-class women, who less often had access to medical care or could not afford to buy effective contraception. In the 1910s, **feminists** like **Margaret Sanger** campaigned for the legalization of birth control.

Changing sexual mores drew attention to a small but noteworthy number of women who sought opportunities to live outside of their natal families without marrying. The practice of two unmarried women sharing a home, often called a "Boston marriage," enabled female professionals to participate in public life. **Vida D. Scudder** and poet Amy Lowell were examples of prominent women in Boston marriages, which may have been lesbian relationships. Working-class women had fewer resources, but some earned enough to live in lodgings with other women. However, women's earnings were typically so low that they exchanged sexual favors with men to gain access to commercial amusements, ready-made clothing, and restaurant meals. Working-class parents, young women, and reformers alike worried about the blurring line between these "charity girls," prostitutes, and women in relationships leading to marriage. Among middle-class people, the new ideal of "companionate marriage" emphasized the partners' equality and emotional commitment. It, along with women's greater economic resources, contributed to rising rates of **divorce**. A few radicals centered in **Greenwich Village**, led by the members of the feminist club Heterodoxy, regarded transformed heterosexual relations as the key to social revolution. **Emma Goldman** was the most notorious spokeswoman for this view.

The increasing visibility of same-sex sexual activities, especially among men, and publicized scandals in Portland, Oregon (1912); Los Angeles and Long Beach, California (1914); and Newport, Rhode Island (1919), brought the existence of what now became known as "homosexuality"—rather than older concepts such as "sexual inversion"—into popular view. The difference is complex, but in general, the term *homosexuality* came to signify a durable personal identity marked by desiring sex with people of the same gender. Stigmatized as deviants, homosexuals suffered more active criminalization and repression than in previous periods, though subcultures colloquially labeled "queer" or "gay" thrived in large cities. *See also* ADOLESCENCE; NEW WOMAN.

SHAW, ANNA HOWARD (1847-1919). Minister and women's suffrage leader. Born in England and raised in Massachusetts and Michigan, Shaw became the first **woman** ordained as a Methodist minister and served as a pastor in Massachusetts in the 1870s and 1880s. After earning a medical degree from Boston University (1886), she discovered a talent for public speaking and threw herself into the temperance and women's **suffrage** movements, becoming a popular lecturer for the **Woman's Christian Temperance Union** and the **National American Woman Suffrage Association**. As president of the latter beginning in 1904, she led a fractured organization that suffered two schisms during her term in office: the formation of the **Southern States Woman Suffrage Conference** in 1913 and the ouster of the Congressional Union in 1914. After **Carrie Chapman Catt** resumed the presidency in 1915, Shaw returned to lecturing. When the United States entered World War I, she worked for the Woman's Committee of the Council of National Defense. She died in 1919 while campaigning for the **League to Enforce Peace**.

SHERMAN ANTITRUST ACT (1890). *See* ANTITRUST.

SHORT BALLOT. A Progressive Era innovation, the short ballot aimed to make local and state elections simpler and more understandable by converting some elective offices to appointive ones. Appointed city clerks or coroners, for example, would no longer be **machine** hacks but trained officials. A characteristic example of the **progressive** stress on expertise and **efficiency**, touted by public administration experts such as **Richard S. Childs** and **Charles Beard**, the short ballot responded to the criticism that the ballot was often cluttered with candidates for obscure offices whom the voters could not know. Many voters, when confronted by a long ballot full of little-known candidates, did not vote for them, voted randomly, or voted for an entire party ticket, a practice that gave independent candidates little chance to defeat incumbents or party regulars nominated by political **bosses**. *See also* AT-LARGE ELECTIONS; AUSTRALIAN BALLOT; STRUCTURAL REFORM.

SIERRA CLUB. Cofounded by **John Muir** in 1892, this organization initially sought to persuade people to preserve California's wilderness. It failed in the famous campaign to preserve **Hetch Hetchy Valley**. But the club succeeded in defeating a ranchers' campaign to limit the size of Yosemite National Park in 1890, and when Muir accompanied President **Theodore Roosevelt** on a trip to Yosemite in 1903, he increased the park's public visibility. The club was so central in the creation of many other national parks, including Sierra National Forest Reserve (1893), Mount Rainer National Park (1899), Crater National Park (1902), and Acadia National Park (1919), that Muir was called the father of the national park system. Another founding member, Stephen Tyng Mather, became the first head of the **National Park Service** in 1916. His efforts to promote public access to and use of the parks while maintaining their wild character exemplify contradictions in the club's strategy. Yet in contrast to the managed development approach of **conservation** advocates such as **Gifford Pinchot**, the Sierra Club persistently argued for limiting use of protected wilderness to recreation. This stance helped to prevent commercial exploitation of some fragile and beautiful places, but it also criminalized existing subsistence practices and often forced **Native American** and white locals out of protected areas. This pioneering club became one of the major environmentalist organizations in the United States.

"SIGNIFICANCE OF THE FRONTIER IN AMERICAN HISTORY." Frederick Jackson Turner, a young historian at the University of Wisconsin, argued, in a renowned essay first presented at the Columbian **Exposition** in Chicago in 1893, that the frontier had played a critical role in shaping American character and institutions. The frontier's closing, reported by the 1890 census, deprived Americans of the difficult conditions that supposedly made Americans self-reliant and resourceful, along with the ready opportunities that

had enabled the republic until now to avoid the negative social consequences of industrialization. Observers such as **Theodore Roosevelt**,
Owen Wister, and **Frederic Remington** feared that without a frontier to conquer, white men would lose their virility. The final defeat
of **Native Americans** in the 1880s, the allotment of the former **Indian Territory**, and the admission of nine additional states between
1889 and 1912 completed the map of the continental United States
and seemed to prove that the frontier no longer existed and that the
country had entered a new, uncertain phase. The idea of a closed or
vanishing frontier overlooked the fact that few Americans yet lived
in the trans-Mississippi West; indeed, the period 1890–1920 became
a great but overlooked age of homesteading. Would-be pioneers also
crossed into Canada to settle its great plains. But contemporaries saw
much truth in the idea and sought new frontiers in Latin America,
the Caribbean, and the Pacific. Turner, however, a mild-mannered,
progressive-minded scholar and teacher, was ambivalent about
the use of his ideas to justify **imperialism**. The Turner thesis had a
profound influence on U.S. historiography, and despite some recent
revisionism, continues to inform historians today. *See also* NEW
HISTORY; RACE SUICIDE; STRENUOUS LIFE.

SIMKHOVITCH, MARY MELINDA KINGSBURY (1867–1951).
Social worker. Born into a wealthy Boston family, Mary Kingsbury
graduated from Boston University (1890) and then studied at Radcliffe College, Columbia University, and the University of Berlin,
where she became interested in **socialism** and Marxism. Taking a
job as head resident of New York's College **Settlement House**, she
married Vladimir Simkhovitch, a Russian scholar at Columbia University, with whom she had two children. In 1902, with the support
of **Jacob Riis**, among others, she founded and directed a new settlement, Greenwich House, in New York's most congested neighborhood; she stayed there for 44 years. Greenwich House offered social
services, a kindergarten, and handicraft and music classes. **John
Sloan** taught **art** classes for a time. The settlement house members
formed the city's first neighborhood association, the **Greenwich
Village** Improvement Society, and by 1916 had the area **zoned** as
a residential district. A leading figure in the New York branch of
the **National Consumers' League** and the **Women's Trade Union**

League, Simkhovitch advocated old-age pensions and public housing, policies she saw enacted during the 1930s. *See also* SOCIAL INSURANCE.

SINCLAIR, UPTON B. (1878–1968). Novelist. Born in Baltimore, Sinclair studied at the City College of New York and Columbia University before becoming a **journalist.** Friendships with leading **socialists** such as **George Herron** and **John Spargo** led to his serializing the **muckraking** novel, *The Jungle,* in the **Socialist Party** newspaper, *Appeal to Reason.* Published in book form in 1906, this exposé of Chicago meatpacking plants contributed to the passage of the **Meat Inspection Act,** although Sinclair expressed disappointment that the public focused on poor sanitation in the packinghouses while neglecting his account of deplorable working conditions. Like *The Jungle,* Sinclair's later novels *Metropolis* (1908), *Oil* (1927), and *Boston* (1928) illustrated his socialist convictions. In 1906–7, he established Helicon Hall Colony, a commune in Englewood, New Jersey. Sinclair played a major role in socialist and **Democratic** politics in California during the 1920s and 1930s, running for governor as a Democrat in 1934.

SINGLE TAX. This panacea for poverty was famously expounded in the popular book *Progress and Poverty* (1879) by reform writer Henry George (1839–97). He argued that society owned all land and created its value; therefore, society should tax the unearned value of the land, but not the improvements made on the land. Advocates believed that eliminating all other levies except those on land would end the paradox of poverty and economic depressions amid economic growth by providing incentives for the productive use of land while penalizing unproductive speculation. While utopian and never put into full practice, this concept affected tax policies and inspired reformers in the United States and other nations. Because land values were highest in cities, where property speculation seemed to drive up rents and confine poorer residents to slums, municipal reformers such as **Hazen S. Pingree, Tom Johnson, Frederic Howe,** and George's son, Henry George Jr., lauded the single tax for its potential effect on housing conditions. Versions of this idea continued to appear throughout the 20th century.

SIXTEENTH AMENDMENT. *See* INCOME TAX.

SLATER FUND. *See* GENERAL EDUCATION BOARD; HIGH SCHOOL; INDUSTRIAL EDUCATION; SOUTHERN EDUCATION BOARD.

SLOAN, JOHN (1871–1951). Artist. Born in Pennsylvania, Sloan studied at the Pennsylvania Academy of Fine Arts and worked as an artist for the *Philadelphia Inquirer* and the *Philadelphia Press* between 1892 and 1902. Sloan's early illustrations also appeared in **mass-circulation magazines** such as *Harper's, Scribner's, Saturday Evening Post*, and *Collier's*. By 1904, he had settled in a **Greenwich Village** studio and produced etchings and paintings of New York City life that gained wide attention in 1908 when he figured prominently in **The Eight** exhibition that launched the **Ash Can School**. A **socialist**, he was **art** editor and cartoonist for *The Masses* from 1912 until 1916, when after a falling-out with editor **Max Eastman**, Sloan moved away from political art. Seven of his works appeared in the famous **Armory Show** in 1913. He also painted watercolors and oils and taught at the Art Students League from 1914 to 1930. Sloan's best-known paintings include *The Coffee Line, McSorley's Back Room*, and *Backyards, Greenwich Village*. *See also* HENRI, ROBERT.

SMALL, ALBION W. (1854–1926). Sociologist. Born in Maine, he studied at the Andover Newton School of Theology in the late 1870s before shifting, like numerous scholars of the era, into secular studies. After studying in Leipzig and Berlin in 1880–81, he taught at Colby College and earned a Ph.D. in history from Johns Hopkins University (1889). In 1892, Small founded the Department of Sociology at the **University of Chicago** and chaired it for 30 years. He founded the *American Journal of Sociology* (1895) and served as dean of the graduate school of arts and sciences (1905–25). A major force in the establishment of this new discipline, Small wrote *General Sociology* (1905), *Adam Smith and Modern Sociology* (1907), *The Meaning of the Social Sciences* (1910), and *Between Eras: From Capitalism to Democracy* (1913). *See also* EDUCATION; PARK, ROBERT E.; UNIVERSITY.

SMITH, ALFRED E. (1873–1944). Politician. Born in New York City, Al Smith left school early to work at the Fulton Fish market to support his widowed mother. As a member of **Tammany Hall** and a protégé of **Charles F. Murphy**, Smith rose to prominence during six terms in the New York State Assembly, where he served as **Democratic** majority leader and speaker. Influenced by his work on the **New York State Factory Investigating Commission**, where he became associated with **progressives** such as **Belle Moskowitz**, Smith emerged as a prominent exponent of **urban liberalism** even before his unprecedented four terms as state governor (1919–20 and 1923–28). Identified with nuts-and-bolts labor and social reforms such as **workers' compensation**, Smith appealed to urban voters as someone who emerged from poverty to champion their issues. Known as the "Happy Warrior," a colorful figure with a derby hat, a cigar, and a distinctive New York accent, Smith in 1928 became the first Catholic to be nominated for president, but his opposition to **prohibition**, his religion, and his big-city political background made him unacceptable to southerners and rural voters; Smith lost to Herbert Hoover in a landslide. Nevertheless, he was a pivotal figure in the transition from early 20th-century progressivism to the liberalism of the New Deal era. *See also* WAGNER, ROBERT F.

SMITH, HOKE (1855–1931). Politician. Born in North Carolina, Smith was educated by his father, an Atlanta educator and former professor at the University of North Carolina. Admitted to the bar in 1873 at age 17, Smith became owner and editor of the *Atlanta Evening Journal* in 1887. He used the paper to express white supremacist views but also advocated reforms for farmers and other **progressive** causes. A **Democrat** like virtually all white southerners, Smith served in Grover Cleveland's second presidential administration as secretary of the interior (1893–96), after which he returned to law and **journalism** in Atlanta. Elected governor in 1906, he supported penal reform, railroad regulation, **prohibition**, and aid to education but also endorsed the 1907 **disfranchisement** of black voters. Losing his 1908 reelection campaign to a candidate backed by **Tom Watson**, an erstwhile ally, Smith returned as governor in 1911 only to resign to take a seat in the U.S. Senate (1911–21). In Congress, he sponsored the **Smith–Lever** and **Smith–Hughes Acts** along with other progressive causes. Defeated for reelection in 1920 by Watson, he returned to practicing law in Atlanta and Washington, D.C.

SMITH–HUGHES ACT (1917). Also known as the Vocational **Education** Act, this first legislation to provide federal aid to **industrial education** was written by Senator **Hoke Smith** of Georgia, chairman of the Commission on National Aid to Vocational Education, and Representative Dudley Hughes, former president of the Georgia State Agricultural Society. The law established a Federal Board of Vocational Education and mandated state boards to train secondary teachers and students in agriculture, industry, trades, and **home economics**. The law helped to increase the number of vocational students from 200,000 to 3.4 million by 1950. *See also* HIGH SCHOOL.

SMITH–LEVER ACT (1914). Sponsored by Georgia senator **Hoke Smith** and South Carolina representative Asbury F. Lever, this federal law vastly expanded cooperative extension services for agriculture, **home economics**, and related fields. Building on several earlier laws, including the 1887 Hatch Act and the 1906 Adams Act, this bill authorized the U.S. Department of Agriculture to work with the state and county governments and land-grant **universities** to support agricultural research and make the results available to the public. In practice, extension agents visited county or state fairs, towns, and farm households to provide pragmatic advice, soil testing, pest control, and other services. In time, Smith–Lever-funded services included community development and the **4-H clubs** or youth and family programs. *See also* COOPERATIVES, FARMERS'.

SOCIAL DARWINISM. Inaccurately named for evolutionary theorist Charles Darwin, this philosophy derived in part from the work of British philosopher Herbert Spencer (1820–1903), who proposed that societies evolved by the same "survival of the fittest" process as did animals and plants in the natural world. American followers of Spencer such as William Graham Sumner and **John W. Burgess** believed that government regulation of the **economy**, philanthropy, and social welfare programs encouraged the reproduction of the unfit and weakened the nation. Together with the related doctrine of "laissez-faire" ("allow to do" in French) economics, social Darwinism justified the wealth and power of corporations and their leaders as the natural outcome of free competition. Social Darwinism also gave a scientific sheen to common ideas about social evolution that sustained white supremacy and **imperialist** expansion. The notion of the "survival of the fittest" implied that the genocide of **Native Americans** and other aboriginal peoples by whites was inevitable and **progressive**. Similarly, the **disfranchisement** and **segregation** of **African Americans** was justified by their supposed evolutionary incapacity to participate in democracy. In Britain Francis Galton formalized these views into **eugenics** in the 1860s, and the Austrian Ernst Haeckel and Americans Madison Grant, **Charles Davenport**, and others popularized them in campaigns for **immigration** restriction and the imprisonment and **sterilization** of "unfit" people.

These views were contested from the start; indeed, proponents of active government used the term *social Darwinist* as an insult. Many scientists argued that Spencer distorted Darwin's main point, that natural selection applied to *species*, not individuals, and that cooperation was as plausible a species survival strategy as competition. Sociologists such as **Lester Frank Ward** elevated this argument into a theory of humanitarian reform by casting humans as a cooperative species whose progress depended on recognition of human interdependence. Ward's quasi-Darwinian concept became an **intellectual** pillar of progressive reform, which proponents saw as advancing civilization's evolution through cooperative action. **Socialists, Social Gospel** advocates, and other sorts of progressives, including many Catholic, **Jewish**, and other immigrant politicians, argued with considerable success that individuals and the government had a moral obligation to assist and protect the poor and redress injustice. Although campaigns against racism and imperialism gained little traction during this era, organizations combating them, such as the **Society of American Indians** and the **National Association for the Advancement of Colored People**, were active, and anthropologists such as **Franz Boas** formulated alternatives to racial understandings of human differences.

SOCIAL GOSPEL. This humanitarian movement in American Protestantism called for the clergy and lay Christians to apply biblical teachings and the example of Jesus to solving urban industrial problems. Social Gospel advocates drew on influences ranging from European and American ideas of Christian **socialism** to **modernist** theology, with its emphasis on the practical application of Christianity. Other influences included transcendentalism, the utopian writings of Edward Bellamy, and even Henry George's **single tax**. Theologically conservative revivalists such as Dwight Moody and **Billy Sunday** also expressed elements of Social Gospel thought. During the depression of the 1890s, William T. Stead's tract *If Christ Came to Chicago* (1894) and Charles M. Sheldon's novel *In His Steps* (1896) influenced many Americans to express solidarity with workers and emulate Jesus as a witness for social justice. Theology professor **Walter Rauschenbusch** became an acknowledged movement leader with works such as *Christianity and the Social Crisis* (1907). Other leaders included W. D. P. Bliss, founder of the Society of Christian Socialists, and Columbus, Ohio, minister **Washington Gladden**. Social Gospel activists established the Federal Council of the Churches of Christ in America in 1908 to oppose **child labor**, improve wages and working conditions, and foster social justice. Although Catholics were not usually associated with this movement, Pope Leo XIII's 1891 encyclical *Rerum Novarum* encouraged the social activism evident in Father **John A. Ryan**'s writing. *See also* ELY, RICHARD T.; HERRON, GEORGE DAVIS.

SOCIAL INSURANCE. Since the colonial era, Americans organized private burial societies and self-help fraternal associations, to which members contributed funds for funeral and emergency expenses, a voluntarist tradition that flourished among ethnic groups in American industrial cities. In 1891, Connecticut alone boasted an estimated 386 mutual aid societies with 127,000 members. Meanwhile, the Progressive Era saw a vigorous campaign for "social insurance," a term that implied compulsory, government-run programs for health and **unemployment insurance** and old-age pensions. In writings such as *Social Insurance* (1911), **Isaac M. Rubinow** drew upon German programs launched in the 1880s, along with Great Britain's National Insurance Act of 1911, in making a case for American schemes. The agitation of Rubinow, **John R. Commons**, and their colleagues in the **American Association for Labor Legislation** influenced **Theodore Roosevelt** to include social insurance in the **Progressive Party**

program in 1912. **Socialists** such as **Eugene V. Debs** and **Meyer London** were natural advocates of such ideas. Despite much debate and numerous state-level proposals, social insurance made little headway before World War I, although many **progressives** lived to see the unemployment and old-age insurance principles enshrined in the 1935 Social Security Act. From the start, compulsory health insurance met resistance from segments of the medical profession and from large **insurance** companies, who were at the time developing a profitable business in employer-run health plans. Insurance industry lobbyists worked hard to stymie debate, thereby ensuring that universal health insurance ended up the most important Progressive Era reform proposal never to have a wide trial in the United States. *See also* AMERICAN MEDICAL ASSOCIATION.

SOCIALISM. Socialism is a term signifying an enormous variety of proposals for the communal or public ownership or management of the means of production. In the pre–World War I decades, the term could encompass everything from the municipal ownership of **utilities** to anarcho-syndicalism. Usually it implied an array of more-or-less radical movements for the replacement of capitalism with some form of democratic collectivism. The dramatically uneven distribution of wealth created by rapid economic expansion, along with a legal and political system highly favorable to private property and enterprise, brought socialism to the apex of its popularity in the United States. By 1886, a Socialist Labor Party (SLP) led the campaign for the **eight-hour day** and, despite being blamed for the Haymarket Riot of that year, continued to grow under the leadership of Daniel DeLeon. The socialist candidate Simon Wing won 21,000 votes when he ran for president in 1892; the SLP increased that to 82,000 votes in 1898. DeLeon's increasingly rigid Marxism and contentious meddling in the **labor union** movement prompted moderates, led by **Eugene V. Debs** and **Victor Berger** to form the rival **Socialist Party of America**, which seemed repeatedly on the verge of attaining national party status until internal divisions and the antiradical purges of the World War I era stymied the movement. Afterward, bitter quarrels over the Bolshevik Revolution and the rival Communist and **anarchist** movements hampered efforts to rebuild American socialism's mass following.

SOCIALIST PARTY OF AMERICA (SPA). In 1901, moderate dissidents from the **immigrant**-backed Socialist Labor Party combined with **Eugene V. Debs**'s Social Democratic Party, whose following was strong among native-born radicals in the Midwest and the Great Plains, to form the Socialist Party of America, the most successful social democratic movement in U.S. history. Although personally more leftist than most leading associates, Debs became the movement's charismatic public face, winning admirers among **progressives** of the mainstream parties and among self-proclaimed **socialists**. Having gained 97,000 votes as the Social Democratic presidential candidate in 1900, Debs pushed his cause in four national campaigns under the SPA banner (1904, 1908, 1912, and 1920). His electoral influence reached its height with 900,672 votes or 6 percent of the popular vote in 1912. He gained 913,935 votes in his last campaign in 1920 while he was imprisoned in the Atlanta Federal Penitentiary for antiwar activities, but the advent of **women**'s **suffrage** and increased population meant this figure accounted for only 3.4 percent of the total vote.

Debs was a national spokesperson for a movement whose strength lay mainly at the local level. SPA candidates won mayoral elections in dozens of municipalities, most famously Milwaukee, where Socialist Daniel Hoan served as mayor from 1916 to 1940. Socialists sat on many city councils and in state legislatures, especially in areas with substantial numbers of **intellectual**, German, Finnish, and **Jewish** voters. Two Socialists held seats in Congress: **Victor Berger** of Milwaukee (1911–13, 1923–29) and **Meyer London** of New York City (1915–19, 1921–23). Socialists also exerted influence in Great Plains states with a populist tradition, especially Oklahoma, where SPA support reached 21 percent in the 1914 governor's race. Published in Girard, Kansas, the Socialist newspaper *Appeal to Reason* had a national readership, with a circulation of 760,000 at its height. This weekly paper attracted prominent contributors, including **Jack London**, **Upton Sinclair**, and **Mary "Mother" Jones**, as well as Debs.

Historians debate the causes for the SPA's faltering electoral support and membership, which reached a high point of 120,000 in 1912, before falling to 80,000 with the expulsion from the party of **"Big Bill" Haywood** and the **Industrial Workers of the World**, and recovering only to 109,000 amid the labor strife of 1919. The outbreak of World War I in 1914 and the Russian Revolution in 1917, with accompanying antiradical purges in the United States, splintered the party, though in other countries social democratic movements rebounded from even worse circumstances during and after the war. Most historians attribute the SPA's decline to a combination of factors, including ethnic and regional splits among American workers, the antisocialist politics of **Samuel Gompers** and the **American Federation of Labor**, and ideological and personality conflicts within the party.

SOCIETY OF AMERICAN INDIANS (SAI). Founded in 1911, this society brought together middle-class **Native Americans** to promote the **education** of Native people, lobby Congress, and combat racism. Prominent members included **Gertrude Bonnin** (Yankton Sioux), who served as secretary between 1911 and 1916; **Charles Eastman** (Santee Sioux); Arthur C. Parker (Seneca), editor of the society's journal between 1915 and 1920; and **Carlos Montezuma** (Yavapai-Apache). At its height in 1913, the society had some 200 active (Native) and about 400 associate (non-Native) members. For several years, the society published the *American Indian Magazine*. It also ran a **settlement house** that provided a model for later urban Indian centers. Unable to raise money from non-Indians and distant from the daily struggle on many reservations, the SAI also suffered internal divisions, particularly over the Bureau of Indian Affairs and whether Indians should accept employment with it. In 1924, the society dissolved even as it achieved a major aim, a bill passed by Congress declaring Native Americans to be U.S. citizens.

SOCIOLOGICAL JURISPRUDENCE. This legal philosophy stresses law as a product of evolving social circumstances and as an instrument of social reform. It originated in the attempts by **Oliver Wendell Holmes Jr.** and others to replace formalistic, abstract interpretations of law with analyses rooted in time and place. The approach gained currency with cases such as *Muller v. Oregon* (1908), where the legal team led by **Louis Brandeis** presented social science data as well as legal arguments in favor of a law limiting the hours of working women. Roscoe Pound, professor and dean of the Harvard

Law School (1910–36), developed comprehensive arguments for this approach. Pound pondered why people obey the law even though norms, customs, and morality change over time and differ between societies. He argued for reforming the law by focusing on its aim, which he believed was to benefit society.

SOUTHERN EDUCATION BOARD (SEB). Founded in 1901, the Southern Education Board coordinated campaigns to improve public **education** in southern states. The SEB also participated in national campaigns against **child labor** and in favor of **compulsory education laws**. The poverty and rural nature of most southern states meant dilapidated, inadequate buildings, short school days and terms, and transient, low-paid, poorly educated teachers. Illiteracy rates were higher in this region than anywhere else in the United States. The SEB helped local reformers, many of them middle-class white **women**, to galvanize public opinion behind property tax increases and special education tax districts for the public schools—but only those serving white children. By 1910, some philanthropies, such as the Jeanes Fund, the Slater Fund, and the Rosenwald Fund, turned to improving schools for **African American** children. The SEB's counterpart, the **General Education Board**, emphasized long-term policy rather than immediate change. *See also* HIGH SCHOOL; INDUSTRIAL EDUCATION; SEGREGATION.

SOUTHERN PACIFIC RAILROAD. Formed from the fusion of railroads converging on California, including the famous Central Pacific, the Southern Pacific (SP) controlled 85 percent of California's rail traffic by 1877. The company's overwhelming power in the West Coast transportation network, along with its immense property holdings and well-documented manipulation of state and federal politics, made it the main target of **antitrust** sentiment in California and a controversial presence throughout the Southwest from Los Angeles to New Orleans, which the railroad reached in 1883. **Frank Norris**'s *The Octopus* (1901), a fictionalized account of the 1880 Mussel Slough shootout between farmers and law enforcement over SP claims to their farmland, summed up the Progressive Era view of the company as a greedy, murderous monster. **Hiram Johnson** became governor by promising to rein in the SP. The SP's acquisition in

1901 by **Edward H. Harriman**, owner of the Union Pacific and Illinois Central, prompted a federal antitrust suit in 1908. Even after its separation from the Union Pacific in 1913, the SP continued to fight federal antitrust pressure into the 1920s. In 1911, the SP purchased the Pacific Electric Railway, the Los Angeles region's extensive **electric trolley** line.

SOUTHERN SOCIOLOGICAL CONGRESS (SSC). Founded in Nashville, Tennessee, in 1912, the SSC created a regional counterpart to the **National Conference of Charities and Correction**. The congress's aims included abolishing **convict leasing**, improving **juvenile courts**, ending **child labor**, adopting **compulsory education laws**, improving the institutional treatment of the feebleminded and insane, regulating alcohol, reforming marriage and **divorce** laws, improving **public health**, addressing the role of churches in social service provision, and ameliorating racial tensions. The final issue received a great deal of discussion, and while **African Americans** did not play leading roles in the SSC, they did participate in its discussions, sometimes in integrated settings. In 1916, the congress adopted a resolution condemning **lynching**, but like other southern white liberal organizations, the SSC promoted racial justice only to the extent that it did not challenge **segregation** and **disfranchisement**. It ceased meeting after 1919.

SOUTHERN STATES WOMAN SUFFRAGE CONFERENCE (SSWSC). Louisiana suffrage leader **Kate Gordon** founded the SSWSC in 1913 to oppose the decision by the **National American Woman Suffrage Association (NAWSA)** to focus on winning **women** the right to vote through an amendment to the Constitution. White southern women's **suffrage** advocates feared that amending the national constitution to give women the vote would empower the federal government to establish qualifications for voting. The right of each state to determine who could vote was a cornerstone of the **disfranchisement** of **African Americans**. Despite the SSWSC's arguments that enfranchising white women would strengthen white supremacy, southern legislators continued to oppose women's suffrage, and most white southern activists remained members of NAWSA. The SSWSC ceased to function in 1917.

SPANISH–AMERICAN WAR. When Spain brutally suppressed a rebellion in **Cuba** beginning in 1895, the **yellow journalism** of **William Randolph Hearst** and **Joseph Pulitzer** sensationalized the news. Due to rising nationalism and growing American power, many Americans resented the remnants of European colonialism just 90 miles off U.S. shores. Urged by Congress, President **William McKinley** pressured Spain to end the brutal treatment of Cuban civilians and reach an autonomy arrangement with the rebels. Fanning the flames in early February 1898, Hearst's *New York Journal* published a stolen letter acquired by Cuban rebels in which the Spanish minister in Washington, Enrique Depuy de Lôme, expressed contempt for McKinley and hinted that Spanish negotiations were insincere. Just a few days later on 15 February, the battleship USS *Maine*, harbored in Havana to protect Americans and their property in Cuba, inexplicably exploded and sank, killing 266 sailors. Spain denied responsibility, but a U.S. Navy court of inquiry concluded—perhaps incorrectly—that a submarine mine was the cause. *New York Journal* headlines made "Remember the *Maine*" into a popular slogan. Still, President McKinley's war message on 11 April did not mention the *Maine*. The war itself resulted from Spain's inability, due to its own domestic political problems, to respond decisively to American pressure, along with American unwillingness to allow the Cuban rebels to win on their own terms. Congress accepted McKinley's war message with a 19 April resolution that demanded Spain's departure from Cuba, authorized the president to use armed force, and in the **Teller Amendment**, denied any intent to annex the island, in effect promising the Cubans independence. Spain declared war on the United States on 23 April, and Congress returned the favor on 25 April.

With only 28,000 men in uniform, the U.S. Army was unprepared, but 200,000 volunteers, like **Theodore Roosevelt's Rough Riders**, quickly swelled the ranks. General W. S. Shafter landed 18,000 soldiers in Cuba in June, and in July the Americans won battles at Siboney, San Juan Hill, and El Caney. Spanish military leaders surrendered on 16 July. However, Cuba was not the only front in the war. In better condition than the army, the U.S. Navy also benefited from advance notice from Assistant Secretary of the Navy Roosevelt, who just before resigning to form the Rough Riders, wired Commodore **George Dewey** to leave Hong Kong as soon as war was declared to attack the Spanish navy in the **Philippines**. On 1 May, Dewey destroyed the Spanish fleet at Manila Bay, and the city surrendered in August. In the Atlantic, Admiral William T. Sampson's fleet destroyed the Spanish navy as it left Santiago, Cuba, on 3 July. General Nelson A. Miles invaded **Puerto Rico** on 25 July, meeting little resistance.

Its last three colonies lost, Spain asked for an armistice on 12 August, and the belligerents signed the **Treaty of Paris** on 10 December 1898; it was ratified by the Senate on 6 February 1899. The United States took over Puerto Rico and Guam and bought the Philippine Islands for $20 million. In ten weeks of one-sided, dramatic, and destructive warfare, over 5,000 Americans died, most from disease. Puerto Ricans lost the autonomy they had recently won from Spain; Cubans found their long struggle for independence hijacked. Filipino nationalists redirected their fight, now against the Americans in the **Philippine–American War** (1899–1902). The Spanish–American War marked the advent of the United States as a great power, owner of overseas colonies, with an increased role in Pacific and Asian affairs. Domestically, the war sparked a raging debate over **imperialism**, and members of the **Anti-Imperialist League** issued stinging critiques of the U.S. suppression of anticolonial struggles. *See also* FOREIGN POLICY; *INSULAR CASES*; PLATT AMENDMENT.

SPARGO, JOHN (1876–1966). Reformer and writer. Born in England, Spargo became a stonecutter, a lay Methodist minister, and a **socialist**. In 1900, he immigrated to New York City, where he became a leader of the **Socialist Party of America**, only to leave when the party opposed American involvement in World War I in 1917. With **Samuel Gompers**, he organized the American Alliance for Labor and Democracy. Founder of a **settlement house** in Yonkers, New York, Spargo was best known as a **muckraking** author. Among his books are *The Bitter Cry of the Children* (1906), which called for an end to **child labor** in mines and quarries, *The Spiritual Significance of Modern Socialism* (1908), *Karl Marx: His Life and Work* (1910), *Applied Socialism* (1912), and *The Jew and American Ideals* (1921). *See also* SINCLAIR, UPTON B.

SPINDLETOP OIL FIELD (1901). Industry giant **Standard Oil** dismissed geologists' claims about potential oil deposits on this hill

outside Beaumont, Texas, leaving the field to independent operators such as Patillo Higgins (1863–1955). The reward for Higgins's
persistence came in January 1901 in the form of a towering jet of
oil spewing 200 feet into the air and spilling nearly a million gal-
lons before it could be capped. The Spindletop field was the first of
many oil discoveries in Texas, Louisiana, Oklahoma, Kansas, and
California. Much of this newfound oil wealth came under the control
not of the **Rockefellers** and other New York–based capitalists but of
exploration and refining companies based in Houston, Dallas, Tulsa,
and other southwestern cities. Spindletop thus marked the emergence
of a dynamic urban economy in the hitherto underdeveloped Southwest. The new fields also encouraged new uses for petroleum, such
as home heating fuel and gasoline for **automobiles**. *See also* HOUS-
TON SHIP CHANNEL.

**SPINGARN, JOEL ELIAS (1875–1939), AND ARTHUR BAR-
NETT (1878–1971).** Civil rights activists. Born into a well-to-do
Jewish family in New York City, the Spingarn brothers are best
known for their lifelong commitment to **African American** civil
rights. A poet, critic, and **literature** professor at Columbia University (1899–1911) and a founder of the Harcourt, Brace publishing
company, Joel joined the board of the **National Association for the
Advancement of Colored People (NAACP)** in 1913. Amid rising
tensions between founding members Oswald Garrison Villard and
W. E. B. Du Bois, he took the chairmanship in 1914 and later that
year established the Spingarn medal, awarded annually to a black
American for outstanding achievement. His brother Arthur, an attorney and member of the New York Vigilance Committee (an
anti-**prostitution** organization) between 1911 and 1915, served as
the NAACP's legal counsel for many years and as its president after World War II. His monumental collection of works by African
American authors now resides at the Moorland-Spingarn Research
Foundation at Howard University in Washington, D.C.

SPRINGFIELD RIOT (1908). Sparked when a white woman falsely
accused an **African American** man of trying to rape her, this **race
riot** ran for two days, 14–15 August, causing seven deaths and
$200,000 in property damage. Thousands of black residents fled the

city as the mob burned 24 black-owned businesses and 40 houses. The violence ended only with the arrival of the Illinois National Guard. The extension of mob violence outside of the South—and to the hometown of emancipator Abraham Lincoln, no less—shocked many white liberals. **William English Walling**, who witnessed and reported on the riot, and **Mary White Ovington**, among others, issued a call for white and black reformers to meet to discuss preventing further violence and promoting racial equality. Among those invited were publisher Oswald Garrison Villard, **Lillian Wald**, **Florence Kelley**, and the members of the short-lived **Niagara Movement**, including **W. E. B. Du Bois**. This interracial group laid the groundwork for the **National Association for the Advancement of Colored People**. *See also* GREAT MIGRATION.

SQUARE DEAL. President **Theodore Roosevelt**'s platform for reelection in 1904, the Square Deal promised fairness for both labor and capital. He adopted this familiar poker term as a slogan during his first term while dealing with issues such as the 1902 **Anthracite Coal Strike**. Roosevelt's insistence that government should be impartial with regard to industry and labor seemed like progress to a **labor union** movement accustomed to public officials and the courts intervening against unions in disputes. In his 1904 campaign, Roosevelt discussed **income** and inheritance taxes, business regulation, tariff revision, and aid to farmers and workers but offered few specifics. The Square Deal permitted him to retain support in the conservative and **progressive** wings of the **Republican Party** and among voters in general. For his unsuccessful 1912 campaign, Roosevelt replaced the Square Deal with the more sweeping notion of a **New Nationalism**. *See also* ANTITRUST.

STANDARD OIL (SO). Incorporated in Ohio in 1870, this company replaced an earlier partnership among **John D. Rockefeller**, **Henry M. Flagler**, and others. By the end of the decade, Standard Oil controlled more than 90 percent of the nation's oil refining capacity, as well as a vast system of pipelines and storage tanks. The company's success made its form and management difficult issues, as the Ohio-based company could not legally hold stock in or partner with other firms. In 1882, the company's top management created the Standard

Oil Trust Agreement, transferring its stock, properties, and interests to a board of trustees. This controversial maneuver helped establish the word *trust* as a euphemism for an overwhelmingly powerful business enterprise. The Ohio supreme court dissolved this arrangement in 1892, and the company spent several years seeking an adequate and legal organization through **interlocking directorates**, finally establishing a **holding company** based in New Jersey in 1899. By that time, SO was a formidable multinational enterprise, doing more than half its business abroad.

The company's organization and its dominance did not go unchallenged. The opening of the **Spindletop oil field** in Texas in 1901 led to a rash of new, independent companies there and in California and the plains states. Oil men in Texas and Kansas used state antimonopoly laws to resist SO's expansion attempts and secure their own position. In *McClure's Magazine* in 1902, **muckraking journalist Ida Tarbell** published a famous exposé of the myriad unethical and illegal tactics that SO had used over decades to absorb or bankrupt rivals. The combination of state legal battles and national publicity encouraged the federal government to step in, first with a **Bureau of Corporations**' report in 1905 and then with an **antitrust** suit begun in 1906. In 1911, after years of appeals, the **U.S. Supreme Court** upheld a ruling in *Standard Oil v. United States* that dissolved the holding company. This decision created competitors such as the Mobil, Esso, and Atlantic Richfield oil corporations. For many Americans, the company and its head, Rockefeller, were among the most loathed icons of corporate capitalism.

***STANDARD OIL V. UNITED STATES* (1911).** Standard Oil's control of most oil refining and sales in the United States and overseas, along with numerous press and government accounts of the company's dubious tactics, prompted **Theodore Roosevelt**'s administration to begin an **antitrust** suit against the company in 1906. The suit argued, among other things, that the **holding company**, Standard Oil Company of New Jersey, had secret agreements with the railroads that gave it favorable rates and treatment of its tank cars. On 15 May 1911, the **U.S. Supreme Court** ordered the breakup of Standard Oil of New Jersey into 34 independent companies. The landmark decision articulated the **rule of reason**, according to which size and market dominance alone did not qualify a business as an unlawful trust; the enterprise had to be engaged in improper behavior or have a clear anticompetitive effect. *See also* ELKINS ACT.

STARR, ELLEN GATES (1859–1940). Social reformer. Born in Illinois to middle-class parents, Starr visited Europe with her college classmate **Jane Addams** in 1888, where they were inspired by the **settlement houses** of British reformers. In 1889, they cofounded **Hull House** in Chicago. Like many settlement workers, Starr was radicalized by her experiences. She helped feed and house strikers as well as picketing with them and writing articles on their behalf. Her support of a 1915 strike by the Amalgamated Clothing Workers of America earned her an honorary life membership in that **labor union**. A founding member in 1904 of the Chicago branch of the **Women's Trade Union League**, she joined the **Socialist Party** in 1911 and ran unsuccessfully for alderman on the party's ticket in 1916. Her labor activism, differences over the management of Hull House, and her search for a satisfying form of Christianity gradually alienated her from Addams. Starr converted to Catholicism in 1920 and, after an operation left her paralyzed in 1929, left Hull House to live in a convent.

STEFFENS, JOSEPH LINCOLN (1866–1936). Journalist. From a prosperous San Francisco family, Lincoln Steffens graduated from the University of California in 1889 and then spent three years traveling in Europe before working as a reporter for the *New York Evening Post* (1892–97), during which time he befriended the police commissioner, **Theodore Roosevelt**, along with **Jacob Riis**. Editor of the *New York Commercial Advertiser* for several years, by 1902 he worked for **Samuel McClure** as an editor of *McClure's Magazine*, where he encouraged the **muckraking journalism** of **Ida M. Tarbell**, **Ray Stannard Baker**, and others. He also published a vivid series of articles on **machine politics** that became the popular book *The Shame of the Cities* (1904). *The Struggle for Self-Government* (1906) turned the same critical eye on corruption and reform in state government. With Tarbell, Baker, **Finley Peter Dunne**, and **William Allen White**, in 1906, he bought the *American Magazine*, which became a leading reform journal. Disappointed by the failure of projects such as the "Boston-1915" movement to put his ideas for civic improvement into practice, Steffens lost faith in reform and pinned his hopes on charismatic leaders. He visited Venustiano Carranza, leader of the **Mexican Revolution**, in 1917 and met V. I. Lenin in Russia in 1919. Impressed with the Soviet Union, he became notorious for pronouncements such as "I have seen the future and it works." Steffens's *Autobiography* (1932) won notice for its memorable insider account of the muckraking movement. *See also* FAGAN, MARK M.; FOLK, JOSEPH W.

STERILIZATION. The **eugenics** movement advocated the surgical sterilization of persons deemed unfit to reproduce and incapable of self-imposed chastity. Between 1907 and 1917, 16 states legalized compulsory sterilization of habitual criminals or those convicted of sex crimes, epileptics, the insane, and "idiots" living in state institutions. Elsewhere, legislatures or governors rejected such laws as cruel and unusual punishment or a violation of due process. Experts as well as the lay public assumed that vasectomies and tubal ligations would diminish sexual appetite in addition to causing infertility. Police and social workers readily labeled unmarried, sexually active working-class girls and **women** as "feebleminded" to have them institutionalized and sterilized against their will. In the 21 years after the enactment of Indiana's 1907 law, between 8,000 and 10,000 people were sterilized, often against their will or without their knowledge. This number included many men and women guilty of nothing more than public, frequent, or interracial sexual activity. Some men were castrated to treat depression or for sexual offenses, including same-sex sexual acts. In the 1920s, the **Supreme Court** endorsed compulsory sterilization, and 24 more states empowered public officials to forcibly sterilize people living in state institutions. *See also* BIRTH CONTROL; SEXUALITY.

STIEGLITZ, ALFRED (1864–1946). Photographer and art dealer. Born in Hoboken, New Jersey, he moved to New York City with his family in 1871. After studying engineering at the City College of New York, he enrolled at the Polytechnic Institute in Berlin in 1881 and became fascinated with photography. He won honors and acclaim for pictures taken at night, in storms, and under other adverse conditions.

Upon his return to New York in 1890, revolutionary photographs of the city and skyscrapers, as well as aerial photography, built his reputation. Having made the camera a new means of aesthetic expression and photography a fine **art**, Stieglitz encouraged this innovation as editor of the *American Amateur Photographer* (1892–96), *Camera Notes* (1897–1903), and *Camera Work* (1903–17). With Edward Steichen and a group known as the photo-secessionists, he opened the famous Gallery 291 on Fifth Avenue in 1905, and in the years before it closed in 1917 he hosted the first U.S. exhibits by Matisse, Picasso, Toulouse-Lautrec, and other European painters and defended modern art and African sculpture to an outraged public and press. He also exhibited the art of Max Weber, Georgia O'Keefe (his future wife), John Marin, and other American **modernists**.

STOKES, ROSE PASTOR (1879–1933). Journalist and radical. Born into a **Jewish** family in Poland, Stokes grew up in poverty in London and Cleveland, Ohio. She supported her family by rolling cigars from age 11. Largely self-educated, a **socialist** from an early age, she began as a **journalist** in 1900 and by 1903 wrote a popular advice column for the *Jewish Daily News*. Her interview with **settlement house** activist and socialite James Graham Phelps Stokes led to their scandalous cross-class, cross-religion marriage in 1905. No longer required to earn a living, Stokes threw herself into political activism, writing and lecturing on behalf of the **Uprising of the Twenty Thousand** and other strikes, socialism, and **birth control**. An outspoken opponent of U.S. intervention in World War I, she was the first person indicted under the Espionage Act in 1917. **Divorcing** her husband in 1925, in part over growing political differences, Stokes pursued radical politics and journalism until her death.

STOREY, MOORFIELD (1845–1929). Lawyer and reformer. Born in Boston, Storey graduated from Harvard College (1866), studied at Harvard Law School, and was private secretary to Senator Charles Sumner (1867–69). Admitted to the Massachusetts bar in 1869, he became a distinguished lawyer and president of the American Bar Association in 1896. The epitome of a proper Bostonian, he served as president of the **Anti-Imperialist League** (1905–21). He championed civil rights for **African Americans** as president of the **National Association for the Advancement of Colored People** from 1909 to 1915 and served as lead counsel in *Buchanan v. Warley* (1917) in which the **U.S. Supreme Court** overturned a Louisville, Kentucky, **segregation** law.

STORYVILLE. This name refers to New Orleans' official **red-light** district, which existed between 1897 and 1917. Before 1897, New Orleans, like many cities, tolerated a vice district, alternately attempting to collect taxes on brothels and suppressing them as nuisances. In that year, city councilor Sidney Story proposed to reduce further the city's official vice district, which had been shrinking since its establishment in 1857. Unlike earlier laws, Story's included no medical inspection, taxation, or licensing clauses, relying instead on the spatial **segregation** of **prostitution**. The city deliberately located the vice district in a heavily **African American** neighborhood and required all sex workers living outside its boundaries to move inside them. "Respectable" property owners and residents within the district's limits protested, while landlords and merchants outside the district objected to the loss of tenants and customers who happened to be prostitutes. Despite these objections, state courts decided lawsuits in the city's favor in 1900, and the ordinance went into effect that summer.

In 1917, after passing a residential racial segregation ordinance, the city announced that it also planned to segregate the vice district and bar white men from frequenting black brothels. This proposal threatened New Orleans' reputation for giving white men easy access to African American **women**, especially light-skinned women who embodied the city's history of racial mingling. Several African American brothel owners and prostitutes sued the city and, surprisingly, won their case before the Louisiana Supreme Court. Later that year, the U.S. Navy demanded that the city close the vice district in order to retain military camps and contracts. Officially, Storyville closed on 12 November 1917, although the brothels operated quietly throughout the war. The end of Storyville was partly responsible for the spread of **ragtime** and **jazz** music because many unemployed brothel musicians joined the **Great Migration** to Chicago and elsewhere.

STRAIGHT, WILLARD D. (1880–1918). Diplomat. Born in New York, Straight graduated from Cornell University (1901) and served in a variety of diplomatic posts in Beijing, Seoul, Havana, and Manchuria, in addition to covering the Russo–Japanese War for Reuters. After working briefly for **J. P. Morgan** & Company, he became acting chief of Far Eastern Affairs for the Department of State (1908–9), a post in which he encouraged U.S. investors to take advantage of the **Open Door** policy in China and President **William Howard Taft**'s **dollar diplomacy**, activities that heightened tensions between the United States and Japan. With Dorothy Payne Whitney, a wealthy New Yorker whom he married in 1911, he underwrote the *New Republic*. A leader of the **preparedness** movement, Straight served in the U.S. Army in France until he died of influenza on 1 December 1918 while working at the Versailles Peace Conference.

STRAUS, OSCAR S. (1850–1926). Public official. Born in Germany, Straus emigrated with his family to Georgia in 1854. After graduating from Columbia College (1871) and Columbia Law School (1873), he practiced law in Manhattan, but by 1881 he joined his brothers in running a chinaware and glass shop within Macy's, the famous New York **department store** that brothers Isidore and Nathan Straus came to own. Oscar Straus meanwhile served three terms as U.S. minister to the Ottoman Empire (1887–89, 1898–1900, 1909–10). President **Theodore Roosevelt** appointed him to the Permanent Court of Arbitration at The Hague and then as secretary of **commerce and labor** (1906–9), making him the first **Jew** to sit in the cabinet. After running unsuccessfully for New York State governor on the **Progressive Party** ticket in 1912, Straus became chairman of the New York Public Service Commission (1915–19) and advised **Woodrow Wilson** at the Versailles peace conference. Active in Jewish and eventually Zionist affairs, he lobbied to protect Jews from persecution in Eastern Europe.

STRENUOUS LIFE. Theodore Roosevelt coined this phrase in 1899 in a speech exhorting American men to take up their duty to govern the lands wrested from Spain in the **Spanish–American War**. Overlapping with the contemporary idea of muscular Christianity, the strenuous life responded to the fear that elite white men had become too civilized and lost their virility. Military life or, failing that, aggressive sports like hunting or **football** would give young men the strength of mind and body to take on the task of bringing civilization to peoples from supposedly less-advanced races. *See also* RACE SUICIDE; SOCIAL DARWINISM.

STRONG, JOSIAH (1847–1916). Clergyman and reformer. Born in Illinois, Strong graduated from Western Reserve College (1869) and was ordained at Lane Theological Seminary (1871). A successful Congregational pastor, he also was a well-known writer, lecturer, and social reformer. In *Our Country* (1885) and *The New Era* (1893), he delineated social and economic problems of an urbanizing, industrializing country, including dangers he saw as posed by Mormons, Catholics, **socialism**, and **immigration**. In Strong's view, a version of Christian socialism would remedy the country's turmoil, which brought him to the forefront of the **Social Gospel** movement. Serving as an officer in a variety of religiously based reform organizations, he was a founder of the Federal Council of the Churches of Christ. *See also* AMERICANIZATION; ANTI-CATHOLICISM.

STRONG MAYOR SYSTEM. One of the **structural reform** plans supported by groups such as the **National Municipal League**, the strong mayor system was meant to make city government more **efficient** and accountable. Under this plan, the profuse semi-independent boards for police, water, health, schools, parks, and other matters operating in many cities would be abolished or subordinated to the mayor, who would also gain powers held in many cities by the city council to appoint and dismiss department heads. The mayor's term of office would increase from two to four years. In some variants, the mayor became chair of a board that formulated or reviewed the budget. The goal was to end the fragmentation that in theory encouraged **machine politics**, while creating an executive clearly accountable to voters. Public administration experts generally recommended this system for large, diverse cities, in preference to the **commission** and **city manager** plans, considered more appropriate for small or medium cities. Virtually all big cities of the Northeast and Midwest—New York, Chicago, Philadelphia, Baltimore, and Boston among them—came to operate under strong mayor charters. Subsequent experience taught that strong mayor systems could create rather than undermine an enduring power base for an astute **boss**. *See also* AT-LARGE ELECTIONS; HOME RULE; SHORT BALLOT.

STRUCTURAL REFORM. Historian Melvin Holli coined this influential term in his book *Reform in Detroit: Hazen S. Pingree and Urban Politics* (1969) to describe **progressives'** emphasis on restructuring political institutions and governmental agencies, especially at the municipal level. Holli argued that in contrast with his subject, Detroit mayor **Hazen S. Pingree**, progressives with a professional or corporate outlook often mistook governmental restructuring as a substitute for social reform. While borrowing Holli's term, many later historians have disagreed with his sharp distinction between structural and social reforms. They note that numerous progressives saw municipal **efficiency** and professionalism as preconditions for durable social reform. Structural progressives pursued civil service and tax reform, improved budgets, and regulation or municipal ownership of **utilities**. They campaigned for **home rule**; **at-large** and **nonpartisan elections**; **strong mayors**, **city managers**, or **commission** governments; **short ballots**; **recall**; **referenda**; and **initiatives**. *See also* BEARD, CHARLES A.; BUREAU OF MUNICIPAL RESEARCH; CHILDS, RICHARD S.; GOODNOW, FRANK J.; NATIONAL MUNICIPAL LEAGUE.

STUDENT VOLUNTEER MOVEMENT (SVM). Methodist evangelist **John R. Mott** founded this organization in 1888 at an intercollegiate summer meeting of 250 student evangelists from 86 colleges convened by evangelist Dwight Moody. Mott's annual summer SVM conferences recruited thousands of young men and women, most recently college graduates, as missionaries in Latin America, Asia, and Africa. Often connected with the **Young Men's Christian Association**, the missionaries originated mainly in the northeastern and midwestern states and Canada, but volunteers came from every state. The SVM was nondenominational; about 85 percent of the first 6,000 volunteers were Presbyterian, Baptist, Methodist, or Congregational, and 30 percent were unmarried **women**. The SVM at times exhibited a military outlook, using the words *conquest, recruits,* and *council of war* in its publications and portraying the missionary as a general commanding local people ("natives") who served as captains and soldiers. Like Mott, SVM missionaries shared Progressive Era values and were also motivated by an older evangelical tradition and a militant form of American Christianity. Most missionaries returned to the United States after a few years of service, many to careers as clergy. The SVM gradually declined after 1925.

SUBWAY SYSTEMS. In the 1890s, many cities replaced horsecar and cable car systems with a network of **electric trolley** lines that grew from 1,300 to 22,000 miles by 1902, but the tracks and wires needed to run these light-rail systems could disrupt other forms of traffic. A few large cities drew on new technology and the precedent of London's Underground (opened in 1863) to construct subway train systems under public regulation. The first to be constructed was in Boston, with a line running under its famous Common in 1897. Hailed as a success from the first, it carried 27 million passengers a year for the same nickel fare charged by the slower streetcars. Success prompted expansion, and by 1902 **Louis D. Brandeis** led Boston reformers to create a unified metropolitan public transit system under public control. Business and professional men, **labor unions**, **settlement house** workers, and a rare Yankee-Irish political alliance supported this effort. The subway line soon reached East Boston (1904) and the suburbs of Cambridge and Dorchester (1912). At a time when many Americans considered municipal government the nation's greatest failure, Boston built an efficient and modern rapid transit system.

Although New York City began planning a subway in 1872 and the state legislature authorized a subway commission in 1891, no private contractor bid on the project. In another rare display of political consensus, in 1894 **Republican Party** state **boss Thomas C. Platt** and **Tammany Hall**'s **Democratic Party** boss **Richard Croker** persuaded the legislature to create the independent Rapid Transit Commission to build the subway. Obstacles created by rival, privately owned streetcar lines and elevated train lines delayed construction until 1900, but the Interborough Rapid Transit (IRT) subway finally opened in 1904. In 1913, the IRT merged with the Brooklyn Rapid Transit, and by 1920 the city had the largest urban transit system in the world with a capacity of 35 million passengers a day. Philadelphia received fewer **immigrants** than Boston or New York City, but nevertheless its population grew from 850,000 in 1880 to 1,500,000 in 1910, making a subway a feasible venture. By 1907, its subway, the third in the nation, supplemented an extensive streetcar network.

Subways and trolleys helped to transform cities. Real estate near rapid transportation lines rose in value and popularity, and the middle class and the prosperous offspring of immigrants moved to new suburban neighborhoods. As city residents moved outward, shops, theaters, churches, and businesses of all types followed, creating new secondary commercial centers near the subway stations. Increasingly the urban core became a work zone with industries, banks, offices, and **department stores** where only the less affluent continued to live, setting the pattern for 20th-century urban development.

SUFFRAGE. The Progressive Era offers the irony of simultaneous, successful campaigns to extend voting rights and to curtail them. The movement to eliminate gender as a criterion for voting gained momentum from the 1890 founding of the **National American Woman Suffrage Association** and triumphed with the ratification of the **Nineteenth Amendment** in 1920. Yet by this time, white supremacists in the South had succeeded in **disfranchising African American** men through pervasive violence and such legal mechanisms as the **poll tax**, **grandfather clause**, **literacy tests**, and the **white primary**. These mechanisms also made it more difficult for **immigrants**, Mexican Americans, and poor white men to vote, and voting rates fell precipitously across the South in the early 20th century. Some southern women, such as those who formed the **Southern States Woman Suffrage Conference**, even portrayed **women**'s suffrage in racial terms, arguing that white women would counter black and immigrant votes.

Moreover, political reforms intended to make elections honest and fair, such as the **Australian ballot**, **at-large** and **nonpartisan elections**, and the **direct primary**, may have led to lower rates of voter participation throughout the country. Through civil service reform and **city manager** and **commission** government, reformers tried to remove partisan politics from many areas of city government, perhaps at the expense of public accessibility. **Efficiency** measures may have had similar effects at the state and federal level. Many people, avowed **progressives** as well as conservatives, openly doubted the capacity of immigrants, especially those from eastern and southern Europe, to exercise the rights of citizenship properly, although only Asian immigrants were legally barred from naturalizing and voting. Many reforms may have had the unintended consequence of alienating people from electoral politics at the neighborhood level, but for the most part progressives intended to replace what they saw as a short-sighted, fragmentary, and self-serving electoral system dominated by **machine politics** with a system that encouraged civic consciousness and engaged people in broad debates over public issues. This explains their stress on devices to simplify and open up the electoral process, such as direct primaries, the **short ballot, initiative, referendum,** and **recall**. *See also GUINN V. UNITED STATES;* STRUCTURAL REFORM; *WILLIAMS V. MISSISSIPPI.*

SULLIVAN, LOUIS (1856–1924). Architect. Born in Boston, Sullivan studied at the Massachusetts Institute of Technology and the École des Beaux Arts in Paris between 1872 and 1875, then worked in the Chicago **architecture** firm of William Le Baron Jenney. Sullivan's partnership with Dankmar Adler (1844–1900), formed in 1881, quickly became renowned for theater designs and experiments in steel-frame construction. They won international fame for Chicago's Auditorium Theater building (1887–89), for which Sullivan's intricate interior design produced perfect acoustics. With the young **Frank Lloyd Wright** as an apprentice from 1887 to 1893, Sullivan and Adler designed the Wainwright Building in St. Louis (1890), the Transportation Building for the Columbian **Exposition** (1893), and the Guaranty Building in Buffalo (1895), as well as many others. Sullivan's professional position declined after Adler dissolved the partnership in 1895. Clients rejected the advanced ideas of Sullivan, who could be difficult to work with. Still, one of Sullivan's masterpieces, Chicago's stunning Carson Pirie Scott department store (1899–1903), came from this later period, as did many banks and smaller buildings. Sullivan continued to lecture and write, elaborating on his dictum that form follows function, a founding idea of **modernist** architecture.

SULLIVAN, TIMOTHY D. "BIG TIM" (1862–1913). Politician. Born in New York City, Sullivan grew up in the Irish tenement district of the **Lower East Side**. He had limited education, sold newspapers by age eight, and became leader of a Five Point gang. One of the many **saloon**-keepers to enter **machine** politics, he relied on **Tammany Hall** for election to the New York state legislature (1886–94), the state senate (1894–1903), and the U.S. House of Representatives (1903–6). One of the most colorful, controversial district leaders (or second-level **bosses**) in New York's **Democratic** machine, he was beloved by constituents for his open-hearted **pluralism** and **urban liberalism**, but he was loathed by reformers for his connections with **prostitution** and gambling. Ownership of saloons, theaters, and a **vaudeville** circuit made him a wealthy man. Reelected to Congress in 1912, he was too ill—probably with **syphilis**-induced dementia—to take his seat and died in a mysterious locomotive accident.

SUNDAY, BILLY (1862–1935). Evangelist. Born in Ames, Iowa, William Ashley Sunday grew up in poverty without his father. After **high school** he joined the Chicago White Sox **baseball** team in 1883 and played for eight years in Chicago, Pittsburgh, and Philadelphia. After a religious conversion in 1887, he worked with the **Young Men's Christian Association** in Chicago. In 1896, he took to the road as a revivalist and was ordained a Presbyterian minister (1903). His sensational, **fundamentalist** sermons attracted large crowds whose contributions made Sunday a rich man. He catalyzed many local reform campaigns, especially those focused on **prohibition** and other moral issues. Sunday's popularity declined after 1920.

SUPREME COURT, U.S. Between 1898 and 1917, 20 men served on the U.S. Supreme Court, two of whom were the chief justice (Fuller and White). They were **John M. Harlan** (1877–1911), Horace Gray (1882–1902), **Melville W. Fuller** (1888–1910), **David J. Brewer** (1890–1910), Henry B. Brown (1890–1906), George Shiras Jr. (1892–1903), **Edward D. White** (1894–1921), Rufus W. Peckham (1895–1909), Joseph McKenna (1898–1925), **Oliver Wendell Holmes** (1902–32), William D. Day (1903–22), William H. Moody (1906–10), Horace H. Lurton (1910–14), **Charles E. Hughes** (1910–16), Willis Van Devanter (1911–37), Joseph R. Lamar (1911–16), Mahon Pitney (1912–22), James C. McReynolds (1914–41), **Louis D. Brandeis** (1916–39), and John H. Clarke (1916–22).

The Court did not have its own offices until the opening of **Cass Gilbert**'s building on 1st Street east of the Capitol in 1935. Since the Civil War, the Court had met in the Old Senate Chamber. Justices had no individual offices and usually worked at home. This informality belied the Court's controversial influence in American **economy**, politics, and society. With some qualifications, a conservative, formalistic outlook dominated the legal profession during the late 1800s. Nearly all justices came to the court imbued with the belief that the judiciary's duty was to discern and apply constitutional principles that did not change even as society evolved. They believed that adherence to fundamental principles of individual rights and private property provided a bulwark against governmental or popular despotism.

Thus, on the great legal issues of the Progressive Era—corporate power and **antitrust**, **labor unions** and workers' protection, **disfranchisement** and **segregation**—the Court seemed often to adhere to abstract notions of freedom and equality that belied everyday reality. Justices turned to the doctrine of "substantive due process" to protect corporate property from state and federal regulation. Abstract doctrines of freedom of contract inhibited public oversight of wages, hours, and working conditions, on the grounds that such regulation interfered with workers' freedom. *Plessy v. Ferguson* (1896) culminated a generation of precedents that sanctioned blatant racial discrimination as long as technically the races were equal.

There were always countercurrents within the legal profession, which in the end did sanction most **progressive** legislation. Only the most inveterately laissez-faire–minded justices consistently questioned state or federal exercise of the "police power," the common-law principle that allows regulation of private property for **public health**, safety, and welfare. Justice Harlan spoke for an old-fashioned perspective in which judges were responsible for the practical consequences of their decisions. Justices Holmes and Brandeis brought to the Court **modernist** perspectives rooted in **social Darwinism**, **pragmatism**, **realism**, and **sociological jurisprudence**. But overall, the Court was vulnerable to charges that it was out of touch, leading to resentment and loss of credibility that culminated in the willingness of **Theodore Roosevelt** and the 1912 **Progressive Party** to consider the legislative **recall** of judicial decisions.

Throughout the tumultuous 1890s, the Court interpreted the 1887 Interstate Commerce Act so as to limit the **Interstate Commerce Commission**'s authority. A series of decisions made the 1890 Sherman Antitrust Act more a burden on labor than on industry. The Court also declared the new federal **income tax** unconstitutional in *Pollock v. Farmer's Loan and Trust* (1895). Having ratified state segregation laws in *Plessy v. Ferguson*, with only Justice Harlan dissenting, the Court unanimously affirmed state authority to disfranchise **African Americans** in *Williams v. Mississippi* (1898).

The ambiguity of the Court's conservatism showed up in the landmark 1904 *Northern Securities* case, when by a 5–4 vote the justices supported the Roosevelt administration's effort to dissolve **J. P. Morgan**'s attempt to create a northwestern railroad combine. In *Lochner v. New York* (1905) the Court struck down a New York state maximum-hour law, with only Justices Harlan and Holmes in dissent, but these dissenting opinions proved persuasive in upholding a 10-hour workday law in *Muller v. Oregon* (1908) and in *Bunting v. Oregon* (1917), decisions based in part on innovative sociological briefs prepared by Brandeis, along with **Josephine Goldmark** and the **National Consumers' League**. Nevertheless, the Court's anti-labor union views were evident in cases such as the 1908 **Danbury Hatters**' decision. Such decisions prompted the **American Federation of Labor** to drop its apolitical stance, promulgate **Labor's Bill of Grievances**, and move toward alliance with the **Democratic Party**. In *Lone Wolf v. Hitchcock* (1903) the Court abrogated U.S. treaties with **Native American** tribes to facilitate the **Dawes Allotment Act**.

When Chief Justice Fuller died in 1910, President **William Howard Taft** broke tradition by nominating Associate Justice Edward D. White as chief justice (1910–21). In *Standard Oil v. United States* (1911), the White Court affirmed the breakup of the **Standard Oil** monopoly, adopting the so-called **rule of reason** as a moderate conservative rationale for federal antitrust activity. The Progressive Era judiciary, like the progressives themselves, was not much preoccupied with civil liberties, but in *Weeks v. United States* (1914), the Court did enunciate a federal exclusionary rule barring illegally obtained evidence. When Justice Hughes, a moderate progressive, resigned to accept the **Republican** presidential nomination in 1916, President **Woodrow Wilson** nominated Brandeis, who was confirmed only after five months of debate over his progressive views and the fact that he was the first **Jew** nominated for the Court. Despite the presence of Brandeis alongside Holmes, the Court reverted to stereotype in the 1918 decision ***Hammer v. Dagenhart***, which by a 5–4 vote struck down the 1916 **Keating–Owen Child Labor Act**. *See also BUCK'S STOVE* CASE; CLAYTON ANTITRUST ACT; ERDMAN ACT; GRANDFATHER CLAUSE; *GUINN V. UNITED STATES*; *HITCHMAN COAL & COKE V. MITCHELL*; *INSULAR CASES*; NATIONAL CHILD LABOR COMMITTEE; *SWIFT AND COMPANY V. UNITED STATES*.

SURVEY. After participating in the **Pittsburgh Survey**, editor Paul U. Kellogg decided to rename *Charities and the Commons*—the social welfare magazine in which excerpts from the innovative Pittsburgh study first appeared—*Survey*, to reflect the increasingly professional and social science orientation of the social workers and **settlement house** workers whom the magazine addressed. Under this name (and from 1921 to 1952 *Survey Graphic*), Kellogg's magazine was a major forum for writing on social problems and social work. Dedicated to illustrations, it popularized the documentary photographs of **Lewis W. Hine**, among others.

SWIFT AND COMPANY V. UNITED STATES **(1905).** In this **antitrust** case, the **U.S. Supreme Court** unanimously ruled in January 1905 against the meatpacking company of Gustavus F. Swift (1839–1903), ordering the breakup of the "Chicago beef trust." The giant meat processing firms of Swift, Armour, Morris, and three others had been indicted for manipulating livestock prices and other conspiracies. With 60 percent of the nation's fresh meat market, the Chicago meat packers made an inviting target for **Theodore Roosevelt**'s administration's antitrust investigations, especially given the public furor that led to the **Meat Inspection Act**. Drawing on the precedent of the 1895 *E. C. Knight* case, Swift claimed that the Sherman Antitrust Act was too vague and did not apply to its activities in different states. Writing for the court, Justice **Oliver Wendell Holmes** asserted that even Swift's intrastate activities were part of a nationwide "stream of commerce," thereby vastly expanding federal authority to regulate big business.

SYPHILIS. In the United States, physician **Prince Morrow** began publicizing the dangers of syphilis to innocent wives and children in the 1880s, but not until 1905 did two German researchers identify the organism that causes the disease. In 1906, August Wasserman and his colleagues developed a diagnostic test, prompting several states to follow Michigan's 1899 lead in requiring men to take blood tests for sexually transmitted diseases before marrying. In 1909, researchers Paul Ehrlich and Sahachiro Hata developed Salvarsan, a cure for the disease. After 1915, many American physicians had learned to conduct the test and administer the cure via intravenous injection, and 20 states mandated premarital blood tests by 1921. Although the Wasserman test revealed that rates of infection were much lower than expected, fears about sexually transmitted disease motivated the campaign against **prostitution** and calls for sex **education** in the schools.

– T –

TAFT, WILLIAM HOWARD (1857–1930). President of the United States and jurist. Born in Ohio, Taft graduated from Yale University (1878) and the Cincinnati Law School (1880). An active **Republican**, he became a superior court judge in 1887, then U.S. solicitor general in 1890, and two years later presiding judge on the federal court of appeals, a position he held for eight years. Although not hostile to **labor unions**, Taft used injunctions to limit union violence and secondary strikes. In 1900, President **William McKinley** appointed him to head the **Philippine** Commission, and he served as the first U.S. civil governor of the islands (1901–4), where he organized a civil government, negotiated with Filipino elites and Catholic leaders, and began economic reconstruction. When President **Theodore Roosevelt** named his old friend secretary of war (1904–8), Taft became a trusted adviser on many **foreign policy** and military issues. Three times, Roosevelt offered Taft, who often expressed a preference for the judiciary over politics, appointment as an associate justice on the **Supreme Court**, but Taft held out hoping for the chief justice's seat and eventually was pressured to run for the presidency. Roosevelt arranged Taft's nomination as the Republican candidate in

1908, and he won the election easily over **Democrat William Jennings Bryan,** earning 51.6 percent of the popular vote (321 electoral votes) to his rival's 43.1 percent (162).

Progressives who expected President Taft to be an ally were very disappointed. The Taft administration was efficient but politically inept. Divisions between **Old Guard** and **Insurgent** Republicans overshadowed the administration's many accomplishments and permitted the **Democrats** to win control of Congress in 1910. Then in 1912, Roosevelt challenged Taft for reelection, first in the Republican primaries and then as the nominee of the breakaway **Progressive Party**. The contest between the two Republicans allowed Democrat **Woodrow Wilson** to win. After his presidency, Taft was a professor of law at Yale until 1921, served as joint chairman of the National War Labor Board during World War I, and advocated for the League of Nations. President Warren Harding appointed Taft as chief justice of the U.S. Supreme Court (1921–30), a job that, as expected, he was well suited to perform. Taft resigned due to poor health and died in Washington, D.C., on 8 March 1930. *See also* ANTITRUST; BALLINGER–PINCHOT CONTROVERSY; CUBA; INTERNATIONALISM; LEAGUE TO ENFORCE PEACE; PAYNE–ALDRICH TARIFF.

TAFT–KATSURA AGREEMENT (1905). Secretary of War **William Howard Taft**, on a mission to Manila, stopped in Tokyo in July 1905 to sign a memorandum with Prime Minister Taro Katsura that reassured Japan about its position in northeast Asia in advance of the **Portsmouth Conference**, in which President **Theodore Roosevelt** mediated an end to the Russo–Japanese War. Japan disavowed aggressive aims on the U.S.-controlled **Philippines**, while the United States acquiesced in Japan's suzerainty over Korea. By November, Secretary of State **Elihu Root** closed the U.S. legation in Korea, accepting the Japanese ambassador's announcement that Tokyo would control Korean foreign affairs. A retreat from the **Open Door** policy, this agreement acknowledged that the United States could not prevent Japan's annexation of Korea without war. Roosevelt's pursuit of a balance of power in the Pacific restored good will between the United States and Japan, at least in the short run. *See also* FOREIGN POLICY; ROOT–TAKAHIRA AGREEMENT.

TAMMANY HALL. This was a nickname for the dominant faction of New York City's **Democratic Party**. It referred to the fraternal society, founded in 1805, that by the Civil War controlled Manhattan Democratic politics. With a meeting hall on Fourteenth Street, Tammany became the archetype for urban **machine politics**, a symbol of patronage, influence peddling, and graft, especially after the scandals caused by **Boss** William M. Tweed during the 1860s and 1870s. Like most political machines, Tammany Hall was in reality a coalition of local bosses with strongholds in wards or state legislative districts, but it generally had more durable citywide leadership than the Chicago or Boston machines before World War I. In 1880, Honest John Kelly, Tammany's first Irish-American, citywide boss, assumed control; his protégé, **Richard Croker**, succeeded Kelly in 1886. By 1902, corruption charges and electoral defeats had driven Croker from politics, with **Charles F. Murphy** succeeding him. Reformers of all sorts demonized Tammany, sometimes excessively but often with grounds. Numerous **muckraking** articles, along with books such as Gustavus Myers's landmark *The History of Tammany Hall* (1901), sought to expose Tammany's chronic corruption, while **journalist** William L. Riordan used *Plunkitt of Tammany Hall* (1905), a series of embellished interviews with Tammany district leader George Washington Plunkitt, to explain the machine from an insider's perspective. Under Murphy, a new Tammany emerged, dedicated to **urban liberalism** and powerful enough to elect **Alfred Smith** governor of New York four times and help him to win the nomination for president in 1928. Nevertheless, Tammany could never put behind its penchant for scandal and its connections to police graft and organized crime. Between the 1920s and 1950s, voter disenchantment and changing New York demographics led to Tammany's decline. *See also* NEW YORK CITY, CONSOLIDATION OF; SULLIVAN, TIMOTHY D.; WAGNER, ROBERT F.

TANNER, HENRY O. (1859–1937). Artist. Born in Pittsburgh, Tanner was the son of Benjamin Tucker Tanner, a bishop of the African Methodist Episcopal church. After studying with Thomas Eakins at the Philadelphia Academy of Fine Arts and working as a painter and photographer in Atlanta, he studied in Paris (1891–96), where he won recognition and honors. By 1900, Tanner had an international reputation, especially for biblical scenes and landscapes. He had exhibitions across the United States and major museums acquired his paintings; his *Destruction of Sodom and Gomorrah* is owned by New York's Metropolitan Museum of Art. Tanner's success inspired many **African Americans** to pursue artistic careers. *See also* ART.

TARBELL, IDA M. (1857–1944). Journalist. A Pennsylvania native, Tarbell earned a B.A. in biology in 1880 at Allegheny College and taught school before becoming the editor of a journal for the **Chautauqua** system and then a popular historian. Her biography of Napoleon doubled *McClure's* subscriptions when serialized in 1894–95. For several years she wrote mostly biographies, but in 1902 *McClure's* published a series of her **muckraking** articles on **Standard Oil**. These articles, published as a book in 1904, helped to prompt the 1906 **antitrust** suit that eventually forced the company's dissolution. Along with coworkers, she abandoned *McClure's* in 1906 to found *The American Magazine*, for which she wrote on topics such as protective tariffs and congressional lobbyists. In the 1910s, she turned her attention to the **women**'s **suffrage** movement and the changing social roles of women, both of which she opposed, despite her own unconventional life. In other works, she advocated **scientific management** as a cure for labor unrest. Retiring from investigative **journalism** after 1915, Tarbell wrote mainly on business and public affairs while serving on several federal commissions. *See also* BAKER, RAY STANNARD; STEFFENS, JOSEPH LINCOLN.

TARIFF COMMISSION ACT (1916). At the urging of President **Woodrow Wilson**, Congress created the Tariff Commission in 1916 as an independent federal agency to advise the president and Congress on foreign trade and commercial policy. It was a bipartisan board with six members appointed by the president and confirmed by the Senate for six-year terms. This commission was innovative in its goal of eschewing politics and instead acting as an unbiased, fact-finding, quasi-judicial agency assessing tariff levels in response to changing trade conditions. Yet the commission also reflected long-standing **Democratic Party** suspicions of protective tariffs and huge changes in international trade during World War I. *See also* UNDERWOOD–SIMMONS TARIFF.

TAYLOR, FREDERICK WINSLOW (1856–1915). Engineer and business management reformer. Born in Germantown, Pennsylvania, the son of wealthy Pennsylvanians, Taylor left Harvard University because of eye strain and became a machinist at Midvale Steel Company in Philadelphia, where he worked his way up the ranks while earning an engineering degree from Stevens Institute. Fascinated by new ideas of **efficiency**, Taylor experimented with time-and-motion studies, systematic work rules, incentive pay, and other methods to increase productivity by rationalizing the informal, custom-driven procedures that had hitherto governed industrial production. After running a paper company for a few years, he became a management consultant, creating an approach he labeled **scientific management**. Hired by the Bethlehem Steel Company in 1898, Taylor introduced innovations in cost accounting and production management that engendered so much resistance from both workers and managers that he was fired in 1901. Nonetheless, he persevered in promoting his concepts as an author and lecturer, and some of his former employees, including **Frank Gilbreth**, made lucrative careers as consultants. At the behest of **Louis Brandeis**, who became enamored with engineer-run enterprise as an alternative to short-sighted, self-serving businessmen, Taylor compiled his lectures into *The Principles of Scientific Management* (1911), one of the best-selling business books of the early 20th century. *See also* WELFARE CAPITALISM.

TAYLOR, GRAHAM (1851–1938). Clergyman and social worker. Born in New York, Taylor graduated from Rutgers College and the Theological Seminary of the Reformed Church in New Brunswick, New Jersey, in the early 1870s. After pastorates in Hopewell, New York, and Hartford, Connecticut, he taught at Hartford Theological Seminary (1888–92) and Chicago Theological Seminary (1892–1924). Inspired by the **Social Gospel** and the example of **Jane Addams**, Taylor founded the Chicago Commons **settlement house** in 1894. Home for his family as well as a nonsectarian social welfare agency, Chicago Commons offered clubs, a day nursery, a kindergarten, and forums open to his working-class neighbors and seminary students. Taylor constructed a larger building in 1901 and two years later founded the Chicago School of Civics and Philanthropy, which became part of the **University of Chicago** in 1920. Active in city politics, he served on the **Chicago Vice Commission** and the **Civic Federation**, among other groups. He also founded a magazine on the settlement house movement, *The Commons,* one of the predecessor publications of the influential *Survey.* His books include *Religion in Social Action* (1913). Taylor retired in 1921 but remained active into the 1930s, while Chicago Commons survived as a neighborhood service center through the 20th century.

TEAMSTERS, INTERNATIONAL BROTHERHOOD OF. Founded in 1903 with the merger of the Teamsters National Union and the Team Drivers International Union, this **labor union** represented men driving horse-drawn vehicles, such as city delivery wagons. A member of the **American Federation of Labor**, with a key position in urban transportation, the Teamsters exercised much influence over local labor councils in large cities. The general strike in San Francisco (1901) and the strike in Chicago against major meatpacking firms (1902) succeeded largely due to the Teamsters' cooperation. But a 1905 Chicago strike, begun against the **mail-order** company Montgomery Ward, spread throughout the city, cost $1 million, prompted clashes between police and strikebreakers in which 21 people died, and weakened the Chicago Teamsters for years. Under the conservative leadership of Boston's Daniel J. Tobin (1907–52), the Teamsters grew steadily from 40,000 members to 500,000 by 1940. In the 1920s, the Teamsters expanded to include chauffeurs, warehouse workers, and dairy employees; more **women**; and interstate truck drivers in most urban centers.

TELLER AMENDMENT (1898). Attached to the joint resolution Congress passed on 19 April 1898 authorizing the **Spanish–American War**, this amendment, proposed by Colorado senator Henry M. Teller, committed the United States to the independence of **Cuba** upon the defeat of Spain. Teller intended this measure to reassure Americans, Cubans, and Europeans who suspected that U.S. intervention in the Cuban revolt was a pretext for annexation. The 1901 **Platt Amendment** enabled the United States to fulfill this commitment while retaining sway over Cuba's affairs. *See also* FOREIGN POLICY.

TEMPERANCE. *See* PROHIBITION.

TENEMENT HOUSE ACT (1901). This New York state law resulted from a campaign by the New York Charity Organization Society's housing expert, **Lawrence Veiller**. In January 1900, Veiller exhibited 1,000 photographs, maps, and charts that documented the poor air and toilet facilities, lack of light, dangerous conditions, and absence of privacy in more than 44,000 deteriorating and overcrowded tenements in Manhattan and the Bronx. The solution, he argued, was enforcement of existing fire, safety, and health laws; repair of tenements; and construction of new model housing. When city officials did not cooperate, the reformers pressed the state for new legislation, which passed in April 1900. The law established a Tenement House Department to enforce new regulations concerning lot and room size, lighting, ventilation, and plumbing. Landlords sued to resist the most important and expensive change, the provision of indoor toilets, a requirement upheld by the **U.S. Supreme Court** in 1906. This law became a model for urban housing regulation around the country, though New York City's problems were so overwhelming that even in 1920 many residents still lived in 100,000 pre-reform or "old law" tenements. *See also* NATIONAL HOUSING ASSOCIATION; RIIS, JACOB.

TENNESSEE COAL AND IRON COMPANY. *See* ANTITRUST; PANIC OF 1907; ROOSEVELT, THEODORE; TAFT, WILLIAM HOWARD; UNITED STATES STEEL COMPANY.

TENNIS CABINET. This term refers to President **Theodore Roosevelt**'s informal group of advisers, with whom he played tennis at the White House. They included General **Leonard Wood**, **James R. Garfield**, **Gifford Pinchot**, French Ambassador Jean Jules Jusserand, and British diplomat Sir Cecil Arthur Spring-Rice.

TERRELL, MARY ELIZA CHURCH (1863–1954). Educator and civil rights activist. The daughter of well-to-do Tennesseans, Mary Eliza Church graduated from Oberlin College (1884) and became a teacher at the leading **high school** for **African American** students in Washington, D.C. Forced to resign in 1891 upon marrying fellow teacher Robert Terrell (who eventually became Washington's first African American judge), she turned to activism. A founder and first president of the **National Association of Colored Women** and an early member of the **National Association for the Advancement of Colored People**, she battled **disfranchisement, segregation, lynching,** and job discrimination and sought better housing and health and child care for African American women. A staunch **Republican,** Terrell served on the Washington, D.C., board of education, the first black **woman** to hold such a position in the United States. A widely published author who represented the United States in international organizations, she lived long enough to participate in the desegregation of Washington's restaurants in the 1950s.

TESLA, NICOLA (1856–1943). Engineer. Born in Croatia to Serbian parents, he studied in Austria and at the University of Prague from 1878 to 1880, worked in Paris as an **electrical** engineer, and arrived in New York in 1884 to work for **Thomas A. Edison** and later George **Westinghouse.** Edison preferred direct current (DC) to the alternating current (AC) that Tesla devised, and the two inventors had a famous dispute that Tesla effectively won. After founding the Tesla Electric Company in 1887, Tesla patented 700 inventions, including the telephone receiver, generators, transformers, and alternating current systems. Renowned as a visionary inventor by the time he illuminated the Columbian **Exposition** in 1893, he made major contributions to wireless communications and electrical transmission. When a mysterious, devastating explosion occurred on 30 June 1908 in remote Tunguska in Siberia, rumors attributed it to a secret death ray test-fired by Tesla. Solitary and eccentric, Tesla lived with his pet pigeons in New York hotels and died in a run-down room in Times Square while appealing to investors to back increasingly outlandish schemes. *See also* GENERAL ELECTRIC COMPANY.

THAW, HARRY K. (1871–1947). *See* WHITE, STANFORD.

THOMAS, M. CAREY (1857–1935). Educator and women's rights activist. Born in Baltimore, Thomas graduated from Cornell University in 1877. Refused permission to attend seminars with male students at Johns Hopkins University, she went to the University of Leipzig, where further discrimination made her move to the University of Zurich, which granted her a Ph.D. in 1882. Family connections led to her appointment as a professor and dean at Bryn Mawr College, whose president she became (1894–1922). A strong, even autocratic leader, she excelled at fund-raising, while shifting the college away from its Quaker origins. A persistent advocate for **women**'s higher **education**, Thomas helped to found a preparatory girls' **high school** in Baltimore, raised money for the Johns Hopkins Medical School on the condition that it admit women on an equal basis with men, and publicly ridiculed Harvard University president **Charles W. Eliot**'s call in 1899 for a simpler curriculum for female students. Active in the **American Association of University Women** and a leader of the College Equal Suffrage League, she went beyond the typical women's rights agenda to endorse a broad **feminist** program of self-expression free of social constraints. This attitude probably developed partly out of her passionate relationships with other women, which led her to define herself as a lesbian as the new concept of homosexuality took shape. *See also* SEXUALITY; UNIVERSITY.

THORPE, JAMES "JIM" (1887–1953). Athlete. Born to parents of Sac and Fox heritage in the **Indian Territory**, Thorpe became a sports star at the Carlisle Industrial Training School, where he shattered school track and field records and, coached by the legendary Glenn S. "Pop" Warner, led the **football** team to several upset victories. He earned All-American honors in 1908, 1911, and 1912. At the 1912 Olympic Games in Stockholm, he won gold medals in both the pentathlon and decathlon, an unprecedented feat. President **William Howard Taft** wrote him a letter of congratulations, and a ticker-tape parade greeted him in New York City. But a year later, the discovery that he had played semiprofessional **baseball** in 1909–10 led the **Amateur Athletic Union** to strip him of his Olympic medals and bar him from future amateur competition. During the next decade he played major-league **baseball** and football, leading his teams in the latter sport to three unofficial national championships. A hero to many Americans, Thorpe was awarded several posthumous honors, culminating with the International Olympic Committee's return of his Olympic medals to his heirs in 1982. *See also* ATHLETICS; INDUSTRIAL EDUCATION; NATIVE AMERICANS.

TILLMAN, BENJAMIN R. (1847–1918). Politician. Born in Trenton, South Carolina, Tillman was educated privately on his family plantation and served briefly in the Confederate Army. Turning to politics in the 1880s, he allied with the upcountry farmers to oppose bankers and lawyers alleged to rule the state. Elected governor in 1890 as a **Democrat**, he used his four-year term to found Clemson and Winthrop Colleges, equalize taxes, regulate railroads, and increase funds for public **education**. Like other white southern politicians of the era, he endorsed **lynching** and oversaw a new state constitution that **disfranchised** black men. Elected to the U.S. Senate in 1895, "Pitchfork" Ben Tillman championed Southern agriculture and vehemently denounced President Grover Cleveland for negotiating with **J. P. Morgan** to protect the nation's gold reserves amid the depression of the 1890s. Despite censure by the Senate in 1902 for assaulting another senator on the Senate floor, he remained influential. Tillman managed the passage of the **Hepburn Act** (1906) and other bills increasing railroad regulation and authored a bill in 1907 that restricted corporate funding in federal elections. Illness diminished his influence after 1909. *See also* SMITH, HOKE; VARDAMAN, JAMES K.

TIN PAN ALLEY. Coined in the early 20th century, this affectionate nickname for the New York City streets dominated by sheet **music** companies was inspired by the cacophony produced by overused, cheap pianos on which songwriters developed and demonstrated their works. Boston, Chicago, New Orleans, and St. Louis also had music publishers, but Manhattan was the major center. Although most Tin Pan Alley songs were initially ballads or comic songs, gradually they included Broadway musical scores, **ragtime**, **jazz**, and blues. Among the best-known and most successful of Tin Pan Alley songwriters were **Irving Berlin** ("Alexander's Ragtime Band," 1911), and **George M. Cohan** ("Give My Regards to Broadway," 1904).

In the era before radio broadcasts and widespread ownership of **phonographs**, song publishers "plugged" or promoted, performed, and sold sheet music on the streets, in dime stores such as **Woolworth's**, cafes, **department stores**, nickelodeons, **saloons**, and **amusement parks**. However, popular songs achieved their greatest success when incorporated into touring **vaudeville** shows. By the 1910s, Broadway theaters were replacing the staple European operettas with Tin Pan Alley songs, launching the new musical comedy genre. The music firms organized the Music Publishers Association in 1895 and lobbied Congress for a new copyright law. In 1914, the formation of the **American Society of Composers, Authors, and Publishers (ASCAP)** solidified the power of Tin Pan Alley music publishers and composers, and most sheet music and phonograph records paid royalties to ASCAP. *See also* POPULAR CULTURE.

TITANIC. The RMS *Titanic* was an Olympic-class passenger liner built in Belfast for the British White Star Line in 1912. The largest, most luxurious passenger steamship in the world, it was one of three sister ships designed to dominate transatlantic travel. Considered the ultimate in modern marine technology, this ship was said to be unsinkable. Carrying thousands of passengers on its maiden voyage, the *Titanic* struck an iceberg on 14 April 1912 and sank in three hours. A U.S. Senate investigation reported that 1,517 people died in this disaster, making it one of the worst peacetime disasters in maritime history and certainly the most notorious. Catalyst for the 1912 **Radio Act**, which began the standardization of wireless communications, along with international efforts to improve ship design, safety, warning, and rescue, the *Titanic* is the subject of at least five **movies**, as well as a play, a Broadway musical, and many books. Discovery of the shipwreck by oceanographers in 1985 renewed interest in this unparalleled disaster.

TREATY OF PARIS. *See* PARIS, TREATY OF (1898).

TRIANGLE SHIRTWAIST COMPANY FIRE (1911). This fire at a garment factory on the **Lower East Side** of Manhattan on 25 March 1911 led to the deaths of 146 people, 125 of whom were girls and young **women**. The 500 workers tried to escape as the fire roared through the cloth, thread, and flammable chemicals surrounding them, but some doors were locked to prevent employees from leaving early or stealing materials, and the one flimsy ladder leading down the nine stories to the ground collapsed. Women plunged from the windows to slam into the pavement below as horrified spectators watched. A few days later, as the victims were laid to rest, tens of thousands of working people led a protest march up Fifth Avenue, home to many wealthy New Yorkers.

The **Uprising of the Twenty Thousand** two years before had targeted the Triangle Company, among others, but the resolution of that strike had not included safety regulations the workers had demanded. After the fire, instead of direct negotiations between workers and employers, reformers and legislators took the lead. The **New York State Factory Investigating Commission** recommended an overhaul in factory safety regulations that other states used as a model. This disaster gave momentum to campaigns for protective labor laws, including **employer liability, workers' compensation**, maximum hours, and health and safety regulation. *See also* INTERNATIONAL LADIES' GARMENT WORKERS' UNION; MOSKOWITZ, BELLE LINDNER ISRAELS; SMITH, ALFRED E.; TAMMANY HALL; URBAN LIBERALISM.

TROLLEYS, ELECTRIC. The **electric** trolley or streetcar transformed urban mass transit in the 1890s when it replaced horse-drawn streetcars. Experiments began and patents were issued for electric streetcar motors as early as the 1830s. **Thomas Edison** and less well-known inventors built prototypes or short lines by the early 1880s, but Frank Sprague installed the first commercially successful electric trolley in Richmond, Virginia, in 1887. Edison's company quickly bought the rights to Sprague's streetcar and soon had a booming business. Within three years, some 200 cities bought or ordered the streetcars, and by 1895 over 850 lines were operating. Sprague went on to invent a multiple-unit control system that allowed streetcars to be run alone or in trains without the need for a special engine car.

Electric cars solved a series of problems for cities. Unlike steam cars, they produced no clouds of black coal smoke, flying cinders, or ash. Unlike horsecars, they produced no urine or manure, nor did they rot if they died along the route. They could move at 10 miles per hour, twice as fast as the typical horsecar. They were easier to stop and start than steam cars, and they handled steep grades and sharp turns better. Electricity was cheaper than horse feed, and the cars lasted far longer than the four-year average for horses. The trolley systems were also more durable, cheaper, and quicker to build than cable cars, the main rival technology. By 1902, private operators had invested some $2 billion in more than 850 electric streetcar systems in the United States, and Americans took 4.8 billion trips and one billion transfers. The industry was highly profitable, producing a new crop of industrial barons. One problem that trolleys did not solve, of course, was traffic congestion; indeed, the nation's first **subway system**, opened in Boston in 1897, was intended to ease traffic by eliminating trolley tracks, poles, and wires from the streets.

The boom in electric trolleys encouraged the growth of steel and copper wire production as well as plate glass and upholstery. Thousands of men worked as streetcar drivers and conductors. Electricity generation vastly expanded to meet the new demands, and the need to find paying customers during off-peak hours led streetcar and power companies (often the same entity) to sell electricity at cut rates to businesses and build **amusement parks** at the end of their lines. The low cost and speed of the cars enabled more people to travel quickly, encouraging both suburbanization and tourist day-tripping. The Bronx, incorporated into New York City in 1898, saw its population more than double in the decade after the streetcars rolled in. Henry Huntington's sprawling Pacific Electric Railway was a central element in the development of Los Angeles as a dispersed city, even before the **automobile** gained popularity there. Downtown **department stores** and theater districts benefited from the growing ease of travel. Towns and rural areas along the trolley lines attracted picnickers, and beach resorts like **Coney Island**, Atlantic City, and Revere Beach hosted huge crowds in the summer months. In the densely settled mid-Atlantic and Midwest, streetcars sometimes replaced steam railroad lines as primary passenger carriers and also handled light freight, such as mail, fruit, vegetables, and milk. Families, churches, and other organizations could rent a trolley car for a run through the countryside, and schools used them to transport students to classes and sports events.

The central importance of the streetcar made it the object of bitter political battles over Sunday operation, fares, transfers, line placement and extensions, ownership, and safety. In an era when only the rich owned carriages or automobiles, the vast majority of city dwellers relied on the trolleys, averaging roughly a single roundtrip every day. Many cities mandated a 5-cent fare and free transfers, yet despite this apparently modest cost, many people spent between 10 and 20 percent of their annual income on streetcar fares. Suburbanization thus was initially only available to the better-off, although working-class streetcar suburbs soon developed. Some communities sued to have the trolleys stilled on Sunday, but courts ruled that the cars constituted interstate travel and were not subject to local Sabbath ordinances. Others agitated for public ownership of this among other **utilities** to avoid the route elimination, price-gouging, bribery, and political deals that operators such as Chicago's **Charles T. Yerkes** engaged in. Strikes among car drivers (often members of the **Teamsters Union**) were among the more widely felt and violent of labor stoppages. The greater speed of the trolleys endangered pedestrians, particularly children playing in the streets, and passengers boarding or departing a car might easily trip and fall under the wheels. For **African Americans**, **segregation** on mass transit became a defining instance of their loss of civil rights, confirmed in the *Plessy v. Ferguson* decision (1896). Outside the South, streetcars were not segregated by law.

The streetcar quickly became the source and subject of both popular and high art. Cartoons, **Tin Pan Alley** songs, and novels addressed its crowding and discomforts as well as the kinetic and panoramic experience of urban landscapes that it allowed. Postcards, **movies**, and guidebooks celebrated sights along the routes and on occasion the rails and cars themselves. **Ash Can School** artists painted crowds waiting for or riding trains or used the sharp lines of rails, wires, and cars to compose their images of the urban landscape. **Advertisers** posted controversial billboards along routes and sometimes turned whole cars into decorative floats celebrating a store or product. *See also* ANNEXATION, SUBURBAN; JOHNSON, TOM L.

TROTTER, WILLIAM MONROE (1872–1934). Journalist. Born in Ohio, Trotter became the first **African American** elected to Phi Beta Kappa at Harvard University when he graduated in 1895. He founded the *Boston Guardian* (1901), a national weekly newspaper famous for biting criticism of **Booker T. Washington**, whose "**Tuskegee Machine**" frequently harassed him. When Washington spoke in Boston in 1903, Trotter protested, was arrested, and spent a month in jail for disrupting a public assembly. He allied with **W. E. B. Du Bois** to found the **Niagara Movement** but refused to join the **National Association for the Advancement of Colored People** because it had a white leadership. Trotter famously argued with President **Woodrow**

Wilson during a White House meeting on **segregation** (1914) and led a protest against the showing of *The Birth of a Nation* (1915) at a Boston theater. *See also* JOURNALISM.

TUBERCULOSIS. This contagious respiratory infection was a leading cause of death in the United States and elsewhere. Although the mortality rate had declined since the 1830s, when some 25 percent of all deaths resulted from the disease, by 1900 tuberculosis still accounted for roughly a quarter of deaths among young adults and 10 percent of deaths in the general population. In 1914, it was the second leading cause of death. Tuberculosis was increasingly an ailment of poverty, as those living in crowded, unsanitary working-class neighborhoods contracted, communicated, and died of the disease more often. The treatment of the "wasting disease" or "consumption," as it was called, changed significantly in the Progressive Era because of the gradual acceptance of germ theory and widespread efforts to improve **sanitary engineering**, water quality, medical care, and housing conditions. German bacteriologist Robert Koch isolated the bacillus that causes tuberculosis in 1882, but physicians continued to attribute the disease to heredity and poor living conditions well into the 20th century, in part because of skepticism about germ theory and in part because environment clearly did play a role. Although there was no cure, physicians offered a number of treatments. Well-to-do patients traveled to sanitariums in places considered especially healthy. Mountainous areas in New York, Colorado, New Mexico, and California all gained reputations as places where the sick could recover through fresh air, regular exercise, and a monitored diet. Some cities and states established public sanitariums for the less well-to-do, but these institutions were often isolated barracks in the rural settings thought to be conducive to cures.

As germ theory gained in favor and the contagiousness of tuberculosis became evident, some physicians called for public registries of those infected with the disease and their isolation to prevent others from getting sick. In some states sufferers were removed, sometimes forcibly, from families and quarantined in sanitaria, and houses might be inspected and fumigated. **Public health** officials also undertook campaigns to ban or moderate such common activities as spitting in public, kissing babies, and sharing drinking cups and utensils. Their agitation against full beards and moustaches contributed, along with the **Gillette safety razor**, to a transformation in men's appearance. The new paper "Dixie" cup (1907) and water coolers began to replace the water fountain and its shared tin cup. The **National Tuberculosis Association** (1904) conducted health campaigns to promote better ventilation, simpler interior décor, and nonporous building materials to prevent dust and bacteria. The National Association for the Study and Prevention of Tuberculosis, founded in 1904 by physicians, later became the American Lung Association. Such measures contributed to a steadily falling mortality rate even before successful treatments and vaccinations became available in the 1940s and 1950s, although a new tuberculosis pandemic since the 1980s has reversed some of these gains. *See also* HEALTH AND MEDICINE.

TUMULTY, JOSEPH P. (1879–1954). Politician. Born in New Jersey to an Irish Catholic family, Tumulty graduated from St. Peter's College in 1899, read law in a Jersey City firm, and began practicing in 1902. Elected as a **machine Democrat** to the New Jersey Assembly (1907–10), he sponsored unsuccessful reform bills to regulate civil service, **child labor**, and railroad and **utility** rates. A vigorous campaigner for **Woodrow Wilson**'s gubernatorial bid in 1910, Tumulty became the new governor's secretary (1911–13), a position he kept when Wilson moved into the White House in 1913. Wilson relied on Joe Tumulty to act as his press secretary and handle public relations, patronage, and political matters, especially with Catholic voters. But Tumulty opposed Wilson's second marriage in 1915, straining their relationship, although he stayed in the administration until 1921.

TURNER, FREDERICK JACKSON (1861–1932). *See* "THE SIGNIFICANCE OF THE FRONTIER IN AMERICAN HISTORY."

TUSKEGEE INSTITUTE. Founded in 1880 by a former slave and a former slave owner united in their desire to provide higher **education** to **African Americans**, this institution was chartered by the Alabama state legislature as a "normal" or teacher-training school in 1881. The school's first president, **Booker T. Washington**, enjoyed great success in raising money and promoting the institution, gaining the patronage of philanthropists **John D. Rockefeller**, **Andrew Carnegie**, and Julius Rosenwald of **Sears, Roebuck**. Following the **industrial education** model, Tuskegee offered a curriculum emphasizing manual labor and vocational skills as well as academic courses. Converted to a private institution in 1892, Tuskegee operated on the assumption, articulated in Washington's **Atlanta Compromise** speech of 1896, that by focusing on self-improvement and economic success, African Americans could prove themselves indispensable to whites and prejudice would diminish accordingly. Because few whites would work under a black president (**Robert Park** was an exception), Tuskegee became the first institution of higher education to have a black faculty, including scientist **George Washington Carver**. After Washington's death in 1915, the school broadened its curriculum and became a **university** offering a range of academic and professional degrees.

– U –

UNDERWOOD, OSCAR W. (1862–1929). *See* FEDERAL RESERVE ACT; UNDERWOOD–SIMMONS TARIFF.

UNDERWOOD–SIMMONS TARIFF (1913). Also known as the Revenue Act of 1913, this act passed after President **Woodrow Wilson** called a special session of Congress in April 1913 and appeared before Congress, the first president to do so since John Adams. He enjoyed a strong position because the **Democratic Party** controlled both houses of Congress for the first time in 18 years. Senator Furnifold M. Simmons and Representative Oscar W. Underwood wrote the bill, which Congress passed in October amid much lobbying and a flood of letters from constituents. A break with decades of **Republican** protectionism, this bill lowered tariff rates by an average of 26 percent, adding to the tax-free list iron, steel, wool, many foods and raw materials, and agricultural machinery. The law also imposed the first federal **income tax** since the ratification of the Sixteenth Amendment. *See also* NEW FREEDOM; TARIFF COMMISSION ACT.

UNEMPLOYMENT INSURANCE. Although some European countries began making payments to the unemployed in the 19th century and Great Britain enacted a dole in 1911, many Americans considered such insurance a dangerous program that would undermine the work ethic and pauperize recipients. Also, **labor unions**, suspicious of too much dependence on government, initially gave it tepid support. When ten countries followed the British example between 1911 to 1930, some U.S. reformers cautiously advocated the idea. It became part of the **social insurance** program promoted by the **American Association for Labor Legislation**, but no American state adopted it before World War I. A model program devised by **John R. Commons** in the early 1920s was finally adopted by the Wisconsin legislature in 1931, the first American state to do so. Not until the passage of the Social Security Act in 1935 did the United States create a national unemployment compensation system.

UNITED DAUGHTERS OF THE CONFEDERACY (UDC). Founded in 1894 and claiming some 100,000 members by 1917, the UDC was an organization of white southern **women** dedicated to commemorating the Confederate past. Its members provided relief to Confederate veterans and needy white women, constructed war memorials, lobbied school boards to ensure that textbooks presented the Civil War from a Southern perspective, and contributed to the establishment of **segregation** by insisting on the righteousness of the rebellion and the horrors of the Reconstruction period. Like the Daughters of the American Revolution, the UDC promoted a conservative version of history and defended existing gender roles. Its numbers declined steeply after 1920. *See also THE BIRTH OF A NATION*; DUNNING SCHOOL; KU KLUX KLAN.

UNITED FRUIT COMPANY. This powerful banana-growing and -shipping company developed from American businessman Minor Keith's railroad-building enterprise in Costa Rica in the 1870s and 1880s. Seeking freight for his railroads, Keith (1848–1929) perceived a huge potential market for the yellow fruit, introduced to Boston society by Lorenzo Dow Baker in 1870. An 1899 merger between Keith's company and Baker's led to the founding of United Fruit Company (later Chiquita Brands International). It soon became known in Central America as "El Pulpo"—the Octopus—for its overwhelming control of land, transportation, and labor. United Fruit was the most visible of the American-owned firms that squeezed out small farmers and converted ever-growing acres of jungle into plantations. These firms developed unsavory connections with authoritarian governments, often with the cooperation of U.S. officials. New refrigeration and freight loading technologies and swift steamships and railroads enabled United Fruit Company to provide bananas to the American market year-round by the early 20th century. The firm defended itself successfully against **antitrust** allegations in 1908 and joined other fruit importers in opposing the **Underwood–Simmons** tariff (1913). By 1915, it operated 95 ships, each with a 5,000-ton freight capacity. In the 1920s, the company imported about half of all bananas purchased in the United States, as well as other tropical products. It also played a key role in expanding tourism to the tropics. As early as 1902, more than 5,000 people bought passenger accommodations on the banana boats each year. The company soon established a separate passenger department with its own fleet. Along with several other steamship companies, United Fruit promoted Caribbean cruises and developed tourist resorts in Jamaica, **Cuba**, the **Panama Canal** Zone, Honduras, Costa Rica, and Guatemala, among other places. By the 1920s, well over 60,000 passengers embarked each year on Caribbean cruises on United Fruit's "Great White Fleet" alone. *See also* DOLLAR DIPLOMACY; IMPERIALISM.

UNITED MINE WORKERS OF AMERICA (UMW OR UMWA). Founded in 1890 and led by **John Mitchell**, the UMWA was the first national miners' **labor union** and the largest craft union in the **American Federation of Labor**. After the Panic of 1893 decreased demand for coal and ruined the union wage scale, the 1894 UMWA strike took 180,000 miners off the job but produced poor results. After a more successful strike in 1897, membership rose from 12,000 to 100,000 by 1900. Mitchell and the UMWA reached the height of their Progressive Era influence during negotiations to end the 1902 **Anthracite Coal Strike** for an **eight-hour workday** and increased pay. The cooperation of the UMWA with President **Theodore Roosevelt**'s efforts at investigation and arbitration contrasted sharply with the belligerence and obstruction of the Pennsylvania mine owners. At least until a new round of angry strikes in 1919, the UMWA retained a reputation for acting responsibly on behalf of workers who truly needed organization. **Muckraker** reports by **Ray Stannard Baker** and others on pro-union violence in the anthracite region only partly tarnished this image. *See also* NATIONAL CIVIC FEDERATION; SQUARE DEAL; WESTERN FEDERATION OF MINERS.

UNITED STATES BREWERS' ASSOCIATION (USBA). Established in 1862 to oppose a federal tax on brewing, the USBA helped member beer producers increase market share, promoted new technologies, encouraged the production of needed raw materials, and lobbied for protective tariffs. Unlike other trade associations, however, the brewers faced a mounting political challenge to their industry's existence from the **prohibition** movement. For a long time, the USBA launched only a half-hearted response to its well-organized opponents, even after 1887, when the **Supreme Court** upheld the right of states to criminalize alcohol production and sale without compensating business owners. Brewers rejected any alliance with distillers, who later formed the National Wholesale Liquor Dealers' Association. The USBA provided covert support for campaigns against **women**'s **suffrage** because women were major supporters of prohibition. The group funded "Personal Liberty Leagues" at the state and local levels and allied with the United Brewery Workers to establish pro-beer political lobbies. The passage of the **Webb–Kenyon Act** (1913) finally moved the USBA to establish a publicity office in 1914. Brewers' bribing of **journalists** and politicians caused major scandals in Pennsylvania, Texas, and New York. These belated and poorly organized efforts failed; Congress approved the **Eighteenth Amendment** in 1917 and three-quarters of the states ratified it by 1919. *See also* LOCAL OPTION; SALOON.

UNITED STATES STEEL CORPORATION. When **Andrew Carnegie** sold his steel business to **J. P. Morgan** and **Elbert H. Gary** in 1901 for $492 million in stocks and bonds in a deal brokered by Carnegie executive **Charles Schwab**, it was the largest financial transaction ever concluded. Federal Steel, Carnegie Steel, and eight other companies merged to form the United States Steel Corporation, with Schwab as president (1901–3). Capitalized at $1.4 billion, the world's first billion-dollar corporation, the sprawling enterprise produced two-thirds of all American steel. Burdened with debt,

U.S. Steel faced accusations from the start of being less innovative and **efficient** than competitors, especially when Schwab left to run Bethlehem Steel. In a lengthy **antitrust** suit begun in 1911, the federal government failed to break up U.S. Steel, which maintained the antiunion policies of Carnegie and **Henry Clay Frick**, with 12-hour shifts, low wages, labor spies, and limited unionization. In 1906, U.S. Steel built the city of Gary, Indiana, making it the site of the largest integrated steel plant in America. *See also* GARY PLAN; GREAT MERGER MOVEMENT; HOLDING COMPANIES; RULE OF REASON.

UNIVERSAL STUDIOS. Founded in 1912 as the Universal Film Manufacturing Company, this firm was a coalition of independent **movie** companies seeking to break the hold of **Thomas Edison**'s **Motion Picture Patents Corporation (MPPC)**. **Carl Laemmle** served as Universal's treasurer and eventually dominated the new company. By 1914, Universal and two other anti-MPPC firms, Mutual and Film Supply, had effectively undermined Edison's company, which also faced **antitrust** lawsuits and was forced by a court decision to dissolve in 1915. Universal became one of the "Big Eight" firms that controlled American movie making in the 1920s.

UNIVERSITY. A wave of reform in higher **education** that began in the 1870s crested and took institutional form at the turn of the 20th century. Between 1870 and 1910, the number of colleges and universities—both public and private—almost doubled from around 560 to 1,000. The federal government encouraged the creation of state universities, intended to offer a more practical curriculum than the classics-based one typical of private institutions, beginning in 1862 with the Morrill Land Grant Act. This law assigned to each state tracts of federal land whose sale would fund so-called land-grant colleges. The Hatch Act (1887) and the second Morrill Act (1890) provided additional federal funds, including some designated for agricultural experiment stations and **segregated** facilities for **African American** students. State universities pioneered secular curricula and the admission of **women** students, often not from any principled commitment to secularism or coeducation but because they needed the tuition. The **Wisconsin Idea** encouraged public institutions of higher education to serve their communities as comprehensively as possible, especially in providing professional expertise to government.

Private institutions were also transformed in this era. Cornell University (1877), which received some public land-grant funds, rejected the denominationalism that had traditionally characterized American private colleges. Cornell also accepted women and working-class students from the start. Drawing on the example of German universities and under the guidance of Daniel Coit Gilman (1831–1908), Johns Hopkins University (1876) became the first full-fledged research university in the United States. Clark (1889), Stanford (1891), and the **University of Chicago** (1892) followed suit. The presidents of existing institutions, such as **Charles W. Eliot** at Harvard and **Nicholas Murray Butler** at Columbia, transformed the traditional curriculum by downplaying classics and religious training in favor of science and modern languages, introducing standardized admission exams and the elective system for undergraduates, and supporting faculty research. Amid well-publicized battles over academic freedom, presidents' power to hire and fire declined and the faculty took an increasing role in university governance. Innovative teachers like economist **Simon N. Patten** and historian **James Harvey Robinson** used primary sources and encouraged discussion, problem solving, and a focus on contemporary relevance. The **pragmatic** emphasis on "learning by doing" made **John Dewey** famous. Like public universities, large private ones began to acquire or create professional schools in law, medicine, business, dentistry, social work, and other fields that either had not existed or had operated independently in the 19th century.

University education remained a rare privilege, but the number of students expanded rapidly, especially at public institutions. About 250,000 people enrolled at postsecondary institutions in 1900, rising to more than one million 30 years later. Women's enrollment increased faster than men's, and by the 1920s almost half of all college students were female. Far more women attended coeducational universities than private, all-women's colleges such as Bryn Mawr or Vassar. Indeed, women's prominence on campus led to many innovations, from the hiring of female administrators and faculty to the addition of **home economics** curricula and efforts to establish enrollment quotas based on gender. Pioneers like Alice Freeman Palmer,

Marion Talbot, **Ellen Swallow Richards**, **M. Carey Thomas**, and the **American Association of University Women** worked to ensure that women had full access to academic and professional training.

Nonwhite students faced significant obstacles in gaining a college education, beginning with the difficulty of getting a good primary and secondary education. Major private universities admitted very few nonwhite students, and many imposed quotas on **Jewish** and Catholic students as well. African Americans had founded colleges and universities in the wake of the Civil War, and some southern states supported agricultural and mechanical colleges for black students, such as the famed **Tuskegee Institute**. Other minority groups, including Chinese and Japanese students, gained entrance to public university campuses in small numbers. The Catholic Church supported its own colleges and universities. Working-class students of all races, especially women, found private business colleges, public municipal and junior (now community) colleges, and normal (teacher-training) schools more accessible than four-year institutions. *See also* ACADEMIC ASSOCIATIONS; AMERICAN ASSOCIATION OF UNIVERSITY PROFESSORS; CARNEGIE FOUNDATION FOR THE ADVANCEMENT OF TEACHING; INTELLECTUAL.

UNIVERSITY OF CHICAGO. *See* CHICAGO, UNIVERSITY OF.

UNTERMEYER, SAMUEL (1858–1940). Lawyer. Born Samuel Untermyer in Virginia, the son of a **Jewish** Confederate officer, he grew up in New York City, attended the City College of New York, and graduated from Columbia Law School in 1878. He became one of the most successful trial lawyers in the United States. In the course of defending major corporations, Untermeyer became interested in the regulation and reform of business. His suit against the Equitable Life Assurance Society helped prompt New York State's **Armstrong Commission** investigation and the strengthening of **insurance regulation**. He expanded his interests to include state and federal regulation of stock exchanges, public ownership of **utilities**, tariff reform, and the **income tax**. His 1911 lecture "Is There a **Money Trust**?" led to his appointment as legal counsel for the **Pujo Committee** (1912–13). Untermeyer remained active in economic reform and public service after World War I, and in Jewish and Zionist causes.

UPRISING OF THE TWENTY THOUSAND (1909). This strike by 20,000 to 40,000 **Jewish** and Italian **immigrant** shirtwaist makers in New York City launched more than five years of unprecedented militancy among **women** workers. The uprising began after months of smaller strikes over the shirtwaist makers' low pay, typically $4 to $6 per week, and long hours, often 65 per week. When some strikers were fired and the women demanded a general strike, the **International Ladies' Garment Workers' Union (ILGWU)** and the **Women's Trade Union League (WTUL)** agreed to a mass meeting on 22 November. Doubting that young women could sustain a general strike, labor leaders, including **Samuel Gompers**, **Leonora O'Reilly**, and **Mary Dreier**, advised against it but were overridden after a fiery speech in Yiddish by striker Clara Lemlich. She and fellow worker **Pauline Newman** helped to coordinate the strike. Garment manufacturers and city officials responded by promoting ethnic divisions, portraying the strikers as sexually promiscuous, and having police beat and arrest picketers. The violence diminished only after the strikers held a press conference to publicize it and well-to-do WTUL members—"the mink brigade"—joined the picket lines. In February 1910, the male ILGWU leadership agreed to a settlement that raised wages and limited working hours to 52 but did not address the strikers' safety concerns. The **Triangle Shirtwaist Fire** revealed the gravity of this mistake. The 1909 uprising transformed the ILGWU into a powerful national force and demonstrated that women could be effective, disciplined, and assertive union members—something male labor leaders had long denied.

URBAN LEAGUE. Organized in New York in 1910 as the Committee on Urban Conditions among Negroes, this group merged with several like-minded groups in 1911 to form the National League on Urban Conditions among Negroes, shortened in 1920 to the National Urban League. The group focused on economic conditions and social services among urban **African Americans**, pressing issues during the **Great Migration**. Urban League chapters, 30 of which operated by 1919, trained black social workers, hired black social scientists to research housing, health, jobs, and other matters, and offered employment counseling and job training to migrants and expert advice to black-owned businesses.

URBAN LIBERALISM. Historian J. Joseph Huthmacher coined this term in a 1962 article to describe the tendency for political **machines** to reach out to **progressives** and take an interest in their urban and labor reform proposals by the 1910s. In response, some reformers replaced their denunciations of **bosses** with tentative praise. For example, in the aftermath of the **Triangle Shirtwaist Fire** of 1911, **Tammany Hall** figures such as **Alfred Smith** and **Robert Wagner**, with the acquiescence of boss **Charles Murphy**, threw themselves into the **New York State Factory Investigating Commission**, which produced nationally emulated labor legislation. Through these activities, Smith developed friendships with reformers, such as **Frances Perkins** and **Belle Moskowitz**, that became central to his liberal agenda as New York governor and presidential candidate in the 1920s. In an influential 1973 book, *Urban Liberalism and Progressive Reform*, historian John D. Buenker used the concept to explain how progressivism, with its tendency toward self-righteous Protestant moralism and technocratic elitism, evolved into New Deal–style liberalism, with its nonjudgmental humanitarianism and strong appeal to urban working-class Catholics and **Jews**. *See also* DEMOCRATIC PARTY.

U'REN, WILLIAM S. (1859–1949). Lawyer and reformer. Born in Wisconsin, U'Ren grew up in Nebraska and Colorado, where he studied and practiced law in the 1880s. After living for a time in California and Hawaii, he settled in Portland, Oregon, where he practiced law and served in the state legislature (1896–97). Associated in the 1890s with Oregon populists and later with the state's **progressive Republicans**, U'Ren became the most prominent proponent of **structural reform** in the Pacific Northwest. As secretary of the Direct Legislation League and leader in groups such as the People's Power League and the Anti-Monopoly League, he was instrumental in winning state constitutional amendments authorizing the **initiative** and **referendum** (1902), the **direct primary** (1904), and **recall** (1908). His most significant accomplishment came in 1906, when he persuaded the Oregon legislature to mandate the direct election of U.S. **senators**, accelerating the national movement that resulted in the Seventeenth Amendment (1913).

U.S. BUREAU OF CORPORATIONS. *See* BUREAU OF CORPO-
RATIONS, U.S.

U.S. CHAMBER OF COMMERCE. *See* CHAMBER OF COM-
MERCE, U.S.

U.S. CIVIL SERVICE COMMISSION. *See* CIVIL SERVICE COM-
MISSION, U.S.

U.S. DEPARTMENT OF COMMERCE AND LABOR. *See* COM-
MERCE AND LABOR, U.S. DEPARTMENT OF.

U.S. DEPARTMENT OF LABOR. *See* LABOR, U.S. DEPART-
MENT OF.

U.S. FOREST SERVICE. *See* FOREST SERVICE, U.S.

U.S. IMMIGRATION COMMISSION. *See* IMMIGRATION COM-
MISSION, U.S.

U.S. RECLAMATION SERVICE. *See* RECLAMATION SERVICE,
U.S.

U.S. SUPREME COURT. *See* SUPREME COURT, U.S.

UTILITIES, MUNICIPAL OWNERSHIP OF. In a period of rapid
urbanization, control of the infrastructure that made life in and movement around modern cities possible became a hotly contested issue.
Already by the mid-1800s, **public health** concerns and huge construction costs legitimated replacing private water companies with
impressive public projects such as New York's Croton Aqueduct,
Philadelphia's Fairmount Waterworks, and the Washington Aqueduct. By the 1920s, only nine of the 69 largest American cities still
relied on private companies to provide water. Other facilities with
health implications, such as market halls, also came under public
control, although often after bitter fights with entrenched corporations. Because street cleaning and sewer systems were unlikely to

generate profits for investors, there was little question that they would be publicly run.

The fiercest battles over public versus private ownership emerged in natural gas, **electricity**, and transit, services for which users could easily be charged fees and in which private enterprise saw the potential for profit. The arguments of free market advocates that cities could expand service and lower rates by granting competing franchises confronted a history that consistently disproved them: After the disruption entailed by the laying of competing lines, upstart companies almost always fell under the control of established ones. This situation led economists such as **Henry Carter Adams** and **Richard Ely** to develop the view that utilities were "natural" monopolies and therefore fit subjects for public ownership or regulation. The high-handed tactics of transit entrepreneurs such as Chicago's **Charles T. Yerkes**, along with allegations of close connections between utilities and **machine politics**, increased sentiment for public control. Urban affairs writers such as **Frederic Howe** and Albert Shaw cited the experience of German and British cities as evidence that what the British often called "municipal **socialism**" could result in better, cheaper services.

From the 1890s until World War I, reform mayors such as Detroit's **Hazen Pingree**, Cleveland's **Tom Johnson** (a former transit operator), and Chicago's Edward Dunne embarked on raucous campaigns for municipal takeovers that for the most part achieved only fare reductions or service improvements, not public ownership. Utility corporations presented city governments with impossible condemnation costs, which would only be followed by daunting capital investment requirements. Such practical concerns dissuaded **structural reform** groups such as the **National Municipal League** from advocating municipal ownership. Until the 1930s and 1940s, when bankrupt transit companies fell into public hands by default, only a few cities boasted municipally owned transit, among them Seattle, Detroit, and San Francisco; New York and Boston did so in part because they had constructed expensive **subway systems**. Chicago, Los Angeles, Seattle, and Cleveland came to operate electric utilities, in Chicago's case alongside the dominant **Commonwealth Edison**. But in the 1920s, only 2 percent of the streetcar tracks, 5 percent of electric power, and 1 percent of gas output were in public hands. These scattered public utilities were often models of sound management and service, but at times, as in the case of Philadelphia's notorious gas company, political **bosses** turned them into sources of political patronage. The relative failure of the municipal ownership movement encouraged cities and states to focus instead on strengthening regulation through expert commissions, after the model of state railroad commissions. *See also* EFFICIENCY; SANITARY ENGINEERING; TROLLEYS, ELECTRIC.

– V –

VAIL, THEODORE N. (1845–1920). Industrialist. Born in Ohio and raised in New Jersey, Vail worked as a youth as a Western Union telegrapher. By 1876, he had been promoted to general superintendent of railway mail in Washington, D.C., and then became general manager of the new Bell Telephone Company in Boston in 1878. He incorporated the **American Telephone and Telegraph Company (AT&T)** in 1885 and served as its president until resigning in 1889. Returning to this job in 1907, he embarked on a campaign to buy out or undercut regional and independent telephone companies. Threatened with **antitrust** prosecution in 1913, Vail reached an agreement with President **Woodrow Wilson**'s administration that allowed AT&T to operate as a regulated monopoly providing uniform long-distance service throughout the United States, an arrangement that endured until deregulation in the 1980s. A proponent of **welfare capitalism**, Vail introduced the first pension plan in the United States. He retired as AT&T president in 1919 but remained chair of the board until his death.

VAN HISE, CHARLES R. (1857–1918). Geologist and educator. Born in Wisconsin, Van Hise earned several degrees from the University of Wisconsin, culminating in a Ph.D. (1892), by which time he was already on the faculty. He helped to transform geology from a primarily descriptive to an analytical science by incorporating principles of physics and chemistry and examining processes of geological change. He also advanced the field institutionally, gaining its recognition by major foundations and serving as president of national and international **academic associations**. In 1903, with the help of his colleague, historian Frederick Jackson Turner, and former classmate and state governor **Robert La Follette**, he became president of the **university**. In this position, he sought to improve faculty qualifications and research, as well as graduate, undergraduate, and adult education. His stress on faculty involvement in policy formation and on research and teaching for the public benefit came to be called the **Wisconsin Idea**, emulated by public universities throughout the country. Van Hise's innovations and his role in convincing the **Carnegie Foundation for the Advancement of Teaching** to include public university faculty in its pension program helped transform state-supported universities into full-fledged research institutions. Van Hise participated in the 1908 **White House Conference on Conservation**, served on the **National Conservation Commission**, and wrote a popular college textbook on the topic. *See also* COMMONS, JOHN R.; EDUCATION; MC-CARTHY, CHARLES.

VARDAMAN, JAMES K. (1861–1930). Politician and **journalist**. The son of Texas planters, Vardaman grew up in Mississippi, where he became a lawyer and newspaper editor. An ardent champion of the **segregation** and **disfranchisement** of **African Americans**, he rose quickly in the state's **Democratic Party** through emotional appeals to white small landowners who felt threatened by local elites, national corporations, and blacks. Like other southern white demagogues such as **Benjamin Tillman**, he promoted reform, but only for whites. As governor (1904–8), Vardaman raised state appropriations for **education**, restricted corporations, abolished **convict leasing**, and advanced penal reform. Despite his racism, he also sought to prevent **lynching** and curb the power of the **Ku Klux Klan**. In the U.S. Senate (1913–19), Vardaman voted in favor of many **progressive** measures, including the **income tax**, **child labor** regulation, **women**'s **suffrage**, the **Federal Reserve Act** (1913), and the **Federal Trade Commission**. Having angered his constituents by resisting U.S. participation in World War I, he lost his seat in the election of 1918.

VAUDEVILLE. A popular form of public entertainment from the 1880s to the 1930s, vaudeville enjoyed its golden age in the early

20th century. Incorporating the older theatrical genres of minstrelsy and burlesque, vaudeville encompassed singing, dancing, comedy, striptease, acrobatics, and animal acts. Comic skits relied heavily on ethnic and sexist stereotypes that parodied the multiethnic, working-class milieu from which vaudeville sprang. Although audiences were **segregated**, black performers did what they called "white time" in white-owned shows, and some **African American** performers and all-black musical shows were very popular. Boston-based entrepreneur Benjamin F. **Keith** probably coined the term "vaudeville" in the 1880s as he cleaned up burlesque to broaden the audience, but the renamed shows retained risqué elements. Municipal governments frequently censored "immoral" acts that featured female partial nudity and sexual innuendo and sometimes arrested performers. Audiences remained mostly male, but this predominance may have reflected **women**'s greater domestic responsibilities and lower wages rather than any objection to the content.

Innovations such as continuous performances from mid-morning to late evening and low ticket prices compared to the "legitimate" theater expanded audiences. Moreover, like other businesses, vaudeville consolidated, forming four major circuits in the 1890s, three in the northeast and one in the west. By 1912, Keith and his partner, Edward Albee, had combined with the western Orpheum circuit to control some 700 theaters nationwide. Each circuit rotated acts through the theaters it controlled. As a result, even people living in small towns saw vaudeville on a regular basis, albeit with second- or third-string acts. About a million people attended vaudeville performances each week in the late 1890s. Initially, the industry's consolidation benefited actors by providing steady work and higher salaries, but soon vaudeville circuit managers tightened control over their workers. In 1906, Keith–Albee established the United Booking Office (UBO) to control both the theaters and the hiring of performers. Two efforts to form a performers' union (1910–11 and 1916–17) foundered on the shoals of the UBO's near monopoly.

While impresario Tony Pastor recruited legitimate stage stars for vaudeville, by the turn of the century vaudeville had its own stars. Some performers, such as comic duo Weber and Fields, dancer Bill "Bojangles" Robinson, and singer Eva Tanguay, commanded huge salaries and enjoyed national celebrity. Magician **Harry Houdini** got his start in vaudeville, as did **Mary Pickford** and dancer Ruth St. Denis. The inclusion of **Tin Pan Alley** songs in vaudeville skits was a key means of music promotion before widespread recording or radio broadcasting. By the 1910s, the **movies** challenged vaudeville's dominance. The movie industry had the great advantage that it was much easier and cheaper to ship a reel of film than to book and move actors through hundreds of theaters. Nevertheless, vaudeville persisted, and its format and many of its star performers made the transition to film and radio and to cabaret and musical stage shows. *See also* MUSIC; POPULAR CULTURE.

VEBLEN, THORSTEIN (1857–1929). Economist. Born in Wisconsin to a Norwegian **immigrant** family, Veblen grew up in Minnesota, graduated from Carleton College in 1880, studied at Johns Hopkins University, and earned a Ph.D. at Yale University in 1884. He worked on his father's farm until he obtained a fellowship at Cornell University (1891) and then taught political **economy** at the **University of Chicago** starting in 1892. Veblen's career flourished; he edited the *Journal of Political Economy* (1892–1905) and wrote two famous critiques of the American economy and the business class, *The Theory of the Leisure Class* (1899) and *The Theory of Business Enterprise* (1904). However, his unconventional private life outraged colleagues and led to his forced resignation in 1906. Veblen then taught at Stanford University for three years, but his affairs with women again led colleagues to demand his resignation. Despite these setbacks, he taught at the University of Missouri (1910–18) and helped found the New School for Social Research in New York City while writing *The Instinct of Workmanship* (1914) and *An Inquiry Into the Nature of Peace* (1917). His highly original writings reflected his hard-bitten rural upbringing and urged a more rational, even technocratic approach to the economy. Veblen is best known for introducing the term "conspicuous consumption" and championing the institutionalist approach to economics.

VEILLER, LAWRENCE T. (1872–1959). Housing reformer. Born in New Jersey, Veiller was a volunteer social worker at the University **Settlement** in New York City and the New York Charity Organization Society in 1890. While working as a plan examiner for the city building department, he decided housing was the key to social uplift. He established and directed the Charity Organization Society's Tenement House Committee (1898–1907) and rose to national attention as secretary of the New York State Tenement House Commission (1900–01). His reports and lobbying led the state legislature to pass the **Tenement House Act** (1901). Veiller founded and directed the **National Housing Association** (1911–36) and wrote numerous path-breaking articles and books on housing reform. *See also* RIIS, JACOB.

VERACRUZ INCIDENT. On 9 April 1914, in the midst of heightened tensions over President **Woodrow Wilson**'s meddling in the **Mexican Revolution**, Mexican soldiers seized a U.S. Navy boat loading supplies at Tampico. The sailors were soon released, but Admiral Henry T. Mayo, commanding the American fleet, demanded a formal apology and a 21-gun salute. Mexico offered the apology but refused the salute, providing the Wilson administration with an occasion to intervene, with the overall goal of blocking arms shipments to military dictator Victoriano Huerta and speeding Huerta's overthrow. The U.S. Navy seized the port of Veracruz on 21 April, at the cost of 19 Americans dead and 71 wounded and 126 Mexicans killed and around 200 wounded. Latin Americans were shocked, and European governments condemned Wilson for overreacting. With 7,000 U.S. forces occupying Mexico's chief port, the Wilson administration accepted an offer of mediation from Argentina, Brazil, and Chile (the ABC powers) with negotiations at Niagara Falls, Canada, from May to July. The collapse of Huerta's government in July 1914 and its replacement by a more acceptable regime under General Venustiano Carranza allowed the United States to claim success and withdraw in November of that year. *See also* FOREIGN POLICY; PERSHING EXPEDITION.

VILLA, PANCHO (1877–1923). *See* MEXICAN REVOLUTION; PERSHING EXPEDITION.

VILLARD, OSWALD GARRISON (1872–1949). *See* NATIONAL ASSOCIATION FOR THE ADVANCEMENT OF COLORED PEOPLE.

VOTING RIGHTS. *See* SUFFRAGE.

– W –

WAGNER, ROBERT F. (1877–1953). Politician. Born in Germany, Wagner emigrated in 1885 with his parents to New York City, where he graduated from the College of the City of New York (1898) and New York Law School (1900). He practiced law until, with **Tammany Hall** support, he was elected as a Democratic state assemblyman (1905–8) and a state senator (1908–18). As chairman of the **New York State Factory Investigating Commission** (1911–15), he and **Alfred E. Smith** oversaw wide-ranging state labor legislation that became a national model. Later, as a justice of the state supreme court (1919–26) and U.S. Senator (1927–49), Wagner emerged as the embodiment, alongside Smith, of **urban liberalism**. He was a key figure in the implementation of the New Deal in the 1930s.

WALD, LILLIAN (1867–1940). Nurse and reformer. Born to well-to-do **Jewish** parents in Ohio, Wald graduated from New York Hospital's **nursing** program (1890). In 1895, she and a colleague founded a **settlement house** initially known as the Nurses' Settlement but later called the Henry Street Settlement for its location. Here Wald launched the Visiting Nurses Service (VNS), which sent nurses into people's homes for only a small fee. By 1913, nearly 100 nurses made some 20,000 home visits annually; **Margaret Sanger** is perhaps the best known VNS nurse. Celebrated for her efforts to improve **education**, professional standards, and licensing for nurses, Wald also helped to found the **Women's Trade Union League** in 1903 and campaigned for **child labor** laws, creation of the **Children's Bureau**, and **women's suffrage**. A pacifist, she chaired the **American Union against Militarism** before U.S. entry into World War I, after which she served with the American Red Cross. *See also* LOWER EAST SIDE.

WALLING, WILLIAM ENGLISH (1877–1936). Journalist and reformer. Born in Louisville, Kentucky, Walling graduated from the **University of Chicago** (1897) and joined the **Hull House** staff while studying sociology with **John Dewey**. He later moved to New York City, worked with **Lillian Wald** at the Henry Street Settlement, and became an official of the **Women's Trade Union League**. In 1906, he married Anna Strunsky, a Russian **Jewish immigrant** and novelist. They became a famous "**socialist** couple," traveling to Russia in 1905 to report on the aborted revolution there. After witnessing and reporting on the 1908 **Springfield Riot**, he became a founder of the **National Association for the Advancement of Colored People**. Walling also wrote for *The Masses* at the invitation of his friend **Max Eastman**, but he quit the magazine and the **Socialist Party** in 1917 because, unlike most socialists, he supported U.S. entry into World War I. His marriage failed for the same reason. An early anticommunist, Walling worked in the 1920s with **Samuel Gompers** for the **American Federation of Labor**.

WALSH, DAVID I. (1872–1947). Politician. Born in Leominster, Massachusetts, the son of Irish Catholic **immigrants**, Walsh graduated from the College of the Holy Cross (1893) and Boston University Law School (1897). He served as a **Democratic** state representative (1900–01), lieutenant governor (1913–14), and governor of Massachusetts (1914–16). Overcoming **anti-Catholic** and nativist prejudices, Democratic **machine politics**, and the entrenched **Republican** control of the state, Walsh was the first Catholic Democrat elected governor and the first Irish Catholic elected to the U.S. Senate (1919–25, 1926–47) from Massachusetts. Walsh, like **Robert F. Wagner** and **Alfred E. Smith**, was an ethnic minority politician respected as a proponent of **urban liberalism**. *See also* FITZGERALD, JOHN FRANCIS.

WALSH, FRANK P. (1864–1939). *See* INDUSTRIAL RELATIONS, COMMISSION ON.

WARBURG, PAUL M. (1868–1932). Financier. Born in Hamburg, Germany, to a wealthy **Jewish** banking family, Warburg began his banking career in London and Paris. After marrying the American Nina Loeb, he moved to New York City in 1901 and became a partner in his father-in-law's Wall Street investment firm. A strong advocate of central banking, Warburg published essays in response to the **Panic of 1907** and provided advice to Senator **Nelson W. Aldrich**'s National Monetary Commission. His involvement with the creation of the **Federal Reserve** in 1913 led President **Woodrow Wilson** to appoint Warburg to the board, despite objections of anti–Wall Street **Democrats**. Vice governor of the board from 1916 to 1918, Warburg played a pivotal role in the central bank's development until clashes with Treasury Secretary **William McAdoo**, along with suspicions of his German connections, resulted in Warburg's leaving the board in 1918. High-minded and taciturn, Warburg became a target for anti-Semitic stereotypes and conspiracy theories regarding Jewish bankers. *See also* MONEY TRUST.

WARD, LESTER FRANK (1841–1913). Sociologist. Born in Illinois, Ward was raised in poverty on the Iowa frontier. He served in the Union Army during the Civil War and, after being wounded and discharged, worked for the Treasury Department (1865–81) while earning law and master's degrees from Columbian College (later George Washington University). His work with the U.S. Geological Survey (USGS; 1882–1905) sparked an interest in paleontology and sociology. His 1883 book, *Dynamic Sociology*, was a pioneer work in evolutionary sociology. Rebutting proponents of individualistic versions of **social Darwinism**, Ward proposed viewing humanity as an inventive species that progressed through deliberate cooperative action, an argument that made him renowned as a formative figure of **progressive** social science. Founding president of the American Sociological Society (1906–7), Ward left the USGS in 1905 for a professorship at Brown University, which he held until his death. *See also* INTELLECTUAL.

WAREHOUSE ACT (1916). Passed by Congress in August 1916, this act, which recalled the Populist Party's subtreasury idea of the 1890s, authorized the Secretary of Agriculture to license warehouses to receive and store cotton, grain, tobacco, and a few other major agricultural commodities. These storage facilities enabled farmers to market commodities throughout the year, not just at harvest times. They used warehouse receipts as currency to obtain credit or loans at lower interest rates on the security of staple crops. Congress expanded the system in 1923 and updated it numerous times thereafter. *See also* COOPERATIVES, FARMERS'; FEDERAL FARM LOAN ACT.

WASHINGTON, BOOKER TALIAFERRO (c. 1856–1915). Educator and politician. Born into slavery on a Virginia plantation, Washington moved after emancipation with his family to West Virginia, where as a boy he worked in the coal mines and domestic service. Encouraged by his mother, he taught himself to read and attended classes at a nearby school. At age 16, he scraped together money to take him by train, foot, and hitchhiking to Virginia's Hampton Institute, a school for former slaves. Working his way through Hampton, Washington found its emphasis on practical skills and personal rectitude congenial and became the protégé of its founder, Samuel Chapman Armstrong. After graduation (1875), Washington tried teaching, studied briefly for the ministry, and considered law until 1881, when Armstrong recommended him to head the new Alabama normal school for **African Americans** that became **Tuskegee Institute**.

Washington won the support of philanthropists **Andrew Carnegie**, George Eastman of the **Eastman Kodak** Company, and **John D. Rockefeller**, among others. His emphasis on character building and hard work, instead of political activism, and his refusal to openly challenge **segregation** and **disfranchisement** made him popular among whites, even in the South. The best known of his speeches on this subject is the famous "**Atlanta Compromise**" (1895). His autobiography, *Up from Slavery* (1901), and many other publications and public lectures spread the message to a multiracial audience. To encourage black economic success, he established the Tuskegee Negro Conferences for black farmers (1892) and the **National Negro Business League** (1900) for business owners. He gained the patronage of leading **Republicans**, including Presidents **William McKinley** and **Theodore Roosevelt**, who faced a firestorm of criticism for inviting Washington to dine at the White House in 1901. As a result of having friends in high places, Washington largely controlled minority political appointments until **Democrat Woodrow Wilson** took office in 1913; but he also refrained from criticizing his patrons, notably in the case of the **Brownsville Raid**.

Washington was a controversial figure among African Americans after 1900. **Ida B. Wells-Barnett, William Monroe Trotter**, and **W. E. B. Du Bois**, among others, criticized his political power, accommodationist agenda, and emphasis on **industrial education**. He used an extensive network of contacts along with covert part-ownership of black-owned newspapers to promote himself and Tuskegee while lambasting his opponents, a system they labeled the "Tuskegee Machine." Privately, he gave considerable sums to legal challenges to discriminatory laws in Alabama and supported **T. Thomas Fortune**'s *New York Age*, a staunch advocate of racial equality. His influence declined after the establishment of the **National Association for the Advancement of Colored People** in 1909, a development he worked hard to prevent. At his death in 1915, the school that had been a church-owned shack in 1881 had 200 faculty, 2,000 students, and an endowment of $2 million. *See also* EDUCATION; LYNCHING; RACE RIOTS.

WATSON, JOHN BROADUS (1878–1958). Psychologist. Born in North Carolina, Watson taught psychology at the **University of Chicago** (1903–8) and Johns Hopkins University (1908–20). In 1912, he turned from studying animal to human behavior. Rejecting theories of the unconscious mind in favor of the observation of behavior and physiological responses to stimuli, he became a leading exponent of **behaviorism**. By arguing that emotions resulted from conditioning and humans were so plastic they could be conditioned to eliminate a neurosis, he had a major impact on behavior therapy. His books include *Psychology from the Standpoint of a Behaviorist* (1919), *Behaviorism* (1925), and the very influential *Psychological Care of Infant and Child* (1928). Forced to leave Johns Hopkins in 1920 when he **divorced** to marry a student, Watson brought his insights to an **advertising** agency. Always hostile to religion, he was a controversial spokesman for experimental psychology.

WATSON, THOMAS E. (1856–1922). Politician. Born in Georgia, Watson attended Mercer University, studied law, and was admitted to the bar in 1875. In 1882, he was elected as a **Democrat** to the state legislature and in 1891 went to Congress as a Farmers' Alliance Democrat. Moving into the Populist Party, he advocated an alliance of downtrodden black and white farmers, to which white supremacist Democrats reacted with violence and fraud, contributing to his defeat for reelection in 1892 and 1894. In 1896, the Populists nominated him for vice president in a vain attempt to preserve their separate identity while backing Democrat **William Jennings Bryan**. Watson continued as an increasingly sour spokesman for a fading small party, whose presidential candidate he was in 1904. After publishing magazines and a newspaper, biographies of Thomas Jefferson (1903) and Andrew Jackson (1912), and an **anti-Catholic** book, *The Roman Catholic Hierarchy* (1910), he lost another bid for Congress in 1918 only to win a seat in the Senate in 1921. By the 1910s, the embittered Watson became infamous for diatribes against **African Americans, Jews,** and **socialists** and inciting the mob that lynched **Leo Frank**. *See also* LYNCHING; RACE RIOTS; SMITH, HOKE.

WEBB–KENYON ACT (1913). Sponsored by **Democratic** representative Edwin Webb of North Carolina and **Republican** senator William Kenyon of Iowa, this act prohibited shipping alcohol across state lines into areas where it was illegal by local or state ordinance. Without such a law, liquor manufacturers could circumvent local and state "dry" or anti-alcohol laws by shipping their products directly through the federal mail, with which states could not interfere. The **Anti-Saloon League**, which lobbied hard for the bill, saw its years of promoting the election of dry men to Congress pay off when, early in 1913, both houses passed the bill. President **William Howard Taft** vetoed it as unconstitutional, but Congress overrode the veto by a substantial margin. Its passage heralded the momentum in favor of nationwide **prohibition**. *See also* LOCAL OPTION.

WEBER, ADNA FERRIN (1870–1968). Urban studies pioneer. Born in upstate New York, Weber graduated from Cornell University (1894), studied in Berlin, and received a Ph.D. from Columbia University (1898). Weber's dissertation, *The Growth of Cities in the Nineteenth Century: A Study in Statistics* (1899), became a classic in American urban studies because of its careful documentation of urbanization—which he famously labeled one of the age's most remarkable social phenomena—and because of his book's emphasis on the huge implications of the shift toward an urban society. Weber continued to write on urban issues while working as a statistician for New York State from 1899 to 1921. Instrumental in promoting **workers' compensation** laws, he was a founding member of the **American Association for Labor Legislation** in 1900. *See also* PARK, ROBERT E.

***WEEKS v. UNITED STATES* (1914).** In this landmark case, the **U.S. Supreme Court** ruled unanimously that the Fourth Amendment protects Americans from all unreasonable searches and seizures by federal officers and excludes evidence obtained illegally without a warrant from federal courts. Justice William R. Day, writing for the court, found unconstitutional the police search of the defendant's home; this decision was the first application of the exclusionary rule. However, state officials continued to perform unreasonable searches and seizures, and state courts admitted evidence obtained without warrant, sometimes providing such evidence to federal officials, until 1961.

WELFARE CAPITALISM. Originating in the Progressive Era, welfare capitalism was the idea that company benevolence, not **labor unions**, would protect workers from the ravages of capitalism. Participating employers offered benefits such as housing, recreation, health care, credit unions, pensions, paid vacations, profit sharing, and company stock. White-collar workers received these benefits first, and only gradually were other workers encouraged to participate. Such programs existed mainly at large, nonunion companies in the Northeast and Midwest. Few employees worked or lived long enough to enjoy the pensions, but this approach marked a new era in labor relations and tended to prevent strikes and reduce turnover. **American Federation of Labor** unions often opposed employer welfare programs, regarding such benefits as proper subjects of labor negotiations. Contrasting with the cynicism with which labor activists tended to view such schemes was the almost utopian zeal with which employers such as **National Cash Register** in Dayton and **Filene's** in Boston pursued them. *See also* AMERICAN TELEPHONE AND TELEGRAPH; EASTMAN KODAK; FIVE-DOLLAR DAY; SCIENTIFIC MANAGEMENT.

WELLS-BARNETT, IDA B. (1862–1931). Journalist and civil rights activist. Born into slavery in Mississippi, Wells-Barnett became the sole support of four siblings at age 16, when **yellow fever** killed her parents and another sibling. She taught in the Memphis, Tennessee, public schools from 1883 to 1891 and wrote for black-owned newspapers. When her criticism of the school board led to her ouster in 1891, she worked full-time for the *Memphis Free Speech and Headlight*, of which she was also part-owner and editor. Her dismissal from teaching was not Wells-Barnett's first confrontation with authorities. In 1884, she refused a train conductor's order to leave the first-class "ladies' car," for which she had bought a ticket, to sit in the smoking car with other **African Americans**. When he threw her off the train, she sued the railroad for violating her civil rights—and won, though the Tennessee Supreme Court overturned the decision in 1887.

Gaining prominence as a **journalist**, Wells-Barnett spoke out for civil and political equality and eventually criticized the accommodationism of **Booker T. Washington**. In 1892, whites lynched three of her friends for the crime of running a successful grocery store that drew business away from a white-owned shop. When white officials failed to punish the killers, Wells-Barnett published extensive research demonstrating that, contrary to the claims of whites, **lynching** did not punish blacks for rapes of white **women** or other incendiary crimes; rather, black assertiveness and economic success provoked most lynchings. She organized a successful streetcar boycott and encouraged nearly 2,000 of her neighbors to emigrate to Oklahoma. She also wrote editorials condemning lynching, including one accusing white men of using the myth of the black rape of white women to conceal consensual sexual relations between white women and black men. This editorial led a mob of Memphis whites to shut down the newspaper. White newspapers published editorials calling for castration, torture, and lynching of the unnamed author, whom they assumed to be male. It is likely that only Wells' absence from Memphis at this moment saved her life, and she did not return to the South until 1922. She moved to New York City, where she wrote for **T. Thomas Fortune**'s *New York Age* and published *Southern Horrors* (1892), the first in a series of vivid pamphlets detailing white southern atrocities toward blacks. Her lecture tours in England and Scotland galvanized public opinion and may have contributed to a decline in lynching.

In 1895, Wells-Barnett married lawyer Ferdinand Barnett, with whom she and Frederick Douglass had published a protest against the **segregation** at the Columbian **Exposition**. Settling in Chicago, she edited a newspaper, continued to agitate against lynching, and helped found the **National Association of Colored Women** (1896) and the **National Association for the Advancement of Colored People** (1910). She participated in numerous civic and political causes, including organizing assistance for participants in the **Great Migration**. *See also* RACE RIOTS.

WESTERN FEDERATION OF MINERS (WFM). This radical **labor union** had its roots in the efforts of the Knights of Labor to organize hard-rock miners in the Rocky Mountain West. Responding to chronic, bitter battles between miners and mine owners as well as the depression of the 1890s, miners founded the WFM that year in Butte, Montana, the company town of **Anaconda Copper**. Violent conflicts in Leadville and **Cripple Creek** in Colorado and **Coeur d'Alene** in Idaho during the 1890s put the WFM on the front lines of a struggle against the growing power of corporations.

At first, the WFM operated within the bounds of the trade unionism espoused by the **American Federation of Labor**, focusing on improving wages and mine safety, cutting hours, and providing health and other benefits. In part responding to WFM activity, several western states enacted mine safety and inspection laws and, despite inadequacies in the laws and their enforcement, fatality rates fell significantly as mines improved ventilation, installed better equipment, and hired better-trained technicians to operate it. Although the WFM exercised considerable power over hiring and wages in the 1890s, it lost ground after 1900 as mining corporations grew larger, more organized, and more politically aggressive. The companies' growing power and the willingness of state governments to use militia and police against strikes encouraged union members to turn to **socialism**. Meanwhile, various disagreements prompted the WFM to break with the AFL in 1897. Growing more radical, the union in 1900 declared its opposition to the wage labor system, calling for the cooperative operation of industry and the public ownership of the means of production. WFM-led efforts to establish an alternative to the AFL culminated in founding the **Industrial Workers of the World (IWW)** in 1905. At the same time that radical WFM men like **"Big Bill" Haywood** became IWW stalwarts, other members continued to work within the mainstream political system and opposed the union's radical turn. Under pressure from moderates, the WFM broke with the IWW in 1907, and by 1911 it rejoined the AFL.

WESTINGHOUSE ELECTRIC COMPANY. This corporation originated in the Westinghouse Air Brake Company that George Westinghouse (1846–1914) founded in Pittsburgh in 1869. By 1886, he established the new company to produce transformers, dynamos, motors, alternating current (AC) power systems, and other equipment used at the Niagara Falls power plant and the rapid transit systems in New York City. The company, with Charles Steinmetz and **Nicola Tesla**, pioneered in the use of AC power in the United States. Although Westinghouse lost control of the company in 1907, he remained its president until he retired in 1911. *See* ELECTRICITY AND ELECTRIFICATION; GENERAL ELECTRIC COMPANY.

WEYL, WALTER E. (1873–1919). Economist and **journalist**. Born in Philadelphia, the son of German **Jewish** immigrants, Weyl graduated from the University of Pennsylvania's Wharton School (1892) and studied in Paris and Berlin. In 1896, he earned a Ph.D. at the Wharton School, publishing his dissertation, *The Passenger Traffic of Railways*, the following year. During the 1902 **Anthracite Coal Strike**, he helped **John Mitchell**, leader of the **United Mine Workers**, to write *Organized Labor: Its Problems, Purposes, and Ideals* (1903). He also wrote articles on **immigration**, and his *The New Democracy* (1912) was hailed as a powerful statement of **progressive** politics and ideas. Weyl was a founding editor of the *New Republic* in 1914. During World War I, he toured Germany and Russia to research the causes and problems of the war and published *American World Policies* (1917) and *The End of the War* (1918). *See also* CROLY, HERBERT D.; LIPPMANN, WALTER; STRAIGHT, WILLARD D.

WHARTON, EDITH (1862-1937). Novelist. Born into New York City's aristocracy, Edith Newbold Jones was educated privately in New York and Europe. Her unhappy marriage with Boston banker Edward Wharton ended in **divorce** in 1913. Like her friend **Henry James**, she lived in self-imposed exile in Europe, financially independent and writing for her own satisfaction. Her novels, *The House of Mirth* (1905), *The Custom of the Country* (1913), and the **Pulitzer**

Prize–winning *The Age of Innocence* (1920), are well-crafted, ironic, and subtle depictions of the social conventions of New York society. She also explored social and moral constraints in rural Massachusetts, where she spent summers, in *Ethan Frome* (1911) and *Summer* (1917). Best known for her novels, she also wrote about interior design and landscaping. Wharton was awarded the Cross of the Legion by the French government for her services in World War I, which included the pro-Allied book *Fighting France* (1915) and two novels, *The Marne* (1918) and *A Son at the Front* (1923). She published a revealing autobiography, *A Backward Glance*, in 1934. *See also* LITERATURE; REALISM.

WHEELER, WAYNE BIDWELL (1869–1927). Prohibitionist. Born in Ohio, Wheeler graduated from Oberlin College (1895) and earned his law degree there three years later. An organizer for the **Anti-Saloon League (ASL)**, he advanced rapidly up the ranks and played a major role in turning Ohio into a **prohibition** stronghold. In 1915, Wheeler worked in the ASL's Washington, D.C., office as general counsel and legislative superintendent. In this position, he helped to draft the Volstead Act that implemented the **Eighteenth Amendment**. Placing his faith in strict laws and their enforcement, he repeatedly clashed with **Ernest Cherrington**, who favored education and individual persuasion.

WHITE, EDWARD DOUGLASS, JR. (1845–1921). Chief Justice of the **U.S. Supreme Court**. Born in Louisiana to a wealthy sugar-growing family, White served in the Confederate Army during the Civil War and then became a lawyer and **Democratic** politician. Elected to the Senate in 1891, he resigned this office in 1894 when President Grover Cleveland appointed him to the Supreme Court. In 1910, President **William Howard Taft** appointed him chief justice (1910–21). A relative moderate on a somewhat conservative court, White wrote over 900 opinions and is best known for applying the **rule of reason** in the **Standard Oil** and American Tobacco **antitrust** cases.

WHITE, STANFORD (1853–1906). Architect. Born in New York City, the son of a noted scholar and literary critic, White studied with Henry Hobson Richardson and **Augustus Saint-Gaudens** and in 1879 formed the famous McKim, Mead, and White firm in New York. Charismatic and ostentatious, White became the firm's star, with designs that included the enormous shingled Casino in Newport, Rhode Island (1881), New York's Washington Square Arch (1892), and the *New York Herald* building (1894). He designed Madison Square Garden (1889) with his own apartment at the top, where the architect held extravagant dinners and pursued affairs with young women, including one in 1901 with model Evelyn Nesbit, only 16 at the time. On 25 June 1906, Nesbit's husband, the jealous playboy Harry K. Thaw, shot White at the Madison Square Garden rooftop theater, leading to a sensational murder trial. *See also* ARCHITECTURE.

WHITE, WILLIAM ALLEN (1868–1944). Journalist. Born in Emporia, Kansas, White attended the University of Kansas and worked as a reporter before purchasing the *Emporia Gazette* in 1895. His editorials, reprinted across the nation, made him a rural spokesman for progressivism in the **Republican Party**. Dubbed the Sage of Emporia, he ridiculed populism in a famous August 1896 editorial, "What's the Matter with Kansas?" In 1906, White joined **muckrakers Ray Stannard Baker**, **Lincoln Steffens**, and **Ida M. Tarbell** to publish the *American Magazine*. A friend of **Theodore Roosevelt**, White endorsed TR's **Progressive Party** in 1912. White's posthumously published *Autobiography* (1946) provides an inside account of Progressive Era **journalism**.

WHITE HOUSE CONFERENCE ON CONSERVATION (1908). President **Theodore Roosevelt** sponsored this meeting at the White House on 13–15 May 1908, following the suggestion of conservationists **Gifford Pinchot** and W. J. McGee. State governors or their delegates, **Supreme Court** justices, cabinet members, and experts met to make **conservation** of natural resources and preservation of natural wonders and historic sites a national priority. Roosevelt increased attention for the conference by inviting celebrities as representatives of the public, including **William Jennings Bryan**, **James J. Hill**, **John Mitchell**, and **Andrew Carnegie**. Among this meeting's recommendations was the creation of a **National Conservation Commission**

to inventory natural resources and create a comprehensive policy for resource management. *See also* ANTIQUITIES ACT; FOREST SERVICE, U.S.

WHITE PRIMARY. In the late 19th century, the **Democratic Party** in most southern states prevented **African Americans** and in some places Latinos from voting in primary elections, which traditionally were more like mass meetings than elections. In the overwhelmingly Democratic South, winning the primary was tantamount to victory in the general election. By 1915, all southern states adopted **direct primary** laws, which implicitly or explicitly gave legal sanction to the exclusion of black voters from primaries. In the 1927 decision in *Nixon v. Herndon*, the **U.S. Supreme Court** ruled that a Texas law barring African Americans and Latinos from voting in party primaries violated the Fourteenth Amendment, but the court permitted state party organizations as ostensibly private clubs to determine who could vote in primaries. The white primary remained common until the Supreme Court banned it in 1944. *See also* DISFRANCHISEMENT.

WHITE SLAVERY. In the 1880s, a panic about **prostitution** swept through England and the United States. Among white middle-class Americans, the notion developed that **immigrant** procurers had created a nationwide network to drug and kidnap innocent, young white **women** to force them into prostitution—in short, to make them "white slaves." The notion of a prostitution trust wildly exaggerated the business's scope and organization during this era. Poverty, family instability, and the narrow range and low wages of jobs open to women led most sex workers to their trade, not pimps and drugs. In the United States, documented instances of trafficking in women were rare. Moreover, the "white" in this term emphasized the innocence of white women as opposed to the assumed promiscuity of women of color, especially **African Americans** and Chinese. In response to this white slavery scare, efforts increased to eradicate prostitution through **red-light abatement** ordinances, police raids, and anti-soliciting laws. The most notable outcome of the panic was the **Mann Act** (1910), which involved the federal government in combating what had been a local law enforcement issue.

WHITLOCK, BRAND (1869–1934). Journalist and diplomat. Born in Ohio, Whitlock was educated privately, became a reporter for the *Chicago Herald*, and often covered **baseball**. By 1894, he had become a lawyer, practicing in Illinois and Ohio until 1905. Influenced by his friends, Illinois governor John P. Altgeld and Toledo mayor **Samuel M. Jones**, Whitlock became interested in urban **progressive** reform. He was legal adviser to Jones, whom he succeeded as mayor of Toledo (1905–11). Disillusioned, he returned to writing and the law until President **Woodrow Wilson** appointed him as ambassador to Belgium (1913–22), a position that put him in the middle of World War I's stormy diplomacy. He also wrote novels, *The Thirteenth District* (1902) and *The Turn of the Balance* (1907); his autobiography, *Forty Years of It* (1914); and *Belgium, a Personal Narrative* (1919).

WHITNEY, WILLIS R. (1868–1958). Chemist. Born in New York, Whitney graduated from the Massachusetts Institute of Technology (MIT; 1890), taught there for four years, and received his Ph.D. in chemistry from the University of Leipzig (1896). Returning to MIT, he did pioneering work in electrochemistry before accepting an offer in 1900 from the **General Electric Company** to establish and direct the first **industrial research laboratory** for basic research in the United States. He held this position for 32 years and was lauded for achievements in lighting, X-rays, and electrical fever therapy. Though often underfunded, his laboratory produced remarkable improvements in **electricity** and electronics.

WICKERSHAM, GEORGE W. (1858–1936). Lawyer and public official. Born in Pittsburgh, Wickersham earned a law degree at the University of Pennsylvania (1880) and practiced corporate law in Philadelphia (1880–83) and New York City (1883–1909). President **William Howard Taft** appointed him U.S. attorney general in 1909. Over the next four years, he oversaw an unprecedented number of **antitrust** cases, pursuing successful suits against the **American Tobacco** and **Standard Oil** companies but failing against **United States Steel** and **International Harvester**. Wickersham also wrote a bill to strengthen the **Interstate Commerce Commission**, which Congress passed as the **Mann–Elkins Act** (1910). He served briefly in President **Woodrow Wilson**'s administration and headed a commission during Herbert Hoover's presidency on the problems of enforcing **prohibition**. *See also* RULE OF REASON; *STANDARD OIL V. UNITED STATES*.

WILD WEST SHOWS. This genre of popular spectacles originated with former U.S. Army scout William "Buffalo Bill" Cody, who in 1883 launched Buffalo Bill's Wild West show to capitalize on his fame and public fascination with the period's warfare between the United States and **Native Americans**. The show became an international hit, spending several seasons in Europe and performing in London for Queen Victoria's 1887 jubilee. The show's performances at the 1893 Columbian **Exposition** enhanced its domestic reputation. Cody kept his show on the road for about 30 years and inspired many competitors. Wild West shows featured displays of riding and calf roping, feats of marksmanship, and reenactments of battles between Native Americans and settlers or the U.S. Army. The shows featured as performers noted Indian warriors, including Sitting Bull, Red Shirt, and Luther Standing Bear. Missionaries and the Bureau of Indian Affairs discouraged Indians' participation, but Native performers preferred making a living with their hunting, riding, and fighting skills while traveling widely and gaining allies for their peoples. Along with the novels of **Owen Wister**, the paintings of **Frederic Remington**, and western **movies**, these shows memorialized a heroic, vanishing West that obscured that region's rapid colonization, resource exploitation, and its racial and ethnic diversity and conflict. *See also* POPULAR CULTURE.

WILEY, HARVEY W. (1844–1930). Chemist. Born in Indiana, Wiley earned a medical degree then studied chemistry at Harvard University and in Germany in the 1870s. After teaching at Purdue University and serving as Indiana state chemist, he became chief chemist of the U.S. Department of Agriculture (1883–1912). During his tenure, Wiley increased the staff from six to 500 and expanded the chemical analysis of agricultural crops and adulterated food products. Aided by **muckraking journalists** and **Upton Sinclair**'s novel *The Jungle* (1906), he lobbied Congress to pass the **Pure Food and Drug** and **Meat Inspection Acts** (both 1906). Wiley wrote a column for *Good Housekeeping* magazine (1912–29), lectured widely, taught agricultural chemistry at George Washington University (1899–1914), and published books on agriculture and food adulteration. *See also* PUBLIC HEALTH.

WILLARD, FRANCES ELIZABETH CAROLINE (1839–1898). *See* WOMAN'S CHRISTIAN TEMPERANCE UNION.

***WILLIAMS V. MISSISSIPPI* (1898).** This **U.S. Supreme Court** case arose over the murder conviction of Henry Williams, an **African American**, by an all-white jury in 1896. Williams appealed, arguing that the Fourteenth Amendment forbade the exclusion of blacks from juries. In April 1898, the Supreme Court ruled 9–0 against Williams, on the grounds that the plaintiff had not sufficiently demonstrated discriminatory intent in the administration of Mississippi's **literacy tests** and **poll taxes**, the means by which blacks had been excluded from juries. This decision gave federal judicial sanction to the **disfranchisement** of African Americans, as long as state laws to accomplish this end worked by subterfuge rather than explicit discrimination.

WILMINGTON RIOT (1898). One of several major **race riots** in the Progressive Era, this riot began with whites' protest against **African American** domination of the government of this North Carolina city, in which blacks were a majority. When a black newspaper editor refused to leave Wilmington with his press, a white mob torched the building and killed 10 local African Americans. The city's elected officials resigned and were replaced by white **Democrats**. This riot was one of the decisive events in the campaign to impose Jim Crow in North Carolina. By 1902, the all-white Democratic Party had **disfranchised** black men and enforced **segregation** of public facilities. *See also* ATLANTA RIOT; LYNCHING; NEW ORLEANS RIOT.

WILSON, HENRY LANE (1859–1932). *See* MEXICAN REVOLUTION.

WILSON, JAMES (1835–1920). Politician. Born in Scotland, Wilson immigrated to the United States with his parents in 1852. After graduating from Iowa College, he was a teacher, farmer, and editor of the

Agricultural Digest. A **Republican** state representative (1867–71), he was elected to the House of Representatives (1873–77, 1883–85). He also served as state railroad commissioner (1878–83) and taught at Iowa Agricultural College while directing its agricultural experiment station (1891–97). As secretary of agriculture for presidents **William McKinley**, **Theodore Roosevelt**, and **William Howard Taft** (1897–1913), he oversaw major expansion of **cooperative** extensions, farm demonstrations, and other federal agriculture programs.

WILSON, THOMAS WOODROW (1856–1924). Political scientist and president of the United States. Born in Virginia, Wilson graduated from Princeton University (1879) and studied law at the University of Virginia before his admission to the bar in 1882. He earned a Ph.D. in government at Johns Hopkins University (1886) and taught at Bryn Mawr (1885–88) and Wesleyan University (1888–90). Returning to Princeton, he was a professor of jurisprudence and political **economy** (1890–1902) and president of the university (1902–10). Wilson was a popular and eloquent teacher, and as president he instituted liberal reforms, though his attempt to democratize the elitist eating club system was thwarted. His prolific writings on government, history, and public affairs made him widely known for explicating academic political science issues to the general public.

With the support of George B. M. Harvey, a New York publisher, and James Smith, **boss** of the state **Democratic Party** machine, Wilson was elected governor of New Jersey in 1910. Breaking with **machine politics** and his own prior conservative inclinations, he advocated an **employer liability law**, the **direct primary**, a corrupt practices law, and reorganization of the state public **utilities** commission. This record earned him the Democratic nomination for president in 1912 after a prolonged convention fight. Against a divided opposition in this dramatic election, he won with 41.9 percent of the popular vote over **Republican** incumbent **William H. Taft** (23.2 percent), **Progressive Party** candidate **Theodore Roosevelt** (27.4), and **Socialist Eugene V. Debs** (6). Reflecting his southern background and allegiances, on taking office Wilson openly sanctioned for the first time racial **segregation** in federal offices in Washington, D.C. On other fronts, he achieved notable success in implementing the reform program labeled the **New Freedom** during his campaign. Working closely with a Democratic Congress, he achieved long-sought tariff reforms, founded the **Federal Reserve** and the **Federal Trade Commission**, and signed the **Clayton Antitrust Act**. His administration also oversaw a variety of innovations in federal labor protection, aid to agriculture, and federal support for public works.

In **foreign policy**, Wilson disavowed the expansionism of Roosevelt, as well as Taft's **dollar diplomacy**. But his belief in America's mission to spread its ideals, whether people wanted them or not, inclined him to be at least as interventionist as his predecessors. His clumsy attempts to guide the **Mexican Revolution** achieved little other than reinforcing Mexico's suspicions about the United States. Continuing the pattern established by earlier presidents of asserting U.S. power in the Caribbean, Wilson sent troops to **Haiti** (1915), the **Dominican Republic** (1916), and **Cuba** (1917). In Asia, Wilson repudiated the Taft administration's dollar diplomacy in China.

When World War I began in Europe in 1914, Woodrow Wilson proclaimed American neutrality but gradually drifted toward tacit support for Britain and France, especially after a series of clashes with Germany over submarine warfare. Though doubtful of his ability to avoid war, he campaigned for reelection in 1916 on the slogan "He kept us out of war," even as public opinion grew increasingly hostile to Germany. Wilson narrowly won a second term, earning 49.4 percent of the popular vote (277 electoral votes) to 46.2 percent (254 electoral votes) for the Republican **Charles Evans Hughes**. Unable to mediate between the belligerent nations, Wilson broke diplomatic relations with Germany in early 1917, when the Germans resumed their unrestricted U-boat warfare. In urging Congress to declare war on Germany in April 1917, Wilson eloquently if ambitiously proclaimed that the United States would fight for the expansion of democracy, rather than the narrow national interests pursued by the other belligerents.

Although pacifists, **socialists**, and Americans of German and Irish descent opposed U.S. entry into the war, Wilson's speeches rallied public opinion in favor of intervention. During the war, the president assumed the role of a moral leader while overseeing an unprecedented mobilization of men and resources that broke the German war effort. His Fourteen Points (1918) became the basis for the peace negotiations ending in an armistice signed on 11 November 1918.

However, Wilson squandered his influence at home and abroad with a series of blunders, and he failed to persuade the European powers or American politicians to accept his idealistic policies. He was felled by a stroke in 1919 while campaigning for ratification of the peace treaty and U.S. membership in the League of Nations. Led by the chairman of the Senate Foreign Relations Committee, Republican **Henry Cabot Lodge**, the Senate twice rejected the treaty, even as Wilson was awarded the Nobel Peace Prize in December 1919. The president retired to a new home in Washington after his term ended and lived quietly his last few years. *See also* EDUCATION; INTERNATIONALISM; VERACRUZ INCIDENT.

WILSON, WILLIAM B. (1862–1934). Labor leader and politician. Born in Scotland, Wilson came to Pennsylvania with his family in 1870 and worked as a coal miner (1871–1898), becoming secretary-treasurer of the **United Mine Workers** in 1900, a position he held for eight years before being elected as a **Democrat** to the House of Representatives (1907–13). President **Woodrow Wilson** appointed him the first secretary of labor (1913–21), making him a hero to the **labor union** movement. In this position, he oversaw the many experiments in federal labor regulation of the Wilson years. *See also* LABOR, U.S. DEPARTMENT OF.

WINNING PLAN. This phrase named the strategy pronounced in 1915 by **National American Woman Suffrage Association (NAWSA)** president **Carrie Chapman Catt** for achieving **women**'s **suffrage** within five years. The plan centralized control over the movement, enabled the national leadership to determine where and when to hold state-level campaigns, and turned the organization's energies toward winning suffrage at the federal level. Catt's plan enhanced the power of the professional staff and diminished the role of the general membership in decision making. Aided by World War I, NAWSA achieved its goal even faster than Catt anticipated. By 1919, Congress sent the **Nineteenth Amendment** to the states, three-fourths of which ratified it a year later.

WISCONSIN IDEA. Articulated in 1904 by **Charles Van Hise**, president of the University of Wisconsin, and explained in **Charles**

McCarthy's 1912 book of this name, this notion called for the state **university** to take an active role in public policy and public service. A typically **progressive** view, this notion supported policy experimentation and activist government. In addition to establishing a strong adult **education** program, the university encouraged faculty to lend their expertise to the formulation and implementation of laws and regulations. Professors such as **John R. Commons** and **Richard Ely** contributed to progressive causes with which the state and its leading politician, **Robert La Follette**, were identified, including civil service reform, **utilities** regulation, labor reform, tax reform, and electoral reform. Less visibly but influentially, scholars also applied the findings of science to improve agriculture and industry. Many other public universities also implemented such programs. *See also* MODERNIZATION; ORGANIZATIONAL SYNTHESIS.

WISE, STEPHEN S. (1874–1949). Clergyman. Born in Budapest, Hungary, Wise came to New York City with his family in 1875, graduated from City College of New York (1892), and received a Ph.D. from Columbia University (1901). Ordained a rabbi in 1893, he led congregations in New York City and Portland, Oregon, before founding the Free Synagogue in New York in 1907, where he remained the rest of his life. The leading Reform rabbi of his generation, the charismatic Wise helped invigorate this movement in the face of challenges from the new Conservative movement and the mass **immigration** of Eastern European Orthodox **Jews**. Active in the Zionist movement as well as Jewish **education**, he was involved with secular causes such as **child labor** and the campaign against New York's **Tammany Hall**. He argued for a **pluralist** vision of Judaism's role in American society, rather than **Americanization**.

WISTER, OWEN (1860–1938). Author. The son of well-to-do Pennsylvanians, Wister graduated from Harvard University (1882), where he became friends with **Theodore Roosevelt**. After studying music in Paris, Wister in 1885 traveled to Wyoming looking for a cure for his frequently poor health. He returned east and earned a Harvard law degree in 1888. While practicing law in Philadelphia, he wrote western stories and novels, becoming nationally known for *The Virginian* (1902), a bestseller credited with setting standards for the western novel. Wister's western heroes exemplify aristocratic, Anglo-Saxon, chivalrous, masculine virtues as much as cowboy grit. His writings regularly deplore the degrading effects of urbanization and industrialization, and he served as vice president of the **Immigration Restriction League**. *See also* REMINGTON, FREDERIC; STRENUOUS LIFE.

WOBBLIES. *See* INDUSTRIAL WORKERS OF THE WORLD.

WOMAN'S CHRISTIAN TEMPERANCE UNION (WCTU). This antiliquor organization began in Ohio in 1873. **Women** across the nation soon adopted the Ohio group's direct action techniques, marching into **saloons**, praying and singing hymns outside them, dumping barrels of alcohol, and forcing shops and bars to close. **Carry Nation** was the most notorious practitioner of such direct action. Formalized as the WCTU in 1874, it quickly became the single largest women's organization in the United States; every state had at least one branch. Under its second president, Frances Willard (1839–98), it grew into a sophisticated and powerful political organization. In the 1880s, Willard led the organization to adopt her "do everything" motto and endorse women's **suffrage** while lobbying as well for penal reform, **industrial education**, **Americanization**, abolition of **prostitution**, and many other issues. In Chicago, it ran homeless shelters, day nurseries, Sunday schools, a free medical clinic, and a low-cost restaurant. Its publishing company produced hundreds of thousands of anti-alcohol tracts, a pioneering model of both issue advocacy and **public health** education.

A critical training ground for female activists, the WCTU welcomed women of all races but typically organized them into **segregated** locals. **Lugenia Burns Hope** and **Susan La Flesche Picotte** were among many women who began reform careers in the WCTU. Men and children also participated in auxiliary groups, indicating their support for temperance by taking the "cold water" pledge. In keeping with the overall atmosphere in the temperance movement, the WCTU remained a largely Protestant organization. Willard's efforts to reach out to **socialists**, populists, Catholics, and other reformers and dissenters sparked considerable dissension and even a split for a time.

The WCTU's program for ending alcohol consumption steadily expanded from its initial focus on individual abstinence to include legal **prohibition**. Despite internal quarrels, the organization wielded considerable political power even though women could not vote in most elections. Members convinced state legislators to mandate temperance instruction in the public schools by 1902. Along with the **Anti-Saloon League**, the WCTU's local activists convinced many city, county, and state officials to enact **local option** laws. These "dry" laws restricted or banned alcohol production and distribution for about half of the nation's population by 1913, especially in rural western and southern areas. In short, the WCTU played a significant role in making possible the **Eighteenth Amendment**. The World WCTU, founded in the 1880s, launched the joint campaign for temperance and women's rights throughout Europe and the colonial empires. *See also* REFORM MOVEMENTS.

WOMEN. At the turn of the 20th century, women faced changing circumstances that varied by class, race, region, nativity, age, and marital status. Growing numbers of young, single women entered the workforce, increasingly as factory operatives and pieceworkers rather than domestic servants. As clerical jobs opened to women, more girls went to **high school** and took business courses to become clerks, while better-off white women attended colleges and coeducational universities in growing numbers, and a few entered the professions. **Department stores**, **cosmetics**, and beauty salons were among the businesses offering women entrepreneurial and managerial opportunities; women also came to dominate **nursing**, teaching, social work, and librarianship in this era, and **home economics** offered some a route into scientific careers.

Especially among middle-class white and black women, the idea of **municipal housekeeping** sustained a large-scale expansion of women's political activism through organizations such as the **Woman's Christian Temperance Union**, the **General Federation of Women's Clubs**, the **National Association of Colored Women**, the **National American Woman Suffrage Association**, the **National Congress of Mothers**, the **National Consumers' League**, and the **Women's Trade Union League (WTUL)**, and others. Women founded and staffed numerous **settlement houses** and participated in movements for **prohibition, suffrage,** the **Americanization** of **Native Americans** and **immigrants,** banning **child labor, conservation,** penal reform, **juvenile** justice, the prevention of **lynching,** public **education,** eradication of **prostitution, public health,** arbitration, and many other Progressive Era causes. Middle-class white women played a major role in founding and staffing the agencies of the emerging welfare state as social workers, police and prison matrons, physicians, nurses, researchers, and administrators. The **Children's Bureau** (1912) was the highest-level agency of this kind.

Women also made inroads into the labor movement via strikes like the **Uprising of the Twenty Thousand,** while a few women gained leadership positions in organizations such as the **International Ladies' Garment Workers' Union.** More leaders rose through the rank of the WTUL. A few women gained prominence in the Populist and **Socialist** Parties as orators and officers, but the lack of the right to vote limited their influence, as it did in the mainstream **Republican** and **Democratic** parties.

Despite the illegality of **birth control** and fears of **race suicide** among middle-class, native-born whites, birth rates fell during this period among all social groups, although unevenly according to region, race, ethnicity, and nativity; they fell fastest among middle-class black women. As laws governing **divorce** eased, women flocked to the courts to demand release from failed marriages. Women's growing, if fragile, economic autonomy and the proliferation of commercial entertainments such as **dance halls, movies,** and **amusement parks** made many people fear—and a few **feminists** and **Greenwich Village** bohemians celebrate—radical changes in **sexuality.**

Immigration and migration from rural to urban areas, including the **Great Migration** of **African Americans,** transformed the circumstances of millions of women. The new **chain stores,** department stores, and **mail-order** catalogs offered a wide array of mass-produced goods and packaged foods that were also **advertised** in the **mass-circulation magazines. Electricity,** indoor plumbing, and the appearance of new home appliances gradually reduced the manual labor housewives performed. *See also* ADDAMS, JANE; AMERICAN ASSOCIATION OF UNIVERSITY WOMEN; BURNS, LUCY; CATT, CARRIE CHAPMAN; EASTMAN, CRYSTAL; GILMAN, CHARLOTTE PERKINS; GOLDMAN, EMMA; KELLEY, FLOR-

ENCE; LATHROP, JULIA CLIFFORD; NEW WOMAN; PAUL,
ALICE; RICHARDS, ELLEN SWALLOW; SANGER, MARGA-
RET; SHAW, ANNA HOWARD; UNIVERSITY; WALD, LIL-
LIAN; WELLS-BARNETT, IDA B.; YOUNG, ELLA FLAGG.

WOMEN'S SUFFRAGE. *See* NATIONAL AMERICAN WOMAN
SUFFRAGE ASSOCIATION; NATIONAL WOMAN'S PARTY;
NINETEENTH AMENDMENT; SUFFRAGE; WINNING PLAN;
WOMEN.

WOMEN'S TRADE UNION LEAGUE (WTUL). Founded in 1903,
the WTUL brought together well-to-do and working-class **women** to
address problems facing female wage workers. Despite rapid growth
in female factory employment, the **American Federation of Labor**
refused to organize women. Indeed, one of the central tenets of the
mainstream **labor union** movement was the "family wage," the idea
that men should earn enough that wives and daughters do not have to
work for wages. Organizer **Mary Kenney O'Sullivan** enlisted prominent reformers, such as **Grace Abbott**, **Jane Addams**, **Sophonisba
Breckinridge**, **Mary Eliza McDowell**, **Vida Dutton Scudder**, and
Lillian Wald, to form a group dedicated to the interests of working
women. Sympathetic men like **William English Walling** were also
supporters. Working-class leaders such as **Leonora O'Reilly**, **Rose
Schneiderman**, and **Pauline Newman** found the WTUL a base for
their activism, though they often disagreed with their well-to-do "allies," as the middle-class and professional activists were called.

Led by sisters **Margaret Dreier Robins** and **Mary Elisabeth
Dreier** from 1907 to 1922, the WTUL achieved national notice for
its role in large garment worker strikes throughout the Northeast
and Midwest, most famously New York City's **Uprising of the
Twenty Thousand**. In the aftermath of the **Triangle Shirtwaist
Fire**, the WTUL led the demand for greater government regulation
of working conditions, and Robins was appointed to the **New York
State Factory Investigating Commission**. In addition to strike
support, the WTUL lobbied for protective legislation mandating the
eight-hour day, a **minimum wage**, and health and safety regulations. It demanded women's **suffrage**, although some **socialists** and
working-class activists pointed out that men's enfranchisement had

not prevented problems that working-class men faced. Despite tensions between well-to-do and working-class members, the WTUL served as an important institutional voice for a working-class **feminism** that demanded **education** and leisure as well as improved pay and working conditions. It called the first International Congress of Working Women in 1919 and maintained a Washington lobby until 1950, when it ceased to exist. *See also* INTERNATIONAL LADIES' GARMENT WORKERS' UNION; LABOR UNIONS; NATIONAL CONSUMERS' LEAGUE.

WOOD, LEONARD (1860–1927). Military officer and colonial official. Born in New Hampshire, Wood graduated from Harvard Medical School (1884) and worked as a U.S. Army contract surgeon, participating in the campaign against Apache leader Geronimo, for which he later received the Medal of Honor (1898). Posted to Washington, D.C., in 1895, he served under President **William McKinley** and organized the 1st U.S. Volunteer Cavalry—the **Rough Riders**—with **Theodore Roosevelt** when the **Spanish–American War** began in 1898. In **Cuba**, Wood became a major general of volunteers and the military governor (1899–1902). Promoted to major general in the regular army, he served as military governor of Moro Province in the **Philippines** (1903–6) and military commander in the islands (1906–8). An avid sportsman, he supported **athletics** in the army to improve morale and physical fitness. An adviser to President Roosevelt in the **Tennis Cabinet**, he became army chief of staff (1910–14) and worked to **modernize** the army. Despite President **Woodrow Wilson**'s disapproval, Wood advocated **preparedness** after World War I began in 1914 and joined Roosevelt in organizing training camps for college-student volunteers. Passed over by Wilson for command of the country's World War I forces in favor of General **John J. Pershing**, Wood lost the **Republican Party** presidential nomination in 1916 and 1920. After retiring from active service in 1921, General Wood returned to the Philippines as governor general until the last year of his life. *See also* GENERAL STAFF, U.S. ARMY; PLATT AMENDMENT.

WOODS, ROBERT ARCHEY (1865–1925). Settlement house worker. Born in Pittsburgh to Scotch-Irish **immigrants**, Woods graduated from Amherst College (1886) and studied at the Andover Theological Seminary (1886–90). During a visit to London he was inspired by Toynbee Hall, and on his return to Boston he founded the South End House (1891) and was its head worker until his death. Woods lectured at the Episcopal Theological School in Cambridge and served as president of the Boston School Union (1908–25). Having helped to found the National Federation of Social Settlements, he served as its secretary (1911–23) and president (1923–25). His many writings include the *Handbook of Settlements* (1911), prepared for the **Russell Sage Foundation**. Woods emphasized social justice, the importance of neighborhood churches, and the value of **industrial education** in public schools. *See also* SOCIAL GOSPEL.

WOOLWORTH BUILDING. Designed by **Cass Gilbert** in the neo-Gothic style, this 55-story office building opened in 1913 at Broadway and Park Place in New York City as headquarters for the **Woolworth's** 5-and-10-cent **chain stores**. It included a Byzantine-Romanesque-Gothic lobby, an Elizabethan bank, a medieval German Rathskeller, and F. W. Woolworth's Second Empire–style executive offices. The lobby had shops, and the entire building had the most modern elevators and electrical, water, heating, cooling, and fire protection systems. Dubbed the cathedral of commerce, it stood near two **subway** lines and had a view of the Brooklyn Bridge. It became an immediate tourist attraction and a symbol of U.S. economic primacy. The Woolworth Building was the tallest skyscraper in the world until 1930. *See also* ARCHITECTURE.

WOOLWORTH'S. This was the colloquial name for the five-and-dime **chain stores** begun in the late 1870s by F. W. Woolworth (1852–1919) and incorporated as F. W. Woolworth & Co. in 1888. The company became F. W. Woolworth Co. in 1912 after a merger that consolidated several firms into a single enterprise with 596 stores nationwide. By 1919, more than 1,000 outlets bearing the familiar bright red storefront and the diamond with a "W" in the center operated in the United States and Canada, making Woolworth's one of the most successful early chains. The company's success rested on exploitation of mass manufacturing and deskilling of the workforce. In contrast to existing dry goods stores, but much like **department stores**, five-and-dimes displayed goods so that customers could inspect and select their own items, rather than relying on the clerk. This approach allowed stores to dispense with knowledgeable clerks, typically men, and employ lower-paid clerks, typically adolescents or **women**. In the 1890s, female salesclerks at Woolworth's earned as little as $2.50 per week, not enough to survive independent of family. **Child labor** laws threatened the chain's labor strategy because, although Woolworth hired girls 15 or older, its learner program included boys as young as 12. Thanks to efforts of **labor union** organizers and consumer advocates like the **National Consumers' League**, counter clerks with more than six months of service earned a 25-dollar Christmas bonus and a one-week paid vacation each year.

The company also ranged far and wide to find cheap goods to sell, importing, for example, Christmas decorations and toys from Germany and Japan and glass from Austria. Global purchasing allowed the company to make a profit on low-priced goods; American consumers thus enjoyed greater choices because of the low wages of foreign workers. The predecessor of later giant discount stores, Woolworth's was the most successful of a range of similar businesses, including S. S. Kresge (1897) and J. C. Penney (1902). *See also* WOOLWORTH BUILDING.

WORKERS' COMPENSATION. This program of **social insurance** for employees injured or killed on the job came to the attention of American reformers through its implementation in Germany (1884) and Great Britain (1897). Promoted by President **Theodore Roosevelt**, the **Russell Sage Foundation**, the **National Civic Federation**, and others, workers' compensation enjoyed quick success, adopted by 22 states between 1910, when New York passed the first thorough law, and 1913. Facing the threat of litigation posed by **employer liability laws**, employers proved surprisingly favorable to workers' compensation schemes, which in some states were directly state run, while other states mandated that companies buy private insurance. The **Kern–McGillicuddy Act** of 1916 extended the principle to all federal employees. *See also* AMERICAN ASSOCIATION FOR LABOR LEGISLATION.

WRIGHT, CARROLL D. (1840–1909). Public official and statistician. Born in New Hampshire, Wright served as a colonel in the Civil War and then practiced law in Massachusetts. He served in the state senate (1872–73) and was director of the Massachusetts Bureau of the Statistics of Labor (1873–85), the nation's first such agency. He carried out innovative investigations of a host of labor issues, including **child labor**, working women, and conditions in textile mills. In 1885, Wright became the first U.S. commissioner of labor, a position he held for a decade; in 1893, he added director of the U.S. Census to his portfolio. He served as president of the American Statistical Association (1897–1909) and Clark University (1902–9). A pioneer in statistical analysis of society and economy, Wright wrote *The Industrial Evolution of the United States* (1897) and *Battles of Labor* (1906).

WRIGHT, FRANK LLOYD (1867–1959). Architect. Born in Wisconsin, Wright studied civil engineering at the University of Wisconsin (1885–87) and apprenticed with **Louis Sullivan** (1887–93) in Chicago before opening his own office in Oak Park, Illinois, in 1893. Disdaining neoclassical, neo-Gothic, and other historical revival fashions as well as the modern steel and glass high-rise style, Wright developed his own unorthodox **architecture**. His much-admired "prairie style" used colors, forms, and natural textures to blend with the expansive horizontal midwestern landscape, producing long, low houses featuring wide windows and terraces. The interior space flowed from one room to another for a unified house with clean, simple lines and broad proportions, often with built-in furniture. Among his famous works were his home and studio in Oak Park (1889); the Frederick C. Robie house (1906) in Chicago; Taliesin (1914), his home in Spring Green, Wisconsin; Falling Water (1935), a house in Bear Run, Pennsylvania; Taliesin West (1937); and the Guggenheim Museum in New York City (1943–59). Wright designed 1,100 projects, of which only half were built, including the Imperial Hotel in Tokyo (1915) and textile block houses in Southern California (1923–29). Despite an ornery disposition and a penchant for personal scandal that nearly destroyed his career several times, he had secured his reputation as the greatest American architect of the 20th century by his death at age 91. *See also* MODERNISM.

WRIGHT, WILBUR (1867–1912) AND ORVILLE (1871–1948).
Aviators. Wilbur was born in Indiana and Orville in Ohio, the sons
of a United Brethren bishop. By 1892, they operated a bicycle shop
in Dayton and seven years later began their efforts to invent a viable mechanical flying machine by building gliders. On the advice
of the U.S. Weather Bureau, they traveled to Kitty Hawk, North
Carolina, in 1900 to make extended glider flights. By 1903, they had
designed an engine to power the glider and made successful flights
on 17 December 1903 over the Kitty Hawk sand hills. In 1906, they
obtained a U.S. patent for the world's first practical airplane. At first,
European governments as well as the United States dismissed the
Wright brothers' invention, but by 1908 both the U.S. Army and a
French syndicate supported their research. The brothers incorporated
the Wright Company in 1909 to build improved airplanes and train
pilots. After Wilbur died in Dayton in May 1912, Orville continued
the company until 1914. During World War I he was a consultant for
the U.S. Army Signal Corps' Aviation Service.

– Y –

YELLOW DOG CONTRACT. This is an agreement between employer and employee in which the employee agrees as a condition of
employment not to join a **labor union**. Starting in the 1870s, such
agreements became widespread in New England's textile mills, Chicago's stockyards, and other industrial centers. Labor unions pressured 16 state legislatures to outlaw the contracts, but a series of court
decisions culminating in the *Hitchman Coal & Coke* case in 1917
negated such state laws. Congress, meanwhile, outlawed the yellow
dog contract for railroad workers in the **Erdman Act** (1898), but in
1908 the **U.S. Supreme Court** overturned this prohibition in *Adair v.
United States*. Justice **Oliver Wendell Holmes** dissented consistently
in such cases, joined in 1917 by Justice **Louis Brandeis**. The yellow
dog contract undermined union organization until Congress banned
it in 1932. *See also* OPEN SHOP.

YELLOW FEVER. Repeated epidemics of this disease and cholera
catalyzed the formation of **public health** boards in many American

cities during the 19th century. However, physicians did not agree on the disease's cause or transmission and had no effective treatment to offer. In 1900, **Walter Reed** led the U.S. Army's Yellow Fever Commission in **Cuba**, where troops occupying the country after the **Spanish–American War** were at risk. Cuban researcher Carlos J. Finlay had argued that the disease was mosquito borne, and epidemiological research and human experimentation by Dr. Reed and his colleagues demonstrated that he was right. This knowledge prompted mosquito-eradication programs and greater use of mosquito netting and screens, dramatically diminishing yellow fever infections and deaths and making the construction of the **Panama Canal** feasible. *See also* HEALTH AND MEDICINE.

YELLOW JOURNALISM. The term may derive from the comic strip *The Yellow Kid* by Richard F. Outcault, which appeared in a color comic section of **Joseph Pulitzer**'s *New York World* starting in 1896. The term referred to the sensationalist reporting identified with the competing newspaper chains of Pulitzer and **William Randolph Hearst**, with lurid depictions of crime, sex, immorality, suicide, and disasters. Critics accused yellow **journalism** of playing a pernicious role in drumming up popular support for the **Spanish–American War**, for example by overstating Spanish atrocities in **Cuba**, publishing the inflammatory De Lôme letter, and rushing to attribute the explosion and sinking of the USS *Maine* in Havana harbor to a Spanish mine. Hearst sent ace reporter **Richard Harding Davis** and the artist **Frederic Remington** to cover the Cuban Revolution, and after the United States entered the war as many as 40 editions of the *New York Journal* appeared in a single day.

YELLOWSTONE NATIONAL PARK. *See* NATIONAL PARK SERVICE.

YERKES, CHARLES TYSON (1837–1905). Financier. Born in Philadelphia, Yerkes went into business at age 16, enjoying both success and failure, including a prison term for embezzlement, before moving to Chicago in 1881. With the help of Philadelphia financiers, he gained control of Chicago's streetcar system over the next decade. Overseeing Chicago transit's **electrification** and the beginnings of the elevated system and the famed Loop, Yerkes demonstrated an unscrupulous approach to labor as well as local and state politics, and the public made him a one-person argument for the municipal ownership of **utilities.** In 1895, Governor John Peter Altgeld thwarted his attempt to manipulate the state legislature into renewing his leases for 50 years. After failing again in 1897 to extend his leases, amid plausible accusations of bribery, Yerkes sold his Chicago holdings. To improve his image, he contributed generously to the Columbian **Exposition** (1893) and also donated funds in 1897 to the **University of Chicago** for the Yerkes Observatory. From Chicago, he moved to London, where he headed the franchise to expand the London **subway,** a project barely begun at his death. **Theodore Dreiser** fictionalized Yerkes as Frank Cowperwood in his novels *The Financier* (1912), *The Titan* (1914), and *The Stoic* (1947). *See also* TROLLEYS, ELECTRIC.

YOSEMITE NATIONAL PARK. *See* NATIONAL PARK SERVICE.

YOUNG, ART (1866–1943). Artist. Born in Wisconsin, Arthur Henry Young supported himself as an illustrator and cartoonist while studying at the Chicago Academy of Design (1884), the Art Students League in New York City (1888), and in Paris (1889–90). He worked for the *Chicago Inter-Ocean* and the *Denver Times* during the 1890s before moving back to New York City. By 1906, he was a **socialist** whose cartoons protested against the injustices of capitalism and racial prejudice and advocated **women**'s rights. In 1912, when he was coeditor of *The Masses*, the Associated Press sued him for libel for his cartoon *Poisoned at the Source*. The federal government prosecuted him unsuccessfully during World War I for his antiwar views. A fixture for decades in radical journals, Young also contributed cartoons to mainstream, **mass-circulation magazines** and newspapers. *See also* ART; SLOAN, JOHN.

YOUNG, ELLA FLAGG (1845–1918). Teacher and administrator. A New York native, Young became a teacher in the Chicago schools before and after her brief marriage. Unlike most **women** teachers in a rapidly feminizing profession, she moved into administration, becoming assistant superintendent in 1887. In this position she supervised reforms that replaced a classical curriculum with a more modern, practical one, substituted active learning for memorization and recitation, and improved teacher training. In the 1890s, she enrolled at the **University of Chicago** to study with **John Dewey**. Receiving her doctorate in 1900, Young taught at the **university** and wrote books on pedagogy. She served as principal of the Chicago Normal School (1904–9) and then became the first woman in the nation to manage a major city's schools as Chicago's superintendent. She served as president of the **National Education Association** (1909–10). Young survived the controversial introduction of a sex education program in 1913 but briefly lost her job in 1914 in retaliation for her recognition of the Chicago Teachers Federation. Mass protests led the school board to reinstate her, though she retired in 1915. *See also* EDUCATION; PRAGMATISM.

YOUNG MEN'S CHRISTIAN ASSOCIATION (YMCA). Originally a British institution, the first American YMCA opened in Boston in 1851 and spread rapidly from there. The respectable older men who established YMCAs aimed to provide safe, Christian havens for young men, often rural migrants, alone in dangerous, vice-filled cities. Although Bible study and prayer services remained central, in the Progressive Era the YMCAs paid increasing attention to men's physical well-being. Club houses expanded to include gymnasiums and helped spread **basketball** and volleyball. Some YMCAs also supported reform activities; the New York City branch supported **Anthony Comstock** throughout his career. Others reached out to working-class men, seeking to foster cross-class Christian brotherhood and eliminate labor unrest. By the turn of the century, the reconceptualization of **sexuality** made suspect the intergenerational male relationships that the institution encouraged. Increasingly the YMCA encouraged its secretaries to marry and involve their wives in the organization's work. Coed activities became more common, and the institution encroached on the **Young Women's Christian Association** by allowing women to use some of its facilities. The YMCA was racially **segregated** from the start, with the first branch for **African Americans** opening in 1853. Its international missionary activities reached young men around the world. *See also* ATHLETICS; BOY SCOUTS OF AMERICA; SOCIAL GOSPEL.

YOUNG WOMEN'S CHRISTIAN ASSOCIATION (YWCA).
Originating in Britain in the 1850s, the first U.S. branch opened
in 1858; this organization took on the YWCA name in the 1870s.
Always smaller and less wealthy than **Young Men's Christian Association**, the YWCA offered working-class young **women** safe,
clean lodging, libraries, sewing schools, and mentoring. The original
organization only served whites; **African Americans** established
affiliated but separate associations by 1870. In the 1880s, female
college students founded a related but more evangelical organization
that became active in foreign missionary work. When the original
YWCA and this student organization united in 1908, the group could
claim more than 180,000 members. Like other female reform organizations, such as the **Woman's Christian Temperance Union** and
settlement houses, the YWCA gave women unusual opportunities
for paid professional work. Like its brother institution, in the 20th
century the YWCA promoted physical exercise and **athletics** and
supported the **Girl Scouts** and the Camp Fire Girls.

– Z –

ZANGWILL, ISRAEL (1864–1926). Writer. Born in England, the
son of a Russian **Jewish** émigré, Zangwill graduated from London
University (1884). Mostly resident in England, though a regular
traveler to the United States, he became widely known for his novel
Children of the Ghetto: A Study of a Peculiar People (1892), which
depicted Jewish life in London. New York City was the setting of his
hit Broadway play, *The Melting Pot* (1908), whose title became a
popular term for fusion of **immigrant** cultures into a new American
nationality. A Zionist who also worked for Jewish colonization in
Canada, Australia, and Uganda, he promoted younger Jewish writers,
including **Mary Antin**.

ZIEGFELD FOLLIES. First staged in 1907, the Follies were a high-
class version of **vaudeville**, combining short acts, musical numbers
performed by 60 marvelously costumed young **women**, comedy,
satire, and tableaux of semi-nude women posed to represent paintings. Initially produced by Klaw & Erlanger of the Theatrical Syn-

dicate, the shows came under the control of director and impresario Florenz Ziegfeld (1867–1932), who named the annual show after himself in 1911. He hired leading set and fashion designers to create the scenery and costumes, contracted with songwriters such as **Irving Berlin** and Jerome Kern, and featured top-name writers, comedians, and dancers. The chorus girls were the show's chief claim to fame, however, and Ziegfeld sought to make them icons of a winsome, physically perfect American womanhood. The show went through 21 versions before failing during the 1930s. *See also* SEXUALITY.

ZONING. An urban planning tool developed in Germany, it spread to the United States, among other countries, at the turn of the 20th century. Zoning involves the division of cities by municipal officials into sections ("zones") reserved for residential, commercial, or industrial activities. In its original form, zoning was intended to protect residential areas from encroachment by industry and other land uses incompatible with a pleasant, healthy home life. In 1909, Los Angeles became the first major American city to attempt a zoning system by designating 27 areas of the city for industry and reserving the rest for residence and commerce. After other experiments and years of advocacy by proponents of **City Practical** planning and by housing reformers such as **Benjamin C. Marsh**, New York in 1916 became the first major American city to adopt a comprehensive zoning ordinance. The New York law assigned different areas to residence, industry, and mixed uses, restricted building height in relation to street width, and limited the proportion of a lot that buildings could cover. One effect of this system was the spread of the setbacks characteristic of New York skyscraper construction.

But zoning was not without its problems. Very quickly, complaints emerged that real estate interests manipulated zoning ordinances to protect property values in a manner at odds with the comprehensive management of the urban environment. A related complaint targeted the manipulation of zoning to enforce racial and ethnic **segregation**, generally through the stipulation of lot sizes and house sizes, because the **U.S. Supreme Court** ruled against the explicit use of race in zoning in 1917. Especially after 1926, when the Supreme Court sanctioned zoning, the practice became the most characteristic urban planning activity. *See also* NATIONAL CONFERENCE ON CITY PLANNING.

ZUKOR, ADOLPH (1873–1976). Movie producer and businessman. Born in Hungary, Zukor immigrated to the United States in 1889 and apprenticed with a furrier in New York City. A successful Chicago businessman by 1903, he invested in the new **movie** technology by opening kinetoscope arcades and then nickelodeons. In 1912, he incorporated the Famous Players Film Company and, with the help of theatrical producers, including **David Belasco**, made films that featured stage stars and told respectable historical and literary tales. Zukor's intention was to raise the reputation and profitability of movies, and his company played a key role in the emergence of feature films and the star system. Within several years of its founding, Famous Players had contracts with leading film stars such as Douglas Fairbanks and **Mary Pickford**.

In addition to innovations in the type of film and film actors, Zukor took advantage of the breakup of **Thomas Edison**'s **Motion Picture Patents Company** to develop new production and distribution arrangements. He joined **Jesse Lasky** (1916) to take over the national distribution company, **Paramount Pictures**, a step toward vertically integrating the film industry. When exhibitors combined to resist the practice of "block booking"—compelling houses to take all of the company's films in order to get those few that had real star power—Zukor responded by convincing Wall Street investors to underwrite the construction of new, ornate theaters in cities across the nation. This move marked the transition of filmmaking for a low-budget business to a large-scale, capital-intensive enterprise. It also launched large ornate downtown motion picture palaces. Other film producers quickly followed Zukor's example, establishing the Hollywood studio system.

Appendix 1:
Presidents and Their Administrations 1893–1921

GROVER CLEVELAND, 1893–97

1892 Election

	% Popular Votes	# Electoral Votes
Grover Cleveland	46.1	277
Benjamin Harrison	43	145
James Weaver	8.5	22

Vice President

Adlai E. Stevenson (1893–97)

Cabinet

Secretary of State

Walter Q. Gresham (1893–95)
Richard Olney (1895–97)

Secretary of the Treasury

John G. Carlisle (1893–97)

Secretary of War

Daniel S. Lamont (1893–97)

Attorney General

Richard Olney (1893–95)
Judson Harmon (1895–97)

Postmaster General

Wilson S. Bissell (1893–95)
William L. Wilson (1895–97)

Secretary of the Navy

Hilary A. Herbert (1893–97)

Secretary of the Interior

Hoke Smith (1893–96)
David R. Francis (1896–97)

Secretary of Agriculture

Julius Sterling Morton (1893–97)

WILLIAM MCKINLEY, 1897–1901 (ASSASSINATED IN 1901)

1896 Election

	% Popular Votes	# Electoral Votes
William McKinley	51	271
William Jennings Bryan	46.7	176

Vice President

Garret A. Hobart (1897–1901)

1900 Election

	% Popular Votes	# Electoral Votes
William McKinley	51.7	292
William Jennings Bryan	45.5	155

Vice President

Theodore Roosevelt (1901) became president at McKinley's death in September 1901.

Cabinet

Secretary of State

John Sherman (1897–98)
William R. Day (1898)
John M. Hay (1898–1901)

Secretary of the Treasury

Lyman J. Gage (1897–1901)

Secretary of War

Russell A. Alger (1897–99)
Elihu Root (1899–1901)

Attorney General

Joseph McKenna (1897–98)
John W. Griggs (1898–1901)
Philander C. Knox (1901)

Postmaster General

Charles E. Smith (1901–02)
Henry C. Payne (1902–04)

Secretary of the Navy

John D. Long (1897–1901)

Secretary of the Interior

Cornelius N. Bliss (1897–99)
Ethan A. Hitchcock (1899–1901)

Secretary of Agriculture

James Wilson (1897–1901)

THEODORE ROOSEVELT, 1901–9

1904 Election

	% Popular Votes	# Electoral Votes
Theodore Roosevelt	56.4	336
Alton B. Parker	37.6	140
Eugene V. Debs	4	0

Vice President

Charles W. Fairbanks (1905–09)

Cabinet

Secretary of State

John M. Hay (1901–05)
Elihu Root (1905–09)
Robert Bacon (1909)

Secretary of the Treasury

Lyman J. Gage (1901–02)
Leslie M. Shaw (1902–07)
George B. Cortelyou (1907–09)

Secretary of War

Elihu Root (1901–04)
William H. Taft (1904–08)
Luke E. Wright (1908–09)

Attorney General

Philander C. Knox (1901–04)
William H. Moody (1904–06)
Charles J. Bonaparte (1906–09)

Postmaster General

Charles E. Smith (1901–02)
Henry C. Payne (1902–04)
Robert J. Wynne (1904–05)
George B. Cortelyou (1905–07)
George von L. Meyer (1907–09)

Secretary of the Navy

James D. Long (1901–02)
William H. Moody (1902–04)
Paul Morton (1904–05)
Charles J. Bonaparte (1905–06)
Victor H. Metcalf (1906–08)
Truman H. Newberry (1908–09)

Secretary of the Interior

Ethan A. Hitchcock (1901–07)
James R. Garfield (1907–09)

Secretary of Agriculture

James Wilson (1901–09)

Secretary of Commerce and Labor

George B. Cortelyou (1903–04)
Victor H. Metcalf (1904–06)
Oscar S. Straus (1906–09)

WILLIAM HOWARD TAFT, 1909–13

1908 Election

	% Popular Votes	# Electoral Votes
William Howard Taft	51.7	321
William Jennings Bryan	43	162
Eugene V. Debs	2.8	0

Vice President

James S. Sherman (1909–12)

Cabinet

Secretary of State

Philander C. Knox (1909–13)

Secretary of the Treasury

Franklin MacVeagh (1909–13)

Secretary of War

Jacob M. Dickinson (1909–11)
Henry L. Stimson (1911–13)

Attorney General

George W. Wickersham (1909–13)

Postmaster General

Frank H. Hitchcock (1909–13)

Secretary of the Navy

George von L. Meyer (1909–13)

Secretary of the Interior

Richard A. Ballinger (1909–11)
Walter Lowrie Fisher (1911–13)

Secretary of Agriculture

James Wilson (1909–13)

Secretary of Commerce and Labor

Charles Nagel (1909–13)

WOODROW WILSON, 1913–21

1912 Election

	% Popular Votes	# Electoral Votes
Woodrow Wilson	41.8	435
Theodore Roosevelt	27.4	88
William Howard Taft	23.2	8
Eugene V. Debs	6	0

Vice President

Thomas R. Marshall (1913–21)

1916 Election

	% Popular Votes	# Electoral Votes
Woodrow Wilson	49.2	277
Charles Evans Hughes	46.1	254
A. L. Benson	3.2	0

Vice President

Thomas R. Marshall (1913–21)

Cabinet

Secretary of State

William J. Bryan (1913–15)
Robert Lansing (1915–20)
Bainbridge Colby (1920–21)

Secretary of the Treasury

William G. McAdoo (1913–18)
Carter Glass (1918–20)
David F. Houston (1920–21)

Secretary of War

Lindley M. Garrison (1913–16)
Newton D. Baker (1916–21)

Attorney General

James C. McReynolds (1913–14)
Thomas W. Gregory (1914–19)
A. Mitchell Palmer (1919–21)

Postmaster General

Albert S. Burleson (1913–21)

Secretary of the Navy

Josephus Daniels (1913–21)

Secretary of the Interior

Franklin K. Lane (1913–20)
John B. Payne (1920–21)

Secretary of Agriculture

David F. Houston (1913–20)
Edwin T. Meredith (1920–21)

Secretary of Commerce

William C. Redfield (1913–19)
Joshua W. Alexander (1919–21)

Secretary of Labor

William B. Wilson (1913–21)

Appendix 2:
Constitutional Amendments

SIXTEENTH AMENDMENT

[Passed by Congress 12 July 1909; ratified 3 February 1913]

The Congress shall have power to lay and collect taxes on incomes, from whatever source derived, without apportionment among the several States, and without regard to any census or enumeration.

SEVENTEENTH AMENDMENT

[Passed by Congress 16 May 1912; ratified 31 May 1913]

The Senate of the United States shall be composed of two Senators from each State, elected by the people thereof, for six years; and each Senator shall have one vote. The electors in each State shall have the qualifications requisite for electors of the most numerous branch of the State legislatures.

When vacancies happen in the representation of any State in the Senate, the executive authority of such State shall issue writs of election to fill such vacancies: *Provided,* That the legislature of any State may empower the executive thereof to make temporary appointments until the people fill the vacancies by election as the legislature may direct.

This amendment shall not be so construed as to affect the election or term of any Senator chosen before it becomes valid as part of the Constitution.

EIGHTEENTH AMENDMENT

[Passed by Congress, 17 December 1917; ratified 29 January 1919]

Section 1.

After one year from the ratification of this article the manufacture, sale, or transportation of intoxicating liquors within, the importation thereof into, or the exportation thereof from the United States and all territory subject to the jurisdiction thereof for beverage purposes is hereby prohibited.

Section 2.

The Congress and the several States shall have concurrent power to enforce this article by appropriate legislation.

Section 3.

This article shall be inoperative unless it shall have been ratified as an amendment to the Constitution by the legislatures of the several States, as provided in the Constitution, within seven years from the date of the submission hereof to the States by the Congress.

NINETEENTH AMENDMENT

[Passed by Congress 5 June 1919; ratified 26 August 1920]

The right of citizens of the United States to vote shall not be denied or abridged by the United States or by any State on account of sex.

Congress shall have power to enforce this article by appropriate legislation.

Bibliography

CONTENTS

INTRODUCTION

The purpose of this bibliography is to enable the reader and the scholar to make a start at virtually any area in this vast field of historical research. The bibliography is, therefore, more comprehensive in listing recent works than older ones. This is not because new scholarship is better, but because newer works cite older ones, while the reverse is impossible. It includes only the most indispensable books published before 1970. Dissertations have been left out, on the grounds that a flood of published books are available to begin virtually any project. For space reasons, the bibliography also omits articles, the most important of which researchers can trace through books.

A major contribution of progressivism to American social thought arose from the way that intellectually engaged reformers and socially engaged scholars sought to examine society as a web of interdependence. The privileged classes, progressives argued, could not turn away from the deplorable working and living conditions that afflicted the poor. Everyone's well-being depended on the health of each part of the social system. At its best, historical scholarship on progressivism reflects this sense of interconnectedness and multiple causation that animated progressive thought and reform. While this makes for subtle, engaging scholarship, it complicates the task of bibliography writing, since bibliographies by their nature dissect and distinguish and unravel the strands of webs. For example, progressive social science explicitly endeavored to create an empirical foundation for social reform. When, therefore, is a work on the social sciences in this period about intellectual history or the academic professions, and when is it about reform itself?

To give another example of how the character of progressivism can create bibliographic confusion, an especially striking change since the 1970s in progressive historiography comes from the application of concepts and methods drawn from women's and gender history. Women's historians generally set as their goal the infusion of all areas of study with an awareness of the role of women and gender. The result is both a multitude of novel perspectives and increased bibliographic confusion. In keeping with what most women's historians would counsel, scholarship on women's roles appears throughout the bibliography. Books on women in movements for social welfare or temperance, therefore, appear under the appropriate subcategory of "Reformers and Reform Movements." Similar considerations governed the dispersal of relevant works in "Women's" subsections of "Labor," "African Americans," "Cities and Urbanism," "The West," and "The South." A limited number of works do appear under a major heading called "Women," to offer a starting point for those interested in women's overall role in society during the early 20th century.

Similar points could be made about labor history, immigration and ethnicity, studies of African Americans, urban history, southern and western history, politics, radicalism, and even foreign relations. Many scholars explicitly endeavor to weave together categories, so it is artificial to treat them separately, though in a bibliography one can do no other. The best advice to the user of this bibliography is to look through the table of contents and consult several relevant categories.

The bibliography includes every historiographic school except that of the progressives themselves. Progressive Era writing on contemporary issues was so profuse and lively that a decent bibliography of it would require a separate volume. The dictionary itself includes entries on Progressive Era authors in the social sciences, public affairs, and the humanities. Major authors and works can thus easily be gleaned from the dictionary and from any number of secondary works listed below.

The modern historiography of progressivism begins after World War II with the efforts of professionals like Harold Faulkner and George Mowry to provide well-researched narrative overviews of the period. The best-known launching point for the modern historiography of progressivism is Richard Hofstadter's 1955 book *The Age of Reform: From Bryan to F.D.R.* Tagged with the misleading label "Consensus School," Hofstadter and people like him endeavored to apply the innovative sociology and social psychology of the 1950s to a sometimes mordant analysis of the reformers and their enthusiasms. To sum up a complex argument, Hofstadter saw the reform movements of the late 1800s and early 1900s—populism and progressivism—as beginning in the so-called status anxieties of farmers in the case of populism and old-line patrician and professional families in the case of progressivism, groups pushed aside by the raucous urban industrial capitalism of the post–Civil War decades.

The 1960s saw the historical treatment of progressivism spin off in several directions, all of which amounted to attacks on Hofstadter. The outlook of the New Left appears in Gabriel Kolko and James Weinstein—and later on in complicated ways in the writings of Martin Sklar, James Livingston, and others. These writers depict progressivism as a reorganization of capitalism toward "corporate liberalism," in which business and government cooperated to seek stable prosperity and to contain some of capitalism's most brutal and self-defeating impulses. A sometimes overlapping but generally competing interpretation acquired the name "organizational synthesis" from the historiographic articles of Louis Galambos, "The Emerging Organizational Synthesis in Modern American History," *Business History Review* 44 (Autumn 1970): 279–90, and "Technology, Political Culture, and Professionalization: Central Themes of the Organizational Synthesis," *Business History Review* 57 (Winter 1983): 471–93. Organizational writers, imbued with the tenets of the then-fashionable modernization theory, saw progressivism as a concerted effort by professionals, academics, managers, scientists, and engineers to build new institutions appropriate for an urban, corporate, industrial society and to adjust politics and public policy to urban industrialism. Samuel Hays's 1957 *The Response to Industrialism* was an early statement of this approach, but the best known is Robert Wiebe's *The Search for Order, 1877–1920* (1967), a book that can be maddeningly vague in its arguments. Again to oversimplify, the New Left's "corporate liberal" school saw progressivism as emanating from an alliance of the business class and government, while the organizational writers saw progressivism as reflecting the optimistic "new middle class" generated by urban industrialism, rather than the defensive "old middle class" stressed by Hofstadter.

In his 1970 essay "An Obituary for the Progressive Movement," *American Quarterly* 22 (Spring 1970): 20–34, historian Peter Filene lamented what he saw as a fatal conceptual error in all such approaches—the effort to impose a false unity on a political tendency that was manifestly multifaceted and multicentered. Henceforth, historians have been reluctant to label any particular line in early 20th-century reform as "the" progressive movement, but the study of progressivism as a loosely defined trend flourished. For example, John D. Buenker's emphasis on urban ethnic politics as a source for the social and labor reform impulse in progressivism, outlined in *Urban Liberalism and Progressive Reform* (1973), built upon the sympathetic reexamination of urban political machines that became popular among political scientists and urban historians during the 1960s and 1970s. Historian Joseph Huthmacher had coined the term *urban liberalism* earlier in his essay "Urban Liberalism and the Age of Reform," *Mississippi Valley Historical Review* 49 (September 1962): 231–41. Meanwhile, David Thelen, in writings such as *The New Citizenship: The Origins of Progressivism in Wisconsin, 1885–1900* (1972), rooted the influential Wisconsin version of progressivism in the consumer-oriented politics that would loom larger and larger over the 20th century. Richard L. McCormick wove together the organizational writers' focus on the rise of "administrative" politics with the careful attention to electoral results characteristic of the so-called New Political History of the 1970s in his book *From Realignment to Reform: Political Change in New York State* (1981) and in the essays collected in *The Party Period and Public Policy* (1986).

Reflecting the then-burgeoning interest in cultural approaches to history, Daniel Rodgers, in his 1982 essay "In Search of Progressivism," *Reviews in American History* 10 (December 1982): 113–32, suggested that Filene and nearly all other commentators erred in seeking the unifying qualities of progressivism in the reformers' social background or political and policy goals. Perhaps what distinguished progressivism and held it together were a set of concepts and "languages" about social justice, efficiency, and antimonopoly. Also in 1982, the American Studies scholar Robert Crunden published a vivid intellectual/cultural study, *Ministers of Reform: The Progressives' Achievement in American Civilization, 1889–1920*. These writings marked the start of a long period of creative work on the intellectual and cultural dimensions of progressivism, until then a glaring gap, given the distinctive place of writers, academics, and experts in progressive activity. The bibliography includes as many as possible of the landmarks of this line of research, ranging from James Kloppenberg's thorough *Uncertain Victory: Social Democracy and Progressivism in European and American Thought, 1870–1920* (1986) to Louis Menand's accessible *Metaphysical Club: A Story of Ideas in America* (2001).

Kloppenberg's book is also an impressive example of a recent trend evident throughout the bibliography, the effort to relate progressive ideas and movements in the United States to social democratic and liberal reform movements in other developing countries. The landmark book on the international context of American progressivism is Daniel Rodgers's *Atlantic Crossings: Social Politics in a Progressive Age* (1998). Two books by Alan Dawley, *Struggles for Justice: Social Responsibility and the Liberal State* (1991) and *Changing the World: American Progressives in War and Revolution* (2003), offer another angle on the international context of American progressivism. Ballard Campbell provides an overview in "Comparative Perspectives on the Gilded Age and the Progressive Era," *Journal of the Gilded Age and Progressive Era* 1 (April 2002): 154–77.

As hinted above, the women's history and gender history movements of the period since 1970 profoundly transformed the ways that historians understand and write about progressivism. The effects of these perspectives on progressive historiography permeate this entire volume, including the bibliography. For a brief introduction, one might start with Elisabeth Israels Perry, "Men Are from the Gilded Age, Women from the Progressive Era," *Journal of the Gilded Age and Progressive Era* (January 2002): 25–48. An especially clear writer on these themes is Maureen A. Flanagan in a series of influential articles along with books such as *Seeing with Their Hearts: Chicago Women and the Vision of the Good City, 1871–1933* (2002) and *America Reformed: Progressives and Progressivisms, 1890s–1920s* (2007), an interpretive textbook that attempts to weave women's history perspectives fully into its narrative.

One very recent line of interpretation stresses those aspects of progressivism that arose from alliance between middle-class professionals and activists and varying segments of the working class. Such writers also emphasize the lively debates during the Progressive Era concerning the theory and practice of democracy at the local and national level, matters that permeated progressive discussions but that writers in the New Left and organizational traditions ignored or explained away. Works reflecting this new approach range from Kevin Mattson, *Creating a Democratic Public: The Struggle for Urban Participatory Democracy during the Progressive Era* (1998), and Leon Fink, *Progressive Intellectuals and the Dilemmas of Democratic Commitment* (1997), to Robert D. Johnston, *The Radical Middle Class: Populist De-*

mocracy and the Question of Capitalism in Progressive Era Portland, Oregon (2003), and Shelton Stromquist, *Reinventing "The People": The Progressive Movement, the Class Problem, and the Origins of Modern Liberalism* (2006). Robert Johnston explains the agenda of this line of writing in "Re-Democratizing the Progressive Era: The Politics of Progressive Era Political Historiography," *Journal of the Gilded Age and the Progressive Era* 1 (January 2002): 68–92.

Many books listed above can serve as introductory texts, though their purposes are generally more interpretive or historiographic. An exemplary text with clear explanations for college students is John Whiteclay Chambers II, *The Tyranny of Change: America in the Progressive Era, 1890—1920,* 2nd ed. (2000). John Milton Cooper, *Pivotal Decades: The United States, 1900—1920* (1990), offers a readable overview based on deep knowledge of the period. Steven J. Diner, *A Very Different Age: Americans of the Progressive Era* (1998), provides a sound introduction to the abundant contributions that social and cultural history have made since the 1970s to research on these decades. For a knowledgeable survey of Progressive Era politics that pays adequate attention to conservatives and other nonprogressives, see Lewis L. Gould, *Reform and Regulation: American Politics from Roosevelt to Wilson,* 3rd ed. (1996). One new survey, Michael McGerr, *A Fierce Discontent: The Rise and Fall of the Progressive Movement in America, 1870—1920* (2003), reflects a recent tendency to root early 20th-century progressivism in the post–Civil War decades and to muddy the distinction, which has seemed sharp to many writers, between the Gilded Age and the Progressive Era. For comparison, see the bibliography in T. Adams Upchurch's *Historical Dictionary of the Gilded Age* (2009).

REFERENCE AND GENERAL WORKS

Reference Works

Buenker, John D., and Joseph Buenker, eds. *Encyclopedia of the Gilded Age and Progressive Era.* Armonk, N.Y.: Sharpe Reference, 2005.

Buenker, John D., and Nicholas C. Burckel. *Progressive Reform: A Guide to Information Sources.* Detroit: Gale, 1980.

Buenker, John D., and Edward R. Kantowicz, eds. *Historical Dictionary of the Progressive Era, 1890–1920.* Westport, Conn.: Greenwood, 1988.

Narrative Texts

Chambers, John Whiteclay, II. *The Tyranny of Change: America in the Progressive Era, 1890–1920*. 2nd ed. New Brunswick, N.J.: Rutgers University Press, 2000.

Cooper, John Milton. *Pivotal Decades: The United States, 1900–1920*. New York: Norton, 1990.

Diner, Steven J. *A Very Different Age: Americans of the Progressive Era*. New York: Hill and Wang, 1998.

Flanagan, Maureen A. *America Reformed: Progressives and Progressivisms, 1890s–1920s*. New York: Oxford University Press, 2007.

Hays, Samuel P. *The Response to Industrialism, 1885–1914*. 2nd ed. Chicago: University of Chicago Press, 1995.

Hofstadter, Richard. *The Age of Reform: From Bryan to F.D.R.* New York: Alfred A. Knopf, 1955.

Jones, Howard Mumford. *The Age of Energy: Varieties of American Experience, 1865–1915*. New York: Viking, 1971.

Klein, Maury. *The Flowering of the Third America: The Making of an Organizational Society, 1850–1920*. Chicago: Ivan R. Dee, 1993.

McGerr, Michael. *A Fierce Discontent: The Rise and Fall of the Progressive Movement in America, 1870–1920*. New York: Free Press, 2003.

Meinig, D. W. *The Shaping of America: A Geographical Perspective on 500 Years of History*, vol. 3, *Transcontinental America, 1850–1915*. New Haven, Conn.: Yale University Press, 1998.

Painter, Nell Irvin. *Standing at Armageddon: The United States, 1877–1919*. New York: Norton, 1987.

Sullivan, Mark. *Our Times: The United States, 1900–1925*. 6 vols. New York: Scribner's, 1926–1935.

Traxel, David. *1898: The Birth of the American Century*. New York: Alfred A. Knopf, 1997.

———. *Crusader Nation: The United States in Peace and War, 1898–1920*. New York: Alfred A. Knopf, 2006.

Wiebe, Robert H. *The Search for Order, 1877–1920*. New York: Hill and Wang, 1967.

Interpretive and Historiographic

Buenker, John D., John C. Burnham, and Robert M. Crunden. *Progressivism*. Cambridge, Mass.: Schenkman, 1977.

Dawley, Alan. *Changing the World: American Progressives in War and Revolution*. Princeton, N.J.: Princeton University Press, 2003.

——. *Struggles for Justice: Social Responsibility and the Liberal State.* Cambridge, Mass.: Harvard University Press, 1991.

Eisenach, Eldon J. *The Lost Promise of Progressivism.* Lawrence: University Press of Kansas, 1994.

Frankel, Noralee, and Nancy S. Dye, eds. *Gender, Class, Race, and Reform in the Progressive Era.* Lexington: University Press of Kentucky, 1991.

Gilmore, Glenda Elizabeth, ed. *Who Were the Progressives?* Boston: Bedford/ St. Martin's, 2002.

Hays, Samuel P. *American Political History as Social Analysis.* Knoxville: University of Tennessee Press, 1980.

Kolko, Gabriel. *The Triumph of Conservatism: A Reinterpretation of American History, 1900–1916.* New York: Free Press, 1963.

Link, Arthur S. and Richard L. McCormick. *Progressivism.* Arlington Heights, Ill.: Harlan Davidson, 1983.

Milkis, Sidney M., and Jerome M. Mileur, eds. *Progressivism and the New Democracy.* Amherst: University of Massachusetts, 1999.

Rauchway, Eric. *Murdering McKinley: The Making of Theodore Roosevelt's America.* New York: Hill and Wang, 2003.

Rodgers, Daniel T. *Atlantic Crossings: Social Politics in a Progressive Age.* Cambridge, Mass.: Harvard University Press, 1998.

Sklar, Martin J. *The Corporate Reconstruction of American Capitalism, 1890– 1916: The Market, the Law, and Politics.* New York: Cambridge University Press, 1988.

——. *The United States as a Developing Country: Studies in U.S. History in the Progressive Era and the 1920s.* New York: Cambridge University Press, 1992.

Stromquist, Shelton. *Reinventing "The People": The Progressive Movement, the Class Problem, and the Origins of Modern Liberalism,* Urbana: University of Illinois Press, 2006.

Weinstein, James. *The Corporate Ideal in the Liberal State, 1900–1918.* Boston: Beacon Press, 1968.

REFORMERS AND REFORM MOVEMENTS

General

Crunden, Robert M. *Ministers of Reform: The Progressives' Achievement in American Civilization, 1889–1920.* Reprint, Urbana: University of Illinois Press, 1984.

Cyphers, Christopher J. *The National Civic Federation and the Making of New Liberalism, 1900–1915.* Westport, Conn.: Praeger, 2002.

Danbom, David. *"The World of Hope": Progressives and the Struggle for an Ethical Public Life.* Philadelphia: Temple University Press, 1987.

Eisenach, Eldon, ed. *The Social and Political Thought of American Progressivism.* Indianapolis: Hackett, 2006.

Forcey, Charles. *The Crossroads of Liberalism: Croly, Weyl, Lippmann and the Progressive Era.* New York: Oxford University Press, 1961.

Haber, Samuel. *Efficiency and Uplift: Scientific Management in the Progressive Era, 1890–1920.* Chicago: University of Chicago Press, 1964.

Rauchway, Eric. *The Refuge of the Affections: Family and American Reform Politics, 1900–1920.* New York: Columbia University Press, 2001.

Sanders, Elizabeth. *Roots of Reform: Farmers, Workers, and the American State, 1877–1917.* Chicago: University of Chicago Press, 1999.

Schäfer, Axel R. *American Progressives and German Social Reform, 1875–1920: Social Ethics, Moral Control, and the Regulatory State in a Transatlantic Context.* Stuttgart: Steiner, 2000.

Steel, Ronald. *Walter Lippmann and the American Century.* Boston: Atlantic-Little, Brown, 1980.

Governmental Reform

Bloomfield, Maxwell. *Peaceful Revolution: Constitutional Change and American Culture from Progressivism to the New Deal.* Cambridge, Mass.: Harvard University Press, 2000.

Goebel, Thomas. *A Government by the People: Direct Democracy in America, 1890–1940.* Chapel Hill: University of North Carolina Press, 2002.

Hirschorn, Bernard. *Democracy Reformed: Richard Spencer Childs and His Fight for Better Government.* Westport, Conn.: Greenwood, 1997.

Piott, Steven L. *Giving Voters a Voice: The Origins of Initiative and Referendum in America.* Columbia: University of Missouri Press, 2003.

Social Reform

Social Welfare, Poverty

Beito, David. *From Mutual Aid to the Welfare State: Fraternal Societies and Social Services, 1890–1967.* Chapel Hill: University of North Carolina Press, 2000.

Brandes, Stuart D. *American Welfare Capitalism, 1880–1940.* Chicago: University of Chicago Press, 1976.

Bremner, Robert Hamlett. *From the Depths: The Discovery of Poverty in the United States*. Reprint, New Brunswick, N.J.: Transaction, 1992.

Coleman, Peter J. *Progressivism and the World of Reform: New Zealand and the Origins of the American Welfare State*. Lawrence: University Press of Kansas, 1987.

Hoffman, Beatrix. *The Wages of Sickness: The Politics of Health Insurance in Progressive America*. Chapel Hill: University of North Carolina Press, 2001.

Igra, Anna R. *Wives without Husbands: Marriage, Desertion, and Welfare in New York, 1900–1935*. Chapel Hill: University of North Carolina Press, 2007.

Kleinberg, S. J. *Widows and Orphans First: The Family Economy and Social Welfare Policy, 1880–1939*. Urbana: University of Illinois Press, 2006.

Krainz, Thomas A. *Delivering Aid: Implementing Progressive Era Welfare in the American West*. Albuquerque: University of New Mexico Press, 2005.

Levine, Daniel. *Poverty and Society: The Growth of the American Welfare State in International Comparison*. New Brunswick, N.J.: Rutgers University Press, 1988.

Lubove, Roy. *The Struggle for Social Security, 1900–1935*. Cambridge, Mass.: Harvard University Press, 1968.

McClymer, John F. *War and Welfare: Social Engineering in America, 1890–1925*. Westport, Conn.: Greenwood, 1980.

Orloff, Ann Shola. *The Politics of Pensions: A Comparative Analysis of Britain, Canada, and the United States, 1880–1940*. Madison: University of Wisconsin Press, 1993.

Skocpol, Theda. *Protecting Soldiers and Mothers: The Political Origins of Social Policy in the United States*. Cambridge, Mass.: Harvard University Press, 1992.

"Maternalism" in Social Welfare

Aiken, Katherine G. *Harnessing the Power of Motherhood: The National Florence Crittenden Mission, 1883–1925*. Knoxville: University of Tennessee Press, 1998.

Boris, Eileen. *Home to Work: Motherhood and the Politics of Industrial Homework in the United States*. New York: Cambridge University Press, 1994.

Curry, Lynne. *Modern Mothers in the Heartland: Gender, Health, and Progress in Illinois, 1900–1930*. Columbus: Ohio State University Press, 1999.

Goodwin, Joanne L. *Gender and the Politics of Welfare Reform: Mother's Pensions in Chicago, 1911–1929*. Chicago: University of Chicago Press, 1997.

Gordon, Linda. *Pitied but Not Entitled: Single Mothers and the History of Welfare, 1890–1935.* New York: Free Press, 1994.

Klaus, Alisa. *Every Child a Lion: The Origins of Maternal and Infant Health Policy in the United States and France, 1890–1920.* Ithaca, N.Y.: Cornell University Press, 1993.

Kunzel, Regina G. *Fallen Women, Problem Girls: Unmarried Mothers and the Professionalization of Social Work, 1890–1945.* New Haven, Conn.: Yale University Press, 1995.

Ladd-Taylor, Molly. *Mother-Work: Women, Child Welfare, and the State, 1890–1920.* Urbana: University of Illinois Press, 1994.

Lovett, Laura L. *Conceiving the Future: Pronatalism, Reproduction, and the Family in the United States, 1890–1938.* Chapel Hill: University of North Carolina Press, 2007.

Children, Child Labor, and Juvenile Justice

Clapp, Elizabeth J. *Mothers of All Children: Women Reformers and the Rise of Juvenile Courts in Progressive Era America.* University Park: Pennsylvania State University Press, 1998.

Holt, Marilyn Irvin. *The Orphan Trains: Placing Out in America.* Lincoln: University of Nebraska Press, 1992.

Knupfer, Anne Meis. *Reform and Resistance: Gender, Delinquency, and America's First Juvenile Court.* New York: Routledge, 2001.

Lindenmeyer, Kriste. *"A Right to Childhood": The U.S. Children's Bureau and Child Welfare.* Urbana: University of Illinois Press, 1997.

Marten, James. *Childhood and Child Welfare in the Progressive Era: A Brief History with Documents.* Boston: Bedford/St. Martin's, 2005.

Macleod, David I. *Building Character in the American Boy: The Boy Scouts, the YMCA, and Their Forerunners.* Madison: University of Wisconsin Press, 1983.

Schlossman, Steven L. *Love and the American Delinquent: The Theory and Practice of "Progressive" Juvenile Justice, 1825–1920.* Chicago: University of Chicago Press, 1977.

Smuts, Alice Boardman. *Science in the Service of Children, 1893–1935.* New Haven, Conn.: Yale University Press, 2006.

Tanenhaus, David S. *Juvenile Justice in the Making.* New York: Oxford University Press, 2004.

Trattner, Walter I. *Crusade for the Children: A History of the National Child Labor Committee and Child Labor Reform in America.* Chicago: Quadrangle, 1970.

Wolcott, David B. *Cops and Kids: Policing Juvenile Delinquency in Urban America, 1890–1940*. Columbus: Ohio State University Press, 2005.

Zmora, Nurith. *Orphanages Reconsidered: Child Care Institutions in Progressive Era Baltimore*. Philadelphia: Temple University Press, 1994.

Labor Conditions

Bender, Daniel E., *Sweated Work, Weak Bodies: Anti-sweatshop Campaigns and Languages of Labor*. New Brunswick, N.J.: Rutgers University Press, 2004.

Graebner, William. *Coal-Mining Safety in the Progressive Period: The Political Economy of Reform*. Lexington: University Press of Kentucky, 1976.

Lehrer, Susan. *Origins of Protective Labor Legislation for Women, 1905–1925*. Albany: State University of New York Press, 1987.

Wikander, Ulla, Alice Kessler-Harris, and Jane Lewis, eds. *Protecting Women: Labor Legislation in Europe, the United States, and Australia, 1880–1920*. Urbana: University of Illinois Press, 1995.

Woloch, Nancy, ed. Muller v. Oregon: *A Brief History with Documents*. New York: Bedford/St. Martin's, 1996.

Moral Reform and Moral Order

General

Foster, Gaines M. *Moral Reconstruction: Christian Lobbyists and the Federal Legislation of Morality, 1865–1920*. Chapel Hill: University of North Carolina Press, 2002.

Parker, Alison. *Purifying America: Women, Culture Reform, and Pro-Censorship Activism, 1873–1933*. Urbana: University of Illinois Press, 1997.

Tate, Cassandra. *Cigarette Wars: The Triumph of "The Little White Slaver."* New York: Oxford University Press, 1999.

Wheeler, Leigh Ann. *Against Obscenity: Reform and the Politics of Womanhood in America, 1873–1935*. Baltimore: Johns Hopkins University Press, 2004.

Sexuality and Prostitution

Alexander, Ruth M. *The "Girl Problem": Female Sexual Delinquency in New York, 1900–1930*. Ithaca, N.Y.: Cornell University Press, 1995.

Connelly, Mark Thomas. *The Response to Prostitution in the Progressive Era*. Chapel Hill: University of North Carolina Press, 1980.

Donovan, Brian. *White Slave Crusades: Race, Gender, and Anti-vice Activism, 1887–1917.* Urbana: University of Illinois Press, 2006.

Langum, David. *Crossing Over the Line: Legislating Morality and the Mann Act.* Chicago: University of Chicago Press, 1994.

Odem, Mary E. *Delinquent Daughters: Protecting and Policing Adolescent Female Sexuality in the United States, 1885–1920.* Chapel Hill: University of North Carolina Press, 1995.

Pivar, David J. *Purity and Hygiene: Women, Prostitution, and the "American Plan," 1900–1930.* Westport, Conn.: Greenwood, 2002.

Rosen, Ruth. *The Lost Sisterhood: Prostitution in America, 1900–1918.* Baltimore: Johns Hopkins University Press, 1982.

Temperance, Prohibition, and Narcotics Control

Blocker, Jack S., Jr. *Retreat from Reform: The Prohibition Movement in the United States, 1890–1913.* Westport, Conn.: Greenwood, 1976.

Clark, Norman H. *Deliver Us from Evil: An Interpretation of American Prohibition.* New York: Norton, 1976.

Hamm, Richard F. *Shaping the Eighteenth Amendment: Temperance, Reform, Legal Culture, and the Polity, 1880–1920.* Chapel Hill: University of North Carolina Press, 1995.

Kerr, K. Austin. *Organized for Prohibition: A New History of the Anti-Saloon League.* New Haven, Conn.: Yale University Press, 1985.

Murdock, Gilbert. *Domesticating Drink: Women, Men, and Alcohol in America, 1870–1940.* Baltimore: Johns Hopkins University Press, 1998.

Musto, David F. *The American Disease: The Origins of Narcotic Control.* 3rd ed. New York: Oxford University Press, 1999.

Rumbarger, John J. *Profits, Power, and Prohibition: Alcohol Reform and the Industrializing of America, 1888–1930.* Albany: State University of New York Press, 1989.

Spillane, Joseph F. *Cocaine: From Medical Marvel to Modern Menace in the United States, 1884–1920.* Baltimore: Johns Hopkins University Press, 2000.

Tracy, Sarah W. *Alcoholism in America: From Reconstruction to Prohibition.* Baltimore: Johns Hopkins University Press, 2005.

Tyrell, Ian. *Woman's World/Woman's Empire: The Woman's Christian Temperance Union in International Perspective, 1880–1930.* Chapel Hill: University of North Carolina Press, 1991.

Zimmerman, Jonathan. *Distilling Democracy: Alcohol Education in America's Public Schools, 1880–1925.* Lawrence: University Press of Kansas, 1999.

Women in Reform

General

Dye, Nancy Schrom. *As Equals and as Sisters: Feminism, the Labor Movement, and the Women's Trade Union League of New York*. Columbia: University of Missouri Press, 1980.

Muncy, Robyn. *Creating a Female Domain in American Reform, 1890–1935*. New York: Oxford University Press, 1991.

Rupp, Leila J. *Worlds of Women: The Making of an International Women's Movement*. Princeton, N.J.: Princeton University Press, 1997.

Sklar, Kathryn Kish, Anja Schüler, and Susan Strasser, eds. *Social Justice Feminists in the United States and Germany: A Dialogue in Documents, 1885–1933*. Ithaca, N.Y.: Cornell University Press, 1998.

Tax, Meredith. *The Rising of the Women: Feminist Solidarity and Class Conflict, 1880–1917*. New York: Monthly Review Press, 1980.

Suffrage Movement

Buechler, Stephen M. *The Transformation of the Woman Suffrage Movement: The Case of Illinois*. New Brunswick, N.J.: Rutgers University Press, 1986.

Finnegan, Margaret. *Selling Suffrage: Consumer Culture and Votes for Women*. New York: Columbia University Press, 1999.

Ford, Linda. *Iron-Jawed Angels: The Suffrage Militancy of the National Woman's Party, 1912–1920*. Lanham, Md.: University Press of America, 1991.

Graham, Sara Hunter. *Woman Suffrage and the New Democracy*. New Haven, Conn.: Yale University Press, 1996.

Harrison, Patricia Greenwood. *Connecting Links: The British and American Suffrage Movements, 1900–1914*. Westport, Conn.: Greenwood, 2000.

Kraditor, Aileen. *The Ideas of the Woman Suffrage Movement, 1890–1920*. Reprint, New York: Norton, 1981.

Lumsden, Linda J. *Rampant Women: Suffragists and the Right of Assembly*. Knoxville: University of Tennessee Press, 1997.

Lunardini, Christine A. *From Equal Suffrage to Equal Rights: Alice Paul and the National Women's Party, 1910–1928*. New York: New York University Press, 1986.

Mead, Rebecca J. *How the West Was Won: Women's Suffrage in the Western United States, 1868–1914*. New York: New York University Press, 2004.

Terborg-Penn, Rosalyn. *African American Women in the Struggle for the Vote, 1850–1920*. Bloomington: Indiana University Press, 1998.

Wheeler, Marjorie Spruill. *New Women of the New South: The Leaders of the Woman Suffrage Movement in the Southern States.* New York: Oxford University Press, 1993.

Antisuffrage Movements

Camhi, Jane Jerome. *Women against Women: American Anti-suffragism, 1880–1920.* Brooklyn: Carlson, 1994.

Jablonsky, Thomas J. *The Home, Heaven, and Mother Party: Female Antisuffragists in the United States, 1868–1920.* Brooklyn: Carlson, 1994.

Marshall, Susan E. *Splintered Sisterhood: Gender and Class in the Campaign against Woman Suffrage.* Madison: University of Wisconsin Press, 1997.

POLITICS AND GOVERNMENT: NATIONAL AND STATE

General

Clemens, Elisabeth S. *The People's Lobby: Organizational Innovation and the Rise of Interest Group Politics in the United States, 1890–1925.* Chicago: University of Chicago Press, 1997.

Gould, Lewis L. *Reform and Regulation: American Politics from Roosevelt to Wilson.* 3rd ed. Prospect Heights, Ill.: Waveland, 1996.

Higgens-Evenson, R. Rudy. *The Price of Progress: Public Services, Taxation, and the American Corporate State, 1877 to 1929.* Baltimore: Johns Hopkins University Press, 2003.

Keller, Morton. *Regulating a New Economy: Public Policy and Economic Change in America, 1900–1933.* Cambridge, Mass.: Harvard University Press, 1990.

———. *Regulating a New Society: Public Policy and Social Change in America, 1900–1933.* Cambridge, Mass.: Harvard University Press, 1994.

Kornbluh, Mark Lawrence. *Why America Stopped Voting: The Decline of Participatory Democracy and the Emergence of Modern American Politics.* New York: New York University Press, 2000.

Link, Arthur S. *Woodrow Wilson and the Progressive Era, 1900–1917.* New York: Harper & Row, 1954.

McCormick, Richard L. *The Party Period and Public Policy: American Politics from the Age of Jackson to the Progressive Era.* New York: Oxford University Press, 1986.

McGerr, Michael. *The Decline of Popular Politics: The American North, 1865–1928.* New York: Oxford University Press, 1986.

Reagan, Patrick D. *Designing a New America: The Origins of New Deal Planning, 1890–1943.* Amherst: University of Massachusetts Press, 1999.

Parties and Electoral Politics

Chace, James. *1912: Wilson, Roosevelt, Taft, and Debs—The Election that Changed America.* New York: Simon & Schuster, 2004.

Edwards, Rebecca B. *Angels in the Machinery: Gender in American Party Politics from the Civil War to the Progressive Era.* New York: Oxford University Press, 1997.

Flehinger, Brett W. *The 1912 Election and the Power of Progressivism: A Brief History with Documents.* Boston: Bedford/St. Martin's, 2003.

Gable, John Allen. *The Bull Moose Years: Theodore Roosevelt and the Progressive Party.* Port Washington, N.Y.: Kennikat, 1978.

Gildow, Liette Patricia. *The Big Vote: Gender, Consumer Culture, and the Politics of Exclusion, 1890s–1920s.* Baltimore: Johns Hopkins University Press, 2004.

Gustafson, Melanie. *Women and the Republican Party, 1854–1924.* Urbana: University of Illinois Press, 2001.

Kleppner, Paul. *Continuity and Change in Electoral Politics, 1893–1928.* Westport, Conn.: Greenwood, 1987.

Lovell, S. D. *The Presidential Election of 1916.* Carbondale: Southern Illinois University Press, 1980.

Reynolds, John F. *The Demise of the American Convention System, 1880–1911.* New York: Cambridge University Press, 2006.

Sarasohn, David. *The Party of Reform: Democrats in the Progressive Era.* Jackson: University Press of Mississippi, 1989.

Sherman, Richard B. *The Republican Party and Black America: From McKinley to Hoover, 1896–1933.* Charlottesville: University Press of Virginia, 1973.

Presidency

Anderson, Donald F. *William Howard Taft: A Conservative's Conception of the Presidency.* Ithaca, N.Y.: Cornell University Press, 1973.

Clements, Kendrick A. *The Presidency of Woodrow Wilson.* Lawrence: University Press of Kansas, 1992.

Coletta, Paolo Enrico. *The Presidency of William Howard Taft.* Lawrence: University Press of Kansas, 1973.

Gatewood, Willard B. *Theodore Roosevelt and the Art of Controversy: Episodes of the White House Years.* Baton Rouge: Louisiana State University Press, 1970.

Gould, Lewis L. *The Presidency of Theodore Roosevelt.* Lawrence: University Press of Kansas, 1991.

Ponder, Stephen. *Managing the Press: Origins of the Media Presidency, 1897–1933.* New York: St. Martin's, 1999.

Congress

Harrison, Robert. *Congress, Progressive Reform, and the New American State.* New York: Cambridge University Press, 2004.

Holt, L. James. *Congressional Insurgents and the Party System, 1909–1916.* Cambridge, Mass.: Harvard University Press, 1967.

Margulies, Herbert F. *Reconciliation and Revival: James R. Mann and the House Republicans in the Wilson Era.* Westport, Conn.: Greenwood, 1996.

Public Agencies and Administration

Breen, William J. *Labor Market Politics and the Great War: The Department of Labor, the States, and the First U.S. Employment Service, 1907–1933.* Kent, Ohio: Kent State University Press, 1997.

Carpenter, Daniel P. *The Forging of Bureaucratic Autonomy: Reputations, Networks, and Policy Innovation in Executive Agencies, 1862–1928.* Princeton, N.J.: Princeton University Press, 2001.

Harden, Victoria A. *Inventing the NIH: Federal Biomedical Research Policy, 1887–1937.* Baltimore: Johns Hopkins University Press, 1986.

Skowronek, Stephen. *Building a New American State: The Expansion of National Administrative Capacities, 1877–1920.* New York: Cambridge University Press, 1982.

Public Finance, Taxation, and the Federal Reserve

Broz, J. Lawrence. *The International Origins of the Federal Reserve System.* Ithaca, N.Y.: Cornell University Press, 1997.

Buenker, John D. *The Income Tax and the Progressive Era.* New York: Garland, 1985.

Kahn, Jonathan David. *Budgeting Democracy: State Building and American Citizenship, 1890–1928.* Ithaca, N.Y.: Cornell University Press, 1997.

Livingston, James. *Origin of the Federal Reserve System: Money, Class, and Corporate Capitalism, 1890–1913.* Ithaca, N.Y.: Cornell University Press, 1986.

Stanley, Robert. *Dimensions of Law in the Service of Order: Origins of the Federal Income Tax, 1861–1913.* New York: Oxford University Press, 1993.

Weisman, Steven. *The Great Tax Wars: Lincoln to Wilson—The Fierce Battles over Money and Power that Transformed the Nation.* New York: Simon & Schuster, 2002.

Wolman, Paul. *Most Favored Nation: The Republican Revisionists and U.S. Tariff Policy, 1897–1912.* Chapel Hill: University of North Carolina Press, 1992.

Government and Business, Regulation, and Antitrust

General

Bringhurst, Bruce. *Antitrust and the Oil Monopoly: The Standard Oil Cases, 1890–1911.* Westport, Conn.: Greenwood, 1979.

Clark, John G. *Energy and the Federal Government: Fossil Fuel Policies, 1900–1946.* Urbana: University of Illinois Press, 1987.

Freyer, Tony. *Regulating Big Business: Antitrust in Great Britain and America.* New York: Cambridge University Press, 1992.

Grant, H. Roger. *Insurance Reform: Consumer Action in the Progressive Era.* Ames: Iowa State University Press, 1979.

James, Scott C. *Presidents, Parties, and the State: A Party System Perspective on Democratic Regulatory Choice, 1884–1936.* New York: Cambridge University Press, 2000.

McCraw, Thomas K. *Prophets of Regulation: Charles Francis Adams, Louis D. Brandeis, James M. Landis, Alfred E. Kahn.* Cambridge, Mass.: Harvard University Press, 1984.

White, Eugene. *The Regulation and Reform of the American Banking System, 1900–1920.* Princeton, N.J.: Princeton University Press, 1983.

Wiebe, Robert H. *Businessmen and Reform: A Study of the Progressive Movement.* Reprint, Chicago: Ivan R. Dee, 1989.

Railroad Regulation

Berk, Gerald. *Alternative Tracks: The Constitution of American Industrial Order, 1865–1917.* Baltimore: Johns Hopkins University Press, 1994.

Caine, Stanley P. *The Myth of a Progressive Reform: Railroad Regulation in Wisconsin, 1903–1910*. Madison: State Historical Society of Wisconsin, 1970.

Hoogenboom, Ari, and Olive Hoogenboom. *A History of the Interstate Commerce Commission: From Panacea to Palliative*. New York: Norton, 1976.

Kerr, K. Austin. *American Railroad Politics, 1914–1920: Rates, Wages, and Efficiency*. Pittsburgh: University of Pittsburgh Press, 1968.

Food and Drug Regulation

Coppin, Clayton A., and Jack High. *The Politics of Purity: Harvey Washington Wiley and the Origins of Federal Food Policy*. Ann Arbor: University of Michigan Press, 1999.

Wolfe, Margaret Ripley. *Lucius Polk Brown and Progressive Food and Drug Control: Tennessee and New York City, 1908–1920*. Lawrence: Regents Press of Kansas, 1978.

Young, James Harvey. *Pure Food: Securing the Federal Food and Drugs Act of 1906*. Princeton, N.J.: Princeton University Press, 1989.

State Politics and Government, and State-Level Progressivism

Abrams, Richard M. *Conservatism in a Progressive Era: Massachusetts Politics, 1900–1912*. Cambridge, Mass.: Harvard University Press, 1964.

Baker, Paula. *The Moral Framework of Public Life: Gender, Politics, and the State in Rural New York, 1870–1930*. New York: Oxford University Press, 1991.

Blackford, Mansel G. *The Politics of Business in California, 1890–1920*. Columbus: Ohio State University Press, 1977.

Brøndel, Jørn. *Ethnic Leadership and Midwestern Politics: Scandinavian Americans and the Progressive Movement in Wisconsin, 1890–1914*. Urbana: University of Illinois Press, 2004.

Buenker, John D. *The History of Wisconsin*. Vol. 4, *The Progressive Era, 1893–1914*. Madison: State Historical Society of Wisconsin, 1998.

Cherny, Robert W. *Populism, Progressivism, and the Transformation of Nebraska Politics, 1885–1915*. Lincoln: University of Nebraska Press, 1981.

Deverell, William, and Tom Sutton, eds. *California Progressivism Revisited*. Berkeley: University of California Press, 1994.

Gould, Lewis L. *Progressives and Prohibitionists: Texas Democrats in the Wilson Era*. Austin: University of Texas Press, 1973.

La Forte, Robert Sherman. *Leaders of Reform: Progressive Republicans in Kansas, 1900–1916*. Lawrence: University Press of Kansas, 1974.

Margulies, Herbert F. *The Decline of the Progressive Movement in Wisconsin, 1890–1920.* Madison: State Historical Society of Wisconsin, 1968.

McCormick, Richard L. *From Realignment to Reform: Political Change in New York State, 1893–1910.* Ithaca, N.Y.: Cornell University Press, 1981.

Pegram, Thomas R. *Partisans and Progressives: Private Interest and Public Policy in Illinois, 1870–1922.* Urbana: University of Illinois Press, 1992.

Piott, Steven L. *Holy Joe: Joseph Folk and the Missouri Idea.* Columbia: University of Missouri Press, 1997.

Reynolds, John F. *Testing Democracy: Electoral Behavior and Progressive Reform in New Jersey, 1880–1920.* Chapel Hill: University of North Carolina Press, 1988.

Sealander, Judith. *Grand Plans: Business Progressivism and Social Change in Ohio's Miami Valley, 1890–1929.* Lexington: University Press of Kentucky, 1988.

Thelen, David. *The New Citizenship: The Origins of Progressivism in Wisconsin, 1885–1900.* Columbia: University of Missouri Press, 1972.

———. *Paths of Resistance: Tradition and Dignity in Industrializing Missouri.* New York: Oxford University Press, 1986.

VanderMeer, Philip R. *The Hoosier Politician: Office Holding and Political Culture in Indiana, 1896–1920.* Urbana: University of Illinois Press, 1984.

Wright, James. *The Progressive Yankees: Republican Reformers in New Hampshire, 1906–1916.* Hanover, N.H.: University Press of New England, 1987.

Individual Politicians

Dual Biography

Cooper, John Milton, Jr. *The Warrior and the Priest: Woodrow Wilson and Theodore Roosevelt.* Cambridge, Mass.: Harvard University Press, 1983.

William Jennings Bryan

Coletta, Paolo E. *William Jennings Bryan.* 3 vols. Lincoln: University of Nebraska Press, 1964–1969.

Kazin, Michael. *A Godly Hero: The Life of William Jennings Bryan.* New York: Alfred A. Knopf, 2006.

Robert La Follette

Thelen, David P. *Robert M. La Follette and the Insurgent Spirit.* Boston: Little, Brown, 1976.

Unger, Nancy C. *Fighting Bob La Follette: The Righteous Reformer.* Chapel Hill: University of North Carolina Press, 2000.

Weisberger, Bernard. *The La Follettes of Wisconsin: Love and Politics in Progressive America.* Madison: University of Wisconsin Press, 1994.

Theodore Roosevelt

Brands, H. W. *TR: The Last Romantic.* New York: Basic Books, 1997.

Dalton, Kathleen. *Theodore Roosevelt: A Strenuous Life.* New York: Alfred A. Knopf, 2002.

Harbaugh, William H. *The Life and Times of Theodore Roosevelt.* Rev. ed. New York: Oxford University Press, 1975.

Jeffers, H. Paul. *Colonel Roosevelt: Theodore Roosevelt Goes to War, 1897–98.* New York: Wiley, 1996.

Morison, Elting E., and John M. Blum, eds. *The Letters of Theodore Roosevelt.* 8 vols. Cambridge, Mass.: Harvard University Press, 1951–54.

Morris, Edmund. *Theodore Rex.* New York: Random House, 2001.

O'Toole, Patricia. *When Trumpets Call: Theodore Roosevelt after the White House.* New York: Simon & Schuster, 2005.

Watts, Sarah. *Rough Rider in the White House: Theodore Roosevelt and the Politics of Desire.* Chicago: University of Chicago Press, 2003.

Woodrow Wilson

Clements, Kendrick A. *Woodrow Wilson: World Statesman.* Boston: Twayne, 1987.

Heckscher, August. *Woodrow Wilson: A Biography.* New York: Scribner's, 1991.

Link, Arthur S. *Wilson.* 5 vols. Princeton, N.J.: Princeton University Press, 1947–1965.

Link, Arthur S., ed. *The Papers of Woodrow Wilson.* 69 vols. Princeton, N.J.: Princeton University Press, 1966–1993.

Thompson, John A. *Woodrow Wilson.* London: Longman, 2002.

Walworth, Arthur. *Woodrow Wilson.* 3rd ed. New York: Norton, 1978.

Other Figures

Braeman, John. *Albert J. Beveridge: American Nationalist.* Chicago: University of Chicago Press, 1971.

Garraty, John A. *Henry Cabot Lodge: A Biography.* New York: Alfred A. Knopf, 1953.

Hodgson, Godfrey. *Woodrow Wilson's Right Hand: The Life of Colonel Edward M. House*. New Haven, Conn.: Yale University Press, 2006.

Leopold, Richard. *Elihu Root and the Conservative Tradition*. Boston: Little, Brown, 1954.

Lower, Richard Coke. *A Bloc of One: The Political Career of Hiram W. Johnson*. Stanford, Calif.: Stanford University Press, 1993.

Morton, Richard Allen. *Justice and Humanity: Edward F. Dunne, Illinois Progressive*. Carbondale: Southern Illinois University Press, 1997.

Rowley, William D. *Reclaiming the Arid West: The Career of Francis G. Newlands*. Bloomington: Indiana University Press, 1996.

Slayton, Robert A. *Empire Statesman: The Rise and Redemption of Al Smith*. New York: Free Press, 2001.

Strum, Philippa. *Louis D. Brandeis: Justice for the People*. Cambridge, Mass.: Harvard University Press, 1984.

LAW AND THE COURTS

General, Legal Practice, and the Legal Profession

Bergstrom, Randolph E. *Courting Danger: Injury and Law in New York City, 1870–1910*. Ithaca, N.Y.: Cornell University Press, 1992.

Beth, Loren. *The Development of the American Constitution, 1877–1917*. New York: Harper & Row, 1971.

Cowan, Geoffrey. *The People v. Clarence Darrow: The Bribery Trial of America's Greatest Lawyer*. New York: Times Books, 1993.

Hobson, Wayne K. *The American Legal Profession and the Organizational Society, 1890–1930*. New York: Garland, 1986.

Hovenkamp, Herbert. *Enterprise and American Law, 1837–1937*. Cambridge, Mass.: Harvard University Press, 1991.

LaPiana, William P. *Logic and Experience: The Origins of American Legal Education*. New York: Oxford University Press, 1994.

Rabban, David M. *Free Speech in its Forgotten Years, 1870–1920*. New York: Cambridge University Press, 1997.

Weinberg, Arthur, and Lila Weinberg. *Clarence Darrow: A Sentimental Rebel*. New York: Putnam, 1980.

Welke, Barbara Young. *Recasting American Liberty: Gender, Race, Law, and the Railroad Revolution*. New York: Cambridge University Press, 2001.

Wiecek, William M. *The Lost World of Classical Legal Thought: Law and Ideology in America, 1886–1937*. New York: Oxford University Press, 1998.

Willrich, Michael. *City of Courts: Socializing Justice in Progressive Era Chicago*. New York: Cambridge University Press, 2003.

Judiciary

General

Bickel, Alexander M., and Benno C. Schmidt Jr. *History of the Supreme Court of the United States*. Vol. 9, *The Judiciary and Responsible Government, 1910–21*. New York: Macmillan, 1984.

Curriden, Mark, and Leroy Phillips Jr. *Contempt of Court: The Turn-of-the-Century Lynching that Launched a Hundred Years of Federalism*. New York: Faber and Faber, 1999.

Ely, James W., Jr. *The Chief Justiceship of Melville W. Fuller, 1888–1910*. Columbia: University of South Carolina Press, 1995.

Fiss, Owen M. *History of the Supreme Court of the United States*. Vol. 8, *Troubled Beginnings of the Modern State, 1888–1910*. New York: Macmillan, 1993.

Kens, Paul. *Judicial Power and Reform Politics: The Anatomy of* Lochner v. New York. Lawrence: University Press of Kansas, 1990.

———. Lochner v. New York: *Economic Regulation on Trial*. Lawrence: University Press of Kansas, 1998.

Pratt, Walter E. *The Supreme Court under Edward Douglass White, 1910–1921*. Columbia: University of South Carolina Press, 1999.

Ross, William G. *A Muted Fury: Populists, Progressives, and Labor Confront the Courts, 1890–1937*. Princeton, N.J.: Princeton University Press, 1994.

John Marshall Harlan

Beth, Loren P. *John Marshall Harlan: The Last Whig Justice*. Lexington: University Press of Kentucky, 1992.

Przybyszewski, Linda. *The Republic according to John Marshall Harlan*. Chapel Hill: University of North Carolina Press, 1999.

Yarbrough, Tinsley E. *Judicial Enigma: The First Justice Harlan*. New York: Oxford University Press, 1995.

Oliver Wendell Holmes

Aichele, Gary J. *Oliver Wendell Holmes, Jr.: Soldier, Scholar, Judge*. Boston: Twayne, 1989.

Alschuler, Albert W. *Law without Values: The Life, Work, and Legacy of Justice Holmes.* Chicago: University of Chicago Press, 2000.
Baker, Liva. *The Justice from Beacon Hill: The Life and Times of Oliver Wendell Holmes.* New York: HarperCollins, 1991.
Novick, Sheldon M. *Honorable Justice: The Life of Oliver Wendell Holmes, Jr.* Boston: Little, Brown, 1989.
White, G. Edward. *Justice Oliver Wendell Holmes: Law and the Inner Self.* New York: Oxford University Press, 1993.

SOCIALISM AND OTHER RADICAL MOVEMENTS

General

Fogarty, Robert S. *All Things New: American Communes and Utopian Movements, 1860–1914.* Chicago: University of Chicago Press, 1990.
Green, James R. *Grass-Roots Socialism: Radical Movements in the Southwest, 1895–1943.* Baton Rouge: Louisiana State University Press, 1978.
Kraditor, Aileen S. *The Radical Persuasion, 1890–1917: Aspects of the Intellectual History and the Historiography of Three American Radical Organizations.* Baton Rouge: Louisiana State University Press, 1981.
Laslett, John H. M. *Labor and the Left: A Study of Socialist and Radical Influences in the American Labor Movement, 1881–1924.* New York: Basic Books, 1970.
Lipow, Arthur. *Authoritarian Socialism in America: Edward Bellamy and the Nationalist Movement.* Berkeley: University of California Press, 1982.
Shor, Francis Robert. *Utopianism and Radicalism in a Reforming America, 1888–1918.* Westport, Conn.: Greenwood, 1997.
Sorin, Gerald. *The Prophetic Minority: American Jewish Immigrant Radicals, 1880–1920.* Bloomington: Indiana University Press, 1985.

Socialism and the Socialist Party

Bissett, Jim. *Agrarian Socialism in America: Marx, Jefferson, and Jesus in the Oklahoma Countryside, 1904–1920.* Norman: University of Oklahoma Press, 1999.
Buhle, Mari Jo. *Women and American Socialism, 1870–1930.* Urbana: University of Illinois Press, 1981.
Critchlow, Donald T., ed. *Socialism in the Heartland: The Midwestern Experience.* Notre Dame, Ind.: University of Notre Dame Press, 1986.

Dick, William M. *Labor and Socialism in America: The Gompers Era.* New York: Kennikat, 1972.

Graham, John, ed. *"Yours for the Revolution":* The Appeal to Reason, *1895–1922.* Lincoln: University of Nebraska Press, 1990.

Miller, Sally M. *Victor Berger and the Promise of Constructive Socialism, 1910–1920.* Westport, Conn.: Greenwood, 1973.

Nash, Michael. *Conflict and Accommodation: Coal Miners, Steel Workers and Socialism, 1890–1920.* Westport, Conn.: Greenwood, 1982.

Pittenger, Mark. *American Socialists and Evolutionary Thought.* Madison: University of Wisconsin Press, 1993.

Pratt, Norma Fain. *Morris Hillquit: A Political History of an American Jewish Socialist.* Westport, Conn.: Greenwood, 1979.

Shannon, David A. *The Socialist Party of America: A History.* Reprint, Chicago: Quadrangle Books, 1967.

Shore, Elliott. *Talkin' Socialism: J. A. Wayland and the Role of the Press in American Radicalism, 1890–1912.* Lawrence: University Press of Kansas, 1988.

Weinstein, James. *The Decline of Socialism in America, 1912–1925.* New York: Monthly Review Press, 1967.

Eugene V. Debs

Morgan, H. Wayne. *Eugene V. Debs: Socialist for President.* Syracuse, N.Y.: Syracuse University Press, 1962.

Salvatore, Nick. *Eugene V. Debs: Citizen and Socialist.* Urbana: University of Illinois Press, 1982.

Young, Marguerite. *Harp Song for a Radical: The Life and Times of Eugene Victor Debs.* New York: Alfred A. Knopf, 1999.

Anarchism

Avrich, Paul. *Anarchist Portraits.* Princeton, N.J.: Princeton University Press, 1988.

Marsh, Margaret. *Anarchist Women, 1870–1920.* Philadelphia: Temple University Press, 1981.

Emma Goldman

Drinnon, Richard. *Rebel in Paradise: A Biography of Emma Goldman.* Reprint, Chicago: University of Chicago Press, 1982.

Falk, Candace Serena. *Love, Anarchy, and Emma Goldman*. New York: Henry Holt, 1984.

Morton, Marian J. *Emma Goldman and the American Left: "Nowhere at Home."* New York: Twayne, 1992.

Wexler, Alice. *Emma Goldman: An Intimate Life*. New York: Pantheon, 1984.

FOREIGN RELATIONS AND MILITARY HISTORY

General

Boyle, Francis Anthony. *Foundations of World Order: The Legalist Approach to International Relations, 1890–1922*. Durham, N.C.: Duke University Press, 1999.

Davis, Calvin DeArmond. *The United States and the Second Hague Peace Conference: American Diplomacy and International Organization, 1899–1914*. Durham, N.C.: Duke University Press, 1976.

Hannigan, Robert E. *The New World Power: American Foreign Policy, 1898–1917*. Philadelphia: University of Pennsylvania Press, 2002.

Koistinen, Paul A. C. *Mobilizing for Modern War: The Political Economy of American Warfare, 1865–1919*. Lawrence: University Press of Kansas, 1997.

Lake, David A. *Power, Protection, and Free Trade: International Sources of U.S. Commercial Strategy, 1887–1939*. Ithaca, N.Y.: Cornell University Press, 1988.

Lafeber, Walter. *The American Search for Opportunity, 1865–1913*. New York: Cambridge University Press, 1993.

May, Ernest R. *Imperial Democracy: The Emergence of the United States as a Great Power*. New York: Harcourt, Brace, and World, 1961.

Rosenberg, Emily S. *Financial Missionaries to the World: The Politics and Culture of Dollar Diplomacy, 1900–1930*. Cambridge, Mass.: Harvard University Press, 1999.

———. *Spreading the American Dream: American Economic and Cultural Expansion, 1890–1945*. New York: Hill and Wang, 1982.

Sparrow, Bartholomew. *The Insular Cases and the Birth of American Empire*. Lawrence: University Press of Kansas, 2006.

Taylor, Arnold H. *American Diplomacy and the Narcotics Traffic, 1900–1939: A Study in International Humanitarian Reform*. Durham, N.C.: Duke University Press, 1969.

Terrill, Tom E. *The Tariff, Politics, and American Foreign Policy, 1874–1911*. Westport, Conn.: Greenwood, 1973.

Veeser, Cryus. *A World Safe for Capitalism: Dollar Diplomacy and America's Rise to World Power*. New York: Columbia University Press, 2002.

Presidents, Secretaries of State, and Policy Leaders

Ambrosius, Lloyd G. *Wilsonianism: Woodrow Wilson and His Legacy in American Foreign Relations*. New York: Palgrave Macmillan, 2002.

Calhoun, Frederick S. *Power and Principle: Armed Intervention in Wilsonian Foreign Policy*. Kent, Ohio: Kent State University Press, 1986.

Clements, Kendrick A. *William Jennings Bryan: Missionary Isolationist*. Knoxville: University of Tennessee Press, 1982.

Clymer, Kenton J. *John Hay: The Gentleman as Diplomat*. Ann Arbor: University of Michigan Press, 1975.

Collin, Richard H. *Theodore Roosevelt: Culture, Diplomacy, and Expansion*. Baton Rouge: Louisiana State University Press, 1985.

Levin, N. Gordon. *Woodrow Wilson and World Politics: America's Response to War and Revolution*. New York, Oxford University Press, 1968.

Marks, Frederick W. *Velvet on Iron: The Diplomacy of Theodore Roosevelt*. Lincoln: University of Nebraska Press, 1979.

Minger, Ralph Eldin. *William Howard Taft and United States Foreign Policy: The Apprenticeship Years, 1900–1908*. Urbana: University of Illinois Press, 1975.

Safford, Jeffrey J. *Wilsonian Maritime Diplomacy, 1913–1921*. New Brunswick, N.J.: Rutgers University Press, 1978.

Scholes, Walter V., and Marie V. Scholes. *The Foreign Policies of the Taft Administration*. Columbia: University of Missouri Press, 1970.

Widenor, William C. *Henry Cabot Lodge and the Search for an American Foreign Policy*. Berkeley: University of California Press, 1980.

Zimmerman, Warren. *The First Great Triumph: How Five Americans Made Their Country a World Power*. New York: Farrar, Straus, and Giroux, 2002.

The Military and Military Reform

Abrahamson, James L. *America Arms for a New Century: The Making of a Great Military Power*. New York: Free Press, 1981.

Challener, Richard D. *Admirals, Generals, and American Foreign Policy, 1898–1914*. Princeton, N.J.: Princeton University Press, 1973.

Coffman, Edward M. *The Regulars: The American Army, 1898–1941*. Cambridge, Mass.: Belknap, 2004.

Cooper, Jerry. *The Rise of the National Guard: The Evolution of the American Militia, 1865–1920.* Lincoln: University of Nebraska Press, 1997.

Johnson, Herbert A. *Wingless Eagle: U.S. Army Aviation through World War I.* Chapel Hill: University of North Carolina Press, 2001.

Lane, Jack C. *Armed Progressive: A Study of the Military and Public Career of Leonard Wood.* San Rafael, Calif.: Presidio Press, 1978.

McBride, William M. *Technological Change and the United States Navy, 1865–1945.* Baltimore: Johns Hopkins University Press, 2000.

Nenninger, Timothy K. *The Leavenworth Schools and the Old Army: Education, Professionalism, and the Officer Corps of the United States Army, 1881–1918.* Westport, Conn.: Greenwood, 1978.

Reardon, Carol. *Soldiers and Scholars: The U.S. Army and the Uses of Military History, 1865–1920.* Lawrence: University Press of Kansas, 1990.

Spector, Ronald. *Admiral of the New Empire: The Life and Career of George Dewey.* Reprint, Columbia: University of South Carolina Press, 1988.

Vandiver, Frank W. *Black Jack: The Life and Times of John J. Pershing.* 2 vols. College Station: Texas A&M University Press, 1977.

Missionaries

Clymer, Kenton J. *Protestant Missionaries in the Philippines, 1898–1916: An Inquiry into the American Colonial Mentality.* Urbana: University of Illinois Press, 1986.

Garrett, Shirley S. *Social Reformers in Urban China: The Chinese Y.M.C.A., 1895–1926.* Cambridge, Mass.: Harvard University Press, 1970.

Hill, Patricia R. *The World Their Household: The American Foreign Mission's Movement and Cultural Transformation, 1870–1920.* Ann Arbor: University of Michigan Press, 1985.

Hopkins, C. Howard. *John R. Mott, 1865–1955: A Biography.* Grand Rapids, Mich.: Eerdmans, 1979.

Hunter, Jane. *The Gospel of Gentility: American Women Missionaries in Turn-of-the-Century China.* New Haven, Conn.: Yale University Press, 1984.

Martin, Sandy D. *Black Baptists and African Missions: The Origins of a Movement, 1880–1915.* Macon, Ga.: Mercer University Press, 1989.

Parker, Michael. *The Kingdom of Character: The Student Volunteer Movement for Foreign Missions, 1886–1926.* Lanham, Md.: University Press of America, 1998.

Rabe, Valentin H. *The Home Base of American China Missions, 1880–1920.* Cambridge, Mass.: Harvard University Press, 1978.

Anti-imperial and Peace Movements

Beisner, Robert L. *Twelve against Empire: The Anti-imperialists, 1898–1900.* New York: McGraw-Hill, 1968.

Chambers, John Whiteclay, II, ed. *The Eagle and the Dove: The American Peace Movement and United States Foreign Policy, 1900–1920.* 2nd ed. Syracuse, N.Y.: Syracuse University Press, 1991.

Johnson, Robert David. *The Peace Progressives and American Foreign Relations.* Cambridge, Mass.: Harvard University Press, 1995.

Kuhlman, Erika A. *Petticoats and White Feathers: Gender Conformity, Race, the Progressive Peace Movement, and the Debate over War, 1898–1919.* Westport, Conn.: Greenwood, 1997.

Marchand, C. Roland. *The American Peace Movement and Social Reform, 1898–1918.* Princeton, N.J.: Princeton University Press, 1972.

Osborne, Thomas J. *"Empire Can Wait": American Opposition to Hawaiian Annexation, 1893-1898.* Kent, Ohio: Kent State University Press, 1981.

Patterson, David S. *Toward a Warless World: The Travail of the American Peace Movement, 1887–1914.* Bloomington: Indiana University Press, 1976.

Tompkins, E. Berkeley. *Anti-imperialism in the United States: The Great Debate, 1890–1920.* Philadelphia: University of Pennsylvania Press, 1970.

Spanish and Philippine Wars and Cuban Occupation, 1898–1902

Berner, Brad. *The Spanish–American War: A Historical Dictionary.* Lanham, Md.: Scarecrow Press, 1998.

Cosmas, Graham. *An Army for Empire: The United States Army in the Spanish–American War.* Columbia: University of Missouri Press, 1971.

Gates, John Morgan. *Schoolbooks and Krags: The United States Army in the Philippines, 1898–1902.* Westport, Conn.: Greenwood, 1973.

Gatewood, Willard B. *Black Americans and the White Man's Burden, 1898–1903.* Urbana: University of Illinois Press, 1975.

Gould, Lewis L. *The Spanish–American War and President McKinley.* Lawrence: University Press of Kansas, 1982.

Hoganson, Kristin L. *Fighting for American Manhood: How Gender Politics Provoked the Spanish–American and Philippine–American Wars.* New Haven, Conn.: Yale University Press, 1998.

Linderman, Gerald. *The Mirror of War: American Society and the Spanish–American War.* Ann Arbor: University of Michigan Press, 1974.

Linn, Brian McAllister. *The Philippine War, 1899–1902.* Lawrence: University Press of Kansas, 2000.

——. *The U.S. Army and Counterinsurgency in the Philippine War, 1899–1902*. Chapel Hill: University of North Carolina Press, 1989.

McCartney, Paul T. *Power and Progress: American National Identity, the War of 1898, and the Rise of American Imperialism*. Baton Rouge: Louisiana State University Press, 2006.

Miller, Stuart Creighton. *"Benevolent Assimilation": The American Conquest of the Philippines, 1899–1903*. New Haven, Conn.: Yale University Press, 1982.

Offner, John L. *An Unwanted War: The Diplomacy of the United States and Spain over Cuba, 1895–1898*. Chapel Hill: University of North Carolina Press, 1992.

Pérez, Louis A., Jr. *The War of 1898: The United States and Cuba in History and Historiography*. Chapel Hill: University of North Carolina Press, 1998.

Silbey, David. *A War of Frontier and Empire: The Philippine–American War, 1899–1902*. New York: Hill and Wang, 2007.

Trask, David D. *The War with Spain in 1898*. New York: Macmillan, 1981.

Mexico, the Caribbean, and Latin America

Benjamin, Jules R. *The United States and Cuba: Hegemony and Dependent Development, 1880–1934*. Pittsburgh: University of Pittsburgh Press, 1977.

Collin, Richard H. *Theodore Roosevelt's Caribbean: The Panama Canal, the Monroe Doctrine, and the Latin American Context*. Baton Rouge: Louisiana State University Press, 1990.

Eisenhower, John S. D. *Intervention! The United States and the Mexican Revolution, 1913–1917*. New York: Norton, 1993.

Findlay, Eileen J. Suárez. *Imposing Decency: The Politics of Sexuality and Race in Puerto Rico, 1870–1920*. Durham, N.C.: Duke University Press, 1999.

Haley, P. Edward. *Revolution and Intervention: The Diplomacy of Taft and Wilson with Mexico, 1910–1917*. Cambridge, Mass.: MIT Press, 1970.

Healy, David. *Drive to Hegemony: The United States in the Caribbean, 1898–1917*. Madison: University of Wisconsin Press, 1988.

——. *Gunboat Diplomacy in the Wilson Era: The U.S. Navy in Haiti, 1915–1916*. Madison: University of Wisconsin Press, 1976.

Katz, Friedrich. *The Secret War in Mexico: Europe, the United States, and the Mexican Revolution*. Chicago: University of Chicago Press, 1981.

Kaplan, Edward S. *U.S. Imperialism in Latin America: Bryan's Challenges and Contributions, 1890–1920*. Westport, Conn.: Greenwood, 1997.

Lafeber, Walter. *The Panama Canal: The Crisis in Historical Perspective*. Rev. ed. New York: Oxford University Press, 1989.

Langley, Lester D. *The Banana Wars: United States Intervention in the Caribbean, 1898–1934*. Rev. ed. Lexington: University Press of Kentucky, 1985.

Langley, Lester D., and Thomas Schoonover. *The Banana Men: American Mercenaries and Entrepreneurs in Central America, 1880–1930*. Lexington: University Press of Kentucky, 1995.

McCullough, David G. *The Path between the Seas: The Creation of the Panama Canal, 1870–1914*. New York: Simon & Schuster, 1977.

Mitchell, Nancy. *The Danger of Dreams: German and American Imperialism in Latin America*. Chapel Hill: University of North Carolina Press, 1999.

Munro, Dana G. *Intervention and Dollar Diplomacy in the Caribbean, 1900–1921*. Reprint, Westport, Conn.: Greenwood, 1980.

O'Brien, Thomas F. *The Revolutionary Mission: American Enterprise in Latin America, 1900–1945*. New York: Cambridge University Press, 1996.

Schoonover, Thomas D. *The United States in Central America, 1860–1911: Episodes of Social Imperialism and Imperial Rivalry in a World System*. Durham, N.C.: Duke University Press, 1991.

Asia and the Pacific

Braisted, William R. *The United States Navy in the Pacific, 1897–1909*. Austin: University of Texas Press, 1958.

——. *The United States Navy in the Pacific, 1909–1922*. Austin: University of Texas Press, 1971.

Brands, H. W. *Bound to Empire: The United States and the Philippines*. New York: Oxford University Press, 1992.

Chey, Jongsuk. *Diplomacy of Asymmetry: Korean–American Relations to 1910*. Honolulu: University of Hawaii Press, 1990.

Hunt, Michael H. *The Making of a Special Relationship: The United States and China to 1914*. New York: Columbia University Press, 1983.

Iriye, Akira. *Pacific Estrangement: Japanese and American Expansion, 1897–1911*. Cambridge, Mass.: Harvard University Press, 1972.

Israel, Jerry. *Progressivism and the Open Door: America and China, 1905–1921*. Pittsburgh: University of Pittsburgh Press, 1971.

Kramer, Paul A. *The Blood of Government: Race, Empire, the United States, and the Philippines*. Chapel Hill: University of North Carolina Press, 2006.

Linn, Brian McAllister. *Guardians of Empire: The U.S. Army and the Pacific, 1902–1940*. Chapel Hill: University of North Carolina Press, 1997.

McCormick, Thomas J. *China Market: America's Quest for Informal Empire, 1893–1901*. Reprint, Chicago: Ivan R. Dee, 1990.

Stanley, Peter W. *A Nation in the Making: The Philippines and the United States, 1899–1921*. Cambridge, Mass: Harvard University Press, 1974.

Thomson, James C., Jr., Peter W. Stanley, and John Curtis Perry. *Sentimental Imperialists: The American Experience in East Asia.* New York: Harper & Row, 1981.

Ye Weili. *Seeking Modernity in China's Name: Chinese Students in the United States, 1900–1927.* Stanford, Calif.: Stanford University Press, 2001.

Great Britain and Canada

Anderson, Stuart. *Race and Rapprochement: Anglo-Saxonism and Anglo–American Relations, 1895–1904.* Cranbury, N.J.: Associated University Presses, 1981.

Coogan, John W. *The End of Neutrality: The United States, Britain, and Maritime Rights, 1899–1915.* Ithaca, N.Y.: Cornell University Press, 1981.

Gardner, Lloyd C. *Safe for Democracy: The Anglo-American Response to Revolution, 1913–1923.* New York: Oxford University Press, 1984.

Kohn, Edward P. *This Kindred People: Canadian–American Relations and the Anglo-Saxon Idea, 1895–1903.* Montreal: McGill-Queen's University Press, 2004.

Perkins, Bradford. *The Great Rapprochement: England and the United States, 1895–1914.* New York: Atheneum, 1968.

Tilchin, William N. *Theodore Roosevelt and the British Empire: A Study in Presidential Statecraft.* New York: St. Martin's, 1997.

Russia

Allison, William. *American Diplomats in Russia: Case Studies in Orphan Diplomacy, 1916–1919.* Westport, Conn.: Prager, 1997.

Saul, Norman E. *War and Revolution: The United States and Russia, 1914–1921.* Lawrence: University Press of Kansas, 2001.

Travis, Frederick F. *George Kennan and the American–Russian Relationship, 1865–1914.* Athens: Ohio University Press, 1990.

World War I: Neutrality to Intervention

Cooper, John Milton. *The Vanity of Power: American Isolationism and the First World War, 1914–1917.* Westport, Conn.: Greenwood, 1969.

Devlin, Patrick. *Too Proud to Fight: Woodrow Wilson's Neutrality.* New York: Oxford University Press, 1974.

Gregory, Ross. *The Origins of American Intervention in the First World War.* New York: Norton, 1971.

May, Ernest R. *The World War and American Isolation*. Cambridge, Mass.: Harvard University Press, 1963.

BUSINESS, ECONOMICS, AND TECHNOLOGY

General

Carosso, Vincent P., with Rose C. Carosso. *The Morgans: Private International Bankers, 1854–1913*. Cambridge, Mass.: Harvard University Press, 1987.

Chandler, Alfred D., Jr. *The Visible Hand: The Managerial Revolution in American Business*. Cambridge, Mass.: Harvard University Press, 1977.

Galambos, Louis. *The Public Image of Big Business in America, 1880–1940: A Quantitative Study of Social Change*. Baltimore: Johns Hopkins University Press, 1975.

Lamoreaux, Naomi, *The Great Merger Movement in American Business, 1895–1904*. New York: Cambridge University Press, 1985.

Porter, Glenn. *The Rise of Big Business, 1860–1920*. 2nd. ed. Wheeling, Ill.: Harlan Davidson, 1992.

Vatter, Harold G. *The Drive to Industrial Maturity, 1860–1914*. Westport, Conn.: Greenwood, 1975.

Whitten, David O., and Bessie Whitten. *The Birth of Big Business in the United States, 1860–1914: Commercial, Extractive, and Industrial Enterprise*. Westport, Conn.: Praeger, 2006.

Corporate Structure and Culture

Davis, Clark. *Company Men: White-Collar Life and Corporate Cultures in Los Angeles, 1892–1941*. Baltimore: Johns Hopkins University Press, 2000.

Levenstein, Margaret. *Accounting for Growth: Information Systems and the Creation of a Large Corporation*. Stanford, Calif.: Stanford University Press, 1998.

Noble, David F. *America by Design: Science, Technology, and the Rise of Corporate Capitalism*. New York: Oxford University Press, 1977.

Nye, David E. *Image Worlds: Corporate Identities at General Electric, 1890–1930*. Cambridge, Mass.: MIT Press, 1985.

Roy, William G. *Socializing Capital: The Rise of Large Industrial Corporations in America*. Princeton, N.J.: Princeton University Press, 1997.

Watts, Sarah Lyons. *Order against Chaos: Business Culture and Labor Ideology in America, 1880–1915*. Westport, Conn.: Greenwood, 1991.

Yates, JoAnne. *Control through Communication: The Rise of System in American Management.* Baltimore: Johns Hopkins University Press, 1989.

Zunz, Olivier. *Making America Corporate, 1870–1920.* Chicago: University of Chicago Press, 1990.

Depression of 1893–1897

Hoffman, Charles. *The Depression of the Nineties.* Westport, Conn.: Greenwood, 1970.

Steeples, Douglas, with David O. Whitten. *Democracy in Desperation: The Depression of 1893.* Westport, Conn.: Greenwood, 1998.

White, Gerald T. *The United States and the Problem of Recovery after 1893.* Tuscaloosa: University of Alabama Press, 1982.

Marketing, Advertising, and Public Relations

Laird, Pamela Walker. *Advertising Progress: American Business and the Rise of Consumer Marketing.* Baltimore: Johns Hopkins University Press, 1998.

Norris, James D. *Advertising and the Transformation of American Society, 1865–1920.* New York: Greenwood, 1990.

Strasser, Susan. *Satisfaction Guaranteed: The Making of the American Mass Market.* New York: Pantheon, 1989.

Tedlow, Richard. *New and Improved: The Story of Mass Marketing in America.* New York: Basic Books, 1990.

Manufacturing

Cortada, James W. *Before the Computer: IBM, NCR, Burroughs, and Remington Rand and the Industry They Created, 1865–1956.* Princeton, N.J.: Princeton University Press, 1993.

Davis, Donald Finlay. *Conspicuous Production: Automobiles and Elites in Detroit, 1899–1933.* Philadelphia: Temple University Press, 1988.

Hounshell, David. *From the American System to Mass Production, 1800–1932: The Development of Manufacturing Technology in the United States.* Baltimore: Johns Hopkins University Press, 1983.

Kane, Nancy Frances. *Textiles in Transition: Textiles, Wages, and Industry Relocation in the U.S. Textile Industry, 1880–1930.* Westport, Conn.: Greenwood, 1988.

Misa, Thomas J. *A Nation of Steel: The Making of Modern America, 1865–1925.* Baltimore: Johns Hopkins University Press, 1995.

Scranton, Philip. *Endless Novelty: Specialty Production and American Industrialization, 1865–1925*. Princeton, N.J.: Princeton University Press, 1997.

——. *Figured Tapestry: Production, Markets, and Power in Philadelphia Textiles, 1885–1941*. New York: Cambridge University Press, 1989.

Electricity and Communications

Aitken, Hugh. *The Continuous Wave: Technology and American Radio, 1900–1932*. Princeton, N.J.: Princeton University Press, 1985.

Douglas, Susan. *Inventing American Broadcasting, 1899–1922*. Baltimore: Johns Hopkins University Press, 1987.

Garnet, Robert W. *The Telephone Enterprise: The Evolution of the Bell System's Horizontal Structure, 1876–1909*. Baltimore: Johns Hopkins University Press, 1985.

Hughes, Thomas P. *Networks of Power: Electrification in Western Society, 1880–1930*. Baltimore: Johns Hopkins University Press, 1983.

Lipartito, Kenneth. *The Bell System and Regional Business: The Telephone in the South, 1877–1920*. Baltimore: Johns Hopkins University Press, 1989.

Moran, Richard. *Executioner's Current: Thomas Edison, George Westinghouse, and the Invention of the Electric Chair*. New York: Knopf, 2002.

Smith, George David. *The Anatomy of a Business Strategy: Bell, Western Electric, and the Origins of the American Telephone Industry*. Baltimore: Johns Hopkins University Press, 1985.

Wasserman, Neil H. *From Invention to Innovation: Long Distance Telephone Transmission at the Turn of the Century*. Baltimore: Johns Hopkins University Press, 1985.

Industrial Research and Invention

Crouch, Tom D. *The Bishop's Boys: A Life of Orville and Wilbur Wright*. New York: Norton, 1989.

——. *A Dream of Wings: Americans and the Airplane, 1875–1905*. New York: Norton, 1981.

Hughes, Thomas P. *American Genesis: A Century of Invention and Technological Enthusiasm, 1870–1970*. New York: Viking, 1989.

Jenkins, Reese. *Images and Enterprise: Technology and the American Photographic Industry, 1839–1925*. Baltimore: Johns Hopkins University Press, 1975.

Millard, Andre. *Edison and the Business of Innovation*. Baltimore: Johns Hopkins University Press, 1990.

Reich, Leonard. *The Making of American Industrial Research: Science and Business at GE and Bell, 1876–1926*. New York: Cambridge University Press, 1985.

Slaton, Amy E. *Reinforced Concrete and the Modernization of American Building, 1900–1930*. Baltimore: Johns Hopkins University Press, 2001.

Tobin, James. *To Conquer the Air: The Wright Brothers and the Great Race for Flight*. New York: Free Press, 2003.

Wise, George. *Willis R. Whitney, General Electric, and the Origins of U.S. Industrial Research*. New York: Columbia University Press, 1985.

Railroads

Hidy, Ralph W., et. al. *The Great Northern Railway: A History*. Boston: Harvard Business School Press, 1988.

Martin, Albro. *Enterprise Denied: Origins of the Decline of American Railroads, 1897–1917*. New York: Columbia University Press, 1971.

Thomas, William G. *Lawyering for the Railroad: Business, Law, and Power in the New South*. Baton Rouge: Louisiana State University Press, 1999.

Usselman, Steven W. *Regulating Railroad Innovation: Business, Technology, and Politics, 1840–1920*. New York: Cambridge University Press, 2002.

Oil and Petrochemicals

Giebelhaus, August W. *Business and Government in the Oil Industry: A Case Study of Sun Oil, 1876–1945*. Greenwich, Conn.: JAI Press, 1980.

Hidy, Ralph, and Muriel Hidy. *Pioneering in Big Business, 1882–1911: History of the Standard Oil Company (New Jersey)*. New York: Harper & Brothers, 1955.

Olien, Roger M., and Diana Davids Olien. *Oil in Texas: The Gusher Age, 1895–1945*. Austin: University of Texas Press, 2002.

Stiles, Jo Ann, Judith Linsley, and Ellen Rienstra. *Giant under the Hill: A History of the Spindletop Oil Discovery at Beaumont, Texas, in 1901*. Austin: Texas State Historical Association, 2002.

Logging

Robbins, William G. *Lumberjacks and Legislators: The Political Economy of the United States Lumber Industry, 1890–1941*. College Station: Texas A&M University Press, 1982.

International Business

Becker, William H. *The Dynamics of Business–Government Relations: Industry and Exports, 1893–1921*. Chicago: University of Chicago Press, 1982.

Davies, Robert B. *Peacefully Working to Conquer the World: Singer Sewing Machines in Foreign Markets.* New York: Arno, 1976.

Wilkins, Mira. *The Emergence of Multinational Enterprise: American Business Abroad from the Colonial Era to 1914.* Cambridge, Mass.: Harvard University Press, 1970.

Biographies

Baldwin, Neil. *Edison: Inventing the Century.* New York: Hyperion, 1995.

Brayer, Elizabeth. *George Eastman: A Biography.* Baltimore: Johns Hopkins University Press, 1996.

Chandler, Alfred D., Jr., and Stephen Salsbury. *Pierre S. du Pont and the Making of the Modern Corporation.* New York: Harper & Row, 1971.

Chernow, Ron. *Titan: The Life of John D. Rockefeller, Sr.* New York: Random House, 1998.

McDonald, Forrest. *Insull.* Chicago: University of Chicago Press, 1962.

Israel, Paul. *Edison: A Life.* New York: Wiley, 1998.

Hughes, Thomas P. *Elmer Sperry: Engineer and Inventor.* Baltimore: Johns Hopkins University Press, 1971.

Kemp, Kathryn W. *God's Capitalist: Asa Candler of Coca-Cola.* Macon, Ga.: Mercer University Press, 2002.

Klein, Maury. *The Life and Legend of E. H. Harriman.* Chapel Hill: University of North Carolina Press, 2000.

Kline, Ronald R. *Steinmetz: Engineer and Socialist.* Baltimore: Johns Hopkins University Press, 1992.

Martin, Albro. *James J. Hill and the Opening of the Northwest.* New York: Oxford University Press, 1976.

Nasaw, David. *Carnegie.* New York: Penguin, 2006.

Nevins, Allan. *Study in Power: John D. Rockefeller.* New York: Charles Scribner's Sons, 1953.

Wall, Joseph Frazier. *Andrew Carnegie.* New York: Oxford University Press, 1970.

Watts, Steven. *The People's Tycoon: Henry Ford and the American Century.* New York: Alfred A. Knopf, 2005.

LABOR

General

Dubofsky, Melvyn. *Industrialism and the American Worker, 1865–1920.* 3rd ed. Wheeling, Ill.: Harlan Davidson, 1996.

Glickman, Lawrence. *A Living Wage: American Workers and the Making of Consumer Society.* Ithaca, N.Y.: Cornell University Press, 1997.

Gutman, Herbert G. *Work, Culture, and Society in Industrializing America: Essays in American Working-Class and Social History.* New York: Alfred A. Knopf, 1976.

Haydu, Jeffrey. *Making American Industry Safe for Democracy: Comparative Perspectives on the State and Employee Representation in the Era of World War I.* Urbana: University of Illinois Press, 1997.

Montgomery, David. *The Fall of the House of Labor: The Workplace, the State, and American Labor Activism, 1865–1925.* New York: Cambridge University Press, 1987.

Shergold, Peter R. *Working-Class Life: The "American Standard" in Comparative Perspective, 1899–1913.* Pittsburgh: University of Pittsburgh Press, 1982.

Labor Markets

Keyssar, Alexander. *Out of Work: The First Century of Unemployment in Massachusetts.* New York: Cambridge University Press, 1986.

Korver, Tom. *The Fictitious Commodity: A Study of the U.S. Labor Market, 1880–1940.* New York: Greenwood, 1990.

Licht, Walter. *Getting Work: Philadelphia, 1840–1950.* Cambridge, Mass.: Harvard University Press, 1992.

Robertson, David Brian. *Capital, Labor, and the State: The Battle for American Labor Markets from the Civil War to the New Deal.* Lanham, Md.: Rowman & Littlefield, 2000.

Women and Labor, General Works

Enstad, Nan. *Ladies of Labor, Girls of Adventure: Working Women, Popular Culture, and Labor Politics at the Turn of the Century.* New York: Columbia University Press, 1999.

Meyerowitz, Joanne J. *Women Adrift: Independent Wage Earners in Chicago, 1880–1930.* Chicago: University of Chicago Press, 1988.

Murolo, Priscilla. *The Common Ground of Womanhood: Class, Gender, and Working Girls' Clubs, 1884–1928.* Urbana: University of Illinois Press, 1997.

Peiss, Kathy Lee. *Cheap Amusements: Working Women and Leisure in Turn-of-the-Century New York.* Philadelphia: Temple University Press, 1986.

Rotella, Elyce J. *From Home to Office: U.S. Women at Work, 1870–1930.* Ann Arbor: University of Michigan Press, 1980.

Tentler, Leslie Woodcock. *Wage-Earning Women: Industrial Work and Family Life in the United States, 1900–1930*. New York: Oxford University Press, 1979.

Craft and Industrial Labor

Bae Youngsoo. *Labor in Retreat: Class and Community among Men's Clothing Workers of Chicago, 1871–1929*. Albany: State University of New York Press, 2001.

Blatz, Perry K. *Democratic Miners: Work and Labor Relations in the Anthracite Coal Industry, 1875–1925*. Albany: State University of New York Press, 1994.

Brody, David. *Steelworkers in America: The Nonunion Era*. Cambridge, Mass.: Harvard University Press, 1960.

Cooper, Patricia A. *Once a Cigar Maker: Men, Women, and Work Culture in American Cigar Factories, 1900–1919*. Urbana: University of Illinois Press, 1987.

Gamber, Wendy. *The Female Economy: The Millinery and Dressmaking Trades, 1860–1930*. Bloomington: Indiana University Press, 1997.

Haydu, Jeffrey. *Between Craft and Class: Skilled Workers and Factory Politics in the United States and Britain, 1890–1922*. Berkeley: University of California Press, 1988.

Mohun, Arwen P. *Steam Laundries: Gender, Technology, and Work in the United States and Great Britain, 1880–1940*. Baltimore: Johns Hopkins University Press, 1999.

Montgomery, David. *Worker's Control in America: Studies in the History of Work, Technology, and Labor Struggles*. New York: Cambridge University Press, 1979.

Peterson, Joyce Shaw. *American Automobile Workers, 1900–1933*. Albany: State University of New York Press, 1987.

Rees, Albert. *Real Wages in Manufacturing, 1890–1914*. Princeton, N.J.: Princeton University Press, 1961.

Office Work and Clerical Services

Benson, Susan Porter. *Counter Cultures: Saleswomen, Managers, and Customers in American Department Stores, 1890–1940*. Urbana: University of Illinois Press, 1986.

Bjelopera, Jerome K. *Office and Sales Workers in Philadelphia, 1870–1920*. Urbana: University of Illinois Press, 2005.

Davies, Margery W. *Woman's Place Is at the Typewriter: Office Work and Office Workers, 1870–1930.* Philadelphia: Temple University Press, 1982.

DeVault, Ileen A. *Sons and Daughters of Labor: Class and Clerical Work in Turn-of-the-Century Pittsburgh.* Ithaca, N.Y.: Cornell University Press, 1990.

Fine, Lisa M. *The Souls of the Skyscraper: Female Clerical Workers in Chicago, 1870–1930.* Philadelphia: Temple University Press, 1990.

Kocka, Jürgen. *White Collar Workers in America, 1890–1940: A Sociopolitical History in International Perspective.* Translated by Maura Kealey. Beverly Hills, Calif.: Sage, 1980.

Kwolek-Folland, Angel. *Engendering Business: Men and Women in the Corporate Office, 1870–1930.* Baltimore: Johns Hopkins University Press, 1994.

Strom, Sharon H. *Beyond the Typewriter: Gender, Class, and the Origins of American Office Work, 1900–1930.* Urbana: University of Illinois Press, 1992.

Labor Management, Scientific Management, and Welfare Capitalism

Aldrich, Mark. *Safety First: Technology, Labor, and Business in the Building of American Work Safety, 1870–1939.* Baltimore: Johns Hopkins University Press, 1997.

Clawson, Dan. *Bureaucracy and the Labor Process: The Transformation of U.S. Industry, 1860–1920.* New York: Monthly Review Press, 1980.

Jacoby, Sanford M. *Employing Bureaucracy: Managers, Unions, and the Transformation of Work in American Industry, 1900–1945.* New York: Columbia University Press, 1985.

Kanigel, Robert. *The One Best Way: Frederick Winslow Taylor and the Enigma of Efficiency.* New York: Viking, 1997.

Mandell, Nikki. *The Corporation as Family: The Gendering of Corporate Welfare, 1890–1930.* Chapel Hill: University of North Carolina Press, 2002.

Meyer, Stephen. *The Five Dollar Day: Labor Management and Social Control in the Ford Motor Company, 1908–1921.* Albany: State University of New York Press, 1981.

Nelson, Daniel. *Frederick W. Taylor and the Rise of Scientific Management.* Madison: University of Wisconsin Press, 1980.

——. *Managers and Workers: Origins of the Twentieth-Century Factory System in the United States, 1880–1920.* 2nd ed. Madison: University of Wisconsin Press, 1995.

Tone, Andrea. *The Business of Benevolence: Industrial Paternalism in Progressive America.* Ithaca, N.Y.: Cornell University Press, 1997.

Working-Class Structure and Culture

Barrett, James R. *Work and Community in the Jungle: Chicago's Packinghouse Workers, 1894–1922*. Urbana: University of Illinois Press, 1987.

Bodnar, John E. *Workers' World: Kinship, Community, and Protest in an Industrial Society, 1900–1940*. Baltimore: Johns Hopkins University Press, 1982.

Cumbler, John T. *Working-Class Community in Industrial America: Work, Leisure, and Struggle in Two Industrial Cities, 1880–1930*. Westport, Conn.: Greenwood, 1979.

Hareven, Tamara. *Family Time and Industrial Time: The Relationship between Family and Work in a New England Industrial Community*. New York: Cambridge University Press, 1982.

Higbie, Frank Tobias. *Indispensable Outcasts: Hobo Workers and Community in the American Midwest, 1880–1930*. Urbana: University of Illinois Press, 2003.

Rosenzweig, Roy. *Eight Hours for What We Will: Workers and Leisure in an Industrial City, 1870–1920*. New York: Cambridge University Press, 1983.

Organized Labor

General

Friedman, Gerald. *State-Making and the Labor Movement: France and the United States, 1876–1914*. Ithaca, N.Y.: Cornell University Press, 1999.

Hattam, Victoria C. *Labor Visions and State Power: The Origins of Business Unionism in the United States*. Princeton, N.J.: Princeton University Press, 1993.

Marks, Gary. *Unions in Politics: Britain, Germany, and the United States in the Nineteenth and Early Twentieth Centuries*. Princeton, N.J.: Princeton University Press, 1989.

McMartin, Joseph A. *Labor's Great War: The Struggle for Industrial Democracy and the Origins of Modern American Labor Relations, 1912–1921*. Chapel Hill: University of North Carolina Press, 1997.

Mink, Gwendolyn. *Old Labor and New Immigrants in American Political Development: Union, Party, and State, 1875–1920*. Ithaca, N.Y.: Cornell University Press, 1986.

Ramirez, Bruno. *When Workers Fight: The Politics of Industrial Relations in the Progressive Era, 1898–1916*. Westport, Conn.: Greenwood, 1978.

Tomlins, Christopher. *The State and the Unions: Labor Relations, Law, and the Organized Labor Movement in America, 1880–1960*. New York: Cambridge University Press, 1985.

Trade Union Movement and American Federation of Labor

Greene, Julie. *Pure and Simple Politics: The American Federation of Labor and Political Activism, 1881–1917*. New York: Cambridge University Press, 1998.

Livesay, Harold C. *Samuel Gompers and Organized Labor in America*. Boston: Little, Brown, 1978.

Phelan, Craig. *Divided Loyalties: The Public and Private Life of Labor Leader John Mitchell*. Albany: State University of New York Press, 1994.

Taft, Philip. *The A.F. of L. in the Time of Gompers*. New York: Harper & Brothers, 1957.

Van Tine, Warren R. *The Making of the Labor Bureaucrat: Union Leadership in the United States, 1870–1920*. Amherst: University of Massachusetts Press, 1973.

Industrial Workers of the World

Carlson, Peter. *Roughneck: The Life and Times of Big Bill Haywood*. New York: Norton, 1983.

Conlin, Joseph R., ed. *At the Point of Production: The Local History of the I.W.W.* Westport, Conn.: Greenwood, 1981.

Dubofsky, Melvyn. *"Big Bill" Haywood*. New York: St. Martin's, 1987.

——. *We Shall Be All: A History of the IWW*. 2nd ed. Urbana: University of Illinois Press, 1988.

Hall, Greg. *Harvest Wobblies: The Industrial Workers of the World and Agricultural Laborers in the American West, 1905–1930*. Corvallis: Oregon State University Press, 2001.

Kimeldorf, Howard. *Battling for American Labor: Wobblies, Craft Workers, and the Making of the Union Movement*. Berkeley: University of California Press, 1999.

Sellars, Nigel Anthony. *Oil, Wheat, and Wobblies: The Industrial Workers of the World in Oklahoma, 1905–1930*. Norman: University of Oklahoma Press, 1998.

Women and Organized Labor

Argersinger, Jo Ann E. *Making the Amalgamated: Gender, Ethnicity, and Class in the Baltimore Clothing Industry, 1899–1939*. Baltimore: Johns Hopkins University Press, 1999.

Cameron, Ardis. *Radicals of the Worst Sort: Laboring Women in Lawrence, Massachusetts, 1860–1912*. Urbana: University of Illinois Press, 1993.

Gorn, Elliott. *Mother Jones: The Most Dangerous Woman in America.* New York: Hill and Wang, 2001.

Norwood, Stephen H. *Labor's Flaming Youth: Telephone Operators and Worker Militancy, 1878–1923.* Urbana: University of Illinois Press, 1990.

Orleck, Annelise. *Common Sense and a Little Fire: Women and Working-Class Politics in the United States, 1900–1965.* Chapel Hill: University of North Carolina Press, 1995.

Van Raaphorst, Donna L. *Union Maids Not Wanted: Organizing Domestic Workers, 1870–1940.* Westport, Conn.: Praeger, 1988.

Local and Case Studies

Fink, Gary M. *Labor's Search for Political Order: The Political Behavior of the Missouri Labor Movement, 1890–1940.* Columbia: University of Missouri Press, 1973.

Fones-Wolf, Ken. *The Trade-Union Gospel: Christianity and Labor in Industrial Philadelphia, 1865–1915.* Philadelphia: Temple University Press, 1989.

Goldberg, David J. *A Tale of Three Cities: Labor Organization and Protest in Paterson, Passaic, and Lawrence, 1916–1921.* New Brunswick, N.J.: Rutgers University Press, 1989.

Greenwald, Richard A. *The Triangle Fire, the Protocols of Peace, and Industrial Democracy in Progressive Era New York.* Philadelphia: Temple University Press, 2005.

Harris, Howell John. *Bloodless Victories: The Rise and Fall of the Open Shop in the Philadelphia Metal Trades, 1890–1940.* New York: Cambridge University Press, 2000.

Kazin, Michael. *Barons of Labor: The San Francisco Buildings Trade and Union Power in the Progressive Era.* Urbana: University of Illinois Press, 1987.

Leidenberger, Georg. *Chicago's Progressive Alliance: Labor and the Bid for Public Streetcars.* DeKalb: Northern Illinois University Press, 2006.

Strikes and Other Conflicts

Adams, Graham. *Age of Industrial Violence, 1910–15: The Activities and Findings of the United States Commission on Industrial Relations.* New York: Columbia University Press, 1966.

Gitelman, Howard M. *Legacy of the Ludlow Massacre: A Chapter in American Industrial Relations.* Philadelphia: University of Pennsylvania Press, 1988.

Golin, Steve. *The Fragile Bridge: Paterson Silk Strike, 1913.* Philadelphia: Temple University Press, 1988.

Schneirov, Richard, Shelton Stromquist, and Nick Salvatore, eds. *The Pullman Strike and the Crisis of the 1890s: Essays on Labor and Politics.* Urbana: University of Illinois Press, 1999.

Schwantes, Carlos A. *Coxey's Army: An American Odyssey.* Lincoln: University of Nebraska Press, 1985.

Steel, Edward M., Jr., ed. *The Court-Martial of Mother Jones.* Lexington: University Press of Kentucky, 1995.

Tripp, Anne Huber. *The I.W.W. and the Paterson Silk Strike of 1913.* Urbana: University of Illinois Press, 1987.

Watson, Bruce. *Bread and Roses: Migrants and the Struggle for the American Dream.* New York: Viking, 2005.

SOCIAL AND CULTURAL HISTORY

General

Batchelor, Bob. *The 1900s: American Popular Culture through History.* Westport, Conn.: Greenwood, 2002.

Blanke, David. *The 1910s: American Popular Culture through History.* Westport, Conn.: Greenwood, 2002.

Leach, William. *Land of Desire: Merchants, Power, and the Rise of a New American Culture.* New York: Pantheon, 1993.

Schlereth, Thomas J. *Victorian America: Transformations in Everyday Life, 1876–1915.* New York: HarperCollins, 1991.

Family Life and Childhood

Apple, Rima D. *Mothers and Medicine: A Social History of Infant Feeding, 1890–1950.* Madison: University of Wisconsin Press, 1988.

Gordon, Linda. *Heroes of Their Own Lives: The Politics and History of Family Violence, 1880–1960.* New York: Viking, 1988.

Macleod, David I. *The Age of the Child: Children in America, 1890–1920.* New York: Twayne, 1998.

May, Elaine Tyler. *Great Expectations: Marriage and Divorce in Post-Victorian America.* Chicago: University of Chicago Press, 1980.

Zelizer, Viviana A. *Pricing the Priceless Child: The Changing Social Value of Children.* Princeton, N.J.: Princeton University Press, 1985.

Ideas, Attitudes, and Practices

Burch, Susan. *Signs of Resistance: American Deaf Cultural History, 1900 to 1942.* New York: New York University Press, 2003.

Dawson, Melanie. *Laboring to Play: Home Entertainment and the Spectacle of Middle-Class Cultural Life, 1850–1920.* Tuscaloosa: University of Alabama Press, 2005.

De Leon, Charles L. Ponce. *Self-Exposure: Human Interest Journalism and the Emergence of Celebrity in America, 1890–1940.* Chapel Hill: University of North Carolina Press, 2002.

Glassberg, David. *American Historical Pageantry: The Uses of Tradition in the Early Twentieth Century.* Chapel Hill: University of North Carolina Press, 1990.

Joselit, Jenna Weissman. *A Perfect Fit: Clothes, Character, and the Promise of America.* New York: Henry Holt, 2001.

Lindgren, James M. *Preserving Historic New England: Preservation, Progressivism, and the Remaking of Memory.* New York: Oxford University Press, 1995.

Litwicki, Ellen M. *America's Public Holidays, 1865–1920.* Washington, D.C.: Smithsonian Institution Press, 2000.

O'Malley, Michael. *Keeping Watch: A History of American Time.* New York: Viking, 1990.

Orvell, Miles. *The Real Thing: Imitation and Authenticity in American Culture, 1880–1940.* Chapel Hill: University of North Carolina Press, 1989.

Rieser, Andrew Chamberlin. *The Chautauqua Moment: Protestants, Progressives, and the Culture of Modern Liberalism.* New York: Columbia University Press, 2003.

Rodgers, Daniel T. *The Work Ethic in Industrial America, 1850–1920.* Chicago: University of Chicago Press, 1978.

Schmitt, Peter J. *Back to Nature: The Arcadian Myth in Urban America.* New York: Oxford University Press, 1969.

Schorman, Rob. *Clothing and Social Change at the Turn of the Century.* Philadelphia: University of Pennsylvania Press, 2004.

Consumer Culture

Bronner, Simon, ed. *Consuming Visions: Accumulation and Display of Goods in America, 1880–1920.* New York: Norton, 1989.

Calder, Lendol. *Financing the American Dream: A Cultural History of Consumer Credit.* Princeton, N.J.: Princeton University Press, 1999.

Gordon, Ian. *Comic Strips and Consumer Culture, 1890–1945.* Washington, D.C.: Smithsonian Institution Press, 1998.

Horowitz, Daniel. *The Morality of Spending: Attitudes toward the Consumer Society in America, 1875–1940.* Baltimore: Johns Hopkins University Press, 1985.

Lears, T. J. Jackson. *Fables of Abundance: A Cultural History of Advertising in America.* New York: Basic Books, 1994.

Matt, Susan J. *Keeping Up with the Joneses: Envy in American Consumer Culture, 1890–1930.* Philadelphia: University of Pennsylvania Press, 2002.

McGovern, Charles F. *Sold American: Consumption and Citizenship, 1890–1945.* Chapel Hill: University of North Carolina Press, 2006.

Technology and Culture

Fischer, Claude S. *America Calling: A Social History of the Telephone to 1940.* Berkeley: University of California Press, 1992.

Flink, James J. *America Adopts the Automobile, 1865–1910.* Cambridge, Mass.: MIT Press, 1970.

Kenney, William Howland. *Recorded Music in American Life: The Phonograph and Popular Memory, 1890–1945.* New York: Oxford University Press, 1999.

Nye, David E. *Electrifying America: Social Meanings of a New Technology, 1880–1940.* Cambridge, Mass.: MIT Press, 1990.

West, Nancy Martha. *Kodak and the Lens of Nostalgia.* Charlottesville: University Press of Virginia, 2000.

Material Culture

Clark, Robert Judson, ed. *The Arts and Crafts Movement in America, 1876–1916.* Princeton, N.J.: Princeton University Press, 1992.

Foy, Jessica H., and Karel Ann Marling, eds. *The Arts and the American Home, 1890–1930.* Knoxville: University of Tennessee Press, 1994.

Foy, Jessica H., and Thomas J. Schlereth, eds. *American Home Life, 1880–1930: A Social History of Space and Services.* Knoxville: University of Tennessee Press, 1992.

Grier, Katherine. *Culture and Comfort: Parlor-Making and Middle-Class Identity, 1850–1930.* Washington, D.C.: Smithsonian Institution Press, 1997.

Kaplan, Wendy. *"The Art that Is Life": The Arts and Crafts Movement in America, 1875–1920.* Boston: Little, Brown, 1987.

Roell, Craig H. *The Piano in America, 1890–1940*. Chapel Hill: University of North Carolina Press, 1989.

Tourism

Aron, Cindy S. *Working at Play: A History of Vacations in the United States*. New York: Oxford University Press, 1999.

Cocks, Catherine. *Doing the Town: The Rise of Urban Tourism in the United States, 1850–1915*. Berkeley: University of California Press, 2001.

Dilworth, Leah. *Imagining Indians in the Southwest: Persistent Visions of a Primitive Past*. Washington, D.C.: Smithsonian Institution Press, 1996.

Rothman, Hal K. *Devil's Bargains: Tourism in the Twentieth-Century West*. Lawrence: University Press of Kansas, 1998.

Shaffer, Margaret S. *See America First: Tourism and National Identity, 1880–1940*. Washington, D.C.: Smithsonian Institution Press, 2001.

Sterngass, Jon. *First Resorts: Pursuing Pleasure at Saratoga Springs, Newport & Coney Island*. Baltimore: Johns Hopkins University Press, 2001.

Expositions

Badger, Reid. *The Great American Fair: The World's Columbian Exposition and American Culture*. Chicago: Nelson Hall, 1979.

Benedict, Burton, et al. *The Anthropology of World's Fairs: San Francisco's Panama Pacific International Exposition of 1915*. Berkeley: Scholar Press, 1983.

Burg, David F. *Chicago's White City of 1893*. Lexington: University Press of Kentucky, 1976.

Gilbert, James. *Perfect Cities: Chicago's Utopias of 1893*. Chicago: University of Chicago Press, 1991.

Muccigrosso, Robert. *Celebrating the New World: Chicago's Columbian Exposition of 1893*. Chicago: Ivan R. Dee, 1993.

Reed, Christopher Robert. *"All the World is Here": The Black Presence at the White City*. Bloomington: Indiana University Press, 2000.

Rydell, Robert. *All the World's a Fair: Visions of Empire at American International Expositions, 1876–1916*. Chicago: University of Chicago Press, 1984.

Entertainment and Amusement Parks

Kasson, John F. *Amusing the Million: Coney Island at the Turn of the Century*. New York: Hill and Wang, 1978.

Nasaw, David. *Going Out: The Rise of Public Amusements.* New York: Basic Books, 1993.

Register, Woody. *The Kid of Coney Island: Fred Thompson and the Rise of American Amusements.* New York: Oxford University Press, 2001.

Sports and Physical Culture

Alexander, Charles C. *John McGraw.* New York: Viking, 1988.

Burk, Robert F. *Never Just a Game: Players, Owners, and American Baseball to 1920.* Chapel Hill: University of North Carolina Press, 1994.

Hardy, Stephen. *How Boston Played: Sport, Recreation, and Community, 1865–1915.* Boston: Northeastern University Press, 1982.

Malloy, Jerry, ed. *Sol White's History of Colored Base Ball, with Other Documents of the Early Black Game, 1886–1936.* Lincoln: University of Nebraska Press, 1995.

Mrozek, Donald J. *Sport and American Mentality, 1880–1910.* Knoxville: University of Tennessee Press, 1983.

Pope, Steven W. *Patriotic Games: Sporting Traditions in the American Imagination, 1876–1926.* New York: Oxford University Press, 1997.

Putney, Clifford. *Muscular Christianity: Manhood and Sports in Protestant America, 1880–1920.* Cambridge, Mass.: Harvard University Press, 2001.

Riess, Steven A. *City Games: The Evolution of American Urban Society and the Rise of Sports.* Urbana: University of Illinois Press, 1989.

———. *Sport in Industrial America, 1850–1920.* Wheeling, Ill.: Harlan Davidson, 1995.

———. *Touching Base: Professional Baseball and American Culture in the Progressive Era.* Rev. ed. Urbana: University of Illinois Press, 1999.

Roberts, Randy. *Papa Jack: Jack Johnson and the Era of White Hopes.* New York: Free Press, 1983.

Robinson, Ray. *Matty, an American Hero: Christy Mathewson of the New York Giants.* New York: Oxford University Press, 1993.

WOMEN

General

Schneider, Dorothy, and Carl J. Schneider. *American Women in the Progressive Era, 1900–1920.* New York: Facts on File, 1993.

Social and Cultural Trends

Abel, Emily. *Heart of Wisdom: American Women Caring for Kin, 1850–1940.* Cambridge, Mass.: Harvard University Press, 2000.

Cunningham, Patricia A. *Reforming Women's Fashion, 1850–1920: Politics, Health, and Art.* Kent, Ohio: Kent State University Press, 2003.

Lowe, Margaret. *Looking Good: College Women and the Body Image, 1875–1930.* Baltimore: Johns Hopkins University Press, 2003.

Marks, Patricia. *Bicycles, Bangs, and Bloomers: The New Woman in the Popular Press.* Lexington: University Press of Kentucky, 1990.

Patterson, Martha H. *Beyond the Gibson Girl: Reimagining the American New Woman, 1895–1915.* Urbana: University of Illinois Press, 2005.

Rose, Elizabeth. *A Mother's Job: The History of Day Care, 1890–1960.* New York: Oxford University Press, 1999.

Rosenzweig, Linda W. *The Anchor of My Life: American Middle-Class Mothers and Daughters, 1880–1920.* New York: New York University Press, 1993.

Shapiro, Laura. *Perfection Salad: Women and Cooking at the Turn of the Century.* Reprint, New York: Modern Library, 2001.

Vicinus, Martha. *Independent Women: Work and Community for Single Women, 1850–1920.* Chicago: University of Chicago Press, 1985.

Intellectual Trends

Allen, Polly Wynn. *Building Domestic Liberty: Charlotte Perkins Gilman's Architectural Feminism.* Amherst: University of Massachusetts Press, 1988.

Cook, Blanche, ed. *Crystal Eastman on Women and Revolution.* New York: Oxford University Press, 1978.

Cott, Nancy. *The Grounding of Modern Feminism.* New Haven, Conn.: Yale University Press, 1987.

Kessler, Carol Farley. *Charlotte Perkins Gilman: Her Progress toward Utopia with Selected Writings.* Syracuse, N.Y.: Syracuse University Press, 1995.

Lagemann, Ellen Condliffe. *A Generation of Women: Education in the Lives of Progressive Reformers.* Cambridge, Mass.: Harvard University Press, 1979.

Rosenberg, Rosalind. *Beyond Separate Spheres: Intellectual Roots of Modern Feminism.* New Haven, Conn.: Yale University Press, 1982.

Sochen, June. *The New Woman: Feminism in Greenwich Village, 1910–1920.* New York: Quadrangle, 1972.

Tumber, Catherine. *American Feminism and the Birth of New Age Spirituality: Searching for a Higher Self, 1875–1915.* Lanham, Md.: Rowman and Littlefield, 2002.

Women in the Professions

Fitzpatrick, Ellen. *Endless Crusade: Women Social Scientists and Progressive Reform.* New York: Oxford University Press, 1989.

Glazer, Penina Migdal, and Miriam Slater. *Unequal Colleagues: The Entrance of Women into the Professions, 1890–1940.* New Brunswick, N.J.: Rutgers University Press, 1987.

Morantz-Sanchez, Regina. *Conduct Unbecoming a Woman: Medicine on Trial in Turn-of-the-Century Brooklyn.* New York: Oxford University Press, 1999.

Rossiter, Margaret W. *Women Scientists in America: Struggles and Strategies to 1940.* Baltimore: Johns Hopkins University Press, 1982.

Silverberg, Helene, ed. *Gender and American Social Science: The Formative Years.* Princeton, N.J.: Princeton University Press, 1998.

Women's Organizations and Philanthropy

Blair, Karen J. *The Clubwoman as Feminist: True Womanhood Redefined, 1868–1914.* New York: Holmes and Meier, 1980.

Gere, Anne Ruggles. *Intimate Practices: Literacy and Cultural Work in U.S. Women's Clubs, 1880–1920.* Urbana: University of Illinois Press, 1997.

Scott, Anne Firor. *Natural Allies: Women's Associations in American History.* Urbana: University of Illinois Press, 1991.

Women and the Arts

Batker, Carol J. *Reforming Fictions: Native, African, and Jewish American Women's Literature and Journalism in the Progressive Era.* New York: Columbia University Press, 2000.

Blair, Karen J. *The Torchbearers: Women and Their Amateur Art Associations, 1890–1930.* Bloomington: Indiana University Press, 1994.

Gover, C. Jane. *The Positive Image: Women Photographers in Turn-of-the-Century America.* Albany: State University of New York Press, 1988.

McCarthy, Kathleen D. *Women's Culture: American Philanthropy and Art, 1830–1930.* Chicago: University of Chicago Press, 1991.

Prieto, Laura R. *At Home in the Studio: The Professionalization of Women Artists in America.* Cambridge, Mass.: Harvard University Press, 2001.

Swinth, Kirsten. *Painting Professionals: Women Artists and the Development of Modern American Art, 1870–1930.* Chapel Hill: University of North Carolina Press, 2001.

Van Hook, Bailey. *Angels of Art: Women and Art in American Society, 1876–1914.* University Park: Pennsylvania State University Press, 1996.

Wexler, Laura. *Tender Violence: Domestic Visions in an Age of U.S. Imperialism.* Chapel Hill: University of North Carolina Press, 2000.

Biographies

Bordin, Ruth. *Frances Willard: A Biography.* Chapel Hill: University of North Carolina Press, 1986.

Brown, Victoria Bissell. *The Education of Jane Addams.* Philadelphia: University of Pennsylvania Press, 2004.

Clarke, Robert. *Ellen Swallow: The Woman Who Founded Ecology.* Chicago: Follett, 1973.

Cook, Blanche Wiesen. *Eleanor Roosevelt.* Vol. 1, *1884–1933.* New York: Viking, 1992.

Costin, Lela. *Two Sisters for Social Justice: A Biography of Grace and Edith Abbott.* Urbana: University of Illinois Press, 1983.

Deacon, Desley. *Elsie Clews Parsons: Inventing Modern Life.* Chicago: University of Chicago Press, 1997.

DuBois, Ellen Carol. *Harriot Stanton Blatch and the Winning of Woman Suffrage.* New Haven, Conn.: Yale University Press, 1997.

Elshtain, Jean Bethke. *Jane Addams and the Dream of American Democracy: A Life.* New York: Basic, 2002.

Garrison, Dee. *Mary Heaton Vorse: The Life of an American Insurgent.* Philadelphia: Temple University Press, 1989.

Grace, Fran. *Carrie Nation: Retelling the Life.* Bloomington: Indiana University Press, 2001.

Hermann, Dorothy. *Helen Keller: A Life.* New York: Alfred A. Knopf, 1998.

Horowitz, Helen Lefkowitz. *The Power and Passion of M. Carey Thomas.* New York: Alfred A. Knopf, 1994.

Lane, Ann J. *To Herland and Beyond: The Life and Work of Charlotte Perkins Gilman.* New York: Pantheon, 1990.

Lumsden, Linda J. *Inez: The Life and Times of Inez Milholland.* Bloomington: Indiana University Press, 2004.

Perry, Elisabeth Israels. *Belle Moskowitz: Feminine Politics and the Exercise of Power in the Age of Alfred E. Smith.* New York: Oxford University Press, 1987.

Sicherman, Barbara. *Alice Hamilton: A Life in Letters.* Cambridge, Mass.: Harvard University Press, 1984.

Sklar, Kathryn Kish. *Florence Kelley and the Nation's Work: The Rise of Women's Political Culture, 1830–1900.* New Haven, Conn.: Yale University Press, 1995.

GENDER AND SEXUALITY

Sexuality: Ideas, Attitudes, and Practices

Birken, Lawrence. *Consuming Desire: Sexual Science and the Emergence of a Culture of Abundance, 1871–1914.* Ithaca, N.Y.: Cornell University Press, 1988.

D'Emilio, John, and Estelle B. Freedman. *Intimate Matters: A History of Sexuality in America.* 2nd. ed. Chicago: University of Chicago Press, 1997.

Maines, Rachel P. *The Technology of Orgasm: "Hysteria," the Vibrator, and Women's Sexual Satisfaction.* Baltimore: Johns Hopkins University Press, 1999.

Ullman, Sharon R. *Sex Seen: The Emergence of Modern Sexuality in America.* Berkeley: University of California Press, 1997.

Masculinity: Ideas, Attitudes, and Practices

Bederman, Gail. *Manliness and Civilization: A Cultural History of Gender and Race Relations in the United States, 1880–1920.* Chicago: University of Chicago Press, 1995.

Carnes, Mark C., and Clyde Griffen, eds. *Meanings for Manhood: Constructions of Masculinity in Victorian America.* Chicago: University of Chicago Press, 1990.

Chudacoff, Howard P. *The Age of the Bachelor: Creating an American Subculture.* Princeton, N.J.: Princeton University Press, 1999.

Kasson, John F. *Houdini, Tarzan, and the Perfect Man: The White Male Body and the Challenge of Modernity in America.* New York: Hill and Wang, 2001.

White, Kevin. *The First Sexual Revolution: The Emergence of Male Heterosexuality in Modern America.* New York: New York University Press, 1993.

Winter, Thomas. *Making Men, Making Class: The YMCA and Workingmen, 1877–1920.* Chicago: University of Chicago Press, 2002.

Homosexuality

Boag, Peter. *Same Sex Affairs: Constructing and Controlling Homosexuality in the Pacific Northwest.* Berkeley: University of California Press, 2003.

Chauncey, George. *Gay New York: Gender, Urban Culture, and the Making of the Gay Male World, 1890–1940.* New York: Basic Books, 1994.

Duggan, Lisa. *Sapphic Slashers: Sex, Violence, and American Modernity.* Durham, N.C.: Duke University Press, 2000.

Terry, Jennifer. *An American Obsession: Science, Medicine and Homosexuality in Modern Society.* Chicago: University of Chicago Press, 1999.

IMMIGRATION AND ETHNICITY

General

Bodnar, John. *The Transplanted: A History of Immigrants in Urban America.* Bloomington: Indiana University Press, 1985.

Daniels, Roger. *Coming to America: A History of Immigration and Ethnicity in American Life.* New York: HarperCollins, 1990.

Debouzy, Marianne, ed. *In the Shadow of the Statue of Liberty: Immigrants, Workers, and Citizens in the American Republic, 1880–1920.* Urbana: University of Illinois Press, 1993.

Handlin, Oscar. *The Uprooted: The Epic Story of the Great Migrations that Made the American People.* Boston: Little, Brown, 1951.

Klapper, Melissa R. *Small Strangers: The Experiences of Immigrant Children in America, 1880–1925.* Chicago: Ivan R. Dee, 2007.

Kraut, Alan M. *The Huddled Masses: The Immigrant in American Society, 1880–1921.* 2nd ed. Arlington Heights, Ill.: Harlan Davidson, 2001.

Nugent, Walter. *Crossings: The Great Transatlantic Migrations, 1870–1914.* Bloomington: Indiana University Press, 1992.

Wyman, Mark. *Round Trip to America: The Immigrants Return to Europe, 1880–1930.* Ithaca, N.Y.: Cornell University Press, 1993.

Multigroup and Comparative Studies

Barton, Josef. *Peasants and Strangers: Italians, Rumanians, and Slovaks in an American City, 1890–1930.* Cambridge, Mass.: Harvard University Press, 1975.

Bodnar, John. *Steelton: Immigration and Industrialization, 1870–1940.* Reprint, Pittsburgh: University of Pittsburgh Press, 1990.

Chan, Sucheng. *Entry Denied: Exclusion and the Asian Community in America, 1881–1943.* Philadelphia: Temple University Press, 1991.

Diner, Hasia. *Hungering for America: Italian, Irish, and Jewish Folkways in the Age of Migration.* Cambridge, Mass.: Harvard University Press, 2001.

Ewen, Elizabeth. *Immigrant Women in the Land of Dollars: Life and Culture on the Lower East Side, 1890–1925.* New York: Monthly Review Press, 1985.

Friday, Chris. *Organizing Asian-American Labor: The Pacific Coast Canned-Salmon Industry, 1870–1942*. Philadelphia: Temple University Press, 1994.

Friedman-Kasaba, Kathie. *Memories of Migration: Gender, Ethnicity, and Work in the Lives of Jewish and Italian Women in New York, 1870–1924*. Albany: State University of New York Press, 1996.

Kessner, Thomas. *The Golden Door: Italian and Jewish Immigrant Mobility in New York City, 1880–1915*. New York: Oxford University Press, 1977.

Morawska, Eva. *For Bread with Butter: The Life Worlds of East Central Europeans in Johnstown, Pennsylvania, 1890–1940*. New York: Cambridge University Press, 1985.

Perlmann, Joel. *Ethnic Differences: Schooling and Social Structure among the Irish, Italians, Jews, and Blacks in an American City, 1880–1935*. New York: Cambridge University Press, 1988.

Ramirez, Bruno. *On the Move: French-Canadian and Italian Migrants in the North Atlantic Economy, 1860–1914*. Toronto: McClelland and Stewart, 1991.

Smith, Judith E. *Family Connections: A History of Italian and Jewish Immigrant Lives in Providence, Rhode Island, 1900–1940*. Albany: State University of New York Press, 1985.

Specific Groups

Canadian

Ramirez, Bruno, with Yves Otis. *Crossing the 49th Parallel: Migrations from Canada to the United States, 1900–1930*. Ithaca, N.Y.: Cornell University Press, 2001.

Caribbean

James, Winston. *Holding Aloft the Banner of Ethiopia: Caribbean Radicalism in Early Twentieth-Century America*. New York: Verso, 1998.

Watkins-Owens, Irma. *Blood Relations: Caribbean Immigrants and the Harlem Community, 1900–1930*. Bloomington: Indiana University Press, 1996.

Chinese

Chan, Sucheng. *This Bittersweet Soil: The Chinese in California Agriculture, 1860–1910*. Berkeley: University of California Press, 1986.

Chen, Yong. *Chinese San Francisco, 1850–1943: A Trans-Pacific Community*. Stanford, Calif.: Stanford University Press, 2000.

Hsu, Madeline Y. *Dreaming of Gold, Dreaming of Home: Transnationalism and Migration between the United States and South China, 1882–1943.* Stanford, Calif.: Stanford University Press, 2000.

Lee, Erika. *At America's Gates: Chinese Immigration during the Exclusion Era, 1882–1943.* Berkeley: University of California Press, 2003.

Lui, Mary Ting Yi. *The Chinatown Trunk Mystery: Murder, Miscegenation, and Other Dangerous Encounters in Turn-of-the-Century New York City.* Princeton, N.J.: Princeton University Press, 2005.

McKeown, Adam. *Chinese Migrant Networks and Cultural Change: Peru, Chicago, Hawaii, 1900–1936.* Chicago: University of Chicago Press, 2001.

Yung, Judy. *Unbound Feet: A Social History of Chinese Women in San Francisco.* Berkeley: University of California Press, 1995.

Dutch

Brinks, Herbert J., ed. *Dutch American Voices: Letters from the United States, 1850–1930.* Ithaca, N.Y.: Cornell University Press, 1995.

Sinke, Suzanne M. *Dutch Immigrant Women in the United States, 1880–1920.* Urbana: University of Illinois Press, 2002.

German

Detjen, David W. *The Germans in Missouri, 1900–1918: Prohibition, Neutrality, and Assimilation.* Columbia: University of Missouri Press, 1985.

Kazal, Russell A. *Becoming Old Stock: The Paradox of German-American Identity.* Princeton, N.J.: Princeton University Press, 2004.

Keil, Hartmut, ed. *German Workers' Culture in the United States, 1850–1920.* Washington, D.C.: Smithsonian Institution Press, 1988.

Keil, Hartmut, and John B. Jentz, eds. *German Workers in Industrial Chicago: A Documentary History of Working-Class Culture from 1850 to World War I.* Urbana: University of Illinois Press, 1988.

Irish

Meagher, Timothy J. *Inventing Irish America: Generation, Class, and Ethnic Identity in a New England City, 1880–1920.* Notre Dame, Ind.: University of Notre Dame Press, 2001.

———, ed. *From Paddy to Studs: Irish-American Communities in the Turn-of-the-Century Era, 1880–1920.* Westport, Conn.: Greenwood, 1986.

Nolan, Janet A. *Ourselves Alone: Women's Emigration from Ireland, 1885–1920.* Lexington: University Press of Kentucky, 1989.

Italian

Baily, Samuel. *Immigrants in the Lands of Promise: Italians in Buenos Aires and New York City, 1870–1914.* Ithaca, N.Y.: Cornell University Press, 1999.

Cinel, Dino. *From Italy to San Francisco: The Immigrant Experience.* Stanford, Calif.: Stanford University Press, 1992.

———. *The National Integration of Italian Return Migration, 1870–1929.* New York: Cambridge University Press, 1991.

Cohen, Miriam. *Workshop to Office: Two Generations of Italian Women in New York City, 1900–1950.* Ithaca, N.Y.: Cornell University Press, 1993.

Gabaccia, Donna R. *From Sicily to Elizabeth Street: Housing and Social Change among Italian Immigrants, 1880–1930.* Albany: State University of New York Press, 1984.

Guglielmo, Thomas A. *White on Arrival: Italians, Race, Color and Power in Chicago, 1890–1945.* New York: Oxford University Press, 2003.

Nelli, Humbert S. *Italians in Chicago, 1880–1930: A Study in Ethnic Mobility.* New York, Oxford University Press, 1970.

Yans-McLaughlin, Virginia. *Family and Community: Italian Immigrants in Buffalo, 1880–1930.* Ithaca, N.Y.: Cornell University Press, 1977.

Japanese

Hayashi, Brian Masaru. *"For the Sake of Our Japanese Brethren": Assimilation, Nationalism, and Protestantism among the Japanese of Los Angeles, 1895–1942.* Stanford, Calif.: Stanford University Press, 1995.

Ichioka, Yuji. *The Issei: The World of the First Generation of Japanese Immigrants, 1885–1924.* New York: Free Press, 1990.

Modell, John. *The Economics and Politics of Racial Accommodation: The Japanese of Los Angeles, 1900–1942.* Urbana: University of Illinois Press, 1977.

Moriyama, Alan Takeo. *Imingaisha: Japanese Emigration Companies and Hawaii, 1894–1908.* Honolulu: University of Hawaii Press, 1985.

Okihiro, Gary Y. *Cane Fires: The Anti-Japanese Movement in Hawaii, 1865–1945.* Philadelphia: Temple University Press, 1991.

Smith, Susan L. *Japanese American Midwives: Culture, Community, and Health Politics, 1880–1950.* Urbana: University of Illinois Press, 2005.

Jewish

Berrol, Selma. *East Side/East End: Eastern European Jews in London and New York, 1870–1920.* Westport, Conn.: Praeger, 1994.

Glazier, Jack. *Dispersing the Ghetto: The Relocation of Jewish Immigrants across America.* Ithaca, N.Y.: Cornell University Press, 1998.

Glenn, Susan. *Daughters of the Shtetl: Life and Labor in the Immigrant Generation.* Ithaca, N.Y.: Cornell University Press, 1990.

Gurock, Jeffrey, ed. *East European Jews in America, 1880–1920.* 3 vols. New York: Routledge, 1998.

Heinze, Andrew. *Adapting to Abundance: Jewish Immigrants, Mass Consumption, and the Search for American Identity.* New York: Columbia University Press, 1990.

Howe, Irving. *World of Our Fathers: The Journey of the East European Jews and the Life They Found and Made.* New York: Harcourt Brace Jovanovich, 1976.

Joselit, Jenna Weissman. *The Wonders of America: Reinventing Jewish Culture, 1880–1950.* New York: Hill and Wang, 1994.

Klapper, Melissa R. *Jewish Girls Coming of Age in America, 1860–1920.* New York: New York University Press, 2005.

Kosak, Hadassa. *Cultures of Opposition: Jewish Immigrant Workers, New York City, 1881–1905.* Albany: State University of New York Press, 2000.

Morawska, Eva. *Insecure Property: Small-Town Jews in Industrial America, 1890–1940.* Princeton, N.J.: Princeton University Press, 1995.

Rischin, Moses. *The Promised City: New York's Jews, 1870–1914.* Reprint, Cambridge, Mass.: Harvard University Press, 1977.

Rockaway, Robert A. *Words of the Uprooted: Jewish Immigrants in the Early Twentieth Century.* Ithaca, N.Y.: Cornell University Press, 1998.

Soyer, Daniel. *Jewish Immigrant Associations and American Identity in New York City, 1880–1939.* Cambridge, Mass.: Harvard University Press, 1997.

Weinberg, Sydney Stahl. *The World of Our Mothers: The Lives of Jewish Immigrant Women.* Chapel Hill: University of North Carolina Press, 1988.

Korean

Patterson, Wayne. *The Korean Frontier in America: Immigration to Hawaii, 1896–1910.* Honolulu: University of Hawaii Press, 1988.

Mexican and Mexican American

Camarillo, Albert. *Chicanos in a Changing Society: From Mexican Pueblos to American Barrios in Santa Barbara and Southern California, 1848–1930.* Cambridge, Mass.: Harvard University Press, 1979.

Deutsch, Sarah. *No Separate Refuge: Culture, Class, and Gender on an Anglo-Hispanic Frontier in the American Southwest, 1880–1940.* New York: Oxford University Press, 1987.

García, Juan R. *Mexicans in the Midwest, 1900–1932.* Tucson: University of Arizona Press, 1996.

García, Mario T. *Desert Immigrants: The Mexicans of El Paso, 1880–1920.* New Haven, Conn.: Yale University Press, 1981.

González, Gilbert G. *Labor and Community: Mexican Citrus Worker Villages in a Southern California Community, 1900–1950.* Urbana: University of Illinois Press, 1994.

Guerín-Gonzales, Camille. *Mexican Workers and American Dreams: Immigration, Repatriation, and California Farm Labor, 1900–1939.* New Brunswick, N.J.: Rutgers University Press, 1994.

Johnson, Benjamin Heber. *Revolution in Texas: How a Forgotten Rebellion and Its Bloody Suppression Turned Mexicans into Americans.* New Haven, Conn.: Yale University Press, 2003.

Rosales, F. Arturo. *!Pobre Raza¡: Violence, Justice, and Mobilization among Mexico Lindo Immigrants, 1900–1936.* Austin: University of Texas Press, 1999.

Sánchez, George J. *Becoming Mexican American: Ethnicity, Culture, and Identity in Chicano Los Angeles, 1900–1945.* New York: Oxford University Press, 1993.

Sandos, James A. *Rebellion in the Borderlands: Anarchism and the Plan of San Diego, 1904–1923.* Norman: University of Oklahoma Press, 1992.

Polish and Other Slavic Peoples

Alexander, June G. *The Immigrant Church and Community: Pittsburgh's Slovak Catholics and Lutherans, 1880–1915.* Pittsburgh: University of Pittsburgh Press, 1987.

Kuropas, Myron B. *The Ukrainian Americans: Roots and Aspirations, 1884–1954.* Toronto: University of Toronto Press, 1991.

Majewski, Karen. *Traitors and True Poles: Narrating a Polish-American Identity, 1880–1939.* Athens: Ohio University Press, 2003.

Pacyga, Dominic. *Polish Immigrants and Industrial Chicago: Workers on the South Side. 1880–1922.* Columbus: Ohio State University Press, 1991.

Scandinavian

Anderson, Philip J., and Dag Blanck, eds. *Swedish-American Life in Chicago: Cultural and Urban Aspects of an Immigrant People, 1850–1930.* Urbana: University of Illinois Press, 1992.

Attitudes toward Immigrants, Nativism, and Restriction

Allerfeldt, Kristofer. *Race, Radicalism, and Restriction: Immigration in the Pacific Northwest, 1890–1924*. Westport, Conn.: Praeger, 2003.

Daniels, Roger. *Not Like Us: Immigrants and Minorities in America, 1890–1924*. Chicago: Ivan R. Dee, 1997.

Fairchild, Amy L. *Science at the Borders: Immigrant Medical Inspection and the Shaping of the Modern Industrial Labor Force*. Baltimore: Johns Hopkins University Press, 2003.

Higham, John. *Strangers in the Land: Patterns of American Nativism, 1860–1925*. 2nd ed. New Brunswick, N.J.: Rutgers University Press, 1988.

Jacobson, Matthew Frye. *Barbarian Virtues: The United States Encounters Foreign Peoples at Home and Abroad, 1876–1917*. New York: Hill and Wang, 2000.

Kinzer, Donald L. *An Episode in Anti-Catholicism: The American Protective Association*. Seattle: University of Washington Press, 1964.

Kraut, Alan M. *Silent Travelers: Germs, Genes, and the "Immigrant Menace."* New York: Basic Books, 1994.

Zeidel, Robert F. *Immigrants, Progressives, and Exclusion Politics: The Dillingham Commission, 1900–1927*. DeKalb: Northern Illinois University Press, 2004.

AFRICAN AMERICANS

General

Southern, David W. *The Progressive Era and Race: Reaction and Reform, 1900–1917*. Arlington Heights, Ill.: Harlan Davidson, 2005.

African Americans in the South

Christian, Garna. *Black Soldiers in Jim Crow Texas, 1899–1917*. College Station: Texas A&M University Press, 1995.

Dittmer, John. *Black Georgia in the Progressive Era, 1900–1920*. Urbana: University of Illinois Press, 1997.

Gordon, Fon Louis. *Caste and Class: The Black Experience in Arkansas, 1880–1920*. Athens: University of Georgia Press, 1995.

Hahn, Steven. *A Nation under Our Feet: Black Political Struggles in the Rural South from Slavery to the Great Migration*. Cambridge, Mass.: Harvard University Press, 2003.

Lamon, Lester. *Black Tennesseans, 1900–1930*. Knoxville: University of Tennessee Press, 1977.

Litwack, Leon. *Trouble in Mind: Black Southerners in the Age of Jim Crow*. New York: Alfred A. Knopf, 1998.

McMillen, Neil R. *Dark Journey: Black Mississippians in the Age of Jim Crow*. Urbana: University of Illinois Press, 1989.

Oshinsky, David. *"Worse than Slavery": Parchman Farm and the Ordeal of Jim Crow Justice*. New York: Free Press, 1996.

African Americans in the North and West and the Great Migration

Gerber, David A. *Black Ohio and the Color Line, 1860–1915*. Urbana: University of Illinois Press, 1976.

Gottlieb, Peter. *Making Their Own War: Southern Blacks' Migration to Pittsburgh, 1916–1930*. Urbana: University of Illinois Press, 1987.

Grossman, James R. *Land of Hope: Chicago, Black Southerners, and the Great Migration*. Chicago: University of Chicago Press, 1989.

Hamilton, Kenneth Marvin. *Black Towns and Profit: Promotion and Development in the Trans-Appalachian West, 1877–1915*. Urbana: University of Illinois Press, 1991.

Henri, Florette. *Black Migration: The Movement North, 1900–1920*. Garden City, N.Y.: Anchor, 1975.

Marks, Carole. *Farewell—We're Good and Gone: The Great Black Migration*. Bloomington: Indiana University Press, 1989.

Trotter, Joe William, Jr., ed. *The Great Migration in Historical Perspective*. Bloomington: Indiana University Press, 1991.

African Americans in the City

Kusmer, Kenneth. *A Ghetto Takes Shape: Black Cleveland, 1870–1930*. Urbana: University of Illinois Press, 1976.

Lane, Roger. *William Dorsey's Philadelphia and Ours: On the Past and Future of the Black City in America*. New York: Oxford University Press, 1991.

Nielson, David Gordon. *Black Ethos: Northern Urban Negro Life and Thought, 1890–1930*. Westport, Conn.: Greenwood, 1977.

Osofsky, Gilbert. *Harlem: The Making of a Ghetto, 1890–1930*. New York: Harper & Row, 1966.

Schneider, Mark Robert. *Boston Confronts Jim Crow, 1890–1920*. Boston: Northeastern University Press, 1997.

Spear, Allan. *Black Chicago: The Making of a Negro Ghetto, 1890–1920.* Chicago: University of Chicago Press, 1967.

Williams, Lillian Spence. *Strangers in the Land of Paradise: The Creation of an African American Community in Buffalo, 1900–1940.* Bloomington: Indiana University Press, 1999.

Wright, George C. *Life Behind a Veil: Blacks in Louisville, Kentucky, 1865–1930.* Baton Rouge: Louisiana State University Press, 1985.

African American Women and Women's Movements

Bunch-Lyons, Beverly A. *Contested Terrain: African-American Women Migrate from the South to Cincinnati, 1900–1950.* New York: Routledge, 2002.

Clark-Lewis, Elizabeth. *Living In, Living Out: African American Domestics in Washington, D.C., 1910–1940.* Washington, D.C.: Smithsonian Institution Press, 1994.

Hendricks, Wanda A. *Gender, Race, and Politics in the Midwest: Black Club Women in Illinois.* Bloomington: Indiana University Press, 1998.

Higginbotham, Evelyn Brooks. *Righteous Discontent: The Women's Movement in the Black Baptist Church, 1880–1920.* Cambridge, Mass.: Harvard University Press, 1993.

Hine, Darlene Clark. *Black Women in White: Racial Conflict and Cooperation in the Nursing Profession, 1890–1950.* Bloomington: Indiana University Press, 1989.

Knupfer, Ann Meis. *Toward a Tenderer Humanity and a Nobler Womanhood: African-American Women's Clubs in Turn-of-the-Century Chicago.* Chicago: University of Chicago Press, 1996.

Neverdon-Morton, Cynthia. *Afro-American Women of the South and the Advancement of the Race, 1895–1925.* Knoxville: University of Tennessee Press, 1989.

Shaw, Stephanie J. *What a Woman Ought to Be and to Do: Black Professional Women Workers during the Jim Crow Era.* Chicago: University of Chicago Press, 1996.

Smith, Susan L. *Sick and Tired of Being Sick and Tired: Black Women's Health Activism in America, 1890–1950.* Philadelphia: University of Pennsylvania Press, 1995.

The Middle Class, Business, and the Professions

Feldman, Lynne B. *A Sense of Place: Birmingham's Black Middle-Class Community, 1890–1930.* Tuscaloosa: University of Alabama Press, 1999.

Gaines, Kevin K. *Uplifting the Race: Black Leadership, Politics, and Culture in the Twentieth Century.* Chapel Hill: University of North Carolina Press, 1996.

Gatewood, Willard B. *Aristocrats of Color: The Black Elite, 1880–1920.* Bloomington: Indiana University Press, 1990.

Kenzer, Robert C. *Enterprising Southerners: Black Economic Success in North Carolina, 1865–1915.* Charlottesville: University Press of Virginia, 1997.

Moore, Jacqueline. *Leading the Race: The Transformation of the Black Elite in the Nation's Capital, 1880–1920.* Charlottesville: University Press of Virginia, 1999.

Summers, Martin. *Manliness and Its Discontents: The Black Middle Class and the Transformation of Masculinity, 1900–1930.* Chapel Hill: University of North Carolina Press, 2004.

Education

Anderson, Eric, and Alfred A. Moss Jr. *Dangerous Donations: Northern Philanthropy and Southern Black Education, 1902–1930.* Columbia: University of Missouri Press, 1999.

Anderson, James D. *The Education of Blacks in the South, 1860–1935.* Chapel Hill: University of North Carolina Press, 1988.

Cooper, Arnold. *Between Struggle and Hope: Four Black Educators in the South, 1894–1915.* Ames: Iowa State University Press, 1989.

Mohraz, Judy Jolley. *The Separate Problem: Case Studies of Black Education in the North, 1900–1930.* Westport, Conn.: Greenwood, 1979.

Civil Rights Movements and Organizations

Kellogg, Charles F. *NAACP: A History of the National Association for the Advancement of Colored People.* Baltimore: Johns Hopkins University Press, 1967.

Luker, Ralph E. *The Social Gospel in Black and White: American Racial Reform, 1885–1912.* Chapel Hill: University of North Carolina Press, 1991.

Reed, Christopher. *The Chicago NAACP and the Rise of Black Professional Leadership, 1910–1966.* Bloomington: Indiana University Press, 1997.

Ross, B. Joyce. *J. E. Springarn and the Rise of the N.A.A.C.P.* New York: Atheneum, 1972.

Weiss, Nancy. *The National Urban League, 1910–1940.* New York: Oxford University Press, 1974.

Intellectual Trends, Literature, and the Arts

Bay, Mia. *The White Image in the Black Mind: African-American Ideas about White People, 1835–1925.* New York: Oxford University Press, 2000.

Bruce, Dickson D., Jr. *Black American Writing from the Nadir: The Evolution of a Literary Tradition, 1877–1915.* Baton Rouge: Louisiana State University Press, 1989.

Curtis, Susan. *The First Black Actors on the Great White Way.* Columbia: University of Missouri Press, 1998.

Horne, Gerald. *Black and Brown: African Americans and the Mexican Revolution, 1910–1920.* New York: New York University Press, 2005.

Katz, Michael B., and Thomas Sugrue, eds. *W. E. B. Du Bois, Race, and the City: The Philadelphia Negro and Its Legacy.* Philadelphia: University of Pennsylvania Press, 1998.

Meier, August. *Negro Thought in America, 1880–1915: Racial Ideologies in the Age of Booker T. Washington.* Ann Arbor: University of Michigan Press, 1963.

Mitchell, Michelle. *Righteous Propagation: African Americans and the Politics of Racial Destiny after Reconstruction.* Chapel Hill: University of North Carolina Press, 2004.

Moses, Wilson Jeremiah. *Creative Conflict in African American Thought: Frederick Douglass, Alexander Crummell, Booker T. Washington, W. E. B. Du Bois, and Marcus Garvey.* New York: Cambridge University Press, 2004.

Sotiropoulos, Karen. *Staging Race: Black Performers in Turn-of-the-Century America.* Cambridge, Mass.: Harvard University Press, 2006.

Zamir, Shamoon. *Dark Voices: W. E. B. Du Bois and American Thought, 1888–1903.* Chicago: University of Chicago Press, 1995.

Biographies

Davis, Leroy. *A Clashing of the Soul: John Hope and the Dilemma of African American Leadership and Black Higher Education in the Early Twentieth Century.* Athens: University of Georgia Press, 1998.

Fox, Stephen R. *The Guardian of Boston: William Monroe Trotter.* New York: Athenaeum, 1970.

Giddings, Paula J. *A Sword among the Lions: Ida B. Wells and the Campaign against Lynching.* New York: Amistad, 2008.

Harlan, Louis R. *Booker T. Washington.* 2 vols. New York: Oxford University Press, 1972, 1983.

Levy, Eugene. *James Weldon Johnson: Black Leader, Black Voice.* Chicago: University of Chicago Press, 1973.

Lewis, David Levering. *W. E. B. Du Bois: Biography of a Race, 1868–1919.* New York: Henry Holt, 1993.

Manning, Kenneth R. *Black Apollo of Science: The Life of Ernest Everett Just.* New York: Oxford University Press, 1983.

McMurry, Linda O. *George Washington Carver: Scientist and Symbol.* New York: Oxford University Press, 1981.

——. *To Keep Waters Troubled: The Life of Ida B. Wells.* New York: Oxford University Press, 1998.

Pickens, Ernestine Williams. *Charles W. Chesnutt and the Progressive Movement.* New York: Pace University Press, 1994.

Rouse, Jacqueline Anne. *Lugenia Burns Hope: Black Southern Reformer.* Athens: University of Georgia Press, 1989.

Schechter, Patricia A. *Ida B. Wells-Barnett and American Reform, 1880–1930.* Chapel Hill: University of North Carolina Press, 2001.

Thornbrough, Emma Lou. *T. Thomas Fortune.* Chicago: University of Chicago Press, 1970.

Anti-black Racism and Segregation

Gillespie, Michele K., and Randal L. Hall, eds. *Thomas Dixon Jr. and the Birth of Modern America*: Baton Rouge: Louisiana State University Press, 2006.

Gilmore, Glenda. *Gender and Jim Crow: Women and the Politics of White Supremacy in North Carolina, 1896–1920.* Chapel Hill: University of North Carolina Press, 1996.

Guterl, Matthew Peter. *The Color of Race in America, 1900–1940.* Cambridge, Mass.: Harvard University Press, 2001.

Hale, Grace Elizabeth. *Making Whiteness: The Culture of Segregation in the South, 1890–1940.* New York: Pantheon, 1998.

Kousser, J. Morgan. *The Shaping of Southern Politics: Suffrage Restriction and the Establishment of the One-Party South, 1880–1910.* New Haven, Conn.: Yale University Press, 1974.

Lofgren, Charles A. *The Plessy Case: A Legal-Historical Interpretation.* New York: Oxford University Press, 1987.

Newman, Louise Michele. *White Women's Rights: The Racial Origins of Feminism in the United States.* New York: Oxford University Press, 1999.

Perman, Michael. *Struggle for Mastery: Disfranchisement in the South, 1888–1908.* Chapel Hill: University of North Carolina Press, 2001.

Roediger, David R. *The Wages of Whiteness: Race and the Making of the American Working Class.* London: Verso, 1991.

Slide, Anthony. *American Racist: The Life and Films of Thomas Dixon.* Lexington: University Press of Kentucky, 2004.

Thomas, Brook, ed. *Plessy v. Ferguson: A Brief History with Documents.* New York: Bedford/St. Martin's, 1996.

Wang, Xi. *The Trial of Democracy: Black Suffrage and Northern Republicans, 1860–1910.* Athens: University of Georgia Press, 1997.

Williamson, Joel. *The Crucible of Race: Black-White Relations in the American South since Emancipation.* New York: Oxford University Press, 1984.

Anti-black Violence, Lynching, and Riots

Brundage, William Fitzhugh. *Lynching in the New South: Georgia and Virginia, 1880–1930.* Urbana: University of Illinois Press, 1993.

Cecelski, David S., and Timothy B. Tyson, eds. *Democracy Betrayed: The Wilmington Race Riot of 1898 and Its Legacy.* Chapel Hill: University of North Carolina Press, 1998.

Godshalk, David Fort. *Veiled Visions: The 1906 Atlanta Race Riot and the Reshaping of American Race Relations.* Chapel Hill: University of North Carolina Press, 2005.

Hair, William Ivy. *Carnival of Fury: Robert Charles and the New Orleans Race Riot of 1900.* Baton Rouge: Louisiana State University Press, 1976.

Haynes, Robert V. *A Night of Violence: The Houston Race Riot of 1917.* Baton Rouge: Louisiana State University Press, 1976.

Mixon, Gregory. *The Atlanta Riot: Race, Class, and Violence in a New South City.* Gainesville: University Press of Florida, 2005.

Pfeifer, Michael J. *Rough Justice: Lynching and American Society, 1874–1947.* Urbana: University of Illinois Press, 2004.

Rudwick, Elliott M. *Race Riot at East St. Louis, July 2, 1917.* Carbondale: Southern Illinois University Press, 1964.

Senechal, Roberta. *The Sociogenesis of a Race Riot: Springfield, Illinois, in 1908.* Urbana: University of Illinois Press, 1990.

Tolnay, Stewart E., and E. M. Beck. *A Festival of Lynchings: An Analysis of Southern Lynchings, 1882–1930.* Urbana: University of Illinois Press, 1995.

Weaver, John D. *The Brownsville Raid.* New York: Norton, 1971.

Wright, George C. *Racial Violence in Kentucky, 1865–1940: Lynchings, Mob Rule, and "Legal Lynchings."* Baton Rouge: Louisiana State University Press, 1990.

NATIVE AMERICANS

Society and Culture and Tribal Studies

Hosmer, Brian C. *American Indians in the Marketplace: Persistence and Innovation among the Menominees and Metlakatlans, 1870–1920.* Lawrence: University Press of Kansas, 1999.

Hoxie, Frederick E., ed. *Talking Back to Civilization: Indian Voices from the Progressive Era.* New York: Bedford/St. Martin's, 2001.

Littlefield, Daniel F., Jr. *Seminole Burning: A Story of Racial Vengeance.* Jackson: University of Mississippi Press, 1996.

Meyer, Melissa L. *The White Earth Tragedy: Ethnicity and Dispossession at a Minnesota Anishinaabe Reservation, 1889–1920.* Lincoln: University of Nebraska Press, 1994.

Osburn, Katherine M. B. *Southern Ute Women: Autonomy and Assimilation on the Reservation, 1887–1934.* Albuquerque: University of New Mexico Press, 1998.

Public Policy, Law, and Reform Movements

Carlson, Leonard A. *Indians, Bureaucrats, and Land: The Dawes Act and the Decline of Indian Farming.* Westport, Conn.: Greenwood, 1981.

Clark, Blue. *Lone Wolf v. Hitchcock: Treaty Rights and Indian Law at the End of the Nineteenth Century.* Lincoln: University of Nebraska Press, 1994.

Hagan, William T. *The Indian Rights Association: The Herbert Welsh Years, 1882–1904.* Tucson: University of Arizona Press, 1985.

———. *Theodore Roosevelt and Six Friends of the Indians.* Norman: University of Oklahoma Press, 1997.

Hatfield, Shelley Bowen. *Chasing Shadows: Apaches and Yaquis along the United States–Mexico Border, 1876–1911.* Albuquerque: University of New Mexico Press, 1998.

Holm, Tom. *The Great Confusion in Indian Affairs: Native Americans and Whites in the Progressive Era.* Austin: University of Texas Press, 2005.

Hoxie, Frederick E. *A Final Promise: The Campaign to Assimilate the Indians, 1880–1920.* Lincoln: University of Nebraska Press, 1984.

McDonnell, Janet A. *The Dispossession of the American Indian, 1887–1934.* Bloomington: Indiana University Press, 1991.

Samek, Hana. *The Blackfoot Confederacy, 1880–1920: A Comparative Study of Canadian and U.S. Indian Policy.* Albuquerque: University of New Mexico Press, 1987.

Shurts, John. *Indian Reserved Water Rights: The* Winters *Doctrine in its Social and Legal Context, 1880s–1930s.* Norman: University of Oklahoma Press, 2000.

Trennert, Robert A., Jr. *White Man's Medicine: Government Doctors and the Navajo, 1863–1955.* Albuquerque: University of New Mexico Press, 1998.

Education and the Indian Education Movement

Adams, David Wallace. *Education for Extinction: American Indians and the Boarding School Experience, 1875–1928.* Lawrence: University Press of Kansas, 1995.

Child, Brenda J. *Boarding School Seasons: American Indian Families, 1900–1940.* Lincoln: University of Nebraska Press, 1998.

Ellis, Clyde. *To Change Them Forever: Indian Education at the Rainy Mountain Boarding School, 1893–1920.* Norman: University of Oklahoma Press, 1996.

Lindsey, Donal F. *Indians at Hampton Institute, 1877–1923.* Urbana: University of Illinois Press, 1995.

Prucha, Francis Paul. *The Churches and the Indian Schools, 1888–1912.* Lincoln: University of Nebraska Press, 1979.

Riney, Scott. *The Rapid City Indian School, 1898–1933.* Norman: University of Oklahoma Press, 1999.

Trennert, Robert A., Jr. *The Phoenix Indian School: Forced Assimilation in Arizona, 1891–1935.* Norman: University of Oklahoma Press, 1988.

Native Americans in Euro-American Culture

Huhndorf, Shari M. *Going Native: Indians in the American Cultural Imagination.* Ithaca, N.Y.: Cornell University Press, 2001.

Jacobs, Margaret. *Engendered Encounters: Feminism and Pueblo Culture, 1879–1934.* Lincoln: University of Nebraska Press, 1999.

Moses, L. G. *Wild West Shows and the Images of American Indians, 1883–1933.* Albuquerque: University of New Mexico Press, 1996.

Smith, Sherry L. *Reimagining Indians: Native Americans through Anglo Eyes, 1880–1940.* New York: Oxford University Press, 2000.

Trachtenberg, Alan. *Shades of Hiawatha: Staging Indians, Making Americas, 1880–1930.* New York: Hill and Wang, 2004.

Biographies

Flood, Renee Sansom. *Lost Bird of Wounded Knee: Spirit of the Lakota.* New York: Scribner's, 1995.

Hagan, William T. *Quanah Parker, Comanche Chief.* Norman: University of Oklahoma Press, 1993.

Iverson, Peter. *Carlos Montezuma and the Changing World of American Indians.* Albuquerque: University of New Mexico Press, 1982.

Kroeber, Theodora. *Ishi in Two Worlds: A Biography of the Last Wild Indian in North America.* Berkeley: University of California Press, 1976.

Mark, Joan. *A Stranger in Her Native Land: Alice Fletcher and the American Indians.* Lincoln: University of Nebraska Press, 1988.

Neeley, Bill. *The Last Comanche Chief: The Life and Times of Quanah Parker.* New York: Wiley, 1995.

Tong, Benson. *Susan La Flesche Picotte, M.D.: Omaha Indian Leader and Reformer.* Norman: University of Oklahoma Press, 1999.

Unrau, William E. *Mixed-Bloods and Tribal Dissolution: Charles Curtis and the Quest for Indian Identity.* Lawrence: University Press of Kansas, 1989.

Wilson, Raymond. *Ohiyesa: Charles Eastman, Santee Sioux.* Urbana: University of Illinois Press, 1983.

INTELLECTUAL HISTORY, SOCIAL SCIENCE, AND THE HUMANITIES

General Works in Progressive-Era Thought

Altschuler, Glenn C. *Race, Ethnicity, and Class in American Social Thought, 1865–1919.* Wheeling, Ill.: Harlan Davidson, 1982.

Blake, Casey Nelson. *Beloved Community: The Cultural Criticism of Randolph Bourne, Van Wyck Brooks, Waldo Frank, and Lewis Mumford.* Chapel Hill: University of North Carolina Press, 1990.

Bramen, Carrie Tirado. *The Uses of Variety: Modern Americanism and the Quest for National Distinctiveness.* Cambridge, Mass.: Harvard University Press, 2000.

Clark, Michael. *The American Discovery of Tradition, 1865–1942.* Baton Rouge: Louisiana State University Press, 2005.

Cohen, Nancy. *The Reconstruction of American Liberalism, 1865–1914.* Chapel Hill: University of North Carolina Press, 2002.

Conn, Peter. *The Divided Mind: Ideology and Imagination in America, 1898–1917.* New York: Cambridge University Press, 1983.

Crunden, Robert. *American Salons: Encounters with European Modernism, 1885–1917.* New York: Oxford University Press, 1993.

Everdell, William. *The First Moderns: Profiles in the Origins of Twentieth-Century Thought.* Chicago: University of Chicago Press, 1997.

Fink, Leon. *Progressive Intellectuals and the Dilemmas of Democratic Commitment*. Cambridge, Mass.: Harvard University Press, 1997.

Gilbert, James B. *Work without Salvation: America's Intellectuals and Industrial Alienation, 1880–1910*. Baltimore: Johns Hopkins University Press, 1977.

Hansen, Jonathan M. *The Lost Promise of Patriotism: Debating American Identity, 1890–1920*. Chicago: University of Chicago Press, 2003.

Kloppenberg, James. *Uncertain Victory: Social Democracy and Progressivism in European and American Thought, 1870–1920*. New York: Oxford University Press, 1986.

Lasch, Christopher. *The New Radicalism in America, 1889–1963: The Intellectual as Social Type*. New York: Alfred A. Knopf, 1965.

Lears, T. J. Jackson. *No Place of Grace: Antimodernism and the Transformation of American Culture, 1880–1920*. New York: Pantheon, 1981.

Levy, David W. *Herbert Croly of the* New Republic*: The Life and Thought of an American Progressive*. Princeton, N.J.: Princeton University Press, 1985.

Livingston, James. *Pragmatism and the Political Economy of Cultural Revolution, 1850–1940*. Chapel Hill: University of North Carolina Press, 1994.

Lloyd, Brian. *Left Out: Pragmatism, Exceptionalism, and the Poverty of American Marxism, 1890–1920*. Baltimore: Johns Hopkins University Press, 1997.

Lustig, R. Jeffrey. *Corporate Liberalism: The Origins of Modern American Political Theory, 1890–1920*. Berkeley: University of California Press, 1982.

May, Henry F. *The End of American Innocence: The First Years of Our Own Time, 1912–1917*. New York: Alfred A. Knopf, 1959.

Menand, Louis. *The Metaphysical Club: A Story of Ideas in America*. New York: Farrar, Straus, and Giroux, 2001.

Oleson, Alexandra, and John Voss, eds. *The Organization of Knowledge in America, 1860–1920*. Baltimore: Johns Hopkins University Press, 1976.

Quandt, Jean B. *From the Small Town to the Great Community: The Social Thought of Progressive Intellectuals*. New Brunswick, N.J.: Rutgers University Press, 1970.

Schäfer, Axel R. *American Progressives and German Social Thought, 1875–1920: Social Ethics, Moral Control, and the Regulatory State in a Transatlantic Context*. Stuttgart: Franz Steiner Verlag, 2000.

Shi, David E. *Facing Facts: Realism in American Thought and Culture, 1850–1920*. New York: Oxford University Press, 1995.

Sklansky, Jeffrey. *The Soul's Economy: Market and Selfhood in American Thought, 1820–1920*. Chapel Hill: University of North Carolina Press, 2002.

Taylor, Bob Pepperman. *Citizenship and Democratic Doubt: The Legacy of Progressive Thought.* Lawrence: University Press of Kansas, 2004.

Thomas, John L. *Alternative America: Henry George, Edward Bellamy, Henry Demarest Lloyd, and the Adversary Tradition.* Cambridge, Mass.: Harvard University Press, 1983.

White, Morton. *Social Thought in America: The Revolt against Formalism.* Reprint, New York: Oxford University Press, 1976.

Darwinian Legacy and Social Darwinism

Bannister, Robert C. *Social Darwinism: Science and Myth in Anglo-American Social Thought.* Philadelphia: Temple University Press, 1979.

Hawkins, Mike. *Social Darwinism in European and American Thought, 1860–1945.* New York: Cambridge University Press, 1997.

Hofstadter, Richard. *Social Darwinism in American Thought.* Reprint, Boston: Beacon Press, 1992.

Numbers, Ronald L. *Darwinism Comes to America.* Cambridge, Mass.: Harvard University Press, 1998.

Pragmatism, Instrumentalism, William James, and John Dewey

Brent, Joseph. *Charles Sanders Peirce: A Life.* Bloomington: Indiana University Press, 1993.

Cotkin, George. *William James: Public Philosopher.* Baltimore: Johns Hopkins University Press, 1990.

Dalton, Thomas C. *Becoming John Dewey: Dilemmas of a Philosopher and Naturalist.* Bloomington: Indiana University Press, 2002.

Diggins, John Patrick. *The Promise of Pragmatism: Modernism and the Crisis of Knowledge and Authority.* Chicago: University of Chicago Press, 1994.

Feffer, Andrew. *The Chicago Pragmatists and American Progressivism.* Ithaca, N.Y.: Cornell University Press, 1997.

Hoopes, James. *Community Denied: The Wrong Turn of Pragmatic Liberalism.* Ithaca, N.Y.: Cornell University Press, 1998.

Martin, Jay. *The Education of John Dewey: A Biography.* New York: Columbia University Press, 2003.

Myers, Gerald E. *William James: His Life and Thought.* New Haven, Conn.: Yale University Press, 1986.

Ramsey, Bennett. *Submitting to Freedom: The Religious Vision of William James.* New York: Oxford University Press, 1993.

Richardson, Robert D. *William James: In the Maelstrom of American Modernism.* New York: Houghton Mifflin, 2006.

Ryan, Alan. *John Dewey and the High Tide of American Liberalism.* New York: Norton, 1995.

Westbrook, Robert B. *Democratic Hope: Pragmatism and the Politics of Truth.* Ithaca, N.Y.: Cornell University Press, 2005.

——. *John Dewey and American Democracy.* Ithaca, N.Y.: Cornell University Press, 1997.

Social and Political Science

Bannister, Robert C. *Sociology and Scientism: The American Quest for Objectivity, 1880–1940.* Chapel Hill: University of North Carolina Press, 1987.

Diggins, John P. *The Bard of Savagery: Thorstein Veblen and Modern Social Theory.* New York: Seabury, 1978.

Fried, Barbara H. *The Progressive Assault on Laissez Faire: Robert Hale and the First Law and Economics Movement.* Cambridge, Mass.: Harvard University Press, 1998.

Furner, Mary O. *Advocacy & Objectivity: A Crisis in the Professionalization of American Social Science, 1865–1905.* Lexington: University Press of Kentucky, 1975.

Haskell, Thomas L. *The Emergence of Professional Social Science: The American Social Science Association and the Nineteenth Century Crisis of Authority.* Urbana: University of Illinois Press, 1977.

Hinkle, Roscoe C. *Founding Theory of American Sociology, 1881–1915.* Boston: Routledge & Kegan Paul, 1980.

Karl, Barry D. *Charles E. Merriam and the Science of Politics.* Chicago: University of Chicago Press, 1974.

Matthews, Fred H. *Quest for an American Sociology: Robert E. Park and the Chicago School.* Montreal: McGill-Queen's University Press, 1977.

Miller, David L. *George Herbert Mead: Self, Language, and the World.* Austin: University of Texas Press, 1973.

Moss, David. *Socializing Security: Progressive-Era Economists and the Origins of American Social Policy.* Cambridge, Mass.: Harvard University Press, 1996.

Raushenbush, Winifred. *Robert E. Park: Biography of a Sociologist.* Durham, N.C.: Duke University Press, 1979.

Ross, Dorothy. *The Origins of American Social Science.* New York: Cambridge University Press, 1991.

Schulten, Susan. *The Geographical Imagination in America, 1880–1950.* Chicago: University of Chicago Press, 2001.

Thorsen, Niels Aage. *The Political Thought of Woodrow Wilson, 1875–1910.* Princeton, N.J.: Princeton University Press, 1988.

Tillman, Rick. *Thorstein Veblen and His Critics, 1891–1963: Conservative, Liberal, and Radical Perspectives.* Princeton: Princeton University Press, 1992.

Weinburg, Julius. *Edward Alsworth Ross and the Sociology of Progressivism.* Madison: State Historical Society of Wisconsin, 1972.

Williams, Vernon J., Jr. *Rethinking Race: Franz Boas and His Contemporaries.* Lexington: University Press of Kentucky, 1996.

Wunderlin, Clarence E. *Visions of a New Industrial Order: Social Science and Labor Theory in America's Progressive Era.* New York: Columbia University Press, 1992.

Experimental Psychology and Intelligence Testing

Brown, JoAnne. *The Definition of a Profession: The Authority of Metaphor in the History of Intelligence Testing, 1890–1930.* Princeton, N.J.: Princeton University Press, 1992.

Chapman, Paul Davis. *Schools as Sorters: Lewis Terman, Applied Psychology, and the Intelligence Testing Movement, 1880–1930.* New York: New York University Press, 1988.

O'Donnell, John M. *The Origins of Behaviorism: American Psychology, 1870–1920.* New York: New York University Press, 1985.

Ross, Dorothy. *G. Stanley Hall: The Psychologist as Prophet.* Chicago: University of Chicago Press, 1972.

History, Philosophy, and the Humanities

Bogue, Allan G. *Frederick Jackson Turner: Strange Roads Going Down.* Norman: University of Oklahoma Press, 1998.

Breisach, Ernst, *American Progressive History: An Experiment in Modernization.* Chicago: University of Chicago Press, 1993.

Clendenning, John. *The Life and Thought of Josiah Royce.* Madison: University of Wisconsin Press, 1985.

Des Jardins, Julie. *Women and the Historical Enterprise in America: Gender, Race, and the Politics of History, 1880–1945.* Chapel Hill: University of North Carolina Press, 2003.

Guttchen, Robert S. *Felix Adler.* New York: Twayne, 1974.

Herbst, Jürgen. *The German Historical School in American Scholarship: A Study of the Transfer of Culture.* Ithaca, N.Y.: Cornell University Press, 1965.

Hofstadter, Richard. *The Progressive Historians: Turner, Parrington, and Beard.* New York: Alfred A. Knopf, 1968.

Kuklick, Bruce. *Puritans in Babylon: The Ancient Near East and American Intellectual Life, 1880–1930.* Princeton, N.J.: Princeton University Press, 1996.

———. *The Rise of American Philosophy: Cambridge, Massachusetts, 1860–1930.* New Haven, Conn.: Yale University Press, 1977.

Roper, John Herbert. *U. B. Phillips: A Southern Mind.* Macon, Ga.: Mercer University Press, 1984.

Rothberg, Morey, and Jacqueline Goggin, eds. *John Franklin Jameson and the Development of Humanistic Scholarship in America.* 2 vols. Athens: University of Georgia Press, 1993–1996.

Smith, John David. *Slavery, Race, and American History: Historical Conflict, Trends, and Method, 1866–1953.* Armonk, N.Y.: M. E. Sharpe, 1999.

Wilson, Daniel J. *Science, Community, and the Transformation of American Philosophy, 1860–1930.* Chicago: University of Chicago Press, 1990.

Literature

Berthoff, Warner. *The Ferment of Realism: American Literature, 1884–1919.* New York: Cambridge University Press, 1981.

Boeckmann, Cathy. *A Question of Character: Scientific Racism and the Genres of American Fiction, 1892–1912.* Tuscaloosa: University of Alabama Press, 2000.

Borus, Daniel H. *Writing Realism: Howells, James, and Norris in the Mass Market.* Chapel Hill: University of North Carolina Press, 1989.

Kaplan, Amy. *The Social Construction of American Realism.* Chicago: University of Chicago Press, 1988.

Labor, Earle, and Jeanne Campbell Reesman. *Jack London.* Rev. ed. New York: Twayne, 1994.

Lee, Hermione. *Edith Wharton.* New York: Alfred A. Knopf, 2007.

Lewis, R. W. B. *Edith Wharton: A Life.* New York: Harper & Row, 1975.

Loving, Jerome. *The Last Titan: A Life of Theodore Dreiser.* Berkeley: University of California Press, 2005.

Lystra, Karen. *Dangerous Intimacy: The Untold Story of Mark Twain's Final Years.* Berkeley: University of California Press, 2004.

McElrath, Joseph R., Jr., and Jesse S. Crisler. *Frank Norris: A Life.* Urbana: University of Illinois Press, 2006.

Michaels, Walter Benn. *The Gold Standard and the Logic of Naturalism: American Literature at the Turn of the Century.* Berkeley: University of California Press, 1987.

Oliver, Lawrence J. *Brander Matthews, Theodore Roosevelt, and the Politics of American Literature, 1880–1920.* Knoxville: University of Tennessee Press, 1992.

Sawaya. Francesca. *Modern Women, Modern Work: Domesticity, Professionalism, and American Writing, 1890–1950.* Philadelphia: University of Pennsylvania Press, 2004.

Toth, Emily. *Kate Chopin: A Life of the Author of* The Awakening. New York: Morrow, 1990.

Wilson, Christopher P. *The Labor of Words: Literary Professionalism in the Progressive Era.* Athens: University of Georgia Press, 1985.

———. *White Collar Fictions: Class and Social Representation in American Literature, 1885–1925.* Athens: University of Georgia Press, 1992.

Bohemians and Cultural Radicals

Abrahams, Edward. *The Lyrical Left: Randolph Bourne, Alfred Stieglitz, and the Origins of Cultural Radicalism in America.* Charlottesville: University Press of Virginia, 1986.

Boylan, James. *Revolutionary Lives: Anna Strunsky and William English Walling.* Amherst: University of Massachusetts Press, 1998.

Clayton, Bruce. *Forgotten Prophet: The Life of Randolph Bourne.* Baton Rouge: Louisiana State University Press, 1984.

Dearborn, Mary V. *Queen of Bohemia: The Life of Louise Bryant.* Boston: Houghton Mifflin, 1996.

Fishbein, Leslie. *Rebels in Bohemia: The Radicals of* The Masses, *1911–1917.* Chapel Hill: University of North Carolina Press, 1982.

Green, Martin. *New York 1913: The Armory Show and the Paterson Strike Pageant.* New York: Collier, 1988.

O'Neill, William L. *The Last Romantic: A Life of Max Eastman.* New York: Oxford University Press, 1978.

Rosenstone, Robert A. *Romantic Revolutionary: A Biography of John Reed.* New York: Random House, 1975.

Rudnick, Lois Palken. *Mabel Dodge Luhan: A New Woman, New Worlds.* Albuquerque: University of New Mexico Press, 1984.

Stansell, Christine. *American Moderns: Bohemian New York and the Creation of a New Century.* New York: Metropolitan, 2000.

Vaughan, Leslie J. *Randolph Bourne and the Politics of Cultural Radicalism.* Lawrence: University Press of Kansas, 1997.

JOURNALISM AND PUBLISHING

General

Campbell, W. Joseph. *Yellow Journalism: Puncturing the Myths, Defining the Legacies.* Westport, Conn.: Praeger, 2001.

Kaplan, Richard. *Politics and the American Press: The Rise of Objectivity, 1865–1920.* New York: Cambridge University Press, 2001.

Lawson, Linda. *Truth in Publishing: Federal Regulation of the Press's Business Practices, 1880–1920.* Carbondale: Southern Illinois University Press, 1993.

Marzolf, Marion Tuttle. *Civilizing Voices: American Press Criticism, 1880–1950.* New York: Longman, 1991.

Milton, Joyce. *The Yellow Kids: Foreign Correspondents in the Heyday of Yellow Journalism.* New York: Harper & Row, 1989.

Publishers, Editors, and Journalists

Cooper, John Milton. *Walter Hines Page: The Southerner as American, 1855–1918.* Chapel Hill: University of North Carolina Press, 1977.

Fanning, Charles. *Finley Peter Dunne and Mr. Dooley: The Chicago Years.* Lexington: University Press of Kentucky, 1978.

Faue, Elizabeth. *Writing the Wrong: Eva Valesh and the Rise of Labor Journalism.* Ithaca, N.Y.: Cornell University Press, 2002.

Griffith, Sally Foreman. *Home Town News: William Allen White and the Emporia Gazette.* New York: Oxford University Press, 1989.

Krabbendam, Hans. *The Model Man: A Life of Edward William Bok, 1863–1930.* Amsterdam: Rodopi, 2001.

Littlefield, Roy Everett, III. *William Randolph Hearst: His Role in American Progressivism.* Lanham, Md.: University Press of America, 1980.

Lubow, Arthur. *The Reporter Who Would Be King: A Biography of Richard Harding Davis.* New York: Scribner's, 1992.

Lyon, Peter S. *Success Story: The Life and Times of S. S. McClure.* New York: Scribner's, 1963.

Nasaw, David. *The Chief: The Life of William Randolph Hearst.* Boston: Houghton Mifflin, 2000.

Seelye, John. *War Games: Richard Harding Davis and the New Imperialism.* Amherst: University of Massachusetts Press, 2003.

Yochelson, Bonnie, and Daniel Czitrom. *Rediscovering Jacob Riis: Exposure Journalism and Photography in Turn-of-the-Century New York.* New York: Free Press, 2008.

Magazines

Cohn, Jan. *Creating America: George Horace Lorimer and the* Saturday Evening Post. Pittsburgh: University of Pittsburgh Press, 1989.

Damon-Moore, Helen. *Magazines for the Millions: Gender and Commerce in the* Ladies' Home Journal *and the* Saturday Evening Post, *1880–1910.* Albany: State University of New York Press, 1994.

Garvey, Ellen Gruber. *The Adman in the Parlor: Magazines and the Gendering of Consumer Culture, 1880s–1910s.* New York: Oxford University Press, 1996.

Ohmann, Richard. *Selling Culture: Magazines, Markets, and Class at the Turn of the Century.* New York: Verso, 1996.

Pendergast, Tom. *Creating the Modern Man: American Magazines and Consumer Culture, 1900–1950.* Columbia: University of Missouri Press, 2002.

Scanlon, Jennifer. *Inarticulate Longings: The Ladies' Home Journal, Gender, and the Promises of Consumer Culture.* New York: Routledge, 1995.

Schneirov, Matthew. *The Dream of a New Social Order: Popular Magazines in America, 1893–1914.* New York: Columbia University Press, 1994.

Steinberg, Salme Harjo. *Reformer in the Marketplace: Edward W. Bok and the Ladies' Home Journal.* Baton Rouge: Louisiana State University Press, 1979.

Muckraking, Muckrakers, and Social Reform Journalism

Bannister, Robert. *Ray Stannard Baker: The Mind and Thought of a Progressive.* New Haven, Conn.: Yale University Press, 1966.

Brady, Kathleen. *Ida Tarbell: Portrait of a Muckraker.* New York: Putnam, 1984.

Filler, Louis. *Appointment at Armageddon: Muckraking and Progressivism in the American Tradition.* Westport, Conn.: Greenwood, 1976.

———. *The Muckrakers.* Enlarged ed. University Park: Pennsylvania State University Press, 1976.

———. *Voice of the Democracy: A Critical Biography of David Graham Phillips: Journalist, Novelist, Progressive.* University Park: Pennsylvania State University Press, 1978.

Fitzpatrick, Ellen. *Muckraking: Three Landmark Articles.* Boston: Bedford/St. Martin's, 1994.

Harris, Leon. *Upton Sinclair: American Rebel.* New York: Crowell, 1975.

Kaplan, Justin. *Lincoln Steffens: A Biography.* New York: Simon & Schuster, 1974.

Wilson, Harold S. *McClure's Magazine and the Muckrakers.* Princeton, N.J.: Princeton University Press, 1970.

VISUAL AND PERFORMING ARTS

Visual Arts

Antliff, Allan. *Anarchist Modernism: Politics and the First American Avant-Garde.* Chicago: University of Chicago Press, 2001.

Bogart, Michele H. *Public Sculpture and the Civic Ideal in New York City, 1890–1930*. Chicago: University of Chicago Press, 1989.

Brown, Milton Wolf. *The Story of the Armory Show*. New York: Abbeville Press, 1988.

Dabakis, Melissa. *Visualizing Labor in American Sculpture: Monuments, Manliness, and the Work Ethic, 1880–1935*. New York: Cambridge University Press, 1999.

Morgan, H. Wayne. *Keepers of Culture: The Art-Thought of Kenyon Cox, Royal Cortissoz, and Frank Jewitt Mather, Jr*. Kent, Ohio: Kent State University Press, 1989.

———. *Kenyon Cox, 1856–1919: A Life in American Art*. Kent, Ohio: Kent State University Press, 1994.

———. *New Muses: Art in American Culture, 1865–1920*. Norman: University of Oklahoma Press, 1978.

Nemerov, Alexander. *Frederic Remington and Turn-of-the-Century America*. New Haven, Conn.: Yale University Press, 1995.

Stange, Maren. *Symbols of Ideal Life: Social Documentary Photography in America, 1890–1950*. New York: Cambridge University Press, 1989.

Todd, Ellen Wiley. *The "New Woman" Revisited: Painting and Gender Politics on Fourteenth Street*. Berkeley: University of California Press, 1993.

Van Hook, Bailey. *The Virgin and the Dynamo: Public Murals in American Architecture, 1893–1917*. Athens: Ohio University Press, 2003.

Zurier, Rebecca. *Picturing the City: Urban Vision and the Ashcan School*. Berkeley: University of California Press, 2006.

Architecture

Baker, Paul R. *Stanny: The Gilded Life of Stanford White*. New York: Free Press, 1989.

Bruegmann, Robert. *The Architects and the City: Holabird and Roche of Chicago, 1880–1918*. Chicago: University of Chicago Press, 1997.

Christen, Barbara S., and Steven Flanders, eds. *Cass Gilbert, Life and Work: Architect of the Public Domain*. New York: Norton, 2001.

Condit, Carl. *The Chicago School of Architecture: A History of Commercial and Public Building in the Chicago Area, 1872–1925*. Chicago: University of Chicago Press, 1964.

Heilbrun, Margaret, ed. *Inventing the Skyline: The Architecture of Cass Gilbert*. New York: Columbia University Press, 2000.

Hines, Thomas S. *Burnham of Chicago: Architect and Planner*. New York: Oxford University Press, 1974.

Jordy, William H. *American Buildings and Their Architects.* Vol. 3, *Progressive Architecture and Academic Ideals at the Turn of the Century.* Garden City, N.Y.: Doubleday, 1972.

Muccigrosso, Robert. *American Gothic: The Mind and Art of Ralph Adams Cram.* Washington, D.C.: University Press of America, 1980.

O'Gorman, James F. *Three American Architects: Richardson, Sullivan, and Wright, 1865–1915.* Chicago: University of Chicago Press, 1991.

Siry, Joseph. *The Chicago Auditorium Building: Adler and Sullivan's Architecture and the City.* Chicago: University of Chicago Press, 2002.

Twombly, Robert C. *Frank Lloyd Wright: His Life and His Architecture.* New York: Wiley, 1979.

——. *Louis Sullivan: His Life and Work.* New York: Viking, 1986.

Music and Dance

Badger, Reid. *A Life in Ragtime: A Biography of James Reese Europe.* New York: Oxford University Press, 1995.

Berlin, Edward A. *King of Ragtime: Scott Joplin and His Era.* New York: Oxford University Press, 1995.

——. *Ragtime: A Musical and Cultural History.* Berkeley: University of California Press, 1980.

Brooks, Tim. *Lost Sounds: Blacks and the Birth of the Recording Industry, 1890–1919.* Urbana: University of Illinois Press, 2004.

Curtis, Susan. *Dancing to a Black Man's Tune: A Life of Scott Joplin.* Columbia: University of Missouri Press, 1994.

Daly, Ann. *Done into Dance: Isadora Duncan in America.* Bloomington: Indiana University Press, 1995.

Davis, Ronald. *A History of Music in American Life.* Vol. 2, *The Gilded Years, 1865–1920.* Huntington, N.Y.: Krieger, 1980.

Kenney, William Howland. *Chicago Jazz: A Cultural History, 1904–1930.* New York: Oxford University Press, 1993.

Kraft, James P. *Song to Studio: Musicians and the Sound Revolution, 1890–1950.* Baltimore: Johns Hopkins University Press, 1996.

Peretti, Burton W. *The Creation of Jazz: Music, Race, and Culture in Urban America.* Urbana: University of Illinois Press, 1992.

Rossiter, Frank R. *Charles Ives and His America.* New York: Liveright, 1975.

Tawa, Nicholas E. *The Way to Tin Pan Alley: American Popular Song, 1866–1910.* New York: Schirmer, 1990.

Tomko, Linda J. *Dancing Class: Gender, Ethnicity, and Social Divides in American Dance, 1890–1920.* Bloomington: Indiana University Press, 1999.

Vaillant, Derek. *Sounds of Reform: Progressivism and Music in Chicago, 1873–1935.* Chapel Hill: University of North Carolina Press, 2003.

Theater, Vaudeville, and Burlesque

Allen, Robert C. *Horrible Prettiness: Burlesque and American Culture.* Chapel Hill: University of North Carolina Press, 1991.
Bordman, Gerald. *The American Theatre: A Chronicle of Comedy and Drama, 1869–1914.* New York: Oxford University Press, 1994.
DiMeglio, John E. *Vaudeville U.S.A.* Bowling Green, Ohio: Bowling Green University Popular Press, 1973.
Erdman, Andrew L. *Blue Vaudeville: Sex, Morals, and the Mass Marketing of Amusement, 1895–1915.* Jefferson, N.C.: McFarland, 2004.
Erdman, Harley. *Staging the Jew: The Performance of an American Ethnicity, 1860–1920.* New Brunswick, N.J.: Rutgers University Press, 1997.
Kibler, M. Alison. *Rank Ladies: Gender and Cultural Hierarchy in American Vaudeville.* Chapel Hill: University of North Carolina Press, 1999.
McArthur, Benjamin. *Actors and American Culture, 1880–1920.* Philadelphia: Temple University Press, 1984.
Mizejewski, Linda. *Ziegfeld Girl: Image and Icon in Culture and Cinema.* Durham, N.C.: Duke University Press, 1999.
Snyder, Robert. *Voice of the City: Vaudeville and Popular Culture, 1880–1930.* New York: Oxford University Press, 1989.
Wertheim, Arthur Frank. *Vaudeville Wars: How the Keith-Albee and Orpheum Circuits Controlled the Big-Time and Its Performers.* New York: Palgrave, 2006.

Early Film Industry

Abel, Richard. *Americanizing the Movies and "Movie Mad" Audiences, 1910–1914.* Berkeley: University of California Press, 2006.
———. *The Red Rooster Scare: Making Cinema American, 1900–1910.* Berkeley: University of California Press, 1999.
Brownlow, Kevin. *Behind the Mask of Innocence: Social Problem Films of the Silent Era.* New York: Alfred A. Knopf, 1990.
Fuller, Kathryn H. *At the Picture Show: Small-Town Audiences and the Creation of Movie Fan Culture.* Washington, D.C.: Smithsonian Institution Press, 1996.
Grieveson, Lee. *Policing Cinema: Movies and Censorship in Early Twentieth-Century America.* Berkeley: University of California Press, 2004.

Hansen, Miriam. *Babel and Babylon: Spectatorship in American Silent Film.* Cambridge, Mass.: Harvard University Press, 1991.

Keil, Charlie. *Early American Cinema in Transition: Story, Style, and Film-making, 1907–1913.* Madison: University of Wisconsin Press, 2001.

Lang, Robert, ed. *The Birth of a Nation.* New Brunswick, N.J.: Rutgers University Press, 1994.

Mahar, Karen. *Women Filmmakers in Early Hollywood.* Baltimore: Johns Hopkins University Press, 2006.

May, Lary. *Screening Out the Past: The Birth of Mass Culture and the Motion Picture Industry.* New York: Oxford University Press, 1980.

Musser, Charles. *The Emergence of Cinema: The American Screen to 1907.* Berkeley: University of California Press, 1994.

Rabinovitz, Lauren. *For the Love of Pleasure: Women, Movies, and Culture in Turn-of-the-Century Chicago.* New Brunswick, N.J.: Rutgers University Press, 1998.

Robinson, David. *From Peep Show to Palace: The Birth of American Film.* New York: Columbia University Press, 1996.

Ross, Steven J. *Working-Class Hollywood: Silent Film and the Shaping of Class in America.* Princeton, N.J.: Princeton University Press, 1998.

Schickel, Richard. *D. W. Griffith: An American Life.* New York: Simon & Schuster, 1983.

Staiger, Janet. *Bad Women: Regulating Sexuality in Early American Cinema.* Minneapolis: University of Minnesota Press, 1995.

Waller, Gregory A. *Main Street Amusements: Movies and Commercial Entertainment in a Southern City, 1896–1930.* Washington, D.C.: Smithsonian Institution Press, 1995.

RELIGION

General

Marty, Martin E. *Modern American Religion.* Vol. 1, *The Irony of It All, 1893–1919.* Chicago: University of Chicago Press, 1986.

Religion in Thought, Culture, and Society

Bowden, Henry Warner. *Church History in the Age of Science: Historiographical Patterns in the United States, 1876–1918.* Chapel Hill: University of North Carolina Press, 1971.

Christiano, Kevin J. *Religious Diversity and Social Change: American Cities, 1890–1906*. New York: Cambridge University Press, 1987.

Handy, Robert T. *Undermined Establishment: Church–State Relations in America, 1880–1920*. Princeton, N.J.: Princeton University Press, 1991.

Ostrander, Rick. *The Life of Prayer in a World of Science: Protestants, Prayer, and American Culture, 1870–1930*. New York: Oxford University Press, 2000.

Seager, Richard Hughes. *The World's Parliament of Religions: The East/West Encounter, Chicago, 1893*. Bloomington: Indiana University Press, 1995.

Szasz, Ferenc Morton. *The Protestant Clergy in the Great Plains and Mountain West, 1865–1915*. Albuquerque: University of New Mexico Press, 1988.

African American Religion

Gregg, Robert. *From the Anvil of Oppression: Philadelphia's African Methodists and Southern Migration, 1890–1940*. Philadelphia: Temple University Press, 1993.

Little, Lawrence S. *Disciples of Liberty: The African Methodist Episcopal Church in the Age of Imperialism, 1884–1916*. Knoxville: University of Tennessee Press, 2000.

MacRobert, Iain. *The Black Roots and White Racism of Early Pentecostalism in the U.S.A.* New York: St. Martin's, 1988.

Sanders, Cheryl J. *Saints in Exile: The Holiness-Pentecostal Experience in African American Religion and Culture*. New York: Oxford University Press, 1996.

Sernett, Milton C. *Bound for the Promised Land: African American Religion and the Great Migration*. Durham, N.C.: Duke University Press, 1997.

Religion in the South

Harper, Keith. *The Quality of Mercy: Southern Baptists and Social Christianity, 1890–1920*. Tuscaloosa: University of Alabama Press, 1996.

Harvey, Paul. *Redeeming the South: Religious Cultures and Racial Identities among Southern Baptists, 1865–1925*. Chapel Hill: University of North Carolina Press, 1997.

McDowell, John Patrick. *The Social Gospel in the South: The Woman's Home Mission Movement in the Methodist Episcopal Church, South, 1886–1939*. Baton Rouge: Louisiana State University Press, 1982.

McMillen, Sally G. *To Raise Up the South: Sunday Schools in Black and White Churches, 1865–1915*. Baton Rouge: Louisiana State University Press, 2001.

Shepherd, Samuel C., Jr. *Avenues of Faith: Shaping the Urban Religious Culture of Richmond, Virginia, 1900–1929.* Tuscaloosa: University of Alabama Press, 2001.

Mainline Protestantism

May, Henry F. *The Protestant Churches and Industrial America.* 2nd ed. New York: Octagon, 1967.

Moorhead, James W. *World without End: Mainstream American Protestant Visions of the Last Things, 1880–1925.* Bloomington: Indiana University Press, 1999.

Smith, Gary Scott. *The Seeds of Secularization: Calvinism, Culture, and Pluralism in America, 1870–1915.* Grand Rapids, Mich.: Christian University Press, 1985.

Szasz, Ferenc Morton. *The Divided Mind of Protestant America, 1880–1930.* Tuscaloosa: University of Alabama Press, 1982.

Modernist Protestantism and the Social Gospel

Curtis, Susan. *A Consuming Faith: The Social Gospel and Modern American Culture.* Baltimore: Johns Hopkins University Press, 1991.

Dorn, Jacob H. *Washington Gladden: Prophet of the Social Gospel.* Columbus: Ohio State University Press, 1967.

Edwards, Wendy J. Deichmann, and Carolyn de Swarte Gifford, eds. *Gender and the Social Gospel.* Urbana: University of Illinois Press, 2003.

Evans, Christopher. *The Kingdom Is Always but Coming: A Life of Walter Rauschenbusch.* Grand Rapids, Mich.: Eerdmans, 2004.

Gorrell, Donald K. *The Age of Social Responsibility: The Social Gospel in the Progressive Era, 1900–1920.* Macon, Ga.: Mercer University Press, 1988.

Hutchison, William R. *The Modernist Impulse in American Protestantism.* Cambridge, Mass.: Harvard University Press, 1976.

Phillips, Paul T. *A Kingdom on Earth: Anglo-American Social Christianity.* University Park: Penn State University Press, 1996.

Smith, Gary Scott. *The Search for Social Salvation: Social Christianity and America.* Lanham, Md.: Lexington, 2000.

White, Ronald C., Jr. *Liberty and Justice for All: Racial Reform and the Social Gospel 1887–1925.* San Francisco: Harper & Row, 1990.

Evangelical Protestantism and Fundamentalism

Dorsett, Lyle W. *Billy Sunday and the Redemption of Urban America.* Grand Rapids, Mich.: Eerdmans, 1991.

Israel, Charles A. *Before Scopes: Evangelicalism, Education, and Evolution in Tennessee, 1870–1925.* Athens: University of Georgia Press, 2004.

Marsden, George M. *Fundamentalism and American Culture: The Shaping of Twentieth-Century Evangelicalism, 1870–1925.* New York: Oxford University Press, 1980.

Martin, Robert F. *Hero of the Heartland: Billy Sunday and the Transformation of American Society, 1862–1935.* Bloomington: Indiana University Press, 2002.

Oberdeck, Kathryn J. *The Evangelist and the Impresario: Religion, Entertainment, and Cultural Politics in America, 1884–1914.* Baltimore: Johns Hopkins University Press, 1999.

Weber, Timothy J. *Living in the Shadow of the Second Coming: American Premillennialism, 1875–1925.* 2nd ed. Chicago: University of Chicago Press, 1987.

Mormonism, Pietism, Pentecostalism, Salvation Army, and Other Protestant Movements

Alexander, Thomas G. *Mormonism in Transition: A History of the Latter-day Saints, 1890–1930.* Urbana: University of Illinois Press, 1986.

Anderson, Robert Mapes. *Vision of the Disinherited: The Making of American Pentecostalism.* New York: Oxford University Press, 1979.

Flake, Kathleen. *The Politics of American Religious Identity: The Seating of Senator Reed Smoot, Mormon Apostle.* Chapel Hill: University of North Carolina Press, 2004.

Gottschalk, Stephen. *The Emergence of Christian Science in American Life.* Berkeley: University of California Press, 1973.

Juhnke, James C. *Vision, Doctrine, War: Mennonite Identity and Organization in America, 1890–1930.* Scottdale, Pa.: Herald, 1989.

Satter, Beryl. *Each Mind a Kingdom: American Women, Sexual Purity, and the New Thought Movement.* Berkeley: University of California Press, 1999.

Taiz, Lillian. *Hallelujah Lads and Lasses: Remaking the Salvation Army in America.* Chapel Hill: University of North Carolina Press, 2001.

Wacker, Grant. *Heavens Below: Early Pentecostals and American Culture.* Cambridge, Mass.: Harvard University Press, 2001.

Winston, Diane. *Red Hot and Righteous: The Urban Religion of the Salvation Army.* Cambridge, Mass.: Harvard University Press, 1999.

Catholicism

Appleby, R. Scott. *"Church and Age Unite!" The Modernist Impulse in American Catholicism.* Notre Dame, Ind.: University of Notre Dame Press, 1992.

Kane, Paula. *Separatism and Subculture: Boston Catholicism, 1900–1920.* Chapel Hill: University of North Carolina Press, 1994.

Moloney, Deirdre M. *American Catholic Lay Groups and Transatlantic Social Reform in the Progressive Era.* Chapel Hill: University of North Carolina Press, 2002.

Nordstrom, Justin. *Danger on the Doorstep: Anti-Catholicism and American Print Culture.* Notre Dame, Ind.: University of Notre Dame Press, 2006.

O'Connell, Marvin R. *John Ireland and the American Catholic Church.* St. Paul: Minnesota Historical Society Press, 1988.

O'Toole, James M. *Militant and Triumphant: William Henry O'Connell and the Catholic Church in Boston, 1859–1944.* Notre Dame, Ind.: University of Notre Dame Press, 1992.

Parot, Joseph John. *Polish Catholics in Chicago, 1850–1920: A Religious History.* DeKalb: Northern Illinois University Press, 1981.

Woods, Thomas E., Jr. *The Church Confronts Modernity: Catholic Intellectuals and the Progressive Era.* New York: Columbia University Press, 2004.

Judaism

Silverstein, Alan. *Alternatives to Assimilation: The Response of Reform Judaism to American Culture, 1840–1930.* Hanover, N.H.: University Press of New England, 1994.

Sorin, Gerald. *A Time for Building: The Third Migration, 1880–1920.* Baltimore: Johns Hopkins University Press, 1992.

Urofsky, Melvin I. *A Voice that Spoke for Justice: The Life and Times of Stephen S. Wise.* Albany: State University of New York Press, 1982.

NATURAL SCIENCES

General

Reingold, Nathan, and Ida H. Reingold, eds. *Science in America, A Documentary History, 1900–1939.* Chicago: University of Chicago Press, 1981.

Life Sciences

Allen, Garland E. *Thomas Hunt Morgan: The Man and His Science.* Princeton, N.J.: Princeton University Press, 1979.

Bowler, Peter J. *The Eclipse of Darwinism: Anti-Darwinian Evolution Theories in the Decades around 1900.* Baltimore: Johns Hopkins University Press, 1983.

Cravens, Hamilton. *The Triumph of Evolution: American Scientists and the Heredity–Environment Controversy, 1900–1941*. Philadelphia: University of Pennsylvania Press, 1978.

Ludmerer, Kenneth M. *Genetics and American Society: An Historical Reappraisal*. Baltimore: Johns Hopkins University Press, 1972.

Maienschein, Jane. *Transforming Traditions in American Biology, 1880–1915*. Baltimore: Johns Hopkins University Press, 1991.

Rainger, Ronald, Keith R. Benson, and Jane Maienschein, eds. *The American Development of Biology*. Philadelphia: University of Pennsylvania Press, 1988.

Physical Sciences

Kargon, Robert H. *The Rise of Robert Millikan: Portrait of a Life in American Science*. Ithaca, N.Y.: Cornell University Press, 1982.

Kevles, Daniel J. *The Physicists: The History of a Scientific Community in America*. New York: Alfred A. Knopf, 1977.

Lankford, John. *American Astronomy: Community, Careers, and Power, 1859–1940*. Chicago: University of Chicago Press, 1997.

Livingston, Dorothy Michelson. *The Master of Light: A Biography of Albert A. Michelson*. New York: Scribner's, 1973.

Osterbrock, Donald E. *Yerkes Observatory: The Birth, Near Death, and Resurrection of a Scientific Research Institution*. Chicago: University of Chicago Press, 1997.

Stranges, Anthony N. *Electrons and Valence: Development of the Theory, 1900–1925*. College Station: Texas A&M University Press, 1982.

MEDICINE AND PUBLIC HEALTH

Medical Practice, Professions, and Institutions

Barney, Sandra Lee. *Authorized to Heal: Gender, Class, and the Transformation of Medicine in Appalachia, 1880–1930*. Chapel Hill: University of North Carolina Press, 2000.

Bonner, Thomas Neville. *Iconoclast: Abraham Flexner and a Life in Learning*. Baltimore: Johns Hopkins University Press, 2002.

Borst, Charlotte G. *Catching Babies: The Professionalization of Childbirth, 1870–1920*. Cambridge, Mass.: Harvard University Press, 1995.

Burrow, James G. *Organized Medicine in the Progressive Era: The Move toward Monopoly*. Baltimore: Johns Hopkins University Press, 1977.

Haller, John S., Jr. *American Medicine in Transition, 1840–1910.* Urbana: University of Illinois Press, 1981.

Howell, Joel D. *Technology in the Hospital: Transforming Patient Care in the Early Twentieth Century.* Baltimore: Johns Hopkins University Press, 1995.

Liebenau, Jonathan. *Medical Science and Medical Industry: The Formation of the American Pharmaceutical Industry.* Baltimore: Johns Hopkins University Press, 1987.

Ludmerer, Kenneth M. *Learning to Heal: The Development of American Medical Education.* New York: Basic Books, 1985.

Numbers, Ronald L. *Almost Persuaded: American Physicians and Compulsory Health Insurance, 1912–1920.* Baltimore: Johns Hopkins University Press, 1978.

Reverby, Susan. *Ordered to Care: The Dilemma of American Nursing, 1850–1945.* New York: Cambridge University Press, 1987.

Rosen, George. *The Structure of American Medical Practice, 1875–1941.* Philadelphia: University of Pennsylvania Press, 1983.

Rosenberg, Charles. *The Care of Strangers: The Rise of America's Hospital System.* New York: Basic, 1987.

Rosner, David. *A Once Charitable Enterprise: Hospitals and Health Care in Brooklyn and New York, 1885–1915.* New York: Cambridge University Press, 1982.

Starr, Paul. *The Social Transformation of American Medicine.* New York: Basic Books, 1982.

Wheatley, Steven C. *The Politics of Philanthropy: Abraham Flexner and Medical Philanthropy.* Madison: University of Wisconsin Press, 1988.

Public Health

Duffy, John. *The Sanitarians: A History of American Public Health.* Urbana: University of Illinois Press, 1990.

Kraut, Alan M. *Goldberger's War: The Life and Work of a Public Health Crusader.* New York: Hill and Wang, 2003.

Leavitt, Judith Walzer. *Typhoid Mary: Captive to the Public's Health.* Boston: Beacon, 1996.

Meckel, Richard A. *Save the Babies: American Public Health Reform and the Prevention of Infant Mortality.* Baltimore: Johns Hopkins University Press, 1990.

Mohr, James C. *Plague and Fire: Battling Black Death and the 1900 Burning of Honolulu's Chinatown.* New York: Oxford University Press, 2005.

Molina, Natalia. *Fit to Be Citizens? Public Health and Race in Los Angeles, 1879–1939.* Berkeley: University of California Press, 2006.

Tomes, Nancy. *The Gospel of Germs: Men, Women, and the Microbe in American Life*. Cambridge, Mass.: Harvard University Press, 1998.

Studies of Specific Diseases

Bates, Barbara. *Bargaining for Life: A Social History of Tuberculosis, 1876–1938*. Philadelphia: Temple University Press, 1992.

Feldberg, Georgina D. *Disease and Class: Tuberculosis and the Shaping of Modern North American Society*. New Brunswick, N.J.: Rutgers University Press, 1995.

Hammonds, Evelynn Maxine. *Childhood's Deadly Scourge: The Campaign to Control Diphtheria in New York City, 1880–1930*. Baltimore: Johns Hopkins University Press, 1999.

Ott, Katherine. *Fevered Lives: Tuberculosis in American Culture since 1870*. Cambridge, Mass.: Harvard University Press, 1996.

Rogers, Naomi. *Dirt and Disease: Polio before FDR*. New Brunswick, N.J.: Rutgers University Press, 1996.

Teller, Michael E. *The Tuberculosis Movement: A Public Health Campaign of the Progressive Era*. Westport, Conn.: Greenwood, 1988.

Birth Control and Eugenics

Chen, Constance M. *"The Sex Side of Life": Mary Ware Dennett's Pioneering Battle for Birth Control and Sex Education*. New York: New Press, 1996.

Chesler, Ellen. *Woman of Valor: Margaret Sanger and the Birth Control Movement in America*. New York: Simon & Schuster, 1992.

Dowbiggin, Ian Robert. *Keeping America Sane: Psychiatry and Eugenics in the United States and Canada, 1880–1940*. Ithaca, N.Y.: Cornell University Press, 1997.

Gordon, Linda. *Woman's Body, Woman's Right: Birth Control in America*. Rev. ed. New York: Penguin, 1990.

Kennedy, David M. *Birth Control in America: The Career of Margaret Sanger*. New Haven, Conn.: Yale University Press, 1970.

Kline, Wendy. *Building a Better Race: Gender, Sexuality, and Eugenics from the Turn of the Century to the Baby Boom*. Berkeley: University of California Press, 2001.

Larson, Edward J. *Sex, Race, and Science: Eugenics in the Deep South*. Baltimore: Johns Hopkins University Press, 1995.

Rafter, Nicole Hahn, ed. *White Trash: The Eugenic Family Studies, 1877–1919*. Boston: Northeastern University Press, 1988.

Stern, Alexandra. *Eugenic Nation: Faults and Frontiers of Better Breeding in Modern America*. Berkeley: University of California Press, 2005.

Psychiatry, Clinical Psychology, and Psychoanalysis

Caplan, Eric. *Mind Games: American Culture and the Birth of Psychotherapy*. Berkeley: University of California Press, 1998.

Dain, Norman. *Clifford W. Beers: Advocate for the Insane*. Pittsburgh: University of Pittsburgh Press, 1980.

Gosling, F. G. *Before Freud: Neurasthenia and the American Medical Community, 1870–1910*. Urbana: University of Illinois Press, 1987.

Grob, Gerald N. *Mental Illness and American Society, 1875–1940*. Princeton, N.J.: Princeton University Press, 1983.

Hale, Nathan G., Jr. *Freud and the Americans: The Beginnings of Psychoanalysis in the United States, 1876–1917*. New York: Oxford University Press, 1971.

Rothman, David. *Conscience and Convenience: The Asylum and Its Alternatives in Progressive America*. Boston: Little, Brown, 1980.

Scull, Andrew. *Madhouse: A Tragic Tale of Megalomania and Modern Medicine*. New Haven, Conn.: Yale University Press, 2005.

EDUCATION

Elementary, Secondary, and Vocational Education

General

Cohen, Ronald, and Raymond A. Mohl. *The Paradox of Progressive Education: The Gary Plan and Urban Schooling*. Port Washington, N.Y.: Kennikat, 1979.

Cremin, Lawrence. *American Education: The Metropolitan Experience, 1876–1980*. New York: Harper & Row, 1988.

———. *The Transformation of the School: Progressivism in American Education, 1876–1957*. New York: Alfred A. Knopf, 1961.

Kliebard, Herbert M. *The Struggle for the American Curriculum, 1893–1958*. Boston: Routledge & Kegan Paul, 1986.

———. *Schooled to Work: Vocationalism and the American Curriculum, 1876–1946*. New York: Teachers College Press, 1999.

Lagemann, Ellen Condliffe. *Private Power for the Public Good: A History of the Carnegie Foundation for the Advancement of Teaching*. Middletown, Conn.: Wesleyan University Press, 1983.

Peterson, Paul E. *The Politics of School Reform, 1870–1940.* Chicago: University of Chicago Press, 1985.

Reese, William J. *Power and the Promise of School Reform: Grassroots Movements during the Progressive Era.* Boston: Routledge & Kegan Paul, 1986.

———. *Education and Women's Work: Female Schooling and the Division of Labor in Urban America, 1870–1930.* Albany: State University of New York Press, 1991.

Sadovnik, Alan R., and Susan F. Semel, eds. *Founding Mothers and Others: Women Education Leaders during the Progressive Era.* New York: Palgrave Macmillan, 2002.

Smith, Joan K. *Ella Flagg Young: Portrait of a Leader.* Ames, Iowa: Educational Studies Press, 1979.

Local and Regional Studies

Brumberg, Stephen F. *Going to America, Going to School: The Jewish Immigrant Public School Encounter in Turn-of-the-Century New York.* New York: Praeger, 1986.

Cordier, Mary Hurlbut. *Schoolwomen of the Prairies and Plains: Personal Narratives from Iowa, Kansas, and Nebraska, 1860s–1920s.* Albuquerque: University of New Mexico Press, 1992.

Hogan, David. *Class and Reform: Schools and Society in Chicago, 1880–1930.* Philadelphia: University of Pennsylvania Press, 1985.

Kantor, Harvey. *Learning to Earn: School, Work, and Reform in California, 1880–1930.* Madison: University of Wisconsin Press, 1988.

Lazerson, Marvin. *Origins of the Urban School: Public Education in Massachusetts, 1870–1915.* Cambridge, Mass.: Harvard University Press, 1971.

Leloudis, James. L. *Schooling in the New South: Pedagogy, Self, and Society in North Carolina, 1880–1920.* Chapel Hill: University of North Carolina Press, 1996.

Link, William A. *A Hard Country and a Lonely Place: Schooling, Society, and Reform in Rural Virginia, 1870–1920.* Chapel Hill: University of North Carolina Press, 1986.

Nelson, Bryce E. *Good Schools: The Seattle Public School System, 1901–1930.* Seattle: University of Washington Press, 1988.

Raftery, Judith Rosenberg. *Land of Fair Promise: Politics and Reform in Los Angeles Schools, 1885–1941.* Stanford, Calif.: Stanford University Press, 1992.

Troen, Selwyn K. *The Public and the Schools: Shaping the St. Louis System, 1838–1920.* Columbia: University of Missouri Press, 1975.

Ueda, Reed. *Avenues to Adulthood: The Origins of the High School and Social Mobility in an American Suburb.* New York: Cambridge University Press, 1987.

Wrigley, Julia. *Class Politics and Public Schools: Chicago, 1900–1950.* New Brunswick, N.J.: Rutgers University Press, 1982.

Universities and Higher Education

General

Barrow, Clyde W. *Universities and the Capitalist State: Corporate Liberalism and the Reconstruction of American Higher Education, 1894–1928.* Madison: University of Wisconsin Press, 1990.

Bledstein, Burton J. *The Culture of Professionalism: The Middle Class and the Development of Higher Education in America.* New York: Norton, 1976.

Diner, Steven J. *A City and Its Universities: Public Policy in Chicago, 1892–1919.* Chapel Hill: University of North Carolina Press, 1980.

Geiger, Roger L. *To Advance Knowledge: The Growth of American Research Universities, 1900–1940.* New York: Oxford University Press, 1986.

Gorelick, Sherry. *City College and the Jewish Poor: Education in New York, 1880–1924.* New Brunswick, N.J.: Rutgers University Press, 1981.

Klingenstein, Susanne. *Jews in the American Academy, 1900–1940: The Dynamics of Intellectual Assimilation.* New Haven, Conn.: Yale University Press, 1991.

Leslie, W. Bruce. *Gentlemen and Scholars: College and Community in the Age of the University, 1865–1917.* University Park: Penn State University Press, 1992.

Marsden, George M. *The Soul of the American University: From Protestant Establishment to Established Nonbelief.* New York: Oxford University Press, 1994.

Reuben, Julie A. *The Making of the Modern University: Intellectual Transformation and the Marginalization of Morality.* Chicago: University of Chicago Press, 1996.

Rosenthal, Michael. *Nicholas Miraculous: The Amazing Career of the Redoubtable Dr. Nicholas Murray Butler.* New York: Farrar, Straus, and Giroux, 2006.

Veysey, Laurence. *The Emergence of the American University.* Chicago: University of Chicago Press, 1965.

Women and Gender in Higher Education

Gordon, Lynn D. *Gender and Higher Education in the Progressive Era.* New Haven, Conn.: Yale University Press, 1990.

Horowitz, Helen Lefkowitz. *Alma Mater: Design and Experience in Women's Colleges from Their Nineteenth-Century Beginnings to the 1930s.* 2nd ed. Amherst: University of Massachusetts Press, 1993.

Palmieri, Patricia Ann. *An Adamless Eden: The Community of Women Faculty at Wellesley.* New Haven, Conn.: Yale University Press, 1995.

Solomon, Barbara Miller. *In the Company of Educated Women: A History of Women and Higher Education in America.* New Haven, Conn.: Yale University Press, 1985.

Turk, Diana B. *Bound by a Mighty Vow: Sisterhood and Women's Fraternities, 1870–1920.* New York: New York University Press, 2004.

PROFESSIONS AND INSTITUTIONS

Professions

Garrison, Dee. *Apostles of Culture: The Public Librarian and American Society, 1877–1920.* New York: Free Press, 1979.

Goebel, Thomas. *The Children of Athena: Chicago Professionals and the Creation of a Credentialed Society, 1870–1920.* Hamburg: Lit, 1996.

Layton, Edwin T., Jr. *The Revolt of the Engineers: Social Responsibility and the American Engineering Profession.* Reprint, Baltimore: Johns Hopkins University Press, 1986.

Lubove, Roy. *The Professional Altruist: The Emergence of Social Work as a Career, 1880–1930.* Cambridge, Mass.: Harvard University Press, 1965.

Miranti, Paul J. *Accountancy Comes of Age: The Development of an American Profession, 1886–1940.* Chapel Hill: University of North Carolina Press, 1990.

Wiegand, Wayne E. *The Politics of an Emerging Profession: The American Library Association, 1876–1917.* Westport, Conn.: Greenwood, 1986.

Cultural, Philanthropic Institutions

Conn, Steven. *Museums and American Intellectual Life, 1876–1926.* Chicago: University of Chicago Press, 1998.

Horowitz, Helen Lefkowitz. *Culture and the City: Cultural Philanthropy in Chicago from the 1880s to 1917.* Reprint, Chicago: University of Chicago Press, 1989.

Lagemann, Ellen Condliffe. *The Politics of Knowledge: The Carnegie Corporation, Philanthropy, and Public Policy*. Middletown, Conn.: Wesleyan University Press, 1989.

Sealander, Judith. *Private Wealth and Public Life: Foundation Philanthropy and the Reshaping of American Social Policy from the Progressive Era to the New Deal*. Baltimore: Johns Hopkins University Press, 1997.

Van Slyck, Abigail Ayers. *Free to All: Carnegie Libraries and American Culture, 1890–1920*. Chicago: University of Chicago Press, 1995.

CITIES AND URBANISM

General

Klein, Maury, and Harvey A. Kantor. *Prisoners of Progress: American Industrial Cities, 1850–1920*. New York: Macmillan, 1976.

Mohl, Raymond A. *The New City: Urban America in the Industrial Age, 1860–1920*. Arlington Heights, Ill.: Harlan Davidson, 1985.

City and Regional Studies

Arsenault, Raymond. *St. Petersburg and the Florida Dream, 1888–1950*. Reprint, Gainesville: University Press of Florida, 1996.

Bixel, Patricia Bellis and Elizabeth Hayes Turner. *Galveston and the 1900 Storm: Catastrophe and Catalyst*. Austin: University of Texas Press, 2000.

Blake, Angela. *How New York Became American, 1890–1924*. Baltimore: Johns Hopkins University Press, 2006.

Cohen, Andrew Wender. *The Racketeer's Progress: Chicago and the Struggle for the Modern American Economy, 1900–1940*. New York: Cambridge University Press, 2004.

Couvares, Francis G. *The Remaking of Pittsburgh: Class and Culture in an Industrializing City, 1877–1919*. Albany: State University of New York Press, 1984.

Crooks, James B. *Jacksonville after the Fire, 1901–1919: A New South City*. Jacksonville: University of North Florida Press, 1991.

Doyle, Don H. *New Men, New Cities, New South: Atlanta, Nashville, Charleston, Mobile, 1860–1910*. Chapel Hill: University of North Carolina Press, 1990.

Fogelson, Robert M. *The Fragmented Metropolis: Los Angeles, 1850–1930*. Cambridge, Mass.: Harvard University Press, 1967.

Fradkin, Philip L. *The Great Earthquake and Firestorms of 1906: How San Francisco Nearly Destroyed Itself.* Berkeley: University of California Press, 2005.

Hanchett, Thomas. *Sorting Out the New South City: Race, Class, and Urban Development in Charlotte, 1875–1975.* Chapel Hill: University of North Carolina Press, 1998.

Hepp, John Henry, IV. *The Middle-Class City: Transforming Space and Time in Philadelphia, 1876–1926.* Philadelphia: University of Pennsylvania Press, 2003.

Hill, Patricia Evridge. *Dallas: The Making of a Modern City.* Austin: University of Texas Press, 1996.

Issel, William, and Robert W. Cherny. *San Francisco, 1865–1932: Politics, Power, and Urban Development.* Berkeley: University of California Press, 1986.

Zunz, Olivier. *The Changing Face of Inequality: Urbanization, Industrial Development, and Immigrants in Detroit, 1880–1920.* Chicago: University of Chicago Press, 1982.

Urbanism and Urban Life and Culture

Adler, Jeffrey S. *First in Violence, Deepest in Dirt: Homicide in Chicago, 1875–1920.* Cambridge, Mass.: Harvard University Press, 2006.

Barth, Gunther. *City People: The Rise of Modern City Culture in Nineteenth-Century America.* New York: Oxford University Press, 1980.

Brandt, Nat. *Chicago Death Trap: The Iroquois Theatre Fire of 1903.* Carbondale: Southern Illinois University Press, 2003.

Chudacoff, Howard P. *Mobile Americans: Residential and Social Mobility in Omaha, 1880–1920.* New York: Oxford University Press, 1972.

Duis, Perry R. *Challenging Chicago: Coping with Everyday Life, 1837–1920.* Urbana: University of Illinois Press, 1998.

Erenberg, Lewis A. *Steppin' Out: New York Nightlife and the Transformation of American Culture, 1890–1930.* Westport, Conn.: Greenwood, 1981.

Goodson, Steve. *Highbrows, Hillbillies, and Hellfire: Public Entertainment in Atlanta, 1880–1930.* Athens: University of Georgia Press, 2002.

Jablonsky, Thomas J. *Pride in the Jungle: Community and Everyday Life in Back of the Yards Chicago.* Baltimore: Johns Hopkins University Press, 1993.

Long, Alecia. *The Great Southern Babylon: Sex, Race, and Respectability in New Orleans, 1865–1920.* Baton Rouge: Louisiana State University Press, 2004.

McFarland, Gerald W. *Greenwich Village: A New York City Neighborhood, 1889–1918.* Amherst: University of Massachusetts Press, 2001.

Nasaw, David. *Children of the City: At Work and at Play*. Garden City, N.Y.: Anchor/Doubleday, 1985.

Noel, Thomas J. *The City and the Saloon: Denver, 1858–1916*. Lincoln: University of Nebraska Press, 1982.

O'Donnell, Edward T. *Ship Ablaze: The Tragedy of the Steamboat* General Slocum. New York: Broadway Books, 2003.

Orsi, Robert. *The Madonna of 115th Street: Faith and Community in East Harlem, 1880–1950*. New Haven, Conn.: Yale University Press, 1985.

Powers, Madelon. *Faces along the Bar: Lore and Order in the Workingman's Saloon, 1870–1920*. Chicago: University of Chicago Press, 1998.

Wingerd, Mary Lethard. *Claiming the City: Politics, Faith, and the Power of Place in St. Paul*. Ithaca, N.Y.: Cornell University Press, 2001.

Women and Cities

Adickes, Sandra. *To Be Young Was Very Heaven: Women in New York before the First World War*. New York: St. Martin's, 1997.

Deutsch, Sarah. *Women and the City: Gender, Space, and Power in Boston, 1870–1940*. New York: Oxford University Press, 2000.

Enstam, Elizabeth York. *Women and the Creation of Urban Life: Dallas, Texas, 1843–1920*. College Station: Texas A&M University Press, 1998.

Flanagan, Maureen. *Seeing with Their Hearts: Chicago Women and the Vision of a Good City, 1871–1933*. Princeton, N.J.: Princeton University Press, 2002.

Hayden, Dolores. *The Grand Domestic Revolution: A History of Feminist Designs for American Homes, Neighborhoods, and Cities*. Cambridge, Mass.: MIT Press, 1982.

Hickey, Georgina. *Hope and Danger in the New South City: Working-Class Women and Urban Development in Atlanta, 1890–1940*. Athens: University of Georgia Press, 2003.

Spain, Daphne. *How Women Saved the City*. Minneapolis: University of Minnesota Press, 2001.

Turner, Elizabeth Hayes. *Women, Culture, and Community: Religion and Reform in Galveston, 1880–1920*. New York: Oxford University Press, 1997.

Urban Space and the Built Environment

Bachin, Robin F. *Building the South Side: Urban Space and Civic Culture in Chicago, 1890–1919*. Chicago: University of Chicago Press, 2004.

Baldwin, Peter C. *Domesticating the Street: The Reform of Public Space in Hartford, 1850–1930*. Columbus: Ohio State University Press, 1999.

Bluestone, Daniel. *Constructing Chicago.* New Haven, Conn.: Yale University Press, 1991.

Fogelson, Robert M. *America's Armories: Architecture, Society, and Public Order.* Cambridge, Mass.: Harvard University Press, 1989.

———. *Downtown: Its Rise and Fall, 1880–1950.* New Haven, Conn.: Yale University Press, 2001.

Landau, Sarah Bradford, and Carl W. Condit. *Rise of the New York Skyscraper, 1865–1913.* New Haven, Conn.: Yale University Press, 1996.

Page, Max. *The Creative Destruction of Manhattan, 1900–1940.* Chicago: University of Chicago Press, 2000.

Stamper, John W. *Chicago's North Michigan Avenue: Planning and Development, 1900–1930.* Chicago: University of Chicago Press, 1991.

Ward, David, and Olivier Zunz, eds. *The Landscape of Modernity: New York City, 1900–1940.* Baltimore: Johns Hopkins University Press, 1992.

Infrastructure, Technology, Urban Sanitation, and the Environment

Davis, Margaret Leslie. *Rivers in the Desert: William Mulholland and the Inventing of Los Angeles.* New York: HarperCollins, 1993.

Elkind, Sarah S. *Bay Cities and Water Politics: The Battle for Resources in Boston and Oakland.* Lawrence: University Press of Kansas, 1998.

Melosi, Martin V. *Garbage in the Cities: Refuse, Reform, and the Environment, 1880–1980.* College Station: Texas A&M University Press, 1981.

———. *The Sanitary City: Urban Infrastructure in America from Colonial Times to the Present.* Baltimore: Johns Hopkins University Press, 2000.

———, ed. *Pollution and Reform in American Cities, 1870–1930.* Austin: University of Texas Press, 1980.

Mulholland, Catherine. *William Mulholland and the Rise of Los Angeles.* Berkeley: University of California Press, 2000.

Platt, Harold L. *The Electric City: Energy and the Growth of the Chicago Area, 1880–1930.* Chicago: University of Chicago Press, 1991.

———. *Shock Cities: The Environmental Transformation and Reform of Manchester and Chicago.* Chicago: University of Chicago Press, 2005.

Rose, Mark. *Cities of Heat and Light: Domesticating Gas and Electricity in Urban America.* University Park: Penn State University Press, 1995.

Tarr, Joel A. *The Search for the Ultimate Sink: Urban Pollution in Historical Perspective.* Akron, Ohio: University of Akron Press, 1996.

Tarr, Joel A., and Gabriel Dupuy, eds. *Technology and the Rise of the Networked City in Europe and America.* Philadelphia: Temple University Press, 1988.

Urban Transportation

Barrett, Paul. *The Automobile and Urban Transit: The Formation of Public Policy in Chicago, 1900–1930.* Philadelphia: Temple University Press, 1983.

Cheape, Charles W. *Moving the Masses: Urban Public Transit in New York, Boston, and Philadelphia, 1880–1912.* Cambridge, Mass.: Harvard University Press, 1980.

Foster, Mark. *From Streetcar to Superhighway: American City Planners and Urban Transportation, 1900–1940.* Philadelphia: Temple University Press, 1981.

Hood, Clifton. *722 Miles: The Building of the Subways and How They Transformed New York.* New York: Simon & Schuster, 1993.

McShane, Clay. *Down the Asphalt Path: The Automobile and the American City.* New York: Columbia University Press, 1994.

———. *Technology and Reform: Street Railways and the Growth of Milwaukee.* Madison: State Historical Society of Wisconsin, 1974.

Housing and Residence Patterns

General

Garb, Margaret. *City of American Dreams: A History of Home Ownership and Housing Reform in Chicago, 1871–1919.* Chicago: University of Chicago Press, 2005.

Hawes, Elizabeth. *New York, New York: How the Apartment House Transformed the Life of the City (1869–1930).* New York: Alfred A. Knopf, 1993.

Simon, Roger D. *The City-Building Process: Housing and Services in New Milwaukee Neighborhoods, 1880–1910.* Rev. ed. Philadelphia: American Philosophical Society, 1996.

The Middle Class and Suburbanization

Ebner, Michael. *Creating Chicago's North Shore: A Suburban History.* Chicago: University of Chicago Press, 1988.

Fogelson, Robert M. *Bourgeois Nightmares: Suburbia, 1870–1930.* New Haven, Conn.: Yale University Press, 2005.

Gowans, Alan. *The Comfortable House: North American Suburban Architecture, 1890–1930.* Cambridge, Mass.: MIT Press, 1986.

Keating, Ann Durkin. *Chicagoland: City and Suburbs in the Railroad Age.* Chicago: University of Chicago Press, 2005.

Marsh, Margaret. *Suburban Lives.* New Brunswick, N.J.: Rutgers University Press, 1990.

Von Hoffman, Alexander. *Local Attachments: The Making of an American Urban Neighborhood, 1850–1920.* Baltimore: Johns Hopkins University Press, 1994.

Wright, Gwendolyn. *Moralism and the Model Home: Domestic Architecture and Cultural Conflict in Chicago, 1873–1913.* Chicago: University of Chicago Press, 1980.

The Working Class and Poor

Bigott, Joseph J. *From Cottage to Bungalow: Houses and the Working Class in Metropolitan Chicago, 1869–1929.* Chicago: University of Chicago Press, 2001.

Day, Jared. *Urban Castles: Tenement Housing and Landlord Activism in New York City, 1890–1943.* New York: Columbia University Press, 1999.

Philpott, Thomas Lee. *The Slum and the Ghetto: Neighborhood Deterioration and Middle-Class Reform in Chicago, 1880–1930.* New York: Oxford University Press, 1978.

Ward, David. *Poverty, Ethnicity, and the American City, 1840–1925: Changing Conceptions of the Slum and the Ghetto.* New York: Cambridge University Press, 1989.

Urban Planning and Design

Blackford, Mansel G. *The Lost Dream: Businessmen and City Planning on the Pacific Coast, 1890–1920.* Columbus: Ohio State University Press, 1993.

Fairfield, John D. *The Mysteries of the Great City: The Politics of Urban Design, 1877–1937.* Columbus: Ohio State University Press, 1993.

Holleran, Michael. *Boston's "Changeful Times": Origins of Preservation and Planning in America.* Baltimore: Johns Hopkins University Press, 1998.

Kahn, Judd. *Imperial San Francisco: Politics and Planning in an American City, 1897–1906.* Lincoln: University of Nebraska Press, 1979.

Lubove, Roy. *The Urban Community: Housing and Planning in the Progressive Era.* Reprint, Westport, Conn.: Greenwood, 1981.

Peterson, Jon A. *The Birth of City Planning in the United States, 1840–1917.* Baltimore: Johns Hopkins University Press, 2003.

Revell, Keith D. *Building Gotham: Civic Culture and Public Policy in New York City, 1898–1938.* Baltimore: Johns Hopkins University Press, 2002.

Schultz, Stanley K. *Constructing Urban Culture: American Cities and City Planning 1800–1920.* Philadelphia: Temple University Press, 1989.

Smith, Carl. *The Plan of Chicago: Daniel Burnham and the Remaking of the American City.* Chicago: University of Chicago Press, 2006.

Sutcliffe, Anthony. *Toward the Planned City: Germany, Britain, and the United States, 1780–1914.* New York: St. Martin's, 1981.

Wilson, William H. *The City Beautiful Movement.* Baltimore: Johns Hopkins University Press, 1989.

Urban Social and Moral Reform

Barrows, Robert G. *Albion Fellows Bacon: Indiana's Municipal Housekeeper.* Bloomington: Indiana University Press, 2000.

Boyer, Paul. *Urban Masses and Moral Order in America, 1820–1920.* Cambridge, Mass.: Harvard University Press, 1978.

Bulmer, Martin, Kevin Bales, and Kathryn Kish Sklar, eds. *The Social Survey in Historical Perspective, 1880–1940.* New York: Cambridge University Press, 1991.

Burnstein, Daniel Eli. *Next to Godliness: Confronting Dirt and Despair in Progressive Era New York City.* Urbana: University of Illinois Press, 2006.

Cavallo, Dominick J. *Muscles and Morals: Organized Playgrounds and Urban Reform, 1880–1920.* Philadelphia: Temple University Press, 1981.

Deegan, Mary Jo. *Jane Addams and the Men of the Chicago School, 1892–1918.* New Brunswick, N.J.: Transaction, 1988.

Elfenbein, Jessica I. *The Making of a Modern City: Philanthropy, Civic Culture, and the Baltimore YMCA.* Gainesville: University Press of Florida, 2001.

Fairbanks, Robert B. *Making Better Citizens: Housing Reform and Community Development Strategy in Cincinnati, 1890–1960.* Urbana: University of Illinois Press, 1988.

Ginger, Ray. *Altgeld's America: The Lincoln Ideal Versus Changing Realities.* Reprint, New York: New Viewpoints, 1973.

Greenwald, Maurine H., and Margo Anderson, eds. *Pittsburgh Surveyed: Social Science and Social Reform in the Early Twentieth Century.* Pittsburgh: University of Pittsburgh Press, 1996.

Lane, James B. *Jacob Riis and the American City.* Port Washington, N.Y.: Kennikat Press, 1974.

Lubove, Roy. *The Progressives and the Slums: Tenement House Reform in New York City, 1890–1917.* Pittsburgh: University of Pittsburgh Press, 1962.

Melvin, Patricia Mooney. *The Organic City: Urban Definition and Community Organization, 1880–1920.* Lexington: University Press of Kentucky, 1987.

Mjagkij, Nina, and Margaret Spratt, eds. *Men and Women Adrift: The YMCA and the YWCA in the City.* New York: New York University Press, 1997.

Recchuiti, John Louis. *Civic Engagement: Social Science and Progressive-Era Reform in New York City.* Philadelphia: University of Pennsylvania Press, 2006.

Schneider, Eric C. *In the Web of Class: Delinquents and Reformers in Boston, 1810s–1930s.* New York: New York University Press, 1992.

Tuennerman-Kaplan, Laura. *Helping Others, Helping Ourselves: Power, Giving, and Community Identity in Cleveland, Ohio, 1880–1930.* Kent, Ohio: Kent State University Press, 2001.

Wedell, Marsha. *Elite Women and the Reform Impulse in Memphis, 1875–1915.* Knoxville: University of Tennessee Press, 1991.

Settlement House Movement

Carson, Mina. *Settlement Folk: Social Thought and the American Settlement Movement.* Chicago: University of Chicago Press, 1990.

Crocker, Ruth Hutchinson. *Social Work and Social Order: The Settlement Movement in Two Industrial Cities, 1889–1930.* Urbana: University of Illinois Press, 1992.

Lasch-Quinn, Elisabeth. *Black Neighbors: Race and the Limits of Reform in the American Settlement House Movement, 1890–1945.* Chapel Hill: University of North Carolina Press, 1993.

Lissak, Rivka Shpak. *Pluralism and Progressives: Hull House and the New Immigrants, 1890–1919.* Chicago: University of Chicago Press, 1989.

Siegel, Beatrice. *Lillian Wald of Henry Street.* New York: Macmillan, 1983.

Stebner, Eleanor J. *The Women of Hull House: A Study in Spiritual Vocation and Friendship.* Albany: State University of New York Press, 1997.

Urban Politics and Government

General

Buenker, John D. *Urban Liberalism and Progressive Reform.* New York: Scribner's, 1973.

Griffith, Ernest S. *History of American City Government: The Progressive Years and Their Aftermath, 1900–1920.* New York: Praeger, 1974.

Urban Political Patterns and Machine Politics

Allswang, John M. *Bosses, Machines, and Urban Voters.* Rev. ed. Baltimore: Johns Hopkins University Press, 1986.

Erie, Stephen. *Rainbow's End: Irish-Americans and the Dilemmas of Urban Machine Politics, 1840–1985.* Berkeley: University of California Press, 1988.

Rosen, Christine M. *The Limits of Power: Great Fires and the Process of City Growth in America.* New York: Cambridge University Press, 1986.

Urban Governmental and Political Reform

Ebner, Michael, and Eugene Tobin, eds. *The Age of Urban Reform: New Perspectives on the Progressive Era.* Port Washington, N.Y.: Kennikat, 1977.

Finegold, Kenneth. *Experts and Politicians: Reform Challenges in Machine Politics in New York, Cleveland, and Chicago.* Princeton, N.J.: Princeton University Press, 1995.

Fox, Kenneth. *Better City Government: Innovation in American Urban Politics, 1850–1937.* Philadelphia: Temple University Press, 1977.

Mattson, Kevin. *Creating a Democratic Public: The Struggle for Urban Participatory Democracy during the Progressive Era.* University Park: Penn State University Press, 1998.

Rice, Bradley R. *Progressive Cities: The Commission Movement in America, 1901–1920.* Austin: University of Texas Press, 1977.

Schiesl, Martin J. *The Politics of Efficiency: Municipal Administration and Reform in America, 1880–1920.* Berkeley: University of California Press, 1977.

Stivers, Camilla. *Bureau Men, Settlement Women: Constructing Public Administration in the Progressive Era.* Lawrence: University Press of Kansas, 2000.

Public Services: Health, Police, and Fire

Escobar, Edward J. *Race, Police, and the Making of a Political Identity: Mexican Americans and the Los Angeles Police Department, 1900–1945.* Berkeley: University of California Press, 1999.

Galishoff, Stuart. *Safeguarding the Public Health: Newark, 1895–1918.* Westport, Conn.: Greenwood, 1975.

Holloran, Peter C. *Boston's Wayward Children: Social Services for Homeless Children, 1830–1930.* Rutherford, N.J.: Fairleigh Dickinson University Press, 1989.

Leavitt, Judith Walzer. *The Healthiest City: Milwaukee and the Politics of Health Reform.* Princeton, N.J.: Princeton University Press, 1982.

Monkkonen, Eric H. *Police in Urban America, 1860–1920.* New York: Cambridge University Press, 1981.

Williams, Marilyn Thornton. *Washing "the Great Unwashed": Public Baths in Urban America, 1840–1920.* Columbus: Ohio State University Press, 1991.

Politics and Government: Individual Cities

Allswang, John M. *A House for All Peoples: Ethnic Politics in Chicago, 1890–1936.* Lexington: University Press of Kentucky, 1973.

Bolin, James Duane. *Bossism and Reform in a Southern City: Lexington, Kentucky, 1880–1940.* Lexington: University Press of Kentucky, 2000.

Connolly, James J. *The Triumph of Ethnic Progressivism: Urban Political Culture in Boston, 1900–1925.* Cambridge, Mass.: Harvard University Press, 1998.

Crooks, James B. *Politics and Progress: The Rise of Urban Progressivism in Baltimore, 1895–1911.* Baton Rouge: Louisiana State University Press, 1968.

Fairbanks, Robert. B. *For the City as a Whole: Planning, Politics, and the Public Interest in Dallas, Texas, 1900–1965.* Columbus: Ohio State University Press, 1999.

Hammack, David C. *Power and Society: Greater New York at the Turn of the Century.* Reprint, New York: Columbia University Press, 1987.

Harris, Carl V. *Political Power in Birmingham, 1871–1921.* Knoxville: University of Tennessee Press, 1977.

Henderson, Thomas M. *Tammany Hall and the New Immigrants: The Progressive Years.* New York: Arno, 1976.

Holli, Melvin. *Reform in Detroit: Hazen S. Pingree and Urban Politics.* New York: Oxford University Press, 1969.

Johnston, Robert D. *The Radical Middle Class: Populist Democracy and the Question of Capitalism in Progressive Era Portland.* Princeton, N.J.: Princeton University Press, 2003.

Jones, Marine. *Holy Toledo: Religion and Politics in the Life of "Golden Rule" Jones.* Lexington: University Press of Kentucky, 1998.

McCaffrey, Peter. *When Bosses Ruled Philadelphia: The Emergence of the Republican Machine, 1867–1933.* University Park: Pennsylvania State University Press, 1993.

McNickle, Chris. *To Be Mayor of New York: Ethnic Politics in the City, 1898–1930.* New York: Columbia University Press, 1993.

Miller, Zane L. *Boss Cox's Cincinnati: Urban Politics in the Progressive Era.* New York: Oxford University Press, 1968.

Paulsson, Martin. *The Social Anxieties of Progressive Reform: Atlantic City, 1854–1920.* New York: New York University Press, 1994.

Tarr, Joel. *A Study in Boss Politics: William Lorimer of Chicago*. Urbana: University of Illinois Press, 1971.

RURAL LIFE AND AGRICULTURE

Agriculture

Danbom, David B. *The Resisted Revolution: Urban America and the Industrialization of Agriculture, 1900–1930*. Ames: Iowa State University Press, 1979.

Lampard, Eric E. *The Rise of the Dairy Industry in Wisconsin: A Study in Agricultural Change, 1880–1920*. Madison: State Historical Society of Wisconsin, 1963.

Vaught, David. *Cultivating California: Growers, Specialty Crops, and Labor, 1875–1920*. Baltimore: Johns Hopkins University Press, 1999.

Woeste, Victoria Saker. *The Farmer's Benevolent Trust: Law and Agricultural Cooperation in Industrial America, 1865–1945*. Chapel Hill: University of North Carolina Press, 1998.

Rural Life, Culture, and Labor

Barron, Hal S. *Mixed Harvest: The Second Great Transformation in the Rural North, 1870–1930*. Chapel Hill: University of North Carolina Press, 1997.

Gjerde, Jon. *The Minds of the West: Ethnocultural Evolution in the Rural Middle West, 1830–1917*. Chapel Hill: University of North Carolina Press, 1997.

Gough, Robert. *Farming the Cutover: A Social History of Northern Wisconsin, 1900–1940*. Lawrence: University Press of Kansas, 1997.

Hahamovitch, Cindy. *The Fruits of Their Labor: Atlantic Coast Farmworkers and the Making of Migrant Poverty, 1870–1945*. Chapel Hill: University of North Carolina Press, 1997.

Kline, Ronald R. *Consumers in the Country: Technology and Social Change in Rural America*. Baltimore: Johns Hopkins University Press, 2000.

Neth, Mary C. *Preserving the Family Farm: Women, Community, and the Foundations of Agribusiness in the Midwest, 1900–1940*. Baltimore: Johns Hopkins University Press, 1995.

Riney-Kehrberg, Pamela. *Childhood on the Farm: Work, Play, and Coming of Age in the Midwest*. Lawrence: University Press of Kansas, 2005.

Rural Women

Fink, Deborah. *Agrarian Women: Wives and Mothers in Rural Nebraska, 1880–1940.* Chapel Hill: University of North Carolina Press, 1992.

Holt, Marilyn Irvin. *Linoleum, Better Babies, and the Modern Farm Woman, 1890–1930.* Albuquerque: University of New Mexico Press, 1995.

Marti, Donald B. *Women of the Grange: Mutuality and Sisterhood in Rural America, 1866–1920.* Westport, Conn.: Greenwood, 1991.

Sharpless, Rebecca. *Fertile Ground, Narrow Choices: Women on Texas Cotton Farms, 1900–1940.* Chapel Hill: University of North Carolina Press, 1999.

Rural Reform Movements and Populism

Argersinger, Peter. *The Limits of Agrarian Radicalism: Western Populism and American Politics.* Lawrence: University Press of Kansas, 1995.

Bowers, William L. *The Country Life Movement in America, 1900–1920.* Port Washington, N.Y.: Kennikat, 1974.

Clanton, Gene. *Populism: The Humane Preference in America, 1890–1900.* Boston: Twayne, 1991.

Goodwyn, Lawrence. *Democratic Promise: The Populist Moment in America.* New York: Oxford University Press, 1976.

McMath, Robert C. *American Populism: A Social History, 1877-1898.* New York: Hill and Wang, 1993.

Postel, Charles. *The Populist Vision.* New York: Oxford University Press, 2007.

Woodward, C. Vann. *Tom Watson: Agrarian Rebel.* Reprint, New York: Oxford University Press, 1963.

ENVIRONMENT AND CONSERVATION

Conservation Movement and Environmental Policy

Dorsey, Kirkpatrick. *The Dawn of Conservation Diplomacy: U.S.–Canadian Wildlife Protection Treaties in the Progressive Era.* Seattle: University of Washington Press, 1998.

Hays, Samuel P. *Conservation and the Gospel of Efficiency: The Progressive Conservation Movement, 1890–1920.* Cambridge, Mass.: Harvard University Press, 1959.

Jacoby, Karl. *Crimes against Nature: Squatters, Poachers, Thieves, and the Hidden History of American Conservation.* Berkeley: University of California Press, 2001.

McCarthy, G. Michael. *Hour of Trial: The Conservation Conflict in Colorado and the West, 1891–1907.* Norman: University of Oklahoma Press, 1977.

Penick, James L., Jr. *Progressive Politics and Conservation: The Ballinger–Pinchot Controversy.* Chicago: University of Chicago Press, 1968.

Tyrrell, Ian. *True Gardens of the Gods: California-Australian Environmental Reform, 1860–1930.* Berkeley: University of California Press, 1999.

Environmental Issues

Kahrl, William L. *Water and Power: The Conflict over Los Angeles' Water Supply in the Owens Valley.* Berkeley: University of California Press, 1982.

MacMillan, Donald. *Smoke Wars: Anaconda Copper, Montana Air Pollution, and the Courts, 1890–1924.* Helena: Montana Historical Society, 2000.

Righter, Robert W. *The Battle over Hetch Hetchy: America's Most Controversial Dam and the Birth of Modern Environmentalism.* New York: Oxford University Press, 2004.

Sauder, Robert A. *The Lost Frontier: Water Diversion in the Growth and Destruction of Owens Valley Agriculture.* Tucson: University of Arizona Press, 1994.

Stradling, David. *Smokestacks and Progressives: Environmentalists, Engineers, and Air Pollution in America, 1881–1951.* Baltimore: Johns Hopkins University Press, 1999.

Environmental Activists and Ideas

Cohen, Michael P. *The Pathless Way: John Muir and the American Wilderness.* Madison: University of Wisconsin Press, 1984.

Fox, Stephen. *John Muir and His Legacy: The American Conservation Movement.* Boston: Little, Brown, 1981.

Dorman, Robert L. *A Word for Nature: Four Pioneering Environmental Advocates, 1845–1913.* Chapel Hill: University of North Carolina Press, 1998.

Miller, Char. *Gifford Pinchot and the Making of Modern Environmentalism.* Washington, D.C.: Island Press, 2001.

Reiger, John F. *American Sportsmen and the Origins of Conservation.* 3rd ed. Corvallis: Oregon State University Press, 2001.

Smith, Michael L. *Pacific Visions: California Scientists and the Environment, 1850–1915.* Berkeley: University of California Press, 1987.

Strong, Douglas H. *Dreamers and Defenders: American Conservationists.* Reprint, Lincoln: University of Nebraska Press, 1988.

Wilkins, Thurman. *John Muir: Apostle of Nature.* Norman: University of Oklahoma Press, 1995.

National Parks and Monuments

Albright, Horace M., and Marian Albright Schenck. *Creating the National Park Service: The Missing Years*. Norman: University of Oklahoma Press, 1999.

Rothman, Hal. *Preserving Different Pasts: The American National Monuments*. Urbana: University of Illinois Press, 1989.

Sellars, Richard West. *Preserving Nature in the National Parks: A History*. New Haven, Conn.: Yale University Press, 1997.

Snead, James Elliott. *Ruins and Rivals: The Making of Southwest Archaeology*. Tucson: University of Arizona Press, 2001.

THE SOUTH

General

Ayers, Edward L. *The Promise of the New South: Life after Reconstruction*. New York: Oxford University Press, 1992.

Rabinowitz, Howard. *The First New South, 1865–1920*. Arlington Heights, Ill.: Harlan Davidson, 1992.

Woodward, C. Vann. *Origins of the New South, 1877–1913*. Baton Rouge: Louisiana State University Press, 1951.

Society and Culture

Benfy, Christopher. *Degas in New Orleans: Encounters in the Creole World of Kate Chopin and George Washington Cable*. New York: Alfred A. Knopf, 1997.

Etheridge, Elizabeth. *The Butterfly Caste: A Social History of Pellagra in the South*. Westport, Conn.: Greenwood, 1972.

Foster, Gaines M. *Ghosts of the Confederacy: Defeat, the Lost Cause, and the Emergence of the New South, 1865–1913*. New York: Oxford University Press, 1987.

Kyriakoudes, Louis M. *The Social Origins of the Urban South: Race, Gender, and Migration in Nashville and Middle Tennessee, 1890–1930*. Chapel Hill: University of North Carolina Press, 2003.

Margo, Robert A. *Race and Schooling in the South: An Economic History, 1880–1950*. Chicago: University of Chicago Press, 1990.

Mixon, Wayne. *Southern Writers and the New South Movement, 1865–1913*. Chapel Hill: University of North Carolina Press, 1980.

Newby, I. A. *Plain Folk in the New South: Social Change and Cultural Persistence, 1880–1915*. Baton Rouge: Louisiana State University Press, 1989.

Ownby, Ted. *Subduing Satan: Religion, Recreation, and Manhood in the Rural South, 1865–1920*. Chapel Hill: University of North Carolina Press, 1990.

Shapiro, Henry D. *Appalachia on Our Mind: The Southern Mountains and Mountaineers in the American Consciousness, 1870–1920*. Chapel Hill: University of North Carolina Press, 1978.

Smith, John David. *An Old Creed for the New South: Proslavery Ideology and Historiography, 1865–1918*. Westport, Conn.: Greenwood, 1985.

Wilson, Charles Reagan. *Baptized in Blood: The Religion of the Lost Cause, 1865–1920*. Athens: University of Georgia Press, 1980.

Rural Labor and Conflict

Campbell, Tracy. *The Politics of Despair: Power and Resistance in the Tobacco Wars*. Lexington: University Press of Kentucky, 1993.

Foley, Neil. *The White Scourge: Mexicans, Blacks, and Poor Whites in Texas Cotton Culture*. Berkeley: University of California Press, 1997.

Marshall, Suzanne. *Violence in the Black Patch of Kentucky and Tennessee*. Columbia: University of Missouri Press, 1994.

Waldrep, Christopher. *Night Riders: Defending Community in the Black Patch, 1890–1915*. Durham, N.C.: Duke University Press, 1993.

Industrialization and Industrial Labor

Arnesen, Eric. *Waterfront Workers of New Orleans: Race, Class and Politics, 1863–1923*. New York: Oxford University Press, 1991.

Eller, Ronald D. *Miners, Millands, and Mountaineers: Industrialization of the Appalachian South, 1880–1930*. Knoxville: University of Tennessee Press, 1982.

Fink, Gary M. *The Fulton Bag and Cotton Mills Strike of 1914–1915: Espionage, Labor Conflict, and New South Industrial Relations*. Ithaca, N.Y.: Cornell University Press, 1993.

Hall, Jacquelyn Dowd, et al. *Like a Family: The Making of a Southern Cotton Mill World*. Chapel Hill: University of North Carolina Press, 1987.

Kelly, Brian. *Race, Class, and Power in the Alabama Coalfields, 1908–1921*. Urbana: University of Illinois Press, 2001.

Kuhn, Clifford M. *Contesting the New South Order: The 1914–1915 Strike at Atlanta's Fulton Mills*. Chapel Hill: University of North Carolina Press, 2001.

Letwin, Daniel. *The Challenge of Interracial Unionism: Alabama Coal Miners, 1878–1921.* Chapel Hill: University of North Carolina Press, 1998.

McHugh, Cathy L. *Mill Family: The Labor System in the Southern Cotton Textile Industry, 1880–1915.* New York: Oxford University Press, 1988.

McKiven, Henry M., Jr. *Iron and Steel: Class, Race, and Community in Birmingham, Alabama, 1875–1920.* Chapel Hill: University of North Carolina Press, 1995.

Rosenberg, Daniel. *New Orleans Dockworkers: Race, Labor, and Unionism, 1892–1923.* Albany: State University of New York Press, 1988.

Southern Women and Women's Reform

Green, Elna C. *Southern Strategies: Southern Women and the Woman Suffrage Question.* Chapel Hill: University of North Carolina Press, 1997.

Hewitt, Nancy A. *Southern Discomfort: Women's Activism in Tampa, Florida, 1880s–1920s.* Urbana: University of Illinois Press, 2001.

Johnson, Joan Marie. *Southern Ladies, New Women: Race, Region, and Clubwomen in South Carolina, 1890–1930.* Gainesville: University Press of Florida, 2004.

McArthur, Judith N. *Creating the New Woman: The Rise of Women's Progressive Culture in Texas, 1893–1918.* Urbana: University of Illinois Press, 1998.

Montgomery, Rebecca S. *The Politics of Education in the New South: Women and Reform in Georgia, 1890–1930.* Baton Rouge: Louisiana State University Press, 2006.

Scott, Anne Firor. *The Southern Lady: From Pedestal to Politics, 1830–1930.* Reprint, Charlottesville; University of Virginia Press, 1995.

Sims, Anastatia. *The Power of Femininity in the New South: Women's Organizations and Politics in North Carolina, 1880–1930.* Columbia: University of South Carolina Press, 1997.

Thomas, Martha Mary. *The New Woman in Alabama: Social Reforms and Suffrage, 1890–1920.* Tuscaloosa: University of Alabama Press, 1992.

Wheeler, Marjorie Spruill, ed. *Votes for Women! The Woman Suffrage Movement in Tennessee, the South, and the Nation.* Knoxville: University of Tennessee Press, 1995.

Southern Politics and Government

General

Anders, Evan. *Boss Rule in South Texas: The Progressive Era.* Austin: University of Texas Press, 1982.

Arsenault, Raymond. *The Wild Ass of the Ozarks: Jeff Davis and the Social Bases of Southern Politics*. Philadelphia: Temple University Press, 1984.

Grantham, Dewey W. *The Life and Death of the Solid South: A Political History*. Lexington: University Press of Kentucky, 1988.

Holmes, William F. *The White Chief: James Kimble Vardaman*. Baton Rouge: Louisiana State University Press, 1970.

Hunt, James L. *Marion Butler and American Populism*. Chapel Hill: University of North Carolina Press, 2003.

Kantrowitz, Stephen. *Ben Tillman and the Reconstruction of White Supremacy*. Chapel Hill: University of North Carolina Press, 2000.

Niswonger, Richard L. *Arkansas Democratic Politics, 1896–1920*. Fayetteville: University of Arkansas Press, 1990.

Southern Legal and Penal Systems

Frey, Robert Seitz, and Nancy Thompson-Frey. *The Silent and the Damned: The Murder of Mary Phagan and the Lynching of Leo Frank*. Lanham, Md.: Madison Books, 1988.

Guthrie, John J., Jr. *Keeper of the Spirits: The Judicial Response to Prohibition Enforcement in Florida, 1885–1935*. Westport, Conn.: Greenwood, 1998.

Lichtenstein, Alex. *Twice the Work of Free Labor: The Political Economy of Convict Labor in the New South*. New York: Verso, 1996.

Mancini, Matthew J. *One Dies, Get Another: Convict Leasing in the American South, 1866–1928*. Columbia: University of South Carolina Press, 1996.

Melnick, Jeffrey. *Black–Jewish Relations on Trial: Leo Frank and Jim Conley in the New South*. Jackson: University Press of Mississippi, 2000.

Miller, Vivien L. *Crime, Sexual Violence, and Clemency: Florida's Pardon Board and Penal System in the Progressive Era*. Gainesville: University Press of Florida, 2000.

Walker, Donald R. *Penology for Profit: A History of the Texas Prison System, 1867–1912*. College Station: Texas A&M University Press, 1988.

Southern Reform Movements and Progressivism

Dennis, Michael. *Lessons in Progress: State Universities and Progressivism in the New South, 1880–1930*. Urbana: University of Illinois Press, 2001.

Ettling, John. *The Germ of Laziness: Rockefeller Philanthropy and Public Health in the New South*. Cambridge, Mass.: Harvard University Press, 1981.

Grantham, Dewey W. *Southern Progressivism: The Reconciliation of Progress and Tradition.* Knoxville: University of Tennessee Press, 1983.

Hoffschwelle, Mary S. *Rebuilding the Rural Southern Community: Reformers, Schools, and Homes in Tennessee, 1900–1930.* Knoxville: University of Tennessee, 1998.

Kirby, Jack Temple. *Darkness at Dawning: Race and Reform in the Progressive South.* Philadelphia: Lippincott, 1972.

Link, William A. *The Paradox of Southern Progressivism, 1880–1930.* Chapel Hill: University of North Carolina Press, 1992.

Noll, Steven. *Feeble-Minded in Our Midst: Institutions for the Mentally Retarded in the South, 1900–1940.* Chapel Hill: University of North Carolina Press, 1995.

State and Local Studies

Buenger, Walter L. *The Path to the Modern South: Northeast Texas between Reconstruction and the Great Depression.* Austin: University of Texas Press, 2001.

Carlton, David L. *Mill and Town in South Carolina, 1880–1920.* Baton Rouge: Louisiana State University Press, 1982.

Cresswell, Stephen. *Rednecks, Redeemers, and Race: Mississippi after Reconstruction, 1877–1917.* Jackson: University Press of Mississippi, 2006.

Ingalls, Robert P. *Urban Vigilantes in the New South: Tampa, 1882–1936.* Knoxville: University of Tennessee Press, 1988.

Keith, Jeanette. *Country People in the New South: Tennessee's Upper Cumberland.* Chapel Hill: University of North Carolina Press, 1995.

Lester, Connie L. *Up from the Mudsills of Hell: The Farmer's Alliance, Populism, and Progressive Agriculture in Tennessee, 1870–1915.* Athens: University of Georgia Press, 2006.

Lewis, Ronald L. *Transforming the Appalachian Countryside: Railroads, Deforestation, and Social Change in West Virginia, 1880–1920.* Chapel Hill: University of North Carolina Press, 1998.

Moneyhon, Carl H. *Arkansas and the New South, 1874–1929.* Fayetteville: University of Arkansas Press, 1997.

Moore, John Hammond. *Carnival of Blood: Dueling, Lynching, and Murder in South Carolina, 1880–1920.* Columbia: University of South Carolina Press, 2006.

Nathans, Sydney. *The Quest for Progress: The Way We Lived in North Carolina, 1870–1920.* Chapel Hill: University of North Carolina Press, 1983.

Wetherington, Mark V. *The New South Comes to Wiregrass Georgia, 1860–1910.* Knoxville: University of Tennessee Press, 1994.

THE WEST

Geography, Economy, and Public Policy

Deverell, William. *Railroad Crossing: Californians and the Railroad, 1850–1910.* Berkeley: University of California Press, 1994.

Friedricks, William B. *Henry E. Huntington and the Creation of Southern California.* Columbus: Ohio State University Press, 1992.

Orsi, Richard J. *Sunset Limited: The Southern Pacific Railroad and the Development of the American West, 1850–1930.* Berkeley: University of California Press, 2005.

Pisani, Donald J. *Water and American Government: The National Reclamation Bureau National Water Policy, and the West, 1902–1935.* Berkeley: University of California Press, 2002.

———. *Water, Land, and Law in the American West: The Limits of Public Policy, 1850–1920.* Lawrence: University Press of Kansas, 1996.

Pyne, Stephen J. *Year of the Fires: The Story of the Great Fires of 1910.* New York: Viking, 2001.

Robbins, William G. *Colony and Empire: The Capitalist Transformation of the American West.* Lawrence: University Press of Kansas, 1994.

Taniguchi, Nancy J. *Necessary Fraud: Progressive Reform and Utah Coal.* Norman: University of Oklahoma Press, 1996.

Thorpe, James. *Henry Edwards Huntington: A Biography.* Berkeley: University of California Press, 1994.

Worster, Donald. *Rivers of Empire: Water, Aridity, and the Growth of the American West.* New York: Pantheon, 1985.

Wycoff, William. *Creating Colorado: The Making of a Western American Landscape, 1860–1940.* New Haven, Conn.: Yale University Press, 1999.

Western Labor

Brundage, David. *The Making of Western Labor Radicals: Denver's Organized Workers, 1878–1905.* Urbana: University of Illinois Press, 1994.

Byrkit, James W. *Forging the Copper Collar: Arizona's Labor–Management War of 1901–1921.* Tucson: University of Arizona Press, 1982.

Clark, Thomas. *Defending Rights: Law, Labor Politics, and the State of California, 1890–1925.* Detroit: Wayne State University Press, 2002.

Daniel, Cletus. *Bitter Harvest: A History of California Farmworkers, 1870–1941.* Ithaca, N.Y.: Cornell University Press, 1981.

Derickson, Alan. *Worker's Health, Worker's Democracy: The Western Miner's Struggle, 1891–1925.* Ithaca, N.Y.: Cornell University Press, 1988.

Garcia, Matt. *A World of Its Own: Race, Labor, and Citrus in the Making of Greater Los Angeles, 1900–1970.* Chapel Hill: University of North Carolina Press, 2002.

Jameson, Elizabeth. *All That Glitters: Class, Conflict, and Community in Cripple Creek.* Urbana: University of Illinois Press, 1998.

Lukas, J. Anthony. *Big Trouble: A Murder in a Small Western Town Sets Off a Struggle for the Soul of America.* New York: Simon & Schuster, 1997.

Mellinger, Philip J. *Race and Labor in Western Copper: The Fight for Equality, 1896–1918.* Tucson: University of Arizona Press, 1995.

Peck, Gunther. *Reinventing Free Labor: Padrones and Immigrant Workers in the North American West, 1880–1930.* New York: Cambridge University Press, 2000.

Schwantes, Carlos. *Radical Heritage: Labor, Socialism, and Reform in Washington and British Columbia, 1885–1917.* Seattle: University of Washington Press, 1979.

Wyman, Mark. *Hard Rock Epic: Western Miners and the Industrial Revolution.* Berkeley: University of California Press, 1979.

Western Social and Cultural Life

Gordon, Linda. *The Great Arizona Orphan Abduction.* Cambridge, Mass.: Harvard University Press, 1999.

McKanna, Clare V., Jr. *Homicide, Race, and Justice in the American West, 1880–1920.* Tucson: University of Arizona Press, 1997.

Van Nuys, Frank. *Americanizing the West: Race, Immigrants, and Citizenship, 1890–1930.* Lawrence: University Press of Kansas, 2002.

West, Elliott. *Growing Up with the Country: Childhood on the Far Western Frontier.* Albuquerque: University of New Mexico Press, 1989.

Western Women and Women's Reform

Butler, Anne M. *Gendered Justice in the American West: Women Prisoners in Men's Penitentiaries.* Urbana: University of Illinois Press, 1997.

Gullett, Gayle. *Becoming Citizens: The Emergence and Development of the California Women's Movement, 1880–1911.* Urbana: University of Illinois Press, 2001.

Haarsager, Sandra. *Organized Womanhood: Cultural Politics in the Pacific Northwest, 1840–1920.* Norman: University of Oklahoma Press, 1997.

Harris, Katherine. *Long Vistas: Women and Families on Colorado Homesteads.* Niwot: University Press of Colorado, 1993.

Moynihan, Ruth, Susan Armitage, and Christiane Fisher Dichamp, eds. *So Much to Be Done: Women Settlers on the Mining and Ranching Frontier.* Lincoln: University of Nebraska Press, 1990.

Pascoe, Peggy. *Relations of Rescue: The Search for Female Moral Authority in the American West, 1874–1939.* New York: Oxford University Press, 1990.

Reese, Linda Williams. *Women of Oklahoma, 1890–1920.* Norman: University of Oklahoma Press, 1997.

Tucker, Cynthia Grant. *Prophetic Sisterhood: Liberal Women Ministers of the Frontier, 1880–1930.* Boston: Beacon, 1990.

The West in American Culture

Eldredge, Charles C., Julie Schimmel, and William H. Truettner. *Art in New Mexico, 1900–1945: Paths to Taos and Santa Fe.* New York: Abbeville Press, 1986.

Gibson, Arrell Morgan. *The Santa Fe and Taos Colonies: Age of the Muses, 1900–1942.* Norman: University of Oklahoma Press, 1983.

Goodman, Audrey. *Translating Southwestern Landscapes: The Making of an Anglo Literary Region.* Tucson: University of Arizona Press, 2002.

Kasson, Joy S. *Buffalo Bill's Wild West: Celebrity, Memory, and Popular History.* New York: Hill and Wang, 2000.

Poling-Kempes, Lesley. *The Harvey Girls: Women Who Opened the West.* New York: Paragon House, 1989.

Stineman, Esther Lanigan. *Mary Austin: Song of a Maverick.* New Haven, Conn.: Yale University Press, 1989.

Warren, Louis. *Buffalo Bill's America: William Cody and the Wild West Show.* New York: Alfred A. Knopf, 2005.

White, G. Edward. *The Eastern Establishment and the Western Experience: The West of Frederic Remington, Theodore Roosevelt, and Owen Wister.* Reprint, Austin: University of Texas Press, 1989.

Wrobel, David M. *The End of American Exceptionalism: Frontier Anxiety from the Old West to the New Deal.* Lawrence: University Press of Kansas, 1993.

———. *Promised Lands: Promotion, Memory, and the Creation of the American West.* Lawrence: University Press of Kansas, 2002.

State and Local Studies

Berman, David R. *Reformers, Corporations, and the Electorate: An Analysis of Arizona's Age of Reform.* Niwot: University Press of Colorado, 1992.

Emmons, David M. *The Butte Irish: Class and Ethnicity in an American Mining Town, 1875–1925*. Urbana: University of Illinois Press, 1989.

Fahey, John. *The Inland Empire: Unfolding Years, 1879–1929*. Seattle: University of Washington Press, 1986.

Goble, Danney. *Progressive Oklahoma: The Making of a New Kind of State*. Norman: University of Oklahoma Press, 1980.

Harris, Charles H., III, and Louis R. Salder. *The Texas Rangers and the Mexican Revolution: The Bloodiest Decade, 1910–1920*. Albuquerque: University of New Mexico Press, 2004.

Miner, H. Craig. *Next Year Country: Dust to Dust in Western Kansas, 1890–1940*. Lawrence: University Press of Kansas, 2006.

Mitchell, Pablo. *Coyote Nation: Sexuality, Race, and Conquest in Modernizing New Mexico, 1880–1920*. Chicago: University of Chicago Press, 2005.

Starr, Kevin. *Inventing the Dream: California through the Progressive Era*. New York: Oxford University Press, 1985.

Stoll, Steven. *The Fruits of Natural Advantage: Making the Industrial Countryside in California*. Berkeley: University of California Press, 1998.

Thompson, John. *Closing the Frontier: Radical Response in Oklahoma, 1889–1923*. Norman: University of Oklahoma Press, 1986.

Watkins, Marilyn P. *Rural Democracy: Family Farmers and Politics in Western Washington, 1890–1925*. Ithaca, N.Y.: Cornell University Press, 1995.

About the Authors

Catherine Cocks is codirector and executive editor of SAR Press, a division of the School for Advanced Research in Santa Fe, New Mexico. After earning a Ph.D. at the University of California–Davis, she taught at the University of California–Davis, California State University, San Marcos, and the State University of New York at Oswego before going into publishing. The author of *Doing the Town: The Rise of Urban Tourism in the United States* (2001), she is currently researching the rise of a resort region ranging from the Caribbean and Florida through Mexico and into Southern California in the early twentieth century. She is a member of the board of the Tepoztlán Institute for the Transnational History of the Americas.

Peter C. Holloran is associate professor of history at Worcester State College in Massachusetts. A specialist in United States cultural history in the nineteenth century, he has served on the board of the American Culture Association and the editorial board of the *Journal of Popular Culture* and as executive director of the New England Historical Association and the Northeast Popular Culture/American Culture Association. With a Ph.D. from Boston University, he is the author of *Boston's Wayward Children: Social Services for Homeless Children, 1830–1930* (1989), the *Historical Dictionary of New England* (2003), and *U.S. Social History in the 1980s* (2008).

Alan Lessoff is professor of history at Illinois State University in Normal, Illinois, where he has been on the faculty since 2000. Before that, he taught at Texas A&M University–Corpus Christi and Dickinson College. A specialist in United States and comparative urban history, Lessoff has since 2004 served as editor of the *Journal of the Gilded Age and Progressive Era*. He has also been on the editorial board of the

Journal of Urban History. With a Ph.D. from Johns Hopkins University, Lessoff has been a Fulbright lecturer at the University of Kassel in Germany and Bilkent University in Ankara, Turkey. He is the author of *The Nation and Its City: Politics, "Corruption," and Progress in Washington, D.C., 1861–1902* (1994), coauthor of *Legacy: A History of the Art Museum of South Texas* (1997), and coeditor of *Adolf Cluss, Architect: From Germany to America* (2005). His articles have appeared in *Planning Perspectives, American Nineteenth Century History*, the *Journal of Urban History*, and the *Southwestern Historical Quarterly*, among other places.